Sitting Ducks at Guadalcanal

The U.S. Navy's Disaster at the Battle of Savo Island in World War II

Lawrence A. De Graw

STACKPOLE
BOOKS

Essex, Connecticut
Blue Ridge Summit, Pennsylvania

STACKPOLE BOOKS

An imprint of Globe Pequot, the trade division of
The Rowman & Littlefield Publishing Group, Inc.
4501 Forbes Blvd., Ste. 200
Lanham, MD 20706
www.rowman.com

Distributed by NATIONAL BOOK NETWORK

British Library Cataloguing in Publication Information Available

Library of Congress Cataloging-in-Publication Data

Names: De Graw, Lawrence A., 1948– author.
Title: Sitting ducks at Guadalcanal : the U.S. Navy's disaster at the
    battle of Savo Island in World War II / Lawrence A. De Graw.
Other titles: US Navy's disaster at the battle of Savo Island in World War II
Description: Essex, Connecticut : Stackpole Books, 2023. | Includes
    bibliographical references.
Identifiers: LCCN 2023019080 (print) | LCCN 2023019081 (ebook) | ISBN
    9780811773836 (cloth) | ISBN 9780811773843 (epub)
Subjects: LCSH: Savo Island, Battle of, Solomon Islands, 1942.
Classification: LCC D774.S318 D43 2023 (print) | LCC D774.S318 (ebook) |
    DDC 940.54/265933—dc23/eng/20230422
LC record available at https://lccn.loc.gov/2023019080
LC ebook record available at https://lccn.loc.gov/2023019081

This book is dedicated to PO1 Daniel J. Galvin and his good friend and shipmate PO1 Clyde Bolton—men of the doomed American heavy cruiser USS *Quincy* (CA-39).

One would survive the night and the battle; the other would not. And only Dan would live on for all the days of his life with a survivor's guilt that was at times overwhelming.

"Why them and not me?" he had continued to ask himself with haunting restlessness.

And so this book is for you, Dan; may you finally find the peace you so richly deserve and know that some of us have not at all forgotten.

Contents

Tables

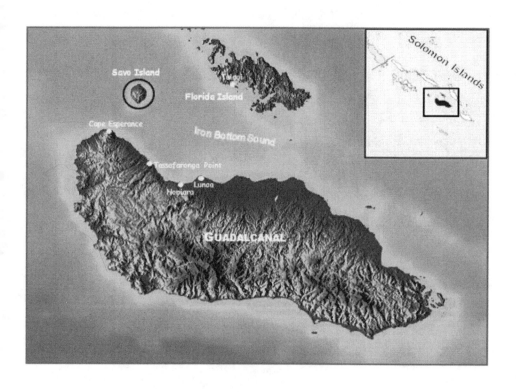

Author's Note

More Than a Compendium of Facts

Decidedly, it could not be enough for this treatise to simply be just another espousal of facts, simply another informed reverberation of previously stated particulars and details, nor even an abstruse technical reiteration of truths known only to a few historians of this period of time in history. The book would not be purposed as just another straight narrative or "textbook"-formatted discourse set only to present dry facts and colorless, unseasoned images of the battle itself. Decidedly, it would need to be more—much, *much* more. It would need to be both factual and concise, yet present substantive arguments to provoke *new* thought and *new* consideration of events as they must have occurred before, during, and even *after* the First Battle of Savo Island (1BOSI). Therefore, it would also need to be objective, and dutifully blend a touch of the real with the fanciful, while still presenting viable new findings for general researcher review, while also delving into the multiple causal factors behind the heavy American and Australian naval losses sustained during the course of this single thirty-one-minute battle that did itself occur but a tick of the clock past midnight on the morning of 9 August 1942.

Quickly spring-boarding up from a detailed review of extant and already known findings, ranging from the two-destroyer "radar picket line" just north of Savo Island not spotting the Japanese ships on approach to the three Royal Australian Air Force Reserve (RAAFR) Hudson reconnaissance planes that did spy the fleet, but were late in reporting those sightings to the Americans, to the absence of Admiral Crutchley himself from the battle main on the very night it occurred in full—the author's extensive review endeavors to address all of these issues and to offer an even greater insight into the actions of the USS *Vincennes* (CA-44), the USS *Quincy* (CA-39), and the USS *Astoria* (CA-34), and their two escort destroyers as well. And, as inevitably he must, based on the events of the night in question, the author will attempt to provide an even deeper view of the sullied and ever-maligned CAPT Howard Douglas Bode himself, and of his actions while in command of the American heavy cruiser USS *Chicago*

(CA-29), during at least the opening salvos of that encounter—as well as his later seeming retreat from that same battle.

The book then moves on to look at both the *aftermath* and the *after-actions* of that same battle: the official reports and damage assessments, the casualty estimates and capital ship losses as well. Compiled from multiple text-based reports, archive files, and online web references, the author hopes to bring a wealth of maps, plotting charts, and even hand-drawn sketches that were called into play from the many long-ago memories of the men who were actually there. And each would itself present a wholly differing view of the battle, the ships, the transitive movements, and even the final resting points for many of those ships that would tragically be lost during the course of this one brief but highly volatile naval night engagement. Some of the chart depictions themselves would actually have been commissioned by the U.S. Navy's own Office of Naval Intelligence (ONI) and would understandably present a far more precise and detailed representation of the open-sea battle areas, and of the general topographic zones that made up the area of Iron Bottom Sound and its Guadalcanal environs. Other map depictions are mere sketches and composites—many dredged up almost entirely from memory—or perhaps only as viewed these many years later by those who had experienced it firsthand and who were actually there, men such as Ohmae, Coombe, and Riefkohl. Others are provided purely as a matter of history and curiosity to those select few who continue, even to the present time, to study the mysterious annals of Naval History and the battle at Savo itself.

Finally, the book would need to be wholly humanistic. It would at all times need to present a first-person look and a driver's-seat view of the events as they must have unfolded on the night of the horrendous attack. To perhaps understand in full, if even for a moment, just what it must have been like to have endured, and to have actually lived through those first terrifying moments of bombardment by the massive 8-inch guns of Mikawa's fast-moving cruisers of the *Rengō Kantai*—the Imperial Japanese Navy's dread Combined Fleet. It is only then that we can even begin to connect the dots and further grapple with the horrors of this single naval night encounter near Savo Island. Only then might we more capably come to grips with the full brutality and swiftness of action, even at its deadliest peak, and all of it made possible by the illuminating orb flares and probing searchlights from the Japanese warships themselves, each critically marking the exact moment of their attack.

Perhaps, then, just to have just been there—at that time and in that place—to perhaps have just been a simple gunner's mate on the *Quincy*, a loader on the *Vincennes*, or a radarman on the beleaguered *Ralph Talbot* itself. Perhaps just to have been there at all, and to have seen the action up close—thence to fully live through it all and return home unscathed. One can only wonder what tales might then have been told and relived by those who could truly say, "And I was there . . ."

Devotion to a Breed Apart: The Average Joes

Into each of our lives there might indeed march many men of great import—truly all good men, of good note, the distinguished reachers and achievers of our times who will command (and well deserve) our collective respect and honor. The wise politicians, insightful historians, brilliant military leaders, brave activists, and sage men-of-state—all worthy indeed of a deferential nod and a tip of our collective political hats, as it were. And then there were the rest of us—the "Average Joes"—indeed, the grunts and groundpounders, the airmen, trenchmen soldiers, and able-bodied seamen of their times all alike, of which I, too, am proud to be counted as one.

But there an end perhaps, as indeed a line must be drawn, for the "Average Joes" of World War II were all truly remarkable men, themselves well a breed apart. And whether a "Leatherneck" Marine during the heated assault on the islands of Tulagi and Tanambogo, or an infantryman at Matanikau—and whether a pilot in a low wavetop-sweeping *Avenger* torpedo plane, or simply a gristled gunner's mate aboard the USS *Astoria* during her final, fateful battle at sea—truly these were the men to be honored here and forever in our minds and in our hearts. These are the stories of the true heroes of the collective battles and small wars of this time, a brave and harrowing tale of aggressors and defenders—of protagonists and villains who populated those wars—and of those who played out their roles with a brilliant performance of both duty and devotion. And in its final analysis perhaps, it is itself a story of the dogged men with an iron will and a glint-of-eye determination, and of the dauntless ships on which they sailed, as well as a tale of the brave few who exceeded even the greatest of expectations to sacrifice their own lives.

These, then, are the men who must be held in best regard, and before whom we—as mere unworthy onlookers and passers-by who can only watch on with admiration—can only stand with doff of hat and a well of cheer to cheerily mark their very passing. The measure of greatness in ourselves is always duty-bound to acknowledge the greatness we find in others first, as well it should be to tell the truth in full. Indeed, then, it was these very men—these same "Average Joes," these brave, brave few who then made it possible for us to live even now, and it is for them that this book must be penned. To put forth the word and set the record straight for the many hell-bent, helmeted mass of soldiers and sailors who cannot and for the regular mates and men who daily affected the triumphant outcome of that war. Long have the Average Joes been a part of America's valiant military history, especially during times of war and greatest conflict . . . and it is for them that the book itself was written.

And as such, a fond regard, a good note, and a very special dedication is extended to:

PO1 Daniel H. Galvin and PO3 Clyde "Leif" Bolton
Brave men of the USS *Quincy* (CA-39)—9 August 1942

CHAPTER 1

The Battle of Savo Island

Antebellum: Background and History

THE WORLD WAS NOT ENOUGH: THE EMPIRE OF JAPAN—
STRATEGIC CONTEXT AND SPHERES OF INFLUENCE

With the onset of hostilities early on the morning of 7 December 1941—America's first Day of Infamy—a stealthy contingent of Japanese air and naval forces embarked on a vicious surprise attack on the United States Navy's Pacific Fleet at Pearl Harbor—and at Ford Island—both on the southern tip of the island of Oahu, Hawaii. Effectively crippling much of the American battleship fleet at anchorage that one fateful morning, the unprecedented attack would precipitate both an open declaration, and later *formal* state of war between the two nations, and the United States and Japan would soon cross over a new threshold of armed conflict, and war itself would be directly on the near horizon.

An always excellent topical discussion point, it could clearly be argued that the initial objectives of Japan's Imperial Navy's leadership of the time might be considered as having been (for the moment) essentially fourfold: that of ❶ fully neutralizing (or at the very least *impeaching*) the credibility and effectiveness of the U.S. naval presence in the Pacific theater; ❷ allowing that aggressor nation (Japan) to seize *outright* possessions and critical natural resources from the many satellite island nations within their purview (and extant sphere of influence) within that Pacific Rim area; ❸ establishing strategic military bases in those areas that could then effectively extend that Japanese "sphere of influence" from its homeland waters well out into the Pacific Basin itself; and ❹ ultimately engulfing all of coastal Asia. To this end—and to the furtherance of each of these quite specific goals—Japan's forces had by mid-1942 summarily captured all of the Philippines, Thailand, Malaya, Singapore, the Dutch East Indies, Wake Island, the Gilberts, New Britain, and Guam, all indeed in very short order, and all in a very patent and unambiguous domino fashion, as approximated in the areas depicted here as plottings ❶ through ❾ in Figure 1.

1

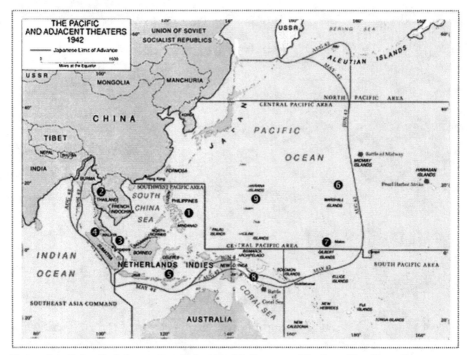

Figure 1.   Extent of Japanese Sphere of Influence: Western/Southwestern Pacific Areas (May-August 1942)

Clearly, some opposing force might soon be needed to stem the brutal tide of that very IJN advance and to attenuate the full momentum of the Japanese encroachment itself. Therefore, joining the United States in a series of unprecedented "preemptive" and retaliatory actions against Japan would be the rest of the Allied powers, many of whom—like Great Britain, Australia, and even smaller New Zealand—had only recently themselves been menaced by the seemingly invincible Empire of Japan.

At least two attempts by the Japanese to maintain the strategic initiative, and to extend their defensive perimeter in the south and central Pacific areas, had already been thwarted by the heated naval engagements at the Battle of Midway and the equally disastrous melee at Coral Sea. As such, it was now but a mauled and badly routed Japanese Navy that could only dolefully lick its wounds and bide its time. Midway, after all, had been more than just a major victory for the Allies against the previously undefeated Japanese; it also had the fortuitous effect of significantly reducing the overall offensive capability of that IJN carrier force. The immutable loss of *four* major aircraft carriers during the course of that one engagement, and yet another light carrier during the later fighting at Coral Sea, would now indeed go on to seal the fate of high-seas dominance for Japan thereafter. And after Guadalcanal itself, decidedly much, much more would befall the IJN—and much of it only to their gross detriment. In fact, up to this point in time the Allies had been strictly on the "defensive" in the Pacific, but these two tandem victories would now alone go a long way to shore up the morale and esprit-de-corps of the American fighting men and provide them with their first opportunity to seize the strategic initiative from a then-foolish and recklessly emboldened Japan.

To this end, the Allied forces specifically chose the Solomon Islands group—then a protectorate of a now-diminishing British Empire—and specifically the southern-most islands of Guadalcanal and cross-channel Tulagi on Florida Island (Nggella Sule), as their first targets. The Imperial Japanese Navy had already made a move to physically occupy Tulagi as early as May 1942 and had in fact already constructed a small seaplane base in that vicinity. Concern grew among the Allied forces when, in early July of the same year, the IJN also began constructing an even larger airfield near Lunga Point at Honiara, on nearby Guadalcanal, that would itself later become the famed (and always hotly contested) Henderson Field airstrip.

By August 1942, therefore, the Japanese had a combined nine hundred naval-borne troops already positioned on almost all of these islands, and nearly three thousand Korean and Japanese construction laborers already in situ and hard at work on precisely that same airstrip. These bases, if allowed to be completed and made fully operational in their own time, could then easily be used to: ❶ protect Japan's major bases at both ends of the Solomons chain, as far south as Tulagi and Tanambogo and all the way up to Rabaul and Kavieng; ❷ protect all of the IJN shipping lanes to and from those locations, and to expedite an unimpeded transport of goods and materiel to its troops already stationed on those islands; ❸ threaten both Allied shippage in the area and its communication and supply lines; and finally ❹ establish a viable staging area for any future offensive actions against the smaller island groups of Fiji, New Caledonia, and Samoa, and even a final targeting push on to the resource-rich Australian mainland itself—the very jewel in the crown of the southwest Pacific at that time.

Quickly, then, did the Allies read the writing on the wall and prepare to meet the enemy's naval approach full on. The American 1st Marine Division, therefore, under the command of the always gruff and bulldoggish Major General Alexander A. Vandegrift, would quickly be put ashore by amphibious reinforcement onto Florida Is-land, Tulagi, Gavutu, Tanambogo, and Guadalcanal itself—all fronting Sealark Lane (Figure 2). Now, under a cover of heavy naval and air bombardment on the morning of 7 August, the first American land offensive of the Pacific war would commence, and the stage was now set for the U.S. Navy's own massive power to be brought to bear in full. The Battle of Savo Island would soon be sparked in the fleet reckoning of a blink on the night of 9 August, and the even greater half-year-long naval battle for Guadalcanal would soon begin in earnest.

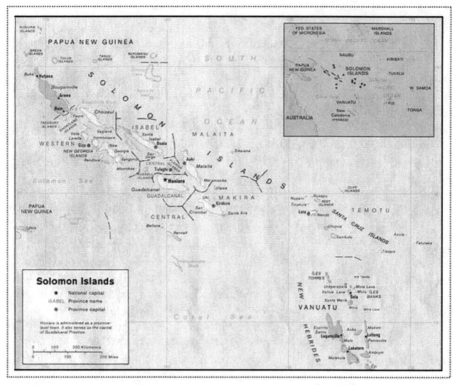

Figure 2.   Area Map of the Solomon Islands and Archipelago (CIA Districting Chart)

EMPEROR OF THE SUN: THE GRAND VIEW

In grand view, all of the spectacular naval battles for Guadalcanal and the greater Solomon Islands—and, more specifically, the First Battle of Savo Island itself—would represent a critical juncture for both the American and Allied naval forces in the Pacific theater of operations and would greatly affect each country's standing in the region (see the Table 1 matrix, *Major Naval Campaigns in the Battle for the Solomon Islands*). In scope and effect, the American defense of the Solomons in 1942 was all about "denial of access"—and "stopping cold" the "Tokyo Express" itself—and the hitherto unchecked advance of the Imperial Japanese Navy in their dogged push throughout the scattered island nations of the South Pacific.

In December 1941, the world would have already witnessed the unprovoked and unparalleled attack on the American naval fleet at both Pearl Harbor and Ford Island, but that same month would also witness the invasion of British Malaya as well, much to the general dismay of a then-astonished global community. Subsequently, the island-hopping tactics used by the Japanese in their accelerated pursuit of both land and sea bases—and the natural resources that were so critically needed just to grind the very gears of war for their vast military machine—found them only too quickly occupying New Britain, New Georgia, and Bougainville by 1942, with each of those advances going virtually unchecked by any real interdiction counterforce. It was therefore only a foolishly emboldened IJN surface fleet that now again began its own slow and steady push to the south and east—now sluicing through a narrowed deep-water passage called the Slot into Iron Bottom Sound itself, only to arrive off Guadalcanal in May of that same year.

This would now undeniably set the stage for perhaps some of the most fierce and most significant naval battles ever joined between two of the greatest superpowers of their time—that of the naval forces of the Americans and their Allied sea defense coalition, pitted against those of the dreaded and already battle-tested Imperial Japanese Navy and the Empire of Japan itself. It would soon become nothing less than a scruff-of-the-neck melee, and a bloody clash of titan navies locked on high seas, often on the very heel of night, in a series of battles that might themselves later be immortalized as "a barroom brawl after the lights had been shot out."*

That place of battle would shortly come to be known as Iron Bottom Sound, and nearly fifty ships of both combined navies would soon be sent to the very bottom of that channel before these hot battles were done . . . and all occurring in but a taut and harrowing six-month time frame between August 1942 and February 1943. A full fifty ships all told, each of them lost in waters fronting the dark and volcanic island of Savo.

ORDER OF BATTLE: FLEET HIERARCHY AND STRUCTURING

Pre-Battle Posturing: Organizational Chain of Command: Allied Forces

Before proceeding into the actual nature of the naval engagement at the First Battle of Savo Island itself, a cursory review of the order of battle from both the IJN and the Allied perspective might well be in order. Shown below and on the following page, therefore, as seen in the *Visio*-based chart illustrations in both Figure 3 and Figure 4, are two hierarchical order of battle command structures for both the Allied and IJN naval powers immediately before (and leading up to) the 1BOSI. This first hierarchical chart presents a high-level overview of the American, British, and Australian (i.e., the "Allied") command elements at the time of the battle.

---

*It was reported that an officer aboard the destroyer USS *Monssen* (DD-436) colorfully likened the heat of the battle, on at least the occasion of the Naval Battle of Guadalcanal, to that of "a barroom brawl after the lights had been shot out." In summation, this insightful (if even somewhat rough) description might indeed be used to also connote virtually *every* night battle that would later take place between the two opposing navies, happening from the battle at Savo Island on. For additional information, see the website at http://en.wikipedia.org/wiki /Naval Battle of Guadalcanal#Action 2.

Table 1. Major Naval Campaigns in the Battle for the Solomon Islands

Solomon Islands Naval Campaign	Also Known As . . .	Dates (To/From)	Decisive Outcome
Battle of Savo Island	❶ To the Allied Navy: **First Battle of Savo Island** ❷ To the Imperial Japanese Navy (IJN): **First Battle of the Solomon Sea**, or *Dai-ichi-ji Soromon Kaisen* (第一次ソロモン海戦)	8–9 August 1942	***Tactical Japanese Victory*** Results (Allies): 3 CAs sunk; 1 CA and 2 DDs damaged Results (IJN): 3 CAs lightly damaged.
Battle of the Eastern Solomons	❶ To the Allied Navy: **Battle of the Stewart Islands** ❷ To the IJN: **Second Battle of the Solomon Sea**, or *Dai-nichi-ji Soromon Kaisen* (第二次ソロモン海戦)	24–25 August 1942	***Stalemate/Tactical Allied Advantage*** Results (Allies): 1 CV damaged; 20 aircraft lost. Results (IJN): 1 CL, 1 DD, 1 AT sunk; 1 CL, 1 AVP seaplane tender heavily damaged; 75 aircraft lost.
Battle of Cape Esperance	❶ To the Allied Navy: **Second Battle of Savo Island** ❷ To the IJN: **Sea Battle of Savo Island** (示島沖海戦)	11–12 October 1942	***Tactical Allied Victory*** Results (Allies): 1 DD sunk, 1 CA and 1 DD damaged. Results (IJN): 1 CA and 3 DDs sunk; 1 CA damaged.

Battle	Date	Results
Battle of the Santa Cruz Islands	25–27 October 1942	**Tactical Japanese Victory/Allied Strategic Advantage**
❶ To the Allied Navy: **First Battle of Santa Cruz** ❷ To the IJN: **Battle of the South Pacific** (南太平洋海戦)		Results (Allies): 1 CV and 1 DD sunk; 1 CV and 2 DDs heavily damaged, 81 aircraft destroyed. Results (IJN): 1 CV and 1 CL heavily damaged; 99 aircraft destroyed.
Naval Battle of Guadalcanal	12–15 November 1942	**Strategic Allied Victory**
❶ To the Allied Navy: **Third Battle of Savo Island Battle of the Solomons Battle of Friday the 13th** ❷ To the IJN: **Third Battle of the Solomon Sea**, or *Dai-san-ji Soromon Kaisen* (第三次ソロモン海戦)		Results (Allies): First Phase (13 Nov): 2 CLs, 4 DDs Second Phase (14–15 Nov): 3 DDs Results (IJN): First Phase: 1 BB, 1 CA, 2 DDs, 7 ATs, Second Phase: 1 BB, 1 DD, 4 ATs beached.
Battle of Tassafaronga	30 November 1942	**Tactical Japanese Victory**
❶ To the Allied Navy: **Fourth Battle of Savo Island** ❷ To the IJN: **Battle of Lunga Point** (ルンガ沖夜戦)		Results (Allies): 3 CAs sunk; 1 CA and 2 DDs damaged. Results (IJN): 1 DD sunk; 1 CA damaged.
Battle of Rennell Island	29–30 January 1943	**Tactical Japanese Victory**
❶ To the Allied Navy: **First Battle of Rennell Island** ❷ To the IJN: レンネル島沖海戦		Results (Allies): 1 CA sunk; 1 DD damaged. Results (IJN): 12 aircraft lost.

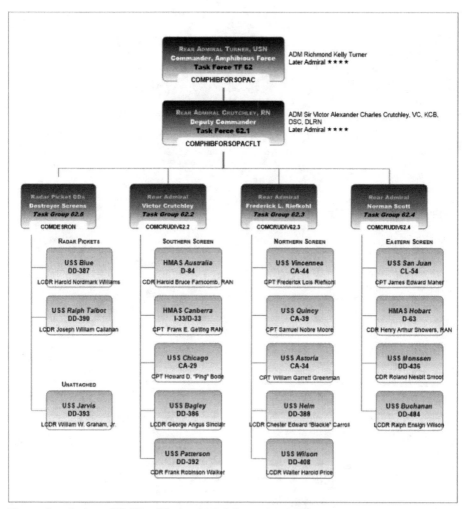

Figure 3. Order of Battle: Hierarchical Command Structure: Allied Forces

Pre-Battle Posturing: Organizational Chain of Command: IJN Forces

In contrast, shown in the organizational chart below is a top-down view of all Imperial Japanese Navy's forces under the able command of Vice Admiral Gunichi Mikawa. The command structure reflects the order of battle for the IJN admiral's combined CRUDIV6 and CRUDIV18 attack forces on the night of 9 August 1942, as both stealthily approached the highly desirable island stronghold of *Gadarukanaru*—the quaintly nominated Japanese linguistic approximation of the name "Guadalcanal" itself.

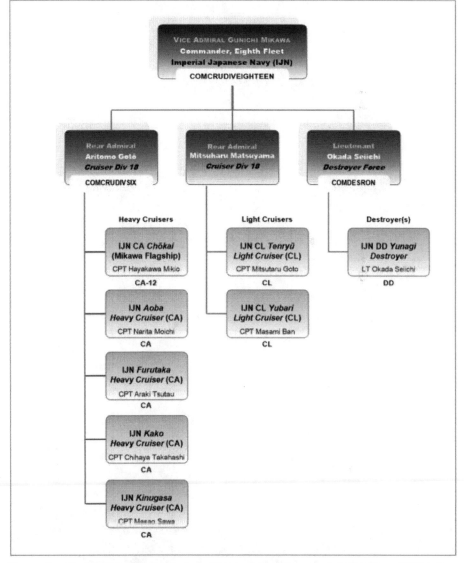

Figure 4.   Order of Battle Posturing: Hierarchical Command Structure: IJN Forces

CHAPTER 2

The Battle Main

Of Gambit and Prelude: Mikawa's First Morning

Early on the morning of 7 August 1942, it was a bit muzzy, and mildly irritated VADM Gunichi Mikawa was too soon roused from sound sleep in his flag quarters at Rabaul—this even as the first of the American Marine divisions began landing at both Tulagi and Lunga Point (and *that* almost to the very minute of his very awakening). At a hardened age of fifty-three, Mikawa was quintessentially both the soft-spoken intellectual and the thinking man's admiral—cautious to a fault, perhaps, but never quick to anger—a man willing to take the calculated risks while also keeping all options before him tabled, open, and available at all times. Now, however, into the emotional mix of anxiety and great disquiet, Mikawa's own communications staff officer, CAPT Teraoka Hadai, himself stepped cautiously out of the shadows of the bridge like a ball of wrangled nerves, weighted down by the very news he knew he carried. And well might he have been reluctant to deliver that news but, as such, also knew he must. Whether conveying that bad news to the good Admiral Mikawa, however, would later itself kill the messenger still remained to be seen.

For now it was but a reserved and heavy-eyed Gunichi Mikawa who quietly read the taut communiqué with seeming confidence and an outwardly calm demeanor. Shortly, the Japanese commander would hand off the incoming report to his advisor and ad hoc chief of staff, CAPT Toshikazu Ohmae—ever standing by the man's side—even as the junior officer himself winced at its very contents. And both men knew on the instant that they did indeed clearly understand the tenor and full import of the message they now held. In full, that message read, "Tulagi under severe bombardment from the air and sea. Enemy task force (sighted as) one battleship, two carriers, three cruisers, fifteen destroyers and 30–40 transports spotted."

At this news, the admiral is said to have bolted upright, enraged at the daring and very audacity of the foolish (and thought to be greatly inferior) Americans and incensed at the very "encroachment" itself by that enemy, into a territory he had hoped to fully occupy himself. On the instant, then, he quickly parsed out the firm action orders that would now fully mobilize his flotilla of warships.

"Wake the staff," was all Mikawa would say. "Arrange for all charts and maps. Find out the disposition of our forces here and at Kavieng!" the admiral ordered. "Be swift, and be thorough!"

Perhaps at this time—and in this very place, Mikawa might clearly have thought to himself, *might it indeed be Japan's final and most decisive showdown with the enemy's own weak and dispirited naval fleet. And I myself shall become the instrument of that very destruction!* In fact, it would gladly be his clear duty to do so—perhaps even his finest hour, to eliminate that force in full, once and for all. And, as always, the *Rengō Kantai*—the great "Combined Fleet" of the Imperial Japanese Navy itself—would lead the naval charge forward and emerge victorious in battle yet again. And, much as expected, the tattered banner of its great "Rising Sun" would once again flutter crisply in the breeze of its own advance, as even now the battle-hardened ships of his mighty Eighth Fleet set forth to skirmish with a soon-stunned and bewildered enemy who only foolishly now lay in the pathway just ahead of them.

Soon to be a formidable foe and opponent to the American naval fleet at Guadalcanal, and already a veteran cruiser commander and an avid proponent of naval night-fighting tactics, Mikawa quickly fired off a series of dispatches to his alerted crews. Irritated by the very impudence of the American "gatecrashers" at Guadalcanal—and by the very encroachment itself—Mikawa quickly deployed a contingency of *Mitsubishi* G4M1 "Betty" bombers and Aichi D3A "Val" dive bombers from his Rabaul-based 25th Air Flotilla, and hotly threw them at the open-sea areas in and around the Sound.

With calculation and a certain dead resolve, the admiral even ordered in what few submarines he had in his command to redeploy to the outskirts of the battle zone to await further orders, then hastily assembled a small force of naval infantry from the Sasebo Special Naval Landing Force as well. All must indeed be made ready, the admiral must clearly have thought. And within but a few hours of having received the mobilization order itself, those very infantry units—and all of their equipment and supplies—were already being put aboard the large troop transport and supply ships and heading south "at best speed" to counter the American landings. And on the instant, Mikawa's great cruisers had already stealthily moved off and quickly put to sea.

Pleased now with both his actions and his decisions, the admiral turned to pensively cast a cautioned look out at the haze and overhang of his gray-lady morning, then summoned together the great IJN cruisers—the "lights" and "heavies" of his own Eighth Fleet—a force known as the Outer South Seas Force, a warship unit that was itself made up of both Cruiser Division Six (CRUDIV6) and Eighteen (CRUDIV18). Now his task group would attack and bring the fight directly to the enemy, with an initial strike force that would boast of his own flagship *Chōkai*, and the CLs *Tenryū* and *Yūbari*. Augmenting this already formidable surface force would be RADM Aritomo Gotō's CRUDIV6 ships as well, as the CAs *Aoba, Kako, Kinugasa,* and *Furutaka* would soon themselves arrive from their own northern portages at Kavieng.

Leaving the perfectly shielded Simpson Harbor in New Britain, the small task force would rendezvous at 1300 hours, with VADM Mikawa converging all ships with only brief ceremony near Cape St. George. Perhaps as a last-minute consideration, even if never a great advocate of the smaller destroyers (DDs) themselves, the good admiral reluctantly added the battered, aging destroyer *Yūnagi* to the flotilla mix as well, soon bringing his surface fleet total up to some eight ships in full.

Mikawa would now himself spearhead the attack and orchestrate the bold thrust to the south. Hoping for the very *best* of all possible outcomes but preparing for the very *worst*, Mikawa quickly boarded his own flagship at 1430 hours on the afternoon of 7 August, and his great *Chōkai* and the other ships of the Imperial armada slowly made for the open waters just off New Georgia Sound. For the IJN, this would be the "head and spring" of a long and circuitous journey to the south, down through the Slot and into Iron Bottom Sound . . . and the First Battle of Savo Island might itself be only hours away.

Of Gambit and Strategy: Mikawa's Best Night

Dawn would find Mikawa's stealthy and formidable force of light and heavy cruisers heading well to the south from points north, from the large IJN naval stations both at Kavieng and at Rabaul, just north and east of the Papua/New Guinea mainland. For now, however, it was but an edgy and ever-watchful Gunichi Mikawa who "only nervously picked at a small bowl of rice and sipped at a cup of lukewarm tea," contemplating a launch of his seaplanes for a quick (and wholly self-assuring) reconnaissance mission. The admiral soon did so, and multiple pontoon-bottomed F1M "Pete" floatplanes were shot at quick speed down their short and stubby catapults and launched from the decks of the massive *Aoba* and *Chōkai*. Then the good admiral waited . . . and waited . . . and waited. The night was stifling and oppressively hot, broken only by its own series of violent and intermittent rain squalls that seemed to loom up again and again just south of Savo, and that already seemed to slash at the very topmasts of his large ships, tossing his fleet rudely about. And yet the ships sailed on, punching through the ruffian waves with but a single fell purpose and dead intent—that of Attack! Attack! Attack! on the great American fleet that was already known to be just ahead of them.

The IJN strike force pushed south over the waves, plowing a heavy trough over the black and roiled seas, and did so for the most part undetected. Mikawa, ever the cunning cruiser commander and tactician and a careful weigher of thought, now nervously paced the bridge, more like a caged panther or shackled tiger—sauntering back and forth, back and forth—while awaiting word from the two groups of scout planes he had sent out seemingly "hours" earlier. Anxiously he awaited the incoming reports from the scout planes themselves, and was soon given to ask the tough questions that he almost feared having answers for: *Where were the American carriers? Indeed, were they even nearby? What was the enemy's strength and force deployment? How close were they? Should he even press on with the attack?* In full, and simply viewed: *What are the stakes, and what is the best gamble?*

A lifelong mariner and career officer of the Imperial Japanese Navy—and a man already well in favor with the good Admiral Isoroku Yamamoto himself—Mikawa was still quite eager to demonstrate the value of his cruiser force in successfully executing its planned series of naval night actions. An avid proponent and a sharp supporter of all such night naval tactics and engagements, the admiral had always been more "architect" than "theoretician"; so now indeed could be his time—his best chance to put all of his theories to good effect and optimal testing. He would move guardedly over the next few hours—and would do so on cat's paws with but a single dread and weighty purpose, the better to increase his own tactical advantage to achieve his greatest of all desired ends: a full element of surprise and the utter annihilation of the American fleet!

By 1000 hours, then, the first of *Aoba*'s reconnaissance floatplanes would finally return with its initial report of "an enemy battleship, four cruisers and seven destroyers," reportedly seen just north of Guadalcanal. Some thirty minutes later, a second plane would return and would itself then report of having seen at least "fifteen transports." The game was now well afoot, the quietly assured Mikawa might clearly have thought to himself even as his great Combined Fleet continued in its stealthy push to the south, as the shrewd Japanese admiral jockeyed his battle fleet into position to carry out only the first of this night's "twin" attacks.

Now other scout planes returned, one after the other, with each soon reporting "two" Allied ship concentrations, split into either two or three formations and set in screening positions both north and south of Savo Island. By 1642 hours, on the eve of the great Savo attack itself, Mikawa signaled his battle plan to all ships in column. That battle plan itself was simple and fourfold: to ❶ execute a force penetration through the passage south of volcanic Savo in a "single-line column-ahead" format, and then ❷ attack the enemy transport and landing ships off Guadalcanal, concentrating on the hotly contested Henderson Field, followed by ❸ a sweep north in the direction of Tulagi and Florida Island to attack any of the enemy's remaining ships by raking them with both gunfire and torpedoes, concluding with ❹ a measured and careful withdrawal back up the Slot through the darkened approaches north of Savo. And all of it—*all* of it—without obvious or undue detection of that force.

The great warships of Mikawa's own CRUDIV6 and CRUDIV18 would sail on in their classic line-ahead format—each warship carefully positioned at short 1,300-yard intervals—each lightly jostled and tossed by the turbulent waters just north of Savo. Of curious note, in the wake of each of his ships trailed the always revealing marine life form *Noctiluca scintillans*—plankton-feeding single-cell organisms that each generated an eerie blue bioluminescence, and the good admiral could only pray that the simple cytoplast "Sea Sparkles" would not at all give away his ships' nighttime positions, but he could not know for sure. In the end, there was little he could do about it, and so Mikawa simply forged ahead at best speed to reach his objective before his position might ever be exposed, even partially, by the biological phenomena that could lead to the very detection of his fleet by any reconnoitering ships or forward scout planes that might have been sent out by that opposing Allied Navy.

Finally, sometime near 1630 on the afternoon of 8 August, purely as a precautionary measure in preparation for the battle that was soon to come, Mikawa ordered all ships to jettison any unneeded topside flammables that might later prove hazardous in battle, should any of his warships be struck by return fire. A few minutes later, the alert signalmen aboard the admiral's great flagship *Chōkai* now clackered out one final message to all ships in convoy: "In the finest tradition of the Imperial Japanese Navy, we shall engage the enemy in night battle. Every man is expected to do his best."

Then the attack would commence almost immediately, with great *Chōkai* leading the *Kaigūn* charge forward herself. At approximately 0112 hours, even as his ships sailed abaft of the northern edge of dark Savo, Mikawa abruptly changed course, setting his convoyed ships into a simple column-ahead formation that then moved his fleet slowly over to a new heading of 160°. Six minutes later, at about 0118, the admiral would do so again, this time steering his attack column over to new heading 180°, by 0120 back to 150°, and again in the next minute all the way back to an even more radical 110°—all of it designed to slip detection by the very enemy forces he knew must still be out there, understanding clearly that he must also desperately avoid the 100-fathom line mark that lay couched just off the southern edge of the bottle-necking, mid-channel island of Savo. After all, the good IJN flag officer might surely have mused to himself, his ships getting bogged down in the shallows off Savo would not at all serve his purpose at the moment, and so the good admiral ensured that all of his prowling cruisers remained well on the alert as they skirted the squat, volcanic island with a wide, wide berth, but continued on to the south and east nonetheless undeterred.

Mikawa's ships would do so for the better part of the next few hours, with seeming ease and no overt detection, then boldly sauntered out into the upper reaches of Iron Bottom Sound to seek out any targets of opportunity. Puzzled by the very ease of his passage and surprised at his "great good fortune" up to this point in time, the admiral found that he need not wait very long at all to find those enemy ships—that is, unless they found him first.

The Juggernaut Clash: Attack on the Southern Screen

The ferocity and quickness of the attack itself would be astonishing; a matter of some deep and reaching study for many years to come. Entire naval strategies would be reengineered because of its outcome; existing naval night-fighting tactics would all go back to their respective "drawing boards" seemingly overnight, and new leading-edge technology in radar detection—that would itself seem incredibly ahead of its time— would be introduced and ushered in quickly on the heels of its very occurrence: that of the defeat of the great Allied naval fleet at Guadalcanal during the course of the battle at Savo. It would at once be that swift kick in the pants and that one harsh wake-up call and—trailing behind only the attack on Pearl Harbor itself—it would also be a sharp blow to the midsection and America's *second* black eye. In fact, it would be the First Battle of Savo Island.

The morning was now that of 9 August 1942—at a stroke of the clock past midnight—even as elements of VADM Gunichi Mikawa's Eighth Fleet had just completed their long journey south, pitching and yawing lightly in low seas as the force boldly moved into New Georgia Sound. The carefully guarded passage was itself but a sluicegate channel that would now carry his force through an area that was already called the Slot—then enter a murky, dark-water zone that would later be known to history by a quite different name—as even now a calm and blissful Sealark Lane would forever be changed to its far more ominous moniker of Iron Bottom Sound.

Fifteen military warships of the U.S.-led coalition fleet now sailed as a deterrence and a sharp counterforce in waters west of Tulagi and sortied out into the Sound. The flotilla moved crisply through the night air, now cruising with a slow and measured push out to the safety of open waters. The contingency of warships would this night include eight light and heavy cruisers of the Allied force—and at least as many destroyers—all tasked with setting a multi-ship screening force to block Mikawa's approach to Guadalcanal and the Sound.

In sharp contrast, Mikawa would commence his attack with only a force of some seven ships, the IJN heavy cruisers *Chōkai*, *Aoba*, *Kako*, *Kinugasa*, and *Furutaka*; the light cruisers *Yubari* and *Tenryū*; and a single destroyer, *Yunagi*. Their sole aim and hot objective would this night be quite simple: conduct probative forays into the Sound and attack the American transport and screening ships at anchor at both Tulagi and Honiara at mainland Guadalcanal, then bomb the hell out of Henderson Field.

Early on the morning of 9 August, therefore, just after a dark, hot, and sodden midnight, Mikawa's fleet would quietly navigate past the radar picket patrols laid out by the American screening ships *Blue* and *Ralph Talbot* and then saunter unchallenged into the Sound. Truly, it was all about timing and sweet opportunity—with only a pepper-sprinkle of surprise and undeniable good luck. And on this night Mikawa clearly had both, and indeed his ships truly owned the night.

The IJN naval forces sailed silently along at 30 knots, slicing through dark, wave-capped seas, past volcanic Savo with little effort, moving in close quarters and pushing forward in a classic line-ahead format. Then up went the distant, red-and blue-lit range-finding shells that were even then being fired from the decks of the IJN ships just over the near horizon. Down came the illuminating flare orbs, dropped from the airborne floatplanes that had been launched from his large cruisers; now rang out the shots in the dark, and the starshell flares began to pop, an action that would itself later be reported as simply "having the lights suddenly turned on, as with the flick of a switch." Mikawa's mighty cruiser force had thus arrived, the fight would now be hotly joined, and the savaging skirmish of the First Battle of Savo Island would be well under way.

From the very outset, the good IJN admiral's orders had been clear and quite specific, and the seasoned naval officer knew precisely what must be achieved, and in

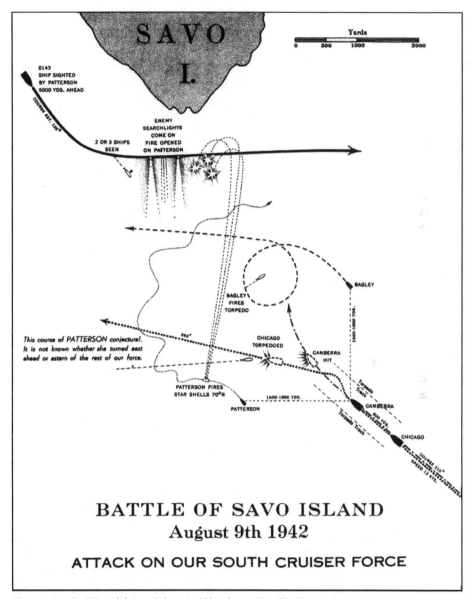

BATTLE OF SAVO ISLAND
August 9th 1942

ATTACK ON OUR SOUTH CRUISER FORCE

Figure 5. Battle of Savo Island: Attack on the Southern Screen

what time frame, and understood clearly what was at stake . . . and by 1600 hours on the eve of the attack, Mikawa would relay the following communiqué to all ships at large within his battle fleet:

> On the rush-in we will go from S. [south] of Savo Island and torpedo the enemy main force in front of the Guadalcanal anchorage; after which we will turn toward the Tulagi forward area to shell and torpedo the enemy. We will then withdraw north of Savo Island. In the finest tradition of the Imperial Navy, we shall engage the enemy in night battle. Every man is expected to do his best.[1]

By 0125 on the morning of 9 August, with his force still fully intact, undetected, and once again relishing a keen element of surprise, Mikawa entered Iron Bottom Sound just south of Savo—the dark, volcanic island now itself some 20° off his ships' port bow—and then slowed his speed from its previous 28–30 knots. With confidence, he pressed the men on to victory and released all ships in his charge, allowing them a greater degree of autonomy and freer movement, the better to operate independently of his own flagship: *Chōkai*. By 0131, Mikawa received the stark warning he had long awaited from his lookouts high aloft the *Pagoda* mast of his own flagship, "Ship's hull down to port!" and then issued his now-famous command of "All ships attack!"[2] By 0138, the ships of his force would spot the first of the Allied heavy cruisers at short distance and steel themselves for the tide of coming battle.

Mikawa's attacking warships swept down deep now into enemy waters, well below the relative safety of blackened Savo, and moved south toward the cargo and transport anchorage areas near Lunga, Honiara, and far Tulagi. Having already sluiced freely past the unawake "gatekeeper" picket lines set by the two radar ships USS *Blue* and USS *Ralph Talbot*, Mikawa trained out all batteries on the first of the two enemy ships, *Blue*, said to then have "more than fifty guns"[3] locked on that lone picket patrol ship at all times. However reluctant the IJN admiral may have been to do so, had either ship twitched or given even the slightest indication that they had spotted his fleet, he would, without hesitation, have blown them both clean out of the water without a second thought.

Moving on to the next leg of their journey, the Imperial Japanese Navy surface fleet now slipped deftly past the crippled *Jarvis*, the lone American destroyer that had been damaged only the day before in a previous action on 7 August, and that was now departing the area for emergency repairs in Australia. There would quickly ensue a minor skirmish and an exchange of gunfire between the exiting *Jarvis* and at least two of the lag-end ships in Mikawa's column, yet none of the ships would later acknowledge any appreciable hits being scored during the course of that brief action. Next would be the *Bagley*-class DD *Patterson*, another of the destroyer escort ships flanking the armored cruisers *Canberra* and *Chicago* as they patrolled the southern reaches of Sealark Lane, close in to Lunga Point and the X-Ray transport area. The attack on the Southern screen would soon be triggered, and the assault would be nothing if not abrupt, well timed, and well executed for almost all of the Allied ships involved.

On this, noted author and naval historian Jack D. Coombe would himself vividly recall the stage being set for just such an attack, in his historical recounting of his own experiences aboard the American destroyer *Patterson* itself—and of the events of the time in his book, *Derailing the Tokyo Express*:

> It was black as pitch, hot and oppressive, with occasional rain squalls jogging through the area, and flickers of lightning dancing in the clouds. It was one of those nights spawned in hell precisely for the kind of trouble that was soon coming.[4]

Already well on the alert, it would in fact be that same *Patterson* that would be first to spot the approaching enemy ships, and as early as 0143 it had already sighted a dusky silhouette of what would later in fact prove to be the *Aoba*-class *Kinugasa* itself—that heavy cruiser then at a distance of some three miles off her starboard bow. In the curt span of minutes only, however, the brave *Patterson* would indeed soon find itself caught up in the fight of her life and compelled to work at a fever pitch to repel the sudden attack by Mikawa's now fast-moving Japanese fleet. Then, as if to add to the *Patterson*'s even greater disquiet, she and the very cruisers she had been tasked with protecting were now all dangerously lit up by the overhead IJN starshells and orb flares, also aided by the shipboard searchlights. Soon the luckless *Canberra* and *Chicago* would become so well illuminated that they were already being hit from just the first barrage of highly accurate HE rounds fired from the large guns of the encroaching Japanese cruisers themselves.

Virtually all of the Allied warships in Admiral Crutchley's Southern screen would be targeted by Mikawa's task force—and this much for the duration of the full battle itself—but it would especially be the combined attacks of the *Chōkai* and the *Furutaka*—both centered entirely on the now-stricken *Canberra*—that would later prove most damaging to that Allied Southern force.

Only minutes after illumination, therefore, the two IJN heavy cruisers opened with all 8-inch guns on their port batteries, scoring direct and impactful hits on the stunned Australian cruiser. These series of attacks would be quick and deadly, impeccably timed and prosecuted with a near-practiced perfection, and only the first series of shots would even be "probative" in nature, set to only locate and zero in on the enemy ships. Then would fall the dread iron hammer itself, in the form of the many dead-on hits from just its second volley alone from the many guns on Mikawa's perfectly positioned ships.

All of these secondary and follow-on attacks were being launched from the two nearest Japanese cruisers only—from the dread *Chōkai* and the *Tenryū*—and were indeed direct hits all. And now two more attacking ships, RADM Gotō's *Aoba* and the *Kako*, also loomed up over a short and darkened horizon at precisely that moment to join in the attack. The brave *Canberra* would not at all stand a chance, even at the moment she was alerted by the sudden evasive actions and offensive posturing of the *Patterson* itself, and she, too, quickly swung into action—but perhaps not quickly enough. Her captain, the experienced Frank Edmund Getting, now brought *Canberra* hard over to port and boldly tried to run a line of interdiction to keep his own ship between the attacking Japanese fleet and those of the other Allied heavies (and the very cargo and munitions ships he had been tasked with safeguarding imprimis).

Sadly, however, before Getting could even train out his own guns to engage the fast-closing enemy fleet, the first of the incoming shells had already quite found him, and began falling near and around his ship, many landing deadly aport of *Canberra*'s current position. The initial assault was led by Mikawa's CRUDIV18 ships, with even deadlier follow-on attacks brought to bear on the hapless Australian cruiser in a renewed action by Gotō's own *Aoba* and even a fourth heavy—the CA *Kako* itself. All were heavily armed with a complement of fourteen 8-inch main and 5-inch second-ary guns, and as many as eight 24-inch torpedo tubes that both housed and fired the dreaded *Type 93* Long-Lance torpedoes. The combined number of ships might easily have involved some seventy guns in full.

All of the IJN attacks would, for the moment at least, be focused on Getting's *Canberra*—the lead ship in the Allied column just ahead of the *Chicago* itself—which in only the first three minutes of the initial attack alone—the enemy had already scored some twenty-four hits combined; at one point even from a distance of only one nautical mile. These early hits alone would take out virtually all of *Canberra*'s bridge and kill the ship's gunnery officer outright, while also leaving Getting himself mor-tally wounded and slumped on the command deck of his own cruiser. Here, history would in fact record the brave captain as refusing to even leave his post and indeed remaining on station, while further insisting that the other wounded men aboard the sinking ship be seen to first, before accepting medical aid for himself. The courageous and selfless captain would finally be evacuated to a nearby American hospital ship but would ultimately succumb to his own grave wounds. Regrettably, the brave captain was only the first of three such senior officers (Getting, Moore, and Greenman) of the Allied fleet who would be lost in the heated actions that would take place that night.

Now little more than a mangled wreck that, through some unseen miracle of fate, still remained afloat, the *Canberra* could no longer train out her own her guns, nor could she engage any of her main batteries. And with no appreciable steerage and little maneuverability, she was now jolted with a severe list to starboard by the severity and harshness of those very attacks. With virtually all of her communications equipment knocked out, the *Canberra* could not warn any of the other Allied screening ships in the Sound of the very action taking place, even at the moment it unfolded. Now, having done with the *Canberra* itself—with an astonishing nineteen torpedoes fired at her, though none recorded as hitting her—the Japanese cruisers left that ship engulfed in flames and reeling from the number of centered hits from the big guns on at least four heavy cruisers within the Mikawa column. Now the massive IJN warships locked their combined 8-inch batteries to port almost in tandem and focused quickly on the second Allied ship in line—Bode's own USS *Chicago*.

Moving rapidly to its highest alert status, *Chicago* snapped to almost on the instant, now quickly alerted by the night-shredding illuminants fired by the IJN ships, and *Canberra*'s own puzzling quick-turn from port to radical starboard only moments before in its lead position just ahead of them. Reportedly, it was even at this point that *Chicago*'s own gunnery officer had offered to open fire on select targets fairly immediately but Bode would himself belay the order on the spot as soon as he arrived on the bridge, opting instead to launch only illuminant starshell flares to obtain a greater survey of the bizarre, time-shuffling events unfolding before his very eyes. To the skipper's greater misfortune, however, many of those 5-inch starshells simply misfired—and neither deployed nor discharged as intended. Even as the ship's gunnery crews scrambled to reload with live shells, all sensed that it might already be too late for *Chicago*.

At 0147, the American cruiser's worst fears would be realized when a single *Type 93* Long-Lance torpedo—later identified as having probably been fired from the *Kako*—would strike the stunned *Chicago* "with a savage jolt" that rocked it to its very hull. The bow-shot torpedo hit would, in and of itself, not be a killing blow to the ship, but Bode and *Chicago* must surely have been fearful when they saw yet a second track from yet another inbound torpedo. With the oft-inconstant, always-fickle Lady Luck standing well on their side, however, that second torp would in fact strike the ship, but would oddly never explode. *Chicago* had been spared a killing fate like that suffered earlier by the vaward *Canberra*, but even that just barely. For the very moments following this same action would now bring about one of the most enigmatic of all events that might unfold, and for which the later battle at Savo would come to be known. The good CAPT Bode—in his enthusiasm to engage any of the enemy ships that were seemingly attacking his column from all sides—apparently began a pursuit of a "phantom contact" he only thought to be that of an IJN warship that had previously fired on him and the Southern force.

Chicago's "ghostly" contact—later thought to have in fact been the destroyer *Yunagi*, at the lag end of Mikawa's exiting column—would inexplicably lead the captain on for some forty minutes as he slowly maneuvered his now-crippled *Chicago* far to the north and west on a curious heading of 2-6-3, chasing only a horizonal blur that either might or might not have been that of a distant enemy warship.

At battle's end, and by the time Bode did return from his mysterious forty-minute trek to the northwest, *Canberra* was already succumbing poorly to her mortal hits, and it was later even suggested that the Australian cruiser might actually have been mistakenly slammed by one or more torpedoes fired by an all-too-nervous *Bagley*—or perhaps even the nearby *Patterson* itself—both of which had been the very escort DDs previously flanking her in Crutchley's initial Southern screening force. On this, even the noted naval historian Samuel E. Morison, in his own studied view of the battle at Savo, would have this to say on the feasibility of this same "*Bagley* Incident":

Bagley, whose crew sighted the Japanese shortly after *Patterson* and *Canberra*, circled completely around to port before firing torpedoes "in the general direction of" the rapidly disappearing Japanese column; one or two [torpedoes] of which may have hit *Canberra*. *Bagley* would play no further role in the battle.[5]

A heavy toll would be exacted, and *Canberra* would alone suffer that payment in full. With a full fifth of her complement of 819 men either killed outright or badly wounded, the Australian ship's end might now fully be in sight. By 0330, the destroyer *Patterson* would slowly pull alongside the stricken *Canberra* and inform the remaining senior officers aboard that ADM Turner, finally reacting to the news of the attacks at Savo, had issued the order that would seal the Australian ship's fate for good: if the now heavily listing *Canberra* could "not repair herself and achieve mobility on her own," she must be scuttled at once and sunk in place. And, despite the best efforts of the men aboard that Australian cruiser to counter the raging fires and check the damage already suffered, all hope was finally abandoned, and the remaining crewmen were removed and simply ordered off the battered warship. The intrepid Australian heavy cruiser must simply be sunk in situ.

An hour later, by 0430, *Patterson* would still be found bustling about her arduous tasks of recovering survivors from the stricken *Canberra*, but would be abruptly pulled away from even those duties by yet another sudden action to the north. The small but plucky destroyer was now again simply doing what she had been tasked to do all along—so she increased speed and pursued the contact with a grave intent to engage. In short order, even though shots had been exchanged between the two ships, oddly all would miss—itself perhaps a clear blessing in disguise, indeed, once the approaching warship was in fact identified only as the wayward *Chicago* herself, just then returning from her imprudent jaunt to the north. She had been gone for the greater part of forty minutes and had truly missed all but the opening gambit of the battle itself. Bode's *Chicago* would now return in time only to see her compatriot Australian ship go down but could do little else to assist the stricken ship itself, and so stood by and prepared to take on as many survivors of the sunken ship as she might be able to rescue.

Patterson, having disengaged from her quickened "false attack" on *Chicago*, now resumed her search-and-rescue activities back near *Canberra* and was soon joined on station by the radar picket *Blue*, both of which then assisted in an even greater recovery operation in and around the location where the Australian ship had last been seen. At sad end, however, the brave *Canberra* could not at all be saved and, on quiet orders from ADM Turner himself, the USS *Selfridge* (DD-357) would draw the short straw and be tasked with sinking the Australian cruiser. The defiant *Canberra*, however—perhaps fixed with her own staunch resolve to survive—would seem to have none of it and would still not be sunk, even after a reported 263 5-inch shells had been pumped into her, and four torpedoes targeted at the ship.

Instead, a second destroyer would need to be dispatched to finish the job that the *Selfridge* could not, and the USS *Ellet* (DD-398) now swept in and fired a spread of torpedoes of her own, this time with maximum effect on the ill-fated Australian heavy cruiser. The *Canberra* would heave a final weighty sigh, its twisted metal creaking and groaning in its own death throes, and sink at a position reported as an estimated 9°12'29" S–159°54'46" E, where the stricken ship remains to this very day.

In so doing, she would be among the first of many Allied and IJN ships that would be sunk in battle, and that would only too soon dot the very bottom of Iron

THE BATTLE MAIN 23

Bottom Sound, indeed becoming the very reason why the name itself would even be applied to the area. Gone now was the sweet and peaceful autograph of Sealark Lane, as once indeed it might have been called by the local nationals, and ushered in harshly in its stead was the ever more sinister name of Iron Bottom Sound.

At end, the attack on the Allied Southern force had been swift and ruthless, yet even it was but an icy forewarning of what was still to come. Both the *Chicago* and the *Patterson* had been damaged, and the *Canberra* had herself been mauled to a point of no recovery. The crafty commander of the Japanese cruiser divisions, Gunichi Mikawa, the calculating and well-fleshed naval night fighter himself, now only cautiously relished his victory over the Allied cruisers, then cautiously swung his still-intact fleet about and began heading back up the channel to his next targets of opportunity, the unsuspecting ships of RADM Riefkohl's own Northern screening force. The American heavy cruisers that made up that secondary screening group had no inkling as to what was just about to befall them, and even fewer could have known that they might not at all survive the battle—or the very night itself. And thus the secondary spiked mace would now also fall and be so effectively used against the unsuspecting ships of the north as well.

Table 2. Southern Screening Force Casualty Assessments

ALLIED SOUTHERN SCREENING FORCE ELEMENTS	
SHIP ASSET	CASUALTY ASSESSMENT
HMAS Canberra (D33) *County*-class heavy cruiser	Of a complement of 819, 84–85 KIA; 109 wounded.
USS Chicago (CA-29) *Northampton*-class heavy cruiser	Of a complement of 1,100, only 2 reported KIA.
USS Patterson (DD-392) *Bagley*-class destroyer	Of a complement of 158, reportedly only 10 KIA; 8 wounded.
USS Bagley (DD-386) *Bagley*-class destroyer	Of a complement of 251, *no* reported casualties; abbreviated contact with enemy only.
HMAS Australia (D84) *County*-class heavy cruiser	Of a complement of 815, no casualties reported. The heavy cruiser *Australia* would remain with RADM Crutchley at the X-Ray transport area after the *McCawley* conference, with no involvement in any of the actions concentrated on either his Southern or his Northern screening forces, on the occasion of the night battle of 8–9 August 1942. Crutchley would return on his CA *Australia* the next morning and played no part in any of the previous night's battles.

The Juggernaut Clash: Attack on the Northern Screen

On the very shank of night, early on the morning of 9 August 1942—but a hot spark after midnight—five military warships belonging to the United States Navy sailed off the coast in waters west of Tulagi, in the Solomon Islands, and moved slowly out into Iron Bottom Sound. The small naval contingency moved crisply off into the night and up through Sealark Lane with a slow and measured push to the northwest, locked on a straight-line nautical heading of three-one-five-True—well on their way to set the Northern screen at Admiral Crutchley's request. It would not be long however, in a mere thirty-one minutes of intense night fighting on the high seas, that of five warships now sauntering into harm's way, only two would survive the battle—and the night. And, with the conclusion of this brief action, it would now constitute much of the battle main and the attack on the Northern screen.

Beginning at about 0150 hours, the five heavily armed warships of the Northern screen, consisting of the American heavy cruisers *Vincennes*, *Quincy*, and *Astoria*—in tandem with two escort DDs, the *Helm* and *Wilson*, bracketing each side—all would come under a sustained heavy naval bombardment and "Long-Lance" torpedo attack from the IJN naval forces that had amassed in the area. Subsequently, all three heavies would suffer crushing torpedo impacts and numerous direct hits from the big guns of the Japanese *Chōkai*, *Kako*, and *Kinugasa*—all now being fired on at near point-blank range and cleverly illuminated by overhead flares, starshell orbs, and shipboard searchlights.

The net effect and tragic outcome of this brief but volatile naval encounter for control of the Slot—and an area that would later come to be known as simply Iron Bottom Sound, as well as all access points into and out of Guadalcanal—would be the critical loss of all three American cruisers (in the Northern action alone), and the loss of the Australian cruiser *Canberra* in the earlier Southern action, as well as the crippling of the *Chicago* itself.

Then, history would ignobly—and almost suspiciously—sweep it all under the carpet, and now only a very few driven souls, surviving veterans, dedicated historians, and researchers alike, can even remember what might actually have occurred at that time, and in that place.

The hapless USS *Quincy* went down, claiming the lives of some 370+ men (see also the later informative endnote). The brave captain, Samuel Nobre Moore, would himself be counted among the many souls that would be lost that night.

The dauntless *Quincy* would perhaps best be remembered for her dogged fighting spirit and her indomitable will in the face of such overwhelming odds. It is said that many of the men simply remained where they were and waited for the waterline to rise up and meet them, before they stepped off the sinking ship into the tepid, dark waters of the Sound, then sight unseen—and indeed with many never to be seen again.

A rudely awakened American fleet was even then still shaking off its torpor and reluctant drowsing and was perhaps a moment too slow in responding to the open-

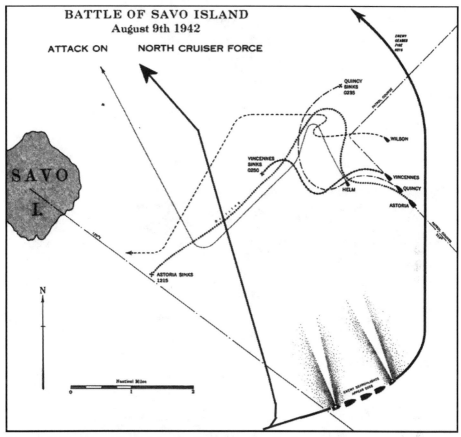

Figure 6. Battle of Savo Island: Attack on the Northern Screen
(Photograph courtesy of the Office of Naval Intelligence)

ing salvos of Mikawa's attack. Concerned that the ships might in fact be elements of Crutchley's other Southern fleet—and thereby indeed "friendlies"—the good Admiral Riefkohl, battling at the helm of the beleaguered *Vincennes* itself, was loath to engage the attacking ships lest in his uncertainty he might also fire on any of his own comrade warships.

Now fading ever deeper into the night, the *Quincy* was itself closely tailed by another of her sister ships, the American CA *Astoria*, with each tagging dutifully behind the already illuminated *Vincennes*. In mere moments, all three ships would be fired on unmercifully by virtually all of Mikawa's heavy cruisers and lost in a mere "minutes-long" battle that would take place on the very shank of night. And, once the dust had settled thick after storm, of four Allied heavy cruisers sunk that very night, the appalling casualty totals would quickly mount to a horrific peak of some 921 men that would all go down with their ships—and this just for the Northern screening force.

Table 3. Northern Screening Force Casualty Assessments

ALLIED NORTHERN SCREENING FORCE ELEMENTS	
SHIP ASSET/CLASS	**CASUALTY ASSESSMENT**
USS *Vincennes* (CA-44) *New Orleans*–class heavy cruiser	Of a complement of 952: reportedly 332 killed.
USS *Quincy* (CA-39) *New Orleans*–class heavy cruiser	Of a complement of 807: reportedly 370–389 killed.*
USS *Astoria* (CA-34) *New Orleans*–class heavy cruiser	Of a complement of 899: reportedly 219 killed.
USS *Helm* (DD-388) *Bagley*-class destroyer	Of a complement of 158: *no* reported casualties.
USS *Wilson* (DD-408) *Benham*-class destroyer	Of a complement of 251: *no* reported casualties.

CHAPTER 3

Piercing the Bamboo Curtain

FACTORS CONTRIBUTING TO THE AMERICAN AND ALLIED NAVAL LOSSES

Findings, Events, and Chronology

After a studied and wide-ranging review of events as they must have occurred during this set time frame, the following findings and observations of the events surrounding the First Battle of Savo Island are offered for both student and collective researcher review. It is also my explicit hope that all such findings can serve as a historical accounting of the great naval defeat suffered by the American and Allied naval force at the hands of VADM Gunichi Mikawa's IJN Eighth Fleet. To this end, a particular emphasis has been placed on the multiple causal factors accounting for the critical loss of the four American and Australian warships, from ❶ a lack of any viable area strategy or fully articulated battle plan to ❷ extant communication factors and means of early-warning notification (or, indeed, perhaps a lack thereof), to ❸ incompetence in captaincy, to ❹ that of just "plain old rotten luck"—all converging in one battle— one brief and highly volatile night engagement at Savo Island itself. What follows, presented in a finely tuned chronological order, is a compendium of discussion points and seemingly "unimpeachable truths," as pointed up in the following twenty-one fact-based observations and findings of what at least is known about the causes and effects of the 1BOSI.

FINDING 1:   AS ABOVE, SO BELOW: THE AMERICAN ATTACK
              SUBMARINE USS *S-38*

7 August 1942, 1800 Hours

*Premise: Failure of the American attack submarine USS S-38 to adequately report
the approach of the Mikawa Task Force in a timely and actionable manner.*

They Were Not Alone: The USS *S-38* and the Detection of the Mikawa Fleet

They were not alone. On the evening of 7 August 1942, VADM Gunichi Mikawa sortied
his CRUDIV18 and CRUDIV6 battle fleets; they were not alone (at least not this day)
and not in St. George's Channel at the very top of the open, churning passage known
as the Slot. Wedged tightly between the Papua/New Guinea islands of New Britain and
New Ireland, the St. George's Channel was literally a "gateway" to the southern Solomons—and to Guadalcanal itself. Clearly, then, the area would be heavily patrolled by
spotter aircraft, surface ships, and submarines lurking in the very deep—both on the side
of the Americans and the IJN. And, much to the advantage of Mikawa's surface force,
even the weather had (up to this point in time, at least) been ideal for his advancing
Japanese attack force, with a moderate to heavy cloud cover that now oafishly collided
with a confluence of intermittent thunderstorms to effectively create a gray and dismal
screen between his ships and any enemy assets attempting to detect his approach.

    Having earlier departed from Rabaul with his own Cruiser Division 18
(CRUDIV18), Mikawa soon joined up with RADM Aritomo Gotō's own CRUDIV6
out of Kavieng, and ordered both groups to rendezvous in the St. George's Channel
for a seemingly threefold purpose: ❶ to rest up and set all of his order of battle formations; ❷ to wisely await an all-enshrouding nightfall to further conceal his ships' very
movements; and ❸ to make final preparations for their all-out attack on enemy shippage in and around Guadalcanal. Mikawa was fairly convinced, and deeply hopeful,
that he had not in fact been detected by any of the enemy's scout planes or surface
ships, since indeed stealth and the masking of his ships' movements would have been
foremost in the commander's mind. He had dodged two Hudson reconnaissance
planes of the RAAFR back at Kavieng and had a safe passage of his strike force up to
his moving through the narrowed straits that skirted the larger islands of New Britain
and New Ireland. His second point of detection would now be an American attack
submarine patrolling the area that could itself only too quickly become his very undoing and foil his entire plan of attack.

    It would, in fact, be LCDR Henry Glass (H. G.) Munson who was in command
of the *S*-class diesel-electric submarine USS *S-38* (SS-143) that night. The *S-38* diesel
"Pigboat" had already been patrolling an area just south of St. George's Channel for
some two days now, between the dates of 7 and 8 August 1942. Cruising on a fixed
patrol corridor, Munson had repeatedly navigated up and down on a straight-line run
from waypoint 320° to 140° (T), with a loop-back to the previous position to repeat

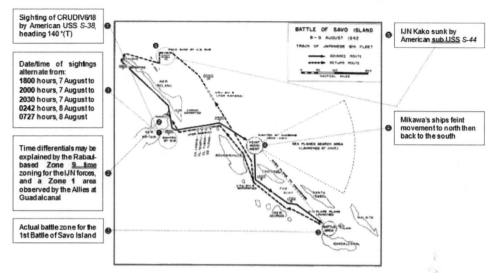

Figure 7. IJN Approach through the Slot: Detection by the Submarine USS *S-38*

yet another patrol leg. The essentially linear search pattern that Munson's sub now followed had been designed specifically to locate and interdict any (and all) IJN fleet traffic passing through the inescapably narrow Channel, whether surface ship or submarine, as so indeed it did on the morning of 7 August.

At about 0600 hours, Munson's alert *S-38* crew began to detect the stealthy approach of a small task force made up of "several unidentified surface ships" some six miles south of the St. George's Channel (seen as ❶ in Figure 7), reportedly so close to the passing convoy as to almost stumble on it. Indeed, it was too close to even fix a target on or to fire on them without carelessly exposing his own ship's position. The captain of the *S-38*, therefore, did the only other thing he could do under the circumstances: he called in the sighting and routed the dispatch to his own command at COMSUBDIV5 (Commander, Submarine Division 5). In fact, Munson's message that day would read in full, "Two destroyers and three larger ships of unknown type, heading one four-zero true at high speed, eight miles west of Cape St. George."[6]

On at least this occasion, Munson could not at all have known that he, too, had been sighted by the Japanese surface fleet, even as the Japanese themselves were not wholly certain whether the American sub had seen them. Yet both had. CAPT Toshikazu Ohmae, at the time a military affairs liaison officer from the Bureau of Naval Ministry, and Mikawa's acting chief of staff aboard the flagship *Chōkai* on the occasion of the battle at Savo, himself noted the following in his own memoir: "As darkness approached, an enemy submarine was detected to the south, and we altered course to the east to avoid it, which we did successfully."[7] Much as the later Naval War College's operational account of the 1BOSI had also observed the reaction of Munson and his *S-38* sub, later alleging in their own discourse that they "could take no offensive action against them [the southbound IJN convoy], for his port motor panel had failed and he was engaged in repairing it in a position clear of the Channel."[8]

With the distance greatly shortened between his sub and Mikawa's passing fleet, the key element of surprise that his sub might previously have enjoyed—and his ship's own damaged port engine affecting his ability to either catch up with or engage that enemy—Munson resigned himself to not investing an attack at that time against the larger surface fleet passing just before him. As a result, he essentially had but two options remaining: shadow or flight. And, since S-38's port engine panel had become compromised in a previous action, he could neither give chase after the fast-moving IJN column nor even depart the area without exposing himself and having to engage that enemy force at that time. As the engine might itself have been fairly stammering with noises—serving only to dangerously reveal his position—Munson's decision to leave the area at once with best speed might in fact have been well founded and was perhaps the skipper's best course of action at the moment.

But what of the message sent by S-38 to its COMSUBDIV5?

Sadly, the lack of "any real urgency" on the part of COMSUBDIV5—and little responsive action by the regional naval commanders at Guadalcanal on receipt of the report from S-38—may have only compounded the fact that the raising of an alarm would be very slow to occur. And if indeed true, could not such an unwary action have contributed to the surprise attack imprimis—and to the later loss of four capital ships within the Allied surface fleet itself? In point of fact, the intel for Admiral Turner—the commander most in need of the information, on which he might fully have based his own reactive defense strategies—would not reach that admiral's desk until 0700 hours on the next morning. By that time, that same intel would now regrettably have been quite stale and would come only long after the attack at Savo itself. In full regard, therefore, perhaps as history would soon itself reveal, it was already far too little, and far too late.

The plucky LCDR Munson, however, would forge on in the many battles across the Pacific, both well before (and even after) the debacle at Savo. For only hours after first sighting Mikawa's cruiser divisions in the St. George's Channel, the brash skipper of the S-38 boat would sight a second surface ship formation surging to the south that same day. This would undoubtedly have been RADM Takatsugu Jojima's own "Reinforcement Force," made up of cargo ships traveling under the aegis of an armed six-destroyer escort commanded by RADM Aritomo Gotō himself.

The good LCDR Munson, on the occasion of that second patrol, was indeed finally able to locate, target, and plot a viable solution out to at least one of the passing ships and would indeed "take the shot," sinking the 5,600-ton auxiliary transport *Meiyo Maru* with a two-torpedo spread as it cruised the narrowed passage through the Channel at a last-reported position of 04°52' S–152°42' E. Pleased with his victory, but also wary of counterattack, Munson would slowly turn his sub back to the south and west and, by 22 August, began a long and arduous trip back to Brisbane, Australia, for much-needed repairs. His arrival there would mark the end of the USS S-38's seventh War Patrol.

For his heroism and unflagging, commendable service aboard the S-38, the later USS *Crevalle* (SS-291), and the USS *Rasher* (SS-269), LCDR Munson would be awarded all of the following medals and ribbons for his unparalleled service as one of the most aggressive and successful of submariners:

- The Navy Cross (with three separate awards that Munson would later option as only one Navy Cross with two Gold Star devices), for combat submarine duty during the heated years of 1943 and 1944
- (1) Presidential Unit Citation (PUC) ribbon
- (1) Navy Commendation Medal
- (2) Letters of Commendation (LOCs)
- (1) Commendation ribbon with two stars and a Combat "V"
- (1) American Defense Service Medal (with Bronze Star device)
- (1) Asiatic-Pacific Campaign Medal with two "Operations" stars
- (1) American Campaign Medal
- (1) World War II Victory Medal
- (1) China Service Medal
- (1) National Defense Service Medal
- (1) Korean Service Medal, and
- (1) United Nations Service Medal

One of the most highly decorated submarine commanders of his time—and perhaps even to our present time—LCDR H. G. Munson would go down in history as perhaps the first American "eyes and ears" to have witnessed the approach of Mikawa's cruiser divisions on the morning of 7 August 1942. That the message back to his COMSUBDIV5 HQs base command would be deemed by his superiors as not being a priority item, and would not be sent in time to save either the men or the ships that would later be lost in the deadly battles south of Savo, would in and of itself be a matter of some mild controversy and dispute for some many years to come, but decidedly none of it could ever be faulted to LCDR Munson.

FINDING 2:   EARLY WARNING: THE AUSTRALIAN HUDSON
             RECONNAISSANCE PLANES

Clearly, no one single event stemming from the First Battle of Savo Island in August 1942, stands out more strikingly than the apparent overflights of two (of three) Royal Australian Air Force Reserve (RAAFR) Lockheed Hudson reconnaissance planes of the 32nd Squadron. Without question, the hot debate and harsh dialogue noted over this one issue seems to be ongoing and has indeed persisted from that time to the present day. Other than the very losses themselves of both the men and the ships in the later battles resulting at Savo, no other salient discussion point of World War II has caused quite as much a stir as this famed "Tea and Crumpets" argument, an argument that would so scandalously rock the world—and a much-angered America in 1942 and 1943—with its heinous implications that elements of an RAAFR airborne search force, sent out to guard Port Moresby, New Guinea, and the many passage points surrounding the great sluicegate at St. George's Channel, would have spotted the Mikawa task force but would not report their sightings until much, much later. In full, that debate would almost always be focused on the sighting of VADM Mikawa's IJN CRUDIV fleet on the morning of 8 August 1942—by at least two of those Australian reconnaissance planes from that RAAFR 32nd Squadron—and their critical delay in delivering that sightings intel.

Figure 8. Australian (RAAF and RAAFR) Lockheed Hudson Reconnaissance Aircraft

8 August 1942, 1025 Hours (1st Hudson—Sighting Reported)
8 August 1942, 1103 Hours (2nd Hudson—Sighting Reported)
8 August 1942, Unknown (3rd Hudson—No Sighting Reported)

Premise: The failure of two (of three) Australian RAAFR Lockheed Hudson reconnaissance planes to adequately report (in a timely and actionable manner) the approach of the Mikawa Cruiser Division Task Force.

ACCEPTED THEORY: Reportedly only two of three Hudson reconnaissance aircraft would actually spot (however inadvertently) the approaching IJN cruiser division force in the vicinity of St. George's Channel—both of which even conducted brief overflights of the sizable surface fleet—with some of the planes even being fired on by those same Japanese warships. In at least one instance (with Flight A16-218), it is known that a brief outgoing radio message was indeed sent back to the Fall River Air Base at Milne Bay, New Guinea; however, the second Hudson sighting—after repeated first-moment attempts to contact its base with the information failed—would allegedly only later report the sighting on its return to that airfield. There would still be no immediate send of the intelligence data, nor any outgoing advisement for some time, and the message would only be received at a much later time—regrettably, well after 2100 hours.

Later, in the face of the highly successful Japanese attacks prosecuted against RADM Crutchley's Southern and Northern screening forces at Savo on 9 August, bitter—often vituperative—accusations would surface about the pilots and crews of the Hudsons themselves, with a vile innuendo of their having placed in abeyance their reporting of the enemy ship sightings until it was virtually too late to prevent the attack at all. Sadly, this would shortly, and seemingly thereafter in perpetuity, result in the infamous "Teacup Controversy"—alternately known as the "Tea and Crumpets Affair." In this latter, rather presumptuous interpretation, it is even alleged that at least one of the Hudson pilots involved was accused of returning to base and "delighting in his tea and crumpets" before routing his critical intel to the Americans at Guadalcanal. It is not surprising, then, that this stinging, insulting innuendo would be so rudely perpetuated for years and would go on to almost develop a life of its own, even to this very day, and would indeed become quite a heated tempest in a teapot—in this event, perhaps with full pun intended.

Still, the difficult but well-mannered arguments continue to the present day among a brave but diminishing band of researchers, remembrancers, and recorders of naval history, and indeed among the few remaining proud veterans who themselves still stand to their former times of good service aboard ships like the *Vincennes*, the *Quincy*, and the *Astoria*. Even after more than eighty years, one can still find ready evidence arguing both for and against the allegations hurled at the two Hudson overflights just prior to Savo, on a number of blogs and discussion fora online. *Technology* is now the new catchphrase and popular buzzword, and much has indeed changed in the ensuing eight decades since 1942, but perhaps some killing half-truths might still remain entirely inescapable.

RAAFR Overflights: Sightings Data

Perhaps to more fully enlarge on any good argument—either for or against any degree of culpability on the part of the Australian RAAFR pilots in not warning the Guadalcanal-based Allied forces of their sightings of Mikawa's ships in a timely manner—clearly a basic understanding of the nature of those overflights might well be in order. The matter of what they saw, or perhaps did not see—and the manner in which that information was digested, handled, and disseminated—could all be of equal importance. Therefore, one might easily infer that it was not just a matter of what they saw but also when they saw it—and what action was taken by those crew members thereafter.

Shown in Table 4, therefore, is a high-level overview of each of the Hudson reconnaissance overflights themselves, with each providing key information for each of those flights, approximate sighting dates and timelines, and even a brief précis of actions taken at the time of the sightings (or as soon thereafter as possible). Following that, the Table 5 matrix will itself provide even greater detail on just what was reported by each of the aircraft back to their Fall River base. Finally, the reader will be further invited to review a concise series of map illustrations that are set to provide an even more solid fix on the actual area of reconnaissance, and of the overflights themselves.

Table 4. RAAFR Hudson Reconnaissance Aircraft Sightings Matrix

RAAFR HUDSON RECONNAISSANCE AIRCRAFT SIGHTINGS OF MIKAWA FLEET (8 AUGUST 1942)					
FLIGHT #	**TIME**	**POSITION**	**COURSE/ SPEED**	**PILOT**	**ACTION**
Hudson Reconnaissance Flight ❶					
A16-218 *32nd Squadron*	8 August 1942 1025 hours	**-4°59' S × 156°07' E**	120° @ 15 knots	*Stutt*	Geddes radios report of sighting at 1026 hours. Allies receive report 2 hours, 16 minutes after sighting.
Hudson Reconnaissance Flight ❷					
A16-185 *32nd Squadron*	8 August 1942 1101 or 1103 hours	**-5°42' S × 156°05' E**	120° @ 25 knots	*Williams*	A16-185 returns to base at 1404 to avoid breaking radio silence. It is 9 hours, 46 minutes before report is received by Allies.
Hudson Reconnaissance Flight ❸					
A16-157 *32nd Squadron*	No sightings report	No sightings report	N/A	*Milne Holland*	Holland attempts radio contact but cannot establish contact due to "skip distance and area."

Table 5. RAAFR Hudson Reconnaissance Aircraft Reporting Matrix

RAAFR HUDSON RECONNAISSANCE AIRCRAFT REPORTS (8 AUGUST 1942)		
HUDSON FLIGHT CREW	**DATE/TIME OF SIGHTING**	**REPORT SENT**
Coastal Reconnaissance Aircraft RAAFR Flight **A16-218** *Stutt, Geddes, Courtis, Bell* Search Mission FR623/Patrol Sector "B"	**8** August 1942 1025 hours	**COMSOWESPAC SitRep #330** *"Three cruisers, three destroyers and two seaplane tenders or gunboat. Course 120°, speed 15 knots."*
Coastal Reconnaissance Aircraft RAAFR Flight **A16-185** *F/O Mervyn Williams* Search Mission FR623/Patrol Sector "B"	**8** August 1942 1101–1103 hours	**COMSOWESPAC SitRep #080947** Upon its departure, the A16-218 Hudson is in fact spotted by the *Chōkai* and assumed to be the same aircraft they had spotted earlier. Williams on the A16-185 Hudson then reports the following: *"Two heavy cruisers, two light cruisers, and one small unknown type (ship)."*
Coastal Reconnaissance Aircraft RAAFR Flight **A16-157** *F/L Lloyd Milne, Holland* Search Mission FR623/Patrol Sector "B"	**8** August 1942 Unspecified	**COMSOWESPAC SitRep # Unknown** Reportedly did not see any IJN cruiser division ships in its patrol sector, but reported: *"Being fired upon on three separate occasions by single Japanese warships, but not a full surface force."*

RAAFR Overflights: Report Filings

Here, for reasons not entirely understood, neither of the first two reports were successfully relayed to the Allied fleet in Tulagi until much later (at about 1839 and 2136 hours, respectively) on the night in question. Oddly, even when finally received by Turner, the reports would still be somewhat discrepant with an earlier report that may also have been confusing to the American commander, which read as follows: "Aircraft reports at 2325Z/7Z: 3 cruisers, 3 destroyers, and 2 seaplane tenders, or gunboats, at position 05°49' S 156°07' E—course 12°(T)—speed 15 knots. At 0027/8Z, 2 subs at 07°35' S 154°07' E—course 15°(T)."[9] The second report itself appears to provide an almost identical presentation of the same information:

> Air sighting 0001Z/8, position 05°-42'-South–156°-05'-East. Two cast, affirm two cast love one small unidentified. One cruiser similar [to] *Southampton* class. When plane attempted correct approach, ships opened fire. At 0120 slant eight, sighted small merchant vessel at 07°-02'-South–156°-25'-East; course 290, speed 10 knots.[10]

Yet, little known to the Americans at the time, or even afterward, a third such report would surface many years later, one based on the observations of CAPT Toshikazu Ohmae himself, the extant Military Affairs liaison officer and acting chief of staff, serving with VADM Mikawa right on the bridge of the great flagship *Chōkai* itself on the morning of 8 August 1942. Here, Ohmae acknowledged not just one but possibly as many as *two* Hudson overflights (although it might appear from his statement that the Japanese were not entirely certain whether it was in fact the same plane) when he noted the following in his own 1957 recounting of events as they occurred:

> While pursuing a southeasterly course some thirty miles northeast of Kieta, we observed an enemy Hudson bomber shadowing us at 0825. We made 90-degree turns to port to throw him off immediately after the sighting, and headed back to the northwest. When the Hudson withdrew to the north, we reversed course at once and at 0845 recovered all seaplanes. While they were being brought on board, we were spotted by yet another Hudson, flying quite low. Salvoes from our eight-inch guns sent this observer on his way, and we resumed [our] course for the Bougainville Strait.[11]

RAAFR Overflights: The Maps

The author was now determined to locate a firm posit on both RAAFR sightings and to fully plot each on a viable map with highly visible reference points. The result was the representation noted in Figure 9—generated both by latitude and longitude, as reported by the crews of the Hudsons. Now, of course, being fully empowered to use present-day Internet researching skillsets, and Google map enhancement technologies, it was indeed possible to posit a good fix on both location reports. The first reported sighting by Stutt on the A16-218 reconnaissance flight is cautiously approximated in the outlay as being plot ❶, while the second A16-185 flight, filed much later in the Flight Officer (F/O) Williams report, is represented here as plot ❷. In either event, it would seem that the accuracy of this first map is in fact clearly upheld by the plotting of a second map as well, as shown in Figure 10.

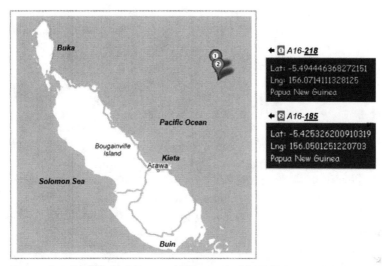

Figure 9. RAAFR Sightings of Mikawa's CRUDIV6 and CRUDIV18

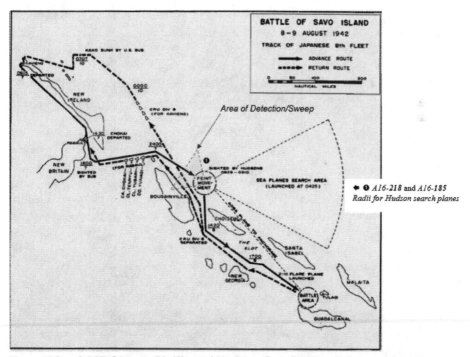

Figure 10. CAPT Ohmae Plotting of Hudson Overflights on 8 August 1942

That map would in fact be the very sketch developed by CAPT Ohmae himself,[12] a senior liaison officer on Mikawa's own *Chōkai* from 1942 to 1943, one who had served with the good admiral, leading charge after charge from the commander's own flagship, and would indeed have been present on the days in question from 7 August to 9 August of that year.

Clearly, this second map could almost be a perfect overlay for the first, and it is quite apparent that, at some point during Mikawa's "rest-up" period off the eastern coast of Kieta, his force was indeed spotted by enemy aircraft—in this event by both the Stutt and the Williams reconnaissance planes, respectively. Also clear from Ohmae's account is the fact that the Japanese apparently also knew of the planes, and had even surmised just what types they were, referring to both sightings as having "observed an enemy Hudson"[13]—and later as having "been spotted by yet another Hudson."[14] Still, the Ohmae map unquestionably provides far greater detail than the previous map, and even incorporates an overlay of the IJN CRUDIV column track as they progressed to the south, as well as the full search radii for both Hudson planes at the time.

RAAFR Overflights: A Dibbling of Wings and the Confounding Delays

The undue delay in the transmission (and receipt) of the sightings intel from the two Hudsons may, in and of itself, not have been wholly causal to the tragedies visited on Crutchley's ships later that night, but it would nonetheless result in the loss of four capital ships of the Allied surface fleet and, regrettably, almost 1,100 men who would also be lost in the stunning surprise attacks launched by Mikawa's undetected cruiser force in Iron Bottom Sound. Had those enemy forces in fact remained undetected, or had they indeed been seen at some far earlier point? This would be among only the first of many such haunting inquiries that would later heatedly be asked in the wake of the debacle at Savo.

It should be noted that each of the RAAFR flight leaders—Stutt, Williams, and Milne—had only loosely been tasked with a critical mission to "search for Japanese submarines and surface craft activity," presumably in and around the Fall River area but extending out in a radial arc that covered all of the narrow choke-points between the islands of New Britain, New Ireland, and Choiseul. According to Stutt and Geddes on the A16-218 flight, they not only had been spotted by the enemy fleet by as early as 1020 but had even been fired on by some of the larger ships. Therefore, allowing for some extremely tense moments that must surely have followed, Stutt had to first wait to clear the zone of attack before he was even able to break his radio silence—which radio silence had already been mandated to all pilots by the Fall River commanders overseeing those very flights.

Once fired on by several of Mikawa's fleet assets—his presence and position now fully compromised to the ships below—Stutt then ordered Geddes to in fact break radio silence and send his message "in the clear." Geddes would do so at 1026 hours. Then, some thirteen minutes later, at 1103—at almost precisely the same lat and long coordinates as the first sighting—F/O Mervyn Williams would spy the same formation of surface ships moving steadily southbound on a projected heading of 120° (T), and he, too, would report having been fired on by at least one of the large Japanese warships. As Ohmae himself would later confirm in his own writings, "we were spotted by another Hudson flying quite low. Salvoes from our eight-inch guns sent this observer on his way, and we resumed [our] course for Bougainville Strait."[15] This could only have been Williams in the second A16-185 flight. When both men sent their messages—or at least attempted to send their messages—both would only receive a delayed response from base headquarters to either acknowledge receipt of the report or seek additional operational instructions. It would later be determined that in great measure this result would be due to several overwhelming (and seemingly unavoidable) reasons, as noted below:

❶ A strict order had just that morning been issued for a total radio blackout by the Fall River base command at Milne Bay, even prior to the planes' departure, which order would have effectively disallowed all of them from initiating any radio contact at all. ❷ From a period of time from 1032 to 1100 hours—based on actual entries in signal logs that are still in archive in Townsville, Australia—the entire radio network at Fall River would have been shut down for some twenty-eight minutes due to an air raid alert that was in progress even at that precise moment. Finally, ❸ the entire air base (and surrounding environs) was for the most part socked in and blacked out by a series of fast-moving electric storms known to have been ravaging the area at the time, which must clearly have exacerbated the nonreceipt of the messages in full. Both flights, therefore, could only do the next best thing possible: depart the immediate area of sighting itself and return at best speed back to their base to report the finding. For Stutt, the return leg of that flight back would take more than *two* hours in total—for Williams, even longer.

After his own harried sighting, Stutt would have been most concerned with dodging the heavy anti-aircraft fire that must have even then been coming at him from the large AA guns on Mikawa's cruisers. Therefore, only once he had successfully averted the attack would he swing his A16-218 about in a tight arc and bank steeply back over the jutting mountains of Bougainville to head for the open waters of the Channel. Regrettably, only moments after having done so, a spotter on his Hudson would take note of two large, unidentified surface vessels moving at speed through the Channel. Deciding to break off his hastened return to base to further investigate the new contact—apparently one or more surfaced subs—Stutt swept down and came in low to cautiously approach both contacts. It would not be long until he and his crew would clearly spot the now all-too-familiar "Rising Sun" insignia emblazoned on the sides of both sub conning towers that appeared to now be coursing slowly on a steady heading of 1-5-0, in a position approximated to have been about at 02°35' S–154°0' E.

Therefore, with critical and time-sensitive intel still in hand, and still waiting to be routed to the Allied forces in the south, Stutt decided to engage either (or both) of the "discovered" submarines—and did so with only mixed success—reportedly dropping two "stick bombs" in the area where the Japanese *I*-class subs had been seen. Only after he had imprudently prosecuted both attacks did Stutt finally turn back to a course that would take him to his home base. Now, accounting for the sixteen-minute delay caused by the attacks on the two subs, Stutt would finally touch down at Milne Bay at 1242, fully two hours and sixteen minutes after the time of the actual sighting of Mikawa's fleet earlier in the day.

So where, then, might that same IJN fleet be by now?

Counterbalanced against Stutt's previous actions, F/O Williams's bearing and conduct in the face of the sightings he had himself noted on his own A16-185 over-flight might equally be called into question when, after repeated attempts to contact his base with the sighting intel, he was censured and told not to break radio silence at that time. Williams would therefore do as he was told by his base command: hold the report in full and simply proceed ahead on his normal patrol course. Whether wholly unfathomable or simply ill advised, the critical delay in the reporting of the sightings data he had in hand would only later become evident. Once back at base, however, it is further reported that F/O Williams would also have an encounter with a particularly scrappy and unconvinced debriefing officer at Milne Bay, which seemed to entirely result in a considerable squabble and a "loud row" between the two. Williams's report would regrettably therefore not get on the air until a full nine hours and forty-six minutes after the fact—and it would not even reach RADM Turner's CTF 62.2 flagship command for some ten hours in full, and even then only after filtering down through other command levels.

Whether through a series of technical problems with area communications, un-avoidable weather factors, power outages, or extant blackouts known to have been plaguing the areas in question, the simplest (and perhaps most convenient) rationale always seemed to come back to some level of benign neglect of the Hudson crews.

Well founded or not, history seems to have continued to walk its way and, with furrowed brow, still casts its stony gaze on the men of A16-218 and 185. In fact, to this very day, it would be a cruel and unforgiving past that would not so soon abort its age-old complaint against the Australian reconnaissance planes that "could have gotten the word out to the Americans in time" but did not. Even if but a simple fail-ure on the part of the pilots to fully understand the consequence and grave import of the very intel they held in their possession, and the absolute time dependency of the reports—and of getting the data to those most in need of it—the event itself would become at once both a lightning rod and a divining rod, with one attracting worldwide criticism and reproach and the other putting forth a finger of *implied* guilt that to this day still foolishly points at the crews of the RAAFR Hudsons. In a later, compiled list of possible causal factors for the tragic defeat at Savo, however, it is curious to note that the "Australian Hudson Overflights" discussion points still rank well within the top-five factor models of true culpability for the later actions and losses, as seen in this summarized fault-finding matrix in Table 6.

RAAFR Overflights: Invective and Scathing Broadsides

Aside from the sharper, more immediate inquiries that would soon be demanded by a disgraced, affronted, and still-grieving U.S. Navy—and truly the nation at large—it would not be long after the Savo attacks that *key* answers to *key* questions would be hotly solicited from those thought to be most responsible for the losses of 9 August. America wanted answers and demanded to know just *what* had happened—and *how*—as, indeed, a taut spectrum of military investigators, naval analysts, government oversight agencies, and even the Average-Joe onlooker in the years between 1942 and 1943 now all slammed a hard fist down on the desk, demanding to know both causation and culpability. Who, after all, was to blame for this—and how could it even happen in the first place? Clearly, heads would have to roll, and all that remained was finding out whose.

Culpability would only too quickly be found with immutable roots to many different causal factors for Savo: from an overall lack of preparedness on the part of the Allied surface fleet to an inability by those forces to sustainably conduct effective naval night engagements to the foremost finding itself—that of an almost total lack of any advance warning or benefit of surveillance discovery. Ships had indeed been sighted on 8 August, it would later be determined, but in almost every event, the reports filtering back about those sightings would either arrive so late as to not at all be "actionable" or were flawed entirely by misrepresented, often understated enemy strength reports coming back from the reconnaissance curtain that had only loosely been drawn around the Solomons. Not only had the two B-17s of Espiritu Santo filed their report (of actually having seen nothing), but the American attack sub USS *S-38* had also done so, as had the two Hudson planes as well—with all of those stale intel reports arriving so late as to essentially be of no intrinsic value.

RAAFR Overflights: At Whom the Finger Points—Laying a Foul Blame

The stage was now set for the delving reports and scathing analyses that would only later surface when released by (then) LCDR Samuel Eliot Morison and as commissioned by the Roosevelt administration and erstwhile Secretary of the Navy (SEC-NAV) William Franklin Knox. The findings would be both far ranging and specific, and they would be grandly titled *A History of United States Naval Operations in World War II*, itself later published over the course of some fifteen volumes during the postwar years between 1947 and 1962. And, indeed, much as the dogged RADM Arthur Japy Hepburn had himself become so obsessed with and distracted by the prosecution of CAPT Howard Douglas Bode in his own deep scrutiny of the *Chicago* skipper's actions years earlier, so, too, would Morison himself become unreasonably fixed on the overflights of the two Hudsons.

Perhaps fully blinded by their own respective and committed dislikes of both the events and the people involved in those events, it is possible that each man could

Table 6. ADM Hepburn Findings: Cause and Degree of Culpability Matrix

#	Factor or Name	Degree of Culpability Findings for the 1BOSI	
		Rating (1-5)	Finding
1	**Australian Hudson Overflights**	1	Assumed perhaps the highest degree of culpability, however unwarranted, in the later Morison investigation, and only less so in the Hepburn report. The stigma of the "Tea and Crumpets" affair would thereafter sadly live on in infamy with most Americans and would render a tainted and somewhat skewed view of the pilots in seeming perpetuity.
2	**USS S-38 Submarine**	2	The report and dispatch sent by Munson's S-38 to his COMSUBDIV5 command occurred in a timely manner (or reasonably so), but would later be quashed for some period of time by that sub base command due to a perceived lack of "any real urgency." The relayed message would thereafter not be received until 0700 hours on the following morning.
3	**Espiritu Santo B-17 Overflights**	2	Two flights of B-17s apparently overflew areas around the St. George's Channel, Bougainville and Choiseul—and extending north from *Kieta*; however, Turner's CTF 62.2 would not receive either of the B-17 sighting reports until 2400, inexcusably some *eleven hours later.*
4	**VADM Robert Lee Ghormley** COMSOPAC Area	1 / 2	Highest commander in the area, and answerable for all operational activities, and the subsequent debâcle at Savo. Ghormley would be relieved of command not long after the 1BOSI itself. Although no one specific reason would immediately be given for his discharge from both his duties and his post, the harsh stigma of Savo itself may have been well evident in Nimitz's decision to replace the admiral. In form and effect, Ghormley was perhaps still a reminder of the "galling defeat" at Savo that would itself never quite go away.

#	Name / Position		
5	**CAPT Howard Douglas Bode** Captain, USS *Chicago* (CA-29)	1	Censured harshly and targeted for further investigation—and possible formal charges—based on his actions (or even *inactions*) aboard the American CA USS *Chicago* on 9 August—and its famed trek to the northwest for an unexplained period of some forty minutes—without fair warning given his own, or even Riefkohl's *Northern* force. In the face of what he clearly saw as an almost-certain tarnishing outcome with the later Hepburn Board of Inquiry, Bode would opt to simply take his own life in April 1943 before any such trial could ever be convened.
6	**RADM John Sidney "Slew" McCain Sr.** COMNAVAIRSOPACFLT	2	Cited for not continuing with the assigned (and *expected*) extended reconnaissance patrols over Iron Bottom Sound and the Slot during 8–9 August, as ordered by ADM Turner himself. He would not only *not* carry out the senior admiral's order but also never inform him that he not done so.
7	**VADM Frank Jack Fletcher** Commander, *Task Force 61*	2	Relieved of command in late August 1942 with a "no-cause" citation, then given a recuperative leave of absence. Later reassigned as COM13NAVDIST (Commander, 13th Naval District), and COMNORWESSEAF (Commander, Northwestern Sea Frontier) in Alaskan waters.
8	**ADM Richmond Kelly Turner** Commander, *Fifth Amphibious Force*	4	Negligible findings by Hepburn inquiry, since Turner had been in charge of cargo and transport unloading and amphibious assault unit deployments both at Tulagi and Guadalcanal on the night in question—and, occupied elsewhere—would have had no direct interaction with the Japanese fleet during the blue-water battle at Savo. The fighting would instead mainly center on the larger escort warships set to guard those same transport and cargo ships at IBS.
9	**RADM Leigh H. Noyes** Commander, *Task Force 18* (09/1942) COMNAVAIRSOPAC (10/1942)	3	Eyed as being only marginally culpable of any wrongdoing at Savo by Hepburn, Noyes would nonetheless later be relieved of command pursuant to the loss of the USS *Wasp* (CV-7) on 14 September of that same year. Assigned to his new COMNAVAIRSOPAC post for that South Pacific area, Noyes would only hold the post for one month, but would never again receive an open-sea command.

have fallen short in their greater assessment of the ill-starred fail-points surrounding the battle at Savo. Morison's churning and intense dislike of the Australian RAAFR Hudson crews—and (in his opinion) their marked failure to report their sightings in a timely manner to the American forces headquartered at Guadalcanal—appear to have become an all-consuming fueling-point for the chronicler Morison, further feeding his deep-seated resentment of the crews of the A16 flights for their seeming inaction—indeed when the critical information both carried might most have been needed—the end result of which would have been the Savo tragedy itself.

Admiral Hepburn indeed had his Bode, and now Morison had found his own scoundrel and fair culprit as well—the Hudson pilots themselves—a viable scapegoat that Morison himself was not at all willing to let go. Therefore, however unjustly, Morison's penned conclusions about the crews of the Hudson A16s would forever tag the Australians as those most deserving of blame for the battle at Savo. His soured findings and scalding invectives would live on in perpetuity to further haunt the crews (and families of those crews) that manned those brave planes. Morison's findings would serve to forever taint the honor of the RAAFR and further slur and disparage the pride and honor of an entire country. Precisely to this end, Hepburn's very first report would itself be nothing if not scornful and deeply inferential:

> The pilot of the Royal Australian Air Force Hudson Plane A16-218 on Search Mission FR623, originating at Fall River Field at Milne Bay, New Guinea, who sighted VADM Gunichi Mikawa's cruiser force headed south, shall remain unidentified and alone with his own conscience, as far as this writer is concerned.[16]

This situation fueled only more finger-pointing rhetoric, as noted again in Morison's continuing hot-button indictment of the A16s:

> Instead of breaking radio silence to report, as he had orders to do in an urgent case, or returning to base which he could have done in two hours, [he] spent most of the afternoon completing his search mission, came down at Milne Bay [tip of Papua], had his tea [and crumpets], and only then reported his contact.[17]

Then, in an even later Richard W. Bates account, reflected in the Naval War College report of 1950 that had itself been titled "The Battle of Savo Island, August 9, 1942: Strategical and Tactical Analysis: Part I," the author himself clearly observes the following:

> All evidence available for this study seems to indicate that the two contact reports were made after the planes returned to their base at Fall River, since both were combined into a single dispatch. The basic instructions required that each [and any] contact be reported by dispatch as soon as it was made by [any of] the planes in flight.
> This dispatch was received by COMSOPACFOR, the action addressee, and by CTF 62 on the HOW Fox schedule between 1843 and 1845. It was received by CTF 62.6 on the BELLS schedule at 1837, and on the HOW Fox schedule at 1843. Thus,

this vitally important contact report was received by the responsible commanders in the SOPAC area about eight hours and twenty minutes after the contact was made.[18]

Yet even here Bates was still not done, as he, too, continued in his detailed assessment of each of the causal factors behind the travesty at Savo:

> The report of the contact made at 1101 [by flight A16-185] was even more incomplete than the 1025 report [of flight A16-218], and did not tend to clarify an already confused situation. Why the pilot did not make a more correct report is not known. However, it may have been due, in part at least, to the fact that all five Japanese heavy cruisers had been recovering planes in widely-separated positions until about 1200, before joining up. It seems logical to assume that the Australian pilot failed to see the five heavy cruisers, but that he did (in fact) sight the *Tenryū*, *Yubari* and *Yunagi*, which latter three ships had not launched planes and had been operating as a unit apart from the other heavy cruisers.[19]

Naturally, such statements continued to provoke only more thought and engender an even greater invective that seemed to now target specific pilots on specific RAAFR flights, such as Stutt on A16-218, whom VADM George C. Dyer—author of the acclaimed *The Amphibians Came to Conquer: The Story of Admiral Richmond Kelly Turner*—heavily faulted with the delay in sending his own cautioning advisory to the otherwise unsuspecting Americans far to the south:

> He [Stutt] quite erroneously identified the seven cruisers and one destroyer that were in the waters below him. . . . [Stutt] had not only failed to identify what he saw, but failed to trail his contact and failed to report promptly. Four of the five Japanese heavy cruisers were sister ships, alike as peas in a pod from a distance.[20]

So, in the end, what did he see, and when did he see it? Furthermore, why was he not able to make a distinction between the ships he had himself already sighted?

Even in our present time, all these years later—now more than eight decades—the author was stunned to find on a modern-day Naval Warfare Simulations website forum,[21] where much indeed might still be inferred from the comments of historian Richard Morgan, as recently as 2008, in his own observation of the activities of both Stutt and Williams's flights on A16-218 and A16-185:

> Couple the two slow [Hudson] reports with the B-17 sightings on August 7th, and it shows that communication networks throughout SouthPac Air Forces to CTF 62.2 were greatly flawed. No true sense of urgency was ever apparent at Townsville, Australia, where these reports would have been received and later forwarded to CTF 63, or to CTF 62.2.

So, where indeed might the rotting carcass of full culpability lie for the losses suffered during the First Battle of Savo Island? Did the fault lie with the general degree of torpor, fatigue, and unwatchfulness on the part of the American naval screening forces at Guadalcanal? Or did it lie with the sub USS *S-38*, the B-17s, or even the two radar pickets USS *Blue* and the *Ralph Talbot*? Or would it—with a far more dangerous and sweeping hand—instead be tied to the Australian Hudson crews, forever broad-stroking and branding them with only an expedient untruth, however unfounded? Perhaps we as historians and researchers of the ships, the men, and the battle at Savo itself may never really know for certain why the myth itself continues to remain so self-perpetuating, seeming to take on a life of its own. Perhaps it is time to simply dispel the blinding myths and resolve the horrid tale of false culpability in full.

RAAFR Overflights: Response and Conclusions

Decidedly, no one hot-button issue would so influence the many topical discussion fora as those soon centered on the controversy of the pilots and crews of the Hudson overflights, even as the questions themselves continued to abound. Had they in fact been derelict in their duties in not ensuring that the extremely sensitive and time-dependent sightings intel they had indeed transmitted to the Allied commanders in the south, who were themselves most in need of that very information? Had the Hudson pilots truly been so cavalier and jaunty as to return to their base only "circuitously" and not report their findings in a more effective and time-appropriate manner? And had the crews of A16-218 and A16-185 in fact not fully recognized the gravity of those same reports, to the extent that they would arrive back at the base at Milne Bay and "seek refreshment" first before ensuring a timely dispatch of the hot intel each pilot held in hand? Indeed, was the very "Tea and Crumpets" finding in and of itself even viable, or at all even true? Or did the men of the two Hudsons simply suffer a "bad rap" over the delays in reporting the sightings of Mikawa's surface fleet? Indeed, were the men of the Hudsons in fact either wrongfully or rightfully laid open to attack and the dark innuendo of slander that they have since had to endure for so many years thereafter . . . or was the claim itself not at all true?

After a studied and cautious review of much of the data made available through multiple reference points that must necessarily include ADM Hepburn's own findings and those of the many celebrated analysts, writers, and naval historians who would follow, such as RADM Samuel Eliot Morison, VADM Joseph Wendell Dyer, RADM Richard W. Bates, CAPT Emile L. Bonnot, CDRE Bruce H. Loxton—and even CAPT Toshikazu Ohmae himself—I still find myself preeminently drawn to the writings and reasoned discourses of (former) LCDR Gregory Mackenzie, watch officer on the HMAS *Canberra* itself on the fateful night of the battle. LCDR Mackenzie (or "Mac," as he seems to prefer on his highly acclaimed *World War 2 in the Pacific* website) is a man who is still wholly assured of the innocence and "absence of malfeasance" on the part of either of the pilots of A16-218 and A16-185, and he has tirelessly devoted himself to recreating the events before, during, and even after the attacks at Savo—and to doing his utmost to amend the historical record once and for all—while simultaneously seeking a full exculpation of charges (implied or otherwise) that have for so long been upheld against the otherwise indefensible RAAFR crewmen of those same Hudsons.

Through exhaustive interviews with several of the surviving ships' complement from the ill-fated HMAS *Canberra* itself, to even those of the remaining original Hudson aircrews, Mackenzie appears both devout and sincere in his push to clear the good names of his fellow fallen comrades, themselves all from a long bygone era that is now itself some eighty-plus years past. To the expectation of LCDR Mackenzie and his modern-day online forum, perhaps only a full exoneration should be sought for the many honorable men he has encountered in his exhaustive studies, men such as Geddes, Stutt, Milne, Courtis, and Bell. Oddly, to this same end, the site even features a copy of the full four-page letter of 2009 to the president of the United States, then sent by an aging but still exasperated Sergeant Eric Geddes, the former navigator of A16-218 on the date of 7–8 August 1942. And indeed, in that same letter, Geddes clearly states his heartfelt case to the American commander in chief in full:

> Sergeants Courtis and Bell are now deceased and Sergeant Stutt—due to [an extended] illness—is a resident of a nursing home. Consequently, it remains with me to make this audacious approach for you to confirm that the real history of that sighting is the one not at all being taught in your schools, bearing in mind that for Justice [*sic*] to be served, the accused must be given the opportunity to present their case to the examining judiciary. To this day, we (the pilots and crew of the RAAFR Hudson reconnaissance planes) have not enjoyed that luxury.

Then Geddes moves on to only more clearly dispute the full absurdity of the age-old "Tea and Crumpets" allegation itself:

> [It was also] reported that when we finally arrived back at Milne Bay, we indulged in "tea and apple pie" before we proceeded to Operations to verbally report our sighting. We were at a loss to understand what war those gentlemen were reporting. It sure as hell wasn't the one we were fighting. Perhaps apple pie was on the menu for them, but we were flying daily missions of up to (8) hours in duration with only in-flight rations of 1x850 gm tin of preserved pears shared between four men, and one packet each of four dog biscuits.

So, who indeed was more correct in their assessment of the Hudsons and their later, indirect involvement in the Battle of Savo Island? Was it Morison, Mackenzie, Bates—or the Naval War College report itself? Were the pilots in fact guilty of some degree of malfeasance in delaying the sending of the advisory report of their sightings? And would a timely sendoff (and receipt) of that information have in fact resulted in a completely different posturing of the Allied naval assets in and around Iron Bottom Sound that night? If received earlier by Turner's own CTF 62.2, could some degree of (i.e., carrier) intervention have even been brought to bear to somehow alter the course of events that were yet to come? And with that sufficient warning, might Crutchley have had a greater luxury of time within which to fully rethink his planned screening deployments, and to center on only the northern approaches to Savo? The three senior in-theater admirals—namely, Crutchley, Turner, and Fletcher—would quite assuredly have had every right to expect that any such reconnaissance and discovery information—whether gleaned by sea, by air, or even by the remotely situated Coastwatchers themselves—might all be expected to indeed have a direct bearing on their strategic planning operations and screening deployments, and clearly should have been passed on to them in a far more timely, expeditious, and "actionable" manner.

Since this was not the case, it was instead left to the ordered misrepresentations and bitter (often vituperative) findings of the later naval historian Morison, who would be among the first to "officially" lay blame on the Hudson crews for not breaking radio silence to report their sightings, taking their time in returning back to base, and having tea and crumpets before debriefing. Decidedly (and quite sadly), Morison's views have more skewed than clarified the issue of the Hudson A16 sightings. His sharp invective and blunt finger-pointing may indeed have done little to ease the injustice foisted on the Australian RAAFR pilots and may have only caused others who followed in his footsteps in their own studies and writings to use an even faultier logic, thereby giving a tacit consent to his findings with an almost carte-blanche treatment, accepting them as almost "confirmed." Perhaps none of us should so slavishly follow in that line, lest we, too, further perpetuate the innuendo and half-truths that even now continue to surround the galling defeats at Savo. Perhaps indeed it is time for us to simply lift the cloak and stigma that have, for far too long, hung over the heads of the Australian Hudson pilots and crews.

During the later recovery years following World War II, it would indeed be much to the surprise of all that a quite tattered and age-worn copy of an old deck-log from Admiral Mikawa's own flagship *Chōkai* would then surface from a cloistered old naval archive in Japan. In it was found a copy of Mikawa's own "0903" time-stamped report from 8 August 1942, of a full interception of Stutt's own outgoing signal (and report) of 1026 that was sent by that pilot to Milne Bay. How odd that the Hudson pilot's own avowed enemy—the great IJN itself—would be the same party that might now bear out its own full truth and provide new evidence that could fully exonerate the Hudson men even all these years later. At long last, Stutt, Williams, Milne—and all of the crews of both A16-218 and A16-185—might at last be somewhat vindicated, and the great Morison conundrum finally perhaps set aside in full, its taut and unforgiving moments of faulty conclusion now set to rest as being entirely untrue.

Update on RAAFR Hudson Reconnaissance Planes

As noted recently by the assistant director of the U.S. Naval History Command, one Greg J. Martin, and as further reported on the Australian Broadcasting Corporation (ABC) television network on 27 October 2014, the following amending statement was released by Martin vis-à-vis the culpability of the Australian search plane pilots. It is expected that this can once and for all perhaps finally dispel the appalling myth of the "Tea and Crumpets" affair of 1942:

> This claim by Morison of the RAAF Hudson crews failing to report their sightings has now been totally refuted by Australian military historian Dr. Chris Clark, and further verified by Japanese intercepts of the signals. It has now been acknowledged by the Assistant Director of the U.S. Naval History Command, Greg J. Martin, as being a figment of RADM Morison's imagination and wholly unwarranted.

Documentation to prove that the signals were in fact sent by the Hudson crews has been found by both the Royal Australian Air Force Archive and the U.S. National Archive—and an official written apology to the last remaining crew member of the RAAF Hudson, F/O Eric Geddes, was issued by the U.S. Department of Navy on 21 October 2014. Greg Martin has unreservedly stated:

> For Mr. Geddes, the blame was not placed on him by the U.S. Navy at all, so I hope that he can rest easy now that, at least from the United States Navy perspective, the Hudson crews did all they could to provide timely and accurate information.

RAAFR Overflights: Additional Reading

For a studied, more in-depth view of the Hudson pilots' accounts, and those of the reconnaissance overflights themselves, refer to the collected information available from the following bibliographical resources:

Bates, Richard W. (1950). *The Battle of Savo Island, August 9, 1942. Strategical and Tactical Analysis.* Part I, Naval War College report (AD/A-003 037) distributed by the National Technical Information Services, a division of the U.S. Department of Commerce, and prepared for the Bureau of Naval Personnel.

Bonnot, Emile I. (1988, February). "Were the Hudsons to Be Blamed for the Naval Disaster at Guadalcanal?" Article by CAPT Emile I. Bonnot (USNR, Ret.). Historian General Emeritus, Naval Order of the United States.

Loxton, Bruce, and Chris Coulthard-Clark. (1997). *The Shame of Savo: Anatomy of a Naval Disaster.* Allen & Unwin Pty Ltd.

Ohmae, Toshikazu (Captain, Ret.). (1957). Edited by Roger Pineau. "The Battle of Savo Island." *Proceedings* 83, no. 12 (December 1957, U.S. Naval Institute). CAPT Ohmae was VADM Gunichi Mikawa's chief of staff from June 1942 to December 1943.

Also, all of the following electronic websites might be expected to provide additional, even more concise information on the RAAFR Hudson reconnaissance planes and their related overflights:

* http://www.ww2pacific.com/hudsonrep.html
* http://www.ww2pacific.com/savoupdt.html
* http://www.ibiblio.org/hyperwar/USN/ACTC/actc-10.html
* http://en.wikipedia.org/wiki/Lockheed_Hudson
* http://forums.navalwarfare.net/archive/index.php/t-449.html

FINDING 3:   EARLY WARNING: OVERFLIGHT OF THE B-17s
OF ESPIRITU SANTO (VANUATU)

8 August 1942, 1215 Hours

Premise: Failure of two overflights of American B-17 heavy bombers from Carrier Task Force 63, from Espiritu Santo, to locate and adequately report (in a timely and actionable manner) the approach of the Mikawa task force.

Never receiving quite as much rabid notoriety as that of the RAAFR Hudson reconnaissance overflights themselves, the flyovers of not one but *two* American B-17 heavy bombers—indeed, occurring not once but twice over the same approximate patrol corridor as the earlier Hudson planes—seem to have escaped the later scrutiny and blameworthiness seemingly shifted in full to the Hudson pilots instead. That there were any B-17 heavy bombers in the vicinity at all was probably as much a mystery to the average fighting man on Guadalcanal as it might have been to the men on the screening ships themselves; both were used to seeing only smaller attack and pursuit aircraft, torpedo bombers, fighters—and even the ever-annoying nightly visits from "Washing Machine Charlie" itself (see later chapter for a greater topical discussion of the latter).

Yet there was indeed a small contingency of "Flying Fortresses" nearby that had been specially adapted for use in the South Pacific, and that had been quickly assembled, deployed, and assigned to special Bombardment Groups in and around Guadalcanal. The Bombardment Groups themselves had been well dispersed throughout the many jungle islands of the southwest Pacific and had but a single operational purpose: that of supporting the overall Allied Operation Watchtower invasion of the Solomons.

Hastily deployed in small (and wholly under-strength squadrons), the B-17s would number only about fifty and were strategically dispersed throughout the region to patrol the open-sea areas around Papua and New Guinea, with bases known to have already been set on Efate, New Caledonia, Nandi, Ndeni, Maramasike Estuary, Samoa, and Tongatabu (alternate spelling of Tongatapu). One of the area's key B-17 station points, however, had to have been the airbase at Espiritu Santo, and it would indeed have been from this one jump-off point that the crews of the B-17s would most operate in patrolling the areas in and around Bougainville, the

**Figure 11.   B-17 Heavy Bombers of COMNAVAIR-
SOPACFOR—Pacific Theater of Operations**
(Image courtesy of Wikimedia Commons; File:B-17E 19 BG.jpg—
Wikimedia Commons)

St. George's Channel, Choiseul—and the sluice area called the Slot. With CTF 63–assigned Task One groups like the 26th, 42nd, 98th, and 431st Bombardment Groups, only one squadron of B-17s would stand out most prominently and—however insignificantly—play a role in the events leading up to the First Battle of Savo Island. That unit would be the 11th Bombardment Group, which indeed seemed to roster the highest number of B-17s at the time, with some ten aircraft overall.

The bomber groups themselves were then broken down into even smaller, more componential task units and further culled out to form even more localized heavy bomber "detachments" as well, such as the 11th, 67th, 68th, 69th, and 70th Bombardment Groups.

To naval historians and studied researchers of the 1BOSI, there still remains a curious flurry of questions—much in the way of discrepancy and deviation from reported events surrounding the B-17 overflights of 8 August, as noted. Item: Were there in fact two overflights, on separate and distinct missions, and two distinct patrol corridors? And what, if anything, did each patrol element see, and what did each plane report to their COMNAVAIR liaison officers on their return to base command? Further, why indeed the confounding inconsistencies found between the actual sighting dates themselves—with some accounts reporting their sightings on 7 August while still others seem to pin the activity as in fact happening on the morning of the 8th instead? Indeed, all of these questions might appear challenging and poorly resolved—enough to ask again even now, all these years later, and we may still be seeking viable answers well into the future. Clearly, none of those answers would come too easily.

What is known is that the deployment of the B-17 heavy bombers detached from CTF 63 would almost certainly have been tasked with conducting aerial patrols of a zone that spanned from the northern edge of Australia, up through the open sea-lanes surrounding Papua and New Guinea, and down into the island passages of an area already known as the Slot. In and of itself, the often-overlapping operational search zones of the Espiritu Santo B-17s on 8 August would essentially not have been any different than those of 7 August, with reconnoitering heavy bombers sent out to cruise their assigned patrol sectors each day as they searched for any significant IJN fleet deployments, force buildups, or even mass movement of ships.

On the day in question, 8 August, it might well be noted that reconnaissance Sectors I, II, V, and VI (shown in Table 7) had all remained essentially the same without much new activity reported. Sector III, however, had been somewhat modified, and Sector IV itself expanded to include an even broader range of patrol that would then run from Espiritu Santo to the Maramasike Estuary on far Malaita Island. And finally, Sector VII would itself have been an entirely new target patrol area for the B-17s, with its planes being sortied out of Espiritu Santo as well. On 8 August, then, each of the B-17 flights would be sent out as normal, with the results of each of those searches occasioning only the results seen on the next page.[22]

From the data seen in the table, therefore—and based on information presented in VADM George C. Dyer's report in his writings in *The Amphibians Came to Conquer*[23]—the B-17 flights were indeed channeled into "patrol sectors," and yet elsewhere

Table 7. Air Operations of Carrier Task Force 63 (CTF 63) for COMNAVAIRSOPACFOR

OPERATIONS OF CARRIER TASK FORCE 63 (CTF 63) AIR OPERATIONS OF COMAIRSOPACFOR—7-9 AUGUST 1942	
SECTOR OF PATROL	**FINDINGS AND DISPOSITION**
SECTOR I	Area not searched on the date in question due to severe inclement weather. No information received.
SECTOR II	Area only partially patrolled. Perimeter edges to the south not searched due to bad weather, and the northern edge searched only to an extent of some 650 miles—in lieu of its planned 750-mile radius—again due to inclement weather and poor visibility. Vector search results would all be negative, but it would nonetheless be through this very sector that Mikawa's cruiser force would later approach on its way to Savo and IBS. Reportedly, even if the B-17 had flown to the very *extremity* of its patrol sector as expected, it might still not have spotted the IJN fleet simply because that force would not even enter the sector until about 1900 on 8 August. In contrast, the B-17 then searching the area well to the south near Tulagi would arrive at that location by sunrise and might have already reached the extent of its own 650-mile patrol perimeter by 0715. Had a second patrol of B-17 reconnaissance planes been sent up with more specific instruction to in fact proceed all the way out to the extremity of their sector, those bombers might have seen Mikawa's fleet at a point somewhere between Choiseul and the New Georgia island group.
SECTORS III, VI, AND V	All areas searched with only negative results. No information received.
SECTOR IV	An area fully stretching from Espiritu Santo to the Maramasike on Malaita was searched by B-17 patrol planes that had been moved to Espiritu Santo to be closer to the operational areas in and around Guadalcanal, Tulagi, and Tanambogo. Both aircraft, however, would also later report negative findings for both patrol corridors.
SECTOR V	Sector V would be searched only to an extent of (and a distance out *to*) some 600 miles at its ultimate extremity and would also report negative sightings. Critically missing from this report is the fact that the *outer* fifty miles of that planned 650-mile track (totaling its proposed and assigned 740-mile range) had not at all been searched by the B-17s as initially requested of the COMNAVAIR by Admiral Turner himself.

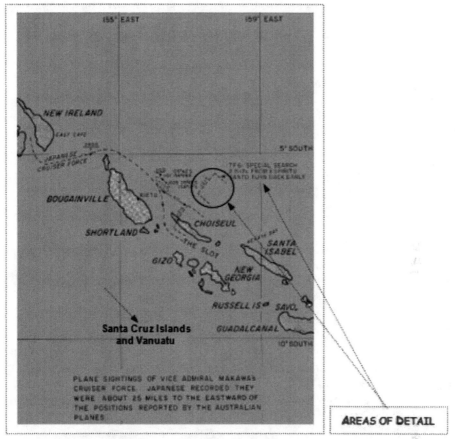

Figure 12. Pre-Action Reconnaissance of Mikawa's CRUDIV Fleet by American B-17s (Map courtesy of VADM George C. Dyer[24])

in the exhaustive 429-page NWC report of Richard W. Bates,[25] these same zones were presented instead as "Reconnaissance Areas"—which areas were tagged therein as Areas "A," B," "C," "D," and "E." That much advanced, the two B-17 overflights that might most have been within the surveillance purview of those enemy forces must indeed have been Reconnaissance Areas "C" and "D" (or II and V in the previous model), as scheduled for that day. Here, the Figure 12 map most clearly reflects the approximated areas for that search zone and the point at which Mikawa's surface fleet might actually have been sighted by those American B-17s.

According to at least the Bates analysis, we begin to get an idea of just how vast a surveillance area the B-17s were expected to cover, and how it may not at all have been unusual for a single reconnaissance plane on a routine intelligence-gathering mission over the St. George's Channel to be assigned an even wider and more circuitous route that might extend out as far as 750 miles. On this, note the following from Bates himself:

One B-17 from Port Moresby reconnoitered Reconnaissance Area "C"; another covered Reconnaissance Area "D", and a third B-17 made a photographic intelligence run over Reconnaissance Area "E"—with a particular emphasis on all access and egress points from Rabaul and Kavieng.[26]

But in the case of at least one B-17, the 750-mile patrol extremity would indeed not be reached, and the aircraft would in fact swing about after only 650 miles, then terminate its patrol route, and head for home. Not having searched the additional 100 miles that morning would have made all the difference, for indeed only 50 miles farther out lay the full strength of Mikawa's surface fleet, and yet none had even witnessed its very passing.

B-17 Overflight Scenario ❶: Detection of the Mikawa Fleet

At about 1215 hours on the afternoon of 8 August, the first of two B-17 reconnaissance planes would indeed spot the fast-approaching Japanese surface fleet then under the combined commands of Admirals Mikawa and Gotō. As borne out by other parallel events—and even Ohmae's own later report of the IJN convoy's movement at the time—the sightings would have occurred off the coast of Kieta, far to the northwestern edge of Choiseul Island, and would probably have been at the precise moment that Mikawa was "resting and reforming" his ships and cautiously waiting for nightfall. The two RAAFR Hudson flights that Mikawa's ships had already seen earlier—and had even fired on with their AA batteries and large 8-inch guns—seemed to themselves know little (if anything at all) of the overflight of the two B-17s. Certainly, the Ohmae account itself seems to bear no mention whatsoever of the sighting of any large planes or heavy bombers—or of even hearing the throaty, deep-engine drone surely each large plane would have made on approach even from the farthest of distances. Ohmae's account would itself only later recall the Hudsons.

And even here, the time of that first sighting seems to be called into question again and again, with Bates as one key source noting the time of the first B-17 sighting as being 1215 hours on 8 August (as upheld and clearly annotated in the area of detail shown in Figure 12). However, this is closely followed by yet other accounts stating that the B-17 only arrived at the extremity of its patrol leg at 1215 but the actual sightings occurred more at 1231 hours. Whichever is more valid, the net effect was that both planes appeared to have had the same sighting of the IJN fleet just south of Kieta, even as that force was moving southeast at a clipped pace.

In addition, both planes would dutifully call in their sightings reports, but neither report would reach RADM Turner until much, much later, nearer 2400 hours. In those reports, the first radio call-in from the crew of the Area C B-17 overflight would itself only vaguely state, "Four cruisers and a destroyer headed westward at 1231," while the second call-in appeared to only more fuzzily report, "Six unidentified ships in the St. George Channel, headed SE." So which report was the more correct report? Perhaps neither.

We could point fingers at the COMSOWESPAC failure to report, in a timely manner, the B-17 sightings of "four cruisers and a destroyer headed westward at 1231" in the afternoon just north of Rabaul; or another group of B-17s who reported "six unidentified ships in the St. George Channel, headed SE". CTF 62 did not receive these reports until 2400 hours, some eleven hours later. We therefore cannot know how more timely reports would have been received, but it might at least have been a reminder to everyone that a potent and resourceful enemy was still lurking at Rabaul, which might have caused them to take some sort of surface action.[27]

But perhaps even this would be only the beginning of the mystery itself . . .

B-17 Overflight Scenario ❷: No Moment of Discovery

So, did the B-17s in fact see something and report it as such to their COMNAVAIR base command back at Espiritu Santo, or, as others seem to suggest, did they in fact simply see "nothing at all" and simply report the same?

While it is well known that ADM Turner, as the extant commander of CTF 63 and overall operations at Guadalcanal—and truly all of the Solomons—had earlier asked RADM McCain specifically to increase "special air reconnaissance" throughout the entire region of Bougainville and Choiseul—centered on an area called the Slot— some seem to purport that not all such recon patrols were carried out as expected. In fact, it is these same reports that seem to imply that nothing at all was seen . . . and that each plane simply returned home with only a "negative" report, even after both patrols.

As alleged, at least one (if not both) of the two B-17s failed to provide a solid contact with Mikawa's cruisers simply because each plane turned back well before the point of extremity within each expected patrol corridor, cutting some 60–100 miles off their anticipated patrol leg. Each B-17, therefore, would seemingly (and inexplicably) terminate its patrol only south of the Japanese surface fleet—indeed, far short of the expected 750-mile search radius each had been tasked to patrol, which the durable B-17s were indeed capable of attaining. Embracing this view in his own writings, historian Richard Bates, in association with the Naval War College, offers up his own view on the reports of those B-17 overflights:[28]

> Sector II was scarcely half searched. The right half was not searched because of bad weather; the left half was searched only out to a radius of 650 miles, rather than [out] to the planned 750-mile radius for the same reason. Results were [therefore expectedly] negative.

He further adds, "Sectors III, VI and VII were searched with negative results," going on to say, "Sector V was only searched (out) to a distance of 600 miles with negative results. The outer 50 miles of the planned 650-mile patrol track was not at all searched." And finally this, perhaps Bates's own scalding observation about the errant flight of B-17s:

There is therefore some doubt as to whether the search of sector 290° to 318° (T) from Malaita Island, which search had been requested the preceding day by CTF 63, was actually made. CTF 63 states in his War Diary that all searches were conducted in accordance with the Basic Operation Plan, yet there is no entry in the Diary concerning a search of this new sector. On the other hand, CTF 63's chief of staff has recently stated that this search was made by two B-17s from Espiritu Santo, which B-17s searched to a distance of about 315 miles beyond Malaita Island, again with negative results.

Assuming that the search was made, and that the planes departed at dawn, they should have reached the outer limit of their patrol corridor at about 1215. At this time, the Japanese cruiser force was still roughly 60 miles to the northwest. It is apparent therefore that this search, as conducted, would necessarily have been ineffective. No special report concerning the results of the search was ever made by CTF 63 to CTF 62.

Have we then only come full circle on the issue of the B-17 overflights, and the sighting of Mikawa's own CRUDIV6 and 18? Just *what* did they see, and *when* did they see it? It would now seem that much better detail, and surviving information from the time itself, both continue to support the idea of a full sighting by both planes—and the later reporting of both sightings in a timely and actionable manner to their base command. That those messages would themselves later be delayed in transit to CTF 62 and CTF63—and not reach Turner's command for some hours yet to come—may not at all have been the fault of either the B-17 pilots or the crews themselves.

B-17 Overflight: Conclusions

The conclusions seem both close-ranging and twofold, and credible scenarios (and supporting data) have been presented for both B-17 overflights, offering views and opinions for both a scenario of "discovery" and one with both planes reporting "no discovery" and returning with only a negative sighting report. But what was the degree of culpability on the part of the pilots and crews of those B-17s, if any at all? Indeed, one could just as easily point fingers at RADM McCain and his manifest failure to follow the explicit orders of RADM Turner himself, whose orders specifically told him to conduct an "extended" air search of the areas in question, and to report to him when done. It would only later be revealed that McCain's reconnaissance assets did not in fact fly the assigned patrol corridors as ordered, nor did they conduct the "extra reconnaissance" flights as charged; then they further aggravated the situation by failing to even inform Turner of that non-action.

Similarly, much blame might rightly be laid at the feet of the RAAFR Hudson crews as well, both for the seeming "lack of urgency" shown the very intel they held in hand, and the unfathomed delay in the forwarding of the data to the intended recipients, the command and control decision-makers well to the south in Guadalcanal. And, when all was said and done, might it all not have been simply as Bates himself later observed as a general and "uniform pattern of slow and ineffective communications between aircraft of the Allied air force in the northeastern area, and the responsible Allied commanders in the SOPAC area"?[29]

With some relief, for at least the pilots and crews of the B-17 reconnaissance squadrons at Espiritu Santo, it would later be determined that little or no culpability could be placed on the doorstep of the B-17s for their reconnaissance operations that day—or for their reporting of that sightings intel—and indeed history would be far kinder to their collective efforts than to those of the RAAFR Hudson pilots. Whether their contribution would later be seen as having been only supplemental—perhaps even "irrelevant"—to the later outcome of the First Battle of Savo Island will probably remain a point of contention for many naval historians and analysts of the battle that was still to come.

After the attacks at Savo, virtually all of the B-17 squadrons stationed in the southwest Pacific area now moved with greater precision almost as one, and the time would indeed see an almost-immediate shift in policy, in attack strategy, and in the group's own revamped resolve and intent. Reconnaissance would now come only secondarily to the B-17's "new" prime mission, that of simply "search and destroy." Now like hounds from hell, the B-17s soon stepped up their attacks and more than made up for any misgivings the Southern command might have had about their viability and effectiveness during their previous surveillance missions. Indeed, they would become the very backbone of many heavy payload missions that would relentlessly pursue the now-retiring Imperial Japanese Navy, and would drive them fully out of the Solomons, feverishly dogging them at the heel all the way back to their northern quarters.

FINDING 4A: EARLY WARNING: THE "RADAR PICKETS":
❶ USS *BLUE* AND USS *RALPH TALBOT*

9 August 1942, 0044–0054 Hours (IJN Spots the USS *Blue*)
9 August 1942, 0058 Hours (IJN Spots the USS *Ralph Talbot*)

Premise: Failure of the "picket" radar ships USS Blue and USS Ralph Talbot to detect the southbound IJN surface fleet, and to effectively sound an alert in a timely and actionable manner.

The two escorts USS *Blue* (DD-387) and USS *Ralph Talbot* (DD-390), serving as "radar pickets" positioned far to the north of the Allied surface fleet, were sailing concurrent and parallel courses north of Savo Island, well above Riefkohl's Northern screen itself. The two ships had been fully outfitted with the latest prototypical radar systems of the day, and what was thought to have been the very best equipment operators in all of the fleet, which was why the two ships had been assigned that radar picket patrol duty imprimis. It must also be said, however, that the Americans may have greatly overestimated the capabilities of that radar, and could not yet have

Figure 13.   Radar Picket: USS *Blue* (DD-387)

Figure 14.   Radar Picket: USS *Ralph Talbot* (DD-390)

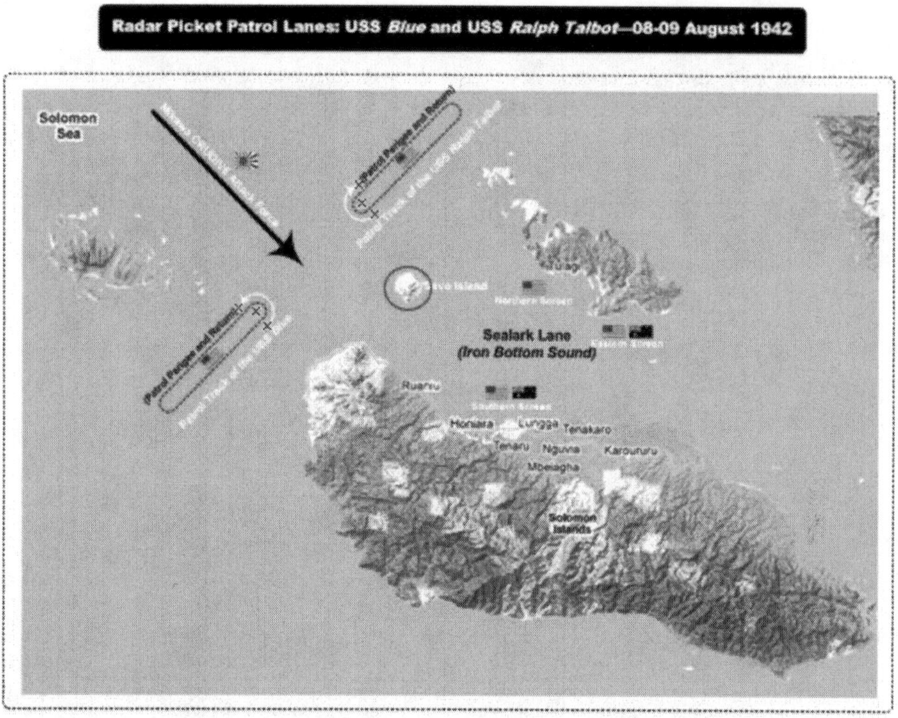

Figure 15.   Diagram of the Patrol Perigees of the USS *Blue* and USS *Ralph Talbot*

fully understood its range, usability, or the inherent limitations of the equipment itself. And in short order would it soon be found that the "new" radar proved to be effective only out to some seven miles in full. Furthermore, since the patrol courses of both the *Blue* and the *Ralph Talbot* were not 100 percent coordinated with any great precision, they effectively left a "gap" of some twenty miles or so, which would thereby remain dangerously unpatrolled (and even more foolishly unguarded), as clearly shown in Figure 15.

It would therefore be here, at precisely at the critical moment of the enemy's approach, that both the *Blue* and the *Ralph Talbot* would reach their normal patrol perigees and were each just turning about and steaming away from the Mikawa passage point—just at the moment of the admiral's entry into the passage—thereby creating a "black hole" through which the Mikawa attack force could now quietly sluice without challenge or threat of engagement. Small wonder, then, that at the point at which Mikawa reached the screening pickets, both the *Blue* and the *Ralph Talbot* were already some fourteen miles apart and the admiral's invading force would only too easily drift between both destroyer pickets completely undetected. The sly passage of Mikawa's attack fleet past the *Blue* and *Ralph Talbot* was even fully documented by crewmen of some of the IJN's own naval forces when, some years later, information was parsed out in a series of releases as part of a Freedom of Information Act (FIA)–equivalent effort in Japan. In part, that newly released IJN report would read:

> To avoid *Blue*, Mikawa changed course to pass north of Savo Island. He ordered his ships to slow to 22 knots to reduce wakes that might make his ships more visible. Four minutes later, his lookouts spied either the *Talbot* about 10 miles away or another vessel of unknown nationality. The IJN battle fleet held their course while pointing more than fifty guns at *Blue*, ready to open fire at the slightest indication that she had even sighted them. When *Blue* was less than a mile away from Mikawa's force she suddenly reversed course, having reached the end of her patrol track and steamed away, apparently oblivious to the long column of large Japanese ships sailing right by her.

FINDING 4B: EARLY WARNING: THE "RADAR PICKETS":
❷ USS *BLUE* AND USS *RALPH TALBOT*

9 August 1942 0040 Hours (IJN Spots the USS *Blue*)
9 August 1942 0050 Hours (IJN Spots the USS *Ralph Talbot*)

Premise: Failure of the USS **Blue** *and USS* **Ralph Talbot** *to detect the southbound IJN surface fleet, or to effectively sound an alert in a timely and actionable manner.*

The destroyers USS *Blue* and USS *Ralph Talbot* had been attached to an Allied-formed naval task group called TG 62.6 and had been posted to two radar picket patrol lines running north and south of Savo Island, to provide an early warning buffer against any Japanese surface ship penetration into any of the areas near the Tulagi and Lunga Roads transport and cargo unloading areas. In earlier training, both of these radar-equipped ships had demonstrated their ability to pinpoint "cruiser-sized" targets at an astounding distance (at the time) of almost ten nautical miles in dead reckoning, but sadly this would not at all be the case on the night of 8–9 August. Here, the David H. Lippman account, as seen on the *World War II Plus 55* website, would itself read in short order:

> At 0040 hours, Mikawa's flagship *Chōkai* spots Savo Island. A lookout spots a ship approaching 30 degrees to starboard. It is the patrolling destroyer USS *Blue*. Mikawa calmly cuts speed to 22 knots to reduce the phosphorescent wakes of his five heavy and two light cruisers. Incredibly, the *Blue* executes a full 180° turn to starboard and moves away, having not at all spotted the passing Japanese ships.
>
> Moments later, *Chōkai*'s lookouts detect another blip on the horizon, and the formation passes what appeared to be a lazing inter-island schooner; and behind that the equally sleepy destroyer USS *Ralph Talbot*. Neither American warship seemed to spot the Japanese convoy.[30]

Now Admiral Mikawa quick-turned all ships to starboard, swinging his force over and into a fold of low-banking clouds—the better to cloak his cruiser division—then cranked the speed of his column of warships up to an accelerated thirty knots. By 0133 hours, Mikawa sat high atop the *Pagoda*-masted superstructure of his great flagship *Chōkai* and had his signalmen clacker out the final message, "All ships attack! All ships attack!" Three minutes later, lookouts on the flagship spotted "three cruisers to starboard," which must itself have been the Southern screen. The Japanese cruiser force then altered course to a new heading of one-two-zero (120°) and ordered "independent firing" for all ships. Minutes later, four Long-Lance torpedoes silently hit the water and began knifing their way toward the unsuspecting *Canberra*. At almost the same time, *Chōkai*'s 8-inch guns opened up on the distressed's Australian cruiser as well, firing repeatedly with good results with full salvos. The battle would soon be joined, and the attack on the Southern screen was now well under way.

Although the *Blue* and *Ralph Talbot* had been tagged as the radar pickets set to patrol north of Savo Island, this was only prior to the attack on the Southern screen. Only once the attack on the *Canberra* and *Chicago* had been successfully prosecuted had Mikawa's task force even considered a second attack on Riefkohl's Northern screen as well. Clearly, the quite advantageous (if accidental) splitting of the Mikawa cruiser column into two (or perhaps even three) battle lanes had to work much in the admiral's favor, as indeed the IJN cruisers *Kinugasa*, *Yubari*, and *Tenryū* broke away and headed off in a more westerly direction, apart from the main body of Japanese warships. This, then, allowed Mikawa to effectively "bracket" the slower-moving American cruisers to the north in a classic, deadly pincer movement, and to virtually corral them all near Savo to begin their new assault on that same Northern screen.

This "trick of luck," and the accidental shift of momentum and good fortune quite aside, Mikawa's brilliance in the stealth and rapid movement of his ships, in all events, clearly pointed up his unquestioned ability to fully slip his warships through the *Blue* and *Ralph Talbot* picket line and to get his ships past that screen without detection, allowing them to ❶ press the attack on both the *Canberra* and the *Chicago* within that Southern screen, ❷ fully attack the Northern screen on their turnabout, and ❸ completely exit the battle area itself while sustaining only minimal damage to his own IJN ships.

The role that the *Blue* and *Ralph Talbot* may have played in "allowing" the passage of Mikawa's CRUDIV fleet was (and may still be) a matter of some great debate even today, but in truth it may never be known in full. Could there in fact have been any degree of culpability found with the two radar pickets? Maybe. Negligence of duty? Probably not. Perhaps in its final outcome, then, it could all just be attributable to little more than excellent timing, good fortune, and an undeniable trick of luck for the admiral himself.

FINDING 5:   EARLY WARNING: USS *JARVIS* (DD-393)

USS *Jarvis*: The "Little Giant" Action of 8 August 1942
9 August 1942, 0134 Hours

*Premise: Failure of the USS **Jarvis** (DD-393) to detect the approaching Mikawa force, and to effectively sound an alert in a timely and actionable manner.*

On the afternoon of 8 August 1942—one day before the unfolding tragic events that would result in the battle at Savo, the aging one-stack *Bagley*-class destroyer USS *Jarvis* would be among the first of the American ships to be attacked and heavily damaged by the land-based Japanese bombers. Swarming down into an area just off the coast of Florida Island, the Rabaul-based Japanese bombers began an almost immediate attack on the heavy cruiser *Vincennes*, this in tandem with a series of follow-on attacks on both the *Jarvis* and the troop transport ship USS *George F. Elliot*. Here, against all odds, the *Jarvis*—or "Little Giant," as she would later be called by the very men who sailed her—would valiantly maneuver to interpose herself between that same *Vincennes* and one of the deadly, air-dropped *Type 93* torpedoes that was already knifing straight for the larger cruiser.

With all main guns firing in tandem, and her AA batteries manned and already working at a fevered pace, *Jarvis* would exact a devastating toll on the attacking Japanese bombers. So deadly was the fire, later observers would note, that "only three planes survived to reach the formation."[31] Bravely had the scrappy little destroyer done precisely what she was supposed to do: to simply "take the hit" to protect the more valuable CA *Vincennes* at all costs—which would soon impact on her own forward fireroom, stopping her dead in the water. The small screening ship was left severely damaged and crippling away from the scene of the attack as soon after the air attack as possible.

After the brief but deadly encounter a sister ship, the destroyer USS *Dewey* (DD-439) would arrive on scene in short order and tow the stricken ship back to home waters and friendly ports off Guadalcanal. The damaged *Jarvis* would anchor in the shallows near Lunga Point, then move cross-channel to Tulagi to discharge her casualties and wounded and to effect emergency repairs in situ, hastily "patching herself up" to a point of being seaworthy enough (even with a 50-foot gash in her starboard hull) to attempt the long and perilous run from Guadalcanal to Efate, New Hebrides—and ultimately all the way to Sydney, Australia. Sadly, *Jarvis* would never recover from her mortal hits and would be severely attacked yet one more time—and the scrappy, battling destroyer would never conclude her final voyage.

USS *Jarvis:* The "Little Giant": Final Action of 9 August 1942

By 0134 hours on the night of the attack at Savo on 9 August, the *Jarvis* would be in for even more catastrophic surprises: that of Mikawa's encroaching surface fleet,

Figure 16.   American Destroyer USS *Jarvis* (DD-393)

which was even then fast approaching Iron Bottom Sound and cruising around the dark shoulder of Savo. Did she in fact see the Japanese ships approaching? And was she in fact even in a position to either intercept or engage that intruding force, and could she not herself have sounded the alarm to warn the other Allied ships of Mikawa's very approach? The answer itself might decidedly have been no—and this in probably all instances.

In fact, as noted earlier, the *Jarvis* had already been mauled and heavily damaged in the first air action of 7 August, and now, limping away battered and gashed with a 50-foot hole in her bow, reportedly had little or no communications capabilities at the time of her sighting of the IJN ships just north of Savo. To this end, even Figure 17 clearly shows a high-level view of the ship's track on the night in question, and might be expected to grant even greater insight into her encounter with that Japanese force and her subsequent actions following that encounter.

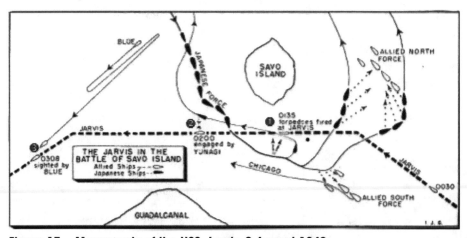

Figure 17.   Movements of the USS *Jarvis*, 9 August 1942

Certainly by at least 0135 hours ❶ *Jarvis* must certainly have seen the Japanese fleet, as indeed she could scarcely have missed them at a very short three thousand yards. She had even been fired on by the IJN CA *Tenryū* with a spread of wide-ranging torps that all ran afoul and wide of their mark due to her slow and underestimated speed (as calculated by the IJN cruisers), with each missing her in sequence. On this very incident, author and naval analyst Commander Robert C. Shaw (Ret.) made the following observation in his USNI *Proceedings* article of February 1950:

> Thus, the seven [IJN] cruisers and a destroyer careened into the Sound just as *Jarvis* was leaving. It was possible that they didn't see the *Jarvis*, and possible that they [only] attacked her briefly. But since the Japanese were engaging the larger American force [Crutchley's Southern fleet] at about the same time, nobody knew for sure.[32]

Antithetically, Robert W. Bates, in his own well-received dissertation titled *The Battle of Savo Island, August 9, 1942. Strategical and Tactical Analysis. Part I*, takes it a step further, noting the following actions of the Japanese ships against the *Jarvis*:

> At 0132, Commander, Cruiser Force on the *Chōkai* [Mikawa] commenced his run in on a course of 096° (T), and at about 0133 signaled the order: "All ships attack!" At about 0134, he sighted an Allied destroyer at a range of about 3000 yards on his port side bearing 76° to the left of his base course, or 19° (T), and moving slowly on an opposite course.[33]

Then he goes on to add the following:

> The Japanese Cruiser Force trained its guns on the *Jarvis*, but withheld its fire. Presumably, the Japanese doctrine was not to open fire until the Flagship had done so first. Commander, Cruiser Force [Mikawa] therefore—mindful of the fact that neither of the previous two destroyers [*Blue* and *Ralph Talbot*] had opened fire—apparently decided to continue on with his basic plan which was to withhold gunfire until after he had fired torpedoes at the Southern force.[34]

And so the admiral's element of surprise held, and his IJN ships' positions remained uncompromised.

Thus the *Jarvis* would only continue. Here it might be worthwhile to note that it would be the selfsame IJN destroyer *Yunagi*, under the command of Lieutenant Okada Seiichi—which Mikawa had earlier turned back from his main force and detached to patrol the rearward passages of his advancing ships—that would soon spot the damaged *Jarvis* in waters north of Savo. ❷ With no communications and most of her guns out of action, locked in train or destroyed entirely, the *Jarvis* could hardly have been spoiling for a fight, and would probably not have been in a position to fully engage any of Mikawa's ships—not even *Yunagi*. Yet by 0200 *Jarvis* would be engaged yet one more time by this same Japanese destroyer, with shots exchanged between the two ships, but with no assured hits on either side.

The two destroyers, on opposing sides of the conflict, would reportedly pass within 3,000 yards of each other, yet other of the accompanying IJN cruisers, such as the *Tenryū* and *Furutaka*, would later also vividly recall having been even closer, reportedly at some 1200 yards—enough indeed to note the following of that passing lone American ship:

> Our ships passed as close as 1100 meters of this lone enemy destroyer; close enough for officers on *Tenryū* to look down onto the destroyer's decks without seeing any crew moving about. If at all *Jarvis* was aware of the Japanese ships passing by, she did not respond in any noticeable way, and simply continued on her own labored journey . . . and we moved on.[35]

Oddly, Mikawa's own chief of staff, CAPT Toshikazu Ohmae—the man who stood beside Mikawa on the bridge of the gallant *Chōkai* during the entirety of the battle—only negligibly mentions the detection and presence of any unusual contacts seen that night just before their attack on Crutchley's Southern force. Was that contact in fact the American destroyer *Jarvis*?

> I stood beside Admiral Mikawa. Before me was a chart on which were plotted the locations of the enemy ships. We peered into the darkness. Then, a voice from a lookout above shattered the tense silence: "Cruiser, 7 degrees to port!"
>
> The shape which appeared in that direction seemed small; it could therefore only be a destroyer. It was still a long way off. Yet we were soon swayed in our observation [of that ship] by the even later call, "Three cruisers, 9 degrees starboard, moving to the right!"[36]

And thus the attack would be initiated quickly against the main body of American cruisers that that night made up the Allied Southern force, with no further mention of either the *Jarvis* or her later encounter with *Yunagi* on her way out of the Sound.

All else aside, in terms of *Jarvis*'s encounter with the enemy's surface fleet that night, it is indeed known that the American destroyer would be spotted at least one last time, this by none other than the American radar picket *Blue* ❸. And once again, as we clearly see in the earlier map, the *Blue* is in fact still continuing on its elliptical patrol pattern just north of Savo—in her role as one of two "gatekeeper" radar pickets—until a point in time between 0308 and 0325 hours.[37] It would be at this time that an alerted crew on the *Blue* would indeed spot the *Jarvis*, even as she limped slowly off to the south and west of their position.

The *Blue* would immediately alert and give sharp pursuit, seeking to close with the as yet unidentified ship with an aim to engage if necessary. Only later would she determine that the ship was in fact a "friendly" and, indeed, none other than the *Jarvis* herself. The attack charge would be quickly aborted and assistance offered to the crippled DD, but it is further recorded that the beleaguered *Jarvis* would in fact decline the assistance offer by that *Blue*, and instead held her course to the south and west with but a single dogged purpose in mind: getting safely to New Guinea (or to her later, alternate destination in Australia) to effect her badly needed repairs. On this point, Bates makes the following curious observation:

> At 0250, when about midway along her patrol line, she [*Blue*] sighted an unidentified ship to the southwest which she noted was rounding Cape Esperance and taking a southwesterly course at average speed. The BLUE increased speed to twenty knots and immediately trailed the contact, closing on it until 0325. She challenged the unidentified ship (visually) and received a response (visually) that the ship was in fact the JARVIS, then withdrawing from the area for repairs.[38]

This, then, is truly our best evidence that the "Little Giant" had in fact escaped the onslaught of the Japanese cruisers—and the *Yunagi*—and was indeed continuing on her life-saving trek toward Australia for dire ship repairs. Later indeed, one final overflight of a lone scout plane from the carrier USS *Saratoga* would also spot the small ship some forty miles west by south of Guadalcanal. Recognizing the dawn-brightened silhouette as being in fact a "friendly," the American pilot dutifully reported seeing the ship "dragging a ribbon of fuel oil, like a painted arrow showing her course, heading SW towards Australia."

This would then be the last time that the courageous *Jarvis* would be seen by friendly forces, as soon the scrappy little destroyer would indeed be no more. For on the very next afternoon, she would come under severe attack by no less than thirty-one Japanese bomber and attack planes, who—mistaking her for a New Zealand *Achilles*-class light cruiser—attacked her with a ferocity and purpose designed to do only one thing—destroy. Succumbing to the several mortal wounds she had suffered during this and the previous afternoon's attack of 8 August, the *Jarvis* simply "split and sank" at 1300 hours on 9 August 1942. Sadly, none of her 233 remaining crewmen would survive this final deadly onslaught, and she would at last be lost—both to her men and to the annals of history forever thereafter.

USS *Jarvis*: Conclusions

So could the "Little Giant" *Jarvis* in fact have been complicit in the untimely demise of both the Southern and Northern screening forces, by not warning them of the enemy's advance? Doubtful. Should any degree of culpability be leveled against the struggling American destroyer on her grueling passage south to Sydney? Probably not. Indeed, she had no means of communicating with the other ships within her own command, nor with the very naval commanders at Guadalcanal who would have most benefited from any such early warning.

The *Jarvis* had therefore essentially been spotted twice by the Imperial Japanese naval fleet on the same date—and during the same time frame—once on the way in, and once on the way out. She had been sighted by at least the *Yunagi* twice, and both the *Tenryū* and the *Furutaka* at least once—this even before the onset of the very hostilities that would later take place at Savo. By the time *Jarvis* was seen exiting the Sound, crippling her own way out that last time, the attack on the Allied Southern fleet was already well under way, and decidedly no alarm raised by *Jarvis* would have made much difference in the outcome of the battle or the night.

USS *Jarvis*: The "Little Giant"—Further Reading

For additional information on the sightings, exploits, and tragic end of the brave American DD USS *Jarvis*, review the following bibliographic material and related electronic weblinks.

Articles and Books

Bates, Richard W. (1950). *The Battle of Savo Island, August 9, 1942. Strategical and Tactical Analysis. Part I.* Naval War College report (AD/A-003 037) distributed by the National Technical Information Services (NTIS) organization, a division of the U.S. Department of Commerce, and prepared for the Bureau of Naval Personnel.

Hornfischer, James D. (2012). *Neptune's Inferno.* Bantam Books.

Loxton, Bruce, and Chris Coulthard-Clark. (1997). *The Shame of Savo: Anatomy of a Naval Disaster.* Allen & Unwin Pty Ltd., 178.

Ohmae, Toshikazu. (1957). "The Battle of Savo Island." *Proceedings* 83, no. 12 (December 1957). United States Naval Institute (USNI).

Shaw, James C. (CDR, USN, Ret.). (1950). "Jarvis: Destroyer That Vanished." *Proceedings* 76, no. 2 (February 1950). United States Naval Institute (USNI).

Electronic Weblinks

Wikipedia, "Battle of Savo Island," at http://en.wikipedia.org/wiki/USS_Jarvis_(DD-393)#Torpedoed

Wikipedia, "USS *Jarvis* (DD-393)," at http://en.wikipedia.org/wiki/USS_Jarvis_(DD-393)

Maritime Quest: Daily Events for August 9, at http://www.maritimequest.com/daily_event_archive/2005/august/09_uss_jarvis_battle_of_savo_island.htm

Opentopia: What Is the USS Jarvis *(DD-393)?*, at http://encycl.opentopia.com/term/USS_Jarvis_(DD-393)

World War II Pacific: Destroyers and Gunboats: Brief Ship Descriptions, at http://www.ww2pacific.com/ships3.html

Dictionary of American Naval Fighting Ships (DANFS) Office of the Chief of Naval Operations, "USS *Jarvis* (DD-393)," at http://www.ibiblio.org/hyperwar/USN/ships/dafs/DD/dd393.html

Finding 6:   EARLY WARNING: USS *PATTERSON*

9 August 1942, 0143 Hours

Premise: Failure of the USS **Patterson** *(DD-392) to effectively sound the alert for the Southern screen in a timely and actionable manner.*

Unlike the tale of the earlier *Jarvis*, the *Bagley*-class destroyer USS *Patterson* (DD-392) would indeed be among the first of the Allied surface ships that would not only see the approaching Mikawa fleet but also be among the first to sound the alarm and engage that fleet as well—this beginning as early as 0143 hours, tragically almost at the moment of attack, just after the starshell illumination flares themselves were fired from the Japanese heavy cruisers. In this event, the *Patterson*'s succinct yet somewhat urgent message would initially be broadcast simply as "Warning! Warning! Strange ships entering the harbor!"[39] That was all she would have time for.

Within minutes of issuing the advisory and clacking her blinkers to warn the other nearby ships, the cruiser floatplanes of Mikawa's fleet were already dropping their aerial orb flares and ship-launched starshells, with quick and live-fire follow-on salvos that would be nothing if not ferocious and deadly accurate. Caught immediately in the crosshairs of the attacking IJN gunners would be not only the *Patterson* herself but also the Australian heavy cruiser HMAS *Canberra* and even CAPT Bode's own *Chicago*—and all with an almost deadly and instantaneous effect.

Probably the most alert of all the fleet screening forces that night, just prior to the attack, would have been the scrappy, high-spirited *Patterson* herself, as she and her never-retreating captain, CDR Frank Walker, and his crew stood well on the alert even at the instant that they saw the approaching enemy fleet. But history itself would later prove that it might have already been too late for her—and for her guarded charges

Figure 18. American Destroyer USS *Patterson* (DD-392)

Canberra and *Chicago*. The *Patterson* would also have the ignoble and harsh claim of being the first ship of that Southern force that would be fired on by Mikawa's fleet, before they abruptly shifted their focus and even greater attack on Riefkohl's prized heavy cruisers to the north. As such, the unfortunate DD would take multiple immediate hits from the first 5-inch salvos fired from at least one of the enemy ships (thought to be the heavy cruiser *Kinugasa*), which tragically resulted in the death of some ten men and the injury of at least eight more. The highly accurate salvos would also take out the ship's number four gun, and soon the tangle was on and the game was soon well afoot.

Now down one battery and reeling from only the first of several hits she would receive, *Patterson* did the only thing she had been tasked to do—protect the "heavies" at all costs—but even that to only slight effect since indeed Mikawa's forces were on the Southern group in an instant—sailing out of the night cloaked in a darkened sheet of rain—and prosecuted their series of attacks on the Allied warships. In the coming moments, *Canberra* and *Chicago* would each take killing hits from the large 8-inch guns of Mikawa's cruisers, but far and away *Canberra* would fare the worst; indeed, a total annihilation would result in her sinking almost in the very spot she had been hit. CAPT Bode's *Chicago* would fare only slightly better, sustaining but a single torpedo strike to her port bow—a hit that would nonetheless leave her staggering off to the north and west with no seeming direction for some forty minutes before Bode could finally correct his ship's own drift.

Unwavering in her support of the two Allied cruisers in her charge, however, *Patterson* did her best to give as good as she got and throughout the entire melee continued to step up her fire with the few remaining guns she still had in operation, obtaining "probable" hits on at least one Japanese ship, thought to be the *Kinugasa* itself. Moments later, however, it was still an all-too-cautious Mikawa who would make the errant (and somewhat misguided) decision to disengage his full attack, and to begin a northward push toward the unsuspecting, target-rich Northern screening group. In short order, the heroic *Patterson* would lose sight of the IJN attack force in full but would continue to fire her guns in that direction nonetheless, even as the enemy slipped back under the cowl of night and moved north to begin their assault on the *Vincennes*, *Quincy*, and *Astoria*.

The battle itself had been fast-paced and ferocious—deadly and all-consuming for many in the Allied Southern group—and especially for the Australian heavy cruiser *Canberra*. But it was also clear that throughout the entire skirmish the *Patterson* had unflaggingly continued to do her job: protecting the fleet's "heavies" and her own flanks, and truly that at all costs.

Unbowed and Undaunted: Conclusions for the *Patterson*

Truly might there be no reasonable level of culpability, therefore, that could be ascribed to the *Patterson*, or to her crew, for their quick-reasoned actions on the night of 9 August in the face of the attack by Mikawa's encroaching cruiser divisions. The courageous destroyer—nicknamed the "Luxury Liner" by her own proud complement of men—had indeed sounded an early alarm and warned the other ships of the Southern and Northern screening groups of that approaching enemy force. Addressing this, even Loxton himself would note the following:

> When Mikawa's ships attacked the Allied Southern force, the captains of all three U.S. Northern force cruisers were asleep, with their ships steaming quietly at 10 knots. Although crewmen on all three ships observed flares and gunfire from the battle south of Savo and had also received *Patterson*'s warning of threatening ships entering the area, it took some time for the crews to go from Condition II to Full Alert. At 0144, the Japanese cruisers began firing torpedoes at the Northern force. At 0150, they aimed powerful searchlights on all three Northern cruisers and opened up with all main guns.[40]

In the end, then, unlike the ineffectual slumbering American radar pickets *Blue* and *Ralph Talbot* just to the north of Savo, the brave *Patterson* had performed her job well and dealt with her adversity head on, and that clearly with a brave intent and a solid sense of duty. When attacked, she responded quickly and paid out in full in her attempt to fend off the enemy attack on the larger ships of her Southern force. Yet, in spite of the destroyer's best efforts to protect both of her charges, the fact that the *Canberra* and *Chicago* would still be so mauled might not entirely have been her fault. The *Patterson* had done all that had been asked of her, sounding an alarm (however sketchy in its wording) to both screening forces in a timely and actionable manner. That the alarm might come at precisely the same moment that the Mikawa attack itself commenced could probably not have been avoided, but it might not at all be owing to any negligence on the part of that smaller DD.

History, and the powers of harsh dissent that would later follow on the heels of the unpardonable defeat of our combined navies at Savo, would indeed grant the *Patterson* a near-exculpation for any of the tragic events that had earlier taken place on the night of 9 August. Indeed, for her very bravery in the face of such overwhelming adversity, the battling destroyer would be well commended and awarded yet another Battle Star for her dogged fighting spirit and valiant efforts. By war's end, the *Patterson* would indeed go on to earn an astonishing thirteen such Battle Stars, placing her almost in a class by herself as the scrappy little destroyer that had, in her own right (on at least that one occasion), fought more like the battleship she was never supposed to be. Other brave ships would come in their own time, such as the USS *Laffey* during the later naval battle of Guadalcanal, and especially the USS *Samuel B. Roberts* itself during the Battle off Samar. But for now, during at least August 1942, it was *Patterson*'s own time to be remembered with highest honors and an eminent regard.

A Hiss of Breath, a Gnash of Teeth, a Flame of Battle: Anatomy of an Attack

To the extent that any first-person account can even be recalled and rendered in full by "one who was there," the captivating, and undeniably haunting, words of Jack D. Coombe—himself serving on that same USS *Patterson* precisely on the night of 9 August 1942—can only forever echo in our minds as a harsh reminder of life aboard the "Tin-Can" destroyers during the campaigns at Guadalcanal and Savo during this time. No amount of weathering or "steeling of nerves" could at all have prepared one for the coming course of battle on the high seas of the South Pacific as it must have been at that time. This chilling account of the battle at Tassafaronga—as indeed it must have been at Savo and virtually all of the other night naval encounters in the Solomons as well—is itself masterfully penned by Coombe as he, too, observes the following:

> You're steaming along in the Slot toward what you know will be a battle area, and your whole universe is concentrated on your ship. The only sounds are the hissing of water past the hull, the muted throbbing of the ship's turbines, and an occasional nervous whisper from a shipmate. You know the enemy is out there, and when you meet no quarter will be given. Your eyes strain to penetrate the darkness until they ache, even though you know that the radar is on the job; you're hoping you spot the enemy first. Your heart pounds so loudly that you're afraid it will betray your ship's position. Your hands grip the gun handles and splinter shields until your knuckles are white. Your mouth is dry, and you long for a tall, tall drink.[41]

Now continuing only to scan the far horizon, the sharp lookouts on the *Patterson* suddenly stood at the alert, even as they were set on by a foe so calculating, so fierce, and so exacting in their naval night-fighting capabilities as to almost replace the dogged resolve in the hearts of the American fighting men and to set there instead a certain feeling of dread and icy fear. Then would come the air-launched orb flares, and the brilliant starshells fired from the hushed decks of the enemy ships, each soon turning darkest night into brightest day:

> Suddenly, the darkness is split by an orange-white flash, followed by a flat-sounding BLAAAP! A streamer of light reaches out to your ship. Your heart seems to stop beating, and you realize that you've been holding your breath. Then there's another flash, and another. Tracers arc across the sky, now coming your way. The enemy has found you first and surely now there will be hell to pay![42]

Soon, the near-in splashes of the high-explosive rounds that were, at the first, only close-in "rangefinders" and "near-misses," now ripped around the ship in thunderous splashes—far too close for comfort—as each of their own gun crews now quickly jumped into action, and even the bedeviled helmsman now struggled to steer clear of the incoming shells:

> Your ship lurches to one side as the helmsman swings her hard over and out of the range of the missiles. Then the fire control people get the range. Orders come from all over the ship's phones to your gun captain: "Range . . . elevation . . . commence firing!" Your gun barks out and you are blinded by the flash because your eyes had only earlier been accustomed to the sheer darkness. Your face is whipped hard by the concussion, and you choke on the very powder fumes. Then you go into a kind of trance—everything is automatic. You load and fire, load and fire, load and fire, until

your fear is temporarily checked by only the tasks at hand. The black universe and your whole world has just been ripped apart.[43]

The anatomy of the attack now complete, it would all be owing to the tenacity, preparedness, and reactionary timing of the crew of the *Patterson* that in the end would spare her life that day, as indeed the hard-hitting destroyer would live on to fight yet another day. The scrappy DD would move on to yet other battles that would indeed carry her bravely through the trials (and tribulations) of the Battle of Lingayen Gulf in the Philippines and later even positioned off the coast of Iwo Jima. In fact, she would survive the war in full and only much later be decommissioned as late as February 1947.

USS *Patterson*: Further Reading

For additional reading on the USS *Patterson* and her exploits during the opening (and later) actions of the First Battle of Savo Island, and other later actions in and around Guadalcanal, review the electronic link resources and collected works available, as noted in the lists below.

Articles and Books

Bates, Richard W. (1950); *The Battle of Savo Island, August 9, 1942. Strategical and Tactical Analysis. Part I.* Naval War College report (AD/A-003 037) distributed by the National Technical Information Services (NTIS). U.S. Department of Commerce, as prepared for the Bureau of Naval Personnel.

Hornfischer, James D. (2012). *Neptune's Inferno.* Bantam Books.

Loxton, Bruce, and Chris Coulthard-Clark. (1997). *The Shame of Savo: Anatomy of a Naval Disaster.* Allen & Unwin Pty Ltd.

Ohmae, Toshikazu. (1957). "The Battle of Savo Island." *Proceedings* 83, no. 12 (December 1957). United States Naval Institute (USNI).

Shaw, James C. (CDR, USN, Ret.). (1950). "Jarvis: Destroyer That Vanished." *Proceedings* 76, no. 2 (February 1950). United States Naval Institute (USNI).

Electronic Weblinks

Wikipedia, "Battle of Savo Island," at http://en.wikipedia.org/wiki/Battle_of_Savo_Island#Action_south_of_Savo

Wikipedia, "USS *Patterson* (DD-392)," at http://en.wikipedia.org/wiki/USS_Patterson_(DD-392)

Destroyers Online, "USS *Patterson*: DD-392 (*Bagley*-Class)," at http://www.destroyersonline.com/usndd/dd392/

Destroyer History Foundation, "USS *Patterson*: DD-392," at http://destroyerhistory.org/goldplater/usspatterson/

NavSource Naval History, "USS *Patterson* (DD-392)," at http://www.navsource.org/archives/05/392.htm

FINDING 7:   CANDLES IN THE NIGHT: THE USS *GEORGE F. ELLIOTT* AND THE USS *JARVIS*

Invasion Landings at Lunga Point

***Premise: The Mystery of the USS* George F. Elliott**

Surfacing yet again, there is the enigmatic and ever-peculiar story of the USS *George F. Elliott* (AP-13), a *Heywood*-class transport ship of its time, which has been repeated time and again, as it related to the onset (and perhaps even the ultimate outcome) of the First Battle of Savo Island.

During the course of her transport, mooring, and unloading duties on the morning of 8 August—almost a full day before the first significant 1BOSI action itself—the *Elliott* (Figure 19) would be found positioned directly offshore slightly north of Lunga Point on the southern end of Sealark Lane, an area itself soon to be renamed to its far more ominous Iron Bottom Sound. The transport ship, under the protective gaze of the American destroyer USS *Jarvis* (Figure 16), began dispatching her amphibious assault ships and supply craft to support the Marine landings at Honiara. Under constant air attack the previous day from a number of *Mitsubishi* G4M1 "Betty" bombers, the strafing and bombing runs had resumed and further stepped up—continuing throughout most of that same 7 August—and resuming by noon of the next day. Despite the increased attacks, however, the men on the transport ship would continue working on late into the night, never knowing that at least for them the worst was yet to come.

Figure 19.   American Transport Ship USS *George F. Elliott* (AP-13)

Premise: The Attack on the *Elliott*

As a result of the increasing number of attacks by Japanese air assets on the morning of 8 August—just at a point when multiple incoming reconnaissance reports seemed to indicate that a squadron of *Betty* bombers were imminently approaching from the north, directly over Florida Island (Nggella Sule), the *Elliott* thought it far better to err on the side of caution and made quick preparations for getting under way to perhaps duck the oncoming assault. The ship's captain may indeed have thought it preferable to make for the open waters of Iron Bottom Sound and to temporarily leave station to draw fire away from the landing Marine forces that were even then disembarking and moving ashore. Better to be a moving target, the *Elliott*'s skipper must surely have thought—now with his ship well under way—than to remain as a sitting duck at a turkey shoot. And so indeed he quickly moved off.

Then, shortly before 1100, both the *Elliott* and her escort *Jarvis* would suddenly come under attack by a swarm of several *Betty* bombers—thought to number twenty-six planes in total. The flight of twin-engined *Bettys* came in fast and low, sweeping in at near-treetop level over the low-slung mountains of Florida Island, then quickly out over the sea. Within seconds, the attacking planes were already skimming the choppy waters of Iron Bottom Sound in loose formation and moving in on final target approach to the starboard side of both ships. The bombers were coming in at an astonishing 25–30 feet over the water, and both crews of the *Elliott* and the *Jarvis* could clearly see multiple attack aircraft closing on them at a high rate of speed. Now making less than 10 knots in the water as she haltingly moved away from shore, the *Elliott* took note of at least one bomber that seemed to zero in on her as it made a short and sweeping turn for its run-in on the American transport ship. The Japanese plane doggedly continued in its push, now approaching with a fierce intent, a deadly dispatch, and a certain terrible resolve.

This would play only too well into the hands of the seasoned gun crews of the *Elliott* and the *Jarvis*, as each turret gang now stood its ground and prepared for the coming onslaught. To no one's great surprise, the incoming torpedo planes were only too quickly met with a deadly torrent of AA fire and heavy shelling from the *Jarvis*—and even the nearby USS *Dewey* (DD-349). Many of the incoming enemy planes simply exploded and splashed in and around the ships; others skirted dangerously close, well ablaze, and mortally wounded, even as they streaked by like flaming deadly comets before their own great impact.

In the end, only nine of the initial twenty-six attack aircraft would even penetrate the ships' defenses and get past the great shroud of fire laid out by the American warships in defense of their positions. The DESRON4 (Destroyer Squadron 4) screening destroyer USS *Bagley* alone would report a total of some fifteen "observed" kills by the combined effect of the heightened AA (Anti-Aircraft) fire, and the dead-on accuracy of her main-gun turrets. Small wonder, then, that it would later in fact be noted that this same DD alone would report having fired some sixty-two shells from all of her 5-inch guns, and over 1,100 rounds from her equally deadly 20 mm antiaircraft batteries. For the Japanese aviators, the toll would have only continued to mount, but almost inevitably—as perhaps it must always be—at least one plane would soon enough slip through.

Here, even with the keyed-in accuracy of the American gunnery crews, and the multiple hits scored on the one incoming *Betty*, the IJN attack plane continued unswervingly in its approach—at various intervals dropping down, and then popping back up almost as quickly, before finally slamming with great impact into the *Elliot*'s 'midships hull, just aft of the starboard superstructure. The lightly framed aircraft would disintegrate fairly immediately into a ball of flames on impact, but large chunks of the very wreckage and shrapnel itself would be strewn violently about the decks of the ship, which, in deadly combination with the spilled fuel, now ignited the wildest of fires. Reportedly, at least one engine (or perhaps both) from the incoming torpedo bomber would even become dislodged with the explosion of the craft itself, and literally punched its way through the lightly armored hull of the rear cargo hold, fully destroying the ship's fire main control.

Soon, from deep within the bowels of the transport itself, massive detonations could be heard throughout the ship and multiple deck fires erupted, which then raged unchecked and threatened to get quickly out of control. Fed by the very ordnance stores and munitions that had been slated for delivery and quick offloading to the waiting Marines at both Lunga and Honiara, the ammunition stockpiles now instead worked devilishly against them and began detonating in situ. The thick, acrid smoke and choking fumes must have been like an asphyxiating mask that cut off all breathing, and the loud report of multiple explosions soon shook the *Elliott* to its very hull, even as great billows of acrid smoke began to black out the sky above the ship, as if to fully mark the crippled and slowly dying ship for further savage attack.

The stage would now be set for perhaps one of the most courageous battles by the crew of the *Elliott* to quell those very fires, and to save their stricken ship. From engine room to deckside standing, all able-bodied hands jumped to and manned hastily convened "bucket brigades" to work the raging fires, but the fight would soon be all but lost. Finally, after all attempts to stem the flow of damage caused by the fires resulting from the single plane impact had failed, the order was soon given to abandon station. Now still under a heavy and seemingly unending attack from above, little aid could be offered by any of *Elliott*'s neighboring ships, as they remained under close assault from the strafing warplanes as well. Save that of the bold venture of the lone American destroyer USS *Dewey*, in her attempt to tow the stricken transport ship out to deeper waters, the *Elliott* would have effectively been just another doomed transport and but a sinking shell of her former self.

Pinned and prevented from receiving even marginal search-and-rescue assistance for her men on deck and in the waters around the ship, the *Elliott* came to a final and abrupt stop in the middle of great Iron Bottom Sound. By 1300 hours, a final order would be given to fully abandon ship. Then, following closely on the heels of the attack on the *Elliott*, the destroyers *Bagley* and *Dewey* were sent in to search for survivors. Forty men would be rescued from the churning waters off Lunga Point, but many others would be lost forever to the choppy and unfathomed maw of that same Sealark

Lane. Later, when the order to do so came down through its normal (circuitous) chain of command, it would be the escort destroyer USS *Hull* (DD-350) that would draw the short straw to scuttle the *Elliott* virtually in situ. Soon enough the deed would be done and the *Elliott* would summarily be sunk in waters off the coast of Lunga Point, at an approximate coordinate fix of 9°20' 45" S–160°8'14" E (or alternate 09°10' S–160°10' E), where she remains to this day.

Further Information: USS *George F. Elliott* (AP-13)

For further information on the USS *George F. Elliott* (AP-13), her history, service record, and TROM events leading up to her sinking on 8 August 1942, see the following highly informative website articles:

http://en.wikipedia.org/wiki/USS_George_F._Elliott_(AP-13)#Final_air_attack_and_sinking
http://www.history.navy.mil/photos/sh-usn/usnsh-g/ap13.htm
http://www.destroyers.org/histories/h-dd-350.htm

USS *Jarvis*: Attack on the Little Giant

The attack on the *Bagley*-class USS *Jarvis* would itself come swiftly, at about the same time the *Elliott* had herself been hit. Tasked with guarding both the *Elliott* and the Australian CA *Canberra*, *Jarvis* had also been ordered to serve as part of the screening force ships that had been set to oversee the unloading of the troop transport and cargo ships off Guadalcanal. The gun crews of the *Jarvis* were understandably edgy and quick to action once they saw the first of the incoming *Betty* bombers coming in at about 1158 hours low out of the north as they came off Florida Island.

Similarly, the *New Orleans*–class heavy cruiser USS *Vincennes* (CA-44) happened to be on station as well in the immediate vicinity of the *Jarvis* and the *Elliott*, patrolling the waters off transport area X-Ray at Lunga Point, when the bombers from Rabaul returned. The new air attack would be even more invigorated, now almost with a near vengeance that must have been carried forward from the previous days' losses on the part of the stunned Japanese, losses that could only now be slaked by the blood of the interlopers—that and the full, unwavering destruction of the American surface fleet just then at Iron Bottom Sound.

It would therefore be an invigorated and greatly emboldened sortie of *Betty* bombers that would soon come menacing out of the north, initiating contact almost immediately with its stepped-up series of torpedo launches and strafing runs on any targets of opportunity that might be found. At various attack intervals, therefore, such "targets of opportunity" would indeed have included the *Jarvis*, *Vincennes*, and perhaps especially the large transport *George F. Elliott*. A sweet bonus—beyond the primary targeting of the capital ships themselves—would also have been the transport and cargo ships that were even then busy unloading their stores and munitions, such that clearly fed the very war effort itself, and that was then facilitating an American military presence on Guadalcanal in the first place.

With all main guns and secondary batteries at the ready and trained to face the near-in threat, the large CA *Vincennes* would be among the first of the warships to open fire on the incoming *Bettys*. From her position covering transport area X-Ray, the great cruiser could clearly see the inbound planes and opened up with all batteries, from her large-bore 8-inch main guns, and her equally deadly 40 mm and 20 mm AA batteries, this even as all assets were clearly and quickly brought to bear.

Vincennes was already laying down a highly effective line of fire, all of it loosed from her heavy 8-inch main batteries. Even the close-in "near-misses" exploding on impact in waters only *near* the attacking planes were enough to erratically force them off course and prevent them from prosecuting any further attacks. As a result, those torpedo planes not directly hit by the cruiser's guns were still in danger of literally "flying into a wall of water," as the detonating shells plumed the rolling surf below into deadly columns right before those IJN attack planes themselves. In fact, just such an event was actually witnessed by crewmen aboard the *Vincennes* and must indeed have been the cause of much heated cheering at the time as the men applauded the downing of each plane.

Fearlessly running the gauntlet between the raiding *Bettys* and the transport ships at Lunga, the *Vincennes* raged on, firing at a white-hot pace and downing seven planes before having to disengage the action in full. A single torpedo launched from one of the incoming bombers did get through, however, slicing through the cold waters and tracking on the cruiser, but would in fact pass harmlessly beneath the stern of *Vincennes*. Later, with almost equal luck and best of timing, she was again able to evade at least one bomb impact off her port quarter—but the ill-fated *Jarvis* would this day not be quite as lucky.

Throughout the course of the opening moments of the attack, the destroyer *Jarvis* was exactly where she should have been: screening the large, heavy cruisers and providing suppression fire to cover the landing ships unloading at X-Ray landing area. At the moment of attack, and after the second explosion off *Vincennes*'s port quarter, *Jarvis* moved crisply to interpose herself between the marauding bombers and the larger cruiser in her keep. Little could she know that there had been a second torpedo launch, and that it was now in fact tracking right for her. Yet, even in the face of such a lethal and withering fire from the smaller ship's AA batteries, the incoming *Betty* was still able to loose its weapon on its last run-in—and even when immediately obliterated by that AA fire—would still drop its single torpedo payload on *Jarvis* that would then slam into the starboard quarter of that ship, effectively stopping her cold in the water and killing some fourteen sailors.

Shortly thereafter, struggling vigorously to control the many raging fires aboard the now-stricken ship, *Jarvis* could only be towed out to shallow anchorage off Lunga Point and only later, under the shrouding cover of darkness, would make for Tulagi for emergency repair, crossing the treacherous waters of Iron Bottom Sound under the watchful gaze of a sister ship, the DD USS *Dewey*. It was with a self-sustaining sigh of relief, then, that she would in fact make the crossing in hours—and would do so under her own power.

Still smoldering, however, and said to now have a "fifty-foot gash" in her starboard quarter, the *Jarvis* was nonetheless cleared and deemed seaworthy enough to attempt the even longer journey back to New Hebrides for the even greater ship repairs she now so desperately needed. Not receiving the order to do so, however (due in part to the communications outages brought on by the loss of their radios), the captain of the *Jarvis*, LCDR William W. Graham Jr., would instead make quick steam for Sydney, Australia, and not at all to the designated New Hebrides location as initially intended. Later that day, therefore, under a canopy of clouds, drizzle, and deepening shadow, the crippled destroyer would—by midnight on 8 August—begin its cautious trek back up Iron Bottom Sound on a northwesterly heading. To a man, each of the crewmen must have prayed for only a safe and uneventful passage, yet sadly this just was not to be.

The radar picket-patrolling destroyer USS *Blue* itself, under the command of LCDR Harold Nordmark Williams, would be the last ship to see the *Jarvis* that night. With only slight speed, no communications linkages, and only a very few of her guns still operational, the "Little Giant"—the bold DD *Jarvis*—exited the area and was last seen "trailing fuel oil and riding low by the bow" as she moved off on a crippled, unsteady heading of north-northwest.

Yet it would still not be over for the hapless *Jarvis*, as indeed by 1300 hours of the following afternoon she would be mistaken for an escaping light cruiser and targeted yet a second time by another wave of torpedo planes, this time by thirty-one *Betty* bombers dispatched from air bases far to the north in Japanese-held Rabaul. Under severe aerial attack, and now overwhelmed by the mortal hits she had already sustained over the course of both days, *Jarvis* would finally succumb to her final attack. The small but intrepid destroyer allegedly "split and sank" in waters just south of Savo Island during the early morning hours of 9 August 1942. She would go down in an area southwest of Savo reportedly in the East Solomon Sea some two hundred nautical miles just southeast of Tulagi. She remains to this day somewhere off the coast of Tangarare, off southern Guadalcanal Island, near Lambi Bay, at a projected coordinate fix of 09°42' S–158°59' E (alternately reported as also being at 09°10' S–160°10' E).

Of the 233 brave souls who had survived the first onslaught in Iron Bottom Sound, none would survive the second. The ship's devoted captain, LCDR Graham, would sadly himself be among those who would perish during her final engagement, and soon both she and all her remaining crew would be lost in battle.

Further Information: USS *Jarvis* (DD-393)

For further information on the *Jarvis*—her service history, TROM movements, and the events leading up to her sinking on 9 August 1942—see the following illuminating website articles:

❶ http://en.wikipedia.org/wiki/USS_Jarvis_(DD-393)#Loss_of_Jarvis
❷ http://www.destroyers.org/DANFS/h-DD-393.htm
❸ http://www.navsource.org/archives/05/393.htm

Premise: The Great Misassumption—Flameout or Discovery?

So what was the great misassumption here—and was it indeed fact or fiction? Could either the *Elliott* or the *Jarvis*—the latter perhaps still on fire from its previous attacks the day before and smoldering well into the darkness of the evening hours of the next day—have been responsible for illuminating the battle area at the time of the later night attacks on either Crutchley's Southern or Northern screens? Could there have been an inadvertent position compromise of the patrolling Allied cruisers on the morning of 8–9 August 1942, brought about by the deadly "back-lighting" set by either (or both) of the fiery wrecks of the *Jarvis* or the *Elliott* itself? Decidedly, probably not for the *Jarvis*, and perhaps even less so for the *Elliott*.

Indeed, the questions themselves are all seeming imponderables—heavy questions that are not to be asked lightly—but questions that must be asked and fielded nonetheless. After a close examination of the facts and narratives surrounding the First Battle of Savo Island, it is still the considered opinion of most researchers that the answer might almost always be a resounding NO. And, while it could have happened—and might indeed have been contributory to the detection (and later attacking) of the cruisers of at least one of the Allied screening forces at the outset of that night battle—it probably never did, and in short order, here perhaps is why:

❶ The USS *George F. Elliott* had already been targeted and attacked very early in the afternoon of 8 August. That she was later scuttled by one of her own ships, the American destroyer USS *Dewey* (DD-349), and sunk at 1300 hours might clearly eliminate the *Elliott* as being one of the ships still on fire in the Sound during the early morning hours of 9 August, especially if she had already been scuttled the day before.

Oddly, at least one account still seems to casually implicate the *Elliott* of doing just this—illuminating the Allied ships in the face of the enemy attack, as Loxton himself avowedly seems to state the following in his book, *The Shame of Savo: Anatomy of a Naval Disaster*:

> Two minutes after sighting *Jarvis*, the Japanese lookouts sighted the Allied destroyers and cruisers of the southern force about 12,500 metres away, silhouetted by the glow from the burning *George F. Elliot*.[44]

How could this be? The approaching cruiser divisions that had been sortied by Mikawa would not arrive in the vicinity of Savo Island until well after midnight on 9 August 1942, with the attack on the American Southern fleet not commencing until about 0138 hours—the attack on the Northern screen occurring no later than 0144. It would seemingly be impossible for the *Elliott* to have even been in the vicinity of the battle itself, as further evidenced in the accounts of the *Dewey*, the *Bagley*, and the other circling destroyers tasked with the *Elliot*'s final disposition. The large transport ship had already been scuttled in fact by no later than 1330 hours on the 8th of August, well before the morning of the 9th itself. How could this same ship, already confirmed as having been scuttled and sunk, reappear and still be afloat by 0138 hours of the following day—at precisely the time of the first attack on Crutchley's Southern force?

❷ The USS *Jarvis* would have been hit at virtually the same time, and during the same skirmish, as the *Elliott* itself. The ship would be attacked repeatedly by a squadron of *Bettys* on the same afternoon and hit by a single torpedo to her starboard bow. She would later be towed out into Iron Bottom Sound, where she would sit at shallow anchorage while undergoing emergency repairs immediately after the attack. She would later even depart the Tulagi area entirely—with little or no forenotice of her intent to do so—and would again do so under her own power, with her new destination then being Sydney instead of the New Hebrides. By midnight on the night of 8 August, therefore, it was only a slightly seaworthy and still badly damaged *Jarvis* that would in fact begin her hobbling trek up Iron Bottom Sound, skirting quietly past Guadalcanal's northern Cape Esperance and soon pass out into the dark of the East Solomon Sea.

Was the *Jarvis* in fact still on fire? Perhaps, but not likely. And did she, at any time during this transit period, truly serve to silhouette and backlight any of the ships of either the Southern or the Northern group just prior to those critical attacks? Was it even causal to the attack, facilitating the sighting of the Allied ships, and could this in fact have even occurred as posited? Again, it might be highly unlikely. All else aside and following her secondary attack by the thirty-one Japanese attack aircraft, the *Jarvis* would still nonetheless become the first destroyer casualty during just the opening days of the Guadalcanal campaign of 1942. Sadly, she would not at all be the last.

In full overview, consider at least the following timeline chart and TROM narratives that perhaps best detail the movements of the ship during 7–9 August 1942, as shown in Figure 20, as well as the Table 8 matrix. In fact, many of the detailed findings recounting the movements and activities of that same *Jarvis* would only come to light in a later series of USNI *Proceedings* articles dating back to the 1950s. As such, however, the following discussion points are in fact only the author's own deductive observations. Perhaps you too might agree.

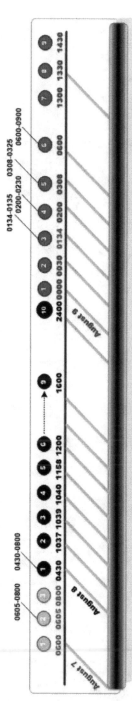

Figure 20. Chronological Timeline of the USS *Jarvis* (DD-393) on 8-9 August 1942

Table 8. USS *Jarvis* TROM and Timeline Narratives and Observations

#	TIME	ACTIVITY
07 August 1942*		
❶	**0430–0600 ±**	The *Jarvis* and accompanying warships that had joined her ranks were initially but a small surface force tasked with guarding (and overseeing) the activities of the arriving transport carriers and supply ships, as they entered into waters that would later be called Iron Bottom Sound. Pushing through mist and light rain, the escort force sailed into clear weather and calm seas, now slashing their speed as they entered the Sound just north of Guadalcanal at dawn on 7 August 1942.
❷	**0700**	Several Marine assault forces under the command of MG Alexander Vandegriff begin landing at staging areas at "Red Beach" near Lunga Point at Honiara, and simultaneously at cross-channel Tulagi as well. Staging activities were already well under way for the most part of 7 August and continued well into the evening hours of that same day. *Jarvis* would be found on station and positioned just off the coast of Lunga Point, and tasked with normal screening and patrol duties as she guarded the quickly unloading utility ships. With her is the aging heavy cruiser USS *Vincennes* (CA-44) and the large armored transport ship USS *George F. Elliott* (AP-13).
❸	**0605–0800 ±**	VADM Gunichi Mikawa is awakened by staff officers and shown only the first of a series of discouraging dispatches hastily sent from IJA commanders on Guadalcanal. He learns first of the presence of the Allied invasion force itself, a landing of American troops—possibly at both Tulagi and Guadalcanal—and receives several urgent messages from the remaining infantry troops still in place on that island. From a Tulagi garrison came the aviso, "0430: Tulagi being heavily bombarded from air and sea. Enemy carrier task force sighted." Then later, an even more ominous, "Enemy force is overwhelming. We will defend our positions to the death."[45]
08 August 1942†		
❶	**0430–0800 ±**	Informed of the presence of enemy ships in the area, Mikawa dispatches a sortie of 37 *Betty* bombers and 15 *Zero* attack fighters. The Rabaul-launched planes all had as their primary targets the transport and cargo ships in and around the port areas of Guadalcanal. To Mikawa and his other subordinate IJN naval commanders, a clear (and viable) secondary bonus would also be any large high-value capital ships of either a CA or BB-class tonnage as well. Simply put, in at least Admiral Mikawa's view, such might indeed be all "icing on the cake."

②	**1037–1039**	On the island of Bougainville, British "Coastwatcher" Jack Read begins a tedious (and somewhat perilous) celestial count as he watches IJN planes pass over *Aravia*, then radios a contact on an adjacent island: "From STO. 27 bombers headed southeast!" Farther off, from another nearby Bougainville locale, British Coastwatcher Paul Mason would report some "45 bombers now going southeast." Obviously, little can now be known about the seeming discrepancy in the reported figures relating to the number of planes seen by both individuals, with each viewing the same event.
③	**1040**	Admiral Turner learns for the first time of the arriving aircraft from Mason's report, and sounds a GQ alarm for all ships in his command.
④	**1158**	Multiple twin-engine *Betty* bombers and *Val* dive bombers begin their attack by concentrating on the ships screening the landing forces and troop transports. With craft and stealth, Mikawa's air attack feints a deceiving push toward Tulagi, then sweeps in low from the north and east over the mountains of Florida Island in a close "V" formation, moving at a quick 180 knots. The planes dropped down and tightened their grouping, then skirted low over the waters of the *Sound* at an altitude estimated to have been an astonishing 25–30 feet. In and of itself, it was an extraordinary feat and a resounding tactical move designed to accomplish three things only: approach, attack, destroy.
⑤	**1200–1600 ±**	The Allied ships again come under attack from twenty-six to twenty-seven *Betty* bombers—an air contingency that seemed to again fly in low from the north at near-treetop-level over the rugged mountains of Florida Island and drop down over *Iron Bottom Sound*.
⑥		The USS *George F. Elliott* (AP-13) is hit by a single torpedo bomber and quickly set on fire.
⑦		*Jarvis* interposes herself between an incoming dive bomber and the heavy cruiser *Vincennes* to protect the larger, more valuable capital ship, and is herself struck by a torpedo from that same enemy bomber. Her turbines falter, the propellers slow, and she grinds to a halt in the water, the 1,500-ton warship now seriously in peril of being lost altogether.
⑧		The destroyer *Dewey* pulls alongside *Jarvis* to offer assistance and tows the stricken *Jarvis* out to a safer shallow-water anchorage near the landing zones just off Lunga Point. *Jarvis* effects some necessary repairs at that location that would then allow her to move at least minimally under her own power to a more protected mooring area closer to Tulagi to effect additional emergency repairs.
⑨		Turner's flagship *McCawley* dispatches thirty men to the *Jarvis* to aid in the ship's repairs. *Jarvis's* captain, LCDR William W. Graham, declares that he does not require assistance at that time; however, with casualties mounting and fourteen men already missing from the previous action alone, he finally capitulates and instructs that the most severely wounded men be transferred to *McCawley* for immediate medical assistance.

(continued)

Table 8. *Continued*

#	Time	Activity
		TABULAR RECORD OF MOVEMENT OF THE USS JARVIS (DD-383, 7-9 AUGUST 1942
	09 August 1942‡	
❶	**2400 ±** **Departure**	The aging destroyer/minesweeper USS *Hovey* (DD-208) is also dispatched by Turner to rendezvous with the stricken *Jarvis*. Turner instructs both ships to proceed "through the eastern passages" of Guadalcanal to avoid detection by the IJN surface fleet that were known to be prowling the area and thought to be already patrolling the western approaches for weakness and opportunistic advantage. Their destination was set to be that of Efate in the New Hebrides.
❷	**2400-0030 ±** **Departure**	❶ *Jarvis* departs Tulagi from its anchorage near Florida Island, and begins her long and erratic journey up through the "western passage," sailing from the northern reaches of Sealark Lane into the Solomon Sea, crossing an already perilous and exposed Channel all alone.
		❷ This then kicks off the continuing debate as to whether the *Jarvis* ever met with, or was engaged by, Mikawa's approaching enemy fleet. Was she still on fire even then while retiring, and was she in fact detected by Mikawa's ships upon their approach *to* Savo, or only *after* their attacks? Or could she have indeed been spied during *both* intervals—in effect, then, being seen both *coming and going?*
		❸ If at all plausible, it might clearly have been at this point during the ship's very passage that she might have been spotted by the advancing Mikawa surface fleet while still retiring from the area. Did she inadvertently serve to illuminate or silhouette the Allied ships of either the *Southern or Northern* screens; and if so, were those fires revealing enough to compromise the other warships' presence and to facilitate that IJN attacks in the first place?
		Questions seem to beget only more questions, and perhaps we may truly never know for certain. One can note, however, the curious time-stamped passage of the *Jarvis*—with its track highlighted above as ❶. Clearly, we see that at some point during her retirement from the battle area, she did indeed cruise past both the *Patterson* and the already stricken *Canberra* and then continued moving north, passing just below the last-known track of the *Astoria* herself.[46]

Note also the curious time posting for the unexplained journey of CAPT Bode's wayward *Chicago* as well ❷, as she moved off on her 40-mile trek to the northwest after having departed the battle area after the attack on her *Southern* screening force. The time-stamp seems to indicate her arrival to the north of Cape Esperance at about 0236, but does not imply that this was the same time interval for the *Jarvis* as well, as she then lumbered past Cape Esperance on her way into the Solomon Sea.

❸	0134–0135 ±	

This map—attributed to an early-on investigative report that was then later chronicled in a USNI *Proceedings* article[47] probing the disappearance of the *Jarvis*—shows an even greater level of detail, with a much more clearly defined timeline of all of the ship's last-known TROM activity. *Jarvis* is fired on just two miles south of Savo Island for the *first* time, with a spread of torpedoes launched from the Japanese destroyer *Yūnagi*, which had reportedly detached itself from Mikawa's advancing cruiser column and pursued the American ship—which the IJN ship had mistaken for a New Zealand *Achilles*-class light cruiser (CL)—as the battered American ship was attempting to exit the area. This would effectively be the American ship's *first* encounter . . . on the way *in*.

(continued)

Table 8. Continued

#	Time	Activity
④	0200–0230 ±	Jarvis is apparently fired on yet a second time as she clears Cape Esperance and reportedly passes only a "hair-raising" 3,000 yards to the south of Mikawa's now-departing ships. She is engaged by the Yūnagi (for a second time?), which IJN ship appears to relentlessly pursue her track for some time. This would effectively be the extent of the DD's second encounter—on the way out.
⑤	0308–0325 ±	Jarvis is sighted by the former picket radar Blue as she (the Jarvis) sails past Savo Island. Though the line-screening Blue had herself failed (along with the Ralph Talbot) to detect the initial approach of Mikawa's attack force, she certainly seemed to have spotted the Jarvis on the latter ship's hobbled trek away from Cape Esperance, as she was now crippled off into the lower reaches of the East Solomon Sea.
		Blue allegedly gives hot chase and prepares to engage the as-yet unidentified target, thinking the ship to be a probing IJN surface contact. The captain of the Blue herself, LCDR Graham, would have his gun crews stand down once the passing ship was determined to in fact be a friendly that is eventually identified as the Jarvis.
		As only the third ship to do so that night, the Blue also offers aid to her slower-moving sister ship, but Jarvis's captain again declines the offer, preferring instead to make directly for a safe passage and repairs at Sydney with all undue haste. After all, the beleaguered skipper of Jarvis might rightly have reasoned, other damaged ships had made port alone. Surely the Jarvis could do so as well.[48]
⑥	0600–0900 ±	By daybreak, the crew of the battered Jarvis is sighted one final time by several USS Saratoga-based reconnaissance planes some 40 miles off the SW coast of Guadalcanal—well within the area of the East Solomon Sea. Reportedly, this would be the last friendly contact the hobbled ship would have, and the last time she would be seen by any American (or Allied) surface ship or plane. By an hour past noon that same day, Jarvis would be attacked one final time in an area in the eastern Solomon Sea.

| ❼ | 1300 ± | Mistaken yet again as an Australian *Achilles*-class light cruiser for the last time some 85 miles SW of Guadalcanal, *Jarvis* is attacked by a hunting pack of thirty-one *Val* dive bombers from the Rabaul-based *Misawa Kokutai* 25th Air Flotilla. It is alleged that a combined total of sixteen torpedoes may have been fired at her, virtually in tandem at the still-smoldering destroyer, as indeed one observer noted: "Noses down (and) throttles forward, the Japanese planes bore in to attack. (The IJN) pilots saw the huge split in the *Jarvis'* side as they closed in. The *Jarvis* had no radio, no speed and a few guns left. Her crew had no boats, no life rafts, and (by and large) no chance at all."[49]

In fact, had it indeed been an *Achilles*-class light cruiser, as calculated by the IJN commanders, it might in fact have been a worthy enough target, and the Japanese bombers would have been dispatched to both "finish the job off" and to deplete that Allied cruiser contingency by at least *one*. Little did they know that *Jarvis* was but one lone destroyer, and not at all a target meriting the number of planes dispatched to intercept and destroy her. In the end, the proud *Jarvis* would go down fighting with all remaining guns in action, yet all much to no avail.[50] |
| ❽ | 1330 ± | *Jarvis* sinks in the East Solomon Sea, going down in an area just SW of Savo, some 200 nautical miles SE of Tulagi. To this very day, she remains off the coast of Tangarare, southern Guadalcanal, near an area called Lambi Bay, at a projected coordinate fix of 09°42′ S–158°59′ E. She would also be the first destroyer casualty in a series of naval campaigns to come at Guadalcanal beginning as early as August 1942. |
| ❾ | 1430 ± | *Yūnagi* radios an abbreviated message to COMCRUDIV6/18. Filled with a sense of false pride and seeming great accomplishment, LT Okada Seiichi, captain of the dogged IJN destroyer itself, quickly contacts Mikawa and reports that his ship had sunk "one cruiser with a great rumble" (the *Chicago* itself?), and one "*Achilles*-class" ship (the *Jarvis*?) damaged while attempting to "escape in the outer bay." Were the two ships sighted in fact one and the same?[51] |

*Time-frame set at 07 August 1942; initial air attack in IBS
†Time-frame set at 08 August 1942; period of repositioning
‡Time-frame set at 09 August 1942; period of highest visibility
Plus or minus (±) stated time interval. Times are understandably sketchy and inexact as regards the final hours of the Jarvis, therefore times might only be estimated by a studiec deductive projection.

Jarvis—Oh, Stricken Warrior: Conclusions

Even with only a cursory view of the visual timeline and supporting narratives presented earlier, a vivid picture begins to emerge regarding the movements of the *Jarvis*, and whether or not she might have served as a critical point of illumination that could have itself compromised the position of the ships of either the Allied Southern or the Northern screens (or *both*) that one fateful night.

Was the *Jarvis* still in fact departing the area just prior to the first-wave attack on Crutchley's *Chicago* and *Canberra*? And, even less likely, was she even in the vicinity of the *Vincennes*, *Quincy*, or *Astoria* at the time of their discovery by Mikawa's surface fleet? Were the destroyers *Bagley*, *Patterson*, *Helm*, and *Wilson*—tasked with escorting those same heavy cruisers—put in harm's way as well by an undue (if even inadvertent) illumination from the stricken *Jarvis*, herself then transiting Iron Bottom Sound while still on fire? After some considerable research and a review of the few known facts available, perhaps one might draw but one conclusion: probably not. But nonetheless consider at least some of following facts listed in Table 9.

Table 9.   USS *Jarvis*: Conclusions and Findings

Premise	Finding / Conclusion
Did the *Elliott* in fact serve as a point of illumination to compromise the position of the Allied ships during at least the outset of the First Battle of Savo Island on 9 August 1942?	
Finding ❶ (1942): USS *George F. Elliott (AP-13)* "A Candle in the Night (I)"	Certainly the premise of a silhouetted illumination (and a possible positional compromise) of the Allied ships can out of hand almost immediately exclude the USS *George F. Elliott*. Clearly, the large transport ship had already been attacked in the same air raid as the *Jarvis* herself that had been launched just two days earlier on 7 August just before the noon hour.
	Indeed, it is already well documented that both ships had been damaged in the same action; however, the *Elliott* was known to have been scuttled by the destroyer *Dewey* shortly after 1300 hours on the afternoon of the 8th, only after it was determined that the ship was in fact unsalvageable.
	In form and effect, therefore, the *Elliott* might clearly be removed from the equation and not found culpable to any degree of any real position compromise that could have resulted in the detection and subsequent attack on any of the Allied screening ships later on the night of 8–9 August.

PREMISE	FINDING / CONCLUSION

Did the *Jarvis* likewise serve as an unwitting point of focus on the night of 9 August, as it, too, made its slow transit across Iron Bottom Sound? Was she in fact still smoldering to the extent that any of the several onboard fires could have illuminated, silhouetted, or otherwise backlit any of the Allied cruisers that were part of Crutchley's Southern and Northern screens?

PREMISE	FINDING / CONCLUSION
FINDING ❷ (1942): USS *Jarvis* (DD-393) *"A Candle in the Night (II)"*	Had the *Jarvis* herself been culpable of the same claim of a position compromise due to her continuing onboard fires, even as the ship retired from the battle area just after midnight on 8 August? And did the crippled ship—*in articulo mortis*—inadvertently light up the night sky in her own move from Guadalcanal as she inched along into the East Solomon Sea? Again decidedly, probably not.
	From the time of the initial attack on the *Jarvis* just before noon on 7 August, there were seemingly only two time frames within which she might have had contact with the Japanese fleet as they approached Iron Bottom Sound from a position north of Savo. Consider the following timeline:
	❶ Between the hours of 2400 and 0030, the DD was known to have been departing the area of IBS.
	❷ Between the hours of 0134 and 0135, she is spotted by several of the ships of the approaching Mikawa force and even fired on by tail elements of that advancing column. She is reportedly attacked less than two miles south of Savo Island for the first time with a spread of torpedoes launched from the IJN DD *Yūnagi*, which had reportedly been detached from Mikawa's column to remain behind and "watch the back door" for that same advancing force.
	❸ Between the hours of 0200 and 0230, *Jarvis* is fired upon once again as she clears Cape Esperance and passes only 3,000 yards of Mikawa's departing ships. At that time, the small ship is again engaged by that same prowling *Yūnagi*.
	❹ Between the hours of 1300 and 1315, the *Jarvis* is attacked one final time and sunk some 85 miles SW of Guadalcanal after being hit by a sortie of some estimated thirty-one *Val* dive bombers.

(continued)

Table 9. *Continued*

Premise	Finding / Conclusion
And Yet the Questions Still Remain . . . Now Some Eighty-plus Years Later.	
Finding ❸ (2023): "*An Insinuation of Doubt*"	Had the *Jarvis* in fact been sighted by the IJN cruiser force both during their initial approach to Savo Island on the night of 9 August 1942 (at about 0135 hours)—*and again* as that same IJN force departed the area at about 0200 hours, this after having successfully prosecuted two surprise attacks on Getting's Southern screening group, as well as Riefkohl's Northern group?
	Was the hapless American destroyer—a brave but battered fighting ship already licking her wounds and nursing a 50-foot gash in her side—essentially therefore attacked *twice* by the same IJN surface fleet: on the way *in* and on the way *out*?
	What role did the *Yūnagi* play in the ultimate demise of the *Jarvis*? Was the Japanese destroyer in fact a prime (or even causal) factor in the sinking of the American ship at that time?
	Was it the *Jarvis* and not the *Elliott* (as previously thought) that might inadvertently have served as a means of silhouetting and backlighting any (or all) of the Allied ships that night?

Truly absorbing questions all, and more than a few of which will continue to drive researchers to further probe into the proceedings of that one night in August 1942 . . . questions for which we may never have truly viable answers. Of needs, the tale of the *Jarvis* and the *Elliott*—and the roles they *may* or may *not* have played in the detection (and subsequent exposure) of the Southern and Northern screening forces by the Mikawa surface fleet—will probably remain a well-closeted truth that may only become more obscured with the passage of time, and the sad passing of the last cadre of veterans who may actually have served in actum during that time, and who might themselves have survived the harsh and violent battles of that night. Yet nothing remains of the *Jarvis* today; there are no tantalizing clues, no evidentiary artifacts, no remnants recovered, and indeed no salvage from the wreckage site itself, where she remains to this day at an estimated position of 09°42' S–158°59' E. Perhaps only the men who sailed her might ever really know her true and final story.

In the playing out of its very tragic end, of the 233 brave souls who had survived the first action in Iron Bottom Sound, none on the *Jarvis* would survive the second. The captain of the ship that would later be called the "Little Giant," LCDR Graham, would himself be counted among the many valiant souls who would perish that day, each taking with them all of the arcane truths surrounding the last moments of that brave American destroyer.

An Alternate Outcome: Illumination and Position Compromise

So what, logically, would have been the most viable alternate outcome here? Could any of the skewed and sketchy accounts of just what happened in fact be borne out and found to be true? And what might such a scenario have even looked like? Decidedly, it could only have been grim and fatalistic indeed, at least for the hapless American cruisers on patrol that night. To such an end, consider the following:

Scenario ❶: A crippled USS *George F. Elliott*, already desperately set on by numerous enemy dive bombers and torpedo planes dispatched from Rabaul and Kavieng by Admiral Mikawa on learning of the American invasion of Guadalcanal. The probative (and unquestionably punitive) force of Japanese attack planes would strike on 8 August shortly after 1100 hours, damage the *Jarvis*, and leave the *Elliott* wholly engulfed in flames. The *Elliott* is still able to move under its own power to at least a temporary moorage in Iron Bottom Sound off Lunga Point. An engine from that lone attacking *Betty* bomber—on being hit by concentrated AA fire from the transport ship—immediately crashed on the *Elliott*'s deck and virtually punched its way through the bulkhead of the transport ship and burst into the aft cargo hold. The rear fire mains soon erupted and massive fires broke out all over the stricken vessel, forcing a final evacuation of the engine room. Most of the men were then compelled to move topside to join the other remaining crew members of the *Elliott* as they valiantly continued to battle the flames well into the night.

Savo Island and steam into Iron Bottom Sound. Mikawa's bold push down the Slot had been fueled both by a reactionary anger and his steeped antipathy for the very "insolence" of the American encroachment itself into the former Japanese stronghold of Guadalcanal. The disabled and still-burning *Elliott* could not by any means make knots enough to either engage or outrun the advancing IJN column that was even then rapidly approaching her position. Now, wary lookouts on the *Chōkai* and the other Japanese warships all come to life with a practiced animation as they spy the fiery hulk of the *Elliott* in Sealark Lane. Behind her can clearly be seen the illuminated silhouettes of multiple American cruiser-class warships and destroyers, their sleek lines and clear profiles now fortuitously shimmering through a curtain of flames already set off on the burning *Elliott* herself.

The attack on the Allied fleet begins almost immediately. The Japanese know only too well that they must strike first before being detected themselves, if betrayed by the very fires they now propose to use to their own end as part of their own attack.

Scenario ❷: The keen-eyed lookouts on the Japanese flagship *Chōkai* are already at a state of high alert, which has been ordered by Admiral Mikawa, commander of the Eighth Fleet cruiser divisions. As Mikawa's attack force sluices through the "open gates" past the two American radar pickets *Blue* and *Ralph Talbot*, they continue sailing southeast and increase speed as they skirt around volcanic Savo Island.

The lookouts easily spy the still-burning *Jarvis* on a shortened horizon, made ever brighter by the burning hulk of the ship, which can be seen quite well for some distance in the darkened night. Behind the fiery silhouette of the still-burning American destroyer, the Japanese can clearly make out at least two—possibly *three*—heavy cruisers from the enemy's fleet but have themselves not yet been seen. These would have been the ships of the Southern screen, most pointedly the heavy cruisers *Canberra* and *Chicago*, and the escort destroyers *Patterson* and *Bagley*. The IJN naval strike force now once again ruthlessly employs its keen element of surprise to spring its steel trap on the unsuspecting enemy.

The attack itself is swift and violent—incredibly well prosecuted, and over in minutes. The silhouetted form of the already crippled *Jarvis* has unintentionally served to only give away the position of the American cruisers that night. This positional compromise would be deadly to the American surface fleet, and when the fog of war had lifted its heavy veil, three heavy cruisers of the line and the Australian pride-of-fleet *Canberra* would all be lost in a single, horrific night battle at sea.

Loxton and the *Elliott*

So which ship, in fact, had the greatest culpability in divulging the position of the Allied ships that night? Loxton purports that this ship had to have been the *Elliott*, but facts do not seem to bear out that assertion. Clearly, the *Elliott* must have been miles away and already scuttled and sent to the bottom of the Sound after its earlier action of 8 August, this by the American DD USS *Dewey* itself.

The only other vessel in the vicinity at the time must have been the *Jarvis* herself. Had the "Little Giant" in fact already transited Iron Bottom Sound that night without detection, or was she encountered—not once but *twice*—by the advancing IJN naval strike force as they moved south past Savo? On this point, research will undoubtedly continue, perhaps as it has enduringly for some eighty-plus years already—and even on to the next generation of researchers and historical analysts as well—as inevitably it did mine. Will viable answers to the ever-ongoing conundrum of the *Jarvis* and the *Elliott* in fact be forthcoming, or will they instead be lost to all posterity with the sly and slow passage of time?

FINDING 8:   THE CRUTCHLEY FACTOR: BRITISH RADM VICTOR A. CRUTCHLEY

8–9 August 1942

Premise: The Crutchley Factor: Departure of British RADM Sir Victor Alexander Charles Crutchley from the area of battle

RADM Victor A. Crutchley's combined fleet screening task force on the night of 8–9 August 1942 would consist of eight Allied light and heavy cruisers and eight American

RADM Victor A. Crutchley

destroyers. In fact, there were another seven destroyers attached directly to Admiral Turner, but Crutchley's units would be stretched to the limit and even further split that night. Already had the American destroyers *Blue* and *Ralph Talbot* been reassigned from him, then wholly sequestered and tasked with covering only the western approaches to Iron Bottom Sound on "radar picket" patrols just north of Savo Island. The small volcanic island of Savo itself virtually split the Slot into two neat and "manageable" halves between the eastern and western Solomon Islands, essentially dividing it into two divergent lanes of approach.

Therefore, to cover both access venues and the eastern approaches through the narrowed channel called Indispensable Strait, Crutchley would decidedly need to divide his ships into three operational forces. Deployed to the east, then, would be the light cruisers *San Juan* and HMAS *Hobart*—plus the destroyers *Monssen* and *Buchanan*—under the overall command of Admiral Scott's Task Group 62.4 (TG 62.4). Covering the northern approaches and emanating from points west between Florida Island and Savo itself, would be RADM Riefkohl's own Northern screen, the fateful TG 62.3, with the American heavy cruisers *Vincennes*, *Astoria*, and the *Quincy*, as well as their two escorts, the DDs *Helm* and *Wilson*. Finally, to their immediate south, Crutchley would himself command the TG 62.2 Southern screening force, with the aging Australian heavy cruisers HMAS *Australia* and *Canberra*, as well as Bode's own *Chicago*, with a combat escort provisioned by the destroyers *Patterson* and *Bagley*.

Crutchley's command deployments within his thinly spread screening forces would not have been easy, given the constraints within which the man would have to work. His force dispositions had been placed with good foresight and planning, his intent was resolute, and his purview of the battle situation—even as it unfolded—could not itself be faulted. His Southern group, for the most part, was considered "seasoned" and well trained, and indeed the *Australia* and *Canberra* had already previously been formed up as a team in the Royal Australian Navy, and *Chicago* had been with them already since early 1942.[52]

By logical extension, therefore, the Northern group had itself been born out of subtle necessity—almost as a "codicil" of leftovers and last-minute assembly. Truly, from at least the admiral's point of view, it made little sense to split up the Southern screen's "experienced" working team; thus the only remaining heavy cruisers left would have been the *Vincennes*, the *Astoria*, and the *Quincy*, and each would tragically fall in together while the lighter forces of Admiral Scott were concentrated only well to the east, where they would remain in place to safeguard Tulagi, Tanambogo, and the lower reaches of Sealark Lane from enemy attack.

It would be within this critical and unrehearsed setting, then, that Admiral Turner would call his ill-advised, late-night meeting and summon several of his senior commanders to Lunga Roads at about 2130 hours aboard his flagship, the armored transport USS *McCawley* (APA-4), for that last-minute powwow. The hastily convened meeting had been set in motion imprimis to discuss the unscheduled withdrawal of Admiral Fletcher's carrier forces, and only secondarily to map out an effective battle strategy for the area. Thirdly, and truly the planning group's most immediate concern, was to set the patrol corridors that would need to be put in place to protect the very troop transport and cargo ships already at anchor in and around Guadalcanal.

Admiral Crutchley, already a key (and integral) part of that strategic planning forum, would of course be obliged to attend the meeting, and so he did. Yet, for some unknown reason, the good admiral would tragically take his entire flagship *Australia* with him to the location where the *McCawley* was situated, rather than use the more discretionary Admiral's Barge (or CAPT's Launch) or indeed any of the nearby escort destroyers that had to have been readily at his very disposal. This crucial, yet at the time seemingly non-impactful, action alone would ❶ serve to further reduce the Southern screening force's firepower by fully one-third; ❷ compromise the response effectiveness of those ships in total; and ❸ entirely remove one capital ship asset from the battle arena itself. Of course, this would later prove to be truly a dooming and ill-timed decision that would only be made worse, as the brief but violent moments ahead would later show that night.

FINDING 9:   THE BODE FACTOR: SO FAR A FALL FROM GRACE— CAPT HOWARD DOUGLAS BODE, 9 AUGUST 1942

Premise: The Bode Factor: A Long Day's Journey into Night

Then, there is the ever-curious account of the ill-fortuned CAPT Howard Douglas "Ping" Bode, commander of the *Northampton*-class heavy cruiser USS *Chicago* (CA-29), during the course of the First Battle of Savo Island. Once RADM Crutchley was called away from the battle arena itself to attend a high-level conference that had been convened by Admiral Turner, Crutchley foolishly withdrew his flagship *Australia* with him as well, this to effectively transport himself to and from that meeting location. This would later prove to be a critical error in judgment and a matter of the very worst of timing. Thus absenting himself from his patrol sector in Iron Bottom Sound—and removing the capital ship asset itself from the potential area of battle—Crutchley further compounded the error by leaving CAPT Howard Bode in charge of that full Southern screening force for the remainder of that night.

Bright Horizons: A Promising Start

Before advancing too far ahead, however, or arriving at any false conclusions regarding Bode himself, one might well be advised to view at least a quick snapshot of the career naval officer's life. CAPT Howard Bode had actually been a quite promising young naval officer—perhaps even an "exceptional" Naval Academy underclassman—with good grade point averages in virtually every area of assumed study. He had already been tagged by many as a true "up-and-comer" in the midshipman ranks, a young fledgling officer well worth a watch, and a man with one foot firmly rooted in the now and the other poised on the threshold of a good and promising future.

It would also be at this point that he would receive the curious moniker "Ping" that would forever follow his name thereafter. Nicknamed for a promising New York Yankees center-fielder from the early 1920s named Ping Bodie, Ping Bode would become a name he neither relished nor shunned thereafter, and by the early 1940s the young officer was beginning to find his stride. He had already held several influential postings to various European capitals, and as an integral (and most fortunate) part of that rapid advancement would go on to serve in many capital cities across the European continent. To his own edification and good advantage, these would include such enviable locations as London, Paris, Berlin, and even Rome, and it would be this very duty that would then make up the bulk of his early "attaché" years. Now on a somewhat accelerated and coveted "fast-track" rise to prominence, Bode would once again move up in the ranks and go on to serve as one of the youngest appointees to head the Foreign Intelligence Division (FID) of the Office of Naval Intelligence (ONI), itself one of the most prestigious investigative arms of all the military services.

Clearly, then, it might well be said that Bode was certainly no one's fool—he just had the luck of a "moke" and the timing of an igniter wick near open flame. And clearly again, he was also no stranger to misfortune; his timing and ill luck were both sadly well known and already a matter of naval record. And already had it begun to plague him for much of his early naval career, beginning in 1941 with a series of certain terrible no-fault incidents.

And the first such incident would happen on a remote tropical island paradise named Oahu, at a place called Pearl Harbor, on a date that would live on well into the future as a day of true "infamy" . . . 7 December 1941.

Command of the USS *Oklahoma* (BB-37)

After a brief and somewhat controversial stint within the ranks of the ONI,[53] Bode would shortly be "promoted up" and out of his intelligence berth and rallied on to actual fleet duty to serve on an actual capital ship of the line, probably at the behest and recommendation of his own immediate superior at the time, Admiral Richmond Kelly Turner himself. He would then be given his first full command of a large battleship of the first order . . . and that command would be none other than the grand old lady USS *Oklahoma* (BB-37) herself. A storybook success by any account, the man's rise to prominence would be exceptional and fast paced, as he now regularly dined with (and sat in the company of) admirals and men of great state. On 7 December 1941, however, all of that would come to an abrupt and somewhat ignoble end. Now obliged to be ashore to meet with his superiors and to attend to the ship's business, the *Oklahoma* would quickly come under immediate attack by the Japanese air strike that began that very morning at 7:48 AM, Hawaii Pacific time.

Bode would stand onshore, in sharp sight of his very own ship—and "first command"—and look on in horror as *Oklahoma* took multiple consecutive torpedo hits—set in a deadly spread of first three, then two—that shuddered through the ship and caused irreparable damage. A mere twelve minutes after the start of the attack, the proud battleship was severely hit again and again—and began to capsize. The men onboard, who had just survived the initial attack, now scrambled from the charred and burning deck areas and were soon ordered to abandon ship. Outboard and alongside the USS *Maryland* herself, *Oklahoma* was anchored at Berth F-5 in that famed "Battleship Row," as indeed both ships would soon be destroyed in mere minutes—entirely put out of commission until each could be repaired and restored to the line almost a year later in 1942.

The good CAPT Bode's lifelong dream of command of a capital ship would in fact be gone in moments and—through no direct fault of his own—placed on hold for several additional months to come. In and of itself, therefore, the event might nonetheless be incontrovertibly called the man's own Strike One. In August 1942, however, Bode would finally again be given another opportunity to command a major ship of the line, when he would be presented with a captaincy of yet another capital ship, this time the aging but still powerful American heavy cruiser USS *Chicago* (CA-29).

USS *Chicago* and the Attack at Sydney Harbor

The ill-starred CAPT Bode's next brush with "no-fault" disaster would come but a year later in Sydney, Australia, where once again he might be found fortuitously comingling with naval brass and dining ashore, this time with the good Admiral Gerard Charles Muirhead-Gould, the senior naval officer in command of Sydney Harbor at the time. The ever-ambitious and self-advancing captain of the *Chicago* could not at all have known that at that very moment a silent and determined enemy had already entered Port Jackson Harbor and now lay in wait, plotting yet another fierce and well-timed surprise attack on several of the Allied capital ships at anchor at that location.

Here, as almost an eerie portent and foreshadow of a time yet to come, two of those ships targeted would inescapably be both the Australian heavy cruiser *Canberra* and his very own *Chicago*. Neither skipper could possibly have known that less than a month later the two ships would meet yet again—for one final mission—far to the north and east in the very heart of the Solomon Islands. For now, however, at least three midget sub-carrying submarines of the IJN *B-1* and *C-1* class had already quietly rendezvoused with a second pack of hunter subs, the *I-29* and *I-21*, some thirty-five miles to the north and east of the inlet itself. All five submarines had slowly approached with stealth and had already been in place since 29 May, and were now set to pull the trigger on their attack some two days later.

On 31 May, therefore, the first of the enemy subs began to probe and penetrate the shallow, lightly guarded entranceway to Sydney Harbor. The small, probative force would in fact be the midget sub *M-14*, followed in a tandem attack column by the IJN's *M-24* and *M-21*, respectively. *M-14*, however, much to her own detriment and sharp surprise, would almost immediately become ensnared in an anti-submarine boom, while a second sub was summarily destroyed by a spread of depth charges (thought to have been fired from the nearby destroyer USS *Perkins* [DD-377]), and a third boat, in its own haste, could only fire wildly at the *Chicago* as the latter began to make turns to depart the area and head for open waters.

Both torpedoes fired at the *Chicago* would miss by a considerable distance, and indeed strike only lesser target assets in the area, oddly including at least one "no-value" target on land,[54] seen here as almost being the amusing equivalent of the torp fired by the USS *Bowfin* (SS-287) some two years later, as it coursed through the waters and hit a "crane and a bus" onshore.[55] This aside, the heavy cruiser would be spared further action (for at least the time being), and the attack would be over almost as quickly as it had begun.

A curious endnote to this attack is the fact that in spite of the initial sightings of the first sub occurring at about 2015 hours—with actual engagement from *Chicago*'s five-inch guns beginning at about 2252—Bode would still not get back aboard his ship until almost 2330—fully more than an hour later. And even then, when informed by a senior watch officer aboard *Chicago* that he had already begun preparations for getting under way, Bode allegedly berated the man for doing so and rescinded the order, ordering the crew to stand down—reportedly even going so far as to accuse his own staff officers of negligence and of "being drunk on duty." This accusation would, of course, be wholly refuted by Bode at the time of the post-incident follow-up and investigation and in the ship's own after-action reports (AARs), presented much later.

In its final outcome, in an incredibly short span of only six months, both of Bode's new command ships had been attacked—with one virtually shot out from under him and attacked twice without his even having been aboard either ship—and in every event, with keen quirkiness, the fault would not be his but infallibly lie elsewhere. Yet he had the luck of a moke, and clearly now might his standing be set as his own *Strike Two*.

The good CAPT Bode would once again resume his command of *Chicago*, and—sailing for a second time in the company of the *Canberra* itself—would prepare for the next leg of his journey, and his final naval exploit: this time far, far to the north in a place of great menace that would itself be called Iron Bottom Sound.

Night Actions: USS *Chicago* and the First Battle of Savo Island

Now, but a few months later, the great *Chicago* would once again become embroiled in yet another action at sea, this one by far the most fiery and brutal of all—more devastating than any she had previously encountered—and that action would be nothing less than the First Battle of Savo Island.

The date would be 9 August 1942, but an hour or so past midnight, when the ever-confident VADM Gunichi Mikawa—commander of the Imperial Japanese Navy's prestigious Eighth Fleet Japanese Striking Force, which was itself made up of RADM Aritomo Gotō's own Cruiser Division 6 (CRUDIV6), combined with his own cruiser assets that then made up his own CRUDIV18—maneuvered both attack forces south with a slow and steady push down the Slot, "sauntering unchallenged" into the upper reaches of Iron Bottom Sound. The swift and stealthy movement of his surface fleet, and the inability of the U.S. radar pickets *Blue* and *Ralph Talbot* to detect them, virtually ensured the admiral an almost impeccable element of surprise. And indeed once again it was simply *old* wine in *new* flasks.

Thirteen U.S. and Allied military ships of the line had been tasked with patrolling the waters around Sealark Lane to the south, to beyond Savo Island to the north, and from Honiara to Tulagi to the west and east, respectively. The flotilla of ships this night would include eight heavy and light cruisers for that Allied force, and at least as many escort destroyers. All of them had specific orders from the task group commander RADM Crutchley and were now set to deploy a screening force that would effectively seal off all of the waterways in and around the Sound and to protect the landing transports now discharging their much-needed troop and munitions cargoes. First and foremost, however, such a blockading action would also be done simply to "deny access" to the interloping Japanese and to impede Mikawa's approach to the Sound.

As early as 0132 hours, therefore, Mikawa's CRUDIV6 and 18 had already found the Allied fleet and were in fact already illuminating them with both flare orbs dropped from cruiser-based floatplanes and from the starshells fired from the 5-inch deck guns. Almost on the instant, then, did they begin launching their torpedo spreads in the direction of the haunting, shadowed hulks that were now the stunned ships of the Allied Southern screen. Under a canopy of cascading starshells, shipboard searchlights, and the still-smoldering silhouette of the burning transport ship USS *George F. Elliott* (AP-13), Mikawa had, by at least 0143, unleashed a ragged hell with salvo on salvo of high-caliber HE shells and Long-Lance torpedoes at each of the ships—seemingly in several different directions at once—while continuing to effectively focus most of that attack on the two heavy cruisers *Canberra* and *Chicago*.

Here at once one can begin to see, in sharp contrast, the difference in command style and reactionary response to a developing emergency situation. On the one hand, CAPT Frank Edmond Getting on the *Canberra* was at first extremely quick to respond, soon ordering an immediate increase in speed and a reversal of the ship's initial turn to port, while continuing to engage the enemy on all sides. By sad comparison, however, CAPT Bode—on his own *Chicago*—had been asleep in his quarters when awakened by the confluence of lights and near-on explosions. He then allegedly made his way to the bridge, immediately rescinded an order set by the senior watch officer to engage the enemy (or at the very least to make preparations to get under way), and berated the man on the spot for being "too precipitous," instead ordering that starshell flares be fired to first identify the attacking ships. The time lost in precisely such pointless bickering and infighting between the ship's senior officers spent countermanding orders and comparing interpretations of the battle unfolding before them would only later prove to be far deadlier than either man might ever have anticipated.

In the short interim, others on *Chicago* observing the ship's own illumination, perhaps brought on by both the burning wreckage of the *Elliott* and the IJN's own searchlights and air-dropped flare orbs, were now also alerted by the sudden turn of the *Canberra* immediately to their front. After what must have seemed an interminable march of moments, *Chicago* finally did come to General Quarters and order all of her crews to full battle stations. The rudely awakened CAPT Bode, startled from a sound but shortened sleep, now ordered his 5-inch guns to fire flares of his own over the passing column of warships, but many such shells simply malfunctioned in place in guns that were otherwise jammed. The captain's failure to execute any effective counteractive response to the attack, and his general lack of preparedness and deadly hesitation in the face of an enemy attack, would indeed all come at a high price. And by 0147, a fast-moving spread of torpedoes, reportedly fired from the Japanese cruiser *Kako*, did indeed sharply impact on *Chicago*'s bow, sending shock waves throughout the ship that would cause major damage, from its main battery directors to the ship's mainmast itself, and even claiming two lives. Then, as abruptly as the attack itself had unfolded, it was over, and the *Chicago* would see no further action in the battle.

What would follow next, however, would curiously become a point of topical discussion thereafter for many years to come: the abrupt departure of that *Chicago* from the battle area in situ. It was precisely at this point that the ship would hurriedly (and quite mysteriously) disengage from the skirmish, turn slowly, and steam north-northwest for a hectic and full *forty* minutes, leaving behind the very cargo and troop transport ships she had been tasked to protect imprimis. The departing American cruiser would last be seen firing a final salvo of shells at the trailing ships bringing up the rear of the Japanese column even as that force withdrew, where she may indeed have hit either the *Tenryū* or the DD *Yunagi*, but the actual success (or nonsuccess) of which action could never quite be confirmed.

In later investigations into the events of that night, it would be noted with great criticism that Bode did *not* assert control over any of the screening assets at his disposal (i.e., the other Allied ships within that Southern screen), and of which he was technically still in command. More significantly, Bode would also make no attempt to warn any of the other Allied ships, or the other commanders in the Guadalcanal area of the attack itself, or to even inform them of his own departure from the area—this as his ship turned abruptly and sped off to the northwest on a quick-time heading of 2-6-3, now well out of the battle zone. He would remain on that course then for some forty minutes, and simply disappear into the storm of night.

So then, *why*? Why would the good CAPT Bode have done this? Why the forty-minute trek on a dash straight north and west to points unknown? And why no communication outreach (of any kind) to any of his own ships or commanders? Was the *Chicago* in fact in hot pursuit of some "phantom" Japanese contact at the lag-end of Mikawa's now-departing cruiser column, and had she indeed engaged either the *Tenryū* or the destroyer *Yunagi*? And what of the ill-fated Bode himself—how might his actions this night be later looked on by those seeking full or even partial culpability? How indeed might the whole affair be viewed by others later seeking fault?

Indeed, the answer would come only too soon, with some now touting his actions on the night in question as being but a minor dereliction of duty, others more stridently calling them a full incompetence of captaincy, or even stupidity. But here there were a salient handful of detractors as well who were bound and determined to be heard, and it would be these men who now began whispering the even harsher words of desertion in the face of the enemy. Far and away, however, the captain's worst and most damning critics would themselves only stop short of categorizing his performance under fire that night as a truly detestable act of cowardice itself and a blatant refusal to join the battle, even at its very height. Had his move to the northwest that night in fact been just a "strategic repositioning" of his fleet asset for better attack vantage while pursuing the ghostly shadow of a Japanese warship only "reportedly" seen in the area? Or was it indeed something else? Was it something far worse and even more sinister—an awful truth that perhaps only helped to bear out the ugly claim and allegation that would later be set against this naval officer? In truth, we will probably never know, since that same truth would soon perish with the good CAPT Bode, even as he made the immutable decision to end his own life less than a year later. And even to the bitter and ignoble end of his life, Bode could never quite forget what had occurred that night, even though Savo itself was soon but a distant memory of his own failed leadership—this as he chose to die by his own hand in Panama City.

The Aftermath: Formal Censure and the Hepburn Investigation

A Voice of Reprimand

As early as 1943, CAPT Bode would be called to a full reckoning and harshly rebuked by none other than the hastily convened "Hepburn Investigation" (alternately referred to as the "Hepburn Report"), a scathing report of findings set forth by an enraged Admiral Arthur Japy Hepburn, who would himself preside over that very Naval Board of Inquiry. On the third day of April of that same year, CAPT Howard Douglas Bode would stand alone to fully answer the hot invective and rank charges, which would themselves only just fall short of incompetence and dereliction of duty then being hurled against him. Now a far uglier innuendo of "cowardice" and even "desertion in the face of the enemy" might be added to the mix. And though there may have been *no* intent to make the report of findings a matter of public record, they would indeed be surreptitiously released and Bode would himself quickly learn of them. He could clearly understand the tenor of the allegations that stood against him, and could easily read the writing on the wall. Bode might himself have clearly seen the long pitch coming in low right over the plate—even before it left the pitcher's glove. And to the hapless captain of the ill-fated *Chicago*, that pitch only too clearly now rang out as a resounding *Strike Three*.

In short order, therefore, would it soon be seen that the initial findings of the well-anticipated Hepburn Report would now seek multiple points of culpability—from Fletcher on down to Turner and Crutchley themselves—and would rebuke those responsible for the unreported sightings of the USS *S-38* sub, the Hudson planes, and even the B-17s out of Espiritu Santo. But always first and foremost in that probative investigation—and always occupying center stage—would have been the ever ill-fated CAPT Howard Douglas Bode. Oddly, though, even with all else aside, there would be yet other factors that would come into play—beyond the ponderous Bode implications—that would in the end also prove contributory (if even only negligibly so) to the routing defeat of the Allied forces during that night's battle, and to the loss of the four Allied heavy cruisers in a single thirty-one-minute action on high seas near Savo.

Shown on the following pages in both the Table 10 and Table 11 matrices, we see only a cursory discussion of those several findings summarized here for collective researcher review. The author has carefully presented here both the formal Hepburn Investigation findings and select inferences of the admiral's own fashioning, adding his own humble opinions as but a "secondary" observation of those primary findings, with which he either concurs or disputes. These latter *Concur/Do Not Concur* notations, as shown, have been added with an intent to further edify the more formalized findings already tabled and perhaps also shed new light on an old topic to offer a more balanced contemporary view and understanding of that First Battle of Savo Island and its tragic fallout and result.

Table 10.   Naval Board of Inquiry: The Hepburn Investigation and Findings

	THE ADMIRAL HEPBURN INVESTIGATION FINDINGS	CONCUR / DO NOT CONCUR
FINDING	**THE HEPBURN OBSERVATIONS**	
(a)	**FINDING:** The primary cause of the overwhelming defeat suffered during the battle at Savo was unquestionably the element of complete surprise achieved by Mikawa's surface fleet.	*Concur*
(b)	**FINDING:** An inadequate state of readiness on the part of many of the Allied screening ships that may have been insufficient to fully mitigate the sudden night attack launched by the IJN surface fleet led by VADM Mikawa.	*Concur*
(c)	**FINDING:** A failure to recognize the very presence and intent of the enemy ships in the vicinity of IBS just prior to the attack itself.	*Concur*
(d)	**FINDING:** A fatal and misplaced confidence in the functional capabilities of the radar screening systems deployed for the first time on the picket ships *Blue* and *Ralph Talbot*.	*Concur*
(e)	**FINDING:** A serious breakdown and failure in the communication protocols used that occurred on many levels, and which directly resulted in the lack of a timely send-and-receive of vital intel on enemy contacts, position, and transitive movements throughout the area.	*Concur*
(f)	**FINDING:** The abrupt and ill-advised withdrawal of Admiral Fletcher's Carrier Task Force on the evening *before* the battle, effectively removing all of those capital ships, and the air assets they could have provided, from the battle area itself.[56]	*Concur*
(g)	**FINDING:** The actions (or *inactions*) of Captain Howard Douglas Bode on the night of 9 August 1942 as being wholly contributive to the resulting capital ship losses during that later battle.	*Do Not Concur*

Here, as much for the edification of the reader as to review the actual findings of the original Hepburn Report—and those additional observations uncovered by the author himself—the following topical discussion points are presented below in the Table 11 matrix, all of which are offered to show both contrast and similarity to many of those discovery results as well, yet indeed the mysteries only continue to abound:

Table 11. Naval Board of Inquiry: Author's Observations

THE HEPBURN INVESTIGATION FINDINGS		CONFIRMED / NOT CONFIRMED
FINDING	**AUTHOR'S OBSERVATIONS**	
(a)	**PREMISE:** *Removal of Fletcher's Carrier Task Force*	**(C)**
	The inopportune withdrawal of Admiral Fletcher's CTF force on the evening *before* the battle of 9 August must have been immeasurably impactful. Citing a weighted concern over ❶ losses already sustained by his carrier aircraft contingency in the earlier battles of 7 August; ❷ the threat of further Japanese air attacks on his still-vulnerable carrier assets; ❸ worries about his ships' collective fuel states; and ❹ a further need to effect emergency repairs for at least some of the ships within his fleet, Fletcher summarily announces his intent to depart the area on the evening of 8 August, and soon does so—and in an instant he is simply gone. In so doing, he would withdraw not only the carrier assets *Saratoga*, *Enterprise*, and the *Wasp*, but the large BB *North Carolina* itself as well.	
	This would now essentially leave the Marine landing forces already entrenched on both Guadalcanal and Tulagi (and even as far south as Tanambogo), with essentially *no* air cover for the duration of their unloading operations. It would also become one of the principal reasons for Admiral Turner's conference on the night of 8 August—which conference would itself pull Crutchley and his own flagship *Australia* away from the main area of battle as well.	
	This action alone would soon develop a life of its own, with an in-service persona that would then stand as a rankling bone of contention between the men of both services, as soon enough the entire affair would later tongue-in-cheek be recalled by the "abandoned" Marines for all time as the "Great Navy Bug-Out" and would easily be forgiven or forgotten by the men.	
(b)	**PREMISE:** *An Element of Surprise*	**(C)**
	The primary cause of the defeat of the fleet assets within both the Southern and Northern screening forces was, and still remains, the full element of surprise achieved by Mikawa's cruiser attack force on the night of 9 August 1942.	

(continued)

Table 11. *Continued*

	THE HEPBURN INVESTIGATION FINDINGS	CONFIRMED / NOT CONFIRMED
FINDING	AUTHOR'S OBSERVATIONS	
	The unhindered passage of Mikawa's cruiser divisions past the radar pickets *Blue* and *Ralph Talbot*—and the successful prosecution of their later attacks on both the Southern and Northern fleets—can all be directly attributable to their unseen passage and *non*-detection as that enemy force moved into (and out of) the surrounding waterways near Savo Island.	
(c)	**PREMISE:** *Early Warning: USS S-38* Failure of the American attack submarine USS *S-38* to adequately report the movement of the Mikawa task force in a timely and actionable manner.	**(NC)**
(d)	**PREMISE:** *Early Warning: Australian RAAFR Hudsons* Failure of the two Australian Hudson reconnaissance aircraft pilots to adequately report—in a timely and actionable manner—the approach of Mikawa's CRUDIV6 and CRUDIV18 task force.	**(NC)**
(e)	**PREMISE:** *Early Warning: Espiritu Santo B-17 Bombers* Failure of the two American B-17 heavy bombers from Espiritu Santo, Vanuatu to detect and report the position (and approach) of the southbound IJN surface fleet, and to effectively "sound the alarm" prior to their actual arrival at Savo and the lower reaches of *Iron Bottom Sound.*	**(NC)**
(f)	**PREMISE:** *Early Warning: Fleet Destroyer USS* Blue Failure of the fleet destroyer USS *Blue* (DD-387)—in its radar picket patrol corridor—to detect the approach of the southbound IJN surface fleet, and to effectively sound an alarm in a timely and actionable manner.	**(C)**
(g)	**PREMISE:** *Early Warning: Fleet Destroyer USS* Ralph Talbot Failure of the fleet destroyer USS *Ralph Talbot* (DD-390)—in its radar picket patrol corridor—to detect the southbound IJN fleet, and to sound an alarm in a timely and actionable manner.	**(C)**
(h)	**PREMISE:** *Early Warning: Fleet Destroyer USS* Jarvis Failure of the fleet destroyer USS *Jarvis* (DD-393) to detect the IJN destroyer *Yūnagi*—or the greater CRUDIV force itself—even as it departed the Guadalcanal area—and again to effectively sound an alert in a timely and actionable manner to either the Southern or Northern fleets.	**(NC)**

THE HEPBURN INVESTIGATION FINDINGS		CONFIRMED / NOT CONFIRMED
FINDING	**AUTHOR'S OBSERVATIONS**	
(i)	**PREMISE:** *Early Warning: Fleet Destroyer USS* Patterson Failure of the fleet destroyer USS *Patterson* (DD-392) to detect the nearby IJN destroyer *Yūnagi*—or the greater CRUDIV surface fleet itself—or to also alert at least the Southern screening force commanders of that sighting in a timely and actionable manner. It should rightly be noted, however, that the *Patterson* would be the first ship to spot the Mikawa force—when indeed it finally did—and would also be the first Allied ship to engage that same enemy force.	**(NC)**
(j)	**PREMISE:** *The Crutchley Factor* The departure of British Admiral Victor Crutchley from the area of battle on the night of 8 August 1942 would in and of itself engender a command scenario in which all the following would occur: ❶ Captain Bode would be placed in charge *pro tempore* of the full Southern screening force; ❷ Crutchley would later himself depart the battle area and not inform the other ships (or ships' commanders) of that absence from his station; and ❸ Crutchley would thereby also remove the one critical capital ship asset, that was in fact the heavy cruiser *Australia* itself, from the battle main. During the course of that later decisive battle, her large guns might indeed have been much needed. (See also Finding **(l)**.)	**(C)**
(k)	**PREMISE:** *The McCain Factor* Admiral John S. McCain Sr.—extant COMNAVAIR at the time—had been given specific orders from Fletcher and Turner to increase aerial reconnaissance in and around the Guadalcanal area—and north past Savo Island—and so moving up the Slot. For reasons unknown, however, the senior McCain would in fact find it more expedient to *not* carry out the order and did not sanction the extra reconnaissance flights needed to conduct the level of aerial surveillance expected by Turner.	**(NC)**

(continued)

Table 11. *Continued*

	THE HEPBURN INVESTIGATION FINDINGS	CONFIRMED / NOT CONFIRMED
FINDING	**AUTHOR'S OBSERVATIONS**	
(l)	**PREMISE:** *Fleet Communications: Crutchley Goes to Tea* Seen as a full breakdown in communications and information exchange, the departure of Crutchley to attend Turner's McCawley Conference was bound to be impactful on that Southern screening force. Other than Bode, it left no clear link to an effective chain of command, and the commander of that SSF simply left the group with only little or no notification. That he would later *remain* in that same X-Ray transport area overnight was in and of itself another matter completely. (See also Finding **(j)**.)	**(C)**
(m)	**PREMISE:** "*Mission Implausible*" No clear mission outline, viable battle plan, or operational strategy appeared to be in place for either Crutchley's own Southern (or Riefkohl's Northern) screening force, on the occasion of 9 August 1942. In fact, little indeed might be gainsaid of the admiral's bet-hedging deployment of the few ships he did have at his disposal on that occasion. As a result thereof, he would have been further compelled to break down those few remaining forces into several barely adequate screening elements that would then patrol the *Sound*, and would become his famed Southern, Northern, and Eastern screening groups—this while also adding a *fourth* safeguard with the two radar picket ships (*Blue* and *Ralph Talbot*) set on a patrol corridor far to the north of Savo.	**(C)**
(n)	**PREMISE:** "*Good Fortune and the Trick of Luck*" From the fortuitous passage through the New Georgia Sound, Mikawa's surface fleet made a stealthy and somewhat undetected push down the Slot and out into *Iron Bottom Sound*—all virtually undetected. As a result, VADM Mikawa had nothing at all if not sweet "Lady Luck" herself riding with favor on his shoulders on at least the night of 9 August.	**(NC)**

	THE HEPBURN INVESTIGATION FINDINGS	CONFIRMED / NOT CONFIRMED
FINDING	**AUTHOR'S OBSERVATIONS**	
	Mikawa's sly surface fleet had that night been made up of seven heavy and light cruisers and one DD, the *Yūnagi*, so indeed how "fortunate" that the American sub *S-38*, the two Australian Hudson scout planes, and even the small flight of B-17s out of Espiritu Santo—all of whom had indeed spotted his ships at various times, in various places—would experience either technical difficulties (or other imponderable delays) in getting the information about those sightings back to their respective base HQs.	
	And what of Mikawa's continued streak of good fortune when he also sluiced past the two radar pickets *Blue* and *Ralph Talbot* as well, where both had been set to guard the northernmost approaches to the Sound from a point just north of Savo? At precisely the time of Mikawa's approach to their position, both American DDs were just then conveniently executing their perigee turns and were circling back and away from Mikawa's approaching column of warships.	
	Clearly, then, "luck" must have sat squarely on the shoulders of the well-favored IJN admiral this one night, and small wonder, then, that the brilliant Japanese cruiser commander would go on to so successfully prosecute his twin attacks on the Allied ships with near impunity.	
(o)	**PREMISE:** *Effectiveness of Japanese Naval Night Operations* The well-known but little-acknowledged ability of the IJN surface fleets to conduct organized (and highly effective) naval night battles, which knowledge would later come at great expense to both the American and Allied forces and at first as somewhat of a surprise to the coalition forces. Surprising also, at least to the men of the Allied ships, was just *how good* they were indeed. The attack at Savo had not at all been a fluke on the part of Mikawa's attacking forces that night, and neither would the later encounters during the Battle of Cape Esperance and final Battle of Tassafaronga itself.	**(C)**

(continued)

Table 11. *Continued*

	THE HEPBURN INVESTIGATION FINDINGS	CONFIRMED / NOT CONFIRMED
FINDING	AUTHOR'S OBSERVATIONS	
	In fact, the IJN most lived for the night—and indeed almost nurtured it—thriving best at night and far preferring the cover of darkness as perhaps their best weapon overall, as indeed it fought its most decisive and routing battles during that time, seeking always to further improve on those very skills. Their deadly system of hit-and-run tactics that they already so freely employed in battle after battle was only further stepped up and made even more effective by its full-time commitment to precisely perfecting those skills through its series of naval night fighting practice drills, and even live-fire gunnery exercises. The fierce night-fighters of Japan's Imperial Japanese Navy might indeed have been the first in the game, and so—for at least that time—they would continue to be the undisputed masters of its trade and practice.	
(p)	**PREMISE:** *Close Encounters and the Cost of Friendly Fire* Of a noted *nine* possible (and well-accounted-for) incidents of "friendly fire" possibly occurring between the frenzied Allied forces during the course of the surprise attacks by the IJN on 9 August—most by far occurred during Mikawa's first-wave attack on Crutchley's Southern screening force. Whether the *Bagley* itself reportedly firing in error upon the *Chicago* at the height of battle, or the *Patterson* perhaps doing the same—*or* simply the dispute over just who fired the crippling torpedo bow shot at *Chicago* that then took that cruiser somewhat out of action—there still remained many questions. In fact, there may indeed have been an inestimable number of like occurrences, with a series of near-in "fire-on" incidents that happened only in the blink of an eye in heated battle, and that either may or may not have been recorded to history. But the number of IFF and mistaken-identity events that *did* occur during the 1BOSI must clearly have been significant enough in its own time, such that it could indeed have played a high-stakes role in that battle. Second only to this concept of IFF and mistaken-identity was perhaps also the number of "near-on collisions" between ships—both enemy and friendlies—again during the course of that battle main.	**(NC)**

Table 12. Naval Board of Inquiry: Captain Howard Douglas Bode Allegations

	THE HEPBURN INVESTIGATION FINDINGS	CONCUR (C) DO NOT CONCUR (DNC)
FINDING	THE AUTHOR'S OBSERVATIONS	
	CAPTAIN HOWARD DOUGLAS BODE: *"SOLA CULPA— UNUM REPREHENDO"*	
(a)	**ALLEGATION:** A failure of Captain Bode to take the lead and initiative following the departure of RADM Crutchley on his flagship *Australia* to attend the Admiral Turner conference aboard the USS *McCawley*	*Concur.* It must have been Crutchley's full expectation that Captain Bode, then in command of *Chicago*, would be competent enough to command the entirety of the Southern screening force in his absence. In full retrospect now, however, this would obviously be a critical mistake in judgment on the part of the commanding admiral.
		Already perhaps known as a man of encumbering caution and tentativeness—and one seemingly plagued with ill luck—Bode would later effectively "drop the ball" during at least the opening gambit of the 1BOSI. The list of things done wrong, protocols ignored, and notification alerts not sent, would go on and on and ponderously. The charges would later stack up against the ill-fated captain of *Chicago*—and remain virtually *sola culpa–unum reprehendo* for this man only—sole blame and sole responsibility for all.
		Those findings and charges would soon echo forth and would be summarized as follows:
		❶ A failure to detect the approach of Mikawa's cruiser divisions themselves;
		❷ A failure to prosecute a viable offensive—or even *defensive*—response to that same attacking surface fleet;
		❸ A failure to protect the Australian heavy cruiser HMAS *Canberra*;
		❹ A failure to mobilize and deploy the escort destroyers (and other fleet assets) at his immediate disposal as the commander *pro tempore* of the Southern screen;
		❺ A failure to notify any of the other commanders of the Northern screen of the attack;
		❻ A failure to notify any of the other commanders of the Eastern screen of the attack;

(continued)

Table 12. *Continued*

Finding	The Hepburn Investigation Findings / The Author's Observations	Concur (C) / Do Not Concur (DNC)
		Captain Howard Douglas Bode: "Sola Culpa— Unum Reprehendo"
		❼ A failure to notify any of the other commanders of his unscheduled departure from the area of battle, then traveling WNW for an unexplained forty minutes;
		❽ A failure to provide protective cover for the very transport and landing ships at Tulagi and Honiara for which he had *imprimis* been tasked to shield.
(b)	**Allegation:** A failure to warn any of the elements of the Northern screening force of Mikawa's approach	*Concur.* Bode's failure to notify the commander of the Northern screening force—under the aegis of RADM Frederick Lois Riefkohl, of that attack—even as it unfolded on the *Canberra, Bagley, Patterson,* and even *Jarvis* and other ships in the vicinity of the Southern screen's patrol sector that night.
		Clearly, Bode must have had ample opportunity—on numerous occasions before, during, and even after the Japanese surprise attack had been prosecuted—to sound an alarm for that Northern contingency, or even RADM Scott's own Eastern group.
		The commander's failure to effectively mount an alert—to any of the ships in the area—would directly (or perhaps even *indirectly*) result in the dreadful losses that the Northern screen would later suffer.
(c)	**Allegation:** A failure to take an immediate command of the appreciable DD (destroyer) force assets at his disposal as commander *pro tempore* of the Allied Southern force	*Concur.* Bode's failure to mobilize and deploy the destroyer assets at his disposal, as Commander *pro tempore* of the Southern fleet in Crutchley's absence, would that night be no one else individual's shortcoming if not his own. Indeed, even casual research of the battle, the deployment scenarios and fleet assets available to Bode on the night of 9 August, would easily show that he had not only his own two escort destroyers *Patterson* and *Bagley* immediately on station, but not far away the Eastern group's own DDs, *Monssen* and *Buchanan* available to him as well.

It must also be a foregone conclusion that had the Northern screen learned of the attack from Mikawa's cruiser division, they too would have altered their current 3-1-5 heading to the NW and immediately reversed course to assist. Had Bode seen fit to communicate the threat of the moment to any of the elements of the other screening forces deployed in the Sound, the outcome might have been measurably different for the Allied forces that night and would indeed have come at a far lesser cost.

| (d) | **ALLEGATION:** Bode's inexplicable course change to west, away from the battle arena itself, might possibly constitute an even more egregious charge of dereliction of duty, or even desertion in the face of the enemy | *Concur.* *Chicago*, under the command of Captain Bode, would—at the very height of the battle itself—suddenly (and inexplicably) make an abrupt turn and begin sailing off on a new heading to WNW, on a straight-line run on 2-6-3; this for a reported forty minutes.

The first torpedo hit targeting *Chicago* would rock the CA with a shudder felt from stem to stern from the impact to her bow. Occurring at about 0147 hours, the single torpedo hit was thought to have been fired from the Japanese cruiser *Kako* at extremely close range, however, discrepancies surrounding just which ship had fired the bow shot would later arise, many accounts of which later seemed at one point to even implicate either (or both) the nearby *Bagley* or the *Patterson*. For additional information on this subject, see the detailed discussion on the controversy of the "bow shot" on the USS *Chicago*, beginning on page 185, along with corresponding endnotes.

A second torpedo would also impact the ship but not at all detonate, although some damage would nonetheless be sustained. A final parting shot to the mainmast, again probably fired from the 5-inch guns of that same *Kako*, would cause *Chicago* to take further evasive measures and to depart the area in full. |

(continued)

Table 12. *Continued*

	THE HEPBURN INVESTIGATION FINDINGS		CONCUR (C)
FINDING	THE AUTHOR'S OBSERVATIONS		DO NOT CONCUR (DNC)
		CAPTAIN HOWARD DOUGLAS BODE: *"SOLA CULPA— UNUM REPREHENDO"*	
			Here, sharply contrasting reports might only inconclusively connote one of two scenarios: ❶ That *Chicago* was pursuing one or more elements of the tail-end of the Mikawa attack column—possibly the *Tenyū* or the *Yunagi*—as they swung about and began moving north for their second-phase attack on Riefkohl's own Northern screen. ❷ That she was following standard *zigzag* course maneuvering in a bid to outdistance the guns and torpedoes that were even then savaging her at the time.
(e)	**ALLEGATION:** A failure to notify any of the other ships in the screening convoy of his unscheduled departure from the transport area		*Concur.* Bode's unexplained departure from the area of battle on *Chicago* that night would in and of itself be bad enough. The removal of his one capital ship asset as well—in this event a single heavy cruiser of the line—from the battle area when *most needed*, could only further exacerbate an already frenzied and deadly attack. With his sudden turn to port to a new WNW heading, the ship's course would change to 2-6-3 as it now moved off at a quickened pace. Regrettably, Bode would do so without formally notifying his own superior, RADM Crutchley, of his intent to leave—nor would he notify any of the other captains, most notably Norman Scott of the *Eastern* screen, or even Frederick Riefkohl at the helm of the Northern group.

It must be concluded then, that the exclusion of the *Chicago* from the battle main early on in its opening gambit—indeed not soon to return—would be much like a limb bitterly lopped from the greater whole. The remaining ships were now simply *down* one cruiser, and indeed that many more guns, because Bode had opted to leave the area on his ship. Fewer resources, and a diminished strength in firepower that could have been brought to bear against Mikawa's attacking cruisers, would have an immeasurable impact on the battle, the men, the ships, and the greater honorific of "stand and fight" that all Americans—then and now—might so easily embrace.

In addition, the time lost during his mysterious "40-minute" trek to the north, is probably little more than an intangible since the full battle at Savo would, in its entirety, only last some thirty-one minutes in its entirety. Even then, the most severe damage would occur within just the first five to ten minutes of the attack itself, as indeed there would be no "prolonged" assault, since Mikawa's attack strategy had all along been to remain fluid at all times. Bode's journey to the WNW—*away* for the battle zone itself—virtually ensured that his ship would see no further action in that battle, as indeed it did not for the remainder of that night.

So indeed was it a self-serving, self-*saving* flight from what he might clearly have seen as certain death, or was it instead but a *bold* pursuit as *Chicago* continued to fire all guns while hot on the heels of the departing *Tenryū*— after its successful attack on the Southern screening force—in which action the Allies sadly witnessed the tragic sinking of the *Canberra* herself?

Truly, the reasons behind the reluctant captain's failure to communicate with any of the other commanders of his screening force (or even other ships in proximity)—or why he departed the area of battle when he did—may never be known in full. Later, in April 1943, a disheartened Bode would take all of those insights and answers with him as he chose to indeed take his own life; and all of those truths would never see the light of day, leaving only dark rumor, theory, and conjectural opinion behind in its harsh, harsh wake.

(continued)

Table 12. *Continued*

	THE HEPBURN INVESTIGATION FINDINGS	CONCUR (C)
		DO NOT CONCUR (DNC)
FINDING	**THE AUTHOR'S OBSERVATIONS**	
	CAPTAIN HOWARD DOUGLAS BODE: *"SOLA CULPA— UNUM REPREHENDO"*	
(f')	**ALLEGATION:** Incompetence in captaincy and an even greater level of inexperience as a combat commander	*Concur.* The author might be inclined to agree to some extent but finds any implied greater charge of cowardice a shade too harsh indeed and would not agree with the "wide-ranging" tenor of that implication.

Something happened to Captain Bode that night . . . something indeed few of us could ever fathom, or even expect to experience. The sudden, violent, and seemingly relentless attack on his Southern screen—all occurring in a span of minutes and right before his eyes—must have been quite a harrowing experience for the as-yet untested Bode.

Indeed it might be said that it is possible that Bode never really had a chance to command a capital ship of the line in battle. In fact, he may indeed have carried himself with the demeanor of a captain but given his largely administrative and Intelligence background with the ONI, it is feasible that the man had never truly been tested under actual combat conditions.

He had twice escaped the mayhem and clutch of an enemy surprise attack, both at Pearl Harbor and again at Sydney Harbor in Australia. In the first scenario, it would be his first command ship, the great BB *Oklahoma*, that would be virtually destroyed before his eyes as part of the 2-wave attack that took place in December 1941. In the second instance, it would be yet another attack of subterfuge and strategy—a minor brush with midget subs firing on both his *Chicago* and the *Canberra* while at anchor in Sydney Harbor. |

But both of these twin attacks were *not* Savo Island, or anything like the attack that would later be prosecuted against the Southern screen. As naval engagements went, the thirty-one-minute battle at Savo was a white-hot magnesium strip on fire that would flash for but a few brief moments only, then almost as quickly would fade and abate as the attacking IJN ships moved out of range, only well after the worst damage had been inflicted.

An encounter of such a type, and of such a magnitude—however brief—could well be expected to strike fear in the heart of any man, but what one *does* with that fear in the face of such adversity will always be the mark of the man—and of the captain of that ship; and so it would be with Bode.

That he would fail to gather and redeploy the ships in his charge, and at his disposal during the course of the attack, the author agrees that the allegation *is* founded.

That he would fail to notify the commanders of the Northern group, or even of the Eastern group of the attack, and thus very easily *combine* those same fleet assets—the author must again agree that the allegation *is* founded.

That he would depart the area of battle, at one of the most crucial and decisive moments of that skirmish, and inexplicably travel some *forty* minutes to the WNW—whether that departure was in fact flight *or* pursuit—with no apparent incentive to do so, the author agrees that the allegation *is* founded.

(continued)

Table 12. *Continued*

	THE HEPBURN INVESTIGATION FINDINGS	CONCUR (C)
		DO NOT CONCUR (DNC)
FINDING	**THE AUTHOR'S OBSERVATIONS**	
	CAPTAIN HOWARD DOUGLAS BODE: *"SOLA CULPA— UNUM REPREHENDO"*	
(f²)	**ALLEGATION:** Incompetence in captaincy . . . *(Continuum)*	*That Captain Bode would* fail to provide continued protective naval cover for the amphibious transport and supply ships then unloading at both Tulagi and Honiara—as ordered by Crutchley and Turner—the author agrees that the allegation *is* founded.
		That the captain would critically (and unnecessarily) expose those lesser transport ships to an unimpeded naval attack from the IJN combined fleet that night—due entirely to his abandoning his station on *Chicago* and departing the area for a set period of time—the author agrees that the allegation *is* founded.
		So, did Captain Howard Bode, in fact, have the stuff to be an effective "wartime" captain? Did the man truly possess the "intestinal fortitude" to act and lead under heavy fire, and to assume tactical control of a hotly developing situation, however unexpectedly? Or, based on his many stateside years in his senior position at the ONI, was the man merely a displaced (or misplaced) Intelligence officer simply in too deep over his head?
		His first command, the grand *Oklahoma* herself, would last only thirty days and would end ignobly with the attack on Pearl; his second (and last) command would effectively end with an unreasoned trek to west for some forty unaccounted-for minutes without explanation or any level of accountability.
		In less than a year's time, Bode would use his own .45 automatic to summarily bring his life to an end in Balboa, Panama Canal Zone, on an afternoon in April 1943 before being able to answer or resolve any of these questions.

(g)	**ALLEGATION:** Dereliction of duty, cowardice, and desertion in the face of the enemy, (i.e., desertion under fire) … perhaps the most egregious of all charges	*Do Not Concur.* These would perhaps be the most serious and most egregious of all charges that might have been hurled at the hapless Bode after the Allied surface fleet would suffer perhaps one of the most smashing naval defeats in all of naval history.
		That Bode failed to remain on station and provide continued cover for the unloading transport and supply ships that he had been tasked to support would not, in and of itself, have been an indication of cowardice or desertion, given the fact that the *Chicago* would later allege that she left only to "pursue several tail elements" of Mikawa's fleet. In fact, that ship would even later be tentatively identified as having been either the IJN cruiser *Tenryū* or smaller DD *Yūnagi*.
		Therefore, if at all true, and the ship was engaging the departing Japanese ships as stated, it would indeed explain both the absence and the missing forty minutes and would effectively mitigate both of the grim charges of cowardice and desertion. How, after all, could such charges be true if the ship was in fact engaged in its own touch-and-go fight with remnants of that fleeing IJN force?
		Could the period of time in which *Chicago* was absent from the primary scene of battle in fact be attributed to the amount of time spent in pursuit? Or, was it something else—something far less commendable, under a completely different guise of fear and flight? Perhaps the world might now never know for sure.

Hepburn's Naval Board of Inquiry would go on to interview virtually all of the Allied commanders and staff officers who may have been even marginally involved in the action of 9 August; that process would continue for a period of some several months beginning in December 1942. At length, and in conclusion, Hepburn's report would then recommend official censure for but one officer only, the good CAPT Howard Douglas Bode. It would take little into account of any of the others involved; nor did it, in its summation, find any significant degree of culpability in others and would only stop short of recommending any formal action against any of the other key players. Those "key players," of course—of good mention—would inevitably have had to have been a full grouping of all the key flag officers involved that night, and as such would need to include the likes of Admirals Fletcher, Turner, McCain, and Crutchley—as well as the beleaguered commander of the cruiser *Vincennes*, CAPT Frederick Lois Riefkohl.

In all events, it would indeed appear that the long and fruitful naval careers of Admirals Turner, Fletcher, and McCain would not at all be adversely affected by the crushing defeats at Savo at the hands of a momentarily triumphant VADM Gunichi Mikawa—or by the contributory gaffes and miscalculations that seemed to have occurred on the Allied side, and which led to its most tragic outcome. Admiral Crutchley—perhaps an "inconvenient victim" of his own decision to depart the battle area at the critical juncture at which he did—would become the target of only marginal criticism from his superiors and peers (perhaps undeservedly so) but would go on to retain a higher level of confidence within his own chain of command than would the good CAPT Bode. Crutchley would in fact continue in his command of the Royal Australian Navy (RAN) Task Force 44 (TF 44) for yet another two years. The much-honored admiral would go on to even later be awarded his country's honored Chief Commander, Legion of Merit medal in September 1944.

As for Captains Riefkohl and Bode, however, neither man would ever command a capital ship of the line again. By October of the same year, Riefkohl would move on to at least some level of commendable attaché duty within the American Embassy at Mexico City for the remainder of 1942. In sharp contrast, however, a far less fortunate CAPT Bode, on learning that the findings of the Hepburn Report might be particularly scathing toward him, and specifically targeted and highly critical of his actions—and seemingly his alone—would go on to take his own life less than a year later in Panama City in 1943.

A "Report" of Suicide

Only a "report" of suicide.[57] Sadly, there would never be any formal congressional investigative committees, no Naval War College analyses, and no full proceedings held against the good CAPT Howard Douglas Bode. There would be no Captain's Board, no call of reckoning, and truly no satisfactory explanation from Bode himself as to the what and why of what did (and did not) occur on that one night in 1942. Understandably quite disturbed by the seemingly career-ending events unfolding before him, a distraught and deeply troubled Bode would return to his Bachelor Officers' Quarters (BOQ) on 19 April 1943, post a carefully penned letter to Admiral Hepburn himself, and then enter his bathroom, place a .45-caliber pistol to his head, and take his own life. By the following day he would succumb to his injuries and die from the single, self-inflicted gunshot wound at Balboa Hospital in the U.S. Panama Canal Zone.

And not a single living soul would ever hear the man's full story of what occurred that night. Instead, he would leave behind a dark and saddening legacy of only shaded events and rank, nagging doubt.

From a Historical Perspective: The Very Now of the Bode Testament

Even this action alone would still not forever close the book and curious chapter on CAPT Howard Douglas "Ping" Bode and his performance on the night in question while in command of the USS *Chicago*. Instead, he would go on to become the focal point of the quasihistorical account of *The Bode Testament*,[58] which would itself be a chronologically accurate, projected historical novel of the alleged "trial" of CAPT Howard Bode—indeed had he even lived.

Ultimately, this lifelong military man would have reached the very pinnacle of his naval career and—having been implicated in perhaps just one catastrophe too many—would decidedly go on no further. History would remember the man with both distaste and disfavor. And, whether a charge of cowardice, desertion in the face of the enemy, stupidity, or just plain incompetence of captaincy, CAPT Bode would forever bear the brunt of the blame for not only the loss of the *Canberra* but also the crippling of his own *Chicago* and the later attack on the Northern screen in full. In the end it would be history, and the very people who would play a role in its making and recording, that would neither forgive nor forget.

And so, what of the hapless CAPT Howard Bode and the bald allegations that might soon have been leveled at him by RADM Hepburn, LCDR Ramsey, and others? What was his true level of guilt, if any? And what of the puzzling equation of the man's overall culpability in the outcome of the battle itself, a fixed equation that seemed only too perfect and too contrived, as seen even then in the very charges that might stand against the forever star-crossed captain? Thus, much like the convoluted and ever-elusive Axiom of Coherent States, were the allegations against Bode just too perfect, too convenient, and simply too targeted—and all indeed to the exclusion of any real culpability found among any of the others?

Or was the good captain in fact guilty of all the charges that Admiral Arthur Japy Hepburn was almost certain to pursue? We may never know for sure.

Further Reading

Should the serious researcher wish to pursue a further course of study on the ill-fortuned CAPT Howard Douglas Bode—his naval career and time served on the *Chicago*—please reference any (or all) of the following research websites:

Domagalski, John J. (2010). *Lost at Guadalcanal: The Final Battles of the Astoria and Chicago as Described by Survivors and in Official Reports.* McFarland.

Hornfischer, James D. (2011). *Neptune's Inferno.* Bantam.

Kilpatrick, C. W. (1987). *Naval Night Battles of the Solomons.* Exposition Press.

Lundstrom, John B. (1977). *First South Pacific Campaign: Pacific Fleet Strategy: December 1941–June 1942.* Naval Institute Press.

Shanks, Sandy, and Tim Lanzendoerfer (2001). *The Bode Testament.* iUniverse, Inc.

Warner, Denis Ashton, Peggy Warner, and Sadao Senoo. (1992). *Disaster in the Pacific: New Light on the Battle of Savo Island.* Naval Institute Press.

FINDING 10:   THE McCAIN FACTOR: RADM JOHN SIDNEY McCAIN SR.

9 August 1942

Premise: A Failure to Launch: The Gaffe at Guadalcanal

On the day before the little-known First Battle of Savo Island, which took place on the night of 8–9 August 1942, RADM John Sidney "Slew" McCain Sr. had been specifically ordered by his superior, RADM Richmond Kelly Turner, to conduct additional (and specific) reconnaissance overflights of all approaches into and out of Guadalcanal. By necessity, this task would have to include all of the upper reaches of Iron Bottom Sound—above *Tassafaronga and Cape Esperance*—and well to the north into a hotly contested area known only as the Slot. For reasons that have hitherto remained uninterpretable or even known, the good admiral would neither carry out Turner's order for that additional reconnaissance nor inform his superiors of his decision not to do so. As a profound consequence of this action—or *"in*action," as it were—the area overflights would not take place, thus preempting the possible detection of IJN VADM Gunichi Mikawa's advancing cruiser divisions and making it next to impossible to engage them with the scant screening ships left at RADM Crutchley's disposal.

The senior McCain was quite an enigmatic figure who would himself engender a curious and historical phenomenon, in that ADM John S. "Slew" McCain Sr. would in fact be the *father* of John S. "Jack" McCain Jr. (also an admiral of the United States Navy). Indeed, these two would set a historical precedent as the only father-and-son twosome in the United States Navy who would: ❶ both serve concurrently; ❷ both serve within the same branch of service; ❸ both serve during the same (war) time period; ❹ both serve in the same theater of operations in the Pacific; and ❺ both go on to achieve the same flag officer rank and status, with each man becoming a four-star admiral. They would also share the honor of being related to yet another McCain, their grandson and son (respectively)—the navy captain, aviator, and erstwhile POW John Sidney McCain III, who would himself later become the senior senator from the great state of Arizona and go on to become the Republican presidential candidate in the momentous 2008 election.

Each of these unique distinctions aside—each with its own attendant accolades and well-deserved honors—RADM McCain Sr.'s failure to carry out Turner's orders that day would later undeniably have a costly effect on the men who had to sail the ships that fought that war. By 9 August 1942, it would be made abundantly clear just how critical an oversight this action was.

From a historical perspective, the good admiral boasted a spotless service record, and indeed the vast majority of his service in the United States Navy was exemplary. However, McCain's lapse in judgment, proactive leadership, and force assessment on the day leading up to the battle at Savo would unquestionably contribute to one of the worst Allied naval defeats of the war. And, short only of Pearl Harbor and Ford Island, Savo would itself result in heavy losses for both the American and the Australian surface fleets. This action would be only the first of many naval battles yet to come that would be centered on the provincial island of Guadalcanal, the narrow deep-water passage called the Slot, and the southern-basined Iron Bottom Sound.

Mikawa's run down the Slot was neither challenged nor detected by the two DD-force American screening groups that had been patrolling that evening far to the north of Savo, on two oval-shaped patrol corridors, as set by ADM Crutchley and his military planners. With caution and near impunity, then, Mikawa and his attack force continued to probe the area, alternatingly running its famed "Tokyo Express" supply-side runs and screening its amphibious forces as it sought to bring badly needed supplies to the area, while simultaneously conducting a series of "punitive" raids on any Allied ships found at anchorage. Emboldened by an ever-increasing need for both resources and munitions, Mikawa stepped up his probative forays into New Georgia Sound and down to an area just south of volcanic Savo and so into Sealark Lane. In fact, this same IJN cruiser force had earlier sailed past CAPT Munson's American attack sub USS *S-38*, avoided two (of three) Australian *Hudson* reconnaissance planes, eluded the *Vanuatu* B-17s, slipped the noose of the *Blue* and *Ralph Talbot*'s radar picket line, and bearded the Allied surface fleet to its very face at Savo Island. It would therefore presumably have been for this very reason that Turner would have requested that McCain—as the appointed COMNAVAIR-SOPAC (or commander of all Allied air assets in the South Pacific region)—conduct the "extra reconnaissance" missions over specific areas in and around Guadalcanal on the afternoon of 8 August. As a troubling consequence of the man's *non*-execution of the order given him by Turner and Crutchley, both of those senior admirals would be mistakenly led to believe that the Slot had indeed already been reconnoitered and swept clean and was in fact under continued Allied observation (and control) throughout that day. But clearly this was not the case.

In clear perspective, then, the senior McCain's gaffe would be more than "mere oversight" and clearly more than a casual error in judgment. His failure to order the stepped-up reconnaissance overflights on the occasion of 8 August, as instructed, would go on to be one of several multi-pronged causal factors underlying the Allied shortfall. To this failure might even be added some degree of negligence, a damnable lack of communications, and the ever-present infernal delays in reporting any sightings intelligence—all of which would culminate in the decimation of the Allied naval forces that would later be surprised and completely overwhelmed during the battle at Savo. In and of itself, then, that defeat would put at risk the entire success of the Guadalcanal campaign for the Allied forces, but would such a loss serve only as a minor setback for the Americans or indeed a crippling blow to our naval posturing in the region? The loss of the four Allied heavy cruisers later that night would be the most telling moment.

At Whom the Finger Points

In the tragic wake of the debacle at Savo on 9 August, would there be any far-reaching recriminations for RADM McCain that might be counted among those targeted for rebuke? Would there be any call of culpability or full accounting for the blatant disregard of Turner's command to set the additional air reconnaissance? *Decidedly not*—by October 1942, the senior Admiral McCain would be unceremoniously "promoted up and out" instead, quietly sent away from any ship-of-the-line forces in the Pacific. In fact, he would return to the United States to assume a new appointment as the chief of a newly formed Bureau of Aeronautics, and by August of the following year he would be promoted to the rank of vice admiral and placed in post as the Deputy Chief of Naval Operations (DCNO). The fortunate McCain Sr. would remain here for the better part of the next two years before returning once again to sea and to his beloved Pacific theater of operations.

It would not be until late October 1944, therefore, that the senior admiral would return to the southern seas battle arena, this time tasked with replacing the outgoing VADM Marc Mitscher as commander of the Carrier Task Force (CTF) known as "Taffy 58." The admiral's unexpected appointment as the new (incoming) commander of the esteemed carrier group might clearly bespeak the level of confidence he had been able to curry with his many superiors, who believed in his ability to lead—*and* to command—the new attack force; the TF 58 force (in consort with its affiliate TF 38 element) would become a first-wave constituent of ADM Raymond Spruance's own Fifth Fleet. Indeed, by this time, McCain had already operated for more than a year in continuous support of the ongoing Allied amphibious operations themselves, and it was no great surprise that he would soon be named the area's COMNAVAIRSOPAC (or, alternately, the COMNAVAIRSOPACFLT). In point of fact, he may simply have been the very best man for the job at hand.

The Navy Cross

In spite of the role he may (or may not) have played in the debacle at Savo, the senior McCain would go on to distinguish himself in a number of participatory roles during the later Marianas campaign, in both the Battle of the Philippine Sea and the Battle of Leyte Gulf. In fact, during this latter campaign he would display his most extraordinary heroism, with skillful command tactics and a dogged determination that would earn him the esteemed Navy Cross and even a Distinguished Service Medal (DSM) with two Gold Star devices. He would receive these citations for actions "above and beyond the call of duty" when in August 1944, off the eastern coast of Taiwan (then Formosa), his CTF (TG 38.1) came to the aid of the stricken USS *Canberra* (CA-70) and the light carrier USS *Houston* (CL-81). Repeatedly interposing his own ship between the attacking Japanese warplanes and the two American ships, McCain's task group effectively fended off the enemy attack while still providing sufficient cover for the two retiring ships, such that they could safely withdraw. The daring forays and bold interposing of his mobile carrier forces would decidedly have much to do with the eventual Allied victory in that battle—itself but a brief and brutal action within the even greater Battle for the Philippines. Throughout it all, the good ADM McCain would remain steadfast at the helm of that same fast carrier task force all the way up to (and including) the Battle of Okinawa.

By war's end in August 1945, the difficulties and demands of sustained combat operations weighed heavily on the senior McCain. After many disquieting years spent at sea, often burdened by the stress of war—with tensions that ran moment to moment and battle to battle—it simply became too much to bear, and the great flag officer took ill over a period of months, soon dropping in weight to a critical one hundred pounds. His doctors advised that the admiral be granted a recuperative leave, but Bull Halsey had other plans for his friend and compatriot of so many years, insisting that the senior McCain be present at the Japanese surrender aboard the great battleship USS *Missouri*, which would take place in Tokyo Bay on 2 September 1945.

Honoring his commander's request, McCain remained on hand for much of the momentous pomp and military ceremony of that formal surrender event, departing only after the ritual had come to its full conclusion. A quite frail and enfeebled ADM McCain Sr. then returned home and passed away only four days later of a sudden heart attack in Coronado, California.

Following his death, and with much befitting honor, VADM John S. McCain Sr. would be posthumously advanced one single final grade to a rank of full admiral; that advancement would be carried forward thereafter into the annals of naval history as his highest-achieved service ranking.

Final Salvos, Parting Shots

So, was it recalcitrance on the part of RADM McCain—an insubordination almost "in defiance of" ADM Turner's order to carry out the extra air searches? Was it in fact a deep-seated obstinacy and determination to simply do things *his* way or only a minor oversight that the naval air officer's mission would fail so miserably? And now the pendulum would swing full circle. In its final analysis, had there been any lingering questions or grievous misgivings about ADM McCain's leadership roles during at least those early years at Guadalcanal—and specifically during the First Battle of Savo

Island itself—those past events would all be eclipsed by what was to come. History would remember the admiral only for his later service and conspicuous deeds of gallantry in the years *after* Savo.

Regardless, the admiral's failure to conduct the "extra reconnaissance" ordered by Turner on the eve of the first battle at Savo would indeed have come at a steep price—four armored cruisers lost during that night's hellish battle. The first of these would have been the Australian heavy cruiser *Canberra*, which would see some eighty-four men go down with their ship, followed in sequence by the American *Vincennes*, which would lose some 332 crewmen; on the *Astoria* the number lost was 216, and on the *Quincy*—perhaps the worst suffering of all—anywhere from 370 to 389 men. Of the nearly 1,200 souls needlessly lost that night, how many might have welcomed the foresight of increased area reconnaissance that had clearly been ordered by Turner but negated by McCain? How many might have lived to tell the greater tale had there in fact been adequate surveillance of the approaches to the Allied area of operation at the northern end of Sealark Lane and sufficient forewarning given of Mikawa's prowling cruisers on the night in question?

Of course, we may never know for certain, but the seeming incongruity of Admiral McCain's continued good fortune and stepladder advancement up through the ranks—even well after the debacle at Savo—in at least this author's estimation, might (for some) continue to serve as a slap in the face and a painful reminder of perhaps the greater iniquities of war. Why *him*, after all, and not others? Why later a Navy Cross for ADM McCain and only a "cross to bear" for the less fortunate CAPT Bode?

With little or no culpability targeted at him (whether real or implied, greater or lesser) for his part in the battle at Savo, ADM John S. McCain Sr. would go on to enjoy an exciting and rewarding naval career. In another quirk of timing, the date of 9 August would be seared into the senior admiral's brain for an entirely different reason, since it was his own date of birth. As such, for at least this one man, the circle must have been entirely complete.

Further Reading

Budge, Kent (2007–2009). "McCain, John Sidney (1884–1945)," *The Pacific War Online Encyclopedia*, http://pwencycl.kgbudge.com/M/c/McCain_John_S.htm.

Drury, Robert, and Tom Clavin. (2006). *Halsey's Typhoon: The True Story of a Fighting Admiral, an Epic Storm, and an Untold Rescue*. Atlantic Monthly Press.

Gilbert, Alton. (2006). *A Leader Born: The Life of Admiral John Sidney McCain, Pacific Carrier Commander*. Casemate.

Timberg, Robert. (1999). *John McCain: An American Odyssey*. New York: Touchstone Books.

Wikipedia account of Slew McCain at http://en.wikipedia.org/wiki/John_S._McCain,_Sr.

FINDING 11:   "CRUTCHLEY GOES TO TEA":
            THE TURNER CONFERENCE

Clearly, one of the most critical of unforeseen blunders that would regrettably be carried out by a full cadre of unwitting commanders of the Allied naval force operating in
and around Guadalcanal would be that of Admiral Fletcher's untimely withdrawal of
his naval carrier force from Iron Bottom Sound. This action would later engender the
"Turner Conference" (or "*McCawley* Conference") that would be convened to discuss
that very withdrawal and even result in Admiral Crutchley's absenting both himself
and his flagship, HMAS *Australia*, from the later battles to attend that very conference.

In full, VADM Frank "Jack" Fletcher, the overall commander of Carrier Task
Force 61, would, on the afternoon of 8 August, make an unusual and unexpected request of his superior, VADM Robert L. Ghormley, the COMSOPAC (Commander,
South Pacific Area) at the time. On that occasion, Fletcher's unusual request of
Ghormley was that he be allowed to withdraw his "exposed" CTF 61 carrier force from
the dangerously confined waters of the Sound and move them back out to the Pacific
to a point well north of Guadalcanal. At length, Ghormley would indeed acquiesce to
Fletcher's request and give in, however reluctantly, releasing the carrier task force from
its expected support role in Sealark Lane. Unfortunately, most of the Allied surface
fleet commanders were not entirely informed of that decision—which effectively left
the small flotilla of troop transport and supply ships (even then unloading at Honiara
and Tulagi) with only minimal screening cover by sea and little (if any) by air. A bad
situation would therefore soon be made even worse, based on a series of decisions
made by virtually each of the individual area commanders at that time.

This one event—this one immeasurably impactful decision to release the carrier
forces from their station off Honiara—would now in turn trigger a deadly chain of
events that, not unlike a concept of lined-up dominoes, would all too quickly begin
to fall one on the other. And the first such falling domino would be Turner's own
McCawley Conference itself, which meeting had been called by Admiral Turner in his
role as Commander, Amphibious Forces, South Pacific Fleet (or COMPHIBFOR-
SOPACFLT), which would be attended by a handful of key commanders in charge of
both the land and sea operations currently under way at Guadalcanal. Two of those
key individuals in attendance at that late-night meeting (scheduled to convene at 2200
hours) would be none other than RADM Victor A. Crutchley himself and MG Alexander A. Vandegrift. The first senior officer would have been the commander of all
naval screening forces at Guadalcanal and surrounding waters, the second the extant
commanding general of the 1st Marine Division itself. And while it might be said
that there could have been several topical discussion points tabled that night aboard
Turner's flagship, undoubtedly all in attendance might already have known that the
one agenda item of greatest interest to all could only be that of Fletcher's departure
and the removal of the carrier task force.

What followed in the wake of Fletcher's decision to further do so would only
result in a full confluence of errors and grave misgivings, as indeed hard lessons were

yet to be learned by the Americans. Fletcher's move to pull the support carriers out of the immediate operations area would now come to be known by many of the disenchanted, disenfranchised Marines already in place on Guadalcanal as the "Great Navy Bugout." *So damn them all to Hell!*, the cry must clearly have gone out . . . and when uttered by such a disgruntled band of men, the tone assuredly must have been one of venom and deep contempt—and this to a man indeed. Crutchley's own later removal of the transport and cargo ships themselves from the area would also not much help, and it was viewed in much the same way.

When Crutchley was summoned to the Turner Conference aboard *McCawley*, he could easily have observed the expected protocols of the time by simply deploying his small-craft gig, "Admiral's Barge," or "Captain's Launch," to shuttle the short distance from his lead position on *Australia*—in the vaward of the Southern screening force—to the X-Ray transport area just off Honiara to meet Turner. Instead, he took with him the *entire* ship—indeed, the entire heavy cruiser *Australia* itself! This action alone would effectively result in a number of seemingly unrelated events that would all too soon come together with only one fearful outcome.

In fact, Crutchley's departure on *Australia* would engender at least the following: ❶ It left the Southern screening force "one ship down" and reduced its force strength capabilities from three to two heavy cruisers left to guard the southern flank of Iron Bottom Sound; ❷ it left that same Southern screening force with no effective or clearly defined chain of command other than a hasty appointment of the greatly inexperienced and as yet untested CAPT Howard Douglas Bode in command of that screening force instead; and ❸ it further compounded the problem by leaving even that commander with no viable battle plan or means of communication with Crutchley himself. The fact that Crutchley would commit such a grave error—in both leaving that Southern screen with his ship and remaining at the X-Ray transport area as he did—without informing any of the other commanders in his group of his intent to do so (and that of taking the *Australia* with him), thereby further exacerbated an already worsening situation tick by tick.

"Crutchley Goes to Tea": A Ruthless Shot in the Dark

By 0138 hours, therefore, when the switches were thrown on the very first searchlights from Mikawa's cruiser division ships and the first deadly volleys had already begun ringing out against the Australian *Canberra* and Bode's own *Chicago*, that screening force was effectively caught with no real leadership at the helm and few (if any) options. *Canberra* would itself be quickly ravaged and sunk in minutes in the wake of the opening salvos, and *Chicago* would also be hit by a single torpedo strike to her bow, effectively causing her to withdraw from the action—and the area. Could Crutchley's third ship asset, his own heavy cruiser *Australia*, have made a difference in the outcome of the first attack that night, or would she simply have been only one more target for the crack IJN gunners and torpedomen who had so superbly manned their stations on Mikawa's own attack cruisers?

Perhaps we will never know, but it would stand to reason that the addition (and mere presence) of the third heavy cruiser might that night have at least slowed down that initial attack, and perhaps have enabled that force to carry out a more viable counteroffensive against those IJN ships or, at the very least, to mitigate the amount of damage that would later be sustained by the Allied ships during that brief but volatile engagement. None of this would come to pass, and indeed Crutchley would neither respond in time nor make any effort to rejoin his Southern screening force that night until well after the damage had already been done. Here, history does tell us that the good admiral had instead opted to remain in the area of *McCawley* until daybreak and stood by on the very deck of his ship where he could even see the faint blooming flashes just over a darkened horizon to the north and hear the muted "thunder" of Mikawa's big guns in the far distance. Falsely assuming that the action was but a minor skirmish perhaps only involving low-flying aircraft (or some other small encroaching force) near distant Savo Island, Crutchley simply remained on-station in that X-Ray transport area, making an already critical error all the more catastrophic.

In his absence, now with the successful IJN attack on the Allied Southern screen already well under way and not being effectively countered, the cruiser forces under Mikawa and Gotō were even more emboldened—now moving north with an even greater resolve—again with no seeming impediment—to attack Riefkohl's Northern screen, which indeed they soon did. And, as is already known from the rote and chronicle of history, the results there would be even more catastrophic for the Americans, soon resulting in the loss of all *three* American heavy cruisers of that screening group—namely, the *Vincennes*, the *Quincy*, and the *Astoria*. To what extent might Crutchley be held culpable for his actions (or inactions) on that night in question? Soon enough, the world would find out in full.

"Crutchley Goes to Tea": Culpability and a Fair Accounting

In the days following the debacle at Savo, and its devastating losses, it would be a quite enraged Allied high command, in the person of the Chief of Naval Operations (CNO) himself, FADM Ernest J. King, that would fairly demand taut and immediate answers for what had occurred on the night of 9 August 1942. How, after all—the good admiral must clearly have reasoned—could both the American and Allied forces be so duped and set on by elements of what was assuredly thought to have been a far inferior Imperial Japanese Navy? And how indeed could those same enemy forces so easily sluice through the carefully set patrol corridors of the two radar pickets *Blue* and *Ralph Talbot*, only to further encroach into an area of operations thought to be wholly controlled by the Americans—and still successfully prosecute both attacks in dead of night—and all seemingly without detection?

It would soon come to pass, therefore, that a rightly incensed CNO King would rap his knuckles on the table and demand firm answers and some unimpeachable truths about the battle. So also would a now-chastened and "face-losing" Roosevelt administration—and an even angrier and grief-stricken American public as well. In the end, some degree of culpability must truly be leveled for the fiasco at Savo, and its sad results. America wanted its pound of flesh and demanded an effigy scapegoat, and that bill would soon enough be filled almost in full.

As for now, however, heads would simply have to roll, and among the first on the CNO's chopping block would be those of Admirals Fletcher, Turner, McCain, and Crutchley—as well as those of both Riefkohl and Bode. Yet later, other than the hapless Bode himself, only Crutchley would receive but a mild rebuke and soft criticism from his fellow flag officers and superiors, many of whom must clearly have thought, as LTC David E. Quantock of the esteemed U.S. Army War College himself would later observe:

> Admiral Crutchley's strategy to defend Guadalcanal was suspect at best. By dividing his combat power, he violated one of the Navy's oldest principles. Placing his two task forces in positions which precluded mutual support, Crutchley allowed Mikawa to destroy his force in detail. Admiral Turner bears a share in the responsibility [as well] because he had reviewed the plan and had approved it in full.[59]

In truth, RADM Crutchley's career, despite the several gaffes and blunders perpetrated either by himself or by others acting on his behalf in his absence, would not suffer greatly. His continued rise through the ranks seemed assured, and new commands and even greater accolades would await the man just around the next bend, despite the soft censures that would come from his peers and superiors of the time. Indeed, the good admiral's name would not be too sullied, his reputation held intact, and his career not greatly besmirched by the events at Savo. Effectively "given a second chance," Crutchley would continue in his career advancement, even to the extent that he would later be awarded the American Legion of Merit in a degree of "Chief Commander":

> In the wake of the disaster, Crutchley was heavily criticized, both for leaving his command, and for an ineffective deployment which allowed the Japanese to get close without being detected by radar.
>
> Crutchley nonetheless retained the confidence of his superiors. He remained with the RAN in the South West Pacific, commanding TF 44 (redesignated TF 74 in 1943) for another 23 months. His command of the Australian Squadron ended on 13 June 1944.[60]

In sharp contrast, however, CAPT Bode—the hapless and unfortunate captain of the American cruiser USS *Chicago* and ad hoc commander of Crutchley's own Southern fleet—would not be quite as lucky. In the days following the opening of a formal inquiry led by the no-nonsense Admiral Arthur Japy Hepburn and his equally contentious pit-bull interrogator, Commander Donald J. Ramsey, Bode would soon enough begin to "read the writing on the wall" and more clearly understand the intent and tenor of the charges that might soon be leveled against him. Now, almost a full year after the Savo event itself, on 19 April 1943, a distraught and quite disheartened Bode would summarily enter the bathroom of his own BOQ and shoot himself in the head in Balboa, in the Panama Canal Zone. The ill-fated captain would never recover from his self-inflicted wound and would in fact perish the very next day at Balboa Hospital.

Ironically, during precisely this same time frame, Crutchley would assume command of Task Force 44—itself a part of the esteemed U.S. Seventh Fleet—and continue on to the next phase of his still-ascending naval career, but the admiral had also learned both hard and valuable lessons at Savo. This was not the case for Bode, who thereafter had to live with the taint of suspicion and a dark cloud of question hanging over his head, with the world never fully knowing the *what* or the *why* of his actions on the night of the battle at Savo. And so thus thwarted in being able to even defend his good name or his honor, Bode was compelled to instead die by his own hand—not at all in a state of grace, but rather in a state of bitter disgrace—this even as Crutchley himself received the Navy Cross. Who might therefore know in full just what was fair, and indeed what was not?

"Crutchley Goes to Tea": Links and Further Reading

For additional information on RADM Victor A. Crutchley's abrupt and unwarranted departure on the evening of 8 August 1942 aboard his own flagship HMAS *Australia* to attend Admiral Turner's late-night conference aboard *McCawley*—and its subsequent effect on the outcome of the First Battle of Savo Island—the reader is encouraged to review any or all of the following titles and electronic weblinks.

Additional Reading: Bibliography and List of Articles

Ballard, Robert R. (Professor Emeritus of Oceanography, University of Rhode Island). (1993). *The Lost Ships of Guadalcanal*. Madison Publishing and Warner Books.

Coggins, Jack. (1972). *The Campaign for Guadalcanal*. Doubleday & Company.

Hornfischer, James D. (2011). *Neptune's Inferno: The U.S. Navy at Guadalcanal*. Bantam Books.

Loxton, Bruce, and Chris Coulthard-Clark. (1997). *The Shame of Savo: Anatomy of a Naval Disaster*. Allen & Unwin Pty Ltd.

Morison, Samuel Eliot. (2010). *The Struggle for Guadalcanal, August 1942–February 1943, History of United States Naval Operations in World War II* (Reprinted). Naval Institute Press.

Newcomb, Richard F. (2002). *The Battle of Savo Island: The Harrowing Account of the Disastrous Night Battle off Guadalcanal That Nearly Destroyed the Pacific Fleet in August 1942*. New Holt Paperbacks.

Stile, Mark (Commander, USN, Ret.). (2009). *USN Cruiser vs. IJN Cruiser: Guadalcanal 1942*. Osprey Publishing.

Additional Reading: Related Weblinks and Electronic Resources

"Crutchley Coat of Arms and Name History," article from *House of Names* website at http://www .houseofnames.com/crutchley-coat-of-arms. Retrieved 30 January 2013.

Quantock, David E. (LTC, USA, Ret.). (2002). *Disaster at Savo Island, 1942*. U.S. Army War College, Pennsylvania, at http://www.ibiblio.org/hyperwar/USN/rep/Savo/Quantock/index.html #illus.

Naval War College report, dated 1950 (AD/A-003 037), titled "THE BATTLE OF SAVO IS-
    LAND, AUGUST 9, 1942. STRATEGICAL AND TACTICAL ANALYSIS. PART I," authored
    by Richard W. Bates and Walter D. Innis for the Naval War College (Department of Analysis),
    and distributed by the National Technical Information Services (NTIS) organization (U.S. De-
    partment of Commerce).
Today's Lessons Learned, "Posts Tagged—Admiral Victor Crutchley" and subsectioned as "Japanese
    Rout Opponents at Savo Island," at http://todayshistorylesson.wordpress.com/tag/admiral-victor
    -crutchley/.
Victoria Cross Trust, "Admiral Sir Victor Crutchley VC, KCB, DSC, DL, RN," at http://www
    .victoriacrosstrust.org/crutchleyvc.php. Retrieved 30 January 2013.
Wikipedia, "HMAS *Australia* (D84)," further subsectioned as "1942," at http://en.wikipedia.org
    /wiki/HMAS_Australia_(D84)#1942. Retrieved 30 January 2013.
Wikipedia, "Battle of Savo Island," further subsectioned as "Prelude," at http://en.wikipedia.org
    /wiki/Battle_of_Savo_Island#Prelude. Retrieved 29 January 2013.
Wikipedia, "Task Force 44," at http://en.wikipedia.org/wiki/Task_Force_44. Retrieved 29 January
    2013.
Wikipedia, "Victor Crutchley," further subsectioned as "Battle of Savo Island," at http://en.wikipedia
    .org/wiki/Victor_Crutchley#The_Battle_of_Savo_Island. Retrieved 29 January 2013.
World War II Database article by C. Peter Chen titled "Victor Crutchley," at http://ww2db.com
    /person_bio.php?person_id=355. Retrieved 30 January 2013.

FINDING 12:   A TALE OF TWO NAVIES: A COALESCENCE OF FORCES

Clearly, some discussion must be tabled on the sometimes disharmonic, often poorly
orchestrated strategies and communications efforts of the two major forces soon to
be locked in deadly conflict with the Imperial Japanese Navy of 1942—namely, the
naval forces of both the United States and Great Britain and its subsidiary states. Not
surprising, then, that what might follow in the wake of such a coalition of forces would
be a classic, internecine struggle to wrest a greater level of control over the day-to-day
area operations in and around Guadalcanal and other areas of the South Pacific, as
well as influence over those general force deployments, and allocation of those assets to
preferred advantage. And while this push-and-pull relationship between the two forces
was at times benign and amusing to the men, at its *worst* it could result in tirades and
table-pounding diatribes as both command structures sought to fully leverage a greater
degree of control for their own best gain. This would occur at both a command level
and, more curiously, at an even more colloquial level; this was almost across the board
with not just the American, British, and Australian navies but also their land forces.

The quiet, desperate struggle to wrest greater operational control of both theater
and area actions and proceedings, in at least this area of the South Pacific, would rage
on between the two superpowers for most of early 1942—and well into that same
year—continuing always to thread its way between both navies like a sparking undercurrent of friendly competition and quasi-contempt, all too often resulting in serious
disjoins and uncoordinated strategies that might not have been entirely cleared by
both sides. Sadly, the impact of these "disjoins" might soon enough be manifested in

a malaise of mistrust and condescension—this perhaps even on both sides. It might at once be but a friendly rivalry that was nothing if not highly competitive and charged with a measure of good-spirited ribbing but could in an instant also become a dividing element, begetting a false and dangerously misplaced feeling of superiority among the naval commanders (and the men) of both countries' naval fleets.

Such a sporting rivalry could indeed be playful one moment and stern and derisive the next, yet almost comically—at least to the men themselves—and it would simply suffice it to know that perhaps the British would always be Brits, the Australians would always be Aussies, and the Americans would always just be Joes. And that was that—or at least that was the accepted norm in 1942. And while a rivalry between the men may itself have been winked at, quietly sanctioned, and almost "understood"—as often large groups of Anglo-American sailors and soldiers would indeed intermingle, laughing and smoke-breaking together while jostling each other during their several chance encounters. Clearly, however, such a counterpoint dissension at a higher command level could indeed result in a far more serious circumstance than imagined.

Massive navies both, the United States Navy was by far the larger and more powerful force; however, Great Britain had further enhanced her naval posturing by augmenting her own force-presence with warships pressed into service from her commonwealth nation-states of Australia and New Zealand. Consequently (and probably much as expected), each force-presence, and each fleet element, would embrace a different philosophy and pursue a divergent course of strategy in the Pacific. Also, perhaps much as expected, each navy would far prefer a reliance on its own trusted (and *proven*) methodologies for conducting naval operations in and around Guadalcanal, and each navy would observe a wholly separate (and distinct) chain of command that was couched within its own, unique organizational structure. Simply put, each of the four navies simply had its own way of doing business and might not at all cherish transformation and integration into some larger force.

It was therefore inevitable that there might indeed be distinct clashes in style and command, attitudes and behavior, and predilections and basic assumptions of just how things should be done within the current Guadalcanal climate and area of operations. And when it came to any discussion of how capital ship assets would be used—and indeed who should command them—the decks would quickly need to be cleared for the resulting gentlemen's fracas that would almost certainly ensue among the contending Allied commanders. And Admiral Crutchley's very handling of the Allied Southern fleet on the night of 9 August might itself be a prime example of just such a conflict of interests and lack of overall communications.

A Tale of Two Navies: A Brief History

It was unavoidable, therefore, that a badly depleted U.S. Navy—still reeling from the devastating surprise attacks at both Pearl Harbor and Ford Island in late 1941—would be compelled to join forces with the bold British (and her own subsidiary commonwealth states) as early as 1942, as had been clearly spelled out in the mutual support clauses of the still-upheld London Naval Conference of 1930. In that conference—and in part based on the terms of its former U.S.-hosted Washington Naval Treaty—the five sovereign countries of Great Britain, the United States, France, Italy, and Japan would all be bound by doctrine to limit the growth and development of all future naval armaments to especially include large battleships, battlecruisers, and aircraft carriers.

That same treaty would go one step further and fully compel the five superpower signatories to abide by certain changes that now harshly redefined maximum "warship tonnage" allowances for those BB-class ships—and effectively altered the tonnage ratios between the United Kingdom, the United States, and Japan. Not at all unexpectedly, then, the conditions would be much to the favor of the two greater Western powers, but to Japan, of course, this would be nothing short of wholly unacceptable, and she would very quickly move on the offensive to grab a much larger piece of that "global pie." Her first stop, therefore, would be to gain a solid toehold in the many fertile and resource-rich islands of Southeast Asia and the Southwest Pacific. For the first time, however, she would now be facing the combined naval forces of both the American and British surface fleets, and for an unsuspecting Imperial Japanese Navy, it might be expected to be anything but a walk in the park.

Beginning with the well-timed invasion and capture of the Solomons by those Allied forces and the combined-force occupation of that same real estate—and the seizing of the highly desirable deep-water naval ports at Tulagi, Tanambogo, and Honiara—the action would be among the first major joint operations in the Pacific War (other than the Coral Sea battle itself) that would be coordinated between both American and British naval forces. And, on at least the morning of 7 August 1942, it was clear that the well-planned, smartly executed actions of both Allied fleets (and ground elements) might indeed bear a promising fruit. The deceptively easy and mainly uncontested assault on the beaches of Guadalcanal—and her cross-channel neighbor of Nggella Sule (Florida Island)—would indeed catch the IJN by sharp surprise and would essentially be over in hours. By nightfall of the same day, all of these port areas—and the prized airstrip at Henderson itself—would rest solidly in the hands of the Allies, but for how long? After a collective sigh of relief, it was clear that this much had at least gone well for the combined forces, but all knew that the real tasks still lay ahead—those of now *holding* the islands against what was already thought to be overwhelming odds and an almost certain retaliatory strike by the now greatly incensed Japanese. And the wise Joint Operations commanders of both the United Kingdom and the United States did indeed take note of such and used the time to strengthen their force-presence and to hunker down for the coming main attack. Indeed, the great generals and admirals seated around their planning tables knew they need not wait too long for the other shoe to drop.

In fact, the attack would come that same day—on 7 August itself—as soon squadrons of Japanese fighters and dive bombers swept down from the north, from cloistered airbases that dotted the areas near Japanese-held Rabaul and Kavieng and were thrown rabidly against the Allied positions with a clear and punitive vengeance. Wave after wave after wave of *Betty* bombers, Val dive bombers, and *Zeke* attack planes soon circled overhead and came in at near-wave-top level to strafe and scorch the supply and transport ships that were even then just beginning to unload their precious cargoes, and now sat vulnerably at anchor at dockside locations at both Tulagi and Guadalcanal. In an instant, a hotly incensed Japanese response would be ferociously mounted against the Allied ground forces—and the ships that guarded them from points offshore. Those air attacks would be nothing if not targeted and swift, calculated and deadly, and all without seeming let-up.

Remarkably, virtually all of the air attacks would abruptly shift in focus and center instead on the larger escort and screening ships that sat in Iron Bottom Sound, carefully couched offshore but still well within range of battery and stepped-up air attack. These would have been, of course, the light and heavy cruisers, the escort destroyers, and the myriad support ships that were all patrolling along in tandem throughout the Sound. Indeed, in just the opening IJN air actions of 7 August themselves—within a span of hours on that same day and leading up to the battle at Savo itself—the American heavy cruiser *Vincennes* had already been fired on several times, the DD *Jarvis* heavily damaged by a single torpedo hit to her bow, and the crippled attack transport *George F. Elliott* virtually sunk in situ almost at the very point of her attack.

Decidedly, then, something *had* to be done—and quickly—to safeguard the precious cargo ships and troop transports that were still attempting to discharge their vitally needed payloads at Honiara and Tulagi. Something indeed had to be done to offset the considerable deadly effects of the sharp IJN air attacks by day and those that came by night in the form of Mikawa's prowling heavy cruisers. In the short run, a hastily conceived decision would be agreed on by Admirals Turner and Crutchley that a series of naval screening corridors must "on the spot" be put in place to ensure that all transfer operations could in fact proceed normally and without further hindrance.

It would be with the deployment of these very screening forces that a minor discord would become a crucial point of variance, and a mild disharmony would soon form the core of a fracturing in the ranks of the naval commanders on both sides. That rifting would begin at a place called Savo Island . . . in a dark expanse of open sea known as Iron Bottom Sound.

A Tale of Two Navies: A Conflict of Style and Command

Truly, it was no great secret of the history, or of the time, that the British admirals assigned to work with the commanders of the U.S. naval forces at Guadalcanal wanted greater involvement—and perhaps even greater control—over the several many-faceted operations going on at the time in the area. Therefore, with no undue contention, a plan was desperately needed, and that plan would soon take shape during the many late-night sessions and at-sea conferences set between Admirals Fletcher, Crutchley, and McCain; their own superior, Admiral Richmond Kelly Turner; and even his, in the person of RADM Frank Jack Fletcher, the extant commander of Task Force 61. And, by 1942, as a result of those same sequestered meetings during at least the outset of operations at Guadalcanal, an undertone of grumble and discord might have already begun to surface among the British naval high command that, on several occasions, might have let slip their candid observations as they perhaps only "thought out loud" and noted that there simply was "no significant representation" of British naval officers in key leadership roles across the board.

Talk quickly sprang up among the flag officers of His Majesty's own South Seas Fleet that now flat out asked the taut, uncomfortable questions about the American-run naval operations and posturing in the region—and many wondered frankly who indeed was in command. Clearly, some of those voiced concerns might easily (and rightfully) have included at least the following impassioned observations:[61]

- Could not an able-bodied and equally qualified British naval flag officer lead a combined naval force into battle in the Guadalcanal area of operations as *ably* as an American of similar rank and station?
- Could not a British naval officer in fact make the same informed decisions and on-the-spot situational assessments in actual battle that an American commander of equivalent rank might make?
- Could not a British naval officer ever be seen (at its least) as not being inherently "less aggressive" (or at its worst) "less competent" than their American counterpart?
- And finally, perhaps at its most logical and telling end, could not a British naval officer in fact command American sailors and even lead American ships in battle?

Aye—and truly therein would lie the rub. An America still reeling from the attacks at Pearl Harbor and Ford Island, and now at its xenophobic worst, would still be quite reluctant to accept any officer *other than* an American in a crucial leadership role—or in any position that sat at the helm of state—or even one that commanded large naval fleets. In at least the clear and unstained American public eye, Nimitz, after all, was Nimitz and could hardly have been replaced by any alternate foreign officer—even one of an equivalent commanding rank. Such a consideration might not at all sit well with the men and, as such, simply might not ever fly.

Remarkably, the good RADM Sir Victor Alexander Crutchley would himself be the clear choice and most obvious answer to finally resolve that two navies conundrum in full. He was the perfect man for the job at hand, and so indeed he was soon given an immediate command of Task Force 62.2, composed of some eight Allied cruisers, fifteen destroyers, and a handful of minesweepers to clear the shipping lanes throughout the Sound. Three of those eight cruisers would be Australian: the heavy cruisers HMAS *Australia* and *Canberra*, and the smaller light cruiser *Hobart*. And, while the good admiral had indeed fought side by side with Fletcher at Coral Sea, he had never fully integrated his forces with those of the U.S. Navy. But soon enough, Crutchley would indeed get his first taste and sharpest wake-up call, beginning on the morning of 7 August 1942, and running straight through the afternoon of the 8th, when he would become incredibly bogged down in his response to the then stepped-up Japanese air attacks of that day—and would in fact suffer the first loss of ships under his direct command. The ill-provisioned British admiral was now called on to devise a "more workable" screening strategy to cordon off all approaches into and out of Sealark Lane (a large expanse of water that would later be renamed Iron Bottom Sound) from the south, and as far north as Savo, the Russells, and even beyond.

With only good industry and quiet due diligence, then, did Crutchley quickly set about the task of doing just that, and thoroughly took stock of the Allied situation at that time. In snapshot, the admiral would quickly note at least the following: ❶ to the far north sat his first screening group, the two American radar pickets *Blue* and *Ralph Talbot*; ❷ to the south and east of that position, the Southern force would sit as tandem guards for both the transport and supply ships that were even then offloading their much-needed troops and supplies at Allied landing points on mainland Honiara, and at Tulagi, Gavutu, and Tanambogo. Then, east of that group ❸ sat a cautious RADM Norman Scott circling in a tight patrol corridor off Florida Island, with the light cruisers *San Juan* and *Hobart*, thereby forming the good admiral's Eastern screening element, patrolling its own guarded transport area called Yoke (directly corresponding to Guadalcanal's own X-Ray). Finally, well to the north and tucked neatly under the chin of Savo itself at ❹ would cruise Crutchley's Northern screen, sailing its full and complete box-like patrol pattern under the able command of RADM Frederick Lois Riefkohl. And on at least this night, that Northern patrol would be made up of the heavy cruisers *Vincennes*, *Quincy*, and *Astoria*, along with a brace of fast-attack destroyers as seen in the *Helm* and *Wilson*. And, to accomplish this seemingly monumental task, Crutchley had a total of some twenty-three ships at hand—only eight of which were actually large cruiser-class warships—but not a single BB. This meager force was now expected to cover an expanse of open water that stretched some eighteen miles across from side to side of great Iron Bottom Sound—a body of water that was so vast as to be mistaken for a small inland sea. As such, the odds must indeed have been well stacked against the good Admiral Crutchley on at least this one occasion.

But the cunning Allied commander would simply steel himself and make do with what he had. It was therefore now a greatly reserved yet quietly optimistic British admiral that quickly set about the business of doing just that—deploying each of those forces—with each screening group seemingly "straining at the leash" with a certain veiled confidence as they readied themselves once again for live combat on the open seas. Soon enough, however, that veiled confidence would most assuredly be shaken to its very core, and the relationship between the split commands of the Americans, the British, and the Australians themselves would come to its worst possible end: the massacre at Savo.

A Tale of Two Navies: A Gaffe at Guadalcanal

By the night of 9 August 1942, even with Crutchley's four Allied screening forces deployed and fully set in place throughout the Sound—with each assigned a differing patrol sector—coverage could still not be wholly complete, and a full interdiction of all encroaching Japanese ships entering the patrol area that night was not at all assured. And, while the light and heavy cruiser commanders might well receive one set of operational orders, it was almost as plausible that the senior officers of the attending DESRONs may have themselves been given other orders entirely. In fact, there would already be several key miscommunications that would soon crop up between Crutchley and his subordinate American forces, such that would continue to plague the precarious, high-wire operational balancing act already being undertaken by the two navies.

The *first* would oddly come with the disadvantaging placement of the two American DDs, the USS *Blue* and the USS *Ralph Talbot*, as the two northernmost radar pickets set well above Savo Island. The *second* gaffe would then be the very disposition of that DESRON4 destroyer force itself—under the command of DESDIV7—and the issuance of a separate set of standing orders (by Crutchley) for that DESRON force to meet north of Savo in the event that any of the "small-boy" DDs became separated from their main screening groups. The *third* miscommunication error to be committed this night by Admiral Crutchley would perhaps have the greatest impact of all: the removal of his own flagship, the heavy cruiser HMAS *Australia*, and the absenting of himself from the battle area only hours before Mikawa's late-night attack (this to attend RADM Turner's own late-night conference). Finally, even as a sad *fourth*, there is the admiral's muddied and questionable decision to remain in the vicinity of RADM Turner even *after* the conference and to anchor in for the night at that X-Ray transport area, with neither his superior Turner nor his own ship commanders knowing of that flawed and (later) fatal decision. The several discussions that follow, therefore, are expected to provide some additional insight into several of these key factors, many of which seem to further point up a general miscommunication between the two navies . . . and between the admirals who commanded those very ships.

Dangerous Decisions: Crutchley's Placement of the Radar Pickets

The two American destroyers *Blue* and *Ralph Talbot* were inadequately tasked by RADM Crutchley to set the northernmost screening line, both of which essentially circled on two elliptical patrol patterns just north of Savo to detect, report on, and intercept any IJN warships attempting to enter the Sound from that approach venue. Unfortunately, in the end they would do none of the above and, in retrospect, some three to four additional screening ships might decidedly have been far more suited to screen those northern reaches above Savo. Indeed, three such ships would have been passably acceptable—two might only be barely sufficient.

The oval-patterned patrol corridors that the two ships pursued (at Crutchley's direction) did—by sheer oversight in design—inherently leave a significant "gap" between the perigees of both DDs on patrol, who simply ran the course of one patrol leg, then spun about on a reverse course to continue on toward their apogee positions. It was precisely during such a moment that the ships of Mikawa's CRUDIV6 and 18 would be lucky enough to sneak past both pickets without firing a single shot, and without ever being detected. This action would effectively "open the gateway" to the intruding IJN surface fleet, which soon thereafter brought on the very violent attacks on the Allied fleets that left both battered and mauled. And, in the IJN admiral's fast-moving wake, only death and destruction would be left behind for both Allied fleets alike.

To this end, even Bates himself would note in his own exhaustive research on the First Battle of Savo Island that the positioning of the two radar pickets—and the general division of forces that Crutchley insisted on to screen the Sound on that one specific night—might indeed not have been ideal, and even he seemed to clearly fault the admiral for not having more optimally positioned the few screening assets he did have:

> Commander, Cruiser Force [Mikawa] authorized his division commanders to operate independently. As a consequence, COMCRUDIVSIX [Gotō] and the *Yunagi* both separated from his command immediately prior to opening fire on the *Chicago* group. However, despite this, Mikawa—who appears to have been constantly advised as to the Allied cruiser formations by his planes—was always able to obtain an appropriate degree of combat superiority over the Allied screening groups at each point of contact. Therefore, his division of forces did not work as a hardship on his command.
>
> CTG 62.6 [Crutchley], on the other hand and as a corollary of the above, not only so divided his forces as to risk combat inferiority at the point of contact but failed to make adequate provisions for the coordination of his own forces. His division of forces therefore almost immediately placed his command at an initial disadvantage.[62]

And that very *disadvantage* would sadly now come at a high price indeed, at least on the night of 9 August 1942, and at least at a place called Savo Island. Indeed, to that end, even in his own later recounting of the battles that took place that night, CAPT Toshikazu Ohmae—Mikawa's own chief of staff on the night of the attacks—would himself note that for the most part his entire naval force had simply regarded the two radar pickets as being wholly ineffective—more a nuisance or inconvenience than anything else—and only far too easy to elude. As Mikawa's ships sluiced quietly through the night, the two picket destroyers would neither take note of their passage nor at all engage the encroaching enemy fleet:

> We passed between the two enemy destroyers unseen, and they soon disappeared in the darkness. It was a narrow escape, but our emphasis on "night battle practice and night lookout training" had paid off. This advantage was later to be increased by the local situation in which the enemy's backdrop was brightened by flames of burning ships, [or as] reflected from clouds, while we ourselves moved out of utter darkness.[63]

Again, the Japanese words did echo forth with a chilling premonition: *Out of a cloud of darkness, we shall attack!* Crutchley had foolishly set his northernmost picket screen with only two ships instead of four, which would tragically make all the difference that night. It is only now that we can look back at leisure with our sharpest 20/20 hindsight and ask ourselves, could not one additional destroyer have been culled from the minor (secondary) screening forces that stood close in to Tulagi and Honiara, dutifully guarding the transport and supply ships even then still unloading?

Could not the DDs *Selfridge*,[64] *Henley*, or even *Mumford* have been more cautiously reassigned for just such a support role to bolster the force-presence of that northern radar screen? A redeployment of just *one* ship from either (or each) of these lesser screening forces could have easily made up for the deficiency in the number of radar picket destroyers available to screen the northern approaches above Savo. Indeed, had such been the case, might that same Mikawa surface fleet have still been able to slip the noose of that same picket screen as they had on the night of the attacks at Savo? History, of course, sits only in the offing, mum and voiceless, to tell us only that we may simply never know of any alternate story to resolve the conundrum of the *Blue* and *Ralph Talbot*.

Dangerous Decisions: Crutchley and the DD Rendezvous Point at Savo

RADM Crutchley had set a dangerous precedent when first he set the (contingency) destroyer "rendezvous point" just north of Savo. Indeed, the admiral had already noted that in the unlikely (but still plausible) event that any task group–assigned DD—operating with any of the cruiser elements themselves—ever became separated from its main screening group (or other assigned zone of operation guarding the transport areas)—however remote the possibility—individual DESRON commanders were instructed to proceed "at best opportunity" to a somewhat arbitrary and obscure rendezvous point just north and west of volcanic Savo.

The assumption here was that this predefined area could then serve as a point of regrouping and redeployment for those straggling ships at the further discretion of the Commander, TF 62.2 (Crutchley) himself. And, for at least two destroyers that night, a run for the rendezvous point is precisely what each would seek to do. The destroyer commanders had apparently misconstrued Crutchley's somewhat beguiling and arcane instruction to assemble on his current position on his own CA *Australia* and assumed that he instead meant to assemble at the previous "Savo-North" rendezvous point. So again—for yet a second time—a basic flaw in communication would result in a less than desirable outcome for the Allied navies. Noted author and naval historian Bruce Loxton perhaps said it best in his insightful commentary in his own book, *The Shame of Savo: Anatomy of a Naval Disaster*, when he himself observed that:

> Crutchley moved *Australia* out from behind the destroyers screening the transports off Guadalcanal to a position seven miles west of those transports, into a position where he could intercept any enemy breakthrough. He also ordered his destroyers to concentrate on *Australia*. Unfortunately, the position given for the concentration was not enciphered in a system familiar to the Americans, so they assumed the rendezvous point was in fact the one specified in Crutchley's earlier instruction for the screening group and headed [straight] for the position north and west of Savo. In the end, this

would be of little or no consequence, but it is further evidence of the difficulties the two navies were experiencing in operating together.[65]

So, why north of Savo—why here? And why a secondary staging area so far removed from the primary Allied area of operation that was itself miles below to the south nearer Tulagi and Honiara? Why north of Savo? For the time being, the Crutchley-assigned rendezvous point behind Savo would not yet be problematic, but by battle's end it would indeed prove to be so, as a number of straggling DDs would in fact set about the business of doing precisely what they thought they had been ordered to do: move at best speed to the reassembly point to await further orders. Regrettably, even those orders would be a while in coming, and would ultimately affect the movement and focus of at least two other DDs—the *Helm* and *Wilson*—the very DDs that had been set to screen Riefkohl's Northern force earlier that same night.

When the enemy searchlights first switched on at about 0150 hours on the night of 9 August, Mikawa's task force almost immediately opened with a deadly barrage that would be wholly centered on the American Northern screening force cruisers—namely, the *Vincennes*, the *Quincy*, and the *Astoria*, in precisely that order. Each of the three ships would be virtually decimated on the spot, with at least two sinking almost in situ at the very locations at which they had been hit. In the startling wake of the sinking of the three CAs, however, it is known that the destroyer *Wilson* did in fact remain in the area of the battle and was even joined by the *Bagley* and the *Buchanan* shortly thereafter to assist in basic SAR (search-and-rescue) operations for survivors from any of the three stricken cruisers. This, then, left only the *Helm*, which—after attempting to engage several of the enemy's ships at the lag end of Mikawa's outbound column, even as they broke off their attack and began exiting the area—herself became detached from her main screening group, which had in fact already been nearly vanquished in full.

Dutifully (if not foolishly) following Crutchley's orders—which were at *best* misguided and at *worst* wholly misinterpreted by the DESRON commanders—*Helm* in fact did not at all return to the area where her group's cruisers had last been seen, instead proceeding (seemingly at best speed) to the "rendezvous point" where she had been previously instructed to regroup with the other DDs. Only hours later would she in fact be joined by her sister ship, the *Wilson*, which had itself inched along at a "leisurely 15-knot pace" on her way to that same assembly point. Once there, the two ships would simply circle on station while awaiting further orders from the responsible DESRON commander at the time. Those orders would in fact not come until much later on the morning of the 9th, only well after the crippling night attacks themselves.

Addressing just such a supposition, Loxton's dissertation on the Naval War College's own findings and post-action investigation did itself grant us some insight into the unusual miscommunication factors that would come into play before, during, and even after the battle at Savo—critical miscues all—that would time and again continue to plague Allied naval operations in and around Guadalcanal:

USN doctrine clearly called for screening destroyers in such circumstances [i.e., with best proximity to the enemy] to attack, but was imprecise as to the manner in which that response should be carried out. Because of this, the Naval War College analysis was highly critical of Crutchley for not having stipulated in his Special Instructions just what those screening destroyers should do.[66]

And indeed, just to be clear, the British admiral's "Special Instructions" guidelines did itself read as shown in Table 13.

Table 13.   Commander, Task Group 62.6: Special Instructions

RADM Victor Alexander Crutchley (CTG 62.6) Special Instructions

The night disposition was drawn up in broad aspect by CTG 62.6 (Crutchley), but the manner in which each of the main groups accomplished its mission within its own area was left to the discretion of the individual group commanders. For their guidance, CTG 62.6 set forth two principles: ❶ that it was essential that an enemy force be beaten off before it was either sighted by or reached the convoy, and that those Allied naval forces be concentrated so as to avoid confusion and night action; and ❷ that it was his aim to meet the enemy to seaward of the area between Savo and Sealark Channel, and that that Allied force which engaged those ships should remain interposed between the enemy and that area. He expected that the extensive Allied air reconnaissance would give him ample warning of any approaching enemy ships. The CTG 62.6 then further stated that:

(a) If both the *Australia* and the *Vincennes* groups were ordered to attack the enemy, it was his (CTG 62.6) intention that the *Vincennes* group should act independently of the movements of the *Australia* group, so as to provide the greatest level of mutual support.

(b) It was his (the CTG 62.6) intention that the destroyers of each group involved should concentrate under their particular senior officer (COMDESRON4 or COMDESRON7) and attack the enemy with torpedoes and gunfire as soon as that enemy was engaged by the Allied heavy cruisers.

(c) If ordered to form a striking force, all destroyers of DESRON4—less the *Blue* and *Ralph Talbot*—should concentrate under COMDESRON4 on the *Selfridge*, some five miles northwest of Savo Island. In the event of any contact with enemy surface units, the striking force would at once attack with a full outfit of torpedoes and maintain touch from westward (sic). The striking force would engage that enemy in gun action when their own cruisers were engaged, provided it was quite clear that their own cruiser forces were not in the line of fire, and that the destroyers must be prepared to illuminate the enemy targets to optimize their own cruisers' gunfire.[67]

At its most tragic end, however, it would be this same Special Instructions directive—issued to the attending DESRON units under Crutchley's command—that would dangerously be confused with the admiral's later miscue for those same DDs to form up on his flagship, the CA *Australia*. Arguably, then, as a result of the misinterpretations of the two conflicting operational orders given by Crutchley to those DD commanders, at least two critical ship assets—the *Helm* and the *Wilson*—would become somewhat lost to the encounter and sequestered from the battle almost in full and would play but a negligible role in its ultimate outcome.

Regrettably, the die had been cast, and Crutchley's often uninspired leadership had once again led to a serious disjoin; his failure to communicate his task group orders to all of his commanders—with unimpeachable clarity—would later have the gravest of consequences overall. Were the recurring gaffes and disconnects due, in some measure, to the bilateral military command structure in place at the time, or were they simply due more to the man—to the British admiral himself—who was so innately disposed to simply doing business his way, this while struggling to carefully orchestrate all of the complex and compartmentalized operations going on among the joint powers of all three countries[68] (and doing so much in the blind)?

Had all gone according to Crutchley's hastily conceived plan, a destroyer rendezvous point might indeed have been ideal as an assembly point for quick turnaround and redeployment of both his individual and combined ship assets then at the admiral's disposal. But to then obscurely set that "northern rendezvous point" in an area that was itself five miles north of distant Savo would in great measure be problematic, since it then fully sequestered those DESRON forces on the far side of Iron Bottom Sound—well away from the primary guardianships they had already been tasked with screening—namely, the troop transport and supply ships still unloading at Lunga/Honiara and Tulagi. One can only speculate that the very location selected by Crutchley might also have been used to further augment the overall number of interception forces in the area and to set those forces closer to the *Blue* and *Ralph Talbot* position as a "first-line of defense" against any IJN ships attempting to enter the Sound from the north. Could Crutchley's decision to do so have itself been influenced by a misinterpretation of his own orders from his American superiors and subordinates?

Could he not have made better use of the scant-numbered screening forces that were then at his disposal? And with whom would he have conferred in setting those forces throughout the Sound to protect the principal ships in his charge? Would that have included the American Admiral Turner? Might he have also spoken with RADM Norman Scott of the Eastern screen? Perhaps then CAPT Howard Bode of Crutchley's own cast-off Southern screen? Or indeed even RADM Frederick Riefkohl's Northern group itself, just then patrolling off the coast of Nggella Sule (Florida Island)? Or was this simply one more example of a grave miscommunication that could further point up the strained (and perhaps even strangling) disjoins each side encountered in attempting to coordinate activities between the two major naval powers? It is possible that we may never know for sure, and Crutchley's full motives and rationale for doing what he did on the night in question may remain but one more puzzle piece that will await its own resolution and posturing in the annals of naval history.

Dangerous Decisions: Crutchley's Removal of HMAS *Australia*

But for the good Admiral Crutchley he would still not be through with his skewed misreads of the situation that seemed to be unfolding even on the night of the 9 August attacks. No sooner had he concocted the errant and unworkable plans that he would insist on for deploying his naval screening forces—his way—than he would again find himself mired in yet other SNAFUs. And throughout the hushed and darkened area of the Sound there still loomed the odds-on possibility that there was still no viable battle plan in place that could effectively be communicated to all of his subordinate ship commanders. The stage was now set for the admiral's *third* (and perhaps most significant) error, one that would begin with the hot action of close-quartered salvo and barrage and end in deadly mayhem for both the American and the Australian fleets. Crutchley's next decision would be momentous—enough to set his name down in the history books thereafter as perhaps both hero and villain, as both a keen strategist and an inept bumbler—and would soon become the admiral's own Waterloo—the *Mc-Cawley* Conference itself—and indeed here is why.

Following closely on the heels of Crutchley's ill-cautioned placement of his naval screening forces on the night of 9 August, the admiral would summarily be called on to attend a late-night meeting with RADM Richmond Kelly Turner, as the extant COMPHIBFORSOPAC, along with the Marine Corps commander, MG Alexander A. Vandegrift. The meeting would take place aboard Turner's provisional flagship, the armed transport USS *McCawley* (APA-4), which was itself anchored at the X-Ray staging area just off Lunga Point on Guadalcanal. The odd hour set for the hastily convened meeting would be 2200 hours, but the conclave forum of senior officers would not actually commence until an estimated 2225 hours.

Each of the attendees at the conference would already have known of the agenda to be tabled that night, and understood that it promised nothing if not taut, high-pressure talks about Fletcher's removal of the CTF 61 carrier task force the day before. Seen as both a critical and highly impactful move on the part of Fletcher, the withdrawal of the senior officer's carrier task force assets would have another effect as well. It would leave the cruiser and destroyer screening force, troop transports, supply ships, patrol craft, and oilers all without sufficient air cover. The Marines would only later grudgingly call it "The Great Navy Bugout," but Crutchley himself might have sniffed priggishly and called it merely a "dashing spate of bad luck." Nonetheless, the attendance of both men at Turner's conference would have been fairly expected—with Crutchley standing in for all of the key naval forces in and around Guadalcanal, and Vandegrift representing the land-based Marines—and indeed such attendance might have been wholly mandated for both senior commanders.

At 2055 hours, therefore, on the night of 9 August, Crutchley simply packed up and moved away from the Southern screening force to proceed to that *McCawley* meeting area. Perhaps again misinterpreting his orders, or simply preferring more the comfort of his own ship, Crutchley had by 2100 hours that night fully withdrawn his flagship *Australia* and left behind a now-reduced force of only two heavy cruisers that still made up that Allied Southern screen. Crutchley's *Australia* would then disappear into the night as he sailed for Lunga Point and Turner's conference aboard his flagship. He would use neither the "Admiral's Barge" nor even the "Captain's Gig," both of which must clearly have been available to him, nor any other shuttle craft that could have been used, instead taking the entire cruiser with him. The admiral's departure aboard that same *Australia*—thought at the time by Crutchley to be negligible, and for the shortest time only—would in fact prove to be anything but negligible and culminate in the crushing outcome and later defeat of his own screening group—and that of Riefkohl's own Northern fleet. For an approximated linear view of Admiral Crutchley's known operational timeline, see the detailed Microsoft *Visio* rendering noted in Figure 21.

Couched within this one momentous and clearly ill-cautioned decision to leave his own Southern screening force, Crutchley would now single-handedly commit three grave errors in a mere span of hours. First, of course, had already been his very departure from that screening element on his flagship *Australia*, thereby reducing that group's force-presence to only two CAs and two DDs. Second, in his absence, he would ill advisedly appoint CAPT Howard Douglas Bode as the screening force commander *pro tempore* and, in so doing, granted the subordinate captain full tactical command of those Southern force ships patrolling the Sound that night. Crutchley had effected the change in command, however temporarily, with only curt ceremony and did not clearly communicate that command change to others in the surface fleet. In and of itself, this action might not have been problematic, at least not initially, but it would quickly become so at the moment of the IJN attack on the Allied ships by Mikawa's battle fleet.

Later, the still somewhat unproven and ham-fisted captain of the American CA *Chicago*, Howard Bode, would soon fail in his ad hoc leadership role, and would not at all coordinate any of the movements or activities of the ships at his disposal, even in Crutchley's absence. Sadly, Bode would not at all rise to the occasion, and would never mount any effective (or even adequate) response to Mikawa's night attack. Indeed, after sustaining some level of damage to his ship's bow from a single torpedo hit from the IJN cruiser *Kako*, *Chicago* would mysteriously sail off on a curious heading of 263° (T), well to the north and west for some forty minutes—away from the area of skirmish—and would play no further role in the battle itself. Crutchley and Bode's worst nightmare was about to come true, and the "Battle of Five Sitting Ducks"[69] would soon be on them in one of the most gritty and telling events of all of World War II: the *First Battle of Savo Island*.

In its third instance, the good admiral would not only leave the area of the SSF in the dead of night but also do so without ample notification being given the subordinate commanders of either the Northern or the Eastern screening groups, essentially keeping both commanders, Riefkohl and Scott, much in the dark as to his movements,

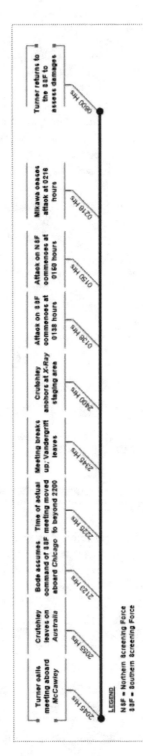

Figure 21. Crutchley Timeline: 2055–0900 Hours, 9 August 1942

his destination, or even a viable timetable for his expected return. With Crutchley now on the move, the meager forces he had left behind to guard the southern flank would indeed now be hard-pressed, and quickly closed ranks in order to offset the deficiency of the admiral's now-absented command ship *Australia*. An already bad decision to leave both his station and the ships of that Southern force was now about to get even worse. The stage was now set for the British admiral's fourth and final gaffe, as the curt and unassuming Crutchley would not even return that night but would in fact simply "spend the night" at his X-Ray anchorage near Turner's *McCawley*. Later, at the time of the battle itself—even as it unfolded in the far northern reaches—it is certain that Crutchley had probably heard the muffled guns and booming from the hot broadsides being fired in anger and could almost see the muted flashes like laser pinpoints of light just over the far horizon.

At the battle's sad end, the haught and portly Crutchley would be seen nowhere near any of the raging battles, as it were, even as the opening salvos to the north began to resound in crescendo. Had there been yet another miscommunication or disjoin between Crutchley and the U.S. naval forces under his immediate command? Commenting on exactly this idea—that of the unacceptably poor communications existing between those same American screening forces and Crutchley himself—Bates would make a parallel observation:

Each screening group command operated independently of the other group commanders. Commander, *Vincennes* group [would notify] the other group commanders of his planned operations, but he was not in turn advised by them as to their own planned operations.[70]

So just how much was Riefkohl on *Vincennes* told—or Getting on *Canberra*, or Greenman on *Astoria*, or even Moore on his own *Quincy*? How many even knew of the good admiral's departure on that occasion or of his further decision to stay overnight? Had Crutchley even previously worked with any of the Northern force screening ships at all, or with their commanders in the past? On closer examination, decidedly not at all:

CTG 62.6 stated that the consideration that the cruisers *Vincennes, Quincy,* and *Astoria* had not operated under his command before they joined him just prior to the rehearsals at Koro Island on July 28, led him to decide to employ them as a separate tactical group. He stated that he had "never had an opportunity to confer with, or even meet the commanding officers of those ships"; nor to issue them the Standing Instructions which he had issued to his own task force. It seems somewhat dubious that no opportunity had presented itself to issue these instructions, or to exercise tactically—at the very least for drill purposes—the forces he would have under his command at Tulagi. Could not the Instructions have been delivered by destroyer, with further explanations then delivered by both voice and visual means? It appears that ample time was available for appropriate tactical exercises while in the vicinity of Koro Island, and while still enroute to their objective. The fault, therefore, must lie mainly with Crutchley.[71]

"The fault, therefore, must lie mainly with Crutchley"—the words would now echo forth, words that would further aggravate the already great difficulty he was experiencing in dealing with his American counterparts. But was this necessarily a full and unimpeachable truth, or might it instead have been an even greater and far more reaching indicator of the Allies' more central problem: that of communication versus miscommunication, that of actual, fact-based intel versus speculation and poor assumption, or that of the compartmentalized ships' activities versus a fully operational and shared command structure? All else aside, Crutchley could not at all have known that his impulsive and risky departure that night would later have such an immeasurable impact on the ships patrolling Iron Bottom Sound during the later battle, as soon he set about the business of committing his fourth and final gaffe: remaining on station at the conference site itself.

Dangerous Decisions: Crutchley Remains at the X-Ray Transport Area

The late-night strategy session aboard *McCawley* between Admirals Turner and Crutchley, and the commander of all Marine forces, MG Vandegrift, had initially been set to convene promptly at 2200 hours, but that time would get pushed back to a time of 2225. Once in full session, however, records of the proceedings of that meeting seem to indicate that it was in fact concluded in less than twenty-five minutes, all told. Within that span of time, however, Turner would have already informed both men of his decision to withdraw the transport ships at first light—this in the face of Fletcher's earlier move to pull the carriers from Guadalcanal on the previous day. Turner's further decision to now remove his own secondary troop transport and supply ships as well would now *stun* Vandegrift, instilling in him a seething anger and a distrust, which must clearly have manifested itself more than once during the edgy, unquiet exchanges at that Turner meeting. Indeed, one might almost hear the gruff and dogged major general of the Marine Corps as he must have growled and pounded hard on the desk to voice his harsh objections.

In fact, Vandegrift's 1st Marine Division was already on shore and well dug in but still desperately in need of the stocks and munitions that were being unloaded from those very cargo and supply ships. And indeed, based on those very decisions made on *McCawley* that night, all of that unloading activity would now have to continue straight through the night—or so at least thought a doubtful Vandegrift—if in fact those supply ships were later being pulled out by Turner at dawn's first light. The debate between the men aboard *McCawley* must at the least have been impassioned and peppered with adamancy and a good measure of resistance—as well perhaps as a sprinkling of well-chosen cusswords—certainly at least on the part of Vandegrift, who stood to lose the most of all the men in the room that night. The ad hoc conference would quickly break up and Vandegrift would make a beeline run back to shore to personally inspect the transport areas to obtain a more informed view of the progress of those unloading activities. The clock was ticking on toward 2345, some fifteen minutes before midnight itself, and in the next instant, Vandegrift himself was gone.

That left only Crutchley.

The admiral's final gaffe would now begin with the false assumption that there would, in fact, be no significant activity by the intruding Japanese for the remainder of that night, and although a single unidentified IJN seaplane tender had earlier been reported to the north of Savo, Crutchley reasoned that such enemy ships (the seaplane tenders themselves) would seldom engage in any ship-to-ship attacks—and even less so at night—and thus saw no real or immediate threat at hand at that time. In its final analysis, however, it would all simply come down to options and the comfort of the good admiral. Should he have returned with all haste to his lead position as flagship of the Southern screening force or simply remained at the X-Ray staging area and hunkered down to wait for the coming morning?

For Crutchley, he would foolishly opt for the latter and so secured his own *Australia* and simply bedded down for the night. He would not return to resume his stewardship of his Southern fleet and would instead leave the command of that group in the untested hands of CAPT Howard Bode. The world would only later find out just how tragically errant a move that would be, and Admiral Crutchley could not at all have known just what earth-shattering trials and tribulations the next few hours would bring to that same screening group. In truth, he would not even learn of their full import until well into the next day.

This would once again serve as a major shortfall for the ill-starred Crutchley, one for which the flag officer would later indeed be only mildly reprimanded. On this, the renowned naval historian Richard B. Frank, in his own studied analysis *Guadalcanal: The Definitive Account of the Landmark Battle*, would himself clearly note the following as well:

> Crutchley elected not to return with *Australia* to the Southern force, but instead stationed his ship just outside the Guadalcanal transport anchorage without informing any of the other Allied ship commanders of his intent to do so . . . or [even] of his final location.[72]

Could a senior naval officer now in fact have four strikes against him—the results of which might taint any senior officer's good name thereafter and only rudely impeach his credibility? At the very first, there had already been ❶ the imprecise issuance of the Standing Instructions for the DESRON forces to (re)assemble/regroup at the obscure Savo rendezvous to the north; then ❷ the inadequate positioning of the radar pickets themselves, utilizing only two ships where four would clearly have been the more cautious screening alternative; then ❸ the untimely departure of the admiral himself on his flagship *Australia* to attend the Turner powwow imprimis; and finally ❹ his remaining at that X-Ray transport area overnight, and not returning to his own screening element until the morning of the next day. In hard truth, the unchecked confusion and often confounding miscues that were only too evident between the naval commanders of all three Allied powers of the time might seemingly know no end indeed.

The SNAFU of the RAAFR Overflights: The Hunting of the Hudsons

Clearly occurring well before Crutchley's later series of indiscretions, there would also have been two forerunner events that would further point up the misinterpretive bungling of intel between the Allied forces and leading up to the First Battle of Savo Island itself. Those events would happen quite early on in the pre-battle timeline, much before Crutchley even entered the picture on the night in question; it would center on the joint operations and communications exchanges between the coalition powers vis-à-vis the Hudsons—the reconnaissance overflights of the Royal Australian Air Force (RAAFR) planes, late on the morning of 8 August 1942.

At that time, three Lockheed Hudson reconnaissance planes from the 32nd Squadron of the RAAFR Fall River Air Base at Milne Bay, New Guinea, would take off on routine surveillance overflights that would take them well out over dangerous waters as they scanned the near horizon for enemy shippage or other unusual (air) activity in the area. In and of themselves, the planes' patrol sectors would be nothing if not vast and would range from as far north as the St. George's Channel—sandwiched between the two large islands of New Britain and New Ireland—to points as far south as Bougainville, Choiseul, and well beyond.

It should be clearly noted that the overall operational activities of the RAAFR planes themselves may (if at all) have been only loosely controlled by Admiral Crutchley himself, and truly only Admiral John S. McCain Sr.—as COMNAVAIR-SOPACFLT of all air operations in the region—might have had dealings with the joint RAAFR forces that were themselves far to the west of Guadalcanal. Instead, the pilots of the Australian search planes had a completely different command structure, one that fed up through its own abbreviated chain to its own upper echelon in the person of the Commander, Southwest Pacific Forces (COMSOWESPACFOR). Crutchley could no more have known about the exact deployments or surveillance activities of the Australian search planes than he could have known about the remote Coastwatchers employed by the local Australians who regularly reported in on any large (or otherwise suspicious) Japanese shipping activity passing through the Channel at any given interval.

That morning, however, flights A16-157, A16-185, and A16-218 would all indeed fly out of Fall River and were not long into their normal patrol circuits when at least two of the planes did in fact spot Mikawa's approaching surface fleet, even as it surreptitiously slipped down the Slot past the remote island of Choiseul. One sighting (Stutt, Geddes, Courtis, and Bell on A16-218) would mistakenly identify the ships of Mikawa's CRUDIV6 and CRUDIV18 force as being "three cruisers, three destroyers and two seaplane tenders or gunboats,"[73] while the second, equally fallacious report (from Williams on A16-185) would note "two heavy cruisers, two light cruisers and one small unknown type."[74] Both reports, therefore, would already obviously be skewed and in error, even as to the type and number of ships sighted. If the squadron's primary task was simply to note and report on the very presence of enemy ships, the situation would fairly demand a quick and timely report be made back to base to alert the Allied naval forces, known to be operating in the southern Solomons at the time of that sighting. But would the RAAFR pilots do as expected? Decidedly, pretty much not at all.

The first report from the A16-218 Hudson aircraft would not be received by the Allied forces in fact for some two hours, sixteen minutes after the sighting, the second A16-185 itself delayed by an even more incredible nine hours, forty-six minutes—this in part due to the pilot's refusal to break a strict radio silence order—such that had earlier in fact been mandated by the individual COMSOWESPACFOR station manager himself.

In either event, the important and "highly perishable" intel each held would not reach the ears of the British and American commanders in the south until late on the evening of 8 August. And, on at least the part of the enemy, the Imperial Japanese Navy's operational clock had already begun ticking down the very hours that would soon give rise to the later savaging attacks at Savo.

And so just where might that IJN fleet be by now?

The combined Allied naval commanders under Turner and Crutchley did not know for sure but, much to their utter dismay, would soon enough find out a terrible and absolute truth.

So, was the delay in the Hudson reports merely a one-time SNAFU—an extraordinary procedural gaffe that only seldom occurred within the notification protocols in place for reporting any such visual sightings—or was it in fact characteristic of an even greater, more deeply rooted problem of communication (and apparent miscommunication) among the British, Australian, and American forces themselves? And while the information from the RAAFR spotter planes would indeed finally channel its way through COMSOWESPACFOR (and various other "handling" waypoints such as Admirals Ghormley and Fletcher), it would in fact reach the Allied commanders at Guadalcanal but would do so barely in time for that intel to still even be relevant.

In its final analysis, therefore, although the RAAFR reporting failures may not have been the fault of the otherwise fairly taciturn Admiral Crutchley, it would nonetheless much concern him later on in the long run, and would create a far more complicated web of dire circumstances and little warning of those approaching ships—all of which would have a direct bearing on the flawed decisions the admiral would later be known to make regarding the placement of his screening ships, before and during the killing attacks that would take place on the very next night.

A Tale of Two Navies: Conclusions

In good premise, then, the fault did not lie with the stars, nor did it alone spring from the communication gaps and gaffes that were themselves quite evident in the integrated service forces of the Americans, British, Australians, and New Zealanders. Of needs, many such problems might almost have been expected to plague the joint operational endeavors of the tripartite navies—especially on an invasion scale of this magnitude. It may indeed have been wholly unavoidable and, perhaps, to great extent even expected. Guadalcanal would be the first such joint operation attempted in the Pacific area by those coalition forces. Indeed, the three powers had already long since partnered in combat in the European theater, but those had all been mainly land-based encounters with an already dug-in enemy. The decisive linking-up of the combined naval forces of all three countries, which would now include their massive light and heavy cruisers and destroyers—from each of the participant countries—into a unified naval force that would then be set to patrol the dark waters of the Solomons, might, at *best*, be ambitious . . . at *worst*, catastrophic.

From the RAAFR Hudsons' failure to report their sightings in a timely manner, indeed only doing so in a most circuitous and delaying manner, to Crutchley's own series of "howlers" and gaffes, it is clear that some level of misinterpretation and confusion might result from the complex interaction of the three naval powers, but certainly few could have thought it might result in the endgame debacle at Savo as much it did later on. Decidedly, time was of the essence to the tripartite league as each of their individual forces soon converged on Guadalcanal, and—but for a series of minor training exercises held by Crutchley off the coast of Koro Island in Fiji itself—there simply was not ample time to conduct the extensive joint naval exercises that might normally have been mandated prior to committing a force of such a size to such a grand undertaking as that of screening the invasion of the Solomons. Take it or leave it, it was clear that the combined forces of the three powers were truly here to stay; they simply had to learn how to quickly integrate those forces and fully work together. Oddly, Savo Island would be precisely that rude wake-up call, and a final weighty lesson for all three.

A Tale of Two Navies: Further Reading

Articles and Books

Loxton, Bruce, and Chris Coulthard-Clark. (1997). *The Shame of Savo: Anatomy of a Naval Disaster.* Allen & Unwin Pty Ltd.

Electronic Weblinks

Cited from the *Adventure Kokoda*, subsectioned as "The Pacific War 1942: The United States Strategy," at http://www.kokodatreks.com/history/thepacificwar1942/unitedstatesstrategy.cfm.

Cited from the website *The Proceedings of the Friesian School, Fourth Series*, subsectioned as "A Guadalcanal Chronology & Order of Battle: 7 August 1942–6 March 1943." See line beginning "the intensity of battle . . ." at http://www.friesian.com/history/guadal.htm.

Cited from the website *Second World War History*, subsectioned as "Battle of Guadalcanal Timeline" at http://www.secondworldwarhistory.com/battle-of-guadalcanal.asp.

Cited from the Wikipedia article, subsectioned as "British Pacific Fleet," under a section titled "Background" at http://en.wikipedia.org/wiki/British_Pacific_Fleet#Background.

Cited from the Wikipedia website, subsectioned as "Naval Battle of Guadalcanal," under a section titled "Background" at http://en.wikipedia.org/wiki/Naval_Battle_of_Guadalcanal#Background.

Cited from the website *U.S. Army Center of Military History*, subsectioned as "Guadalcanal: The U.S. Army Campaigns of World War II," under "Guadalcanal: Strategic Setting" at http://www .history.army.mil/brochures/72-8/72-8.htm.

Cited from the website *The Pacific War*, under a title of "The Pacific War from Pearl Harbor to Guadalcanal, sub-sectioned as America Fights Back," and further categorized as "Despite Pearl Harbor, America Adopts a 'Germany First' Strategy" at http://www.pacificwar.org.au/Germany First/GermanyFirst.html.

FINDING 13:   GOOD FORTUNE AND A TRICK OF LUCK

A Fateful Turn of the Cards

As VADM Gunichi Mikawa formed up his ships and sailed south from the Japanese-held ports of Kavieng and Rabaul, he silently channeled his cruisers through the narrows of New Georgia Sound, past New Britain, and New Ireland, and out into the sprawling open waters fronting the larger island land mass Choiseul. With overall command of the cruiser force at large, Mikawa had just converged all light and heavy cruisers of his Eighth Fleet CRUDIV18 force, with those of RADM Gotō's own CRUDIV6, the latter formation emanating from a coastal point near Rabaul. The heavily armed flotilla of attack ships continued sailing south, down the Slot to a point just north of volcanic Savo Island, where his lead ships soon spotted the two patrolling radar pickets, the American DDs USS *Blue* and the USS *Ralph Talbot*.

In fact, neither American screening ship would even note Mikawa's passing fleet in dead of night, as indeed the good admiral's luck would hold yet one more time, with his force simply "threading the eye of the needle" and moving with speed and continued stealth, sluicing easily past the two "gate-keeper" destroyers of Crutchley's ill-formed northernmost screen. On the very shank of night on 9 August 1942, Mikawa's cruiser force moved forward with hastened speed, already battle hardened and now battle ready, and sailed south to Savo waters with a deadly purpose and a firm resolve. The force was now arrayed in its standard "column-ahead, in-line" formation that soon topped speeds between 22 and 30 knots; then, quietly skirting around an already darkened Savo Island, the keen-eyed lookouts on the *Chōkai* and *Kako* soon spotted a small contingent of unidentified ships just over the near horizon. Those unidentified ships would be none other than those of Crutchley's Southern fleet, itself a small, four-ship element led by two cruisers under the reluctant command of a still untested CAPT Howard Douglas Bode.

By 0138, the lights were switched on and the starshell flares were lofted high above the American ships from the decks of the IJN cruisers, now illuminating the night and peeling back the masking shroud of darkness. And there, right before Mikawa's well-positioned fleet, lay the enemy's ships, now some 12,500 meters distant, and all quite in his range and at his mercy. Having none, Mikawa did what he had been trained to do—he attacked! And that attack would indeed be nothing if not swift and violent, decisive and timed with great precision, and then executed with a near-mechanical accuracy that still stands in awe even to the present day.

With signal ensigns and the colored flags of the Rising Sun fluttering crisply in the breeze of their own advance, Mikawa arrayed his forces into three spaced groupings in a classic line-ahead format, which would now include Mikawa's flagship *Chōkai* in the vanguard position, followed by the second lead ship—Gotō's own flag *Aoba*—in consort with the IJN heavy cruisers *Kinugasa*, *Kako*, and *Furutaka*, in that order. Bringing up the rear of the battle formation was the third group, made up of the only two remaining light cruisers, *Tenryū* and *Yubari*—and the group's lone destroyer, *Yunagi*, which had already been detached by Mikawa to remain back near Savo to "guard the back door" against surprise enemy attack on his ships' return. Curiously to exactly this end, author Jack D. Coombe almost jokingly referred to *Yunagi*'s station as indeed being that of the element's "Tail-End Charlie."[75]

Soon, in the wake of the attack on the *Canberra* and *Chicago*—and the DDs *Patterson* and *Bagley*—Mikawa would abruptly break off his attack only after leaving two Allied heavy cruisers heavily damaged and left in smoldering heaps behind him. As a direct result of these attacks, and those still to come from Mikawa's second cruiser group—made up of the *Furutaka*, *Yubari*, and *Tenryū*—and walloped by the increasing number of hits from the high-caliber shells fired from both *Chōkai* and *Furutaka*, the *Canberra* was compelled to sharply turn to port to escape the sudden, violent secondary attack. It would be precisely then that this same secondary group of IJN ships would—perhaps to avoid a perceived imminent collision with the crippled and now retiring *Canberra*—now take a significant turn to west, effectively causing each ship in sequence to column up in yet a secondary formation behind and away from the Mikawa main force of ships. First to veer off would have been the light cruiser *Furutaka*, followed quickly by her sister ship, the *Yubari*, and even the still-engaging *Tenryū* itself, which simply closed up ranks and followed suit with the two ships to her front, and so also steered to west. These three ships—forced off course simply by the *Canberra*'s own sudden death-throe turn to port—would be that one event that would bring about the quite fortuitous "two-pronged" pincer assault that was now headed straight north toward Riefkohl's own unsuspecting fleet. It would be this critical, if accidental, splitting of the primary Mikawa column into *two* viable attack forces that would then effectively "bracket" the Northern screen . . . again with only the most devastating results.

And now Mikawa's trap would be sprung for yet a second time.

The splitting of Mikawa's forces on the occasion of the night battle at Savo would oddly not be the admiral's only piece of good luck, as, seemingly aided by the very American forces he sought to attack, he could indeed do no wrong. As such, the good admiral continued only to dance with "Lady Luck" in the darkened moonlight, even as the dominoes and obstacles that stood before him toppled one by one. His tactic of approach—that of penetrate, strike, and withdraw—had succeeded far better than anticipated. He had effectively eliminated *four* heavy cruisers from the enemy's meager arsenal of large capital warships in one fell swoop, a "swoop" that cost him but thirty-one minutes in his own hourglass of time. But even this would not be all, since Mikawa's fortune on at least this night would seemingly know no end, as we might more clearly see in the further topical discussion in Table 14.

Table 14. Good Fortune and a Trick of Luck: Dancing by Moonlight with Lady Luck

"TRICK OF LUCK"	EVENT	EXPLOITATION / RESULT
❶ Removal of Carrier Task Force: CTF-based assets removed by VADM Fletcher just prior to the battle	The advancing Mikawa force is at no time attacked by any American planes before or even during the attack. The sole casualty suffered was that of the *Kako*, brought on by a single American S-class diesel sub, the USS *S-44 (S-155)* on 10 August.	ADM Fletcher's removal of the American carrier force brought about a lack of close-air combat support by any of the carrier-based planes, allowing Mikawa to prosecute both attacks, and later even withdraw his forces, without significant challenge. Still fearful of an air attack nonetheless, Mikawa would indeed cut short his attack and beat a hasty retreat back to the north and out of *Iron Bottom Sound*. **RESULT:** Mikawa breaks off his attacks and does not go after any of the primary cargo or troop ships at either Honiara or Tulagi.
❷ No detection of the Mikawa strike force by the American S-class submarine USS *S-38* near New Britain	The American diesel sub USS *S-38* spots the advancing IJN cruiser force but cannot line up a (viable) shot with any torpedoes. CAPT Munson can only call in the contact to his COMSUBDIV5 base command.	Message sent is deemed to *not* be of any great import and is inexplicably delayed. Message is hours late in reaching the southern-based Allied command at Guadalcanal. **RESULT:** Mikawa continues on unchallenged in his slow and calculated move south.
❸ No detection of the Mikcwa strike force by RAAFR Hudson overflights	Not one, not two, but as many as *three* separate reconnaissance overflights by RAAFR Hudsons fly near the approaching IJN convoy at a point just west of Choiseul.	One Hudson reports having seen nothing. One Hudson reports sighting but the report routed to Allied commanders at Guadalcanal is 2 hours and 16 minutes late. One Hudson reports sighting but the report to commanders at Guadalcanal is 9 hours and 46 minutes late. **RESULT:** Mikawa force continues wholly unimpeded.

Table 14. *Continued*

"TRICK OF LUCK"	EVENT	EXPLOITATION / RESULT
❹ No detection of the Mikawa strike force by a reconnaissance squadron of B-17s	A squadron of B-17s out of Espiritu Santo spots the Mikawa fleet near Kieta.	By 1215 hours on 8 August, the planes report to their base HQs to advise them of "four cruisers and a destroyer headed westward at 1231."[76] Sighting Intel is then slowly routed through COMSUBDIV5 to COMSOWESPAC but would not reach CTF 62 (Turner) until almost 2400 hours. **Result:** Mikawa continues in his approach unimpeded and wholly undetected.
❺ No detection of the Mikawa strike force by the American radar picket ships north of Savo	Neither the *Blue* or the *Ralph Talbot*, on picket radar patrol sailing parallel courses in waters north of Savo, would detect Mikawa's advancing fleet.	Mikawa braces for action from either picket ship with allegedly "fifty guns trained out on both ships at all times" during their passage through, but neither ship is ever engaged. **Result:** Mikawa force continues on still unchallenged.
❻ No detection of the Mikawa strike force by ships of the Southern screening force	The two escort ships flanking *Canberra* and *Chicago*, the DDs *Bagley* and *Patterson*, both spot the IJN force, but the alarm sounded is seconds too late.	Mikawa's forces illuminate the American ships and fire on the *Patterson*, then attack all ships in that Southern force. **Result:** Mikawa successfully prosecutes crippling attacks on the *Canberra*, sinking her virtually in situ; and *Chicago* is badly damaged with a single torpedo shot to her bow. Mikawa continues on unimpeded to launch his second attack on the Northern screen as well.

#		
7 No detection of the Mikawa strike force by ships of the Northern screening force	All five ships of the Northern screening force are engaged by the Mikawa surface fleet.	The *Vincennes*, *Quincy*, and the *Astoria*—along with escort DDs *Helm* and *Wilson*—all soon spot the IJN force only after illuminants were deployed and the initial attack was already under way, at which time it was indeed already too late. **Result:** Mikawa successfully prosecutes crippling attacks on the *Vincennes*, the *Quincy*, and the *Astoria*, sinking all three in a matter of minutes (or hours). Mikawa's cruisers break off without further assault, and prepare to simply exit the area.
8 Withdrawal of the Mikawa strike force after the twin attacks at Savo	The well-fortuned attack ships in Mikawa's CRUDIV6 and 18 force now exit the area after prosecuting their primed attacks on both Crutchley's Southern and Northern screening forces at Savo Island just west and north of Guadalcanal.	Mikawa's force essentially leaves the area much as it had come in, sailing straight north past Savo and rejoining the on-station DD *Yūnagi*. The force briefly engages the *Ralph Talbot* and a crippled (and still-retiring) *Jarvis* on their way out, but there are again no real challenges to their departure. **Result:** Mikawa escapes back up the *Slot* toward Rabaul and Kavieng,[77] again remaining essentially unchallenged.
9 Return to Kavieng and Rabaul	Nearing home ports, Mikawa releases Gotō's CRUDIV18 ships back to his command, who then embarks his (Gotō's own) ships off to the north to far Kavieng, where the *Kako* is attacked by the prowling USS *S-44* on the morning of 10 August.	The American sub *S-44* fires four torpedoes in a spread at a stunned *Kako*, three of which impact with devastating effect. The *Kako* sinks almost *in situ* in waters just NE of Kavieng near Simberi Island, at a reported 2°28'0" S–152° 11'0" E). **Result:** Mikawa's streak of good luck now suffers its first and perhaps most devastating setback of his entire attack itinerary to that point. The loss of the *Kako* at Kavieng, for at least VADM Mikawa, must indeed have besmirched the commander's otherwise untarnished reputation, and greatly dialed down the man's savoring of his earlier victories at Savo, all of which were now tempered with the loss of one of his own heavy cruisers.

A Certain Trick of Luck: The Two-Pronged Split

Of interest to both readers and researchers, it should be noted that there are indeed many maps of the times—as well as those drawn after the action itself—that seem to tell two different stories: that of a two-pronged split and that of a three-pronged split of Mikawa's forces that night, all occurring within approximately the same time frame. By 0144 hours, Mikawa was already concluding his attack on Bode's Southern fleet and beginning to move to the north in pursuit of additional targets of opportunity. The splitting of his forces into two deadly columns may in fact have been only accidental, but it also played quite well into the hands of the wily Mikawa and would itself only be caused by the sudden turn to port by a dying *Canberra* as she sought only to escape the killing barrages of the Japanese gunners once she had been attacked.

Therefore, the Northern split-column force would now consist of the errant *Furu-taka*, *Yubari*, and *Tenryū*—each forced off-course by the straggling *Canberra*—while the Southern force carried in its group the remaining heavy cruisers still under Mikawa's immediate command—namely, his *Chōkai*, the *Aoba*, the *Kako*, and the *Kinugasa*. Shown here, in the somewhat oversimplified rendering noted in Figure 22, is a clearly delineated

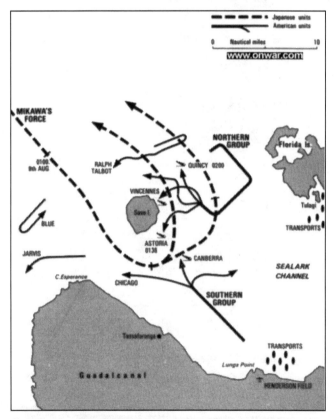

Figure 22.   The "Splitting" of VADM Gunichi Mikawa's CRUDIV6 and CRUDIV18 Forces: The Two-Pronged Formation

line of advance for each of the twin assault columns from both ship groups. Mikawa was having perhaps his best of all days and may not even have been aware of the unfathomable depths his great good fortune would so sweetly enjoy that night.[78]

A Certain Trick of Luck: The Three-Pronged Split

Conversely, we see in this map crafted by Toshikazu Ohmae, Mikawa's own chief of staff on the night in question, evidence of what appears to be a three-pronged split of Mikawa's forces—itself a sufficient force to carry out the next phase of their planned attack in full—on the American Northern screen. Therefore, we now see in the map a clear delineation of yet a *third* line of attack—shown here as Mikawa's own flagship *Chōkai* itself—which by now had taken up the outermost track and began flanking the other ships of his own CRUDIV force. Also curiously noted, however, is the fact that in both events these column splits were not immediately corrected by any of the ships' commanders, and the ships were simply allowed to continue on their tracks even well after the closing of the attack on Riefkohl's Northern fleet. In either column-split scenario (two- or three-pronged), however, it is clear that the divided forces under Mikawa's command did not reconverge and order up until already well past Savo— and perhaps even the Russell Islands themselves, and well into New Georgia Sound fronting the southernmost tip of Choiseul.[79]

Perhaps in its final outcome, therefore, it might not have mattered much whether the sly splitting of Mikawa's cruiser division columns was in any way divine or providential; nor would it have mattered whether that attacking force was either a two- or a three-pronged assault column, save that of knowing it had come to pass at all—and only that at great expense to the Allied fleet. Much like the admiral's initial approach to Savo, his stealthy push past the sluggish American pickets, and the later well-timed attacks on all the ships in Iron Bottom Sound, this, too, would simply be another trick of luck (and a good twist of fate) for the reservedly jubilant Admiral Mikawa. And on this night, in this battle, and on these seas, the twin victories carried off by the crafty cruiser force under the IJN admiral's shrewd command would go down in history as one of the most truly remarkable feats of strategy, planning, and sound execution, as well indeed had bold Mikawa danced well with Lady Luck by moonlight . . . and truly survived his ordeal.

FINDING 14:   EFFECTIVENESS OF JAPANESE NAVAL NIGHT OPERATIONS

Clearly, had there been but one stand-out element—one single, componential ingredient that most allowed VADM Gunichi Mikawa and his CRUDIV surface fleet to prosecute their attacks so successfully on both the Allied Southern and Northern screening forces on the night of 9 August 1942, it must surely have been his ships' ability to fight at night. And, if viewed correctly, in terms of fully optimizing one's

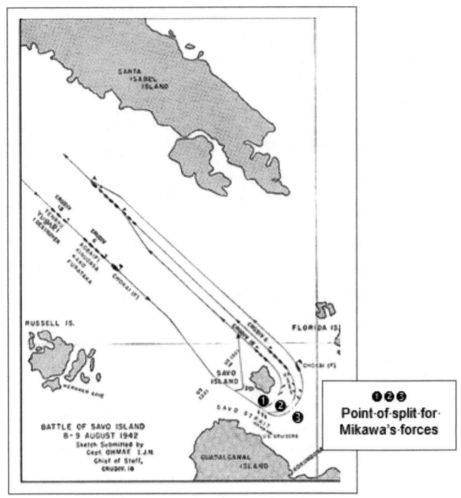

Figure 23. The "Splitting" of VADM Gunichi Mikawa's CRUDIV6 and CRUDIV18 Forces: The Three-Pronged Formation

tactics, battle regimen, and plan of execution, few could this night have surpassed Mikawa or the Imperial Japanese Navy in its demonstrated ability to conduct all such highly effective night-fighting engagements . . . this with results that almost always came at great cost to the enemy's fleets, and almost always *far* exceeded even the IJN's greatest expectations.

Kurayami no kumo no uchi, wareware wa kōgeki shinakereba naranai! avows the Japanese adage: "Out of a cloud of darkness, we shall attack!" So indeed it would come to pass, and by early 1942 virtually all of ADM Isoroku Yamamoto's dread Combined Fleet was already quite proficient in the strategies and good uses of the night attack.

In form and effect, then, this Japanese night attack—or *Yashū*, as it might also be known—would almost always consist of five prime operational components: ❶ detection; ❷ illumination; ❸ identification; ❹ engagement; and finally ❺ withdrawal. By early 1942, the IJN had nearly perfected all of these strategies with an almost studied and second-natured approach, and it would continue to further "fine-tune" those night-fighting skills through a combination of at-sea trials, planned simulations, and accelerated night gunnery and torpedo exercises.

It might be said, therefore, that the Americans would operate by day; truly the IJN owned the night.

In fact, historically it had earlier been only a rigid and unwavering IJN high command that, in its own time, had soon realized that Japan had not built nearly enough "capital ships" (i.e., cruisers, battleships, and CV-class vessels) in the intermediate years between the two World Wars, and that that country's naval forces must now be compelled to focus mainly on keeping those few assets they did have intact. Therefore, the Japanese navy would now fervently and quietly go about the business of perfecting their optical sighting systems; training their keen-eyed and specially selected ship lookouts to always remain alert and well focused; and refining their ability to not only identify COMNAVAIRSOPACFLT potential enemy threats but also render first-sighting target estimates out to those ships.

Far and away, however, Japan's greatest weapon in its arsenal of many must clearly have been its technically superior *Type 93* torpedo, one that—at least to the Allies and Americans alike—would only too soon come to be known as the "Long Lance." This killing torpedo carried a massive (490kg)[80] warhead and could home in on its target at speeds that now full-out approached almost 38 knots and—defying all belief at that time in 1942—had an awesome range of some 24.9 miles. Compared to anything the Americans might have had during this same time frame, it would soon have been the equivalent of bringing a switchblade to a deadly, blazing gunfight—at least on the part of the Americans. On the IJN's practiced and demonstrated ability to conduct all such naval night battles with exacting success, Ohmae's own words would soon ring out with exactly this same sentiment of "assumed superiority" in naval night battle, at least on the part of the IJN:

> If somehow a thrust from the enemy carriers could be avoided, we felt assured of reasonable success against those enemy ships because we had complete confidence in our night battle capabilities. Therefore, the time set for our penetration of the Guadalcanal anchorage would be at midnight, and would not waver.[81]

It would only later be found out by the Americans just how much the Japanese had trained up their forces in naval night maneuvers, who were themselves set specifically for open-sea, blue-water battles. For the Americans and their Allies at Guadalcanal, that "discovery" would be nothing less than astounding, and would tragically come too little, too late . . . and at extremely high cost. With almost clinical precision (and seemingly much "good luck"), the crews of both the IJN cruisers and fast-attack destroyers would train extensively in the operational use of all their weapons: the gunnery teams, the even deadlier long-range torpedo crews—and the detailed timing of the very assault itself. The IJN would simply not stop and in fact sought only to further fine-tune those skills to an even greater precision.

In the face of the overwhelming defeat of Crutchley's screening forces on the night of 9 August 1942 at Savo, it might clearly be said that the primary reason for the Japanese victory that night—aside from the Allied "gaffes and blunders"—would inevitably have been the sweet element of surprise, the IJN's proven and already tested skills in night fighting, and the highly effective use of their "Long Lance" torpedoes. These new torpedoes could each carry a one-ton warhead full-on for an astonishing 25 miles straight to their target—and cover shorter distances at speeds nearly up to 49 knots. Conversely, the Allied naval forces had little night-fighting savvy and virtually no experience in covering large transport and amphibious assault ship landings, since the invasion and occupation of Guadalcanal was itself the first such large-scale landing operation in a coalition led by the United States Navy to date. And this was but the opening gambit of many more years to come in the great Pacific war . . . as even then a far distant shore at Normandy beach was nothing more than an unhatched concept that was itself still some two full years in the offing.

Through the careful and orchestrated use of ❶ excellent (and state-of-the-art) optics of the time; ❷ trained and cycle-refreshed lookouts; ❸ flare orb and starshell illuminants; ❹ effective single and group-attack formations; and ❺ variations in concentrations of fire by those cruiser forces, the Imperial Japanese Navy would probably have been *second to none* in their practiced ability to engage an enemy in either an open-sea or a narrow-water battle—and even more so at night. From the calculated deployment of their ship assets to the coordination of joint tactical activities, to the independent tasking of the ships in that force itself, all these strategies would have been of the highest importance to the IJN admiralty. And each in its time would serve as a key linchpin that would underlie the quintessential success of those very night attacks.

By the time the American and Allied naval units did arrive at Guadalcanal to wrest control of the island chain from the hunkered Japanese, it was already a well-trained and thoroughly practiced IJN naval force that awaited them. After the debacle at Midway and other key battles that took place early in the Pacific War, Japan had learned some hard and valuable lessons and was now itself "itching for a fight"—eager for another opportunity to assert her superiority in naval warfare. Not surprising, then, that the IJN specialty and strategy of choice would soon enough become that of a "hit-and-run, strike-and-withdraw" tactic, especially as seen in the ship-to-ship, and fleet-to-fleet, surface engagements the Imperial Japanese Navy knew they were most likely to encounter in the coming months. Guadalcanal would now become that very make-or-break point for the powerful Japanese navy, and many within the imperial high command already knew precisely that. Japan and its mighty "Combined Fleet" must simply now make a stand, and that stand would need to begin right here in the Solomons.

If, after all, Japan could not herself rule the high seas, who else might be so bold as to even try?

Effectiveness of IJN Naval Night Fighting: Specifications Tables

Clearly, certain clarifying rules of engagement (ROEs) and operational tactics in battle would need to be in place in order for the Imperial Japanese Navy (of that time) to fully carry out its mission of supremacy on the high seas, and its goal of backing Japan's already voracious expansionist policies in the South Seas. Cruising from island chain to island chain—and from stronghold port to stronghold port—the Japanese Empire would soon boast of an incredible expanse that included spheres of influence ranging from the Paracel Islands in the South China Sea to the edges of Mili Atoll and Kwajalein in the Marshalls and even as far south as Makin in the southernmost Gilberts. Presented in the table matrices that follow is a brief overview of several such ROE battle tactics, and training scenarios from an IJN perspective, as utilized by that naval force before, during, and even after the battle for Guadalcanal.

Table 15. Naval Night-Fighting Tactics: Performance and Rules of Engagement (ROEs)

NAVAL NIGHT-FIGHTING TACTIC	DOCTRINAL STATEMENT
General Action—Rules of Engagement IJN Light and Heavy Cruisers: *Operational Mandate*	"The cruiser forces shall be responsible for screening the battle force and reporting enemy dispositions to facilitate the deployment of the battle force, [while also] exploiting any gunnery and torpedo opportunities. If the enemy battle line is observed, a wide spread of torpedoes should be fired across the enemy's line of advance to confuse or destroy the enemy battle line early on in the action. After deployment, the heavy cruisers' primary function shall then be to *attack* the enemy cruisers with all main guns, and to cover the destroyers in their own torpedo attacks on that enemy. Torpedo opportunities against the enemy battle line are also to be seized, and in case of enemy cruiser pressure becoming too great, then spreads of torpedoes should be fired against them as well."[82]

Table 16. Naval Night-Fighting Tactics: Night Action Scenarios and Responses

Naval Night-Fighting Tactic	Doctrinal Statement
Night Action— **Open Sea Attack** IJN Cruiser night attack on single or multiple targets: *Open Sea format*	As darkness approaches, cruisers must do their utmost to make contact and to close with the enemy, attacking and breaking through that enemy outer screen. They are to fire starshells and use searchlights to assist destroyers in their attacks. The cruisers are also to take advantage of the confusion created by the destroyers, and to fully exploit all gunfire and torpedo opportunities as presented. If the IJN fleet is under attack by only *light* enemy forces, the cruisers shall be charged with defeating those enemy cruiser and destroyer forces.[83]
Night Action— **Narrow Waters Attack** IJN Cruiser night attack on single or multiple targets: *Narrow Waters format*	In a narrow waters battle format, starshells, flare orbs, and searchlights shall be used freely in a close-in "melee"-type action. Ships are to be constantly prepared for all and any rapid changes that may be brought on by the very movements of the target ships themselves.
Night Action— **Cruiser Gunnery Attack** IJN Cruiser night attack on single *or* multiple target(s)	Cruiser and destroyer gunfire is to be opened at 18,000 meters (±11.18 miles) when starshells are used for illumination, while 10,000 meters (±6.21 miles) will be the optimum opening range when searchlights are used (12,000 meters (±7.45 miles)) in proximity.

Table 17. Naval Night-Fighting Tactics: Other Concomitant Factors

NAVAL NIGHT-FIGHTING TACTIC	DOCTRINAL STATEMENT
Enhanced Naval Night-Fighting Ability *Improved Optics*	From a naval perspective, an enhanced optics capability would clearly play well into the hands of the IJN and their night-attack forays. The large 20cm IJN "Big Eyes" binoculars that they used were *so* large and unwieldy that most had to be bracket and stanchion-mounted on the very decks of the cruisers themselves. These long-distance sighting instruments would soon prove to be invaluable to the Japanese and would already be far superior to any sighting systems being used by either the Americans or other Allied naval forces at the time.
Enhanced Naval Night-Fighting Ability *Trained Lookouts*	The IJN lookouts were far better equipped to carry out their observation tasks than were their American counterparts. Serving as confirmed petty officers, and later as "Masters of the Lookout," these men trained tirelessly day and night, working closely with all of the gunnery and torpedo crews in tandem. The men not only "spotted" for the ships but also had a keen ability to accurately identify targets by "silhouette" only and to track those targets with only "line-of-sight" estimates on ranges out to those targets. No comparable specialized group ever existed within the ranks of either the American or Allied navies of that time.
Enhanced Naval Night-Fighting Ability *Night Gunnery Drills*	In "back-channel" areas that, by design, were well sequestered from global view, Mikawa's cruisers would have already conducted extensive night gunnery drills and torpedo runs in and around the Paracel Islands in the South China Sea—and in the deep inlet waters on the sheltered side of the Sea of Japan. All of these live-fire gunnery exercises would have been but dry rehearsals for the real thing, but would indeed have already covered many of the engagement scenarios and battle arrays like those shown on the following pages in the gunnery deployment diagrams seen in the Figure 30–Figure 32 *Visio* configurations.

(continued)

Table 17. *Continued*

Naval Night-Fighting Tactic	Doctrinal Statement
Enhanced Naval Night-Fighting Ability **Night Torpedo Run Exercises**	Night torpedo runs and practice drills would not vary greatly in practice to that of a day action. Extant operational orders for both cruisers and DDs in the use of the *Type 93* (Long-Lance) torpedo mandated at least the following: "The center ship in the enemy's lead division shall be the point of aim for all such torpedo attacks, and when an enemy division contains two or four units, the number *two* ship shall be chosen as the point of aim." Indeed, so fast and deadly accurate were the IJN Long-Lance torpedoes that the American and Allied warships at which they were targeted could neither outrun nor outmaneuver them once they were launched by the IJN cruisers and destroyers.
Enhanced Naval Night-Fighting Ability **Illuminants**	Virtually all of the live-fire gunnery drills and torpedo runs would involve the use of both starshell illuminants fired from surface ships, and orb flares air-launched from the ships' floatplanes that would themselves be catapulted off the decks of the IJN heavy cruisers. Put to incredibly effective use and deployed at precisely the right moment before initiating a surface attack, these illuminants would over time spell a certain end to any American or Allied ships unfortunate enough to be caught in their cascade of lights. Once lit up, the full, blunt force of all of the large 8-inch and 5-inch gun platforms on the Japanese heavy cruisers would then be concentrated with deadly effect and quickly brought to bear on the unsuspecting (and often doomed) target ships—preeminently our own American (and Australian) warships themselves. The Allied naval coalition would learn hard lessons the hard way *once*, then roar back with an almost rabid fierceness, a raw determination and a dread resolve that had not previously been seen in the war up to that point.

Table 18. Naval Night-Fighting Tactics: Doctrine for Standard Opening Ranges for IJN Heavy Cruisers

TYPE OF SHIP(S) BEING ENGAGED	OPTIMUM RANGE FOR FIRING
If opposing enemy CV, BB or CA (with spotting/identification)	25,000 meters (±15.53 miles)
If opposing enemy CV, BB, or CA (without spotting/identification)	23,000 meters (±14.29 miles)
If opposing enemy CL	18,000 meters (±11.18 miles)
If opposing enemy DD	12,000 meters (± 7.46 miles)

Effectiveness of IJN Naval Night Fighting: Cruiser Gunnery Engagement Scenarios

Feared and already well respected for their acute naval gunnery skills, the Imperial Japanese Navy might at all times have been able to boast of having perhaps the most highly trained, highly capable, and highly accurate of all ships' gunnery crews during a specific time frame that encompassed much of early World War II in the south and west Pacific. Unquestionably, these crack gunnery teams would irrefutably (and almost consistently) show a deadly expertise during both their practice drills and in actual combat situations. Clearly, this would most be seen at the very outset of the attack on RADM Crutchley's Southern and Northern screening forces on the night of 9 August 1942, where we see the encroaching Japanese warships scoring massive hits on the Allied heavy cruisers, this to the latter force's utter amazement and ultimate demise. If indeed the attack itself began with an IJN illumination of the area at a time beginning at 0138 hours—and the attack on both screening forces ended at a time no later than 0216—the fact that *four* Allied heavy cruisers would be lost in such a short span of minutes was, at the time, both stunning and unfathomable—yet indeed it had just occurred, to the dismay of all and precisely as noted.

That the IJN gunnery teams practiced their craft with due diligence and good application must in some measure account for their overwhelming successes in pitched battle, but they would take it a step further in the very engagement formats and tactics they used as well. Study the *Visio*-based[84] diagrams presented in subsequent illustrations to obtain a better understanding of each of the variable cruiser-based gunnery actions that might have been undertaken by the practiced Imperial Japanese Navy during this time. Each of the attack formats shown, however, depict only generic and nonspecific engagement tactics that were probably used interchangeably by Mikawa's cruisers—but always to good effect.

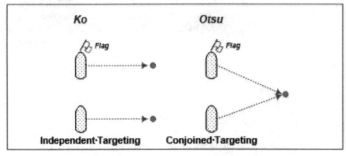

Figure 24. IJN Cruiser Gunnery Engagement Scenario (2-Ship Permutations)

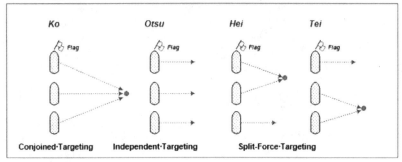

Figure 25. IJN Cruiser Gunnery Engagement Scenario (3-Ship Permutations)

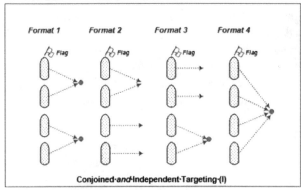

Figure 26. IJN Cruiser Gunnery Engagement Scenario (4-Ship Permutations)

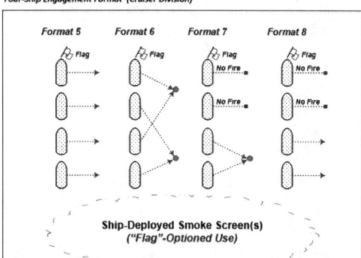

Figure 27.   IJN Cruiser Gunnery Engagement Scenario
(4-Ship Flag-Discretionary Permutations)

Effectiveness of IJN Naval Night Fighting: Noted Naval Night Battles Led by the IJN at Guadalcanal

It might well be said that virtually every battle fought by the Imperial Japanese Navy during its campaign to reoccupy the Solomon Islands—with a particular eye on Guadalcanal, Honiara, and Lunga (and its coveted Henderson Field)—would have been fought at night. Taking full advantage of both a keen element of surprise and the ever-camouflaging mantle of night, the Japanese naval forces repeatedly encroached deep into Iron Bottom Sound and launched their attacks in a time frame that often ranged between 2300 and 0200 hours. For them, it was likely their most optimal striking time and very best witching hour, and once again in almost every early-on campaign in the Solomons did the IJN emerge victorious over the American and Allied fleets. In fact, it might not at all be a stretch to note that the IJN surface fleet—led alternately by its seasoned officers' cadre of tacticians and crafty admirals such as Mikawa, Gotō, Jojima, and Tanaka—would in almost every event come away practically unscathed—or, at the most, suffering only negligible damage to its own surface force.

Shown here in the Table 19 matrix, we can clearly get a glimpse of the several naval battles that would all be centered on the Solomon Islands, and which were in fact all battles that had been fought at night. During at least the opening two years of World War II and throughout much of 1942, the very concept of this night battle would in fact become the IJN's "calling card"—and arguably their most effective weapon.

Table 19. Noted IJN Night Engagements during the Battle for the Solomons

	NOTED IMPERIAL JAPANESE NAVY NIGHT ENGAGEMENTS (EARLY PACIFIC CAMPAIGNS OF WORLD WAR II)		
NIGHT NAVAL ENGAGEMENT	DATE/LOCATION	FORCES	OUTCOME
First Battle of Savo Island[85]	8–9 August 1942 *Iron Bottom Sound Savo Island*	USN: 6 CAs; 2 CLs: 15 DDs IJN: 5 CAs; 2 CLs; 1 DD	**Time: 0138:** Highly successful IJN night attack prosecuted against both the American Southern and Northern screening forces in *Iron Bottom Sound.* **Result:** ❶ 4 Allied CAs sunk; 1 CA, 2 DDs damaged **Result:** ❷ 3 IJN CAs, 11 DD damaged
Second Battle of Savo Island[86] *Battle of Cape Esperance*	11–12 October 1942 *Cape Esperance Russell Islands*	USN: 4 CAs; 5 DDs IJN: 3 CAs; 8 DDs; 1 Seaplane Tender	**Time: 2300:** IJN CRUDIV6 forces under the command of ADMs Gotō and Jōjima lead an IJN surface fleet into an area near Cape Esperance and Savo. The intent is once again to set a night attack, with a two-prong strategy to implant fresh Japanese troops on Guadalcanal and to bombard Henderson Field, now fully under American control. Both were moderately successful, but at great cost to both Gotō and Jōjima, and might therefore actually be seen effectively as an American victory. **Result:** ❶ 1 Allied DD sunk, 1 DD, 1 CA damaged **Result:** ❷ 1 IJN CA, 3 DDs sunk; 1 CA damaged
First Naval Battle of Guadalcanal[87]	13 November 1942 *Cape Esperance*	USN: 2 CLs; 4 DDs IJN: 1 BB; 2 DDs; 7 Transports	**Time: 0125:** Moderately successful IJN night attack on American naval forces near Savo Island (1st Phase). Attack repelled by U.S. forces, again with heavy losses inflicted on the IJN, as noted in ❷: **Result:** ❶ 2 Allied CAs, 1 DD damaged **Result:** ❷ 1 IJN BB, 2 DDs, 7 transport ships damaged or lost

Battle	Date / Location	Forces	Details
Second Naval Battle of Guadalcanal[88]	14–15 November 1942 *Savo Island* *Cape Esperance*	USN: 2 CLs; 4 DDs 1 BB; 2 CAs; IJN: 2 CLs; 9 DDs	**Time: 2300:** Moderately successful IJN night attack on American naval forces near Savo Island (2nd Phase). Attack repelled by U.S. forces, imposing heavy losses for the IJN, as noted in ❷ below: **Result:** ❶ 3 DDs damaged or lost **Result:** ❷ 1 IJN BB sunk; 1 DD, 4 transport ships damaged or lost
Naval Battle of Guadalcanal[89] *Third and Fourth Battles of Savo Island*	12–15 November 1942 *Savo Island* *Cape Esperance*	USN: 1 CV; 2 BBs; 2 CAs; 3 CL; 12 DDs IJN: 2 BBs; 6 CAs; 4 CL; 16 DDs	**Time: 2255:** Highly unsuccessful IJN night attack on American naval forces at Guadalcanal. would be *extremely* costly to Admiral Kondo. The great BB *Kirishima* and the smaller DD *Ayanami* would both be lost during the course of the battle, in addition to numerous IJN transport ships, some of which were compelled to actually beach their ships (while still remaining under fire from the DD *Meade*). Seen effectively as a U.S. strategic victory: **Result:** ❶ (Allied *1st Phase*): 2 CLs, 4 DDs lost **Result:** ❷ (IJN *1st Phase*): 1 IJN BB, 1 CA, 2 DDs, 7 transports sunk **Result:** ❶ (Allied *2nd Phase*): 3 DDs lost **Result:** ❷ (IJN *2nd Phase*): 1 IJN BB, 1 DDs, 4 transport ships sunk **Result:** ❶ (Allied Air, *Both Phases*): 36 aircraft losses **Result:** ❷ (IJN Air, *Both Phases*): 64 aircraft losses
Battle of Tassafaronga[90] *Tassafaronga,* *Guadalcanal*	30 November 1942 *Tassafaronga Point*	USN: 4 CAs; 1 CL; 4 DDs IJN: 8 DDs	**Time: 2306:** Highly successful IJN night attack on American naval forces off Cape Esperance near Savo Island. Surprise attack again inflicts significant losses on U.S. fleet, as noted in ❶: **Result:** ❶ 1 CA sunk; 3 CAs damaged **Result:** ❷ 1 IJN DD sunk

Effectiveness of IJN Naval Night Fighting: Conclusions

What, then, might truly be said of the Imperial Japanese Navy's uncanny ability to conduct sustained night naval warfare unlike any military power before her? Might it be due in part to her technical prowess and effective use of her naval forces, made up of both her surface fleet and attack submarines? Or indeed was it the practiced gunnery and torpedo drills that the IJN ran almost incessantly, always in dead of night and always with best success? Or again the repeating, fortuitous element of surprise that was seemingly always used to best advantage at their disposal, this in combination with her exploitative use of fogbanks, inclement weather, and the general shrouding cover of night? Truly, it might be all of these factors, and more.

For, only all too soon would ADM Yamamoto's Imperial Combined Fleet—with its avowed emphasis on utilizing its light and heavy cruiser forces always to best advantage—incorporate all of these componental elements into a single aggressive strategy to strike again and again at the American and Allied surface ships then operating in and around Guadalcanal . . . this with a clear aim to drive them out once and for all. And, for at least most of 1942, they would do so with an almost rabid determination and a dogged will. Soon, much to the utter dismay of the American and Allied navies that would be hard hit in the battles yet to come, those navies would be compelled to suffer those mounting losses at the hands of an entirely "night-friendly" Imperial Japanese Navy.

Sworn to drive the interloping Americans out of their "toehold" Guadalcanal territory, the Japanese had in fact nearly completed the airstrip at Honiara on the main island when they were abruptly attacked and routed from those locations—both on Guadalcanal and at Tulagi. It was now therefore only a furious VADM Gunichi Mikawa who would strike back at the encroaching western naval forces with a vengeance and ultimately resort to the one proven tactic he knew best: the night attack by his own heavy cruisers. In the ensuing naval actions set by the Americans to deny the Japanese that very same toehold, the Allies would soon find that the price for such action would indeed be quite high; indeed, the very first encounter between the two forces on 9 August 1942 at the Battle of Savo Island would witness the loss of Australia's own *Canberra* and three American heavy cruisers, the *Vincennes*, *Quincy*, and *Astoria*.

As a direct result of the deadly and disastrous attacks at Savo, and throughout all of Iron Bottom Sound, both America and its British and Australian allies would soon find an immediate need to improve on their critically lacking night-fighting skills—this to rapidly enhance each navy's ability to conduct at-sea night operations with a greater surety and allow them to repel the very attacks that were repeatedly being brought on by the cunning and unshakable Japanese. On this subject, even author and noted naval historian Richard B. Frank would have the following to say about the disparity in night-fighting capabilities of both naval forces:

> Unlike U.S. Naval forces, the Japanese Navy drilled and practiced night fighting extensively, as well as conducting frequent night gunnery live-fire drills and exercises,

and that experience would be telling in not only the coming encounter(s), but several other surface fleet actions off Guadalcanal in the months to come.[91]

Or, even as paraphrased here in the highly rated PBS.org presentation of *The War* (subtitled "Guadalcanal (August 1942–February 1943)"), in its own summation:

> A Japanese cruiser squadron overwhelmed an Allied force of equal size, sinking one Australian and three U.S. Navy cruisers, and damaging several destroyers, [while] losing none of its own ships. The battle clearly showed the superiority of Japanese night-fighting techniques . . . and was the worst defeat ever suffered by the U.S. Navy in a fair fight, but for them it was only an actual tactical success, because the Japanese failed to go after the vulnerable American troop transports off Guadalcanal and Tulagi.[92]

Even at the very outset of hostilities—long before they had departed their well-protected IJN ports at both Kavieng and Rabaul in the far northern waters fronting Papua and New Guinea—the Japanese were almost certain of victory in virtually any night engagement scenario and did not at all fear facing an enemy force of equal (or even unequal) size that they held only in slight regard. Indeed, even CAPT Ohmae would himself cheerfully note precisely this same sentiment in his own recounted narrative:

> Admiral Mikawa and his staff boarded *Chōkai* with all possible speed, and the flagship sortied from the harbor at 1430, accompanied by light cruisers *Tenryū* and *Yubari*, and the destroyer *Yunagi*. It was a fine clear day, the sea like a mirror. Our confidence of success in the coming night battle was manifest in the cheerful atmosphere on the bridge.[93]

Perhaps they simply could not lose. But much was yet to be learned, even by an already proficient Imperial Japanese Navy, as regarded its continued fine-tuning of its own night naval operations and tactics—and perhaps no one individual might have known this better than Mikawa's own chief of staff, CAPT Ohmae himself:

> Just before dark our ships had assumed night battle formation, following the flagship in a single column with 1,200-meter intervals between ships. At 2110, the cruiser planes were again catapulted for tactical reconnaissance and to light the target area. The pilots had had no experience in night catapulting, so this was a risky business, but the risk had to be taken.[94]

This with the exception of only Admiral Mikawa himself, the very master architect and avowed proponent of just such night-naval operations, who would later note the following in his own response to Ohmae's account in a later USNI *Proceedings* article:

> As soon as the U.S. landings at Guadalcanal were reported on August 7, and the invasion strength was apparent, I determined to employ all the forces at my command in destroying the enemy ships. My choice of a night action to accomplish this purpose was made because I had no air support on which to rely—and reliable air support was vital to anything but a night action.

On the other hand, I had complete confidence in my ships and knew that the Japanese Navy's emphasis on night battle training and practice would insure [*sic*] our chances of success in such an action, even without air support.[95]

Finally, such a concept was further aptly summed up by LTC David E. Quantock in his own dissertation on the First Battle of Savo Island:

> In the end, it was the night-fighting ability of Mikawa's Strike Force that won the battle. Examination of Japanese firing records for the morning of 9 August reveals that they fired a total of (1844) shells, with (159) definite and (64) likely hits for a total of (223) hits. In sharp contrast, the Allies fired (471) shells with only (10) hits. In fact, the Americans had indeed lived up to their billing in a Japanese training manual, which stated:
> Westerners—being very haughty, effeminate and cowardly—intensely dislike fighting in the rain or mist, or in the dark. They cannot conceive night to be a proper time for battle—though it is excellent for "dancing". It shall be in these weaknesses that our greatest opportunities will lie.

Perhaps truer words could not be spoken about the "haughty" Americans during at least the outset of battle in the Solomons, but those "Westerners," as it were, would indeed learn quickly—much to the astonishment of the IJN high command.

So in the end was it in fact, as noted in H. P. Wilmott's contemporary assessment of the night-fighting capabilities of the heady Japanese, that "The Allies were simply outfought by an enemy that had paid for the advantages it possessed in terms of torpedoes and night-fighting capabilities by years of preparation"? The answer, unquestionably, would have to have been definitely, since that IJN force did indeed train incessantly—most often during the darkest hours just before dawn—this clearly to further fine-tune their already precise skills and to ensure certain victory as their surface forces moved throughout the islands of the South Pacific. The year was 1942, and the Imperial Japanese Navy was still seemingly all but invincible—and almost always deadly accurate—and perhaps it was most then that they truly "owned the night."

Effectiveness of IJN Naval Night Fighting: Bibliography and Additional Reading

In the event the reader might require further information pertaining to the overall effectiveness of the Imperial Japanese Navy's unquestioned superiority over the Americans and their allies to conduct both open-sea and narrow-channel night battles quite to their own advantage, refer to the following bibliographical references and electronic weblinks.

Coombe, Jack D. (1991). *Derailing the Tokyo Express*. Stackpole Books.

Hara, Tameichi (Captain, IJN Ret.). (1961). *Japanese Destroyer Captain*. Edited by Fred Saito and Roger Pineau. Naval Institute Press.

Hornfischer, James D. (2011). *Neptune's Inferno: The U.S. Navy at Guadalcanal*. Bantam Books.

Kilpatrick, C. W. (1987). *Naval Night Battles of the Solomons*. Exposition Press.

Loxton, Bruce, and Chris Coulthard-Clark. (1997). *The Shame of Savo: Anatomy of a Naval Disaster*. Allen & Unwin Pty Ltd.

Morison, Samuel Eliot. (1958). *The Struggle for Guadalcanal, August 1942–February 1943*. Vol. 5 of *History of United States Naval Operations in World War II*. Little, Brown and Company.

Newcomb, Richard F. (2002). *The Battle of Savo Island: The Harrowing Account of the Disastrous Night Battle off Guadalcanal That Nearly Destroyed the Pacific Fleet in August 1942*. Holt Paperbacks.

Ohmae, Toshikazu. (1986). Edited by David C. Evans. *The Battle of Savo Island: The Japanese Navy in World War II: In the Words of Former Japanese Naval Officers*. 2nd ed. Naval Institute Press.

Stile, Mark. (2011). *USN Cruiser vs. IJN Cruiser: Guadalcanal 1942*. Osprey Publishing Books.

Tzu, Lao (1994). *The Art of War*. Basic Book.

Effectiveness of IJN Naval Night Fighting: Weblinks and Electronic Resources

IJN Combined Fleet (*Rengō Kantai*), http://www.combinedfleet.com/kaigun.htm

Wikipedia, "The First Battle of Savo Island," http://en.wikipedia.org/wiki/Battle_of_Savo_Island #Operations_at_Guadalcanal

Wikipedia, "Battle of Savo Island," subsectioned as "Background—Operations at Guadalcanal."

Wikipedia, "The Second Battle of Savo Island (The Battle of Cape Esperance)," http://en.wikipedia .org/wiki/Second_Battle_of_Savo_Island.

Wikipedia, "The First Naval Battle of Guadalcanal," http://en.wikipedia.org/wiki/Naval_Battle_of _Guadalcanal#First_Naval_Battle_of_Guadalcanal.2C_November_13.

Wikipedia, "The Second Naval Battle of Guadalcanal," http://en.wikipedia.org/wiki/Naval_Battle _of_Guadalcanal#Second_Naval_Battle_of_Guadalcanal.2C_November_14.E2.80.9315.

Wikipedia, "The Naval Battle of Guadalcanal," http://en.wikipedia.org/wiki/Naval_Battle_of_Guadal canal.

Wikipedia, "Battle of Tassafaronga," http://en.wikipedia.org/wiki/Battle_of_Tassafaronga.

World War II Multimedia Database, http://www.ww2incolor.com/forum/archive/index.php/t-9681 .html

Information subsectioned as Imperial Japanese Navy (*Nihon Kaigūn*) and presented in four pages, each with quite excellent collections of vintage black-and-white photographic images embedded at Mechanisms of Imperial Japanese Navy Warships in 3-D: http://www.ijnwarship.com/index.html

The website offers curious and detailed narratives and pictorial resources from a model ship-building perspective for both the IJN cruisers *Tone* and *Mogami*. The website may be of interest to the casual reader, the serious naval historian, and the general researcher.

Clash of Arms, http://www.clashofarms.com/ATReadinglists.html

Access the *Clash of Arms* website; locate subsection Admiralty Trilogy Reading List, and follow the directing link IJN Cruiser and Battleship Doctrine to locate the .pdf-based article by W.D. Dickson, titled "Battleship and Cruiser Doctrine, Imperial Japanese Navy," subsectioned as II.B. DOCTRINE GENERAL, followed by: ❶ Day Action; ❷ Dusk Action; ❸ Night Action; ❹ Dawn Action; ❺ Immediate Action, and ❻ Narrow Waters.

WW2 in Color History Forum, http://www.ww2incolor.com/forum/archive/index.php/t-9681.html

Expected navigational flow: *WW2 in Color History Forum* (World War II British Military) (Naval Night Combat. British vs. Japanese).

David's IJN Homepage, https://sites.google.com/site/davidijn/home

FINDING 15:   A CONFIDENCE UNTESTED:
AN UNFOUNDED CERTAINTY

Assured victory was not so well assured, and dominance in the Pacific was not yet a given, although it may have been assumed to be so. Was it cockiness, arrogance, or simply untested confidence? No one can know for sure, but the road to those "expected" victories would be long and arduous, and viciously instructive.

School was in session that day, and the lessons taught—and the lessons learned— would be harsh, violent, and wholly unforgiving. The toll was great, the "instruction" brutal, and, as the task group commander Admiral Richmond Kelly Turner himself would note in his own later assessment of just why the Allied surface fleets had been so roundly defeated during the First Battle of Savo Island:

> The [U.S.] Navy was still obsessed with a strong feeling of technical and mental superiority over the enemy. In spite of ample evidence as to enemy capabilities, most of our officers and men despised the enemy and felt themselves sure victors in all encounters under any circumstances. The net result of all this was a fatal lethargy of mind which induced a confidence without readiness, and a routine acceptance of outworn peacetime standards of conduct. I believe that this psychological factor, as a cause of our defeat, was even more important than the element of surprise.[96]

A lethargy of mind? Probably not so much. But were the men not indeed already possessed of a heady and unwarranted confidence, and exuberant to a fault, as they hastily sought to engage the enemy once more on open seas? Was there in fact a bit of a false swagger and an untested assurance that they (the U.S. military) must and would *always* emerge victorious—and this in all events? Perhaps. On precisely this thought, historian Richard B. Frank was good enough to present his own take on "attitude and assumption" on the part of the Americans, when he, too, observed the following:

> This lethargy of mind would not be completely shaken off without some more hard blows to [U.S.] Navy pride around Guadalcanal; but after Savo, the United States picked itself up off the deck and prepared for the most savage combat in its history.[97]

United States

American Heavy Cruiser USS Vincennes *(CA-44), The* Maggie V *(The Magnificent* Vincennes; ca. 1930s) at http://www.his tory.navy.mil/photos/sh-usn/usnsh-v /ca44.htm

American Heavy Cruiser USS Quincy *(CA-39), The* Mighty Q *(February 1937) at* http://en.wikipedia.org/wiki/File:USS _Quincy_CA-39_ncal.jpg

American Heavy Cruiser USS Astoria *(CA-34),* Nasty Asty *(ca. 1942) at http://www .history.navy.mil/photos/sh-usn/usnsh-a /ca34.htm*

American Heavy Cruiser USS Chicago *(CA-29; ca. 1934) at http://en.wikipedia .org/wiki/USS_Chicago_(CA-29)*

Australian Heavy Cruiser HMAS Canberra *(D33; ca. 1930s) at http://en.wikipedia.org /wiki/HMAS_Canberra_(D33)*

American Bagley-class *DD radar picket ships USS* Blue *and* Ralph Talbot *at https:// en.wikipedia.org/wiki/Bagley-class_de stroyer*

VADM Frank Jack
Fletcher, USN

RADM Richmond Kelly
Turner, USN

RADM Sir Victor Alexander
Crutchley (VC, KCB, DSC,
CCLM, CG, DL, RN)

RADM Norman N. Scott,
USN (Commander of the
Eastern Screening Force)

RADM Frederick Lois
Riefkohl, USN (RADM,
USS Vincennes)

CAPT Samuel Nobre Moore,
USN (Captain, USS Quincy)

RADM John Sidney
McCain Sr., USN

CAPT William Garrett
Greenman, USN
(Captain, USS Astoria)

CAPT Howard Douglas
Bode, USN (Captain,
USS Chicago)

Japanese

The IJN Takao-*class heavy cruiser* Chōkai *(1942; by Ueda Kihachiro and courtesy of Hasegawa Seisakusho) at http://www .combinedfleet.com/chokai_t.htm*

The IJN Furutaka-*class heavy cruiser* Aoba *(ca. 1930s; Hasegawa Seisakusho) at http://www.combinedfleet.com/aoba _t.htm*

The IJN Furutaka-*class heavy cruiser* Kako *(2001, courtesy of Terry Manton) at www .pinterest.com/pin/448671181604834454/*

The IJN Furutaka-*class heavy cruiser* Kinugasa *(ca. 1930s; Hasegawa Seisakusho) at http://www.combinedfleet.com /kinugasa_t.htm*

The IJN Furutaka-*class heavy cruiser* Furutaka *(Ueda Kihachiro and courtesy of Hasegawa Seisakusho) at http://www .combinedfleet.com/furuta_t.htm*

The IJN Yubari-*class light cruiser* Yūbari *(Ueda Kihachiro and Hasegawa Seisakusho) at http://www.combinedfleet .com/ships/tenryu*

The IJN Tenryū-*class light cruiser* Tenryū *(Ueda Kihachiro and Hasegawa Seisakusho) at http://www.combinedfleet .com/Yūbari_t.htm*

Admiral Isoroku Yamamoto,
IJN Combined Fleet

VADM Gunichi Mikawa, IJN CRUDIV6/18
Task Force (Eighth Fleet)

RADM Aritomo Gotō, IJN CRUDIV6
Task Force

FINDING 16:   CLOSE ENCOUNTERS AND THE COST
OF FRIENDLY FIRE

Friend or Foe: Firing at Close Quarters

Could it not with reason and fair assumption be said that friendly fire might long have been a part of every war and every armed conflict? And if granted, is it not a sad and seemingly unavoidable consequence of all such encounters in combat—serving only perhaps as its own contemptible evil? An unfortunate failing that could occur in virtually every battle, and plague every act of heroism and battlefield bravado? And if further true, might it not be a purely reactionary event, triggered to occur only in the heat of battle? And again, if so accepted, might it not have been much like it was for these very men on this day: locked in a fight for their very lives, with an unseen enemy, on blackened seas, in dead of night?

Sadly, the answer to all these questions is probably yes. In every battle situation, every conflict scenario—whether a heated ground-based infantry assault, a coordinated close-air combat attack strategy, or simply full naval broadsides brought to bear at the very lip of midnight—each would have the potential for just such losses due to exactly these friendly-fire incidents that might unfortunately occur at any time during the course of any such pitched battle. Thankfully, that number would be low, and the number of incidents of casualty by friendly fire throughout all of the 1BOSI might, on the surface at least, appear to have been minimal . . . and therefore marginal enough to officially be negligible. However, this could also be due to the possibility that seemingly unrelated incidents may not have been reported with any great immediacy, or with any degree of accuracy—or even with any linking to other events. This aside, the inescapable consequence of all such friendly fire events, and the role they played (or might nearly play) in the conflict, is still a topical discussion point that should merit some closer inspection.

Second only to the deadly hazard and consequence of friendly fire would be the ever-present danger of collision events—or even near-collision events—that could easily be brought on by the orchestrated mayhem of the attack itself. Seemingly at least the first such occurrence of a near-miss situation might not have involved shots fired, or ships' volleys at all, but rather might have been between the actual surface ships themselves.

Presented below and on the following pages, therefore, in a flowing narrative format are a series of topical discussions about both such encounter scenarios. Some would be but the harrowing close calls of the men aboard the ships themselves—such that would vex and coil a man's soul; others would indeed be incidents that would truly have a far deadlier consequence.

❶ The *Blue, Ralph Talbot,* and the Mikawa Task Group

USS Blue *(DD-387), USS* Ralph Talbot *(DD-390), and the Mikawa Task Group: 9 August 1942, 0056 Hours*

Near-Encounter (First Account). At some point after 0054 hours, just as Mikawa's hot cruiser divisions were making their stealthy approach into the northern reaches of Iron Bottom Sound, his task group would spy the USS *Blue* on an apparent patterned patrol course just north of Savo Island. At the time, the distance between the IJN cruiser force and the *Blue* might have been estimated to be no more than five and a half miles ahead of the advancing Japanese column.

To avoid detection by the American radar picket ship, Mikawa had all ships in column change to a more optimal course heading that would then allow his column to pass well north of Savo. The cunning admiral wisely ordered his ships to reduce speed from their former 30 knots to a far slower 22 knots to trim his ships' phosphorescent wakes, which might fully compromise his very position or even dampen his full element of surprise. A short four minutes later, lookouts high atop the *Pagoda* mast superstructure of his great *Chōkai* flagship would indeed spot the patrolling *Ralph Talbot* as well, the second of the fast-moving American picket destroyers, itself then cruising some ten miles off to port.

Mikawa's attack force continued to hold fast on its "eye-of-the-needle" course, boldly pushing on through the night and now with more than fifty guns deadly trained on the *Blue*, ready to open fire with the slightest twitch or indication that she might have detected their presence. Finally, at a distance of no more than a mile from the IJN strike force, *Blue* abruptly reversed her course—having reached the full perigee of her assigned patrol track—and began moving back away, following her set patrol pattern and seemingly blind to the long column of warships that were even at that very minute sailing right past her.

It should, however, still be noted that shortly after the *Talbot* did note the flares, searchlights, and gunfire erupting during the later attack unfolding now well to the south, she reportedly did move at battle speed to engage that enemy. And, as she approached the upper reaches of Iron Bottom Sound, she was allegedly even "shelled by a friendly destroyer"—this at about 0215 hours. Clearly, speculation here might seem to indicate that this second destroyer would have to have been the *Helm*, the only other destroyer in the immediate area of the *Talbot* at that time.

A short time later, a Japanese cruiser would again light up the *Talbot* with searchlights and fire once again on her position. A single shell landed near the ships' charthouse, destroying radar equipment and fire control circuits; then had three more hit close in and in close succession, soon also hitting the wardroom, much of the starboard quarter, and almost all of gun turret 4. Sadly, eleven crewmen on the *Talbot* would be killed outright in the action, including the ship's doctor and chief pharmacist's mate. Whether or not any of the casualties were in fact related to the "unidentified" opening salvo fired at *Blue* just prior to engaging Mikawa's fleet will (in and of itself) remain but a notion that history may never fully resolve.

❷ The *Jarvis* and the *Yunagi*

USS Jarvis *(DD-393) and IJN* Yunagi *(DD-17): 9 August 1942, 0131 Hours*

Near-Encounter (Second Account). A short time after 0131 hours—very near the hour of Mikawa's attack on the Southern screen and specifically on the *Canberra* and *Chicago*—the Japanese destroyer *Yunagi* would have already fully detached itself from the single line-column ahead format of the IJN cruiser force, and abruptly reversed her course. Here, a curious division of theory and speculation seems to exist, with some factors seeming to indicate that the *Yunagi* may have effectively "lost her visual" on the other Japanese ships to her front or that she may have specifically been tasked by Mikawa earlier with providing a "rear screening guard" for the cruiser line as it probed farther south and into the uppermost reaches of Iron Bottom Sound.

Less than a minute later, lookouts posted on at least two of the fast-moving Japanese warships would sight an "unknown ship" well out to port. The ship seen that night, and at that time, might have been the American destroyer USS *Jarvis*, which—already heavily damaged in an action from the previous day—was now attempting to depart the Solomons area under her own power, heading for portage and repair in far Australia. Whether the *Jarvis* had in like manner also spotted the Japanese ships is unknown, since much of her communications capabilities had by that time been fully knocked out, and no alarm (or other alerting call) was believed to have ever been sent from that crippled American DD.

The Japanese convoy of warships would close to within 3,500 feet of the *Jarvis*—astonishingly close enough for officers on the bridge of the IJN CA *Tenryū* to peer down onto the destroyer's decks without seeing any of her crew moving about. Indeed, if the *Jarvis* was at all aware of any of the passing Japanese ships, she seemingly did not indicate anything of the kind, nor did she respond in any noticeable way. Instead, the Mikawa strike force, secure in the knowledge of both a silent and unchallenged passage straight through the radar picket lines, would now simply continue on and begin forming up for the first of their crucial attacks on the pride-of-fleet *Canberra* and the *Chicago*, which they had already begun to prosecute with deadly precision, perfect stealth, and complete and utter success by 0144 on the morning of 9 August 1942.

❸ The *Wilson* and the Mikawa Task Group

USS Wilson *(DD-408) and the Mikawa Task Group: 9 August 1942, 0149 Hours*

Adjusting the Angle of Fire. As the IJN surface fleet continued its stealthy approach to Iron Bottom Sound, they knew that the dark and hilly land mass to starboard had to be Savo Island. Of a sudden, the searchlights aboard the attacking ships were snapped on, fully illuminating a force of at least three heavy cruisers in close proximity. This would indeed have been the American Northern screen, the CAs *Vincennes*, *Quincy*, and *Astoria*. Quickly noting the ship lights and fiery blooms emanating from the large deck guns of the Japanese cruisers, the destroyer *Wilson* would itself begin a hard turn to port (this to effectively bring all guns to bear) and then opened fire all at once and without hesitation. She would therefore have continued to turn and fire at a rapid pace until one or more of her own cruisers inadvertently crossed her path and essentially "fouled the range," momentarily preventing her (the *Wilson*) from keeping up her suppressing fire. At that moment, the range was estimated to have been only 12,000 yards from those target-confirmed enemy ships.

Reacting to the new development, however—and not to be daunted by the erratic and confused movements of the "heavies" *Vincennes* and *Astoria* as they struggled to disengage and fight off the violent attack—*Wilson*'s gunners simply raised the angle of trajectory of those deck guns and fired their shells over the three passing cruisers—a feat that in and of itself was no small matter. For now, however, the enemy salvos continued to impact and explode in the waters between the *Wilson* and the nearest friendly ships—some 1,000 yards off her port beam—but by that time all three of the American heavy cruisers had already been savaged by Mikawa's surface force and left cautiously adrift, without even good steerage, and fully enveloped in flames. In less than an hour's time, two of those same ships would go down; by noon of the next day, the last American cruiser would sink in waters south and west of Savo Island.

Yet, even as the *Wilson* turned, she would have yet another near-encounter with one of her own. Having noted that enemy searchlights were still on and focusing on several of the ships within her screen, the *Wilson* stepped up its fire from a distance of 9,600 yards. It would be at this point, then, that another unidentified friendly destroyer (thought to have been the DD *Helm*) would reportedly maneuver between the first American destroyer and the enemy, forcing the *Wilson* to momentarily check its fire. The *Wilson* would then later resume its accelerated fire at the searchlights until the IJN force finally ceased its own assault, soon perhaps satisfied that they had indeed destroyed in full the enemy Allied force opposing them. At the close of hostilities that night, after a mere thirty-one-minute engagement of truly the greatest ferocity, Mikawa's two cruiser divisions would have sunk three American heavy cruisers of the line—and Australia's own "pride-of-fleet" *Canberra*.

Sadly, much like salt on a wound, a fourth American cruiser, *Chicago*, would also be hit and crippled as well by heavy damage to her bow from a single torpedo hit. Whether that single torpedo impact was in fact fired from the IJN cruiser *Kako*, or erroneously launched (in the chaos of the moment) by the nearby American DD *Bagley*, might indeed be a matter for a further investigation in its own right.

❹ The *Astoria* and the Mikawa Task Group

USS Astoria *(CA-34) and the Mikawa Task Group: 9 August 1942, 0150 Hours*

A Rumor of Friendly Fire. From a series of concise (if somewhat casual and laconic), web-based fora and archive databases presented on many key online reference sites, comes the curious report of the opening salvos between the *Astoria* and Mikawa's surface fleet. At the point when the Japanese opened fire, the *Astoria*'s gunnery officer, LCDR William H. Truesdell, is alleged to already have had all guns trained out in full and ready to fire, but the order was quickly belayed by first the watch commander, one LCDR James R. Topper, and then the *Astoria*'s own skipper himself, CAPT William Greenman, who had at precisely that moment just stepped onto the bridge. Both senior officers then demanded to know just who had given the order to commence firing. "Topper," the good captain, was reported to have said, "I think we are firing on our own ships. Let's not get excited and act too hasty. Cease firing!"[98]

And so they would . . . but the captain's second-in-command would do so only reluctantly, quickly ordering the cease-fire while simultaneously turning on the ship's navigation lights. A few short minutes later, however, a second request to resume the battle came back from a harried ship's gunnery officer, Truesdell, now with a redoubled urgency, when he blurted out the quite anxious, "For God's sake, give the word to commence firing!"

Long and interminable minutes would then pass as CAPT Greenman and the crew of his ship would begin to see the incoming shells, presumably fired from Mikawa's own nearby cruiser *Chōkai*, that now began splashing dangerously close in and between the *Vincennes* and *Quincy*. Still with a measure of reservation, Greenman would finally relent and yell back to his second-in-command, "Whether our ships or not, we will have to stop them. Commence firing." Sadly, that moment's very pause of indecision had effectively lost the Allied cruiser force some four minutes of precious reactionary time; time that, in just such a battle scenario would soon prove to be a fatal eternity. The incoming shells from the Japanese attack force had all so far been short of the mark and slightly off-target; the precious (and unrecoverable) four minutes lost to the Americans had now given Mikawa's batteries just enough time to find and correct their range out to those American ships. The shrewd Admiral Mikawa would now decidedly not miss that same shot again—and indeed did not—as the high-caliber shells soon tore in and began landing with deadly effect some short seconds later.

❺ The *Bagley* and the HMAS *Canberra*

USS Bagley (DD-386) and HMAS Canberra (D33): 9 August 1942, 0143 Hours

A Shot in the Dark. At about the same moment that the *Patterson* sighted *Kinugasa* and the Japanese fleet, she also immediately went into action, while overhead the Japanese floatplanes, on orders from Mikawa, began dropping aerial flares directly over the darkly silhouetted shapes they only thought might be elements of the American surface force. The Australian *Canberra* would respond decisively and immediately, with CAPT Frank Getting ordering an increase in speed and a reversal of his initial turn to port—which turn now juxtaposed *Canberra* between the Japanese and the Allied transports—clearly giving him the further advantage of allowing all gun batteries to be trained out, allowing him full vantage and enabling his ships to provide optimum fire on all targets of opportunity, even at the very moment they were spotted.

Less than a minute later, the *Canberra's* heavy guns would take aim at several sil-houetted ships in the Mikawa force but could not fix a good target before *Chōkai* and *Tenryū* split column and opened fire on her in return, scoring numerous hits within the first few seconds of their opening fusillade. The *Aoba* and the *Kako* would soon join in the furious melee as well, and within a deadly span of mere minutes *Canberra* would have already endured a total of some twenty-four large-caliber hits.

Early impacts would soon find both CAPT Getting and the ship's gunnery officer mortally wounded; then they destroyed both boiler rooms and knocked out power to the entire ship before the *Canberra* could even return fire with any of her own guns, much less signal a warning to any of the other Allied ships. The Australian cruiser, mercilessly pummeled by Mikawa's own attack force and now well on fire, would soon glide to a stop with a 5°–10° list to starboard, and was no longer able to quell the fires that now threatened to rage out of control. The problem would be made worse by a critical loss of power as well, as soon the doomed ship could no longer even pump water out of any of its already flooded compartments.

Since all of the Japanese warships appeared to be on the port side of the *Canberra*, the damage to the ship's starboard side occurred either from those shells entering low on the port side of that CA, and exiting below the waterline on the starboard side, or from one or more torpedo hits on the starboard side. Of interest here is the fact that *if* the torpedoes did hit the *Canberra* on her starboard side (and not the port), there was indeed a good possibility that they may have come instead from a nearby Allied ship; the only Allied ship in the immediate vicinity at the time would have been the DD *Bagley*, which had admittedly just fired a spread of torpe-does moments earlier. Though unplanned and wholly unintentional, could "friendly fire" have played some contributory part, however small, in the ultimate demise of at least this one ship, the *Canberra*?

❻ The *Chicago*, Southern Screening Force, and the Mikawa Task Group

USS Chicago *(CA-29) and HMAS* Canberra *(D33): 9 August 1942, Duration of Attack*

A Shot Too Far. The calamitous result and tragic outcome of the First Battle of Savo Island on the night of 9 August 1942 might have had a significantly different conclu-sion, even with the gaffes and errors in judgment suffered by the Allied surface fleet up to the point of the attack on the *Chicago*, if only the over-reluctant CAPT Bode had seen fit to alert the Northern force that he was under attack; perhaps then the outcome of the battle that night may have been significantly different and much more to the favor of Crutchley's own Southern screening force.

When the probative IJN cruiser force finally did circle about and hit the Northern screen, virtually all of the ships of the *Vincennes* group thought they were only errone-ously under attack by friendly forces, and even fired a series of warning volleys and flares at what they thought were "friendlies." Sadly, this action would serve to mark the very ships of the northern line for their own follow-on fire, which was at once heavy, deadly accurate, and now unrelenting. Further, if such action might have been considered costly in damage, it would be equally costly in time, effectively allowing the IJN attack force a greater measure of time in which to find its range, and to zero in on those target assets with maximum effectiveness.

The good CAPT Bode would later be severely (perhaps almost meanly) brought to task by an enraged RADM Arthur Japy Hepburn—the very investigator who sought to preside over the official review panel that might ultimately have sought to indict him—and who seemingly might already have held the man as guilty on multiple accounts for at least some of the following: ❶ failing to warn the ships of the Northern group of their attack (or very presence of the CRUDIV force in their screening area); ❷ turning his ship away from the Mikawa task force and departing the area for some forty minutes, and effectively abandoning the landing ships and transports that he had been tasked to guard at both Tulagi and Honiara; and ❸ ultimately "opening the door" and providing Mikawa's surface fleet almost full and unimpeded access to the rest of the surface ships within RADM Riefkohl's secondary *Vincennes* group.

The captain of the *Chicago* would indeed later be sternly admonished in a Naval Court of Inquiry that would be convened and presided over by Hepburn, and, although an official report of findings would itself be sealed to public disclosure, and truly never intended for release, Bode would himself quickly learn of its "tenor" and implication. It was therefore a quite stunned and disbelieving Bode who would then return to his BOQ at Balboa, in the Panama Canal Zone, raise a .45-caliber pistol, and shoot himself once in the head on a date of 19 April 1943. The beleaguered career naval officer would linger for less than a day, sadly expiring on the following afternoon.

History would go on to almost entirely vilify the man in full, and to cast both his character and his command performance skills, on at least that one night in question, into only deeper shadow and a more profound suspicion.

❼ The *Patterson* and the *Chicago*

USS *Patterson* (DD-392) and USS *Chicago* (CA-29): 9 August 1942, Duration of Attack

In the Line of Fire. Following on the heels of the Mikawa assault on the Allied Southern fleet, the sinking of the Australian *Canberra*, and the crippling of the *Chicago*, the *Patterson* immediately set out to conduct standard search-and-rescue (SAR) operations for the two stricken warships in her charge, as indeed many surviving crewmen were still left stranded and floundering in the fired and oil-soaked waters around their sinking ships. At that same instant, the *Patterson* would herself come under a combined heavy attack, with concentrated fire centered on her from virtually all of the IJN task force, to include the *Chōkai, Aoba, Kako, Kinugasa,* and *Tenryū*. In minutes, therefore, the flanking escort DD *Patterson* would reportedly be hit by several incoming shells, even while continuing to engage the attack force with all guns trained out and firing as rapidly as her worn batteries could be reloaded by their harried and fast-moving gun crews.

The defiant but staggered ships of Bode's own beleaguered Southern screen—namely, the *Chicago*, *Patterson*, *Bagley*, and *Canberra*—had by now fully opened up with all main batteries, furiously seeking an effective range out to the Japanese ships in column. *Chicago* was busy providing fire support to aid the stricken *Patterson*, which was by now locked in a deadly "dueling dance" with the light cruisers *Yubari* and *Tenryū*. It was during this brief but violent interlude, while *Chicago* was still providing fire support for the *Patterson*, that she may have either fouled the range of the small DD by crossing to her front or directly fired on that DD in the mayhem of the moment. In any case, no significant damage was inflicted on either of the ships, and once a hastily offered handshake protocol (an identification confirmation procedure similar to the current-day IFF [Identification Friend or Foe] format) between the two ships had been clearly established, there was an immediate correction of fire, and the brief incident would be resolved without casualty (or great damage) to either ship. Yet the horrid incident had indeed occurred, even if only for a brief period of time.

❽ The *Astoria* and the *Quincy*

USS Astoria *(CA-34) and USS* Quincy *(CA-39): 9 August 1942: Duration of Attack*

Crossed Paths. The tragic nature and dire results of the First Battle of Savo Island might that night truly have had a quite different outcome had one final path-crossing, range-fouling incident been allowed to occur in full. During the course of the brief but violent action that was even then unfolding near Savo Island, the enemy would be reported as having been some 6200 yards off in the distance, with a solid bearing of two-three-five.

Mikawa's CRUDIV attack force, having once closed on the estimated range of the *Astoria*, now stepped up their accelerated barrage against her and the other American cruisers. During the short interval in which the Allied ships began a rapid shift to port, *Astoria*'s gunnery officer LCDR William Truesdell would later be heard to have observed at least the following:

> All ships turned too slowly, and the increase of speed was too slow to clear the next astern. As a result, the *Astoria* found itself coming quickly into the *Quincy*'s line of fire and had to sharply turn to starboard—across her stern—to clear the ship without collision. This rapid shift to starboard brought the enemy bearing astern more abruptly, so that after one or two more salvos neither the gun directors (nor the turrets themselves) could bear or train out—by which time the Japanese had already fully exacted their range of fire.[99]

Now swinging well to starboard to avoid an imminent collision with her sister ship *Quincy*, *Astoria* quickly sailed northward for several minutes under a sustained and heavy concentration of enemy fire. Her engine rooms had essentially all been abandoned because of the number of unchecked fires raging throughout the ship, and she began to rapidly lose both speed and momentum. *Astoria* did later successfully manage a quick maneuvering swing to port, however, and so sped off on a southwesterly course, where a beleaguered *Quincy* could clearly be seen off her port bow, reportedly already "blazing fiercely from stem to stern."[100] *Quincy* would now herself pursue a standard evasive zigzag course but appeared to be listing severely to starboard. For at least this one moment, then, it looked as if a collision might be inevitable, but at the very last instant *Astoria* would in fact push hard over to port and swing clear, enough to avoid a certain collision with her equally battered companion ship *Quincy*. Sadly, the latter ship would last be seen coasting astern of *Astoria* and traveling well to the north and east; soon thereafter, it appeared to simply detonate in situ and go down where last seen by the men of the *Astoria* that night.

The dauntless *Quincy* would sink in less than ten minutes in waters east-northeast of Savo Island with a crippling (and discrepant) loss of between 370 and 389 men.

❾ The *Ralph Talbot* and Mikawa Task Group

USS Ralph Talbot *(DD-390) and the Mikawa Task Group: 9 August 1942, 0215 Hours*

Flaming Target, Parting Shots. Perhaps one final incident involving either a near-miss scenario or one of friendly fire would occur toward the end of the battle itself, again involving the *Talbot* (for yet a second time) during the final salvos of the melee. Almost as if to render a row of parting shots after their highly successful attacks on both the Southern and Northern screening forces, Mikawa's quickly departing cruiser force met up with yet another American warship for one last time, as it were, on their way out of the Sound. By chance, that warship would again be the USS *Ralph Talbot*—the scrappy DD from the earlier radar picket line north of Savo—and this encounter alone would include elements of both near-collision and even a sniff of friendly fire.

To properly set the stage, the *Talbot* had been assigned to Task Group 62.6 (TG 62.6), as one of two radar picket destroyers set to run the northernmost screen (the *Bagley*-class USS *Blue* being the other), each positioned well north of darkened Savo. The two ships had been ordered to run concurrent and parallel patrol courses looping roughly northeast to southwest, and recycling back on a perigee return. After having failed to detect (or at all intercept) the encroaching Mikawa force coming down the Slot past Savo, the *Blue* and *Ralph Talbot* began a sharp turn to south seeking to engage that same IJN fleet—well after it had stealthily slipped by—and that was by this time already attacking Crutchley's screening forces just to the south of their own patrol corridor.

At about 0150 hours, then, the first of starshell flares could already be seen, followed almost immediately by a heavy bombardment and concentration of gunfire coming from the direction of Honiara and the Southern screen. The *Talbot* could not at all have known that she was in fact actually witnessing an attack on the *Canberra* and *Chicago*, and even at that very moment was reporting in and falsely stating that "nothing was in sight north of Savo."[101] As such, she simply stood close-in to the island and held steady her course at a cruising speed that was now at a brisk 25 knots.

Now *Talbot* was just centering up on her patrol course at about 0215 hours, when she too was abruptly lit up by searchlights off the port bow—at a distance of some 10,000 yards. The light from the unidentified ship momentarily swung away but was quickly brought to bear yet a second time to more fully illuminate the ship, this time from an alarming 7,000 yards off her port beam, at which time she commenced firing. That same "unidentified ship" had, at that time, reportedly managed to get off some six salvos at least—with all but two falling short of their target. So, who indeed was she, and what ship was it that had fired at the *Talbot* at that time?

The captain of the *Talbot*, LCDR Joseph William Callahan, was convinced that the other ship might indeed have been a "friendly"—a fellow destroyer from Tulagi perhaps, and so did not immediately return fire. *Talbot* continued, therefore, on its westward track at best speed, again pursuing a series of standard zigzag maneuvers to avoid the continued hot shelling and unchecked incoming fire. Simultaneously flashing running lights and broadcasting over her own Talk Between Ships (TBS) system, the ship would in fact contact the second ship to report that she was under attack and possibly being fired on by a "friendly." Oddly enough, in response to those same extended TBS calls and her own ship's warning lights, all firing did indeed stop almost immediately.

In its later after-action report, the *Talbot* would go on record indicating that she indeed had a "high degree of certainty" of having been both "lit up and fired on by a friendly destroyer from Tulagi"[102] just before her contact with the IJN cruiser. Here, in all likelihood, it would seem that such an observation could have been erroneous since other warships in the area—namely, the DDs *Ellet* and *Henley*—did not similarly recount any such close encounter (or friendly-fire incident) at the time and may themselves not even have been in the vicinity of the *Talbot* at the time of either of her alleged attacks. Indeed, the only other accounted-for destroyer in that area at the time of that friendly-fire incident was the ever-mysterious *Helm* itself. Could that second "unidentified" warship have in fact been her?

FINDING 17:   THE MYSTERY OF THE *HELM*

USS *Helm*: Search and Rescue—or Absentee Warrior?

Perhaps there is even more damning and pejorative evidence about the *Bagley*-class destroyer USS *Helm* (DD-388), raising heated questions and discussions about the destroyer's post-action dispositioning on the night of 9 August 1942, during the First Battle of Savo Island. From a historical perspective, the *Helm* was only one of two DDs escorting a small American cruiser force on routine patrol in the central Solomons at a place called Guadalcanal, and the actions this night would in fact kick off what would later alternately become known to history as "The Battle of Five Sitting Ducks."

The fast-attack destroyers *Helm* and *Wilson* (DD-408) had both equally been tasked with escorting RADM Frederick Lois Riefkohl's force to patrol the northern reaches of Iron Bottom Sound, just north and east of Savo Island. The slow-moving

American Task Group 62.3 would this night consist of the aging American heavy cruisers USS *Vincennes* (CA-44), USS *Quincy* (CA-39), and USS *Astoria* (CA-34). Under the brackish cowl of night, and riding extremely low in the water, the fleet escorts were set to flank either side of the patrol column some 1,500 yards out from the main body of "heavies" in their charge. Sleek and fast-moving, the two

destroyers maneuvered unerringly forward on a steadied course to the south and west—probing the darkness about them and pacing slightly ahead and off the port and starboard beam of the advancing cruiser column.

The five ships had been set on a routine screening patrol within an imagined "box-like" area that was designated as the Northern screen some five miles square on each patrol leg. For RADM Crutchley, it would have been a pressing imperative that he split his meager naval assets at Guadalcanal into three subgroups to fully create his Southern, Northern, and Eastern screening forces that night. Of these, perhaps the most significant and heavily tasked screening force of all must clearly have been that of the Northern screen—the *Vincennes* group—under the able command of Admiral Riefkohl. It would be in the company of this group, then—this ill-starred and ill-fated group—that the mysterious USS *Helm* would sail on the fateful night of 9 August 1942.[103]

Now cautiously sluicing past the southern edge of their patrol corridor, Riefkohl's small surface force made its slow turn onto the northbound leg of their patrol route, on new course heading 3-1-5° (T), and sailed under condition "Readiness II/Condition Zed." Outside, the night was dark and muffled, deeply overcast, and peppered with a slow pelt of rain that fell in a misted sheet all around them. By 0130, winds were still light but agitated, with a distant squall that had been persistent in its push up from the southwest, bringing with it a reduction in ceiling to only a very slight 1,500 feet, rendering good visibility to only about 10,000 yards. In the distance, far to the north and west, the quiet but subvolcanic Savo Island sat like a gray lady wrapped in a wool shawl, hunched in a shroud beneath a heavy cloudbank that extended for some miles.

The stage was indeed now set for a calculated disaster . . . and that disaster would come in the person of none other than VADM Gunichi Mikawa himself.

For even at the very moment, as suddenly as it might itself be kindled, the battle would begin. Shortly after midnight, commencing at a time nearing 0138 hours, illuminating starshells dropped from the deck-launched seaplanes catapulted from the Japanese warships—and those fired from the large guns of the heavy cruisers themselves—began shredding the mantle of night and dangerously exposing the passing American cruisers. The American ships were now only too vulnerable to attack, and Mikawa knew it. Soon, the searchlights from his IJN ships lit up the near horizon as well, as soon the great *Chōkai*, the *Kako*, and *Kinugasa* opened up with all guns brought to bear and found their range out to Riefkohl's ships. What followed next was the unleashing of a certain hell and fury not often seen in any open-sea battle of its type: the quick-fire blooms of distant light bursting from the 5- and 8-inch guns on the Japanese cruisers and the heavy "ship-concentrated" salvos of deadly accurate fire being laid out on the American surface fleet in full.

As a result, in a taut, thirty-one-minute battle in dead of night, *Vincennes* would be hit a staggering seventy-four times from the repeated volleys of HE shells fired from the guns of Mikawa's CRUDIV6 and 18, and several fatal waterline hits from their far-reaching Long-Lance torpedoes. Closely following on the heels of these opening salvos, a shattered USS *Quincy* would itself be likewise barraged, suffering no less than thirty-six hits as she too now crippled slowly off to the northeast. And even brave *Astoria* was forced to retire after she received some sixty-five impactful hits of her own from the combined actions of the fluid and fast-moving Japanese attack force.

The *Quincy* would be first to sink, however, drifting to a position east-northeast of Savo Island at about 0238 hours, where she would go down (and remains to this day); the *Vincennes* would sadly join her soon thereafter at about 0250; and finally the *Astoria* itself, which by this time was left helplessly adrift to the southwest and fully disengaged from the fray. She would survive another eight hours until noon of the following day, at which time she would be sunk virtually in situ by the American DD USS *Ellet* (DD-398). In full scope, these heavy cruiser losses would only be in addition to the preceding Japanese attack that had already savaged Crutchley's Southern screening force, during which the Australian cruiser *Canberra* had been decimated and sunk, and the *Chicago* seriously damaged by that same Mikawa force. The net effect and harsh outcome of this brief but intensely violent skirmish was the critical loss of all four Allied heavy cruisers; the damaging of a fifth American cruiser and two of its attending escort destroyers as well . . . clearly a high price to pay.

USS *Helm*: A Search for the Truth

A closer examination of these facts then brought this researcher to a critical juncture in his study, where it was curiously found that irrespective of ❶ the amount of time spent in mapping each of the battle scenarios as they unfolded; ❷ interpreting and understanding fleet dispositions, angles of approach and attack, and the close-quarter movements of both the IJN and Allied forces at the time of the battle; ❸ understanding and fully appreciating the quite fortunate splitting of the Mikawa attack column by sheer luck, just prior to the attack on the Northern screen, which then allowed them to trap that cruiser force in a deadly "twin-axial" pincer attack; ❹ charting the transitive movements of each of the ships in their moment-to-moment engagement scenarios; and ❺ following those ships on to their final dispositions—all seemed to culminate in a need for a silent accounting and tallying of those few ships that would survive the battle . . . and those that would not. Curiously enough, the *Helm* would be one that would in fact survive.

In and of itself, of course, this would not be particularly miraculous—or even remarkable—since so had the *Ralph Talbot*, the *Wilson*, and even the *Astoria* herself— at least initially. Likewise, both the *Bagley* and the *Patterson* would escape relatively unscathed as well—and all of RADM Scott's Eastern screening force, made up of the two light cruisers *San Juan* and the Australian *Hobart*, and the two escort destroyers *Monssen* and *Buchanan*. Yet it is here that only the *Helm* comes into question time and again in my findings. Where was the *Helm*? And what was the disposition of the ship before, during, and after the sudden night action itself? But always circling back inevitably to the same precise question: *Where* was she in the heat of battle?

And so I continued to conduct the research and to scour the findings, reports, and after-action analyses; continued to ask the uneasy questions and to seek the uncertain answers—perhaps simply to research and compile those findings—but more at knowing with some level of certainty what actually might have transpired that night during the thirty-one-minute "bare-knuckles brawl" on the high seas at the very lip of dawn, at a haunting place called Iron Bottom Sound.

And so of myself I could only ask the question again and again: Where was 3-8-8 . . . where was the *Helm*?"

This is by no means a question meant to disparage the ship or its brave crew—or to impeach the integrity of its stewardship under the able command of LCDR Chester Edward "Blackie" Carroll (Figure 28) at the time of the battle. Nor is it in any way intended to call into question the battle spirit of the *Helm* itself—the scrappy little destroyer that sailed almost in a class by itself and boasted of a nearly unprecedented eleven Battle Stars for her many naval campaigns. What it does beg to question is why no substantive data can be found to pinpoint the exact position of the *Helm* throughout the full duration of the battle. Extant narratives and accounts of the time seem to suggest that the *Helm* did in fact circle back after the attack and did indeed remain in the area on provisional SAR patrol, working to pull men from the waters and to recover survivors from the *Vincennes*, *Quincy*, and *Astoria*. Curiously enough, however, is the fact that far too many roads diverge from this one account, and many of the plotting maps—both then and now—seem to say something completely different. The maps do not all uphold the purported movements of that ship, and therein lies the rub—therein lies perhaps the even greater tale.

Figure 28.   LCDR Chester Edward "Blackie" Carroll, Captain: USS *Helm* (Midshipman Cadet Years)

At the onset of hostilities on the night of 9 August, the *Helm* rode silently some 1,500 yards due west off the port bow of *Vincennes*[104] as she and the *Wilson* spearheaded a probative force of five ships set to screen the northern reaches of Iron Bottom Sound, close in to Florida Island (Nggella Sule). The attack began imprimis with starshell flares fired from the Japanese cruisers, with follow-on Long-Lance torpedo attacks, and fully enlarged by the stepped-up bombardments from the IJN heavy cruisers' 5- and 8-inch guns.

Alerted to the unfolding action by the very illuminants that now dangerously exposed their position, the intrepid *Helm* and *Wilson* responded fairly immediately to the flares being set off from Mikawa's ships, and even the *Helm*'s fire control officer quickly opened fire with a four-gun salvo directed at the ship-based searchlights—and at the ships themselves. But here, for some reason, whether due to problems in identifying the enemy targets themselves, or simply due to an instance of adjusted range-finding out to that enemy, the *Helm* ceased all fire at a point when her target, *Chōkai*, was estimated to have only been some 7,000 yards away from her, and oddly did *not* engage at that time. Perhaps overcautiously awaiting further instructions from the screening force commander himself, RADM Riefkohl, CDR Carroll on the *Helm* guardedly continued on for some four additional minutes as he held fire, awaiting orders and jockeying forward on a course that soon took him farther away from the Japanese warships that were even then beginning to prosecute their attacks on the American cruisers—which ships both the *Helm* and the *Wilson* had been critically tasked with protecting.

By 0152 of the clock, after some delay—due certainly to the severity of the attack on his own *Vincennes*—Riefkohl would finally issue his operational orders to the two destroyers, ordering them to an immediate fast attack on the Mikawa force with full torpedo spreads to be laid out from the port side of the column and out to the enemy ships . . . but reportedly gave *no* bearing data on those ships. Yet, even in the absence of such data, the *Helm* and *Wilson* still dutifully moved off to try to plot effective firing solutions for their initial torpedo attacks, but they would in effect only be firing "in the blind." As the senior officer of the two DD commanders that night, Carroll should have himself orchestrated the movements of both destroyers, but appeared to make no attempt to do so, with (for all appearances) each destroyer operating independently of the other.

As the lead commander of the destroyer task element that night, Carroll might indeed have had several options available to him—the first and foremost of which would be the most aggressive and head-on approach—that of turning abruptly toward the enemy muzzle-flashes and searchlights on the large Japanese cruisers, increasing his ship's speed for an all-out torpedo run on that CRUDIV force, and ordering the *Wilson* to do essentially the same. Oddly, Carroll did not do this. Secondary only to his protecting the heavy cruisers in his immediate charge, at no time did the *Helm* ever appear to be moving in the direction of the transports or landing ships, this with an aim to provide them with a defensive umbrella even as they continued unloading troops and supplies at Tulagi and Honiara. In lieu of this, the mysterious *Helm* instead continued on a fixed heading for the next two minutes before turning back to the south at about 0154. Now moving at a measured speed of only 15 knots (up from its previous 10 knots), the enemy had by now already moved to a point far to the southeast of *Vincennes*'s current position, as even then the *Helm* moved away from the Northern screening group at good speed past distant Savo. The IJN hit-and-run tactic had worked flawlessly indeed and had been prosecuted to maximum effect by Admiral Mikawa and his deadly flotilla of heavy cruisers. And now the deed was done.

In its sad wake, the *Vincennes* had been sunk almost immediately in situ, the *Quincy* following in quick order—having meandered to the northwest in its final death throes—and *Astoria* herself surviving both the battle and the night, only to sink the following day by 1215 hours.

USS *Helm*: Rendezvous or Mad Dash?

Pursuit or Quick Way Out: Engagement or Quick Run for the Border?

While it cannot firmly be determined just where the *Helm* was for much of the battle, several substantive points appear abundantly clear: ❶ the *Helm* did not know precisely where the enemy ships were; ❷ unable to fix a specific point of focus for her fire, she was probably also uncertain of a best angle of attack and may have been firing in the blind at only "calculated" targets in the near distance; ❸ it would later be reported that she may not have been aware that she had even been fired on—even though she had been targeted multiple times. As with virtually all of the American naval vessels operating in and around Guadalcanal at the time, the scrappy *Helm* was also itching for a fight, but could this night not find one. In his own comprehensive 377-page analysis, *The Battle of Savo Island, August 9, 1942. Strategical and Tactical Analysis. Part I*—as prepared for the Naval War College—author Richard W. Bates probably best summed up the activities of the hapless, "come-up-empty" *Helm* for the duration of the battle, when he, too, observed:

> While yet in his turn to the south at 0155, he [Carroll] became aware of the fact that the Japanese gunfire was extremely accurate, for all three Allied [American] cruisers had topside fires raging. Five minutes had elapsed since the force that he was screening had been taken under fire by the enemy, but he had accomplished nothing that might have forced the Japanese fire to be less effective. Because of the futility of his visual observations, the question arises as to why he did not request from his division commander [RADM Riefkohl] such vital information as the bearing of the enemy.[105]

This point is further exacerbated by a continuation of that same narrative when Bates notes in the very next paragraph:

> This [southerly] course brought him under fire intermittently during the next five minutes from both the AOBA and KINUGASA. The fire of these ships was evidently very inaccurate, because the HELM was not only completely unaware of it but was also unaware of [even] the presence of the firing ships, which by this time were no longer even using their searchlights. The Japanese cruisers each claimed sinking the HELM, but it is probable that she disappeared from their view into the [very] mist that was making it impossible for [her] to even locate that enemy.[106]

This, then, almost begs to question just what in fact the *Helm* was doing at the time of the attack. Unable to initially identify either the source of the enemy's scanning searchlights or even the IJN ships themselves during the course of the attack, *Helm* could apparently help neither herself nor the very cruisers she had been tasked with screening. Her torpedo attacks would have been thwarted and somewhat ineffective at the range from which she proposed to fire, especially with no fixed targets in play and little to slake the thirst of the stepped-up gunfire from her deadly 5-inch batteries. A ghastly pall might indeed have fallen over both the ship and her crew even as they observed, as Bates described, "all three American cruisers with topside fires raging"[107] on them—this as each ghastly ship passed off into the night, now battered and slowly dying.

By 0200 hours, a mere ten minutes after the onset of the full attack itself, the *Helm* was reportedly continuing on a bearing of 102° (T) at a distance estimated to be some 10,500 yards from dead center of Savo Island. By 0210, Mikawa's cruiser divisions had already fully circumnavigated most of Iron Bottom Sound, struck a deadly blow to the Allied surface fleet twice, and were now making fast turns to withdraw from the area as quickly as possible as his warships moved to the north. In full, the entire battle would have lasted some thirty-one minutes only, but again, where exactly might that same *Helm* have been found?

One account[108] seems to provide at least the following observation of the later actions of the mystery ship when it states:

Helm, on the port bow of *Vincennes*, turned back to help the stricken cruisers. She stood by *Astoria*, brought survivors to transports off Guadalcanal, and withdrew with the remainder of the force to Nouméa on 13 August.

Other accounts affirm that DD-388 rapidly moved off to Crutchley's predetermined secondary "destroyer rendezvous point" just north of Savo Island (Figure 29) and seem unclear as to whether she in fact ever did meet up with any other ships at that location, other than possibly in a "probative" brush with the still-patrolling radar picket ship *Ralph Talbot*.

In fact, even Jack D. Coombe himself would be compelled to make the following observation, centered on the erratic movements of CDR Carroll's *Helm*:

> One of the Northern Force's screening destroyers tried to close on the enemy column, but did no damage. Mikawa ignored her. The other, the *Helm*, did not get into action. She wandered around as if in a daze.[109]

Also quite clear not just from the *Opentopia* account[110] but also from the DANFS (Dictionary of American Naval Fighting Ships) reference source[111]—and even the very Report of Loss in Action Report from the Navy Department's own Bureau of Ships in 1943[112]—only four ships were known to have responded in situ to the troubled *Quincy*, *Astoria*, and *Vincennes*. Those ships—destroyers all—were notably the *Bagley*, the *Hopkins*, the *Wilson*, and the *Buchanan*, the latter of which had been released from RADM Scott's own Eastern screening group and dispatched north at best speed to assist. Other than a cursory one-line notation in the Wikipedia account of the 1BOSI,[113] no account appears to contain much mention of the "post-action" movements of the *Helm*, other than that which is plotted on old maps of the time. And even if this much could be resolved, there is still one final discrepancy shadowing her later disposition with the fleet at Guadalcanal, one that seems to indicate that she "withdrew with the remainder of the force to Nouméa on 13 August,"[114] this even in the face of other reports that seemed instead to identify Brisbane as that later port of call:

> For the next few weeks, *Helm* remained in dangerous waters near Guadalcanal, escorting transports and patrolling. She sailed to Brisbane on September 7, and departed the next day to provide escort protection for transports between Australia and New Guinea.[115]

Fortunately, there is another, more "pictorial" side that can shed much additional light on the follow-on events of the ship, such that can capture in full the movements of the USS *Helm*—at least for the duration of the battle and shortly thereafter—that of the navigational tracks shown on extant maps of the times, all of which seem to refute rather than support the claim that the destroyer remained in waters near the area of attack to carry out even basic SAR for survivors from the stricken American cruisers. Perhaps, then, the key to disentangling the Gordian Knot of the movements of the *Helm* is to be found in these maps, many of which paint a wholly different mural of events as they may have unfolded before, during, and after the attacks at Savo.

USS *Helm*: The *Helm* Maps

Guadalcanal must indeed have been a topographer's nightmare and a bald dilemma: a none too easily plottable stretch of land and water that was at once a teeming archipelago comprising some 892 islands in an ecological wonderland made up of extensive land masses, lush rain forests, upland mountain regions, capes, inlets, promontories, and even a still-active conic volcano on Savo Island itself. Small wonder, then, that maps of the time (indeed those that have survived to date) would be accurate to within feet in their depiction of the island groupings and large land masses that dotted the areas in and around Guadalcanal and the greater Solomons. The oceanographic maps of the waters and open-sea areas encompassing those islands, however, may have been another matter entirely, and many were found to be of a less exacting quality, often dismissably unreliable, and subject to the individual mapping analyst plotting their own interpretive grid of the battle, as upheld by extant record and opinion. Whether the initial deployment of both the IJN and Allied forces at the outset of the battle, the transitive movement *of* those forces during the action itself, or the final dispositioning of the ships after the deadly encounter, much is left to the viewpoint and interpretive notion of the map-makers themselves.

The end result, of course, was a swimming multitude of maps, plotting charts, and illustrations from multiple sources that must include not just the American Naval War College itself but also the Department of the Navy's own Bureau of Ships, the Office of Naval Intelligence (ONI), and even individual mappings only "recalled from memory" or pieced together from the few surviving combatants who were actually there. This would have to include individuals like LCDR Mackenzie J. Gregory on the *Canberra*, PO1 Dan Galvin from the *Quincy*, RADM Riefkohl on *Vincennes*, and even CAPT Toshikazu Ohmae, the extant chief of staff serving with VADM Gunichi Mikawa himself on his flagship *Chōkai* on the night of the battle.

Perhaps, then, the maps can be allowed to truly tell their own story . . . so indeed a quick look at some of these very images might well be in order.

Map #1: The first map to be analyzed is prized as being perhaps one of the finest chart depictions of the First Battle of Savo Island itself and fully showcases the meticulous chart-crafting skills of CDR W. D. Innis of the Naval War College. The map itself was only published years later by LTC David E. Quantock in a larger work titled *Disaster at Savo Island, 1942*, for the U.S. Army War College—this as recently as the year 2002.[116] In it, we clearly see the full and purported track of the USS *Helm* from a period of time ranging from her initial cruiser escort position at 0150 on a north-westerly heading of 315°, to her last-known position at a rendezvous point just north of Savo between 0220 and 0224 hours. How she got there, however, is perhaps the tale's even greater mystery. . . .

Shown in Figure 29, one can immediately note the *Helm*'s sharp turn to south after the commencement of the attack on the Allied fleet ❶—presumably to press an attack on the passing *Yubari*, as shown. This feint would quickly be followed by a brief

Track of USS *Helm* in Action—9 August 1942

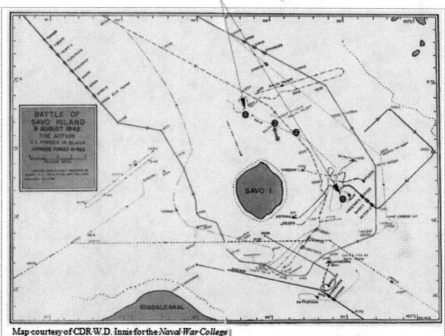

Map courtesy of CDR W.D. Innis for the *Naval War College*

Figure 29.   Engagement/Post-Action Track of the USS *Helm* (Innis/Quantock)

jaunt to west, then almost a beeline run directly to the north and west to the destroyer rendezvous point behind Savo. Clearly, this track also appears to take the *Helm* quite close to a convergence point that must have crossed the paths of at least two of the three stricken American cruisers that night—the lead ship *Vincennes* and its sister ship *Quincy*. But did she in fact see the ships? Did she stop? Did she assist in any of the SAR tasks at that time or later?

Citing Richard B. Frank's own finding in his book, *Guadalcanal: The Definitive Account of the Landmark Battle*, some sources[117] seem to indicate that the "*Helm*, on the port bow of *Vincennes*, did indeed turn back to help the stricken cruisers"[118] and that she later "stood by *Astoria*, brought survivors to transports off Guadalcanal, and withdrew with the remainder of the force to Nouméa on 13 August."[119] Yet this begs the question of just how any of this could have been possible if by 0224 she was already on station behind Savo. If the *Quincy* was itself sunk at 0236, and the *Vincennes* by 0250, how could the *Helm* have even been in a position to assist either ship or be able to effect any SAR activities and still be at the rendezvous point by 0224? Truly a "poser" indeed—but let's look at the timeline anyway.

At a point in time just past 0210 hours, the Innis map already seems to depict the *Helm* crossing the northbound track of the withdrawing IJN column ❷— specifically that of the cruisers *Yubari* and *Tenryū*—which ships had earlier split off from Mikawa's main column to form yet a second attack prong. Did the ships in fact see each other, was the *Helm* fired on by the passing IJN cruiser column at this time, and did she in return engage them as well?

Extant records seem to identify that the lone radar picket destroyer *Ralph Talbot* was the only American ship spotted and savaged by the Japanese warships "on their way out," with again no mention of the *Helm*. Here, however, some sources seem to cite a possibility of the *Helm* sighting the *Ralph Talbot* while the latter was still on its elliptical patrol course well to the north with the USS *Blue* ❸, but she (the *Helm*) did not in fact engage at that time lest that contact later be tagged as a "friendly." In the end, it was well indeed that she did not fire her guns at that time, which in and of itself would have been only the gravest of errors.

Then, by 0220, according to the Innis map, we see the *Helm* in a position of some proximity to the *Yubari* force once again ❹, this time only minutes after that IJN force had prosecuted its third (and final) attack of the night on the still-patrolling *Ralph Talbot*. Was the *Helm* aware of the attack being launched at that time . . . and could she in fact see the action taking place even at her distance? Did the *Helm* attempt to assist or investigate, or simply continue straightaway on her northward track to the rendezvous point past Savo? At its final resting point, the Innis map seems to estimate an approximated position for the *Helm* at that destroyer reassembly point as being at 159°42' E–9°08' S ❺.*

For the dauntless American DD, therefore, this northward trek had been long and fraught with perils unimaginable, yet it would appear that the ship did indeed finally make it to the destroyer assembly point, and the *Helm* would now remain on station until other ships arrived. And one of those other ships would be none other than the straggling *Wilson* itself. So, might it with fairness be said that the two fateful destroyers had in fact failed miserably in their charge to at all costs protect the contingency of heavy cruisers that had made up Riefkohl's Northern screen? And had they not also been tasked with screening the very troop transport and landing ships that were still busy unloading at Tulagi and Honiara? Had both ships failed to do either?

MAP #2: This second map image is far less complex and has a far greater linear sharpness to it but might otherwise be almost simplistic to a fault. It shows little in the way of date or time stamping (other than the sinking of the American ships), nor does it do much to highlight any of the detailed areas of the conflict occurring during the night's engagement itself. Surprisingly enough, this image (Figure 30) was in fact commissioned by the Office of Naval Intelligence (ONI) itself, and in it we clearly see the final resting points of each of the three American heavy cruisers, depicted here as the *Vincennes* ❶, the *Quincy* ❷, and the *Astoria* ❸. This would effectively constitute the bulk of the American Northern screening force itself.

---

*Note also the curious difference between the Innis plotting position of 159°42' E–9°08' S and the later Loxton mapping fix that would place that same "destroyer rendezvous point" at 159°44' E–9° 05' S instead.

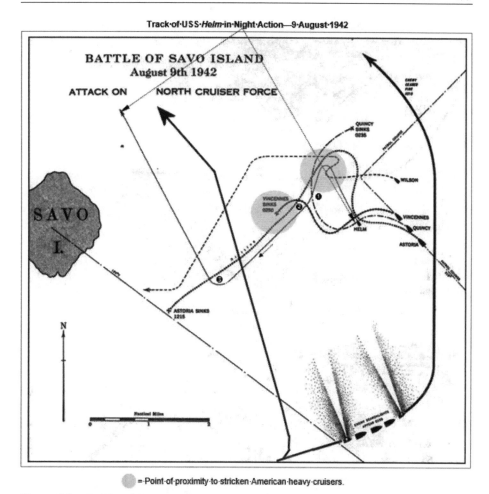

Figure 30.   Battle of Savo Island: Attack on the Northern Fleet (ONI Plotting)
Photograph courtesy of the Office of Naval Intelligence (ONI)

Note also that there appear to have been at least three trajectory passage points for the *Helm* that night (shown here as ❶, ❷, and ❸), which might indeed have brought her close enough to one or more of the beleaguered ships to perhaps render some assistance to carry out some measure of SAR activity. Instead, it would appear that she merely continued on in her quickened northward push to the rendezvous point set by Crutchley as a contingency redeployment area, should any of his ships become separated from their screening groups during any unforeseen scenarios that might have unfolded during the course of that night's battles. Perhaps indeed they never even saw it coming.

Based on the findings of this particular map, however, we only too quickly note that the only two warships she might have passed close enough to assist would have been either the *Vincennes* or the *Quincy*, or both (again at ❶ and ❷ on the map). Without a "fixed" time parameter display shown on the map, however—other than the referential times of the final ship sinkings themselves—it is markedly more difficult to determine the *Helm*'s interaction with either of the two ships during this time frame. Indeed, what can be seen is the almost parallel track that seemingly paces that of the *Astoria* (❸), even as she herself crippled off to a point south and west of the battle zone, where the next day she, too, would be sunk almost in situ.

In addition, note the two highlighted circle areas shown on that same ONI map, as those later added by the author to depict the two "most feasible points of contact and closest passage" for the *Helm*, if indeed she even met up with either warship at all. Yet, rapidly on the heels of this point, we nonetheless see the same beeline run noted in the Innis map, with the *Helm* now coursing straight to the north and west of Savo to Crutchley's predetermined reassembly point. It might reasonably be asked, therefore, just what indeed the *Helm* did do—or, perhaps more scathingly, what did she *not* do during (and right after) the actual attack.

Perhaps history will never yield up the well-kept secrets centering on the precise movements of the *Helm* that have remained dormant for some eighty years or more, and perhaps only the crew who manned the ship that one fateful night can really know with certainty what occurred.

MAP #3: Perhaps the most optimal rendering of all of the extant maps alluding to the 1BOSI, the chart in Figure 31 was quite excellently crafted by the well-respected Bruce Loxton, and would be derived from his larger work, *The Shame of Savo: Anatomy of a Naval Disaster.*[120] In its depiction, it clearly shows a proximity positioning of the *Helm* to the *Vincennes* and the *Quincy* only, and probably not at all to the *Astoria*—which by that time had already begun moving away from the area as early as 0200 hours—well away from the *Helm*. Clearly, in at least Loxton's rendering here, the screening DD *Helm* does appear to approach within an appreciable distance to both the *Quincy* and the *Vincennes*, enough to perhaps render aid to either warship at that time—but, in fact, did she?

For a best referencing of the above, we can simply "walk through the numbers" and begin at map position ❶, where we clearly see that the time stamp is marked as 0200 hours—only minutes after the commencement of the surprise Japanese attack, which was known to have started at about 0150. By about 0207 hours ❷, we see that both the *Vincennes* and the *Quincy* have in fact disengaged from their attacks—with the former cruiser dropping quickly to the south and west—while the crippled *Quincy* curved up on a course that would take her well to the north and east, with both ships seeking only safe refuge from the maelstrom of Mikawa's sudden and complete attacks. In sharp contrast to all of the above, however, we also see that the *Helm* is shown as unquestionably still on her northern track, on what appears to be a dead-on run for the destroyer rendezvous point itself. By 0208, the *Helm* is then curiously shown in an area on the

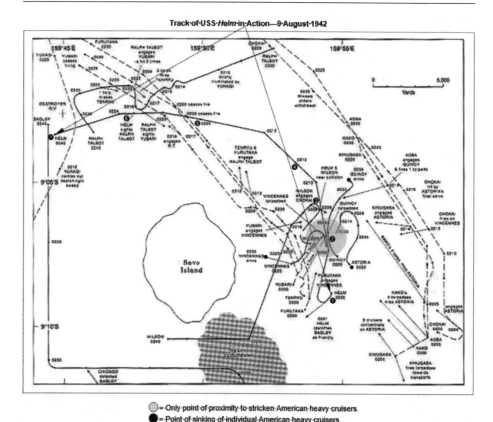

Figure 31. Attack on the Northern Fleet: Transitional Record of Movement and Coordinates (Loxton Plotting)

map simply tagged as "HELM & WILSON—Near Collision" ❸, this presumably happening while the *Wilson* was still itself seeking to engage the now-exiting *Chōkai*.

For the crew of the *Helm*, however, the next 0212 waypoint on her jockey north past dark Savo (❹) must indeed have been interesting, since almost precisely at that same time the IJN heavy cruisers *Yubari* and *Tenryū* were both just spotting and firing on the still-distant *Ralph Talbot*. Loxton's detailed mapping clearly shows that both Japanese warships must have initiated their "confidence-low" attacks at about that time, firing a spread of Long-Lance torpedoes from an extreme distance while at the same moment the *Helm* loitered in waters only slightly north of their position. So did the *Helm* either see or hear anything, and was she even aware that an attack on the *Ralph Talbot* was in fact in progress at that time?

Later, with a spot-check at 0221 hours (❺), even as the *Helm* continued to press northward on her trek to Crutchley's "reassembly point," we see that for the first time she might indeed have crossed the track of Mikawa's own withdrawing ships, or at least those in the second-prong force—namely, the CLs *Yubari* and the CA *Tenryū*—where indeed she would pass behind and through the wake of that same trailing *Tenryū*. It would also be at this point that Mikawa would issue his final "cease-fire" order in his attack on the American ships, even as his own cruiser divisions slunk back under the mantle of fog and night. But had the *Helm* in fact seen the passing IJN ships even at that time? And if in fact she did, did she attempt to engage any of them at that time, or did she simply forge ahead with great resolve, on a mad dash for the redeployment area? Tough, tough questions all . . . and truly none with easy answers to be found.

In its next phase of passage, at approximately 0223 hours (**❻**)—as largely upheld in other accounts of the battle—the *Helm* at some point did spot the *Ralph Talbot* cruising well to her north, but could not immediately identify the ship. Bracing for the very worst of heavy action, and preparing for her best angle of attack, the *Helm* moved at best speed to intercept the contact, and to plot a viable firing solution out to the unidentified warship. Virtually at the very last minute, however, before initiating a launch of her own torpedoes, she was finally able to identify the other ship as a friendly—which "friendly" was indeed the *Ralph Talbot* itself. The hapless *Helm*, therefore, would immediately break off the attack and resume her course for Crutchley's rendezvous point behind Savo. Lastly, with a final time plot set some nineteen minutes later at 0242 (**❼**), Loxton seems to then depict the *Helm* as having in fact arrived at that reassembly point—approximated as being at a position near 159°44' E–9°05' S. She would thereafter remain on station until joined much later by the *Wilson*.

Note, however, that there are still many inconsistencies between the Innis Map 1 image and that of Loxton's own Map 3, with each depicting completely different final destination points for CDR Carroll and his ambiguous *Helm*, at least in relation to its position behind Savo Island. In fact, that northernmost position for that DD at its final rendezvous point is markedly different in each of the maps presented thus far, so which location might be considered the more accurate depiction . . . and how indeed can we know for sure?

USS *Helm*: The Innis/Loxton Maps

To further point up the essential differences in plotting the movements and track of the DD USS *Helm* on the night of 9 August 1942, one might be invited to look at only some of the timeline disparities found between the W. D. Innis/NWC–sanctioned map, and that of the respected author and naval historian, Bruce Loxton. Of interest here, at least, is the exactness in timing of both researchers in their plotting of the near collision between the *Helm* and *Ralph Talbot*, with each connoting the same 0208 time frame. These might in fact have been the only two-time tags that fully coincide between both these key timeline accounts.

MAP #4: Perhaps one of the more obscure and least viewable of maps touching on the actions and movements during the 1BOSI, this appears to be an undated chart based on a drawing by N. W. Grosen,[121] simply titled "The Battle of Savo Island: 9th August 1942," as shown in Figure 32. Truly, this is probably one of the more detailed yet least

Table 20. Actions/Maneuvering Track of the USS *Helm* during the 1BOSI (9 August 1942)

#	Time	ACTIONS AND OPERATIONAL MANEUVERS TRACKING OF THE USS *HELM* DURING THE 1BOSI (9 AUGUST 1942)	Time	
		INNIS / NWC MAP INTERPRETATION		LOXTON MAP INTERPRETATION
❶	0200	With *Vincennes*, *Quincy*, and *Astoria* only minutes after the commencement of the attack by Mikawa's CRUDIV elements at 0150.	0200	*Helm* sights the *Bagley* off her starboard bow at a range of about 4 miles and moves to identify and engage with torpedoes. Momentarily (and quite fortuitously for the *Bagley* itself) illuminated by a flash of lightning at precisely the moment, the *Helm* stays her attack, having quickly identified her sister ship as indeed being in fact a "friendly."
❷	0207	At the height of the attack by the Japanese, both *Vincennes* and *Quincy* split off to the SW and NE, respectively. *Helm* continues on undeterredly to the predetermined destroyer rendezvous point.	0201	After Mikawa's attack, *Helm* reverses course, increases her speed to 25 knots, and moves north. Does she in fact pass by the smoldering hulks of *Vincennes* and *Quincy*, sling-shotting ahead on an almost beeline run for Crutchley's rendezvous point?
❸	0208	0208 is cited by Innis as the time of the near-collision of the *Helm* and *Wilson*, after the prolonged action against Riefkohl's Northern screen by that attacking IJN cruiser force.	0206	*Helm* sights an action unfolding to the northwest and moves to investigate, while also increasing her speed up to 30 knots.
❹	0212	At 0212, while the *Helm* may not have been in the same location as the IJN column consisting of *Yūbari*, *Tenryū*, and *Furutaka*, this appears to be precisely the time that one or more of the IJN cruisers fired upon the still-distant *Ralph Talbot*.	0208	0208 is the time cited by Loxton as the moment of near-collision with *Wilson*. In and of itself, this would not corroborate the 0208 Innis timeline at all.

(continued)

Table 20. *Continued*

	ACTIONS AND OPERATIONAL MANEUVERS TRACKING OF THE USS *HELM* DURING THE 1BOSI (9 AUGUST 1942)			
#	**TIME**	**INNIS / NWC MAP INTERPRETATION**	**TIME**	**LOXTON MAP INTERPRETATION**
⑤	0221	The *Helm* crosses the wake of the passing IJN cruiser column and continues on her westward trek. Several of the Japanese ships fire upon *Helm*, but it is not clear whether she saw them or even knew she was being fired on.	0225	Loxton clearly states that "at 0225, *Ralph Talbot* was identified but, as all firing ceased, *Helm* continued towards the rendezvous point, passing close to the badly-damaged destroyer without asking if assistance was needed" (Loxton).
⑥	0223	A passing *Helm* now sights *Ralph Talbot* and turns to investigate as she prepares to engage. She later determines that the contact is a *friendly*.	0430	Loxton cites this time as the point when the *Wilson* finally arrives at the rendezvous point, said to have been near 159°42' E–9°08' S, to join an already circling *Helm*.
⑦	0240	At 0240, the Innis map shows *Ralph Talbot* moving rapidly south and crossing the path of the *Helm*, but no AARs seem to suggest any near-collision scenario as being reported.		*No further timeline recordation noted for Loxton, however, note the unusual time of the passing of the Helm and the Wilson, which is not at all supported in the Innis map itself, which seems to end at 0242, while the Loxton map concludes at 0430.*
⑧	0242	Arrives at Crutchley's predetermined DD rendezvous (and reassembly) point just north and west of Savo; estimated by the Innis map as being near or at 159°44' E–9°05' S, a clear discrepancy to the Loxton fix.		

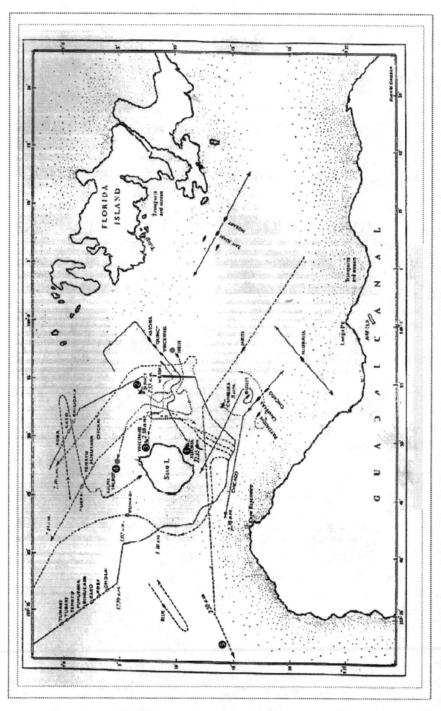

Figure 32.   N. W. Grosen Map: The Battle of Savo Island—9 August 1942 (Position at (±)159°30' E-9°02' S)

desirable of maps that researchers will find, due entirely to its somewhat obscured and darkened background, lack of any clear date or time stamping, and even its questionable end-state plottings for the American cruisers *Vincennes*, *Quincy*, and *Astoria*, all lost during that action.

Although it might on the surface appear to be smartly rendered, the Grosen map is decidedly far less reliable than any of the previous illustrations. In it, we see that the position shown here as the final-state location where *Astoria* went down is ❶ clearly incorrect—as is the location shown for *Vincennes*—at least as far north as shown here at marker ❷. Less controversial, in at least the author's estimation, is the plotting of a last-known position of the *Quincy* ❸, and again the northernmost location of the *Helm* ❹, as indeed both appear to be much more accurate to actual known final positions. However, in the absence of any viable (or even legible) timeline for the interaction of all of these ships, it becomes more difficult to accurately plot the movements and end-state positioning of either the Allied or the IJN fleets.

To its credit, however, the Grosen map is impeccably crafted with a high degree of linear exactitude and displays a good knowledge of topography and scale. We clearly see, for instance, the full-on "approach track" of Mikawa's CRUDIV6 and CRUDIV18 forces at 1239 hours; their interaction (or noninteraction) with both radar picket destroyers *Blue* and *Ralph Talbot*; the commencement of the actual attack on Crutchley's Southern and Northern screening forces; and the detached HMAS *Australia* and all of Scott's own Eastern group as remaining essentially unscathed and entirely uninvolved in any of the battles throughout. Perhaps most curious of all, however, is the superimposing track of the destroyer *Jarvis* (❺), as through it all she forges doggedly along in her southerly exit from Iron Bottom Sound and past the promontory of Cape Esperance, on her way for emergency repairs in Brisbane, Australia.

Inconclusively enough, we also see that there is no final time stamp shown at all for the *Helm* arriving at the destroyer rendezvous point, which might indeed make this map even less useful to the serious researcher seeking a virtual timeline for that DD.

MAP #5: The curious "action" chart shown in Figure 33 is merely an extracted "screen capture" of the actual variable flow of battle for the 1BOSI, as noted on the History Animated website online. Fully animated in its presentation, and cleverly structured in multiple and separate battle phases that encompass nearly all of the naval encounters centered on Guadalcanal, this insightful, modern-day depiction graphically displays the course of battle for not just the First Battle of Savo Island itself but also the later Naval Battle of Guadalcanal, the Battle of Cape Esperance, and even the later Battle of Tassafaronga. Even as a serious and dedicated researcher, I nonetheless found myself drawn to the site, seemingly mesmerized by the color-coded tracks, points of contact, and fleet engagements—and even "last-knowns" for those ships that in fact did not survive. It is therefore with only mild misgiving that I might still recommend the site for viewing by both the devout researcher and even the casual studier of the 1BOSI events. The animated presentation may be seen in full in the video posted to the website *Battle of Savo Island 1942: America's Worst Naval Defeat*.

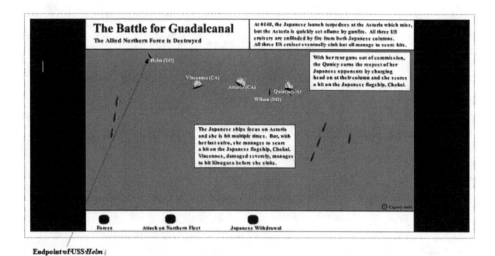

Endpoint of USS *Helm*

Figure 33.   Historical Animated Map: Attack on the Northern Fleet and Final Dispositions Battle of Savo Island 1942: America's Worst Naval Defeat (Bing Video Animation)

Even though cloaked in a shroud of relative inexactitude and only "approximated" position plots for the American cruisers, there is still much to be derived from the animated historical sequences shown on this site, to include those of other select battle animations for many other World War II actions in the Pacific, North Africa, and Europe, as well as some even more obscure links for select video animations for several Revolutionary and Civil War actions as well.

As for the somewhat dubious actions of the *Helm* itself, her end-state position remains obscured and unreferenced in this map, due to the absence of any topographical features being displayed. There are clearly no major land masses shown, nor is Savo itself even depicted in relation to the *Helm* and the other ships that night. That point notwithstanding, we still see that she is far to the north and west of the position of all of the sinking cruisers and would probably indeed not have been in a position to fully render assistance to any of them at that time. It is known, however, that shortly after 1200 hours on the lag end of the morning of 9 August—some eight hours after the action itself—the *Helm* did finally come alongside the now-abandoning *Astoria* to offload what few remaining survivors she could, and to rescue any additional stragglers from the American cruiser only minutes before she went down.

USS *Helm*: A Final Encounter—The *Helm* and the *Ralph Talbot*

From at least the official ONI account of the 1BOSI, perhaps the last known American ship to have seen the *Helm* was the *Ralph Talbot* herself, the second of the two American radar picket ships that had been on patrol just north of Savo Island that night—this in a time frame occurring sometime between 0215 and 0220 hours on the morning of 9 August. For, even as Mikawa's cruiser divisions withdrew from the area, after delivering their punishing blows to both the Allied Southern and Northern screening groups, that same force did indeed encounter at least one last American destroyer on their way out—the *Ralph Talbot*—at about 0215.

Abruptly illuminated by probing searchlights that were at the time estimated to have been some 10,000 yards off her port bow, the *Ralph Talbot* upped her alert status fairly immediately and dutifully moved to battle stations, but refrained from firing lest the target ship in fact later prove to be a "friendly." Having been savaged by a combined attack from the 5-inch guns of a single Japanese destroyer (probably the *Yunagi*), and a second ship mistakenly identified as a *Tone*-class cruiser, the *Ralph Talbot* would take three quick-succession hits to the wardroom, number 4 gun mount, and starboard torpedo battery. Soon sluicing to port with an almost 20° list, the battered American DD had all she could do to limp off to the westward side of Savo Island. Many of the torpedoes she had attempted to fire herself had malfunctioned in situ, or else the weapons' firing tubes themselves had been knocked out by the heavy dead-on bombardment from Mikawa's ships. It would not be until noon of the next morning that the now-stricken destroyer would even be able to rejoin the main battle fleet, and—when the dust had settled thick after storm—she had lost some twenty-one men in only a three-minute action.

Later queried about this very encounter, and her reluctance to (at least initially) respond to the probing searchlights and directed fire, the *Ralph Talbot* remained adamant in its claim that the offending fire could indeed have come from a friendly and was the very reason for the check-fire imprimis. The Bates/ONI account addresses this in part when it states:

> Although the *Talbot*'s report speaks with apparent certainty of her being illuminated and fired upon by a friendly destroyer "from Tulagi" just before her contact with the IJN cruiser, it seems very probable that this identification was a mistake, and that it was no accident that the searchlight remained on her until the cruiser could pick her out. Neither the *Ellet* nor the *Henley*, our two destroyers from the Tulagi area, recount any such incident, and neither was near *Talbot* at the time. The only one of our destroyers in the area was the *Helm*.[122]

That statement is only too closely followed by this observation:

> She [the *Helm*] reported observing a ship illuminated and firing at 0220. She headed for the scene of action at 30 knots, but in about 5 minutes a flash of lightning revealed the destroyer as "one of our own". The firing, according to the *Helm*, lasted for only a few salvos. It seems clear that the *Helm* was merely an observer of the action and neither illuminated nor fired upon the *Talbot*.[123]

One might only imagine the possible tragic outcome had there not indeed been a fortuitous flash of lightning at precisely the moment when it was perhaps most needed.

Yet, in the greater overview of these two significant maps charted by Innis and Loxton, which indeed might be the more accurate account? The only viable conclusion one can infer is the fact that many such dangerous encounters between "friendlies" did in fact occur more often than bears cautious mention here—and not always with the most pleasant of outcomes. Arguably, the *Helm* and the *Ralph Talbot* were not the only two beleaguered ships involved in such that night.

USS *Helm*: Conclusions

"Regarding your analysis of the actions of the [USS] *Helm* on the night in question," a colleague and fellow naval historian quite recently stated, "I object to your major, and urge you to be fair-minded, tread lightly and proceed with good caution in your conclusions about DD-388." And so indeed I have, but I still seem to arrive at the same nonspecific conclusions. So what, if anything, might be said of the fleet, high-spirited USS *Helm* . . . or of her actions on the night of 9 August 1942? Was the order from RADM Crutchley instructing the destroyer captains to rendezvous at a predetermined reassembly point north of Savo so pivotal a mandate that it would override even the more immediate need for her to remain on station in the area of the stricken heavy cruisers to render first-line assistance, as demanded by the state of affairs at that precise moment? And why indeed would she pursue her straight-line run to the north with such unflagging resolve? Did she in fact not see the three American cruisers on fire even at the time of the attack? Clearly, in at least the Bates account they must have, since he himself cites the *Helm* as later commenting that they did indeed see those ships passing, noting that "all three Allied cruisers had topside fires raging."[124]

What, then, was the *Helm*'s greater mandate and objective at this point? Should she have stood by the stricken American cruisers to dutifully carry out normal SAR activities, or should she have in fact moved to a secondary position nearer to the landing and transport ships she had been equally tasked with screening—which were even then still unloading men and supplies ashore? Or should she have just continued on to the destroyer rendezvous point, as apparently indeed she did?

Perhaps, then, the best conclusion one might infer from the *Helm*'s involvement in the deadly skirmish at Savo—however negligible and limited—is that she could probably have seen the battle raging all about her but could not herself identify any viable targets or otherwise enter the fray. For almost the full duration of the night engagement itself, *Helm* could neither launch an attack of her own (due to technical malfunctions with her launch tubes) nor at any time fix a firm target near-in or on the far horizon. Truly perhaps damned if she did and damned if she didn't, the scrappy little DD—like each of the other American and Allied ships that night—was also "fixing for a fight" but could never quite find one, even as she continued to fire only blindly at the probing searchlights and hulking silhouettes that seemed to loom all around her. Here again, author and naval historian Bates makes his own observation:

At about 0154, the AOBA directed the fire of her port dual-purpose battery at the destroyer (HELM) standing to the southward. Not only did the shells all miss, but they must have missed badly, for the HELM was entirely unaware that she was being fired on.[125]

To this same discussion thread, yet another source found in Richard B. Frank's own comprehensive work, *Guadalcanal: The Definitive Account of the Landmark Battle*, provides us with the following insight into the battle status of the two DDs as they zigzagged across the area of concentrated battle:

> During the engagement, the U.S. destroyers *Helm* and *Wilson* struggled to see the Japanese ships. Both destroyers briefly fired at Mikawa's cruisers but caused no [apparent] damage, and received no damage to themselves.[126]

Later, even Loxton would have his say in his own widely acclaimed historical narrative, *The Shame of Savo: Anatomy of a Naval Disaster*:

> When *Chōkai* extinguished her lights at 0216, *Wilson* was already headed for the rendezvous point at a leisurely fifteen knots, passing south of Savo Island. She [the *Wilson*] would later arrive at about 0400 and eventually, at 0430, joined the [already onsite] *Helm*. Thus, at its end, both the *Helm* and the *Wilson* had been totally ineffective in the defense of the cruisers they were screening.[127]

Did the *Helm* in fact fail miserably in its assigned mission to ❶ effectively screen the American heavy cruisers that made up the bulk of the Northern screening force that night; ❷ safeguard the troop deployment and unload activities under way at both Honiara and X-Ray areas by screening those forces secondarily—especially in the wake of the attacks at Savo; and ❸ successfully locate, identify, and engage any attacking enemy ships as well? Perhaps she did in some manner fall short—if not fail altogether in her primary mission—or was the ship's only mandate that night that of reaching the destroyer rendezvous point behind Savo, only to await further deployment instructions from Crutchley? It is difficult to accept that the *Helm*'s hastened "run to the north" would have been entirely intentional, and as such was probably not the expected outcome for the ship—or even her mission at that time.

This aside, however, it would seem that in both later reviews of the 1BOSI and its tragic outcome—neither Crutchley nor Hepburn himself would have much to say of the negative or positive about either the *Helm* or the *Wilson*—or the role that either may (or may not) have played in the battle. Many ships that night would also not factor in the campaign, whether before, during, or even after the attack, truly calling to mind ships like Crutchley's own *Australia* and all four ships of RADM Norman Scott's Eastern screening force.[128] In and of itself, to simply not have been present in the battle would not have been the more weighted issue in this instance, but rather the actions and later disposition of those ships that were embroiled in the fight. Only the actions of Bode alone, on his errant northward-bound *Chicago*, would this night raise a greater degree of question and disquiet than those of the *Helm*, but hard questions would still be closely asked—questions for which viable answers must indeed be fairly sought out.

USS *Helm*: Still A Proud Legacy

From the time of its arrival in waters around Guadalcanal and the greater Solomons in March 1942, to the final naval campaigns that would be fought to win those very islands, the brave *Helm* had truly been there every step of the way. Performing in her usual close-support roles as both a screening ship and an escort for the larger warships she accompanied, the plucky DD would at long last "find its fight" much later, at places like Milne Bay, Australia, and New Britain, this throughout much of 1943.

By 1944, the *Helm* would again briefly return to the United States while escorting the damaged battleship USS *Maryland* (BB-46) to the Bremerton Navy Yard in Puget Sound, Washington State, for general overhaul, and to fully repair the gun liners of her scorched Turret 1. Having then seen the *Maryland* safely into port at Bremerton, *Helm* would soon have stops in San Francisco, Hawaii, and finally at Kwajalein, and she would soon indeed have all the fight she had wished for earlier—and more. The *Helm* would go on to serve well, with distinction and honor, throughout a frenzied year in which she saw taut and fevered action in places like the Marshall Islands, the Marianas, Palau, and even Formosa (modern-day Taiwan). Indeed, she would almost fearlessly go on to serve in numerous naval campaigns that would almost all center on the recapture of the Philippine Islands—and, much to her credit, would fight side by side with other warships during the Battle of the Sibuyan Sea, the Battle off Samar, Battle of Leyte Gulf, Battle of Surigao Strait, and—by late November of that year—the extended Battle of Lingayen Gulf itself.

In fact, for the battle-worn *Helm*, 1945 would clearly be among her finest of hours in her entire service history, as she would again find herself embroiled in actions that included (in that year alone) the Battle of the Sulu Sea, the assault on Iwo Jima, and preparing for amphibious operations just off the coast of Okinawa. From 19 February straight on through 7 March of that same year, the *Helm* would indeed stand fast and hold her ground against overwhelming odds and numerous suicide plane attacks, and would also serve a key role in the SAR efforts that took place after the untimely sinking of the American escort carrier USS *Bismarck Sea* (CVE-95). By August 1945, the *Helm*, the *Madison*, and the *Helm*'s old battle-mate from Savo Island itself, the *Ralph Talbot*, would converge one last time on 30 July in an all-out search for the hapless USS *Indianapolis* (CA-35) in the deadly waters just off the southern tip of the Philippine Sea. Allegedly reported at a last-known 12°02' N–134°48' E, *Indianapolis* was thought to have had a crew of 1,196; however, once torpedoed by the IJN submarine *I-58*, at least 300 were known to have been killed outright (or went down with the ship). Of the remaining 880 men thought to have survived the sinking, some 321 would indeed go on to survive the hypothermia and shark-infested waters of the area, yet only 314 would later in fact be rescued by the *Helm* and its SAR contingency that day.

After a brief stint in waters around Okinawa—and at Sasebo Bay in mainland Japan—the *Helm* was then routed back to Pearl Harbor and quietly decommissioned without ceremony on 26 June 1946. Sadly, the valiant ship's final disposition would be that of serving as part of a target array for the Operations Crossroads atomic bomb tests at Bikini Atoll in the Railik Island chain. Though only negligibly damaged in the resulting blast from the Baker test, both the USS *Helm* and her sister ship of old, the *Wilson*, would survive the underwater detonation that had been set some 90 feet down in waters known to be only 180 feet deep. With both ships deployed outside a 1,000-yard radial point from the area of the Baker test explosion itself, both *Helm* and *Wilson* would survive the blast from this second atomic bomb test, and would later even be "cleaned," purportedly to sanitize base surge contaminants deposited by the resulting radioactive fission products released by the bomb. Clearly, by the more exacting standards of today, it would have been highly doubtful (at best) that either ship would ever be totally free of all such contaminants, and neither ship would ever be serviceable again.

All such considerations aside, it would still be a now "patched-up" *Helm* that would soon join ranks with two other destroyers for their final journey home. Towed in array by a group of ATF-class fleet Ocean Tugs, the three retired DDs would now make their way home, silently and swiftly, back to the United States.

Seen above in perhaps one of the last known photographs[129] of arguably one of the most battle-worn and pugnacious of fighting ships within the entire American destroyer fleet during all of World War II, this image shows the *Helm* en route back to the United States in late 1947. She would by this time have already earned multiple campaign awards and served in virtually every naval campaign from Pearl Harbor to Guadalcanal—and from Okinawa to the very home islands of Japan itself at the very close of the war. Seen here at close quarters are three *Bagley*-class destroyers being towed from Pearl Harbor back to the West Coast for final decommissioning and scrapping.

The remnant hulk of one of the most aggressive fighting ships in all of the Pacific War would then be sold to the Moore Dry Dock Company in San Diego, California, and cannibalized for parts and metals before being destroyed shortly thereafter. From left to right, the three towed ships shown above are the USS *Craven* (DD-282), the USS *Bagley* (DD-386), and the dauntless *Helm* itself. Odd that even now on this final leg of their journey together, at least two of the ships (the *Helm* and *Bagley*) had already served side by side as screening elements for the very cruiser forces that had much earlier sailed (and been lost) at Iron Bottom Sound on that fateful night in August 1942. The two ships had come full circle, and, once again, were seemingly facing one last terrible fate together.

The plucky, spirited USS *Helm* would then (only too ignobly, it might seem) be sold for scrap in Oakland, California, on 2 October 1947, thus bringing to a close nearly a half decade of gallantry, dedication, and exemplary performance that, in and of itself, had always been above and beyond the call of duty in naval service.

For her gallant efforts and dogged determination to fight and endure virtually every campaign in which she fought, the *Helm* had now come full circle in her battle forays—from Pearl Harbor to Okinawa and beyond—and much to her good repute, she would receive an astounding eleven Battle Stars for her unflagging service during the years of 1941 all the way through 1945.

As for the good LCDR Chester Edward "Blackie" Carroll (known in close circles as simply "Chet"), the extant captain of the battle-scarred USS *Helm* at the time of the calamity at Savo Island, he would go on to have a long and good-fortuned naval career that eventually saw him assume command of the newly formed Destroyer Division 96 (DESDIV96), and by 1944 find him in fact leading an entire Task Unit into battle. That Task Unit, TU 94.3.9, would soon be assigned the devilish task of becoming the Bonin Islands Anchorage Occupation Unit, this even as the American carrier task forces themselves sought to close and knock at the very back door of Japan.

Carroll would command the operation from his new flagship, the old *Benham*-class destroyer *Wilson*, the same again of Savo fame. In effect, this meant that the commander had come full circle from *Helm* to *Wilson* in only a matter of years. And both ships had served as escorts at Savo on that one fateful night of 9 August in 1942.

Before his retirement in 1954 from active service, LCDR Carroll would have one final distinction when posted to a naval liaison position as a military advisor in Taiwan. Soon, however, after some thirty years of service to his country, to his men, and to the ships on which he served, Carroll would retire as a full rear admiral from the United States Navy. He would live on for many years to come and settle in the vicinity of San Diego, California, where he would pass away in June 1987 at the age of eighty-six. RADM Chester Edward Carroll was thereafter interred with his wife, Ruth Harriette Carroll, at a burial site overlooking East San Diego Bay at the prestigious Fort Rosecrans National Cemetery at Point Loma, San Diego.

To fully commend his good service and excellence in command, the United States Navy would award him both the Silver Star and the Bronze Star, this in fact after the United States Army would itself have awarded him a Victory Medal for his actions in both the army and the Washington National Guard during the final months of World War I. In this regard, with an array of awards that now spanned two World Wars, RADM Chester E. Carroll must indeed have been one of a very few cadre of officers who could make such an unchallenged claim.

As the skipper of the *Helm* on 9 August 1942, he may have been guilty of only minor missteps and miscalculations, but those same miscalculations had been deadly and had indeed come with some heavy and fatal consequences—namely, the loss of the three American cruisers at Savo. Carroll, on his flagship *Helm*, might have escaped by the skin of his teeth that night, and had indeed been favored enough to have his ship emerge unscathed, but in the years following he would further redeem himself and his perceived inactions that night. One can only imagine the lingering and evocative images of the debacle at Savo Island that must have haunted the man thereafter for the rest of his life.

USS *Helm*: References and Further Reading

For the reader interested in further researching the history and chronology of the USS *Helm* herself, or who wishes to see at least an abbreviated account of the naval career of LCDR Chester Edward "Blackie" Carroll, her captain at the time of the battle at Savo, the following reference websites are offered for collective review:

Opentopia account (USS *Helm*): http://encycl.opentopia.com/term/USS_Helm_(DD-388)
Opentopia account (USS *Astoria*): http://encycl.opentopia.com/term/USS_Astoria_(CA-34)
LTC David E. Quantock Report: http://www.ibiblio.org/hyperwar/USN/rep/Savo/Quantock/in dex.html#illus
Historical Animated Map: Attack on the Northern Fleet: http://www.historyanimated.com/Guadal canal_Savo_Island.html
Wikipedia account of the Battle of Savo Island, subsectioned as "Action North of Savo": http://en.wikipedia.org/wiki/Battle_of_Savo_Island#Action_north_of_Savo
LCDR Chester Edward "Blackie" Carroll (time in command of the *Fletcher*-class USS *Abbot* [DD-629]): http://abbot.us/DD629/captains/carroll.shtml

USS *Helm*: Video History and Chronology

Apparently not at all disposed to being camera shy, the USS *Helm* would be the subject of numerous short films and naval documentaries during the course of World War II, and indeed there appear to be no shortage of chronicling photographic evidence of the ship at various ports of call, as well as her many actions in the South Pacific. To further amplify the point, modern-day researchers may now easily go online and access a full series of unique (yet oddly colorized) vintage videos of the dashing USS *Helm*, which indeed honor her distinguished service career. The film clips themselves, though disputably numbered as shown, appear to be presented in a date-sequenced, five-part series, as noted here:

USS *Helm* Commemorative Video (Part 1 of 5): http://www.youtube.com/watch?v=wN0rdFxLJuM
USS *Helm* Commemorative Video (Part 2 of 5): http://www.youtube.com/watch?v=WHzj7U0ktRw
USS *Helm* Commemorative Video (Part 3 of 5): http://www.youtube.com/watch?v=g6nOSVhh71o
USS *Helm* Commemorative Video (Part 4 of 5): http://www.youtube.com/watch?v=iTn3cAU6R2A
USS *Helm* Commemorative Video (Part 5 of 5): http://www.youtube.com/watch?v=iTn3cAU6R2A

FINDING 18:   IN THE BLINK OF AN EYE—
THE STATE OF FLEET COMMUNICATIONS

Certainly, in a scenario in which the combined navies of three major powers were desperately attempting to unify their disparate forces and work together in now a "Pacific" theater of operations, it would be expected that there might indeed be some level of discord and disunity among those navies in the coordination of those joint activities that was still to be resolved among all of the groups involved. Clearly, one of the most crucial of elements that would be found missing among the men, and especially the commanders on all sides, would be that of a sound, intact, and fully uncompromised communications network. The events leading up to the First Battle of Savo Island would be fraught with miscues, miscommunications, delayed advisories, and even misrouted, "perishable" intel—all of which would go on to plague the Allies in their every endeavor and lay their ships open to the savaging attacks of the Imperial Japanese Navy's mighty surface fleet—and this seemingly time after time.

From the reporting SNAFUs brought on by the delinquent Australian RAAFR Hudson reconnaissance planes' own reports, early on the morning of 8 August, to the delayed report of the prowling American *S-38* attack sub that had itself been patrolling the waters south of St. George's Channel: all would at one time or another have seen the advancing Mikawa fleet, but would experience "technical difficulties" in routing that "hot and consumable" intelligence back to the naval commanders in the south, who were indeed those most in need of the information. Clearly, then, there must already have been an almost-observable breakdown in communications between the multi-force ships then operating in and around Sealark Lane, and some of those breakdowns would have the most fateful of outcomes for both the Allied ships and the men who sailed on them.

That indeed at least two of the major powers, Australia and the United States, had earlier fought side by side at the Battle of the Coral Sea would be somewhat advantageous, and it would have at the very least established an operational history between the two, since indeed elements of the joint-operation Task Force 44, led by the Australian RADM John Crace, had already brought together ships like the HMAS *Australia* and *Hobart* and paired them up with the likes of the USS *Chicago* and other American heavy cruisers of the line. Later, that same Allied Task Force would meet up with RADM Aubrey Fitch's own Task Force 11 and again set a clear precedent and history for collaboration between the two diverse navies. Therefore, with that shared history, it became clear that indeed they could (and must) work together to see their common task through to a successful conclusion—and to the mutual benefit of each— this, whatever the mission itself. But only too soon both sides would learn that, while the joint operations in play at Coral Sea (however complex and diffused) had been one thing, the Naval Battle of Guadalcanal was to be quite another.

The later collaborative operations of the three naval forces now patrolling the waters around Guadalcanal in mid-1942 would be quite the opposite of any of their previous co-opted endeavors, and would soon become overtaxed by individual operational issues, questionable and meanly exchanged intel, and a repeating series of deadly information routing disconnects. And key to this discussion would be the viability of overall fleet communications, in and of itself, such as it was at the time of the Battle of Savo Island. It would begin and end with how quickly—and how accurately—the word could get out if enemy ships or planes were ever seen. In its most risk-free form, that word could be as simple as a directive governing the unloading of ships or the deployment of troops; at its most crucial, it might be the one and only warning any of the ships would ever get before the actual moment of attack by the Japanese interloper.

Sketchy Data—Stale Intel: The Effect on Communications

By the time both the COMAMPHIBFORSOPACFLT (Turner) and the COM-SOPACFOR (Ghormley) finally did receive the full intel and details of the first A16-218 RAAFR Hudson reconnaissance sighting from the morning of 8 August 1942—that of an unknown naval force consisting of several large ships moving south through the Slot past Choiseul—it was already well past 1800 hours on the evening of 8 August. By the time the same two commanders received the second A16-185 overflight report—similarly noting a large Japanese naval element in the same vicinity and time frame—it was almost already beyond its point of usefulness, its point of final receipt now being closer to 2200 hours.

Therefore, the *first* report would indeed have been more than two hours late, the *second* a dreadful nine hours and forty-six minutes overdue, both now received only well *after* the time of both sightings. Yet both reports had one thing in common, and both undeniably spoke to the same point: bold Mikawa was once again on the prowl and approaching the Sound even at that very moment, with a combined force of heavy cruiser-class ships, most of which would probably be made up of his most powerful *Chōkai*, the *Aoba*, and *Tenryū*-class fighting ships. And later, although the intel would arrive in time, it would do so by little, and even then it did not agree at all with one of the other reports. The Allied commanders had once again been dished up only sketchy data and stale intel and would now be expected to mount a viable defense based on that very perishable data.

The ability of the three naval powers to effectively communicate with each other across all lines seemed to have been most hampered by command indecision, poor intelligence screening, and *insufferable* delays in the handling and processing of that intel—to include the endless "hold-and-review" stopover points that must have dotted that information chain up and down, like twisted links that would all too soon compromise the whole. That the high admiralty at Guadalcanal would not hear of the IJN surface fleet's approach to the Sound for some two to ten hours after their sighting was unthinkable. That the primary and probably most vulnerable targets of any such large enemy force would be nothing if not the prized Henderson Field itself and the well-guarded American troop transport and supply ships even then still offloading, was already clearly understood. That the subordinate commanders of the screening force itself, then cruising the waters of Iron Bottom Sound trying to shield those very cargo vessels, would know nothing of the IJN fleet's expected arrival until almost too late, was unforgivable—this due entirely to the number of lives lost, and the number of ships sunk due to the later receipt of that intel . . . and the confounding delays in getting it to those most in need of it.

Addressing this very communications issue in one of his later modules on *Battle Lessons*, naval historian Robert Bates would note the following in his own course of study titled *The Battle of Savo Island, August 9, 1942. Strategical and Tactical Analysis (Part I)*:

The communications system in the SOWESPAC [Southwest Pacific] area was so operated as to enable the direct flow of information from SOWESPAC aircraft, and from SOPAC [South Pacific] aircraft in flight to COMSOWESPAC area via the Headquarters, North Eastern Area at Townsville, and via the Headquarters, Allied Air Forces at Brisbane. The TF 63 common frequency (Net "C") was employed to obtain prompt reports from SOPAC aircraft in flight, but as employed in the north-eastern area it did not serve, in practice, to provide a direct flow of information from SOWESPAC aircraft to the officer in tactical command in that SOPAC Area. Such a communication arrangement would have been proper had the strategic responsibility for the operations of the Solomons lain with the COMSOWESPAC—with the supporting cooperation of the COMSOPAC area . . . Sadly, the two responsible and supporting roles would (in all actuality) be assigned in reverse order.[130]

All of which oddly might only add to an already circuitous and rambling communications network that grew even more ponderous with each passing day. Therefore, beginning with those very RAAFR sighting accounts themselves, the reporting venue for those Australian reconnaissance planes alone was already itself an incomprehensible, multi-tiered network of intelligence handling and processing, and later routing and re-routing tasks—all done on an "as deemed necessary" basis—and involving not just the Australian network but the American communication venue as well. Indeed, no wonder it might be so difficult to follow the "breadcrumb" trail of comm linkages and message routing:

About sundown, August 8, the vital information was finally sent to Townsville, which originated a dispatch to General MacArthur's headquarters at Brisbane. From that moment there was prompt action; "Radio Canberra" at 1817 put the contact report on "Bells," from which Admiral Crutchley got it at 1839; Canberra also sent it to Pearl Harbor, where it was placed on "Fox"; from which Admiral Turner got it at 1845. THUS, it took over eight hours to pass ultra-hot intelligence only 350 miles from a search plane to the Allied flagship.[131]

Should we not at all be surprised, then, that there might be a crippling delay in the sending of all those advisory messages? An almost identical report of the two RAAFR sightings was sent out over two networks almost simultaneously, the first of which would travel on its longest possible track from Townsville to Brisbane, to Canberra (the Australian city, not the ship), and thence to Crutchley, miles below in the Sound on his flagship *Australia*. The second transmission would be sent out only shortly thereafter, this time reporting the sighting data to intelligence sources way off in "Pearl Harbor" rather than directly to the commanders most closely on the ground at Guadalcanal or sailing the seas around that zone in support of those infantry operations.

Oddly, it would be Pearl Harbor (perhaps now more clearly understanding the import of the crucial intel they now had in hand) that would send out the secondary communiqué to Turner, who might otherwise have not found out, other than through a more roundabout flow that might have come through Crutchley. In either event, it was clear from the outset that two intelligence-reporting protocols were in play, as observed by both sides (the Australian and the American), and with each classically trusting more to its own network, however flawed, than to any other collaborative endeavor that might or might not work, involving more than one player. Could there have been resistance to the idea of a *combined* communications network . . . and how, indeed, might that network have functioned?

> The necessity for the maintenance of a reliable, rapid and secure communications network is vital and cannot be over-emphasized. Commanding Officers should real-ize that no more important duty exists than that of obtaining and delivering to the Officer in Tactical Command timely information of the enemy forces. Therefore, communications must be so organized as to ensure that vital information, positive or negative, such as contact reports, can get through with minimum possible delay.[132]

Did Bates have a particularly targeted, or more *privileged*, insight here than oth-ers? Did he in fact possess a clearer understanding of the importance of solid intel, its swift and proper handling, and its rapid movement on to its correct endpoint—more so than the very commanders themselves? Or was it effectively only 20/20 hindsight after all? Decidedly, few could have known more then, and only now may we at leisure fully critique the communication networks and methodologies of that time with full detachment, and the cool "embroidering" eye of hindsight.

What indeed might we have done differently, given a chance to relive those same dread events, had solid communications in fact played a more significant role? And how indeed might the timely receipt and exchange of information have changed the outcome of the battle? How might the American and Allied forces have been more empowered to offer up a more rousing victory for its own surface fleet over the Imperial Japanese Navy forces that night, instead of the crushing defeat that same force would later suffer at their very hands? The questions themselves seemed endless and the list itself ran long, with each question begging answer or simply demanding a sharp dismissal.

Slipping the Noose: Communication Missteps

Many of the most evident communication gaffes that would plague the combined Al-lied navies at Guadalcanal—and that would later be found to be even contributory to the surprise attacks on (and defeat of) the Allied cruiser forces at Savo Island on the night of 9 August 1942—might be viewed categorically in levels: ❶ that of intelligence information, or "perishable" intel being sent that was then either held or circuitously routed to its intended recipient, thus negating its very usefulness; and ❷ those of even the most basic operational orders that would not get communicated at all, as specifically noted in the lack of notification with both Crutchley and McCain. In fact, the mounting errors noted in the loosely linked Allied communications networks would soon put the ratio at a virtual 50/50 rating, in dead certainty, that the two most inhibiting factors for the operational forces under Crutchley's command were related to either intelligence SNAFUs and the nonreceipt of vital information in a timely manner—or those of a wholly operational nature. But clearly, even those communications slippages might extend far beyond even Crutchley, and would in fact have included all of the following as well:

Trickle, Trickle: Data Filtering and the Allied Information Hierarchy

Truly, it might be less than remarkable to even be able to determine what the average lifespan of a normal (or even a *flash emergency*) dispatch order might have been—even as it circled about through its various "processing channels" and "handling waypoints" up and down the chain of command to its final receiving endpoint. Could one even know for sure or in full with any certainty? Logically, most such command-level orders would have been grouped into lesser classifications, such as those of perhaps a logistical or operational nature, even as others might clearly involve more critical and time-sensitive intelligence data either gleaned from or provided by aerial sightings, outpost watchers (i.e., the "Coastwatchers"), and other field, sea, and air operatives. How long should it take, in fact, for information—once in the hands of those intelligence handlers—to find its way to an intended endpoint recipient without undue delay? Minutes—hours? And what indeed might have been considered as "acceptable"?

That all incoming raw intel data must first be vetted and "scrubbed" by the intake analysts themselves, and further assessed for relevance, validity, source, and content, is a given . . . but what might an accepted processing norm have been at Guadalcanal right before the attacks at Savo Island—this based solely on the frailty and imperfectness of the very system in place at that time? Might it not at all surprise us, then, that a single piece of intelligence of a large sighting of enemy ships a mere 350 miles up the Slot, from the current position of the Allied fleet in Guadalcanal, would take some ten hours to reach the ears of Turner and Crutchley? Indeed it might not, and here's probably why, as we observe a spider-webbed tangle of hierarchical commanders shown here in Table 22, each with their respective operational titles, and each with their own procedures for managing the critical data they might receive. Just *who*, after all, would decide *what* was important and what was not, and who would decide what went *where* and to which relevant commander?

Table 21. Allied Communications-Related Incidents during the 1BOSI (with Outcomes)

Communication Incident	Action	Status/Result
Removal of the CTF 61 carriers	ADM Frank Jack Fletcher, fearing that his Carrier Task Force (CTF-61) was far too exposed in the confined waters between Guadalcanal and Florida Island, withdraws that task force on the afternoon of 8 August 1942	Fletcher would do so without duly notifying all commanders of that action and would cause a trickle-down effect that would then cause Turner to pull out his own transport ships the next morning as well. **Result:** The Marines are left with only the supplies they had up to the point of halting the unloading operations and Turner pulling out his stream of supply ships. To the dismayed but stout-hearted men of the 1st Marine Division, the event would not soon be forgotten and would thereafter be known to both the men and to history as the "Great Navy Bugout."
USS S-38 sighting of Mikawa fleet	LCDR H. G. Munson reports sighting a large naval force near St. George's Channel, and further estimates that force to be *two destroyers and three larger ships of an unknown type*	Report sent by the lone American sub to its COMSUBDIV5 HQs in fact does occur in a timely manner but would later be stalled for an undetermined period of time by that sub base commander due to only a perceived "lack of real urgency." **Result:** The report is delayed some hours before being received and viewed by either Turner or Crutchley.
RAAFR Hudson A16-218 overflight ❶	Crew member Geddes sends a report to Milne Bay of *three cruisers, three destroyers, and two seaplane tenders or gunboats*	The sightings data are radioed to Fall River Air Base at Milne Bay; thence to Townsville, Brisbane, and Canberra—and only *then* to Crutchley on his flagship cruiser *Australia*. **Result:** The perishable sighting data are now stale to a point of no longer being relevant and over *two* hours late in their receipt.

RAAFR Hudson A16-185 overflight ❷	Crew member Williams refuses to break radio silence even after spotting *two heavy cruisers, two light cruisers, and one small unknown type ship*	Flight A16-185 does not immediately radio their report to Fall River and continues on. Only once completed with its full and normal patrol circuit does it finally return to base. Williams would later recall having "bickered with" his debriefing officer over the validity of the sighting. The data are again held for some indeterminate period of time before being passed on to Pearl as their next (illogical) recipient. Only then would Pearl finally route that Intel back to Turner at Guadalcanal. **Result:** The sighting Intel is stale, over *ten* hours late in receipt.
Coastwatcher ❶ (No sighting)	Bougainville-based British *Coastwatcher* Jack Read	No report of sighting on the night of 9 August; however, the overall reporting venue would in all events probably have been through "local assets" only, with no quick or official pass-through *of* that sighting info to commanders at Guadalcanal, save that of radio linkages.
Coastwatcher ❷ (No sighting)	Bougainville-based British *Coastwatcher* Paul Mason	No report of sighting on the night of 9 August; however, the method of dissemination and means of reporting were probably much the same as above.
Espiritu Santo B-17 overflight of fleet	CTF 63-assigned squadron of B-17s out of Espiritu Santo spot the Mikawa fleet near Kieta, and report in at 1215 hours on 8 August to advise their base of *four cruisers and a destroyer headed westward at 1231*	Sighting Intel is initially sent to air command elements at COMSOWESPAC, but would not reach Turner (as CTF 62) until much later, closer to 2400 hours. **Result:** The report is delayed by *some* hours before being received by either COMNAVAIRSOPAC (McCain), or his superior Turner.
McCain failure to conduct air searches	Turner requests that McCain conduct effective and far-reaching air searches of the Guadalcanal operations area, and north beyond Savo Island. McCain in fact does *not* carry out the order and later further compounds the error by failing to inform his commander that he had not done so	ADM Turner continues on with the deployment of his screening forces under the wrongful assumption that his ships would be operating under the "safe umbrella" of McCain's redeployed air assets. Sadly, this was not the case at all. **Result:** Turner and Crutchley proceed on with fleet asset placements and screening operations, falsely assured that air-lanes had been properly patrolled and fully swept and affirmed as being cleared.

(continued)

Table 21. *Continued*

Communication Incident	Action	Status/Result
Crutchley leaves the SSF for meeting	RADM Crutchley departs from the Allied SSF late on the night of 8 August and leaves Bode in command *pro tempore* of that force in his expected "short" absence to attend the Turner Conference	Crutchley does so with only cursory notice to Bode on *Chicago* and Getting on *Canberra*; and no notice at all to either the Northern or Eastern screening forces under the individual commands of RADMs Riefkohl and Scott. **Result:** The Northern screening force, under Riefkohl, have no idea that Crutchley has departed the area and removed one heavy cruiser asset from the defending forces then guarding *Iron Bottom Sound.* Little could they have known that they would later be asked to pick up the slack—and even that with little or no success.
Crutchley remains at X-Ray overnight	Crutchley, not wishing to navigate dangerous and unfamiliar waters by night, opts to *remain* at the X-Ray transport area near Turner's flagship *McCawley,* the site of the latter's late-evening conference	Not returning to his SSF and reassuming command was critical; Bode's mishandling of operations in his absence would later be found to be quite flawed and fatally miscalculated, and charges against the latter were indeed being contemplated. **Result:** The absence of Crutchley on *Australia* would play a key role in how much of a defense the Southern screening force could mount in the face of Mikawa's night attack at Savo. Being down one heavy cruiser (the *Australia*) with which to engage the enemy—and with *Chicago* damaged and *Canberra* fully savaged almost *in situ*—there was little the Southern screen could do to fend off the attack. As a result, many lives would be lost in the mêlée that would only later come to be known to history as the "Battle of the Five Sitting Ducks."

Table 22. Fleet Communications: Command and Reporting Hierarchy (USN, 1942)

FLEET COMMUNICATIONS: INFORMATION "FILTERING" HIERARCHY (1942)		
COMMAND LEVEL: ACRONYM TITLE	**COMMAND LEVEL: PERSONA**	**COMMAND LEVEL: IN FULL**
CINCUSPACFLT	FADM Chester William Nimitz ★★★★★	Commander in Chief, U.S. Pacific Ocean Fleet
CINCPOA		Commander in Chief, Pacific Ocean Areas
COMSOWESPACFOR	GEN Douglas MacArthur ★★★★★	Commander, Southwest Pacific Forces
COMSOWESPACOA		Commander, Southwest Pacific Operations Area
COMSOPACFOR	VADM Robert Lee Ghormley ★★★	Commander, South Pacific Forces
COMSOPACOA		Commander, South Pacific Operations Area
COMAMPHIBFORSOPAC	VADM Richmond Kelly Turner ★★★	Commander, Amphibious Forces South Pacific
COMTASKFOR61	VADM Frank Jack Fletcher ★★★	Commander, Task Force 61
COMPACFLTSTRIKEFOR		Commander, Pacific Fleet Striking Force
COMEXFOR		Commander, Expeditionary Forces
COMNAVAIRFORSOPAC	John Sidney ("Slew") McCain Sr. ★★	Commander, Naval Air Forces South Pacific Area
COM\PHIBFORSOPACFLT	RADM Victor Alexander Crutchley ★★	Commander, Amphibious Forces South Pacific Fleet

As a result, one thing would soon be abundantly clear: the (classic and often mutually exclusive) "right-hand, left-hand" arrangement that seemed to pass for Fleet Communications at the time of the battle at Savo was, at best, only marginally effective. The archaic and often heavily taxed networks then in use were already stretched too thin, and more than a little unworkable. Between the Australian and American ships at Guadalcanal, for instance, each communication network was simply too diffused and too decentralized, overtaxed, and operated with the grunt and lethargy of a cold and wintering bear. And each system would generally only be effective out to the shortest of ranges between ships, all of which seemed to further hamper the timely send-and-receive of data to those most in need of it. In 1942 and 1943, the communications options available for use between most such ships would have been limited to radio, TBS, encrypted coding sequences, semaphore flags, and signal lamp–based optical communication—and simple "old-school" methodologies such as the inter-fleet courier ship. A quick look at each might show us why each was important in its time, and how limiting each must have been in its scope and application.

Communications: Talk Between Ships (TBS) Networks

Talk Between Ships (or TBS) was the established radio network most used by American naval ships of the line during the early part of World War II and was commonly used to pass information "in the clear" and communicate over very short distances from ship to ship. Each American warship would have been tasked to use this TBS network for inter-fleet communications, and to dutifully maintain logs for most (if not all) of those key communications, with specific and dated entries made for major surface actions, if encountered. Those log entries would later then be set as an addendum to that ship's official action report. Therefore, a report emanating from RADM Crutchley after the Savo Island debacle itself could indeed have been included its own Report Addendum: TG 62.1/COMAMPHIBFORSOPAC TBS log entry for 09/08/42 in that same report, and which would certainly go on to include the "bad news" and full report of the two attacks themselves.

On this, the inquisitive and ambitious young author, Robert Jon Cox—whose great-uncle served in the USN in World War II on the *Casablanca*-class escort carrier USS *Gambier Bay* (CVE 73), during the heated Battle off Samar (BOSAMAR) in the Philippines in October 1944—would himself have these insights to lend us on the topic of TBS.[133]

" TBS transmissions were made using a standard encoded terminology for certain words. A few of the less obvious variants used in the log entries are shown in the table matrix below.[iv] "

CODE WORD ENTRY	INTERPRETATION		CODE WORD ENTRY	INTERPRETATION
Slingshot	Catapult launch aircraft		Fish	TBM or Torpedo
Pancake	Land-based aircraft		Chicken	FM-2

Figure 34.   Talk Between Ships Coding Variants and Meanings

Here again, it must be remembered that the code variant that Cox is citing here is only an example of what may at the time have been relevant to the Taffy 3 CVE operations force off Samar during that specific battle. The somewhat cryptic example he presents here is perhaps even more abstruse than the encrypted message format itself:

Demonstrated Use:
Great Danes v Taffy 3: "LOAD AVAILABLE FISH WITH TORPEDOES AND MAKE ATTACK ON THE ENEMY. OUT."

Interpreted as:
CTU 77.4.3 directs the CVEs to load TBM torpedo bombers with torpedoes.

Communications: Shackle-Unshackle Coding Sequences

Decidedly, this "shackle code" was itself initially set up simply as a low-tech and alphanumeric message encryption system that could be passed by voice by a radio operator over a standard TBS network between ships in convoy (or as otherwise formed up). And, since the very nature of these often-vulnerable TBS networks would entail passing information "in the clear," some level of encoding would have been demanded to both keep the IJN forces fully "in the dark" on Crutchley's screening force intentions, and to purposefully send disinformation tidbits to them, this with a clear intent to cautiously mislead the enemy with bad intel if at all possible. As a result, these *shackle* and *unshackle* codes would primarily be used to relay course and waypoint changes, as well as other messages that required a full (or even partial) use of numbers, such as when to initiate a timed event such as a coordinated course heading change, such that must be executed by an entire surface fleet at once.

In all such usage events, however, the elemental core data would always be held and bracketed within the shackle code itself, and generally displayed in a format that would contain the actual words *shackle* and *unshackle* in full, before and after the message body of text. This might best be exampled in the following code sequence—again offered by Cox in his "241201Z-251201Z" presentation—again, as it might actually have been used by the American warships that would have made up that TG 77.4 battle group at the time of the BOSAMAR:

Demonstrated Use:
Mercury 3 v Taffy 3: "SIGNAL EXECUTE UPON RECEIPT SHACKLE NAN GEORGE EASY UNSHACKLE TURN. FIDO ACKNOWLEDGE." . . . "FIDO, "WILCO, OUT."

Interpreted as:
CTU 77.4.3 directs the Task Unit to turn to new course 220° (T).

So, could these shackle-unshackle codes have been used within these Code-Talker coding sequences themselves?

Table 23.   BOSAMAR "Shackle-Unshackle" Code Sequencing Table (241201Z-251201Z)

BOSAMAR "Shackle-Unshackle" Code												
A	B	C	D	E	F	G	H	I	J	K	L	M
7	0	4	5	0	3	2	6	1	8	0	00	5
N	O	P	Q	R	S	T	U	V	W	X	Y	Z
2	6	4	7	5	9	00	9	1	8	00	1	3

A curious footnote to the author's continued research on the subject soon also uncovered a possible clear link between these same shackle-unshackle codes and those of the Navajo Code-Talkers of World War II. Forever immortalized in the 2002 MGM film *Windtalkers* (starring Nicholas Cage and a cast of many), it was perhaps a quite enthusiastic Hollywood that sought to finally honor these Native American Code-Talkers, who had themselves created a surprisingly simplistic code that would later become a marvel of cryptographic innovation. In fact, it would also go on to remain the *only* unbroken code in all of World War II—and throughout much of modern military history. This arcane and curiously unknowable code series did in fact, time and time again, simply confound the Japanese through virtually all of the later battles across the Pacific (and perhaps for the full duration of the war).

Using this code format, innate phonic sounds that were already native to the Navajo tongue were cleverly paired up with words and phrases that deliberately offered "double meanings" or that would have been couched in a shackle format. The code structure itself would soon become quite an enigma—one that never would lend itself to interpretation by the still-befuddled Japanese code warriors.

Oddly enough, according to at least the carefully archived website hosted by the well-honored U.S. Marine Corps–World War II Navajo Code-Talkers Association (USMCNCTA),[134] these codes would often incorporate the unlikeliest of phrases, many purposefully laced with double entendre-type meanings, like those shown in Table 24.

The very linguistics of the Navajo Code-Talkers would stand entirely on their own merit and native structure and, in combination with the shackle-unshackle patterns mentioned earlier, might cause only mild concern should a message in fact be sent in the clear—the Americans could now do so with near impunity and never fear any deciphering of that code or message. The theoretical data and formats examples shown in Figure 35

Table 24.   Code-Talker Coding Phraseology and Interpretations

Code-Talker Phrase	Primary (Actual) Translation	Military Interpretation
"Chay-da-gahi"	Tortoise	Tank (Armored)
"Gini"	Chicken Hawk	Dive Bomber
"Besh-lo"	Iron Fish	Submarine (any class)
"Lo-bec-ca"	Iron Knife (?)	Torpedo

> *Example¹:* **STANDING EAGLE** speaks: **SHACKLE** BESH-LO LO-BEC-CA **UNSHACKLE** might translate from its couched message format to "submarine launching torpedoes in area".
>
> *Example²:* **ELK SITTING** speaks: **SHACKLE** TKAL-KAH-O-NEL **UNSHACKLE** might translate to "convoy moving on water".
>
> *Example³:* **RED BEAR DANCING** speaks: **SHACKLE** DA-AH-HI-DZI-TSIO **UNSHACKLE** might connote a "battle of some scale".

Figure 35.   Navajo Code-Talker Coding Sequences (with Shackle-Unshackle)

might not be very different from the actual coding events themselves and, though not at all irregular to the men uttering the phrases, would have a far more profound effect on the clearly befuddled Japanese, who might at every turn attempt to intercept Allied message traffic, especially if sent in the clear. For the Americans, this no longer mattered.

Although not clearly substantiated, it is thought that some such coding sequences may have been exclusively used by those same Code-Talkers to communicate over long distances with other Native American recipients at other stations and that the Talkers would further "block" their code in a standard and expected shackle-unshackle format. In the robust intelligence arena, information relating to an enemy's current (or even last-known) position—its current movements, intent, and strength—might always be of keen interest to many in the Naval Intelligence groups, but the control and marshaling of our own outgoing message traffic would have been equally important. The best method found for encrypting sensitive data that needed to be protected and sent during this time frame must clearly have been this shackle-unshackle variant.

Fleet Communications: Conclusions

In conclusion, what might indeed be said of the combined operations between the Australian and American naval forces under the command of British Admiral Victor A. Crutchley? And what of the communication networks supporting both? Clearly, compared with the exacting benchmark standards we see in today's communications capabilities with our own present-day military forces, what the Allies had at their disposal at the time of the incident at Savo must have been wholly inadequate and only marginally a step above "two tin cans and a string." On this subject, LTC David E. Quantock of the U.S. Army War College, in his own celebrated narrative on the Battle of Savo Island,[135] had this observation to make regarding the tenuous Australian–American communications systems:

> For improbable reasons of security, the Royal Australian Navy avoided the very-short-range radios (TBS) used by the Americans. Communication between ships in the Northern group was no better. Their dependence on TBS so overloaded the circuits that the tactical voice radio became more or less useless, delaying or completely preventing the dispatch and receipt of critical signals. When the attack began, panic took hold and nothing (much) of importance got through (over the TBS).[136]

In fact, all of the RAN ships—the *Australia*, *Canberra*, and *Hobart*—would be piloted by RAN commanders (as indeed it might be expected), but the communication links between those ships, and those tied to the American contingent, were almost nonexistent and dangerously outdated to a fault. For alleged security reasons, none of the Australian cruisers assigned to work with either the Southern or the Eastern screening forces set by Crutchley would even use short-range radios, and basically communicated with other ships in the fleet through dispatch and courier, or silently with semaphore and signal flags, and through the clack and clatter of their own ship-to-ship shutter lamps.

FINDING 19:   "DEAD ON"—THE EFFICACY AND EFFECT OF THE JAPANESE NAVAL SALVOS DURING THE 1BOSI

Clearly, a few words must be said about the ferocity and deadly accuracy of the ships' gunners on the decks of the attacking Japanese Cruiser Division 6 and 18 (CRUDIV6 and 18) fleet that night. VADM Gunichi Mikawa began his approach to Savo Island in a single-line, column-ahead attack posture that was made up of his flagship, the *Chōkai*, and the other IJN heavy cruisers—along with Admiral Gotō's *Aoba*, the *Kako*, the *Kinugasa*, and several smaller surface ships—and as early as 0054 hours had already spotted the American radar picket ship, the destroyer USS *Blue*, some 5.5 miles ahead of the advancing Mikawa column. Shortly thereafter, even as the contingency of Japanese warships slipped stealthily through the picket defenses of both the *Blue* and the *Ralph Talbot*—virtually threading the eye of the needle—the gunners on each of the IJN ships reportedly had more than *fifty* guns trained on the *Blue* at all times as they passed her. Had she but twitched or given any indication that she had noted the presence of any of his ships, Mikawa would have had them open fire unmercifully, with full salvo brought to bear on her position, and simply blown her clean out of the water. One can only imagine that at that range, they could hardly have missed their mark.

The Japanese task force skimmed boldly past Savo Island and silently entered Iron Bottom Sound—as yet wholly undetected—and by 0125 Mikawa had already issued his inspiring order: "Every ship attack!" Minutes later, by 0138, the Japanese fleet had already commenced its ruthless and accelerated attack on Crutchley's Southern fleet. Of the eight known ships in the Mikawa surface fleet that night, no less than four of these attack ships would have already begun to engage the first of the Allied ships and concentrate their fire on the hapless Australian cruiser *Canberra*. She would be the first and one of the most savaged victims of the surprise night attack.

An exacting and highly concentrated fire, emanating from the combined firing of the large 8-inch guns on the heavy cruisers *Chōkai*, *Aoba*, *Tenryū*, and *Kako*—and the focused attack from many of the lesser ships' smaller 5-inch guns—would quickly take its toll on the Allied heavy cruisers. The die had been cast, and the *Canberra* would be first to suffer its terrible fate. Initially able to avoid the first of the incoming torpedoes fired from the Japanese ships, the *Canberra* would quickly find that she was no match for their large guns. Indeed, the first two salvos alone had already slammed into the bridge, disabled both engine rooms, crippled one of the ship's only remaining 4-inch gun platforms, and either wounded or killed outright some seventy-four crewmen, including many senior staff officers who had been standing on the bridge at the time of the attack. Within *two* minutes of the IJN ships' opening salvos, the *Canberra* had already been hit some twenty-four times.

Declining to engage any of the other ships, or to pursue the fleeing *Chicago*—by this hour well on its way on its unexplained forty-minute track to the northwest, with Bode at the helm—and unwilling to further prosecute its attack on any of the nearby escort destroyers, Mikawa's ships simply broke off the action and moved on. The good-fortuned Mikawa would even go on to inadvertently have his battle main split into a two-pronged assault column (page 156) and shortly stumble on the second target group in his seeming twin-axial assault on the Allied forces that night, that of RADM Riefkohl's own Northern screening group—namely, the USS *Vincennes*, the *Quincy*, and its sister ship, the *Astoria*. Once again, sadly, the die would have already been cast, and the Americans would indeed be on the side of the losing toss.

The attack by the Japanese on these three ships alone would be nothing if not swift and astonishingly accurate. The first volleys of shots would fall short of their mark by mere yards, exploding in the waters in and around the *Vincennes*, then the *Quincy*, and then the equally beleaguered *Astoria*. By the time the second and third salvos had begun landing around the first ship in the patrol column, the *Vincennes*, they were already bracketing either side of the ship, scoring incredibly direct hits that caused the great heavy cruiser to virtually shudder underfoot.

Even as the heavy armor-piercing rounds began to breach the plating surrounding the ship's turrets and hull, the first of the volleys would already have impacted almost every nerve center on the ship. Tables 25–27 will show a studied recap and summarization of damage sustained on each of the four Allied ships lost during the opening gambits of the 1BOSI and the range-enablement factors that made it so effectively possible.

Effect and Accuracy: Engagement Range Estimates and Initial Damage Assessments

It has already been noted that Admiral Mikawa's CRUDIV surface fleet were well able to prosecute their opening attack on the Allied force from a far greater distance than might have been anticipated by the Americans. And they were able to do so without detection—at least initially. At the range at which Mikawa's ships did open fire— again, with the full element of surprise on their side—it was almost a foregone conclusion that a successfully high kill ratio would be expected. If, after all, an attacking ship can plot its first series of torpedo launches at 13,000 yards without fully disclosing their own position, they may already have essentially won that battle de facto. Here are just some considerations in support of this theory, shown in Table 25.

Table 25. Ship-to-Ship Comparative Armament Assessments

Ship/Ship Type	Specifications/Armament	Comments
IJN Heavy Cruiser: Ship-to-Ship Comparative Armament Assessment		
IJN *Chōkai*	**Takao-class heavy cruiser** Commissioned: 1932 Displacement: 15,781 tons 10 × 8-inch (200 mm) guns 4 × 4.7-inch (120 mm) guns 8 × 24-inch tubes for *Type 93* torpedo 66+ × 25 mm anti-aircraft gun platforms	The *Chōkai* would serve as Mikawa's flagship and lead the charge into Iron Bottom Sound on the night in question in early August 1942. Clearly outgunning its near-counterpart American cruiser *Vincennes* with a measurable degree of greater firepower, the *Chōkai* also brought to bear its formidable array of *Type 93* Long-Lance torpedoes. Particularly lethal at both short- and long-range launching, the *Type 93s* were deployed quite effectively against Riefkohl's Northern screen during the 1BOSI.
American Heavy Cruiser: Ship-to-Ship Comparative Armament Assessment		
USS *Vincennes*	**New Orleans-class heavy cruiser** Commissioned: 1937 Displacement (Light): 9,850 tons Displacement (Standard): 10,000 tons 9 × 8-inch (200 mm) guns 8 × 5-inch (130 mm) guns 2 × 3-pounder (37 mm) guns 8 × .50 cal machine guns (@ 12.7 mm)	In great contrast, *Vincennes*—and most of her class—were considerably more lightly armed than their IJN counterparts. Several of the smaller escort ships, however—namely, the fast-attack destroyers *Bagley, Patterson, Helm,* and *Wilson*—would have somewhat offset this disparity with their unquestioned speed and multiple-launch, medium-range torpedoes. In and of itself, however, this still might not take into account the overwhelming superiority of the *Type 93s* being used by the Japanese, which could be fired from a *far greater* distance—and with *far greater* accuracy than the equivalent (and highly problematic) American *Mark 14s*.
Australian Heavy Cruiser: Ship-to-Ship Comparative Armament Assessment		
HMAS *Canberra*	**Kent sub-class heavy cruiser** Commissioned: 1928 Displacement: 9,400 tons 4 × 2 – 8-inch guns (4 Twin-turret units) 4 × 1 – 4-inch Anti-Aircraft guns 4 × 1 – 2-pounder quadruple *Pom-Poms* 4 × 1 – 3-pounder Saluting guns 12–16 .303-inch Machine guns 2 × 4 – 21-inch Torpedo tubes 4 × Multiple *Pom-Poms* (installed 1942) 5 × 1 – 20 mm *Oerlikon* guns	While still well armed, the *Canberra* might clearly be seen as perhaps having been the least equipped of all of the Allied heavy cruisers that would later engage the seven light and heavy cruisers that made up Mikawa's surface fleet on 9 August 1942. In theory, however, her more than sufficient array of small-caliber guns and torpedo tubes might otherwise offset her generally being outgunned by the significantly larger IJN ships that would have been stalking her that night.

Table 26. 1BOSI: Northern Screen Opening Salvos: Commence-Fire Engagement Range Estimates

TARGET ALLIED VESSEL	DISTANCE WHEN SIGHTED/FIRED UPON	ACCURACY AND EFFECT	COMMENTS
USS *Vincennes*	13,000 yards (*Chōkai*)	See known initial damage assessment reports presented in the Table 27 matrix.	Initial spread of four torpedoes fired from the *Chōkai*, also with shelling from her 8-inch main guns.
USS *Astoria*	❶ 7700 yards (*Chōkai*) ❷ 10,500 yards (*Kako*)		❶ Shelling from 8-inch main guns—*Chōkai* ❷ Shelling from 8-inch main guns—*Kako*
USS *Quincy*	±9,200 yards (*Aoba*) ±9,200 yards (*Furutaka*) ±9,200 yards (*Tenryū*)		Shelling from 8-inch main guns from the *Aoba*, *Furutaka*, and *Tenryū*. *Quincy* is also reportedly hit by two torpedoes fired initially from a nearby "undetected submarine" but more likely fired from the *Tenryū* itself.
HMAS *Canberra*	4,500–900 yards		Initial spread of four torpedoes fired from the *Chōkai*, also with shelling from the *Aoba*, *Furutaka*, *Kako*, *Kinugasa*, and the Mikawa flagship *Chōkai* itself.

Table 27. 1BOSI: Allied Heavy Cruisers: Initial Damage Assessments

		ALLIED HEAVY CRUISERS DAMAGE ASSESSMENTS
HEAVY CRUISER NAME	DATE OF ATTACK	SCENARIO AND DAMAGE ASSESSMENT
HMAS Canberra (D33/I33)	9 August 1942	The Australian heavy cruiser would be severely damaged by superior gunfire from the IJN surface fleet and *possible* hits from her own escort ships *Chicago* or *Bagley*. Other than the destroyer USS *Patterson* itself, the *Canberra* would be virtually the first ship fired on by the attacking Mikawa surface fleet. All of the following initial damage assessments would be noted:
		Immediate (In Situ) Damage Assessment
		• Salvos 1 and 2 claimed multiple casualties among many senior officers occupying the bridge, all killed as a result of the first volley. Sadly, this would even include the gunnery officer and Captain Getting himself.
		• Salvos 1 and 2, from both 5- and 8-inch main guns on Mikawa's ships, now disabled both engine rooms, ravaged at least one of the 4-inch gun platforms and flooded the magazine area of at least one 8-inch battery.
		• Within the first two minutes of engagement, the *Canberra* would have already been hit some twenty-four times, but only two of the nineteen torpedoes allegedly fired that night were ever recorded as having hit their target.
		• Sustained enemy fire from numerous incoming high-caliber shells razed the ship's boiler rooms and knocked out power to virtually the entire ship.
		• *Canberra* would suffer hits from a combined (20+) salvos fired from the large 8-inch guns of the *Chōkai, Furutaka, Aoba,* and the *Kako*.
		Canberra would glide to a slowed stop, well ablaze, and listing 5°–10° starboard. No longer able to combat the raging fires, and without the power resources to fully pump her flooded compartments, D33 simply went dead in the water.

(continued)

Table 27. Continued

ALLIED HEAVY CRUISERS DAMAGE ASSESSMENTS		
HEAVY CRUISER NAME	**DATE OF ATTACK**	**SCENARIO AND DAMAGE ASSESSMENT**
HMAS *Canberra* (D33/I33) (*continued*)		There was also a curious point of contention of a possible *friendly-fire* incident involving either the USS *Bagley* or Bode's own *Chicago*. At the time of the attack, *Canberra* had been sailing to the northwest with the rest of the Southern screen as Mikawa's ships approached. In short order, this position would invariably expose her *port* side to the enemy ships, yet most of the damage to her bow appeared to be on the *starboard* outside. Evidentiary damage assessments at the time seemed to indicate one of two "starboard-impact" theories:
		• Numerous incoming 5- and 8-inch projectiles fired from the large cruisers hit the *Canberra* just below the waterline. Entering low on the ship's *port* side, it is conceivable that the projectiles then completely punched through and exited the ship on its starboard side. Alternatively, the two starboard side impacts could instead have come from a spread of Long-Lance torpedoes launched from another of the IJN surface ships.
		• If, however, the most damaging impact was in fact from the starboard side, then perhaps it could have been from torpedoes known to have been fired from both the *Bagley* and the *Chicago* at about that same time. Consider the following:
		—The *Canberra* may have inadvertently been torpedoed to her starboard side by the USS *Bagley* (see the full topical discussion on page 183).
		—The *Chicago* may have inadvertently been torpedoed to her starboard side by the USS *Bagley* (see the full topical discussion on page 183).
		The Australian pride-of-fleet, *Canberra*, would later be sunk by tandem shellfire and a single torpedo launched from the American DDs *Ellet* and *Selfridge*, at about 0800 hours on the morning of 9 August 1942.
		The ship itself would suffer many casualties, a firm number of which would stand in controversy for many years to come and would alternately be cited in a range from seventy-four to eighty-four dead; however, still other sources have set this number as being perhaps as high as 193: http://www.navy.gov.au/w/index.php/HMAS_Canberra_%28%29.

USS Chicago (CA-29)	9 August 1942	The USS *Chicago* would be the *second* heavy cruiser screening ship in column on the night of 9 August, directly behind Riefkohl's *Vincennes*—and only *after* the untimely departure of ADM Crutchley on *Australia* to attend ADM Turner's hastily convened conference aboard the armed transport ship *McCawley*.
		By 0143 that night, Mikawa had already deployed his ships—probably at 1,000-yard intervals—and ordered that illuminants be fired. Thus, both the aerial flares dropped from the cruiser floatplanes, and those fired from the ships' large 5-inch guns, would soon light up the night sky and surrounding environs, truly affording not a patch of darkness within which to hide.
		At the time of the attack, she would also have been flanked by the two American fast-attack destroyers, the *Patterson* and the *Bagley*. Indeed, it would be the *Patterson* that would first spot the suspected enemy activity, even as Mikawa's CRUDIV force circled stealthily around dark Savo Island. Caught fully by surprise—and now illuminated by the Japanese flares themselves—the *Chicago* would fairly immediately come under attack right after *Canberra* and would be pounded by the large-caliber shells fired from the 8-inch guns of the IJN heavy cruisers *Chōkai*, the *Kinugasa*, *Aoba*, and the *Kako*. It would be this latter cruiser, the *Kako*, that would fire a two-torpedo spread at *Chicago*, though impacting only with her first shot. It would be sufficient to cause the *Chicago* to fully retire from the battle—and indeed she would play no further role in the brief night action that made up the First Battle of Savo Island.
		Of curious note, however, is the later disposition of the captain of that cruiser, one Howard Douglas "Ping" Bode, who apparently without forenotice or other declaration of intent, summarily took off for some forty minutes on a last-known track far to the north and west, allegedly in pursuit of a *phantom* contact suspected of being a Japanese destroyer. Bode would later be severely censured for both his actions and *inactions* on the night in question, and—in the face of *certain* rebuke and possible charges being brought against him—he would take his own life with a single gunshot wound to the head.
		As for *Chicago* herself, she would indeed survive the action (and indignity) of Savo Island and would be fully repaired and quickly redeployed, only to become yet another sad casualty at sea during the later hotly contested Battle of Rennell Island in January of 1943.

(continued)

Table 27. Continued

		Allied Heavy Cruisers Damage Assessments	
Heavy Cruiser Name	Date of Attack	Scenario and Damage Assessment	
USS *Vincennes* (CA-44)	9 August 1942	On the *Vincennes*, the first salvo would already be one of the most deadly, serving only as the herald of many more high-caliber shells to come, quite a few of which impacted directly on the bridge of the ship. Commencing at about 0155 hours—immediately after being lit up by the enemy searchlights—the 8-inch guns from Mikawa's heavy cruisers had already found their mark and converged all fire directly on Riefkohl's flagship, *Vincennes*.

Immediate (In Situ) Damage Assessment

· Sky aft and sky forward areas both hit, with the after director completely blown overboard.
· All fire main risers critically ruptured.
· Fires in cane fender, ship's movie locker, and searchlight platforms.
· Number one fireroom out of action from single torpedo hit fired from a possible contact thought by turret gunners on *Vincennes* to have been an "enemy submarine."
· Left-side range-finder hoods on both turrets 1 and 2 struck and put out of commission.
· Numerous hits during the early part of the action takes most guns from secondary battery offline as well.
· Turret 2 struck on faceplate by 8-inch projectile penetrating the turret area without explosion, but later set the exposed and concentrated powder on fire.
· Turret 1 barbette hit on starboard side jamming turret in train, resulting in the loss of the battery.
· By 0211 hours, all turrets and secondary battery—with the sole exceptions of turret 3 and gun number 1—are placed out of action with fully all power lost.
· RADM Riefkohl's final order to abandon ship is about to be given, when the enemy searchlights were almost as abruptly doused; all firing ceased; and Mikawa's warships simply disengaged their attack and began moving away. Then, indeed, as if reeling from her wounds, the *Magnificent Vincennes* would begin to list severely to port and go down in the turbulent waters off volcanic Savo Island

The *Maggie V* would suffer an inconceivable eighty-five impact hits—truly the worst of all the heavy cruisers that night—then cripple roughly off in a westerly direction. Shortly thereafter, the great ship would roll and sink by the bow at about 0250 hours on the morning of 9 August 1942. She would go down some 2½ miles due east of Savo Island in an estimated 500 fathoms (3,000 feet) of water. With her to her watery grave, the *Vincennes* would sadly take with her some 332 shipmates. | |

USS *Quincy* (CA-39)	9 August 1942	According to the Navy Department's Bureau of Ships report,[137] dated 2 September 1943, "enemy searchlights were trained the *Quincy* from abaft her port beam" as early as 0155, even as her main batteries trained out and commenced firing on the approaching ships. The *Mighty Q* would sustain the following damage, as reported by the senior surviving officer of the ship:

Immediate (In Situ) Damage Assessment

- Main deck gun mounts aft reportedly struck by first salvo alone.
- Subsequently, at least two additional nine-gun salvos are fired on the *Quincy*.
- *Quincy* takes immediate evasive action, turning abruptly to starboard and perilously (almost foolishly) bringing her stern directly through the enemy's line of fire. While *in* this swing maneuver, *Quincy* is hit fore and aft by both small- and large-caliber shells, all of which began igniting primary and secondary fires in planes tethered down on the hangar deck.
- The bridge of the *Quincy* is hit by both secondary and tertiary salvos;
- The clipping room in the foremast, Battle II and Turret 3 are now also hit—presumably by a grouping of 8-inch armor-piercing projectiles fired from yet another six-gun salvo from Mikawa's heavy cruisers.
- Turret 3 jams in train, requiring that turrets 1 and 2 now promptly be trained out to starboard to compensate, and rapidly brought to bear to engage the attacking enemy.
- While maneuvering into another evasive turn, *Quincy* is struck on the port side by two torpedoes (again curiously reported as having been fired from a "submarine contact" in the area), each of which impacted firerooms 3 and 4, and the IC room at frame 45.
- Director I is now jammed in train, its forestay blown off, which would further damage the nearby radar antenna.
- *Quincy's* bridge is hit one final time, killing outright most of the sailors on deck at that time. Sadly—and perhaps well by design—this would even include the ship's commanding officer, Captain Samuel Nobre Moore.

Quincy would suffer a punishing thirty-six impact hits all told and would perish with almost a full complement of crewmen, such that numbered (with mild controversy) from 370 to 389 men lost in total.

(continued)

Table 27. *Continued*

HEAVY CRUISER NAME	DATE OF ATTACK	SCENARIO AND DAMAGE ASSESSMENT
USS Astoria (CA-34)	9 August 1942	By 0138 hours on 9 August, Mikawa's ships had already begun to launch their attack on the Northern screening group. Multiple Long-Lance torpedoes splashed into the water and knifed their way toward the target ships. The *Astoria* would be the last of the three heavy cruisers to be hit that night but would oddly be the only ship not sunk immediately *in situ*. She would indeed survive the night and only scuttled and sunk the next day at 1216 hours. The first series of opening salvos to be fired by the attacking Japanese warships were used to only find and set a range out to the Allied ships, which, when once obtained, allowed them to unleash the full fury of their later attack. **Immediate (In Situ) Damage Assessment** • At 0156 hours, yet a fourth salvo of large shells landed near the bow of *Astoria*. • A fifth salvo onslaught of 8-inch shells would pass completely through the paint locker areas, igniting small fires in that storage area. • Yet another salvo hits the cruiser full amidships setting several launch craft on the boat deck on fire, and several planes lashed to the ship's hangar deck. • Service ammunition by gun turret 8 is also hit, destroying the gunnery mount and engulfing the area in flames, which would itself result in that loss of the battery. • Salvo number six was perhaps deadliest volley of all, the most critical of impacts thereof being on the faceplate and barbette near turret 1—putting that service battery entirely out of action and claiming the lives of the battery crew that had been manning the station as well. Clearly from a period of time from 0200 to 0206 hours on the morning of 9 August 1942, the *Astoria* remained under heavy attack, with significant and severe actions brought to bear upon her from Mikawa's attacking ships. *Astoria* would suffer a staggering 65–70 impact hits from a combination of torpedoes launched and the highly successful night gunnery tactics involved. The great American ship would list some 10°–15° before its slow roll to port and then began to settle by the stern, capsize, and disappear completely by 1216 hours on the afternoon of 9 August 1942. At the time of her loss, the dauntless *Nasty Asty* would have taken with her some 216 (perhaps as many as 268) men who were still onboard at the time of her sinking. She would be no more, her proud service now fully spent.

Effect and Accuracy: Conclusions

Making Every Shot Count

The brilliant career naval officer, Admiral Arthur Japy Hepburn (chairman of the General Board of the Navy, erstwhile director of Naval Intelligence, and chief of staff for the entire American battle fleet for a period of time from 1927 to 1930—and indeed the very man who would later sit in harsh judgment of CAPT Howard Douglas Bode's actions after the enigmatic *Chicago* incident during the battle at Savo) was once reported as himself having made the following astute observation regarding general fire superiority and first-contact engagement effectiveness:

> It has long been recognized that lightly-armored ships of any type not designed for "corresponding protection" can only exert the designed offensive power before they have received substantial damage. [In cause-and-effect, therefore] it means that all things being equal, victory rides with the first effective salvo.

And so it would be that night—at least for the Japanese—and at least so on the night of 9 August 1942.

Indeed, the good Admiral Mikawa had done little wrong—and much had gone right—during the course of his attack on the Allied surface fleet in Iron Bottom Sound. Not only had his own flagship *Chōkai* performed brilliantly in its own combat endeavors, but the other heavy cruisers under his command had done so as well—namely, the *Aoba*, *Kako*, *Tenryū*, and *Kinugasa*—each performing admirably and with precision in their surprise attack on both Crutchley's Southern and Northern screening forces that night.

And so just how proud must he have felt for at least those moments, as clearly Mikawa might indeed have had good cause to celebrate his decisive twin victories that night? Might he not have indulged himself enough perhaps to glory in his exploits, content in the knowledge that he had clearly demonstrated (yet one more time) the assured advantages and overall effectiveness of naval night fighting? And, as a staunch advocate of such practices, would he not have also shown that the ultimate success of any such night engagement might always guarantee still other victories like those seen that night, if carried out fully, with a good element of surprise, a commanding exactitude, and impeccable timing—all qualities that could easily be brought to fruition by only the most cunning and exceptional of the IJN naval commanders? And might he not have meant no one else *if* not himself?

So, did the big guns of the Imperial Japanese naval fleet in fact simply outmatch those of the Allied surface force that night? Or, as evidenced on numerous other occasions, was it all simply a matter of great fortune and a good element of surprise? Decidedly to the first point, it might only too quickly be resolved that both naval forces were probably not on equal footing—at least not in a true ship-to-ship ratio—or in terms of ship type and armament—clearly with the scales tipping in many instances far more in favor of the Japanese than the Allies.

At the time of the attack at Savo Island, the Japanese task group that night would only consist of seven heavy cruisers and one escort destroyer, the latter ship added only as an afterthought at the very last minute by a somewhat dubious VADM Mikawa. In mild contrast, the Allied surface fleet—itself only "newly arrived" to the hotly contested waters surrounding Guadalcanal—easily equaled this number as well, and then some. So what, then, would make the difference? Decidedly, a single torpedo type . . . the IJN *Type 93*.

Launch of the IJN Long Lance

Can it in fact be argued that the American warships were simply outgunned and out-maneuvered on the night of 9 August 1942 during at least the opening salvos of the 1BOSI? Maybe. Would they have been so in any engagement with the IJN up to that point in time? Perhaps, but not for long. And did the IJN surface fleet in fact have a higher degree of fire supremacy already factored in due simply to the overwhelming number of guns that could be brought to bear in the battle? Probably. Clearly, then, in addition to the considerable number of large 5-inch and 8-inch guns carried by Mikawa's heavy cruisers, the IJN naval force would have yet another trick up its sleeve. That "trick" would be none other than the dreaded *Type 93* Long-Lance torpedo. And for the greater part of 1942, this factor alone would itself threaten to greatly tip the scales in favor of the Japanese, as all too soon the foredoomed Allied surface fleet that night would soon discover.

An Inside View: The *Type 93* Long Lance versus *Mark 14* Torpedo

Without question, the profound disparity between the Japanese *Type 93* Long-Lance torpedo, and the less-equivalent American *Mark 14*, would make all the difference in at least the early part of the Pacific war. What this now meant is that it essentially all came down to range, speed, stealth, and ultimate accuracy . . . in other words, a truly reliable weapon, and indeed the *Type 93* brought all of that directly to the combat arena.

Figure 36. Japanese *Type 93* Long-Lance Torpedo
❶ From Wikipedia at http://en.wikipedia.org/wiki/Type_93_torpedo (Actual)
❷ From Fleeting Guns website at http://www.fleetingguns.blogspot.com/ (Conceptual)

Table 28. *Type 93* versus *Mark 14* Torpedoes:
Comparative Technical Specifications

TORPEDO TYPE	TECHNICAL SPECIFICATIONS
Imperial Japanese Navy (IJN)—Type 93	
Weight:	2.8 tons
Length:	9 meters
Range (Effective):	22,000 meters (@ 48–50 knots)
Range (Maximum):	40,400 meters (@ 34–36 knots)
Speed:	52 knots (96 km/h)
Warhead Type and Weight:	490 kg High Explosive
Weapon Variants:	*Type 95, Type 97*
United States Navy (USN)—Mark 14	
Weight:	3,280 lbs.
Length:	6.25 meters (20' 6")
Range (Effective 4500):	4,500 yards (4.1 km) (@ 46 knots)
Range (Effective 9000):	9,600 yards (8.2 km) (@ 31 knots)
Speed:	46 knots (85 km/h)
Warhead Type and Weight:	292 kg (643 lbs.)—*Torpex* magnetic pistol
Weapon Variants:	*Mark 15, Mark 16*

Far and away, the clear advantage of being able to engage an enemy's surface fleet at an optimum distance—prior to detection by that fleet—could only work to the furtherance of the attacker's ultimate goal of not just the surprise attack itself but also a solid assurance of a higher first-kill ratio. And the Allied force saw precisely that at Savo Island on the night of that first encounter. Perhaps here's one reason why, as we see in this comparative side-by-side view in Table 28 of both launch weapons and their overall capabilities.

Mark 14: A Flawed Performance and a Dangerous Failure

For some years—even well after the American *Mark 14*'s initial development in the early 1930s—it was already becoming quite the buzz within both the industry sector and the military that it might indeed be problematic and "riddled with untenable programmatic glitches." In other words, the weapons just didn't work. And much to our collective national embarrassment, certain new and gloomy catchphrases such as "plagued with problems," "dangerous duds," and "shaking hands with St. Peter" were already being bandied about on more than one occasion (and probably with good cause).

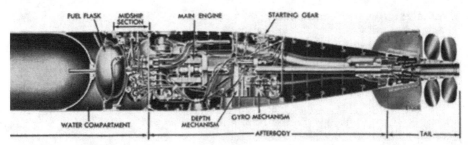

Figure 37.   Cross-Section View of Torpedo *Mark 14* Type (with Interior Mechanisms)
(Cited from *Department of the Navy, BOP-635, Torpedoes: Mark 14 and 23 Types*, page 11.)

Stemming from as far back as December 1941, suspicions had already begun to surface regarding the effectiveness and accuracy of the new "sub-keel" exploding weapon known as the *Mark 14*. In fact, many commanders of the early-stage *SS*-class submarine groups[138] that were already using this type of torpedo were themselves beginning to report any number of frustrating issues when trying to deploy those weapons. And preeminent among those findings would be the concerned reports coming back from those submariners, in several such live-fire scenarios, that had to experience many of these problems first-hand, and this very often in the heat of battle, precisely when most needed. Of note, as presented here in Table 29, is a high-level view of only some of the "found" issues and more pivotal problems with that American *Mark 14* torpedo.

Table 29.   *Mark 14* Torpedo: Noted Deployment Deficiencies

OPERATIONAL FLAW	DESCRIPTION
RUNNING TOO DEEP	The *Mark 14* torpedo was reported as having a tendency to run about ten feet "deeper" than its initial (or desired) setting. This might wholly compromise a valid plotting solution for the firing ship and be most problematic if the track went too deep, causing the weapon to simply *pass under* the keel of the target ship without full impact (or often any impact at all).
	Not surprisingly, this problem would not be as quickly noted by the American destroyer crews as it would be by the submariners, whose primary weapon was, by default, that very *Mark 14*.
PREMATURE DETONATION	The *Mark 14*'s magnetic influence exploder—a mechanism set to correctly trigger the weapon—often malfunctioned, causing a "premature" detonation of the torpedo, yielding little or no effect on the target ship itself. As such, and again much to the detriment of the firing ship, this would only serve to alert the target ship that they were in fact being fired upon and severely compromise the very element of surprise the attacking ship in fact might so adamantly wish to maintain.

OPERATIONAL FLAW	DESCRIPTION
FAILURE TO DETONATE	The *Mark 14*'s contact exploder—designed to set in motion both the arming and triggering of the torpedo itself—were also continuing to malfunction as well. Reported torpedo actions on numerous occasions were often hailed as being essentially "dud" hits, heard often as a mere dull *clang* when impacting the target ship itself. To the amazement of the commanders on the ships firing, the *Mark 14*s, the torpedoes would simply strike their targets and either glance off in full or simply lodge themselves in the ship's hull without detonating at all.
	Aside from the ever-present fear of the "loop-back circulars," this was probably one of the most preeminent *Mark 14* problems of its time.
"LOOP-BACK CIRCULARS"	Truly a worst-case scenario for any warship using the *Mark 14*, this problem had to be perhaps the most significant for all of the early submarine force commanders operating in the Pacific. In such a scenario, the *Mark 14* would run true only for a short period of time and then erratically circle back on the firing vessel itself, however erroneously, as evidenced in the very sinking of the *Gato*-class submarine USS *Tulibee* (SS-284) that occurred near Palau on 26 March 1944.
	On at least that one occasion, responding to numerous radar contacts detected by the sub, the *Tulibee* reportedly fired two *Mark 14*s at an intended surface contact, missed with *both* shots, then shortly had at least one of the torpedoes falter in track, then arc and run a circular course back, ultimately impacting upon the firing ship itself.
	In form and effect, this would essentially mean that the *Tulibee* had sunk herself, though indeed such would not be known until much later—well after the close of World War II. Worth noting, however, is the fact that by the time the next-generation *Mark 15*s were deployed, large metal "retaining collars" had already been added to the torpedo body to prevent just such a circumnavigational hazard from happening again. Once installed, the new *Mark 15*s seldom malfunctioned after such a correcting fix.

So, was the famed *Type 93*, in fact, simply a notch above our *Mark 14*? Perhaps. Even with all other factors being equal, the astounding successes that would mark the use of the Imperial Japanese Navy's formidable, long-range, and deadly accurate *Type 93* torpedo could only be termed remarkable and would tragically come at an extremely high price to the Americans. Shown in Table 30 is a minor summarization

Table 30. Successes and Effectiveness: *Type 93* Long-Lance Torpedo

EFFECTIVENESS AND SUCCESSES OF THE TYPE 93 "LONG-LANCE" TORPEDO		
DURING THE BATTLE OF SAVO ISLAND (9 AUGUST 1942)		
Sunk by *Type 93* Long-Lance firings (and combined volleys/launches) from the IJN heavy cruisers *Chōkai, Aoba, Kako, Kinugasa,* and *Furutaka*:		
USS *Quincy* (CA-39)	American heavy cruiser	*Sunk,* 9 August 1942
USS *Vincennes* (CA-44)	American heavy cruiser	*Sunk,* 9 August 1942
USS *Astoria* (CA-34), and	American heavy cruiser	*Sunk,* 9 August 1942
HMAS *Canberra* (D33)	Australian heavy cruiser	*Sunk,* 9 August 1942
DURING THE OTHER SIX BATTLES OF THE SOLOMONS TASSAFARONGA (1942–1943)		
Sunk by *Type 93* primary and combined launches from IJN heavy cruisers and destroyers:		
USS *Blue* (DD-387)	Destroyer	Sunk on 22 August 1942 by IJN destroyer *Kawakaze*
USS *Hornet* (CV-8)	Carrier	Sunk on 26 Oct 1942 by IJN destroyers *Akigumo* and *Makigumo*
USS *Atlanta* (CL-51)	Light Cruiser	Sunk on 13 November 1942 by IJN destroyer *Akatsuki*
USS *Barton* (DD-599)	Destroyer	Sunk on 13 November 1942 by multiple IJN destroyers
USS *Laffey* (DD-459)	Destroyer	Sunk on 13 November 1942 by multiple IJN destroyers
USS *Walke* (DD-416)	Destroyer	Sunk on 14 November 1942 by IJN destroyers, including *Ayanami*
USS *Benham* (DD-397)	Destroyer	Scuttled by USS *Gwin* on 14 November 1942 after attack by multiple IJN destroyers
USS *Northampton* (CA-26)	Cruiser	Sunk on 30 November 1942 by IJN destroyer *Oyashio*
USS *Helena* (CL-50)	Light Cruiser	Sunk on 5 July 1943 by IJN destroyers *Suzukaze* and *Tanikaze*
USS *Gwin* (DD-433)	Destroyer	Sunk on 12 July 1943 by (unspecified) IJN destroyer
USS *Chevalier* (DD-451)	Destroyer	Sunk on 6 October 1943 by IJN destroyer *Yugumo*
USS *Cooper* (DD-695)	Destroyer	Sunk on 3 December 1944 (probably by IJN destroyer *Take*)

of only some of the many successfully targeted Long-Lance torpedo hits, as seen from the Japanese standpoint. It represents a very specific window of time and accounts for only those *93*s fired from the IJN surface ships, *not* those deployed (with even greater accuracy and success) by its more clandestine submarine fleet.

It would take an additional twenty-one months of accelerated catch-up development work for the United States to achieve a level of parity with its counterpart IJN torpedo technology and development. Noticeable improvements would, however, immediately be seen in the new *Mark 15*'s guidance and propulsion systems, particularly in its arming and detonation control mechanisms. Later, a series of trial-run successes came about as a result of adding some new pin blocks and electric switches installed to control inertial force fluctuation to set proper depth restrictions. In less than a year's time, American engineers had thankfully (and quite fortuitously) resolved at least three of the four primal defects found to be affecting the American ships' ability to use the *Mark 14* when attempting to engage enemy surface ships. Now, finally, serious solutions to serious problems that had so plagued the *Mark 14* seemed to be well at hand, and this moment would clearly mark yet another turning point in the war. Much would change for the Americans by that time—luckily, much of it to their advantage.

But in mid- to late 1942, however—in theory and practical application—this would not be the case, or at least not in this one critical battle or at this one critical moment. The IJN's ability to develop and successfully deploy an effective, long-range, and dead-on torpedo would truly have placed them at the top of the food chain, in that instance—and for that time only. Their unquestioned ability to wreak havoc on enemy shipping nearly at will when combined with their famed "night attack strategies," could easily be pointed up in the number of Allied capital ship losses in just the opening salvos of the First Battle of Savo Island alone. A combination of both the Long-Lance torpedoes, and the highly accurate fire from both the 5-inch and 8-inch guns of the IJN heavy cruisers, would combine this night and ring a muted death knell for the four Allied heavy cruisers.

The battle would be over almost as quickly as it had been joined. In full duration it would in fact last only thirty-one minutes.

FINDING 20:   TRAINED LOOKOUTS AND OPTICAL AIDS

The ability to see at greater distances at sea—and to clearly discern an enemy's fleet well before their own detection—would clearly have been an excellent tactical advantage that might have been more favorably enjoyed by the Japanese than the Americans. During at least the opening salvos of the First Battle of Savo Island, this would be a clear advantage that would only too nicely play into the hands of the Imperial Japanese Navy. Equipped with their new 20 cm stanchion-based, bracket-mounted binoculars—and handheld equivalents—it would indeed be this corps of alert lookouts on Mikawa's own flagship *Chōkai* that would first note the presence of enemy ships on the night of 9 August 1942. Those first ships, of course, would be the USS *Blue* and the *Ralph Talbot*.

The duties of the lookout were simple and twofold: sight and report, but it was also well understood that it must always be the full charge of the "lookout" to perform no less than the following as well: ❶ conduct surveillance operations of all surrounding waterways; ❷ remain on the alert for obstructions and other unexpected navigational hazards; ❸ note and observe other passing ships (whether friend or foe); and finally ❹ note and report any identifying land masses that might help the ship posit a fix on a specific location, at a specific time, if needed.

Far and away, however, the lookout's most critical job would always have been that of "spotting, identifying and reporting contacts." Trained lookouts, like those on Mikawa's heavy cruisers that night, were quickly able to provide all such crucial information to the ships' commanders, such that could then readily be used by those captains to optimize and fine-tune their attack strategies. Such key information as bearing of the object, direction of the object, calculated target and position angles out to the object, and even first-sight estimates as to what type of ship that contact might appear to be could only have proved invaluable to the naval commanders of Mikawa's attack force, as inevitably they prepared to spring their trap on the "interloping" Allied forces.

All such considerations set aside, however, it could still clearly be said that these men were not ordinary lookouts, nor were they ordinary seamen. Consider the following insight from Loxton's own discussion of the near-privileged class status these men seemed to have enjoyed aboard many of the Japanese warships:

> They developed optical equipment, notably binoculars with 20 cm lenses, and selected personnel to use them. These men, as Petty Officers, then became "Masters of the Lookout." They trained day and night and developed the ability to accurately estimate range. No comparable specialist group existed in the British or American navies.[139]

Here, on smaller ships like the fast IJN DDs, there might typically be a series of three lookouts posted, with two set forward and one positioned aft. Each in turn would have had a sweeping observation vector that would have been set and assigned—for the starboard forward at 225°–045°, the port forward at 315°–135°, and the aft forward at 90°–270°, thus creating an almost full 360° arc surveillance radius around them at all times. "Overlap" was obviously the order of the day and was already well factored into the reconnaissance equation, so that if one lookout failed to detect an approaching enemy, the other would catch it.

Of note, these IJN lookouts would almost always have been fresh to their posts, the men well rested and revitalized, with each assuredly performing a notch above their American equivalents. The men would have been rotated in regularly scheduled shifts on the clock, and no man would have been tasked with standing a watch more than a single shift at a time. Indeed, if such a fixed routine was not observed, it was thought, clearly very critical and costly mistakes could almost too readily occur. Case in point: the lookouts stationed on the ships of the Allied fleet that night.

In direct and sharp contrast to their Japanese counterparts, the American look-outs—on virtually all of Crutchley's screening ships—would have had little or no sleep between duty postings, sometimes standing a repetitive and tiresome watch for hours at a time, and—on many occasions—even double-shifting through yet another watch cycle as needed. All too soon, the Allied forces would learn the daunting truth: "tired eyes" might far more readily see the imagined; might well envision the false contact in a mirage-like shimmer of surf; or, in the worst-case scenario, not see anything at all—until indeed it might already be too late.

Clearly, then, the higher degree of conditioned and responsive training for the keen-eyed lookouts on Mikawa's ships must surely have been a factor as well, that might again tip the scales even less in favor of the Americans and their allies, since far fewer men on that side might have been capably trained enough imprimis to expertly man such a post with acumen and true dutifulness.

In the end, it would probably indeed be a combination of both an alert posturing and a readiness capability that would weigh most heavily on at least this one night. This and the very fire supremacy, the chilling accuracy, good range-finding, and target-acquired hits all virtually guaranteed victory with major hits on each mark. The American screening forces at Guadalcanal would suffer great setbacks all in all that night—and suffer the saddening loss of four capital ships. Would the Allied naval forces be caught with their guard down yet other times as well?

Starlight, Star Bright: Effectiveness of Naval Night Fighting and Illumination

Certainly, the vast majority of the Imperial Japanese Navy's ongoing night-fighting training exercises would take place under a secret shroud of darkness in the more remote corners of the Western Pacific and waters surrounding Japan proper. In fact, each exercise would be nothing if not a series of real-life, rapid-fire drills that would clearly have included multiple surface ships and involved the use of "illumination" devices when attacking a specific target ship (or group of ships) at night, and truly any such exercise must indeed have been a sight to behold.

In several remote and carefully selected training areas in and around the Sea of Japan, and its southern deep-sea inlets, the IJN would conduct numerous live-fire training exercises that would inevitably employ the use of both starshell illuminants fired from its surface ships—and those that would be air-launched, in the form of orb flares that could very effectively be deployed from any number of land or even cruiser-based reconnaissance aircraft. With naval training zones extending from Japan's own interior Sea of Japan to as far south as the Tsushima Basin and the Western Channel—to even more secluded training areas well off to the South China Sea areas near the Paracels—Japan continued with its night training exercises sans interruption—and sans detection by the Allies.

By the early 1940s, Japan's naval high command was already fully exploring the viability of such attack formats and would have been keenly aware of the significance of both the surprise attack and the night naval attack in concert as one. And even though the several schools of thought would be factioned and divided in principle, most would actively promote the idea of the use of just such a naval tactic to both initiate and prosecute a fleet commander's attack successfully. The idea may have had its beginnings in 1941, but its true practice must clearly have been fine-tuned in the latter half of 1942. It was a naval tactic and strategy—however grim and fatalistic to the Allies—that would be quite effectively used during the Naval Battle of Guadalcanal and on the night of 9 August 1942 during the battle at Savo as well.

Stemming from a basic, almost Mahanian[140] naval philosophy of stealth, ship movement, and positioning—and ultimate engagement of an enemy's surface fleet at night (when they might least be prepared to fight)—the idea was tantalizing, effective, and an already proven winner. And for at least the Japanese, key to that night naval fighting vision would always be "illumination." Light up the horizon, locate the enemy ships, set the range, and summarily open fire . . . a simple four-fold equation that seemingly never failed time and again. At the first it might be but a horizonal shimmer of light followed almost immediately by the *coup de grâce* deathblows that would only too quickly be delivered at the hands of the 8-inch and 5-inch shells fired by the already deadly accurate gun crews on the Japanese heavy cruisers and destroyers that night.

The IJN crew members had by now trained and drilled thoroughly, by now crisply executing their maneuvers with a practiced and almost mechanical precision. The Japanese naval commanders were learning quickly and developing their attack strategies with a nearly consummate ease. When it came to naval night fighting and the element of "illumination," it would later be said that only the very first volley fired from the massive guns would bracket and miss, the second and third salvos would already be scoring direct hits on any ship . . . and all of it fully enabled by "illumination."

So, did Crutchley's Allied warships in Iron Bottom Sound that night really have a chance in light of all this? Perhaps not. So, what exactly were these starshells, and how were they used to best advantage by the Japanese?

Initially, the type of illuminating shell being used by the Imperial Japanese Navy—and certainly Mikawa's CRUDIV6 and 18 task group that night—was essentially a type of carrier shell, or cargo munition, with an auto-triggered fuse that then discharged an air-launched "candle." This candle would itself be a type of semi-pyrotechnic flare that would then discharge a white (or yellowed) illuminant at a predetermined altitude level. At the point at which the flare ignited, it would descend in slow cascade supported by a heat-resistant parachute, while fully illuminating a wide circumferential area below. This would inevitably have been the type of flare that was used during the First Battle of Savo Island, and that would later come to be known as the "starshell" flare. Other starshell variants would also include colored flare shells that would have been used for target marking initiatives, and even the later "burning pot" flare—itself a carryover design from the early days of World War I, and which would essentially eject a shrapnel-pattern dispersion of small luminous orbs, or "pots."

A typical (and vintage) 1943 British 4-inch illumination shell was essentially made up of multiple codependent stages: a fuse stage; multiple priming composite platforms that contained the illuminant compound itself; a 5–6-inch parachute storage partition; and finally the flare's hard-case shell housing unit itself. All of Mikawa's ships would have the capability to deploy these starshell orbs—these "burning pots"—and indeed did that night, fully lighting up the entire area and simultaneously opening up on the American screening ships with perhaps their most severe attack ever.

In the end, it would indeed be a fully working combination of both stealth (element of surprise) and the swift illumination of the battle zone itself that would, at least on the night of 9 August 1942, spell a certain and terrible disaster for RADM Riefkohl and his Northern screening group. When the smoke had cleared, with Mikawa's attack forces already departing the area to move back up the Slot, only the burning hulk and wreckage of the three American heavy cruisers would remain, and the now-silenced night would toll the tragic end of the CAs *Quincy*, *Astoria*, and *Vincennes*. With 370 men lost on the first ship, 216 on the second, and 332 on the third cruiser *Vincennes*, almost 1,100 men would have been lost in this raging thirty-one-minute battle . . . with each never to be seen again.

Starlight, Star Bright: "Washing Machine Charlie"

For both the beleaguered infantryman entrenched at Henderson Field on Guadalcanal and the weary-eyed gunner's mate on any of the great warships that patrolled the waters offshore, there seemed to always be one constant, and that one constant was the nightly visits by Washing Machine Charlie, a single Japanese reconnaissance aircraft that appeared to make nightly forays over Guadalcanal and much of Iron Bottom Sound.

Over the course of time, and after a series of by now all-too-familiar flyovers by this cunning Japanese reconnaissance plane, it became eminently clear that the overflights appeared to have been fourfold in purpose: ❶ area reconnaissance and passing on its report of findings back to its IJN command center; ❷ harassment and disruption of enemy activities; ❸ occasionally bombing the airfield (and/or Allied shipping and land-based installations); and most often ❹ "illumination"—that is, dropping colored flares over Allied positions to support Japanese naval and land batteries operating on or near those patrol areas. This small aircraft, and those like it, would oddly come to generically be called "Washing Machine Charlie," so called due to the often loud and highly distinctive staccato sound made by the old aircraft's syncopated engines as it approached the Americans below who burrowed, sat, and listened each night on its overflight arrival.

The small and lightly framed Japanese aircraft was known to routinely fly its perilous and solitary course each night—seemingly without fail and without falter—and repeatedly conducted its nightly runs over key areas such as the newly captured Henderson Field, Tulagi, Savo, and much of the vast Iron Bottom Sound itself. The vexing drone was a sound that would come to unnerve the already edgy men dug in on Guadalcanal itself, and those on the support ships sailing Sealark Lane.

Throughout the course of the early naval campaign for Guadalcanal, the Japanese seemed to only step up their dispatch of these solitary aircraft on their recurring nighttime missions. In short order, these planes would be looked on with what might even be called near-amusement by the Allied forces but were nonetheless considered a very real menace to the Americans whenever they were heard to be flying overhead. One might envision men in a foxhole on more than one occasion tapping a buddy on the shoulder with a casual "Here comes Washing Machine Charlie again" kind of gesture as they pointed to the sky almost without undue alarm.

The aircraft used in this role by the Japanese forces, and by the surface ships that made up Mikawa's task force that night, could generally include cruiser-launched or shore-based single-engine seaplane types, and occasionally twin-engine aircraft of the *Betty* bomber class. It is even further suggestive that "inventive" ground crews that serviced the Japanese planes had somehow deliberately tampered with the piston-firing ratios, knowingly causing a displacement of the regular and near-metrical accent of the aircraft's running engines, purposely causing them to run loudly and slightly out of synch . . . perhaps indeed to simply harass and annoy the entrenched Americans below.

The resulting drone and vibration of these engine "enhancements," of course, would wake most men out deep sleep and generally disrupt all routine while also causing each man to virtually hunker down and wait for the bomb-drop that might in fact never even come at all. Later that same year, between late 1942 and early 1943, the United States had already begun to countermand this "minor annoyance" factor by launching a new series of American-piloted "night fighters" themselves, whose primary mission was to interdict and fully quash these lone night-flying raiders. Soon, the harrying drones of night would indeed begin to taper off and then disappear altogether as the planes ceased their forays—never to be seen (or missed) by any of the American troops on the ground or sailors cruising the many ships in Iron Bottom Sound.

Washing Machine Charlie would be no more; however, a curious European variant—a near-reincarnation of the Japanese version itself—would also come about when lone German planes, then called *Bed Check Charlie*, would themselves buzz the forward lines of battle over both U.S. and Allied ground forces. And, much like the Japanese prototype used so effectively in the Solomons, the effect and intent would pretty much be the same here as well—to disarm and disrupt the enemy—much like an errant and probative artillery round fired only randomly into an encampment in dead of night. Sleep deprivation, along with a terror tactic of being "buzzed" or having live ordnance dropped on you at night, it seemed, was clearly the order of the day.

So, what role (if any) did the sly and devious Washing Machine Charlie play in the greater campaign for Guadalcanal and the Solomons, and specifically during the First Battle of Savo Island? In full overview, probably a most negligible one, but one that would nevertheless have been alternatingly fraught with both mild hilarity and a most stark, disquieting terror.

FINDING 21:   THE FOG OF NIGHT:
A FACTORING OF HEAVY WEATHER

Based on numerous first-person accounts and observations of the First Battle of Savo
Island on the night of 8–9 August 1942, one can clearly see that weather must in fact
have played at least a contributory role and might itself have been at least marginally
impactful on operations in and around Iron Bottom Sound that night. Therefore,
some note must be paid to the underlying weather conditions that would later have
some bearing on the battle itself. In researching material on the 1BOSI, and for both
CAPT Howard Douglas "Ping" Bode and his stint as commander of the USS *Chicago* (CA-29)—and again for LCDR Chester Edward "Blackie" Carroll on the USS
Helm—the author was able to find only negligible mention of weather as a factor in
the engagement. In fact, the only extant map of its time that even remotely points up
weather as a key item of mention—enough to plot it on a map—was this curious yet
crudely crafted map, an unattributed chart that is identified only as "Plate 'X': Battle
of Savo Island: Action with the *Chicago* Group: 0143 to 0144, 9 August 1942."

And while no attributive information could at all be found for the hand-drawn
map shown above, in it we still clearly see a large, obscuring cloud formation just to
the south and east of Savo Island ❶ at a time stamp approximating 0143 hours, as
shown. This pattern appears to fully repeat itself (to a lesser degree) with the plotting
of three additional line squalls to the south and east in Iron Bottom Sound ❷. Alternately referred to as both a "rain squall" and a "heavy cloudbank," we can see that
there was definitely (if not entirely to scale) some series of semi-obscuring weather
events taking place at the time of Mikawa's encounter with the Allied surface fleet
on the night in question. The IJN cruiser force would have been transiting the
Sound through moderate to heavy cloud cover that oafishly collided head-on with a
confluence of regional thunderstorms over and again, the result of which created a
gray and dismal screen between Savo Island and much of the northernmost reaches
of Iron Bottom Sound.

Savo, and most of its environs on the night of 9 August 1942, must itself have
been uncharacteristically dark and overcast, with occasional light mists of rain pelting
the ships below. A mild breeze from the southwest allowed for a ceiling between only
1,500 and 1,800 feet, and average visibility was estimated to have been good out to
almost 10,000 yards. The night was cool and relentlessly rainy, but not at all enough
to impede the forward progress of the ships in VADM Mikawa's two cruiser divisions. Here, even CAPT Toshikazu Ohmae, extant chief of staff for the IJN admiral
aboard his great flagship *Chōkai*, would himself later make only minor mention of any
weather factors plaguing the area in his own first-person account in the year 1957,[141]
when he said of the IJN surface fleet, "we encountered only sporadic squalls at 2130,
but these did not interfere with our advance."[142] In yet another observation from a different vantage point, crew members of the Australian heavy cruiser *Canberra* had duly
noted a "visibility that was out to 2 to 6 miles with rain in the area."[143]

However negligibly, weather that night would indeed have been some kind of factor—whether major or minor—and would later (if somewhat inadequately) be pointed up as such in the works of noted collaborators Bates and Innis. The two authors, both well-regarded scholars and naval historians closely affiliated with the Naval War College's Department of Analysis, would later speak of it in their own comprehensive, 396-page treatise titled *The Battle of Savo Island, August 9th, 1942: Statistical and Tactical Analysis: Part I.* And even there, in its own, full account of the battle, we find only minor mention of this factor, as shown here in the following quotes:

> Weather conditions in the north channel area were about as follows: night dark and overcast with occasional light mists and rain; light breeze from the southeast; ceiling about 1,800 feet; average visibility at 10,000 yards, and heavy clouds around and to the south of Savo Island; sea smooth.[144]

In a further elucidation presented in the book's narratives, both historians seem to cite the following:

> At 0145—immediately after the Task Group had settled on the new course—both the *QUINCY* and the HELM endeavored to fix their positions by cross-bearing on Savo Island. The resulting fixes were considerably in error, since both ships mistook the edge of the heavy cloudbank south of Savo as the actual left tangent of that island, and as a result both [ships] found the right tangent somewhat obscured by the haze in that direction.[145]

And yet a third time, in this alternate observation from the deck of the Australian heavy cruiser *Canberra*:

> The general surface visibility to the eastward, through a semi-circle from north to south, was one mile; however, the visibility in the westward semi-circle—though very poor, was somewhat better—increasing out to three miles. The group passed through no rain squalls after 0000 August 9th, although many squalls occurred in close proximity and the clouds in the area remained low.[146]

Evidence indicates that there was a minor clustering of lesser rain squalls situated well to the south and east of Savo Island in the vicinity of the *Chicago*, *Canberra*, and *Bagley* at the time of the IJN attack on Crutchley's Southern fleet, known to have begun at about 0143 hours. Curiously indeed, this is in sharp contrast to the map image seen earlier in Figure 31, where we distinctly see only a gray-patterned area below Savo that is tagged only as a "heavy cloudbank," with no other problematic patches of weather depicted anywhere else. Were those ancillary stormfronts noted to the south so negligible as to simply invite omission from the Loxton map shown here?

In full extent, if Loxton's map is to be taken at face value here, we clearly see a plotting of a weather front to the south of Savo that ❶ appears to be the size of Savo itself, and that might well indeed have provided excellent cover for both enemy

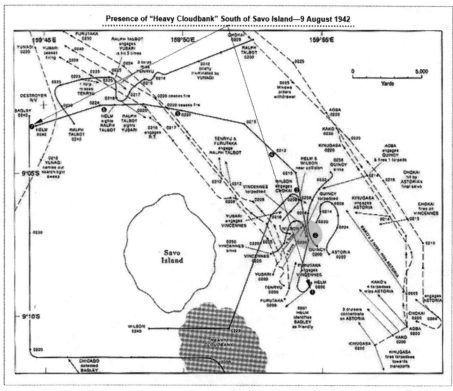

Presence of "Heavy Cloudbank" South of Savo Island—9 August 1942

Figure 38.   1BOSI Weather Elements: Position of Savo Island Cloudbank (Loxton Map Plotting)

ships on approach—and on attack—as well as to serve as a quick escape route for the besieged American ships then seeking a rapid withdrawal from the devastating fire to which they were all being subjected on that occasion. If viewed rightly, therefore, we can clearly see at least the *Helm* ❷ making for a direction toward the masking cloudbank, perhaps in a feint maneuver before turning about and swinging back off to the north, as well as both the *Wilson* and the *Bagley* (❸ and ❺) in fact entering and transiting through it on their way to points west ❹. Whether to fully escape the withering dead-on fire from the IJN cruisers themselves, or to simply reposition themselves to a point of better vantage, the cloudbank would have played an immeasurable role in the hide-and-seek battle that seemed to be unfolding that night.

Already known to be a widely accepted naval battle tactic to fully exploit extant weather conditions to one's advantage in just such a situation, these ships seemed to make some good use of both the cloud and the fogbank elements, sufficient to either successfully reorient themselves for further sustained battle or simply exit the area in full. In either event, weather elements might have unquestionably played a role of some great significance throughout much of the course of this first battle for the Solomons.

ADMIRAL MIKAWA'S LOST OPPORTUNITY

A Failure to Prosecute

Admiral Gunichi Mikawa was the commander of the critically underestimated cruiser attack force of the Imperial Japanese Navy (IJN) that carried out its stunning series of victories over the American (and Allied) naval forces at the First Battle of Savo Island (1BOSI). The battle would take place in Iron Bottom Sound, Guadalcanal—itself in the Solomon Islands group—on the night of 8–9 August 1942. In the true context of this battle, Mikawa's naval contingency—simply identified as the Eighth Fleet "Japanese Striking Force" and made up of both RADM Aritomo Gotō's Cruiser Division 6 (CRUDIV6) and Mikawa's own CRUDIV18—would consist of five heavy cruisers, two light cruisers, and a single destroyer.[147] And it would be this same surface fleet that would go on to sink three American heavy cruisers of the line and the Australian *Canberra* itself.

Of note is the fact that throughout the course of the encounter, Mikawa's forces would suffer few (if any) losses in the battle, although the admiral's own flagship *Chōkai* was known to itself suffer minor structural damage, and the cruiser *Kako* sunk only later, on 10 August, by the American attack sub USS *S-44* on its return trip to Kavieng after that same Savo attack. Although noted as a brilliant tactician and a dutiful proponent of open-sea night naval warfare—for which the Imperial Japanese Navy was now becoming far more well known—Mikawa's later career would be marked by only mixed success, and in the course of history he would later regrettably be reassigned to lesser posts as a result of the disastrous Battle of the Bismarck Sea in March 1943 and the "dishonorable loss" of several critical troop convoys that had been set in his charge that had been destined for New Guinea.[148]

Well after the short but violent clash at Savo, and the near-concurrent attacks on both Crutchley's Southern and Northern screening forces, Admiral Mikawa conferred with his cadre of staff officers about whether he should "press the advantage of the attack" against any of the other surviving enemy warships and indeed go after the prized Allied transport and supply ships that might have been his central targets imprimis—this while those ships were still vulnerable and anchored in two key ports. It is said that several factors may have influenced the man's final decision *not* to further engage the American ships, the first and foremost of which may have been the fact that his own ships had by now become dangerously scattered and dispersed, and it might indeed take some considerable time to form them up to full battle strength again. The slightly battered contingency of ships would also need time to replenish their ammunition stores, reload their torpedo tubes, and effect any repairs that might now have been made necessary from the damaging salvos his ships had suffered (if only lightly) at the hands of the countering American fleet during the heated battle that night.

The good admiral may indeed have scored a major victory at sea that night, but not entirely without price. As a simple matter of course, all of this labor-intensive work would take time, and it was truly this very element, *time*, that Mikawa did not have at leisure. Not wholly certain, therefore, of the size of the Allied naval presence, its composite makeup, or the very location of any of the enemy's remaining warships—specifically Fletcher's carriers—the IJN admiral quietly excused himself from the bridge and walked out onto the compass platform of his great flagship *Chōkai*. By 0216 hours, the admiral had already made his decision—he would not further engage the Allied fleet and instead set an immediate course for home with no undue delay.

Perhaps also fostering Mikawa's decision not to attack the American transport ships must have been the fact that he also had limited (or no) air cover, and he resolutely believed that a contingency of U.S. aircraft carriers, under the aegis and command of Admiral Frank Jack Fletcher, were still near to (or already in) the battle zone bracketing Sealark Lane. A man of sharp foresight and intellect, but one also imbued with an inhibiting caution, Mikawa must have been aware that the Imperial Japanese Navy had very few heavy cruisers of the line still in service—and even fewer in production at that time. It might indeed be that much more difficult to replace any he might lose to air attack that day—or especially from a prolonged surface engagement should he in fact remain in the area of the Sound. He could not at all have known that Fletcher's carriers had already come and gone, having withdrawn from the battle zone in full, and that they no longer presented any appreciable threat to his task force that night. Against the wishes of his own senior staff officers on hand that night—each of whom heatedly urged a reversal of decision and an immediate and decisive attack continuance—a general capitulation soon swept across Mikawa's bridge, as each man dutifully acquiesced and yielded to the admiral's point to withdraw from the battle area with purposefulness and best speed. And so indeed he did precisely that. Better to savor the twin victories at Savo, the senior IJN officer might clearly have thought, than to foolishly perish in a dispiriting and unplanned-for battle somewhere else.

Four minutes later, now a tick closer to 0220 hours, Admiral Mikawa would in fact issue his final order, "All forces withdraw. Force in line ahead, course 320, speed 30 knots."[149] And with that the attack force simply quick-turned as one and began its sly and cautious push back through the Sound and up through the Slot, heading north toward Bougainville and the far ports of Rabaul and Kavieng.

As a young man and midshipman cadet in the 38th class of the Imperial Japanese Naval Academy in 1910, Mikawa would have ranked third in a class of 149—*third!*—and go on to launch a distinguished career as a naval strategist, an exacting tactician, and a careful orchestrator of the great "naval night battle" itself. History might later neglect the good admiral, but for at least this one night of victory he had been brilliant, both in his foresight and in his planning—and in his force's acuity and decisive performance during at least this one hotly contested blue-water battle. The Americans might go on to win the "war" at large, but clearly on this single first occasion the good admiral and his indefatigable cruiser divisions had indeed won the "battle" at Savo.

Admiral Gunichi Mikawa would himself go on to survive the war and retire back to his native homeland (and by then war-torn) Hiroshima, Japan. He would die on

25 February 1981 at the remarkable age of ninety-two. Most curious of all, perhaps, might be the fact that the good admiral would go on to outlive virtually all of his wartime adversaries by some many years—and indeed most of his counterpart American military commanders, against whom he had so fiercely battled in 1942, would perish long before his own demise.

For additional insights and a more detailed biographical account of this unique Japanese commander, as one of Japan's most preeminent Eighth Fleet cruiser force leaders, see the section on VADM Gunichi Mikawa, IJN.

Mikawa and the Factors Contributing to the "No-Attack" Decision

Clearly, history can never really know each and all of the influencing factors that must have taken shape in the mind of the brilliant cruiser commander Gunichi Mikawa on the night of the 9 August 1942 attacks at Savo. Coming at an extremely critical moment in time, in the midst of a heated naval night engagement in a haunting place called Iron Bottom Sound, Mikawa would remain calm throughout much of the battle, in spite of being passionately urged on by his aides and staff officers to again press the attack on the remaining Allied ships. In the end, however, Mikawa would in fact allow all of the Allied troop transport and supply ships to remain wholly intact. His overwhelming force superiority, his keen element of surprise, and the quick dispatch of four Allied heavy cruisers in an estimated thirty-one minutes, might in brief have been enough to make any heady commander preempt an order for any further attack, as indeed what the sly admiral had already accomplished might itself have been enough.

A man of keen foresight and sharp intuition, Mikawa stood transfixed on the bridge of the *Chōkai* and weighed all options available to him at that one stellar moment and then turned on his heel and unceremoniously informed his command officers that he would in fact disengage the attack and retire his cruiser force at best speed, back to safe haven and points north. Undoubtedly, there must indeed have been many stark and sobering thoughts that disquieted the cunning IJN commander that night: matters of force and counterforce, of action and counteraction; of strength against strength, and even that of pondering the very imponderables of a failed effort—or, worse, a failed strategy—should such ever come to pass. And thus the inhibiting thoughts and nagging doubts would soon find their way to the admiral's mind, peppering him with a clouding degree of tepid caution, as indeed he had come full circle. *Better to withdraw with my force still fully intact, and savor the victories already netted,* he must have thought, as opposed to remaining and foolishly risking it all in the face of the American carriers that he believed might indeed still be in the area.

Therefore, among the several considerations that Mikawa must have had to weigh that night in the face of the unfolding sea battles, without question, many might have included at least some of the following key discussion points, as those presented in the Table 31 matrix.

Table 31. Vice Admiral Gunichi Mikawa: Factors Contributing to the "No-Attack" Decision

Mikawa's Decision Point	Result of Decision	Comment
❶ **American Carrier Task Group(s):** Mikawa could not know exactly where Fletcher's carrier group might be, and greatly feared an attack on his cruisers from any of its deck-launched aircraft and dive-bombers.	Mikawa would not commit his surface fleet to further press the attack on any of the other American ships at anchor. Therefore disengaging his forces and exiting the battle zone, he would simply turn his force about and begin the long passage back up the Slot to ports in both Kavieng and Rabaul.	Having seen up close both the crushing effect of his ships' collective large guns and their deadliness in range and accuracy, Mikawa might well have been more than content with his "measured" victory at Savo that night.
❷ **Heavy Cruiser Construction and Availability:** Mikawa knew that Japan's industrial might could be severely compromised should the 1BOSI result in the loss of any (or all) of his heavy or light cruiser force. He was therefore reluctant to press the attack on the troop transport and supply ships lest a retaliatory air strike on (or further naval interaction with) his ships might be imminent.	A heightened and characteristic degree of caution encumbered the admiral's decision to commit his ships' heavy-gun assets to a prolonged engagement with the Allied surface fleet. It would be far better to withdraw all of his warships intact than to recklessly lose one or more in an otherwise unanticipated turn of battle when he might least expect it.	Mikawa knew that the loss of any of his large ship assets would set the IJN back significantly, perhaps even irrecoverably so. Production of these large-scale, almost obsolete heavy cruisers was at an all-time low in wartime Japan that was itself already struggling under her own great losses, a paucity of supplies, and the sharp constraints of war.
❸ **Repair Assessments and Damage Control:** Mikawa's forces would indeed suffer some negligible damage, and ironically most would be heavily centered on the bridge of his own flagship *Chōkai*.	Mikawa's retirement from the area of battle—having already inflicted much serious damage on the Allied fleet during the twin attacks at Savo—would actually work to the advantage of the IJN cruiser task group. In fact, some considerable damage had been inflicted on the bridge of the *Chōkai*, as much to the *Kinugasa* and the *Tenryū* as well, in their own encounters with the Allied Southern and Northern screening elements that night.	Mikawa knew that both his flagship, and the other damaged ships within his CRUDIV6 and 18 force, would need immediate repair, and so left the battle area quickly after completing his highly successful twin attacks. *Better to strike and run, the good admiral might clearly have thought, than to prolong the engagement and risk further damage to any other ships.*

(continued)

Table 31. *Continued*

Mikawa's Decision Point	Result of Decision	Comment
❹ **Replenishment and Resupply of Arms:** Mikawa had very probably exhausted a massive amount of flares, torpedoes, and ammunition stores in his pursuit of (and attack on) Crutchley's Allied Southern and Northern screening forces.	During the course of the attack on the Allied Southern and Northern screens, literally hundreds of rounds would have been expended from the ships' combined 5-inch and 8-inch batteries. This would also not factor in the smaller 20mm and 40mm AA guns, or the number of torpedoes launched by his ships against the Allied forces that night. **Note:** See the detailed information presented in Tables 44–46 (beginning on page 410) for a fuller review of all such ammunition expenditures—both for the Allies and for the IJN on the occasion of that battle.	Though not entirely depleted, clearly Mikawa would have been eager to quickly replenish his weapons stockpiles and ammunition stores before re-engaging the enemy fleet on any future date. It would be far better for Mikawa to exit the battle area when he did than to remain and fully exhaust his remaining stores and depleted ammunition stores.
❺ **Provide Medical Help/Aid Wounded:** Mikawa would indeed have been concerned about his wounded receiving immediate medical attention, and as much about the greater honorific of seeing to his dead, especially toward the close of the battle.	Mikawa's cruiser elements had been hit multiple times during their exchanges with both Bode's Southern fleet and Riefkohl's Northern force. As a direct result of both encounters, many of the ships in the admiral's task group would suffer multiple casualties and would each need to tend to their injured onboard.	During her brief but violent clashes with both the *Quincy* and *Astoria* during their attack on the Northern screen, Mikawa's flagship *Chōkai* would be hit multiple times during the melee.

Among the Northern ships to have had first contact with the IJN fleet, the *Astoria* would already have been firing all of her 8-inch and 5-inch guns and was also reported to have scored multiple impact hits on the *Chōkai*, *Kinugasa*, and *Tenryū*.

Later, *Quincy* would likewise score an almost direct hit on the bridge of the admiral's flagship, nearly killing Mikawa outright in that very exchange.

Vincennes would also have engaged the *Kinugasa* as well, and even the *Ralph Talbot*—the last ship to be attacked on their way out of the *Sound*—would have fired on at least the *Tenryū* as the marauding ships departed the area north of Savo and moved back up the *Slot*.

Truly, there had been hits on the Japanese fleet that night, and they would not escape entirely unscathed in the battle, as truly blood for blood would have been drawn. It might, therefore, clearly have been of *major* importance to Mikawa, as the commander of the Eighth Fleet Striking Force, to break off the fight and cut his losses on at least that one occasion.

The pressing need to obtain medical attention for all of these men—and to perhaps more properly accommodate the even grimmer task of tallying his own casualty figures—might surely have dictated that he then fully disengage from the battle, not prosecute the attack any further, and exit the area at best speed under the cover of darkness while his own losses were still light.

(continued)

Table 31. *Continued*

MIKAWA'S DECISION POINT	RESULT OF DECISION	COMMENT
❻ **REUNITE SPLIT-COLUMN FORMATION OF SHIPS:** Mikawa's CRUDIV attack force had become inadvertently dispersed and split into two (or even three) columns after their attack on Bode's Southern screen. Then, after launching their attacks on Riefkohl's Northern group, Mikawa still had the problem of reunifying his scattered ships back into its normal single column, line-ahead format before returning to Rabaul and Kavieng.	Mikawa, sailing cautiously away on an already slightly damaged *Chōkai*, must have had to reduce speed to allow the three lagging ships to catch up. Every moment spent in the confirmed hostile waters of Iron Bottom Sound would at least in theory have been a moment too perilous for both him and his escaping surface fleet.	At the point at which the Australian cruiser *Canberra* came under attack by Mikawa's cruisers, as part of their general strike on the Allied Southern screen, the cruisers *Tenryū* and *Yūbari*—in tandem with the late-following *Furutaka*—would all veer sharply around the *Canberra*, possibly to avoid an imminent collision with that stricken ship. This most fortunate "trick of luck" would thereby create a secondary attack column that would then sail around the starboard side of the Northern fleet and attack in force (and in tandem) with Mikawa's other ships. This deadly "pincer" approach and attack would spell almost certain doom for at least four of the Allied cruisers within both the Southern and Northern screening groups.

<table>
<tr><td>

❼ PARTING SHOTS AND A CHART ROOM:
The Chōkai's Operations Room is decimated by a naval barrage fired from two American cruisers at the lag end of the night battle at Savo. VADM Mikawa is almost killed outright, and most of the flagship's charts and maps are lost in the resulting Ops Room fires.

</td><td>

Mikawa is compelled to abort his plans for an even greater attack on the American transport ships at anchor near Guadalcanal. Now lacking any viable navigation charts, and not entirely familiar with the territorial waters just off the coast of the large island, the admiral is hesitant to navigate his deep-draft ships through any of the shoals and shallow waters of the area.

</td><td>

During the violent clashes with the two American cruisers Quincy and Astoria during Mikawa's secondary attack on RADM Riefkohl's Northern screen, the flagship Chōkai would be hit multiple times during the melee.

Astoria was already engaging all of her 8-inch and 5-inch guns—as was the Quincy—and both ships were reported to have scored multiple impact hits on the Chōkai, the Kinugasa, and Tenryū as well.

Later, the Quincy would likewise score a series of direct hits on the bridge of the IJN flagship, virtually obliterating its Operations Room (and with it much of the ship's maps and charts stored there). Without those charts and maps, the IJN task force, under the command of VADM Mikawa, would essentially have been running blind and placed at an immediate disadvantage in their attack.

</td></tr>
</table>

CHAPTER 4

The Commanders
THE GENTLEMEN WARRIORS OF GUADALCANAL

VICE ADMIRAL FRANK JACK FLETCHER, USN

VADM Frank "Jack" Fletcher was perhaps one of the most distinguished admirals to have served in the United States Navy with great prominence, even as early as the Mexican Revolution, and for much of the first half of the twentieth century. In his time, Fletcher would serve with merit and distinction in both World War I and World War II; by that time, he would have already been awarded the Medal of Honor (MOH) for his above-and-beyond heroism during the little-known pre–World War I naval encounters during the Battle of Veracruz in April 1914.

For the good admiral, it would only be in the latter half of his career that most of his naval enterprises would become more and more focused on fleet operations in the South Pacific, and in fact culminate at its exhaustive peak in 1942 with the fierce Battle for the Solomons. Indeed, with each new and challenging exploit, and with victory on victory attained, Fletcher might have been the only logical choice to lead the charge against the Japanese naval forces, which Combined Fleet had even now literally "hop-scotched" its way across the great Pacific, island by island, and chain by chain. And expecting that just such a time might come, the American naval command wisely knew that with Fletcher at the helm of its own vast navy, they might sooner (rather than later) be able to counter and face down the massive threat posed by the advancing Imperial Japanese Navy—the dread *Kaigūn*. And indeed Admiral Fletcher would be only too happy to go forward and meet them bravely and full-on, in battle after battle in places like Midway, the Coral Sea, and soon enough bloody Guadalcanal itself.

And who might expect anything less from "Jack," as he favored being called by his peers, since here indeed was a career naval officer who in his time had commanded vast flotillas of fast-attack destroyers and who had already proudly served on no less than seven major battleships of the line—not the least of which would have included the great WWI battleship USS *Maine* (BB-10); the *Rhode Island* (BB-17); the *Ohio*

(BB-12); the *Florida* (BB-30); the *Kearsarge* (BB-5); the grand *New Mexico* (BB-40); and even the newer, more cutting-edge *Colorado* (BB-45)?

Without question, then, Fletcher was probably one of the most preeminent and well-respected operational commanders in-theater at the time, especially during the keystone battles in the Coral Sea and at Midway. Having been advanced in grade some several times since, the newly promoted rear admiral would (at least for the moment) be placed in command of Carrier Task Force 11 (CTF 11) in late 1941—which would now be centered on his great flagship, the *Lexington*-class USS *Saratoga* (CV-3)—itself now preparing to rendezvous with VADM Brown's own Task Force 12 (TF 12), centered around the *Lex* at Wake Island. Like stepping-stones across the vast Pacific, Fletcher's fleet would meet, engage, and repel the enemy in almost every encounter, even as early as June 1942. Later, the good ADM Fletcher would again be appointed to yet another CTF command—sadly this time to the USS *Yorktown* (CV-5), which would be sunk in actions just northwest of Midway Island later that same month. But before he could even arrive there, he would first have to face even more deadly encounters with Yamamoto's vast navy . . . at the Battle of the Coral Sea.

VADM Fletcher: The Battle for the Solomons

By mid-1942, an increasingly disquieted Admiral Nimitz was most concerned about developments in the south and western Pacific. The awesome might and power of the ships of the Imperial Japanese Navy had been openly sailing these waters with swagger and aplomb—with near impunity—and then landing ground forces at strategic locations almost at will, and all of it mainly unchecked. Nimitz, not having been fully apprised of Admiral Fletcher's state of near-exhaustion from his own series of recent intense area battles in the Pacific—much of it without rest—only knew he now needed his most experienced carrier commander to strongly lead America's naval forces through the next phase of the war. Which, in and of itself by quiet default, meant that he needed Fletcher.

To this point in time, Nimitz must indeed have had much on his mind, along with a swirl of options to weigh, and even the enemy's own strategies to anticipate and counter. The beleaguered Americans had been both hammered and spiked, their carrier task forces now greatly reduced in number by the actions at both Coral Sea and Midway. And now, to his great dismay, only the *Saratoga*, the *Wasp*, and the great *Enterprise* remained fully operational and ready for redeployment, as a badly damaged *Hornet* still laid to at Pearl Harbor for emergency repair. Admiral Bull Halsey—Nimitz's "number-one" man and best choice for the new operation—was still laid up in the hospital and said to be "recovering miserably" from dermatitis. The senior admiral had also just learned of the plight of MG Vandegrift's own 1st Marine Division, who were reportedly cut off, besieged, and dug in hard on Guadalcanal, men who quickly needed all the help they could get from him and his ships, and that sooner rather than later.

Nimitz would also learn of what he thought were enemy battleship-class vessels and heavy cruisers that reportedly lay offshore, or simply sailed about unchecked and unopposed, operating without fear or direct challenge. This all the while, of course, as they continued to rain deadly bombardments down on the hapless American defenders at Henderson Field, Honiara, and Tulagi.

Surely, an enraged Nimitz might clearly have thought in this, his darkest hour, enough was by far enough. Japan's unrelenting attempts to both introduce and continually reinforce their land-based troops on both Guadalcanal and cross-channel Tulagi were now seen as being so prevalent and ongoing as to be tagged with the somewhat taunting nickname "Tokyo Express" by the Allied soldiers and sailors operating in the area at the time. Nimitz knew he must not waver in resolve in his response to the Japanese invasions at Guadalcanal and that he must emphatically act now. Fletcher would be ordered back in again and would sail at top speed for southern waters to ride to the rescue of the Solomon Islands.

At bloody Guadalcanal, a self-assured Admiral Fletcher knew from the outset that he would be facing another of his greatest challenges, and again prepared to clash with the might of the Imperial Japanese Navy . . . virtually ship to ship, and gun to gun. What the man could not know, however, was that he would once again be pitted against yet another brilliant nemesis, in the personage of VADM Mikawa, the clever strategist and commander of Japan's great Eighth Fleet. Sadly, as a direct result of that encounter, the United States and its allies would later suffer grave and inestimable losses during the first encounter alone, an encounter that history would remember tragically as the First Battle of Savo Island.

By August 1942, on orders from Admiral Nimitz, Fletcher had already begun to transit his surface ships into the waters adjoining Guadalcanal. With dutifulness and great purposefulness, elements of his Taffy 61 surface fleet already patrolled the dangerous and hotly contested waters separating Guadalcanal and Florida Island, extending as far north as volcanic Savo and as far down as the southern reaches of Sealark Lane. After the unopposed success of the Allied invasion and landings on Guadalcanal, an ever-cautious Fletcher now sought to withdraw his carrier task groups from the general support area to a point northeast of Florida Island. Concerned about possible returning air attacks by the IJN, and his own mounting losses, the admiral decided he would err on the side of caution—which would once again come at a high price indeed.

Convinced that his actions were indeed appropriate, he approached the commander of all theater operations, VADM Robert L. Ghormley, and asked for permission to disengage his CTF from the Sound, being of no further good, which permission was imprudently granted by the senior admiral. The release of Fletcher's ships, however, would have an almost immediate ripple-down effect on several codependent operations that were, at that very moment, still very much in play.

The very least of these operations must certainly have included shielding the still-offloading troop transport and supply ships in the harbor, and those moored at the docks. Much of this "drop-off" work was still in progress—with munitions, supplies, and heavy equipment being put ashore as rapidly as the shore crews could move—and as quickly as the ships could cycle into their next docking. The date was 8 August, even then as Fletcher now sailed his ships out of harm's way and well to the north and east of the coming battle zone. By 9 August, for at least the men and ships below in Savo, the tide would turn yet one more time—and not at all in favor of the Allies.

With undue haste, Fletcher and his carrier support groups would already have departed the area by nightfall on 8 August, as would most of Turner's transport ships by the next day, which, without viable air cover, felt they could no longer safely carry out their own unloading operations. It was therefore much against the heated and incensed objections of the commander of all U.S. Marine forces on Guadalcanal, MG Alexander Vandegrift, that Admiral Turner would leave. The stranded Marines, infantry soldiers, and artillerymen were virtually left with only the basic weapons held in hand and but a modicum of short-lived supplies. This, even as many of their larger 155mm heavy artillery pieces they so critically needed still sat locked aboard the ships, along with pallets of ammunition, unit medical supplies, and key rations. But none of this was to be, at least for the time being, and with little or no forenotice of an intent to do so, the large cargo and support ships abruptly ceased all operations, weighed anchor, and simply pulled out.

For the Marines, and the other men seemingly "left in the lurch," this action alone would later be dubbed the "Great Navy Bugout" and often spoken of with venom and distaste. Up the chain of command, for VADM Fletcher—himself wholly responsible for both Turner and Crutchley's actions that night—this would clearly be *Strike One* . . . but would itself only leave the door open for even greater dangers and far worse disasters.

VADM Fletcher: Turning a Blind Eye (9 August 1942)

Following closely on the heels of the Great Navy Bugout, the cagey admiral would already have left the patrol area of Guadalcanal and the Solomons and had redeployed his carrier task force in full far to the northeast, well out of harm's way, at least for the time being. By nightfall, even as 8 August rolled over to a warm and mostly over-cast morning, Fletcher's luck might appear to have already begun changing radically . . . and none of it for the better. Even at that moment, VADM Gunichi Mikawa and his CRUDIV6 and 18 forces were pressing their advance through the narrow, island-fringed channel called the Slot and down toward Guadalcanal.

This was to be the spearhead of a bold counterstrike set wholly as a "punitive raid" against the interloping Allied naval forces that had so effortlessly supplanted his operations in and around Guadalcanal. The Japanese commander's calm demeanor could hardly bespeak the rage and deep-seated antipathy he must have harbored to-ward the American incursion into these formerly Japanese-held waters and territories. Therefore, on the morning of 8 August, a most determined Admiral Mikawa set forth from both Rabaul and Kavieng with two force elements, and moved forward in a typi-cal line-ahead, column-forward format with seven heavy cruisers and one destroyer.

Their mission would again have been quite simple: track them, hunt them, find them, kill them. And to also engage and fully decimate those Allied warships right there at Iron Bottom Sound—or, barring all else, to at least severely disrupt operations enough to "persuade" the unwelcome American forces to leave. This essentially meant that the Japanese would either invite the Americans to opt out entirely on their own or simply annihilate them in full should they decide to remain.

The eight Japanese warships forged on through a darkening mantle of night, with Mikawa's forces now approaching from the northwest and "threading the eye of the needle" as they sluiced down from points north. Shortly after midnight on 9 August, then, within a ten-minute window of opportunity that simply could not be lost, Mikawa's great ships would have already sighted the first of two U.S. radar pickets, the destroyers USS *Blue* (DD-387) and *Ralph Talbot* (DD-390).

Each patrol ship ran an elliptical patrol course just north of Savo, both equally equipped with a new "leading-edge" radar technology that had been touted as having great long-range-detection capabilities. Each DD would just have completed its patrol perigee—signaling the point of closest contact, while cruising only miles apart—and each was already pulling away on the outer leg of its patrol pattern—at precisely the moment the IJN cruisers steamed right toward them. Each would miss the approaching surface fleet, even as they stalked through the screening point and moved undetected into waters surrounding moonlit Savo. Mikawa did not wish to engage either

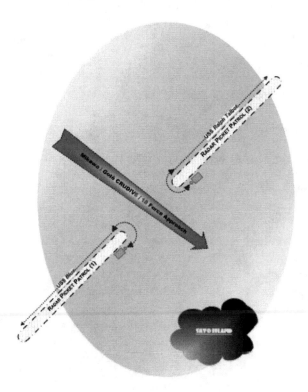

ship at that time for fear of disclosing his own position, and so he sailed with muffled sound and at reduced speed with lights blackened. Timing would have been essential to the shrewd Mikawa, and he had indeed used it fully to best advantage. Quietly, then, he let the two ships pass by and to simply proceed on to their next patrol perimeters without intercept.

From his elevated perch of bridge high atop the *Pagoda* mast of his great *Chōkai* flagship, Mikawa was also no one's fool, and it is truly said that he would have had more than fifty guns trained on the silent *Blue* at all times as she passed . . . just in case. Had she but "twitched" or given any indication of having seen his transiting fleet, the admiral would have, by instinct, simply blown her clean out of the water—and indeed any other takers as well.

For Admiral Fletcher, however, this single event would usher in all else that would follow and even allow those secondary events to occur. The failure of either of the radar pickets to detect and fully halt the IJN advance that night (and at that point) would be the result of a lapse in judgment by then-British RADM Victor A. Crutchley, the overall naval commander of all screening operations being conducted throughout the Sound that night. Later, the events themselves would be attributed to an inadequate screening force deployment, and a misallocation of ship assets. But more important, it would have happened on his "watch—his shift" and would provoke a full and expected "ripple-up" effect that would soon find its way back to Fletcher's own doorstep. To those who might recall Fletcher's somewhat spotty past and dubious actions during the still-fresh debacle at Midway, the admiral had to be walking on thin ice, and to those who could still sharply recall the horror and loss of the *Yorktown* itself, this was nothing if not *Strike Two*.

Iron Hammer: Attack on the Southern Fleet

Admiral Mikawa's eight warships now circumnavigated the waters around Savo Island with caution, even as the *Blue* now slowed to a measured 22 knots while passing just north of the island, within the upper reaches of Sealark Lane. His crew steeled themselves and readied for contact with the enemy surface fleet, which could indeed come at any time. It would be mere minutes before Mikawa's lookouts would spot the *Ralph Talbot* as well—the second of the two American radar pickets—coursing slowly on its own patrol corridor away from his passing ships. Once again, the Japanese commander's luck had run impeccably clean and without falter. Neither ship had even seen his approach. Yet, firm in the mind of the great IJN commander, had the oblivious *Talbot* shown any sign of detection, or had she foolishly chosen to engage any of his ships, her fate, too, would have been sealed by the certain blow of his iron-fisted warships.

The seven heavy cruisers that made up the vice admiral's Eighth Fleet task force would this night include not just his own flagship *Chōkai* but also the light cruisers

Tenryū and *Yubari*, plus the destroyer *Yunagi* and additional heavy cruisers under the command of Rear Admirals Gotō and Matsuyama themselves. That force would then be embodied in both CRUDIV6 and CRUDIV18, boasting of the large warships *Aoba*, *Furutaka*, *Kako*, and *Kinugasa*.

The massive IJN force traveled en masse, surging south in a calculated search for "hard targets" and silhouettes in a rough order that included first the large American battleships; then their screening heavy cruisers; then the destroyers—however found. Far and away, however, Mikawa's ships would also set a particularly high and focused aim on the troop transport and supply ships unloading even then. Soon, the two DDs *Jarvis* and *Patterson* would be the first ships seen by that IJN force and engaged by them in the very dead of night, but they would certainly not be the last.

The resulting major skirmish would be brutal and unrelenting, moment-quick, and decisive. It was in fact the Iron Hammer that Mikawa had now let fall on the Allied surface fleet that night, in a tactical move that would be so impeccably executed as to make one's own enemy sit up and take note. With flawless timing, precision, and ultimately just a sprinkle of "plain old good luck," Mikawa's attack force had swooped down past Savo Island and spotted the larger Allied ships, then prepared to engage them in full.

By 0138 hours, they began their attack on the Australian warship *Canberra*, and the *Northampton*-class *Chicago*, both heavy cruisers of the first order. Damaged in this nighttime surprise attack would also be the DDs *Jarvis* and *Patterson*, and even the *Bagley*. The attack would in fact be less than ten minutes long, but in its wake a battered *Chicago* would be left limping guardedly off to the north with a torpedo-chewed bow, and the *Canberra* sunk outright with a loss of some eighty-four men. The entire action would effectively constitute the attack on Crutchley's Southern fleet.

Pausing in his series of quick and rabid strikes, and soon indeed reining in his violent main-gun and torpedo attacks on the targeted Allied Southern force, Mikawa would now almost as quickly reverse his course and issue the then ill-advised decision to disengage his ships from the fray, and the attack fell away almost as abruptly as it had begun. With soft voice and no great elaboration, the good admiral simply ordered all cruiser columns to make a quick and coordinated turn to the north and to begin their northern exit from the battle area. Yet, even before they could do so, his ships would cross paths with the stricken *Canberra* one more time as she hobbled past in nearby waters.

Each of Mikawa's ships slid dangerously by the ship and off into the night, except only three of the tail element of that IJN column—namely, the *Furutaka*, *Yubari*, and *Tenryū*—all of which had swerved at the last moment and split away from the main advancing column to avoid an apparent collision with the still-blazing *Canberra*. These three ships would then fork out to a point beside and behind Mikawa's main body, and they soon closed on the admiral's starboard flank. Purely a masterstroke of genius and of only the greatest good fortune, this one event now effectively created a two-pronged assault column that soon spearheaded a "combined attack" by almost the full cruiser might of the entire Imperial Japanese Navy. By 0159 hours, then, having finished with Crutchley's Southern force, Mikawa would already have had fresh targets in sight, and those targets would be nothing else if not Riefkohl's own Northern screening ships . . . and few there would fare much better—or even outlive the night.

Spiked Mace: Attack on the Northern Fleet

Only minutes before two in the morning—having just arrived from points south, where they had already encountered and fully destroyed the Allied Southern force— the Japanese task group (under the aegis of VADM Gunichi Mikawa) seemed out for blood, now seeking fresh targets just over the horizon. Those fresh targets would become the very ships of the Allied Northern screen, under RADM Frederick Riefkohl. Unlike the Southern group, this screening force would be made up entirely of American ships and would include the three heavy cruisers the *Vincennes*, the *Quincy*, and the *Astoria*, in addition to their two escort destroyers the *Helm* and the *Wilson*. Only one of these ships might expect to escape great harm this night, and that ship would be the *Helm*.

Having already given the order to his subordinate ships to operate independently of each other, Mikawa now instructed his ships to launch their starshell flares in dead of night—which, coupled with those dropped from the overhead floatplanes sent up from the *Chōkai* and the other cruisers, soon lit up a wide expanse of sea even as his ships advanced at battle speed. Then, soon enough right before them, and fully lit up and trapped in a two-pronged bracketing maneuver, lay the three American cruisers and their escorts, sharply silhouetted by the still-smoldering wreckage of the large transport ship, USS *George F. Elliott* (AP-13), that had been damaged in a previous action. The inadvertent, luck-driven splitting of Mikawa's column now quite fortuitously came into play as well, as virtually all of his ships were then able to launch a bold, twin-axial attack on that Northern group.* The attack itself would be over in minutes and would be little else if not swift and final.

Savaged almost immediately in the resulting sudden attacks would be the proud *Vincennes*, soon itself repeatedly hit by spreads of torpedoes and volleys of high-caliber shells fired from the large 8-inch guns on the Japanese cruisers. This same heated assault would almost at once be followed up by a full barrage on the next ship in column,

---

*On the night in question (9 August 1942), reliable evidence has surfaced over the years that points to a possible "three-pronged" split of Mikawa's forces. This may have been caused by a split-column element that first swung to the north that consisted of the *Furutaka*, *Yubari*, and the *Tenryū*. Mikawa's secondary split force would then constitute a southern force made up of the *Chōkai*, *Aoba*, *Kako*, and *Kinugasa*. Later, even within this latter group, the admiral's own flagship *Chōkai* may have split off to form yet a third (one-ship) column on her own, sailing far to the east. The when and why are entirely unclear, and one might only speculate on Mikawa's actual intent at that time. For an even greater discussion on precisely this two-column–three-column split, see the discussion presented earlier, beginning on page 156.

the *Quincy*, nor would they spare the *Astoria*, as she, too, would soon be hit by several cross-ship attacks. At the very peak, therefore, each of the American warships was being targeted one by one with full broadsides coming from both columns of Mikawa's cruiser division force.

This would effectively constitute the attack on Crutchley's Northern screen. And, much like the Australian *Canberra*, so would it be with the American *Vincennes*, with each ship sinking almost immediately and with great loss of life.

Astoria had herself also been outnumbered and outgunned . . . surprised by the vicious combined attack from the large guns on not just the *Chōkai* but also the *Aoba*, *Kinugasa*, and *Kako*. *Astoria*, too, would be ravaged by the assault and would live on but a few hours more before sinking by 1215 of the next day. Lastly, even *Quincy*'s guns would soon fall silent in the face of the forced attacks of Gotō's *Aoba* and the *Tenryū*, and she would be hit by no less than three torpedoes fired from Mikawa's cruisers. *Quincy* would cripple off from the battle zone, now a mere shell of her once-great self, and would summarily upend and sink in waters far to the northwest of Savo Island. By 0238 on the morning of 9 August 1942, then, the *Mighty Q* would slip under the sea's surface and go down. Her loss would also claim the lives of some 370+ souls.

Mikawa's Spiked Mace had now fallen in full and would be a grievous counterpoint to the Iron Hammer of his earlier attack. Truly, however, the net effect of both would probably have been the same: the loss of all four American and Australian heavies in a single encounter with Mikawa's mighty naval fleet now made it all that much more personal.

RADM RICHMOND KELLY TURNER, USN

Born the son of a rancher/farmer and printer on May 27, 1885, in Portland, Oregon, Richmond Kelly Turner was almost preordained to be a standout navy man and a natural leader; by 1904, due in great measure to the quiet and considered intercession of a local district congressman, he had already been appointed to the U.S. Naval Academy at Annapolis. He would attend the USNA with an arduous zeal and apply himself well to his studies and then go on to actually graduate mid-term in his fourth year in 1908. Over the course of the next four years, he would go on to serve on several smaller ships, and by 1913 the now-LJG (Lieutenant Junior Grade) Turner would obtain his first command ship—however briefly—with the *Bainbridge*-class destroyer USS *Stewart* (DD-13).

RADM Turner: Guadalcanal Diary and the Rude Awakening

The battle for Guadalcanal (and for control of the Solomon Islands) would be understatedly quite rough, and by mid-1942 it would see some of the most historic and most fierce fighting found up to that point in the prolonged Pacific war. It would be terribly costly—not only in terms of men, materiel, and critical ship assets lost—but would also be physically taxing on the American fighting forces already there on station, whether at sea, in the air, or on the ground. Admiral Fletcher may himself have been settled safely some miles away with his carrier task group (and thus absented from the true seat of the action), but Admiral Turner would truly be found right in the thick of it, and by August of that same year he would have already set a number of "safeguards" in place to ensure the security of the entire area then in dispute.

It was therefore a highly motivated Admiral Turner who soon arrived at Guadalcanal and assumed full operational command of the Allies' amphibious force. In short order, the junior admiral would have already set up a series of patrol corridors for his surface ships, wholly made up of at least two heavy cruisers each, and accompanying fast destroyers, to serve as a deterrent screening force to guard the northern, southern, and eastern sectors of Iron Bottom Sound, and truly all approaches to Tulagi, Florida Island, and Guadalcanal itself. Coming directly from Nimitz, Turner would now be tasked with a twofold responsibility that included not just a full command of the amphibious assault ships then landing at Tulagi and Honiara but also the supply and support ships, troop transport vessels, and fleet oilers.

But far and away, however, the admiral's prime directive would always have been that of commanding the main battle fleet that even then busied itself with screening the supply ships' offloading activities. Therefore, the actions of every cruiser, every destroyer, and every oiler and armed transport ship present would indeed be directly reportable to Turner and his leadership role during the heat of battle. Soon, the good admiral would indeed be sorely tested in this new role, and by the evening of 8 August he would have already briefed his cruiser commanders and quickly deployed a vast array of his forces as best he could. Throughout the entire vastness of Iron Bottom Sound, therefore, the sum total of the end-goal screening element that he would quickly piece together would resemble that shown in Table 32.

RADM Turner: The Crutchley Deployments

Soon, Admiral Turner would make the acquaintance of the Allied force's ranking British Royal Navy commander, one Admiral Sir Victor Alexander Charles Crutchley, himself already sailing his own flag on the well-known pride-of-fleet HMAS *Australia*. Assured of the man's earnest competency, and his results-oriented approach to dealing with complex problems, Turner would indeed feel comfortable with placing him in overall command—with full operational control—of all screening forces in and around the Solomons at that time. Turner's decision to do so would be key later on, but for now, however, all large warship deployments seemed well in order (or at least under way), even if both admirals thought their screening forces to be far too inadequate to cover the expansive patrol corridors they were being assigned.[150]

Table 32. Admiral Turner's Decisive Screening Force Deployment (8 August 1942)

Screening Force	Force Composition	Force Element Commander
Southern Group **(Task Group 62.2)**	**Two Heavy Cruisers:** HMAS *Canberra* (D33) USS *Chicago* (CA-29) **Two Destroyers:** USS *Bagley* (DD-386) USS *Patterson* (DD-392)	*Force Commander:* **Admiral Sir Victor Alexander Charles Crutchley, RN** (Departed area on the HMAS *Australia*)
Northern Group **(Task Group 62.3)**	**Three Heavy Cruisers:** USS *Vincennes* (CA-44) (Flag) USS *Quincy* (CA-39) USS *Astoria* (CA-34) **Two Destroyers:** USS *Helm* (DD-388) USS *Wilson* (DD-393)	*Force Commander:* **Rear Admiral Frederick Lois Riefkohl, USN**
Eastern Group **(Task Group 62.4)**	**One Heavy Cruiser:** HMAS *Hobart* (D63) **One Light Cruiser:** USS *San Juan* (CL-54) (Flag) **Two Destroyers:** USS *Monssen* (DD-436) USS *Buchanan* (DD-484)	*Force Commander:* **Rear Admiral Norman Scott, USN**
Radar Pickets **(Task Group 62.6)**	**Two Destroyers:** USS *Blue* (DD-387) USS *Ralph Talbot* (DD-390)	*Force Commander:* **Commander Harold Nordmark Williams, USN**
Unassigned/Detached (?) **(Task Group 62.2)**	**One Heavy Cruiser:** HMAS *Australia* (D84) (Flag for Southern)	*Force Commander:* **Admiral Sir Victor Alexander Charles Crutchley, RN**

In the end, Turner and Crutchley would simply make do with the hard assets they had available to them at the time—which, in this event, meant nothing less than the large heavy cruisers and destroyers immediately at hand. With less than ten heavy cruisers, no carrier or battleship-class assets available at all, and only a handful of "Tin Can" destroyers, Turner was now fully expected to "hold down the fort" and face the almost-certain superior forces that all knew might soon be thrown at them, and which were in fact already en route. For even at that very moment, Mikawa's own Cruiser Divisions 18 and 6 were fast approaching Savo Island, and Turner only knew about the what, but not at all about the when or the how. Both Allied admirals would simply have to bide their time and wait for the certain coming onslaught.

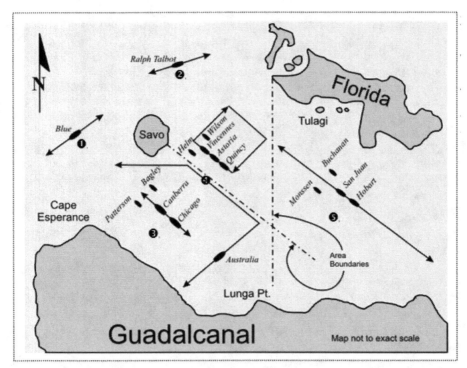

Figure 39.   Admiral Turner's Screening Force Deployments on 9 August 1942

RADM Turner: The *McCawley* Conference

Truly might it be said that Admiral Turner's first pitfall might have been as innocuous as the inopportune convening of a command-level meeting between himself and his high-ranking staff at the time, late on the evening of 8 August 1942. After a busy day of troop landings and cargo unloading, coupled with the activities of the naval screening forces offshore, and further capped by the withdrawal of Fletcher's carrier fleet, there was now every indication that a new strategy for the defense of the area in dispute would be needed—and that sooner rather than later. The good admiral had therefore summoned both of his subordinates—RADM Victor Crutchley (representing all current amphibious forces and screening elements operating in and around Guadalcanal) and MG Alexander Vandegrift (the senior-ranking Marine Corps commander in charge of all landing and land-based operations currently under way). Though vitally important to all men concerned, the meeting itself could not have come at a worse time for each of them, as only hours later Turner's entire fleet would itself come under its most profound and violent attack ever.

The afternoon of 8 August 1942, therefore, would find Admiral Crutchley riding his flag high atop the great HMAS *Australia* as part of the larger Southern screening force, along with her sister ship the Australian *Canberra*, with both heavy cruisers in the company of their allies' USS *Chicago* and a gathering of escort destroyers in the *Bagley* and *Patterson*. Being mandated to attend Turner's hastily convened meeting, Crutchley would do so but would not commute to that meeting by either low transport or Admiral's Barge; he would instead opt to take the entire flagship *Australia* with him. This action would now effectively reduce the force-presence of that Southern fleet to only two heavy cruisers and lessen that screening force's firepower potential by fully one third.

By 2300 hours, therefore, both Crutchley and Vandegrift would have already arrived to meet with Admiral Turner aboard his ship, the heavily armed attack transport USS *McCawley* (APA-4), which also *pro tempore* carried Turner's flag. Had any of the three men in conference that night known of the impending peril that lurked just to their northwest, they would each have insisted on terminating the meeting and returning immediately to their primary duty stations to brace for a full enemy contact. As it was, they were not so informed and would learn only later, well after the quick unfurling of events yet to come. And so, in full measure, they did indeed meet aboard the *McCawley*, where they discussed matters of weight, contemplated their deployment options, and several variable perimeter screening strategies available to them, all the while carefully nursed by refreshment. Yet only a few miles away, VADM Mikawa was now forming up his bold CRUDIV forces into a standard line-ahead column format and already beginning his push into the Sound.

This one conference—this one meeting aboard *McCawley*—had now effectively pulled each of the key commanders away from their assigned duty stations—however momentous and meaningful it might have seemed at the time—but that would in the long run be quite costly to the Allied fleet later that night. And far and away, most critically noted of all would be Crutchley's foolish decision to have even withdrawn his *Australia* from the line when he did, effectively removing one additional asset that might well have turned the tide at the outset of that battle. Later, it would indeed be much to the chagrin of all three commanders that they would have been found "busied elsewhere" when the surprise attack on Crutchley's Southern fleet had itself commenced.

RADM Turner: Radar Pickets and the Attack on the Southern Fleet

The admiral's next shortfall—aside from the thinned and scattered deployment of his ships throughout the Sound, as cited earlier—would now be the failure of either the USS *Blue* or the *Ralph Talbot* to detect or interdict the advancing Japanese surface fleet as it moved south just out of the Slot. The furtive IJN cruiser force, under Mikawa's admiralty, had virtually unraveled the Gordian Knot of it and slipped through the noose of the two American radar picket ships, and simply moved on unchallenged. Neither radar picket would ever spy Mikawa's passing ships until it was already far too late, and it would only be with the onset of actions south of Savo that it would even become apparent that something was horribly wrong.

Having passed the loose blockade of the two radar pickets, Mikawa's ships now quickly identified the silhouetted shapes of the Allied ships in Iron Bottom Sound, and immediately began to prosecute their attacks to their best advantage. Caught unawares and truly stunned by the quickness, ferocity, and dead-on accuracy of Mikawa's surface fleet gunners and torpedomen, the Allied Southern force would be the first group hit. And the heavy cruisers *Canberra* and *Chicago* would be the first hit and mercilessly savaged by as many as four IJN ships each, with all ships attacking in tandem both with their large main guns and each ship's torpedoes.

The Allied screening force stood not a chance, and the *Canberra* would be lost almost immediately, sinking in situ with great loss of life. The *Chicago*—and at least one of her accompanying destroyers, the *Patterson*—would also be hit repeatedly and soon forced to retire from the battle zone, each ship staggering off to lick its rankled wounds and to fight the major deck and bulkhead fires that had resulted. *Chicago* would sustain particular damage to her bow and soon inexplicably shuttle off far to the northwest on a forty-minute trek away from the area of battle. Admiral Crutchley was alleged to have later been furious with CAPT Howard Douglas Bode, the skipper of *Chicago*, for his actions during the attack at Savo Island. He might indeed have been glad to have had the man's head on a platter . . . much as Turner might have had his.

The "slipping" of the Mikawa cruiser force past the two American radar pickets north of dark Savo, so assuredly placed there under the guise and aegis of Admiral Crutchley's overall screening strategy, would that night indeed trickle up the chain of command and move on to haunt Turner for at least this time. And it would wallop him good and leave him with a minor black eye for the first time in his career.

RADM Turner: Attack on the Northern Fleet

The ensuing swing-around of Mikawa's surface fleet after their violent clash with Crutchley's *Canberra* and *Chicago* now fortuitously lined up all of the admiral's ships for a secondary assault, inadvertently set as a two-pronged attack column targeting RADM Riefkohl's Northern screen. In dead of night, with unwary and exhausted lookouts on the American heavies *Vincennes*, *Quincy*, and *Astoria*, Riefkohl's ships could not at all have known what hit them until indeed it did, and by 0150 hours on the morning of 9 August, they would have already come under critical attack from the now-northbound Mikawa force. The resulting savaging twin-axial push past the trapped ships of the Northern screen is today a matter of record, and in short order each of the large American heavy cruisers would be hit and sunk by the fierce IJN warships operating in both columns. The *Quincy* would be first to go down, at 0238, with the *Vincennes* likewise sinking by 0250 and the *Astoria* lingering for an excruciating eight additional hours before herself sinking at 1215 that same morning.

The loss of almost 1,100 men in a combined total for all ships sunk would be nothing if not stunning and dramatic news—of the *worst* order—to the ears of the admiralty and commanders who had formerly been locked in conference on the *Mc-Cawley*. The full Japanese attack on Crutchley's ships would begin and end in a span of minutes; the attack on the Southern and Northern fleets even more fractional than that but would be most impactful when compounded with the mounted casualty rates and utter loss of ships of the line.

Admiral Richmond Kelly Turner, not unlike Fletcher and the many others who were involved either directly or indirectly in the debacle at Savo Island, would also live to see another day. He would go on to later triumph in even greater sea battles yet to come, while only a marginal stain might be cast on either his leadership role or his force-readiness capability, though it would not be enough to flag the overall confidence that Turner's commanders seemed to have had in him. Surprise attacks or not, he was still the best man for the dangerous job at hand and would indeed go on to survive both the trial and travail of Guadalcanal and all of the messiness of the Solomons. History, it would seem, would have far greater plans for the admiral.

It was now indeed this very Admiral Turner who would then become the impetus and driving force behind almost every amphibious landing operation thereafter, a "go-to" aggressor known to his men as "Terrible Turner." He would go on to serve proudly in places like Kwajalein, Saipan, the Marianas, and even the Ryukyus during the battle for the heavily reinforced Okinawa. In later years, by 1945, had a full invasion of Japan's homelands even been warranted—at whatever cost such a battle might have entailed for the Allied force—it was already well known that Turner's amphibious assault ships would be the ones that would lead from the front—as the very tip and spearhead of that invasion force. Of course, it would never come to that end, and the war would soon enough be brought to its horrific and abrupt end because of the sudden (and wholly unforeseen) events at both Hiroshima and Nagasaki.

Admiral Turner would now turn his attention to an even higher command within the Washington short-list circle itself, with an appointment to the Navy Department's own General Board. Far and away, however, perhaps his most crowning achievement must clearly have been his final appointment as U.S. Naval Representative, and prestigiously serving as a liaison officer on the United Nations' Military Staff Committee. Turner would work within that esteemed body for some two additional years before his retirement in 1947, after which he quietly returned to Monterey, California, where he later passed away in 1961.

By prearrangement among the four great men who had been lifelong friends, compatriots, and fellow flag officers of the United States Navy, Admiral Richmond Kelly Turner would be buried in the National Cemetery in San Bruno, California, alongside his wife and interred with other men of great naval renown, such as Admirals Chester A. Nimitz, Raymond A. Spruance, and Charles A. Lockwood. Full military honors would be smartly rendered at the time of the admiral's well-observed burial, and many would regard the passing of this one great man, and flagship commander, as a significant loss both to humanity and to the United States Navy.

RADM SIR VICTOR ALEXANDER CHARLES CRUTCHLEY, RN

If there would be any culpability for the disaster at Savo at all, some of that blame might clearly find its way to the good admiral's feet. Admiral Sir Victor Alexander Charles Crutchley, the operational commander for all screening forces at Guadalcanal at that time, would indeed have held a prime responsibility for the deployment of his own Southern group ships (with which group he would proudly ride his flag), as well as those tasked to form both the Northern and Eastern screens on the day just before the attack at Savo Island.

For, even as Fletcher might himself be unavailable for any accounting of what exactly would later occur at Savo—that senior admiral now cruising well asea some miles to the north and east of Guadalcanal with his own withdrawn carrier forces—there would be no easy escape or quick port of call in the maelstrom of the storm for the less fortunate Crutchley. And life got just a bit more difficult with the resulting close scrutiny and muffled condemnation that would now be targeted at the man, and his subordinates, for their actions (or inactions) on the battle night in question. And, unlike his lofty superior Admiral Turner, still on his sleek transport ship *McCawley*, Crutchley would not be as adept at artfully dodging the bullet as some others might.

As the sole operational commander for all screening forces assigned to escort and shield the transport/landing ships, no one but he would have been tasked with defining and executing a series of workable plans for an effective defense of the sea-lanes in and around Iron Bottom Sound, and extending well up to points even farther north. Only he would retain the stressful and thankless job of setting the patrol corridors for his very few heavy and light cruisers, fast-attack destroyers, and radar pickets. And only he would be asked to assume the slightly more than monumental task of taking those ten ships and having them now do the work of twenty. And indeed he would almost pull it off without a hitch.

In his time, the quite formal Admiral Victor A. Crutchley had indeed been a recipient of not only the esteemed Victoria Cross but also the Knight Commander of the Bath (KCB) award, the Distinguished Service Cross (DSC), and the French Croix de Guerre (CG), and he had been conferred with the honor of Chief Commander, Legion of Merit (CCLM). He was also a well-established senior officer in the British Royal Navy, a man on consultative loan to the Australian commonwealth, a man proud to be in His Majesty's service, and a man glad enough to have simply been a sailor's sailor.

As for the First Battle of Savo Island, however, Admiral Crutchley—and his Marine Corps counterpart, General Alexander Vandegrift—would have both been inopportunely sequestered in Turner's meeting aboard the flagship *McCawley* at the senior admiral's request. Both subordinate officers were therefore absent from the main area of battle precisely at the moment of the attacks themselves, but only Crutchley's attendance at that now-famous *McCawley* Conference would be nothing less than plain rotten luck. Timing would have been essential in both battles, especially as it had so rapidly unfolded and developed; yet Crutchley's absence and apparent ill preparedness even in advance of the attack would ring a heavy toll on the man's perceived command abilities. The unreasoned withdrawal of his own flagship *Australia* just prior to the attack, to attend that very meeting, would at best have been ill advised and at worst incautious and costly. Perhaps a naval commander most wrongfully reviled, he would nonetheless work on under only a slightly blackened cloud for some period of time, but soon enough it might be seen that his sun might continue to shine.

RADM Crutchley: Culpability at Guadalcanal?

To what extent the good Admiral Crutchley would be responsible for the events of 9 August 1942 might not be entirely clear to most researchers and analysts of the period and the battle; however, it might also be speculated that the British commander of all naval forces that night might indeed bear the brunt of the blame game that was sure to follow in the wake of Savo—perhaps even more so than others—and excepting only Bode himself, to great extent Crutchley would receive his own lion's share of the finger-pointing once the dust had settled after the storm.

By later in the day on 9 August 1942, a warm sunrise would be coldly eclipsed by the still-fresh losses of the four Allied heavy cruisers from just the night before . . . and by the even heavier casualty figures that were mounting by the hour to now well over a thousand men. Who indeed, then, should be responsible for the devastating losses suffered at the hands of Mikawa's bold cruiser division attacks? From RADM Turner on down, all fingers began to point at the hapless RADM Crutchley as perhaps being most culpable. After all, had he not been appointed commander of all Allied warships, both American and Australian, that were then operating in and around Iron Bottom Sound? Had he not been solely responsible for the ships' deployments, their composite makeup, and for setting the patrol corridors themselves, all while attempting to coordinate and juggle all of the interdependent actions of over fifteen ships? High aloft and certainly at pay grades much higher than his own, would the great naval high command in fact be "forgiving" of the man's seeming indiscretions at Savo—or would they instead kill at the root the very career of that same man? Would they, in a single instance and a minor stroke of pen, simply let fall the great hammer of condemnation on the British naval commander's head, or might they instead offer but a mild reprimand tempered with lenience and absolution? Decidedly, much would indeed work to the favor of the admiral.

For within hours of the fiasco at Savo, Crutchley would have already heard from both Turner and Fletcher, in their urgent pleas to more clearly understand what had happened, how so quickly, and how such an attack might even have been possible in the first place. Crutchley's leadership ability was now being called into serious question by his superiors, most notably with Turner as the COMAMPHIBFORSOPACFLT (Commander, Amphibious Forces, South Pacific Fleet) force leader, who would express perhaps the greatest disbelief. This point aside, one might well be compelled to walk a mile in the man's shoes, however, and to also consider the moral dilemma of

Turner himself, as the now-conflicted senior commander who could not at all fault Crutchley or Vandegrift for being away from their duty stations at the time of the attack, since it had been precisely at his behest to convene that meeting on the *McCawley* that would pull both men away in the first place.

In the end, several of the senior commanders (certainly not to exclude Crutchley) would be harshly faulted for the actions at Savo, and the subordinate British admiral would indeed share in some of the blame. Had he more ships and a greater force-presence at hand, and time perhaps to more effectively deploy the scant and scattered ship assets available for use that night, the tale might have had a much different ending. As it was, he did not, so it did not . . . and for a time might the world see only that the disaster at Savo Island, in great part, had indeed happened on his watch.

On a kinder and gentler note, in the years following the events of 9 August 1942, the British naval high command would in fact reinvigorate its level of confidence and trust in Admiral Crutchley, and the man would remain with the Royal Australian Navy (RAN), and operate throughout much of the southwest Pacific, while still continuing his command of TF-44 for almost another two years. All might be forgiven, though not wholly forgotten (nor would the role ADM Crutchley had either played or not played during the course of the horrific First Battle of Savo Island).

Valuable lessons would have been learned by the Allied naval commanders as a result of Savo, and certainly Crutchley's best takeaway from the battle would have been that of standing with good force, an ever-increased level of readiness, and a more cautioned command of all of his ship assets. By late September 1944, an already distinguished Admiral Crutchley would have yet another high honor bestowed on him—that of the esteemed American Legion of Merit—which would then be awarded him in the degree of chief commander.

In 1986, Crutchley would pass on at the ripe old age of ninety-two, having far outlived many of his contemporaries and fellow admirals with whom he had so proudly served. His archrival and fellow combatant—the great VADM Gunichi Mikawa himself, who had so valiantly led his own brilliantly performing forces to victory that night—would actually precede RADM Crutchley in death by only five years, passing away in 1981 when he, too, had reached his ninety-second birthday. It is highly doubtful that the two men would ever even have met except on the field of battle.

RADM NORMAN NICHOLAS SCOTT, USN

RADM Norman N. Scott would not play any essential role in the First Battle of Savo Island, but the cruiser commander would later serve with distinction in other major battles in and around Guadalcanal. Scott was no stranger to either hazard or heroism, and the young ensign's very first assignment would be aboard the great battleship USS *Idaho* (BB-24). Later, a highly motivated Scott would go on to spend much of his early career as a "Tin Can Sailor," and proud of having been such, served on a variety of fast-attack destroyers like the USS *Jacob Jones* (DD-61), the USS *Paul Jones* (DD-230), and the USS *MacLeish* (DD-220) before moving up to the big leagues of the light (CL) and heavy (CA) armored cruisers. By early 1940, then, CAPT Scott would again be the skipper at the helm, this time commanding the massive USS *Pensacola* (CA-24), a first-of-her-class heavy cruiser of the finest order. He would be commanding this very ship when the attack on Pearl Harbor unfolded on the morning of 7 December 1941. But, like so many others who might have been only marginally caught up in the surprise aerial attacks of that morning, the admiral would himself play no significant role in that action.

Shortly after the devastating blow at Pearl Harbor, CAPT Scott would have put his command on hold, and instead quite fortuitously rotated back to shore duty where he would reach yet another milestone in his career (and in his life), being assigned to work for the then Chief of Naval Operations (CNO) back in Washington, D.C. Many eyes were now fixed on the young up-and-comer Scott, much for the duration of his tenure here, and in short order he would cross the threshold and attain the rank of a full flag officer of the USN at the age of fifty-three, with his promotion to rear admiral. The new admiral's first assignment would probably also be his roughest, and even perhaps his *last*. That assignment, of course, would be nothing other than that of the invasion of Guadalcanal.

RADM Scott: Commanding the Eastern Screen

Desperately needing a commander of his caliber, the navy brass quickly took note of his standing and invited RADM Scott to the Solomons, as soon he would be dispatched from his CNO duties to now lead several units of the invasion force's screening ship element. The new brass stars on the man's shoulder-boards had scarce been tacked on, therefore, when a determined Scott would have indeed arrived at Guadalcanal in May 1942. His first order of business would be that of commanding a fire support element of cruisers and destroyers during the initial invasions of both Guadalcanal and cross-channel Tulagi in the early part of August 1942. There, he would head up one of Crutchley's four hastily conceived screening force elements, Task Group 62.4,[151] that, by 9 August, would make up the Eastern screening group (Figure 39) and would wholly consist of only two light cruisers, the USS *San Juan* (CL-54) and an Australian equivalent in the HMAS *Hobart* (D63), along with the two escort destroyers *Monssen* (DD-436) and *Buchanan* (DD-484).

At the time of VADM Gunichi Mikawa's arrival at Savo Island, just prior to his highly successful attacks on Crutchley's Southern and Northern screens, RADM Scott would be found well to the south in Sealark Lane, tasked with patrolling the hazardous waters off Tulagi and the Florida Island (Nggella Sule) coastline. For the full interval of the attacks themselves, therefore, he would be occupied with his own primary screening tasks: that of watching over the Marine landings at Tulagi, and riding shotgun for the still-emptying cargo ships crammed with materiel and supplies at both locations.

Quite as a matter of record, neither Scott nor any of his Eastern screening force would see any action that night and would play no significant role in the overall First Battle of Savo Island. The good admiral and his screening ships might well have seen and heard the battle looming far to the west that night, but neither would engage nor even leave station in any attempt to intercept any of Mikawa's surface ships. Scott's ships might indeed have mercifully dodged a big bullet, and his force would sustain no injury or damage. Each of the Eastern screening force ships would live on to fight another day, and to triumph in other heated battles yet to come, both in the Solomons and beyond. One such encounter would earn the dogged RADM Scott nothing less than the Medal of Honor (MOH), this for conspicuous gallantry shown while under heavy enemy fire during the Battle of Cape Esperance (BOCE), and the later Naval Battle of Guadalcanal.

RADM Scott: With All Our Battlewagons Toe to Toe

During the initial night action of the Naval Battle of Guadalcanal—also known as the Third and Fourth Battles of Savo Island—in what would shortly become one of the most chilling and most violent of naval encounters seen thus far in the battle for Guadalcanal, Scott would earn his stripes and deal in hot lead with his Japanese counterparts. In fact, only three months after the disaster at Savo itself, he would once again meet with the forces of a still-determined Imperial Japanese Navy under the admiralty of an only recently promoted vice admiral, one Hiroaki Abe.

Therefore, on the very shank of night on 13 November 1942, massing naval forces under the overall command of Admiral Isoroku Yamamoto began assembling in an area 80 miles north of the Indispensable Strait, a larger body of water just northeast of Guadalcanal that narrowly channels its way into what would soon be called Iron Bottom Sound.

Yamamoto would this night also have been shrewd enough to split his forces into two functional command structures: ❶ a slower-moving convoy of troop transport and cargo ships, placed under the aegis and command of VADM Raizo Tanaka, commander of the destroyer task force; and ❷ a flotilla of fast and armed-to-the-teeth attack ships that had been set to protect the slower-moving vessels until all were fully in place. The convoy itself would have had but one objective: running the "Tokyo Express," a quick and effective means of expediting the landing of fresh occupation troops from Japan's rugged 38th Infantry Division onto the island fortress of Guadalcanal. The secondary group—by far the more fierce and bully aggressors of the entire surface fleet itself—would be the large warships commanded by VADM Hiroaki Abe, which warships would be used to very good purpose, that of screening the landing and unloading activities of Tanaka's troop transport and supply ships. It was essentially this work, then, that needed to get done—by Japan's own estimates—at any cost.

Therefore, already formed up in Admiral Abe's surface fleet would be no less than two massive battleships, the IJN *Kirishima* and his own flagship the *Hiei*; a single light cruiser, the *Nagara*; and as many as eleven escorting destroyers. In and of itself, this complement would constitute only Abe's "screening" force and did not at all factor in the eleven transports with their own twelve-destroyer screen as well, all now traveling under Tanaka's command and set to rendezvous on the morning of 13 November. All told, greater than thirty-eight ships would therefore soon be converging on a single concentrated area just west-northwest of Guadalcanal, near a promontory called Cape Esperance—a small and protuberant outcrop of land jutting out into Iron Bottom Sound. Soon enough, however, the battle main would be joined. This time the Americans would not be caught by surprise, and the overwhelming bravado of the American fighting men would this night entirely save the day for the Allied fleet. In no small measure, Admiral Norman N. Scott could be counted as one of those heroes.

RADM FREDERICK LOIS RIEFKOHL, USN

RADM Frederick Lois Riefkohl may actually have been one of the more unique characters of the First Battle of Savo Island and would in fact be the only cruiser commander of the Northern screen to even survive Admiral Gunichi Mikawa's twin attacks on the night of 9 August 1942. Harsh and valuable lessons would quickly be learned by the competent admiral, who could not at all have known just how much his mettle would be tested during the course of this one event. His reactions under fire this night would soon be the head and spring for several such heroic deeds and a cause-célèbre for later stern rebuke in the battle's aftermath. For now, however, the young Riefkohl's curious story would itself begin to unfold in the year 1911.

Frederick Lois Riefkohl would have the clear distinction of being the first graduate of the United States Naval Academy of Puerto Rican descent, a fact that did not go unnoticed by the author, being of close descent. Of note, he was a man indeed to be quite proud of, both for his academic achievements and for his valor on the field of battle. And by 1917, at the still-tender age of twenty-eight and while serving as a sub-lieutenant aboard the early cruiser USS *Philadelphia* (C-4), he was instrumental in the ship's successful detection—and later full *engagement*—of an enemy submarine stalking his ship. For his actions that day in the throes of battle as Commander, Armed Guard, Riefkohl would be awarded the coveted Navy Cross. It would be one of many awards and commendations that, in its time, would be bestowed on the man but must clearly have always remained his most cherished.

In the years between armed conflicts, it would now be an older and far more experienced Riefkohl who would jockey and prod his way from station to station, finally arriving at a series of senior posts that would eventually include serving as district communications officer for the 15th Naval District in the Panama Canal Zone; being tapped as an aide on the staff of the Commander, Destroyer Force, Atlantic Fleet (DFAF); and being assigned as the executive officer (XO) aboard the aging *Bainbridge*-class destroyer USS *Preble* (DD-12). By 1923, the well-accomplished Riefkohl would have reached an even higher personal goal, that of becoming aide and flag secretary to the Commander-in-Chief of the Asiatic Fleet (CINCAF), a sharp honor in its time. But far and away, it might still have been the man's well-earned Navy Cross that would most continue to open doors for him, and by 1926 he would receive his first command of a ship of the line when he boarded the *Clemson*-class destroyer USS *Corry* (DD-334).

During his more active years, from 1926 to 1931, the ever-ambitious Riefkohl would hold down a series of interim assignments throughout the Caribbean waters in locations like Port-au-Prince, Haiti; Guantanamo Bay, Cuba; San Juan, Puerto Rico; and even St. Thomas in the Virgin Islands—all conceivably due to his native "bilingualism." His years of leisure and intellectual pursuit, however, would soon be over, and an older and more care-worn Riefkohl would soon be shaken out of his professional torpor and forced onto the center stage of activities during the opening salvos of the naval battle for Guadalcanal.

By April 1942, he would finally assume full command of his first heavy cruiser, the *Maggie V*—or the Magnificent *Vincennes* (CA-44). Her destiny and destination would both imponderably be tied together in a small and little-known piece of real estate called Guadalcanal. And Riefkohl could not at all have known that both Admirals Mikawa and Gotō would at that very moment also have had the same intent, and greatly coveted the same area for their own military purposes. The die, it would seem, had already been cast and conflict between the two vast navies was now all but inevitable.

RADM Riefkohl first arrived on the *Vincennes* in early 1942—proud, assured, and fully capable of commanding the graceful, yet aging, American heavy cruiser. With the United States' military forces now secretly planning an invasion of the Solomon Islands (and specifically Tulagi and Henderson Field), Riefkohl would summarily be assigned to serve in direct support of RADM Richmond Kelly Turner's larger task force (see page 271) to effectively screen that concentrated landing effort. By 7 August, then, his intrepid *Vincennes* was already laying to off the coast of Guadalcanal and unleashing her flagging but still powerful 8-inch guns to soften up any resistance encountered from the Japanese infantry forces already dug in near Henderson Field.

Having lent her full fire support to both the landing of the American forces and the unloading of critical supplies and materiel needed to support the effort, *Vincennes* would soon return to normal patrol duties in the Sound guarding the highly exposed (and ever-offloading) cargo and transport ships. Later that same day, the heavy cruiser would be released from station and banded together with a small screening task group with two other heavy cruisers and a brace of destroyers to form Crutchley's new Northern screen. For Riefkohl, of course, it would perhaps be the beginning of the end, in a horrid scenario in which an attempt would be made on his life and a later loss of the very ship he had been so proud to earlier command.

RADM Riefkohl: The *Maggie V*—Attack on the USS *Vincennes*

On the night in question, 9 August 1942, the good Admiral Riefkohl would have already been tasked by his superior, Admiral Victor A. Crutchley, to head up a Northern screening element, which would be dubbed Task Group 62.3. TG 62.3 would itself essentially be only a loose and hastily formed array of surface ships that had been charged with guarding the northern reaches of Iron Bottom Sound, while screening against any sorties of IJN warships coming from that direction. And north was already a very "active" direction indeed, one seething with enemy cruisers and destroyers by night and prowled regularly by Japanese *I*-class submarines at any time.

It was an area that fed into a channel called the Slot, itself a narrow inter-island passage point that ran the entire length of the New Georgia Island chain, and it was already only too well known that if the Japanese were coming at all, they would almost always approach from that direction. And thus it would be that from far to the north would indeed come Mikawa's probative naval force, and Gotō's own CRUDIV6, each emanating from the Japanese-held naval air stations that already dotted the coastlines throughout the northern Solomons, cropping up in places like Rabaul and Kavieng—as far north as the large main islands of New Britain and New Ireland.

On the night of 9 August, then, Riefkohl would ride his admiral's flag high atop his proud *Vincennes*, leading a column of three heavy cruisers, including itself and the bold *Quincy* and *Astoria*. Now steeled for any deadly encounter with the enemy, the men probably could not anticipate the *worst*, and none of the aging battle cruisers could have known what that worst might actually be . . . but by 0153 hours of that same morning, the *Vincennes* was certain to find out.

Viciously set on in a series of violent, near-flawless, and deadly accurate attacks carried out by Admiral Mikawa's split-column, twin-axial formation set around the American warships, *Vincennes* would be among the first targeted in her lead position ahead of *Quincy* and *Astoria*. Sailing on a predetermined patrol corridor that had them moving roughly north-northwest on a fixed heading of 315°, the three ships would all too soon be fully illuminated by a combination of searchlights, seaplane-launched orb flares, and starshells fired right from the decks of the IJN cruisers. In a short time, the IJN flagship *Chōkai* would locate and lock onto the *Vincennes* . . . then indeed all hell would break loose in a mere span of minutes.

Moving in a standard line-ahead patrol column, the *Vincennes* would be ruthlessly savaged again and again from virtually all sides, and seemingly all at once. Firing with excellent advantage from their two-pronged assault columns, one of Mikawa's heavy cruisers, the *Kako*, was probably first to fire, unleashing her massive 8-inch main guns almost immediately on the heavily illuminated lead American cruiser. The high-caliber incoming armor-piercing shells would land with deadly impact in minutes, while also raking the ship's bridge, Battle Main II and general ship's superstructure.

A startled Riefkohl, hurriedly rising out of a shortened sleep and arriving on deck to an already damaged bridge, would later report that he immediately ordered an increase in ship's speed to 25 knots, but with most of her communication systems offline or fully knocked out, it was doubtful that the admiral's order was ever even received belowdecks. Therefore, the stunned *Vincennes* continued on her steadied course at a slowed speed of only 19 knots . . . still a moving target, and moving never quite fast enough, as soon a second and third incoming salvo would make absolutely clear. Nor could the *Maggie V* outrun the fast and ever-stalking Long-Lance torpedoes that had even then been launched by Mikawa's own *Chōkai*. The time now crept past the hour of 0155, and yet more deathblows were delivered by another torpedo that slammed into the big ship's number 4 fireroom. No surprise, then, when in short minutes the reports already began to filter back to Riefkohl that uttered these ominous words: "Both engine rooms, black and dead!"[152]

Soon, the Japanese cruiser *Kinugasa* would join its sister ship *Kako* in the bombardment of *Vincennes*, firing in tandem with an already stepped-up fusillade still pouring in from the *Chōkai* as "primary." What resulted was a veritable free-for-all melee on the high seas, and a blue-water bare-knuckles brawl, as all four ships joined forces in an unrelenting attack on Riefkohl's flame-engulfed ship. Staggering to a slowed pace from the previous twin-impact torpedo hits alone, the American cruiser continued to reel from the repeated poundings from Mikawa's warships and their large-bore guns at extremely close range. A single follow-on shot—thought to have been fired with finality from the light cruiser *Yubari* as she departed the battle area—would then fatefully seal her doom, as recalled in this most solemn of narratives:

> Having lost power and all steering control five minutes later, *Vincennes* was dead in the water within minutes. The glare of burning fires attracted additional incoming shells which quickly put the ship's own guns out of action. *Vincennes* shuddered to a halt. Hit at least (85) times by 8-inch (200 mm), and 5-inch (130 mm) shells, the ship gradually began to list.[153]

Mikawa's dauntless attack ships, now having visited untold damage on the American surface fleet in a mere span of thirty-one minutes, would almost as abruptly now disengage their assault and begin moving back to the north by about 0210 hours. Their offensive itself had been well prosecuted and impeccably timed, leaving in its horrid wake only the smoldering wreckage of three American heavy cruisers and the Australian *Canberra* as well. Mikawa's CRUDIV warships simply slipped back into the velvet fog of night and disappeared almost as quickly as they had come, as they sailed back up the Slot to safe haven. Aboard the crippled *Vincennes*, a full twenty minutes would interminably tick by before an order to abandon ship was finally issued by Riefkohl at 0230. At final count, his ill-fated *Vincennes* had been hit a staggering eighty-five times from the combined and concentrated fire from the four IJN cruisers, and soon the torpedo strikes that had fully smashed her bulkheads hit with significant impact and snapped her very spine in two.

At long last, at 0240 hours, a harrowed and stunned Riefkohl would descend a final time to the main deck of his command ship, the *Maggie V*, and would himself step off into the darkened waters just east of Savo Island. Unlike his two counterpart captains, Greenman and Moore,[154] Riefkohl would not go down with his ship and was instead compelled to simply strike his colors, relieve his flag, and disembark from the sinking ship. In moments, the great *Vincennes* would keel up, roll over, and slowly sink, taking with her some 332 souls to the very bottom of Iron Bottom Sound.

For wounds suffered during the course of the heated naval night battle that night, Riefkohl would receive a Purple Heart award, but he would never command a U.S. Navy capital ship of the line again. In his own later writings, in recounting the events of that one fateful night at Savo Island, the good RADM Riefkohl had only the following statement to make:

> The magnificent *Vincennes*, which we were all so proud of, and which I had the honor to command since 23 April 1941, rolled over and sank at about 0250, 9 August 1942, about 2½ miles [5 km] east of Savo Island, in the Solomons group, in some 500 fathoms 900 m of water.[155]

Further amplifying Riefkohl's statement, the great author and naval historian Samuel Elliot Morison would later pen his own observation of the man when he stated, "RADM Riefkohl, who had made about as many mistakes as a commanding officer could make, was broken in spirit by the loss of his ship."[156]

The sad aftermath of the battle would soon enough also find its way to the good admiral's doorstep, and in short measure Riefkohl would find himself entangled in a web of official after-action reports and analyses, subjected to the often stern and sober scrutiny of the later Naval Boards of Inquiry. He would become the unenviable focus of an endless innuendo of culpability to some extent, the coarse whispers of which seemed to relate both to the overall command of both his own ship, and that of the greater task group that had made up Crutchley's former Northern screening fleet, almost all of which had been lost on that one night alone.

By October 1942, only months after the battle itself—RADM Riefkohl would summarily (perhaps even thankfully) be returned to more desk-bound duties, with an assignment that still at least bespoke the man's dignity, at the Office of the U.S. Attaché, located at the American Embassy in Mexico City. He would serve out the remaining years of his otherwise illustrious naval career in various enviable ports of call throughout Mexico, the Caribbean, and Argentina.

The good RADM Riefkohl would retire with full honors from the United States Navy on 1 January 1947, and would live on in retirement for some twenty-two years longer, enjoying life in Brevard County, Florida, where he would pass away at the age of eighty. At the time of his interment on grounds near the prestigious U.S. Naval Academy itself, the harrowed survivor of the battle in 1942 might be remembered as one who had not only fought at Savo but also outlived Savo. In death, as in life, the rear admiral would be accorded the tribute and deep respect that he had earned during the course of his naval career, and that he indeed so richly deserved, and fine honors would now be smartly rendered over him and would stand him well even after his passing.

CAPT SAMUEL NOBRE MOORE, USN

Arguably the least experienced of the three commanders of the American heavy cruisers that would later make up Admiral Crutchley's Northern screening force, CAPT Samuel Nobre Moore may indeed have had only a short and somewhat unremarkable history in the United States Navy.

Born in Washington, D.C.—the very seat and capital of our own great nation—Moore would kick-start his naval career with a stint at the USNA, beginning as early as 1909. Graduating two years after his counterpart, RADM Frederick Riefkohl (1911), Moore would close out his senior year in 1913 with only a mid-class rating. New "Ensign" Samuel Moore would then embark on a series of assignments to effectively learn the ropes on a variety of smaller surface ships that would include the *Bainbridge*-class destroyer USS *Hopkins* (DD-6), the *Clemson*-class USS *Flusser* (DD-289), the *Tucker*-class USS *Jacob Jones* (DD-61), and even the early *O'Brien*-class USS *Nicholson* (DD-52). Clearly, his first notable move up would come with the entry of the United States into global conflict of World War I, where a young and inexperienced Moore would serve with distinction aboard two early class battleships, the USS *Minnesota* (BB-22) and USS *Michigan* (BB-27).

Seen as a man of few words and larger actions, CAPT Moore was nonetheless known to many as having both a steady hand with his ship and a stern but reassuring smile for his men. It was even reported that the man in fact sported a quick sense of humor, but he remained at all times firm and resolute with all naval affairs and command leadership responsibilities. By 1928, he was ready for his first command, and was now set to serve as commanding officer for the *Clemson*-class USS *MacLeish* (DD-220); the *Wickes*-class destroyers USS *Hazelwood* (DD-10) and USS *Lamberton* (DD-119); and eventually even his first light cruiser (CL) command as captain of the USS *Omaha* (CL-4), at the time the lead ship in her class.

For all intents and purposes, therefore, the new LCDR Moore's outlook could not have been any brighter at that moment in time, and truly things would appear to have been looking up for the middling but still-aspiring naval officer, now at the age of forty-one. By 1934, already some two years and several noted commands later, Moore would reach an even greater benchmark, this time that of being promoted to the rank of full commander, an honor that would have taken him twenty-one years to realize and delight in professionally. But Moore also knew that to really get ahead and advance his career to the next logical flag officer command level, a return to his beloved USNA (and the Naval War College itself) might well be in order. And so he would return in that same year to attend the requisite Senior Course at the NWC, an advanced course of instruction for those few senior naval officers who might be tagged and fast-tracked for an even greater naval honor. And would the man's next step in fact take him up to that coveted rank of rear admiral?

Decidedly not . . . or at least not for CMDR Moore, and not at this juncture. For at that very moment, and a far world away, trouble was already darkening the global horizon and menacing storm clouds were gathering in the skies over Europe as a new and even more fearsome tyrant began his nascent rise to power in Germany: a young Austro-Hungarian corporal from the Bavarian Reserve Infantry's Regiment 16 by the name of Adolf Hitler. By September 1939, it was therefore a cautious and quite troubled world that now held its collective breath at the outbreak of World War II.

For the newly promoted CAPT Moore, however, this was perhaps his one chance to serve both country and career equally, and indeed he would set the bar high to excel in the eyes of many. The year was now 1940, and Moore would soon leave behind the cushy and celebrated CNO posting at Washington, D.C., and roll the dice with Lady Luck to enter the war. By 1942, he would get his long-awaited wish and was given yet another new command, this time of an aging but still regal heavy cruiser of the line. That fateful ship would be none other than the USS *Quincy* (CA-39), and tragically Moore's next stop would be a small South Seas island called Guadalcanal. Sadly, it would also be the man's very last assignment.

CAPT Moore: The *Mighty Q*—Attack on the USS *Quincy*

Now well under way with his new command ship, CAPT Samuel Nobre Moore could never have known, even at the time of his departure for the Solomons, that the landscape would forever thereafter change for him and more than a thousand other men. He could no more have known of the terrible naval night attacks that were yet to come, than he could have known that his own name might itself be marked and held within the moldering maw of death. The date was fast approaching— 7 August 1942—and Moore's flagship, the *Mighty Q,* along with the other heavy cruisers and destroyers of ADM Turner's newly formed Task Group 62.3, would be tasked with screening the Sound in support of the troop landings and offloading of supplies. CA-39, CAPT Moore's own USS *Quincy*, would be one of the principal assault ships that would have been clustered off the coast of Honiara and Lunga as they "softened up the beaches" and cleared the assault lanes that would then serve as the very inroads for an all-out attack on the garrison-size forces of Japanese infantry already dug in on Guadalcanal.

The Allied assault on Guadalcanal, and the landing of U.S. Marines and support personnel, would indeed catch the Japanese by surprise, and General Vandegrift would exploit the advantage to its full extent, leading his rugged 1st Marine Division through a series of landings and large-scale offensives that would encounter little or no resistance from the Japanese. For all intents and purposes, the IJN ground forces appeared to have fled and abandoned the bases and airstrips they had labored so hard to build. By nightfall on 7 August, therefore, both Gavutu and Tanambogo inlets, flanking the Tulagi harbor, would have already been secured by the Americans, and a series of coordinated and highly successful attacks carried out against the Japanese troops near Lunga, in and around the makeshift airstrip at Honiara, itself even then still under construction on the main island.

Clearly, CAPT Moore would have been in the very thick of the battle but would also have been somewhat sequestered offshore in his slow-moving patrol column, sitting well out of range of coastal artillery. For the time being, both he and the *Quincy* might have been safe, but he was still very much concerned about attacks both by air and by sea and would surely have posted lookouts on all quarters of the heavy cruiser, each with a cautious eye peeled to the north—the most logical point of entry for any Imperial Japanese Navy surface ships if indeed they did come. And CAPT Moore and the fighting *Quincy* did not need to wait long at all before the first of Admiral Mikawa's retaliatory airstrikes began to unfold.

Commencing on the afternoon of 7 August, therefore, even as the stepped-up landings and offloading tasks feverishly continued—shielded by Admiral Crutchley's surface ships—a quite enraged Admiral Gunichi Mikawa would begin to make his presence known. Vexed and almost personally offended by the "interloping" Allied forces that were now occupying the stronghold areas of his Guadalcanal and Florida islands, Mikawa was in a stew over both the bald intrusion and the very presence of the American forces, and thus embarked on a series of offensives that were clearly set as punitive raids down into the southern Solomons from his naval air stations in Rabaul and Kavieng. The admiral's attack plan would be hastily contrived but well executed, and lucky almost to a fault . . . indeed, the game was still afoot.

First-wave attacks would begin shortly before 1100 hours on 7 August, when a bevy of *Betty* bombers—thought to number some twenty-six planes in total—did then approach Crutchley's screening fleet parked in Sealark Lane. The flight of twin-engined *Betty* bombers came in fast and low, sweeping in over the treetops of Florida Island and quickly out over the dark waters of the inland sea. In seconds, the attacking planes were skimming the choppy waters of Iron Bottom Sound in loose formation and moving in on final target approach to the starboard side of two ships. Those two ships were the large *Heywood*-class transport, the USS *George F. Elliott* (AP-13), and her aging escort, a *Bagley*-class destroyer, the USS *Jarvis* (DD-393). Both would immediately come under severe attack by the squadron of dive bombers and torpedo planes.

Aboard the harried *Quincy*, CAPT Moore, in tandem with the *Vincennes* and the other heavy cruisers and destroyers, immediately engaged the incoming flight of attack planes, bringing all guns to bear and exacting high kill rates on her first and second engagements with the incoming sorties. Clearly, Moore would have seen the incoming Japanese planes almost as quickly as the others and would have opened up with virtually every gun at his disposal—from *Quincy*'s large 8-inch main guns to her lethal 40mm and 20mm antiaircraft (AA) batteries—all assets would have been ranged out on all targets with apparent deadly accuracy. For, of an original twenty-six Japanese aircraft that had initiated the attack, only nine would even survive the encounter long enough to breach the defensive curtain that had been drawn ever so tightly by that very screening force.

Crutchley's heavy cruisers and destroyers would now have, either directly or indirectly, shot down some seventeen enemy planes, some of which splashed harmlessly into the waters in and around the ships, while still others only ruthlessly found their way to impact on the hulls and superstructures of some of the American ships themselves. Might not at least a primordial concept of the "Divine Wind of the Gods" *kamikaze* attack itself have been born at precisely that moment?

In the wake of this initial attack, and those further follow-on airstrikes that would later ensue throughout much of the day, and well into 8 August, there seemed to be no end in sight—and perhaps nothing at all to slake the embittered Mikawa's driven passion to exact a full revenge on the Americans for the loss of his foothold in the Solomons. Roughly ousted from their entrenched positions by General Vandegrift's own 1st Marine Division early on the morning of 7 August, the Japanese infantry troops were still smarting from those clashes, and clearly still licking their wounds from their first encounters with the American fighting Marines. Instead of an expected outcome of a full routing victory, Japan's infantry forces had instead been sent in rude scatters farther up into the lowland mountains themselves or forced deeper into the dense underbrush of subtropical Guadalcanal. The IJN's infantry elements were now even more desperate for resupply and reinforcement, and simply could not hold their positions against the heated Allied advance. As a direct result of all of these compounded failures—and all else that had transpired in the mere span of two days—Admiral Mikawa would become only more and more irritated and sorely disenchanted with the performance of his men and ships.

By 9 August, then, the two great commanding naval officers, Gunichi Mikawa and Samuel N. Moore, would meet on opposing sides yet one more time on a field of battle. And of two hot combatants locked in conflict, always must one victory see, and the other must vanquished be . . . and so it would be this day as well. By nightfall, Admiral Crutchley had already begun forming up and deploying all his naval screening elements and assigned each of the task groups to fixed "patrol corridors" within which they would now cruise in search of enemy contact. With scant resources and limited (even negligible) ship assets available to him, Crutchley could only do his best with the little he had on hand.

Crutchley would therefore place the two heavy cruisers, *Chicago* and Australia's own pride-of-fleet HMAS *Canberra* (along with two escort destroyers, *Patterson* and *Bagley*), to serve as his force's Southern screening force, patrolling an area roughly shaped like a trapezoid, and extending south almost to Honiara on the main island, then crossing south of Savo and back to the tip of Guadalcanal even as far north as Cape Esperance. A secondary force would then be assigned as Crutchley's Eastern screening force and would itself consist of the light cruisers USS *San Juan* and the Australian HMAS *Hobart*, along with their two escort destroyers, the *Monssen* and *Buchanan*. Each ship in this unit would be tasked with patrolling the waters on the eastern edge of Iron Bottom Sound fronting Florida Island, as these ships perused the coastlines off Tulagi and as far east as Tanambogo. Crutchley's third screening element, the Northern screening force, would consist of CAPT Samuel Moore's very own *Quincy*, RADM Riefkohl's *Vincennes*, and CAPT Greenman's *Astoria*, each of which would be flanked in tandem by their own fast-attack destroyers, the *Helm* and *Wilson*.

At the outset of hostilities, even as bold Mikawa's CRUDIV6 and 18 skirted deftly around Savo and entered the Sound, Moore's own *Quincy* would undoubtedly have been the number two ship in Riefkohl's standard line-ahead column-ahead formation. By 0138, the Japanese heavy cruisers had already detected the ships and quickly launched their ship-based seaplanes, instructing them to drop illuminating orbs over the enemy ships, while the cruisers themselves began to simultaneously fire their own starshell flares to light up vast areas of the blackened sea before them. A curtain would now be drawn and reveal the "stark nakedness" and vulnerability of Riefkohl's Northern fleet standing in harm's way.

Beginning about 0210 hours, *Quincy* would be attacked immediately after the initial assault on *Vincennes* and was herself now fully illuminated and taking heavy fire from all quarters. It was then that CAPT Moore would sharply quick-turn the ship and train out all guns, and by miscalculation, erroneously brought the ship's stern directly through the enemy's line of fire. *Quincy* would be ruthlessly attacked by the large 8-inch guns on the Japanese CAs *Aoba*, *Kako*, and *Tenryū*, as well as a second CL, the *Yubari*. Those two Long-Lance torpedoes would both now impact the *Quincy* on her port side, smashing the bridge, number 1 and 2 gun turrets, and much of the ship's aircraft hangar area.

Perhaps one of the closest and most personal accounts of what happened, precisely at the moment it did, must be this chilling narration of events as noted by an assistant gunnery officer aboard the *Quincy* at the time of that night attack. Ordered to the ship's bridge to seek further instructions from the captain, the man would arrive only seconds after the destructive impact of the two torpedoes and later report on exactly what he experienced:

> When I reached the bridge level, I found it a shambles of dead bodies with only three or four people still standing. In the Pilot House itself, the only person standing was the Signalman at the wheel who was vainly endeavoring to check the ship's swing to starboard [and] to bring her to port. On questioning him, I found out that the Captain, who at that time was laying [sic] near the wheel, had instructed him to beach the ship, and he was trying to head for Savo Island, distant some four miles (6 km) on the port quarter. I stepped to the port side of the Pilot House, and looked out to find the island and noted that the ship was heeling rapidly to port, [and] sinking by the bow. At that instant the Captain straightened up and fell back, apparently dead, without having uttered any sound other than a single moan.[157]

By no later than 0215, the *Mighty Q* was all but doomed. Now with virtually all guns out of action and fires raging through most of the major areas of the ship, with water cascading over the upper deck, and casualties mounting rapidly by the minute, CAPT Moore did all he could to save his ship, but it could only stagger off to the north and east, pursuing an evasive zigzag course to avoid further bombardment and trailing oil and smoke as she retired from the battle arena.

Inclined to an almost 45° list, *Quincy* would settle at the bow and nose over—sinking in less than ten minutes—at about 0238 hours. The ship would suffer an astounding thirty-six deadly hits all told and perish with a complement of crewmen that—with only mild controversy—would range from 370 to as many as 389 souls lost. The good CAPT Moore would indeed have been one of those men killed almost outright by any number of incoming large-caliber shells being hurled at him from Mikawa's opening salvos. CAPT Moore would soon die from injuries sustained, perishing in the heat of battle. Honoring the old, time-preserved, and perhaps extraordinary tradition, Moore—not unlike his Allied counterpart CAPT Getting on *Canberra*—would go down with his ship.

On 23 February 1944, almost a full two years after the loss of the USS *Quincy* and its brave captain, the United States Navy would commission a fast-attack destroyer of the *Allen M. Sumner*–class and name that ship the USS *Samuel N. Moore* (DD-747).[158] She would go on to honor the good captain's legacy and name, receiving some five Battle Stars for World War II alone, three Battle Stars for her participation in the Korean War, and no less than seven Battle Stars for her active roles during the later Vietnam conflict. The men who served on this ship would soon come to know her by yet another name: "Rammin' Sammy," a nickname the author cannot help but think CAPT Moore would have been quite proud of (and indeed he would have had good cause to think so).

For additional reading on the good CAPT Samuel Nobre Moore—the skipper of the lost *Quincy* on the night of 9 August 1942—both the Wikipedia and *Together We Served* accounts were found to be perhaps the best of all online resources for such information.

❶ Wikipedia account: https:::://em.wikipedia.org/wiki/USS_Samuel_N._Moore
❷ USNA account: https://usnamemorialhall.org/index.php/SAMUEL_N._MOORE ,_CAPT,_USN
❸ Hyperwar Online Library account: https://www.ibiblio.org/hyperwar/OnlineLibrary/photos/pers-us/uspers-m/sn-moore.htm

CAPT WILLIAM GARRETT GREENMAN, USN

Long before CAPT William Garrett Greenman would take the helm of the stately USS *Astoria*, the ship itself would already have enjoyed a celebrated and memorable past, long before her ultimate demise during the opening gambit of the battle at Savo. Indeed, no one aboard her at that time could have known of the sinking and smashing defeat that would later come at the hands of VADM Gunichi Mikawa and his Cruiser Division 6 and 18 attack force.

As early as 1934, only a year after her launching from the Puget Sound Navy Yard in Washington State, the *New Orleans*–class heavy (armored) cruiser USS *Astoria* would have made its "big splash" with multiple ports of call in Pacific waters during a series of somewhat lengthy shakedown exercises that took place during most of that summer. Thus, adding to her now-robust profile of worldliness and travel, the "state-of-the-art" ship would have already visited Nouméa, New Caledonia, the Hawaiian Islands, Samoa, and Fiji, even venturing as far south as Sydney, Australia.

The great *Astoria*, it would appear, was destined to be a ship of "friendly ports" and safe harbors—perhaps. But before she could become a fighting ship, she must first assume her far more distinguished role as an ambassadorial ship . . . and soon, it would be apparent just why.

During the pre-conflict years of 1934 through 1937—but leading inevitably up to the outbreak of World War II—the *Astoria* would be assigned to the aging but still-formidable Cruiser Division 7 (CRUDIV7) flotilla, which was then operating in Pacific waters. On assignment to the senior Scouting Fleet—shortly to be renamed the Scouting Force—and consisting of many older, near-mothball-fleet battleships, some naval training operations (and exercises) would logistically be moved from the Atlantic to the Pacific waters. By February 1937, *Astoria* would be reassigned yet one more time . . . to new CRUDIV6, based out of San Pedro and nestled on the southern California coastline. Few at that time could have known that yet another such CRUDIV6—from another time and another place—would later be this ship's very undoing or that the great *Astoria* would perish at the violent hands of Admiral Gunichi Mikawa's brutal surprise attack of 9 August 1942. On that one night alone, the wily Mikawa would also be leading his own CRUDIV6 at the time of his attack, some five years hence. Truly, indeed, there could be no overlooking the almost obvious irony of both similarities.

But before *Astoria* could even arrive at that juncture in time, she would first be asked to carry out yet another mission of mercy in peacetime. It would in fact be one of her most solemn and celebrated of ceremonial undertakings, for in 1939, the stately and well-received Japanese ambassador to the United States, one Hiroshi Saito—an official of good standing who had long been posted to Washington, D.C., as an emissary for his country—would suddenly take ill and die. And proud *Astoria* would be granted the high honor of carrying the remains of the famed diplomat back to his beloved homeland in Japan. This would also be the last time the great American ship would sail in Japanese territorial waters on a peacetime mission and not under battle colors with her many guns trained out.

CAPT Greenman: *Nasty Asty*—The Attack on the USS *Astoria*

CAPT William Garrett Greenman's time on the *Astoria* would be short-lived but suspenseful—and it would ultimately be his finest hour and perhaps his most valiant sea trial while in command of a capital ship of the line. With the outbreak of World War II and the onset of hostilities in an Axis-dominated Europe, Greenman would actually first have been assigned to serve as part of the Atlantic Squadron, then later refitted and redeployed to full command duties in the southern waters of the Pacific. CAPT Greenman would come by the *Astoria* as late as May 1942, having previously served with distinction as a commander of several destroyers, at different times, having captained both the fast-attack DDs USS *Preston* (DD-327) and USS *Brooks* (DD-232). By 1942, the man might arguably indeed have earned his first cruiser command and was so acknowledged by the naval high command. That first-command heavy cruiser would be none other than the fateful USS *Astoria* herself.

By August of that same year, the intrepid *Astoria* could already be found in the thick of the action, along with several of her other sister ships—heavy cruisers all—that were then stationed in situ in waters near the Solomons and fronting the island havens of Tulagi and Guadalcanal. *Astoria*, by this time, had already become fully embroiled in numerous actions in and around the landing zone areas at Lunga, Honiara, and the X-Ray transport areas that included ❶ the bombardment of entrenched Japanese stronghold positions on the main island of Guadalcanal; ❷ protecting the offloading troop landing craft and supply ships; and ❸ screening Iron Bottom Sound to interdict and engage any Japanese incursions from the north. All of this activity would have occurred in a time frame that would include both August 7 and August 8—but by the ninth day of that month few could have known that their ship would soon engage in the fight of her life—a fight that she might indeed not survive.

As for CAPT William Garrett Greenman, now at the age of fifty-three—said to be a humble man from Utica, New York, with a contagious sense of humor and a quick smile—the sad tale would, in the end, play itself out with but a small cast of characters that would include himself, a subordinate gunnery officer, and the supervisor of the watch aboard that same *Astoria*, both of whom were on the bridge with the captain at the moment when the ill-fated attack unfolded.

In cause and effect, therefore, the ship's very survival—or imminent vanquishment—would rest on a sum total of *four* minutes . . . a critical and foolishly squandered four minutes that could not be taken back even at the very instant they were lost. The battle would reach its full and frantic peak at precisely the moment of Mikawa's secondary attack on Riefkohl's Northern screen.

Only minutes after his bold, single-column attack on Crutchley's Southern screening force, the IJN circled back to the north, leaving in its hot wake but a smoldering mass of iron and steel—the flaming wrecks that had only minutes ago been the *Canberra* and *Chicago*. The clever Mikawa now steadied himself and prepared to usher in his even deadlier secondary attack, now navigating his CRUDIV attack column to the leeward edge of the mid-Channel Island, "J-hooking" widely across Iron Bottom Sound, then sluicing northward toward that very same Savo. Ship captains Riefkohl, Moore, and Greenman (each respectively on the *Vincennes*, the *Quincy*, and *Astoria*), along with most of their respective crews, had all been fast asleep by 0144 hours, the time of the initial attack. Cruising at a measured 10 knots on a steady course of 315°, the three American heavy cruisers quietly sailed northward on the outbound leg of their box-square patrol corridor, and none knew they were sailing to their own doom. *Then all hell broke loose.*

In her lead position, flanked by the fast-attack destroyers *Wilson* and *Helm*, *Vincennes* would inevitably be first to be barraged by the bracketing, twin-axial attack set up by the sly Mikawa. Fully illuminated by "teardrop" orb flares and starshell illuminants, *Vincennes* would be mercilessly pounded again and again by the lead elements of the passing IJN naval column. That column, consisting of seven heavy cruisers, would prosecute an attack on the American fleet that would be nothing if not precise, calculated, and fully concentrated. Virtually every ship in the Mikawa surface fleet would fire unrelentingly on the American ships: first on the *Vincennes*, then the *Quincy*, and finally the great *Astoria*. Not one of the American ships would stand a chance, and yet each would fight long and hard, right up to the bitter and tragic end.

The *Astoria*, being the *third* heavy cruiser to wake in the line-ahead formation, would suffer as cruel a fate as her other two sister ships in that screening group. Indeed, within a span of only minutes and commencing at a time somewhere between 0149 and 0152 hours on the night of 9 August—and at a point just east-northeast of Savo—no less than four heavy cruisers of the Imperial Japanese Navy would only too soon pinpoint the American cruiser's track, light her up with starshells and flares, and ruthlessly visit a most harsh fury on her. By 0215 of the clock, the *Kako*, *Aoba*, and *Kinugasa* would also join with Mikawa's own *Chōkai* to simultaneously orchestrate a now even deadlier attack on the outgunned and overpowered *Astoria*. Repeatedly pounded by any number of large 8-inch shells fired by the IJN warships, the American cruiser would fight back as valiantly as she could, and with as much strength as she could, now in her very death throes, muster in full.

In the end, much like a dying lion might rake out its claws feverishly at the earth to strike at that which struck it dead, so *Astoria* would perish in its own blaze of glory, with all guns nearing meltdown, firing rapidly right up to the moment the waterline rose up to swallow whole their ship. In fact, the scrappy *Astoria* would itself have scored some major hits on at least the *Chōkai* and had also violently attacked the *Kinugasa*, firing to virtually all compass points with all batteries hotly engaged. Sadly, however, even the ship's very best might not be enough this time around.

CAPT Greenman: Fight or Check-Fire—The Lost Four Minutes

With the onset of the initial IJN attack, CAPT William Greenman was not present on the bridge and was in fact nurturing a well-deserved sleep in his quarters nearby. Standing in the senior officer's stead, then, was a single relief officer and a Supervisor of the Watch (SOW)—one LCDR James Topper—and *Astoria*'s capable Senior Gunnery Officer, LCDR William Truesdell, who was even then alone manning the helm in the captain's absence. By 0144 hours, just as "the lights came on and the thunder let roar its throaty rumble," *Astoria* would also come under harsh attack by the marauding IJN naval force, as had her two sister ships the *Vincennes* and the *Quincy*.

At the very instant Mikawa opened fire, *Astoria*'s Gunnery Officer Truesdell was still busying himself with training out his guns, while SOW Topper barked, "Stand by to sound General Quarters!"[159] Disregarding the apparent "stand by" part of the order, a subordinate QM3 on the bridge in fact pulled the alarm rattlers anyway. The harm already done, Truesdell could ill afford to waste much time and ordered all batteries to commence firing immediately. And it would be precisely at that moment that

CAPT Greenman would finally step onto the bridge and, on his arrival, would take immediate note of the situation—and of the full attack in progress—and would belay the order, asking, "Who gave the order to commence firing?"

SOW Topper replied in the negative, not implicating Truesdell or his earlier command to do so, as Greenman steadied the men and cautioned them against possible "friendly-fire" incidents. The commander's exact words at the moment were "Topper, I think we are firing on our own ships. Let's not get excited and act too hasty. Cease firing!" Topper, compelled to follow his captain's orders without question, dutifully complied. The senior gunnery officer in fact ordered the cease-fire and then had the ship's nav lights turned on to see whether they could identify any of the attacking ships. Sadly, this action alone would critically be its own tragic misstep, a grave error that might now only beget a grave consequence.

Astoria's Truesdell, unable to contain himself any longer, now shouted over to Greenman, "For God's sake, give the word to commence firing!" But Greenman still would not. Overly concerned about firing on one of his own, the captain was still loath to commit any of his batteries or main gun assets and in effect had the guns train out but did not fire. Soon Greenman could only watch in horror and greatest alarm as the high-caliber 8-inch shells from Mikawa's CRUDIV ships now began to range out to the lead cruiser, *Vincennes*, then out to the *Quincy*, and soon indeed out to the luckless *Astoria*. With exasperation, the skipper was finally heard to yell back to his men, "Whether our ships or not, we have to stop them. Commence firing!"

In so doing, the good captain had now wasted some four minutes . . . four minutes of a fatal eternity. The red and green-tinted rangefinder shells fired from the Japanese heavy cruisers had so far been short. Greenman's four minutes of indecision and "chatter" with his subordinates on the bridge had given Admiral Mikawa just enough time to edge up and correct his range, which the deft Japanese gunnery crews now did—impeccably. Flanked on both sides by Mikawa's twin columns of pounding heavy cruisers, and with all ships seemingly firing on her at the same time, *Astoria* would amazingly receive no direct hits from the first four incoming salvos from the fast-closing enemy ships. Indeed, most of the incoming rounds fell short of the mark and only "bracketed" the American cruiser, but the Japanese admiral's luck was on the rise and soon changed for the better, even as the American's would soon shift far to the worse.

By 0156 hours, entire salvos of 8-inch shells began to impact the waters near the bow of *Astoria*. In short measure, those near-in shots were followed by a fifth salvo of projectiles that now passed completely through the paint locker area, igniting several small fires in and around those storage units. Further follow-on salvos would hit full amidships, setting other areas ablaze and destroying the ship's hangar deck. Service ammunition by gun turret 8 was soon also hit and set off as well, engulfing the entire area in flames, destroying the gunnery mount, and resulting in the loss of the entire battery. A follow-on sixth—and perhaps deadliest salvo of all—now mangled the ship's faceplates and barbette near turret 1, putting even that battery fully out of action and claiming the lives of the many unlucky crewmen who must have been manning that station at that time.

Clearly, then, from a period of time extending from 0200 to 0206 hours on the morning of 9 August, the great *Astoria* would remain under heavy attack, with significant fire brought to bear from almost all of Mikawa's attacking ships. The cruiser would suffer staggering sixty-five to seventy impact hits from a combination of torpedoes launched—and from the many high-caliber HE shells that had already been fired at her. The great ship would literally have reeled from the number of impact hits received, and soon began to list at a dangerous 10°–15° incline. Staggering ahead on an uncertain course that took the ship almost due north in her escape attempt, she was almost as soon seen sharply swinging back to the southwest in confusion.

The good *Astoria* would not perish right away; in fact, she was the only ship to immediately survive the 9 August onslaught that night. With little or no workable steerage, virtually all main guns out of commission, and now ruthlessly mauled by Mikawa's combined force, the great American cruiser would linger on until noon of the next day. In waters just southeast of volcanic Savo, the *Astoria* would then almost seize up and grind to a halt before she began a slow and mournful roll to port. Soon settling by the stern and capsizing, she would in fact no longer be seen, and by 1216 hours of that same fateful day, the *Astoria* would disappear completely on the morning of 9 August 1942.

At the time of her loss, the dauntless *Nasty Asty* would have taken with her some 216 (to as many as 268) men still aboard her at the time of her sinking. Full event duration, and an estimated period of time for the entire action, would only have been from 0155 to 0215 hours . . . in effect, then, twenty minutes.

CAPT Greenman would have fought to the bitter end and allegedly remained "on station" for the duration of the battle. Having received multiple wounds from jagged shards of shrapnel that must have flown in and around the bridge area, the courageous captain would later be evacuated from his sinking *Astoria* and rescued by the *Gleaves*-class destroyer USS *Bagley* (DD-386). This ship, and the nearby USS *Alchiba* (AKA-6), would have arrived on-scene only moments before the *Astoria* actually sank, and each ship quickly set their whaleboats and rescue craft out into the fired waters to fish many survivors out of the water and to shunt them off for medical attention for those most in need. In this circumstance, that might indeed mean the vast majority of the men.

Two days now passed, and the seriously injured captain could still be found recovering aboard the large attack-transport USS *President Jackson* (APA-18), where he and countless other men lay suffering from their grave wounds and even life-threatening injuries. At 1000 hours local time, on the date of 11 August, the gallant CAPT Greenman began (to his own best recollection) to recount his last minutes aboard *Astoria*. And from his ship-side berth, a then-recovering Greenman would set pen to paper and leave all posterity the following definitive dispatch:

110200 (Mailgram) URGENT

Vincennes, *Quincy*, and *Astoria* while on patrol in Channel eastward of Savo Island about 0155 LOVE [local time] 9 August were attacked by an enemy force of unknown number, presumably four CAs [heavy cruisers] and an unknown number of DDs [destroyers].

At time of attack, our cruisers were in column. Order of ships: *Vincennes*, *Quincy*, and *Astoria*, on course 315, speed 10 with two DDs as A/S [anti-submarine] screen. First indication of enemy action was indicated by four aircraft flares seen about 5000 yards bearing 135 to 155 true from this vessel.

Enemy apparently came in under the shadow of Savo Island, and made their initial attack from our port quarter, bearing about 190°–195° true, and on easterly courses concentrating on ships in the van. Shortly after flares were dropped and searchlights seen to right of flares appeared and the enemy opened fire.

Fire was returned to port immediately by *Astoria*, *Vincennes* and *Quincy* in that order. *Astoria* FC [Fire Control] radar gave range at 5640 yards. Preliminary conclusions are that the enemy ships were in two separate sections, for shortly after, fire was observed to port. Ships also received fire from starboard quarter which placed column under a deadly crossfire.

Then, as if to further amplify the heroics and brave efforts put forth by his dauntless crew, Greenman continued:

110200 (Mailgram) URGENT

At about 1130, forward five-inch magazine exploded, blowing a hole in port side of ship below waterline. At about this time, *Buchanan* [DD-484] attempted to come alongside to pump water, but because the ship had started to take on a heavy list to port, she was directed to take station close aboard starboard quarter to rescue personnel.

At about 1200, the salvage group was directed to abandon ship; men sliding down lines and jumping into water. At 1215 *Astoria* capsized and sank.

Buchanan and *Alchiba* [AK-23] rescued all salvage crew. Out of a total of 83 officers, 990 enlisted men, and one civilian newspaper correspondent, Joe J. Custer, onboard, incomplete information now at hand indicates 61 officers, the news correspondent and 629 men were rescued. Of this number, 7 officers and 78 men were wounded, many seriously. 20 officers known dead, 2 unaccounted for, and 138 enlisted men are known to be dead.

Greenman's time on *Astoria* would sadly have been brief, ill fated, and fairly inauspicious, yet the officer nonetheless survived the dreadful action at Savo and would even go on to receive a Legion of Merit award for his brave actions while attempting to save both his men and his ship on the night of 9 August. Only he and the *Vincennes*'s own RADM Riefkohl would survive this night's horrid slaughter and live to speak of it thereafter. One can only imagine, however, that neither man would really ever wish to speak of it in full again, and perhaps most understandably so.

CAPT William Garrett Greenman would survive the brutal attacks suffered during the battle at Guadalcanal and returned to the United States, reporting for duty in Washington, D.C., at the prestigious Office of the Chief of Naval Operations (CNO). There he would distinguish himself yet again and receive a second award of the same Legion of Merit for outstanding service as the head of the Advanced Base Planning Section, or ABPS. This same planning section was mandated with the general logistics planning and coordination for establishing all advanced bases throughout the central Pacific area, this for both the CINCPAC (Commander-in-Chief, Pacific) and the CINCPOA (Commander-in-Chief, Pacific Ocean Area) commands. He would serve in this position for only a short period of time, between 1943 and 1944. By 1945, however, now nearing retirement, Greenman would continue in service to his country one final time, this time oddly as the director of an admittedly obscure entity called simply the Office of Naval Petroleum and Oil Shale Reserves—a curious and highly cryptic title for a posting that, in and of itself, must have been equally as clandestine. This posting would also be the man's last call, and he would retire shortly thereafter with yet another advancement in grade, to the rank of Commodore, Rear Admiral–Lower Half.

CDRE William Garrett Greenman would pass quietly at his home in Utica, New York, in February 1956, even as a grateful nation sadly mourned his passing. At the time of his death, the author himself would have been only eight years old.

CAPT Greenman: "The Vengeance Ships"

"Vengeance is sweet; vengeance is ours," sayeth a now-outraged U.S. Navy, and following closely on the heels of the loss of the great *Vincennes*, the *Quincy*, and the *Astoria*—and even Australia's own *Canberra*—there would indeed be a new series of "vengeance ships" soon rolling down the chutes and slips of naval shipyards across the continental United States. In quick succession, an already accelerated defense sector would hurriedly go about the business of launching a series of brand-new ships that would bear the names of those that had so valiantly perished at Guadalcanal. In short, these became known as "the vengeance ships of Savo," and for good reason. Shown in Table 33, we see a high and cursory view of only some of those "retribution" naval ships—each built to be faster, more maneuverable, and far more heavily armed than any of their predecessors.

For indeed, between the short years of 1943 and 1944, the U.S. Navy would witness the (re)commissioning of a new *Vincennes*, a new *Quincy*, and a new *Astoria*—and an even more enigmatic and new *Canberra*, the latter of which would be the first American naval vessel named for either a foreign ship or a foreign city (see Table 34). And the very first of these new "vengeance ships" would be the great *Astoria* herself, which, unlike her famed predecessor, would be a light rather than a heavy cruiser, though she would nonetheless go on to serve with distinction in her five extended years of service.

Table 33.   The American "Vengeance Ships": A Breed Apart

THE VENGEANCE SHIPS				
PREDECESSOR SHIP NAME	OLD CLASS	NEW SHIP NAME/ HULL DESIGNATION	DATE LAUNCHED	BATTLE STARS AWARDED
USS *Vincennes* (**CA-44**)	*Cleveland*-class	USS *Vincennes* (**CL-64**)	July 1943	**6** ★
USS *Quincy* (**CA-39**)	*Baltimore*-class	USS *Quincy* (**CA-71**)	June 1943	**4** ★
USS *Astoria* (**CA-34**)	*Cleveland* -class	USS *Astoria* (**CL-90**)	March 1943	**5** ★
✦ A new *Cleveland*-class CL USS *Wilkes-Barre* was nearing the end of its production cycle when the navy ✦ stepped in and ordered the renaming of the new ship to a *new* USS *Astoria* designation. She would be the first of the Savo "vengeance ships" to roll off the production line, but she would by no means be the last.				
HMAS *Canberra* (**I33/D33**)	*Baltimore*-class	USS *Canberra* (**CA-70**)	July 1943	**7** ★

To the officers and men who served on the new *Astoria*, CL-90, she would only too quickly be nicknamed the *Mighty Ninety* . . . and she would be hell-bent on payback for the loss of the first *Astoria*. And by June 1944, the scrappy, reborn *Astoria* would be back in the war, and would soon enough get her second chance to fight. The Table 34 model shows only an extracted series of known U.S. Navy ships that were named for either a specific foreign dignitary or a foreign city (or campaign area) during World War II. Though perhaps rare, history would nonetheless show us that the naming of the "USS" *Canberra* after the stricken "HMAS" *Canberra* might not have been that unusual after all.

CAPT Greenman: Legacy for *Nasty Asty*: *Mighty Ninety*—The *New* USS *Astoria*

On the morning of 25 October 1944, a small and dwindling cadre of ordinary seamen and surviving officers of the former USS *Astoria* (CA-34) would line the dockside areas at the Mare Island Navy Yard, some 25 miles northeast of the famed San Francisco skyline, to now witness the launching of a new USS *Astoria* (CL-90). The proud CL, having fully undergone her succession of sea trials and a full Bermuda shakedown, a primed, confident, and ready-to-fight *Astoria* would now embark on her first "war cruise" deep into the troubled and roiled waters of the South Pacific. And her very first destination would be to a small grouping of sea-swallowed islands called the Philippines.

The great General Douglas MacArthur, on his own abrupt and mournful departure from those same islands in 1942, had already uttered the immortal words "I shall

Table 34. American Naval Ships Named after Foreign Dignitaries, Cities, and/or Campaigns

USS Vessel	Named for . . .	The Vengeance Ships	Comments
USS *Anzio* (CVE-57)	*Battle of Anzio* 22 January 1944 Anzio/Nettuno, Italy		*Casablanca*-class escort carrier. Served exclusively in the Pacific
USS *Coral Sea* (CV-42) USS *Coral Sea* (CV-43) USS *Coral Sea* (CVE-57)	*Battle of the Coral Sea* 4–8 May 1942 NW of Australia	-42 -43 -57	Later renamed to USS *Franklin D. Roosevelt* Active until 1990 with forty-plus years of service Later renamed to *Anzio* (above)
USS *Iwo Jima* (CV-46) USS *Iwo Jima* (LHD-7) USS *Iwo Jima* (LPH-2)	*Battle of Iwo Jima* 19 February–26 March 1945 Bonin Islands	-46 -7 -2	Ordered in 1943; cancelled in 1945. Still active at Mayport Naval Station, Mayport, FL An amphibious assault ship, served from 1961 to 1993
USS *Okinawa* (CVE-127) USS *Okinawa* (LPH-3)	*Battle of Okinawa* April to June 1945 Ryukyu Islands	-127 -3	Ordered in June 1945; cancelled in 1945. An amphibious assault ship, served from 1962 to 1992
USS *Saipan* (LHA-2) USS *Saipan* (CVL-48)	*Battle of Saipan* 15 June–9 July 1944 Marianas Islands	-2 -48	Commissioned as CVL in 1946; later renamed to new command ship Arlington in 1966. Served until 1970 An amphibious assault ship, served from 1977 to 2007
USS *Savo Island* (CVE-78)	*Battle of Savo Island* 9 August 1942 Solomon Islands		*Casablanca*-class escort carrier; c Commissioned from 1944 to 1946

USS *Shangri-La* (CV-38)	*Mythical Location*, based on FDR's comment on the Doolittle Raid of April 1942 as launched from the USS *Hornet* (CV-8)	One of 24 *Essex*-class aircraft carriers Served from 1944 to 1947: Decomm, then Recomm Served from 1951 to 1971: Recomm, then Decomm Also nicknamed the *Tokyo Express* and saw action during assault on Okinawa in 1945
USS *St. Lô* (CVE-63)	*Battle at St. Lô* 15 June–9 July 1944 Normandy, France	*Casablanca*-class escort carrier; c Commissioned from 1943 Sunk by *Kamikaze* aircraft on 25 October 1944
USS *Tarawa* (CV-40) USS *Tarawa* (LHA-1)	*Battle of Tarawa* 20–23 November 1943 Gilbert Islands	–40 *Essex*-class CV commissioned in 1945; to new Served from 1945 to 1949: Decomm, then Recomm Served from 1951 to 1960: Recomm, then Decomm –1 An amphibious assault ship, served from 1976 to 2009
USS *Tulagi* (CVE-72)	*Battle of Tulagi* 7–9 August 1942 Nggella Sule (Florida Island)	*Casablanca*-class escort carrier; First named *Fortaleza Bay* (ACV-72); redesignated CVE-72 Renamed to *Fortaleza Bay* and finally to *Tulagi* in 1943 Commissioned from 1943 Decommissioned by 30 April 1946
USS *Wake Island* (CVE-65)	*Battle of Wake Island* 23 December 1941 Territory of the U.S.	*Casablanca*-class escort carrier; c Commissioned from 1943 and served until 1946
USS *Winston S. Churchill* (DDG-81)	Winston S. Churchill Personage and PM (1874–1965)	*Arleigh Burke*-class Guided Missile Destroyer Commissioned in 10 March 2001; still active

return!"—and so indeed he would, bringing with him the fullness of the United States Navy to help fulfill that promise—and with special payback to deal it out in spades. The USS *Astoria*—*Mighty Ninety* herself—would therefore soon enough be found rightly riding her flanking position alongside the great carriers and other attack ships, as both the men and the ships forged dangerously ahead to bring the battle ever closer to Japan's own doorstep. But first there would need to be a return to the Philippines, for both MacArthur and the navy, and the dauntless *Astoria* would indeed be one of those ships leading that approach.

Mighty Ninety sortied in good company with Admiral Halsey's own fast-carrier task force as early as December 1944, serving now as part of an antiaircraft screening element for designated Task Group (TG) 38.2, a smaller component of the admiral's larger fleet that would soon consist of nine CV carriers and eight CVL light-carrier ships.

Their destiny and destination would both have been clear and unwavering, and so they traveled in tandem, now some 18 CVE escort carriers, 12 battleships, 24 light and heavy cruisers, and over 140 DD and DDE fast-attack destroyer units, all converging "at best speed" on a single point of contact with the Imperial Japanese Navy, then led by the indomitable Admiral Takeo Kurita himself. That single point of contact would be no place other than the Philippine Islands.

Divine Wind—Striking Cobra

Having already fleshed herself on—and been bloodied by—several successful engagements with the enemy's land- and sea-based forces, *Astoria* had cleared the baritone throats of its big guns and answered back fiercely when fired on herself. By December 1944, she was near done—her missions both completed and well accomplished—and soon made preparations to get under way and depart the area for other points now far to the north. Then, however, as fate will so often have it, Nature would intervene in full force and with a hell-bent fury, unleashing a sudden typhoon that would quite aptly be named *Cobra*. By the night of 17 December, therefore, all fueling operations for the carrier task force would need to be halted in the face of the fast-approaching Category 4 storm. Conditions only more rapidly deteriorated and soon slipped from Typhoon Condition 1–*Normal*, to 1–*Caution*, to 1–*Emergency* in a mere span of hours—or perhaps only minutes that seemed like hours to the men trapped on the smaller escort ships.

Now with gale-force winds bristling with high velocity and approaching wind gusts at almost a deadly 90–100 knots, three of TG 38's smaller escort DDs that had themselves been in the middle of their own fueling operations soon began to have trouble. The *Fletcher*-class USS *Spence* (DD-512), and the two *Farragut*-class destroyers, the *Monaghan* (DD-354) and the *Hull* (DD-350), each in its own way struggled valiantly to fight the heavy "troughing" between the giant surging waves that rose up on either side to bash at their very hulls. Yet all would be to no avail, as soon none of the ships would shake off the heavy consequence of being "locked in irons" as they rode the cresting waves.

Now virtually all of the ships began to roll and shallow, floundering their way through gulley-like troughs and white-capping waves on two sides. Soon, one of the ships' electrical equipment was abruptly knocked out by the massive amounts of sea water being taken on by each series of tossing waves. Now, for at least three of the lightly built American destroyers, this would truly spell a certain doom, as quickly each took on a graduating roll from starboard to port, with extreme yaw and counter-yaw movements that could have been measured in their extreme at a 70° to near 100° rate of pitch. Lights went out, pumps stopped cold, rudders jammed—all affecting even basic ship maneuverability. And soon enough, after a single deep roll to port at about 1100 hours on the morning of 17 December 1944, *Spence* did herself capsize and sink in waters some 300 miles east of Luzon. And, in short order, both the *Monaghan* and the *Hull* would likewise be overwhelmed by the sudden surge of storm and soon followed suit, suffering a similar harsh fate.

When the dust had settled after the storm, 790 brave souls would have perished in the freakish and all-consuming storm. There would only be a total of some sixty-two survivors from the *Hull* who would be fished out of the waters where the ship had last been seen. The *Spence* would herself have spared the lives of only some twenty-four men, who, soon clear of the sinking ship, still clambered for a lifeline clutch at anything that could yank them out of the water, and yet only six of *Monaghan*'s full crew complement would survive—that out of a possible one hundred officers and enlisted men combined who had earlier been on the destroyer.

Such a typhoon event had happened only two times previously in known Japanese history—at least with such impact and extent of damage—and both had been associated with the attempted Mongol invasions of the Japanese homelands in the year 1274 and again in 1281. On both occasions, the enemy's entire naval fleet would be repulsed and almost decimated in full by an "otherworldly" intervention of wind and rain—a "divine wind of the gods," as it were, that would itself have been the very first notion of Japan's invulnerability, perhaps even her very "unassailability" . . . the *kamikaze*. And again, in both instances, the great fleets of the much-feared Mongol warrior Kublai Khan and the Korean admiral of his naval fleet, Kim Bang-gyeong would perish within sight of land due to a sudden and all-ravaging typhoon—the Japanese could only immortalize both events as the *Divine Wind of the Gods*.

What is inconceivable, however, is that this event could occur for yet a third time in history or, unthinkably further, that such an event might involve any "ships of the line" belonging to our own U.S. Navy—certainly not in the year 1944. But sadly enough it would indeed occur at its worst, and now some 790 men of the sea lay rigid in the grasp of a watery Neptune, all having perished by the terrifying circumstance of the unexpected storm swells.

But brave *Astoria* was not so affected and had thus dodged a heavy bullet from the ferocity of the storm and would indeed survive the night and tempest. For the next two days, she and the countless other naval ships that made up the still-bestraggled Task Group 38 busied themselves with their stepped-up search-and-rescue (SAR) duties as each probed the murky waters for hapless men still at sea. Satisfied enough that they had in fact recovered as many souls as could be found, the great CTF force—with most of her assets still fully intact—soon resumed its slow and measured push to the north and west to seek out other engagements, and yet other targets of opportunity. And, for the moment, the great *Astoria*'s next stop would now in fact be the Carolines.

Over the course of the next (and final remaining) year of World War II, the new *Astoria* would have already served in the Philippines, South China Sea, Cam Ranh Bay, Hong Kong, and Hainan Harbor, and she had even allegedly forayed down through the near-in Bonins just south of Japan, this allegedly "to just poke a stick at 'em" as their convoy went by.

But by far her finest hour must have come during the fierce Battle for Okinawa itself, with RADM Spruance's own Taffy 58. Providing constant fire support and unwavering AA screening cover for the large carriers that made up the bulk of that TF's force-presence, *Astoria* would remain on station some eighty consecutive days "without rest or spelling," holding to her task at hand and standing her ground while still protecting the massive flattops.

The year now curbing on to 1945, the world would soon indeed see an end to the war that had gone on for nearly five years. The grand reincarnation of the earlier dauntless *Astoria*, the reinvigorated CL-90 would still have had much fight yet left in her, and so continued to aggressively patrol the waters off Honshū in tandem with her other TF elements, this from August to September of that same year. Finally, with a cessation of all hostilities between Japan and the United States, the new *Astoria*—the reinvigorated and reborn spirit of her former great self at Savo Island—retired to home waters and friendly ports, and on 15 September 1945, she anchored at San Pedro, California, for a well-deserved and well-earned rest. At the time of that anchorage, then, old *Mighty-Ninety* would have earned the five Battle Stars that she so proudly displayed, and indeed a world away and a time ago one might almost imagine that the brave men of the older *Astoria* might have sat up and taken note of her proud service.

CAPT HOWARD DOUGLAS "PING" BODE, USN

Then, there is the ever-distressing tale of the ill-starred and often overcast CAPT Howard Douglas Bode . . . a saddened and largely condemned man who would later become but an ugly and distasteful undercurrent that would run throughout and beneath the entire Savo incident—and its devastating outcome. And for at least this one man it would not "bode" well. Was he in fact nothing more than a mere pawn in an opening gambit that set him far out of his own element and comfort zone, or was he simply a hapless victim finding himself in the wrong place at the wrong time? Indeed, in its greater view, was the luckless commander of the USS *Chicago* (CA-29) but a vanquished foe fleeing for his very life—or, as he in fact later stated himself, one in hot pursuit of an ever-elusive contact that always seemed to be "out of reach," just over the far horizon, on the night of 9 August 1942?

Indeed, though a ship was never actually seen, the captain would continue to follow the IJN "ghost ship" contact nonetheless, with *Chicago* allegedly now moving far to the northwest for some forty minutes in total—away from the area of conflict even once the battle had been joined. So again, was he simply a man who, at the time of the surprise attack by Mikawa's CRUDIV fleet—now heavily outgunned, outmatched, and outmaneuvered—simply followed a native instinct to save both his ship and his men . . . or even just himself? Was CAPT Bode in fact hero or villain? Were his actions on the night of the battle those of fight or flight, and was he in fact a man vanquished, or simply a staunch aggressor in command of an American heavy cruiser hot on the trail of one of Mikawa's own ships as it sped northward to exit the area? In effect, then, was the good captain champion or rogue—coward or combatant?

As with all scholars, naval tacticians, and historians of battles long past who have struggled to understand the course of these events, we may never truly know the answers in full to any of these puzzling questions surrounding both the man's character and judgment on that one fateful night in question. For it has rightly been said that both heroism and cowardice can often be determined in exactly the same instant—how one responds to a specific element of danger, an impending threat, or simply the deadly pitch of battle itself must surely be a measure of the man himself thereafter. Could a later-sanctioned (or at least considered) charge of "dereliction of duty" and "desertion in the face of the enemy" in fact have been lodged against the star-crossed captain, and could it have held up in a later Naval Board of Inquiry? And, with those dread words so soon pronounced in open forum for all to hear, indeed, what in good conscience might be said of the ill-fated CAPT Bode himself?

Decidedly very little. Cloaked in relative indistinction as perhaps one of the most cryptic and enigmatic of characters during the course of the First Battle of Savo Island—and perhaps throughout naval history in full—the author found it astonishing just how little was known about the man or his background. It would literally take the better part of a year to simply locate a photographic image—and that only through a series of fine-tuned search arguments across the Internet—and even that only after a course of online "bartering" with other key naval historians on various websites and blog media. So why indeed is so little known about Bode, even during his pre-Savo years in Naval Intelligence?

At best, the information we find will only be sketchy, incomplete, and wholly inconclusive—at worst, virtually nonexistent. And, other than the fictional insights so capably fashioned in Sandy Shanks's treatment of the captain's "projected" court-martial trial in his excellent book *The Bode Testament*[160] (had the man even lived), there is little to provide an unbiased or even adequate glimpse of Bode, the man—or of his career as a U.S. Naval officer. This aside, however, this much at least is known . . .

CAPT Bode: A Bloodied Nose—Attack on the *Chicago*

A year would pass with yet other thorny incidents now seemingly set to stain the man's otherwise spotless record, and before Bode could even reach the waters surrounding Guadalcanal, he would have a second brush with disaster, narrowly dodging an attack in Sydney Harbor, Australia. It was indeed when his new *Chicago* and Australia's own pride-of-fleet *Canberra*—heavy cruisers both—would come under direct attack by a pack of stealthy Japanese "midget" subs that had intruded into the harbor. At Guadalcanal, his flirtation with doom and disaster would reach its pinnacle and have far more fatal consequences—consequences that would gravely affect so many, and so quickly. For Bode, however, it would unquestionably all begin and end with Savo Island, where Bode's entire world would unwind and forever change—at least from 9 August forward—and both the man's life and his ever-flourishing naval career would forever thereafter be lost to the cruelest wrench of fate.

Although Bode's great flagship *Chicago* had already arrived in the Solomons as early as 7 August 1942, and soon became a part of RADM Crutchley's newly formed Task Group 62.2 fleet, it would not really be until the night of 9 August that his worst fears would be realized. For on that night, less than two hours past midnight, while patrolling the deep and blackened waters of Iron Bottom Sound just off the northern coast of Guadalcanal, Bode's *Chicago*—in company with the Australian *Canberra*—would come under attack by Mikawa's own Cruiser Divisions 6 and 18.

That CRUDIV task force would consist of eight warships of the Imperial Japanese Navy, composed of five heavy cruisers, two light cruisers, and a single destroyer, the *Yunagi*. And it was this same attack force that now made its cautious approach down the Slot, circumnavigating the two radar picket ships and volcanic Savo as it entered the Sound with stealth, and a superb element of surprise that had remained largely intact.

At the time of the first attack, CAPT Bode's *Chicago* was to have been the third ship in line directly behind CAPT Frank Getting on *Canberra*, which was itself tailing Crutchley's own flagship *Australia*. Flanking all three heavy cruisers in tandem, some 1,000 yards abeam to starboard and port of the lead ship, would have been the fast-attack destroyers *Patterson* and *Bagley*. Soon to be absent from this formation, however, was Crutchley's own *Australia*, which was now foolishly being detached from that screening force to allow the commanding admiral (Crutchley) of that Southern screening force to attend Turner's hastily convened "powwow" aboard the armed transport ship USS *McCawley*. This would effectively leave that same Southern screening force "one ship down" and reduce that force's overall firepower by one third. Yet Crutchley would make yet another grave error that evening, that of leaving CAPT Howard Bode in overall command of that Southern group for the duration of his (Crutchley's) ill-advised (and poorly timed) absence. This would later prove to be quite a flawed decision for both the admiral and the captain—and soon everyone's worst nightmare.

Now in temporary command of that Southern force, Bode's first decision seemed to be resolving whether or not he should jockey his position from third in column to that of the *first* position, effectively leap-frogging past *Canberra* to the vaward Slot, since he now indeed carried the interim flag for that screening group, at least in Crutchley's absence. Bode would decide against doing so, reluctant to even attempt such a maneuver in the unfamiliar and potentially hostile waters while slinking along in the dark and dead of night. The decision not to assume the lead column position for that Southern force is what probably later saved the man's life . . . and those of many of his men on the *Chicago*.

Uncertain of Crutchley's return either way, Bode could only assume (perhaps rightfully so) that the senior officer would return immediately after his *McCawley* meeting and resume his vaward flag position. History would of course later tell us that Crutchley would in fact *not* return at all, and after that Turner Conference simply remained in the vicinity of *McCawley*, "nestled in" with the other force ships already gathered in and around that X-Ray transport area, berthing there for the night rather than risking navigating his way back to his original TG 62.2 screening group. The good CAPT Bode, of course, could not have known any of this, however, or even of the admiral's decision not to return at all, until it was already too late.

Mikawa's force advanced with stealth and an excellent element of surprise from points north. Skillfully had the IJN cruiser commander slipped the very noose of the two American radar pickets *Blue* and *Ralph Talbot*, each American DD still running their unaltered parallel tracks just north of Savo itself. At 0125 hours, Mikawa released all ships in his command and issued an order for full area illumination. By 0131, the IJN vice admiral then issued his now-historic (and somewhat terse) command, "Every ship attack!"[161] Then, by 0138 the starshell illuminants—both those dropped from his airborne floatplanes and those deployed by the 5-inch shells fired from the heavy cruisers themselves—fired the firmament and lit up the night sky, rudely plucking back the securing shroud of darkness, now making night most unholy day.

Caught fully off-guard and locked in the sights of the expert and well-practiced gunnery crews and torpedomen of the Japanese fleet, both the *Chicago* and the *Canberra* were little else than sitting ducks on a calm, open sea. Decidedly, these would be only the first targets of Mikawa's well-coordinated single-column assault, even as later official accounts did capture the full essence of the admiral's intent and attack strategy, as noted in the Naval War College's own report:

CRUDIVSIX followed in general the movements of the *Chōkai*, although it did not follow in the same water. At 0139, COMCRUDIVSIX [Gotō] on the *Aoba*, which at the time appears to have been on course 110° (T) rather than the 120° (T) being steered by *Chōkai* [and its CRUDIVEIGHTEEN], sighted another destroyer four degrees on his starboard bow on opposite course at a great distance.

This destroyer would have been the *Bagley*, which at the time was some 9500 yards away. At 0140, COMCRUDIVSIX sighted three ships—thought to be one battleship and two heavy cruisers—but which were later identified as *London*-class cruisers bearing a few degrees off the starboard bow of *Aoba*, at a range of about 9000 yards. Undoubtedly then, these were the ships of the *Chicago* group themselves.[162]

Or again even here, as CAPT Toshikazu Ohmae—Mikawa's ad hoc chief of staff, who also rode aboard the admiral's flagship *Chōkai*—would so ably state in his own later recounting of the events on that one fateful night:

> For incredible minutes, the turrets of [the] enemy ships remained in their trained-in secure positions, and we stood amazed, yet thankful that they did not bear in on us.
>
> Strings of machine-gun tracers wafted back and forth between the enemy and ourselves, but such minor countereefforts merely made [for] a colorful spectacle, and gave us no [real] great concern. Second by second, however, the range decreased, and now we could actually distinguish the shapes of individuals running along the decks of the enemy ships. The fight was now getting on to extremely close quarters.[163]

Back aboard *Chicago*, as indeed it must have been on *Canberra*, and each of the other ships that night, most of the officers and men would already have bedded down belowdecks for the night, enjoying the comforts of a well-deserved rest after two consecutive days of standing Condition One watches for most of their days and nights. By the evening of the same day (8 August), a state of Condition Two had at long last been declared, allowing the men to stand down a degree, and would also require that only half the watch be on duty during those nighttime hours. Within such a purview, then, Bode would have been no exception, and he was known to have been resting in his cabin just behind the bridge at the time of Mikawa's first attack. And he, too, would have been one who would be rudely jostled from sleep, as he immediately sprang to his feet and dashed to the bridge to find out what was unfolding even at the instant it was.

Bode would arrive at his station just in time to countermand a previous order given by his watch officer to engage the firing ships, and instead ordered only illuminating flares be fired from his 5-inch guns at first, presumably to firmly identify the attacking ships. *Might this in fact be a "friendly-fire" incident*, Bode must surely have thought to himself, *or are we in fact under attack by enemy ships?*—this even as he continued to contest the previously issued attack order.

This wrangling tiff between the two men on the bridge—at precisely that moment, at precisely that location, and under the harshest of circumstances of the unexpected IJN attack itself—might have been measured in seconds but felt more like hours for the Allied sailors now under such ruthless attack. Fully illuminated by the IJN cruiser floatplane orb flares and the ships' own starshell rounds, the two besieged Allied heavy cruisers, and their escort DDs, were now only sheep for Mikawa's pack of hungry wolves. Veteran navy man Jack Coombe, himself serving aboard the scrappy American destroyer USS *Patterson* at the time of those very attacks, had himself observed the action first-hand as he also noted:

> It is a strange and frightening thing to have one's ship lit up by enemy searchlights. Everything [is] splashed white, creating a bas-relief of surroundings, including the chalk-white faces of your shipmates—a nightmare![164]

Farther south in the channel on his own *Australia*, Crutchley must himself have been awakened by the distant roll of thunder, which was indeed not thunder at all, but rather a massive duel and a great naval barrage unfolding even then between his very ships and the Japanese attackers then entering Iron Bottom Sound. Indeed, from Crutchley's vantage point, the good admiral might have seen the muted flashes of light from the night's action, even then shimmering in the far western sky. Even in his current state of near-exhaustion, Crutchley scurried to the bridge and clearly heard the deep-throated report of the enemy's big guns far out, along with the explosions emanating just west of his current position. The admiral's first concern at this point was clearly that of contacting the patrol ships of his former Southern screening force as quickly as possible, as indeed he attempted to do by radio. Sadly, even after repeated attempts to hail his own ships, Crutchley would receive no response from any of the TG 62.2 elements, and neither the cruisers themselves nor the fleet destroyers that escorted them were answering any of his calls.

Only later, after the heated actions of the initial attack—precisely at a time when the commander of *Australia* was preparing to order his remaining DDs to form up and launch a full-on torpedo attack on that enemy surface fleet—was he finally able to hail Bode on *Chicago*. Crutchley queried the captain of the American cruiser, asking, "Are you in action at this time?" Then he waited for the reply. Bode's classically terse (and wholly inadequate) reply would not, surprisingly, be anything more than "Was, but not now." To Crutchley, this information would have been both cryptic and utterly useless to his (the admiral's) immediate purpose. One can only assume, therefore, that at the time of Crutchley's initial radio contact, Bode must indeed have had his hands full just fending off the attack that was even then still in progress and already well on him.

As noted earlier, it would in fact be the *Patterson* that would be first to react at the moment of the attack—even commendably so—with the ship's alert captain, CDR Frank Walker, flying into action almost on the instant as he quickly warned the others in the screening group both by radio and signal clacker with a shortened aviso that was both simple and to the point: "Warning! Warning! Strange ships entering the harbor!"[165] This even while preparing to engage all targets of opportunity and moving quickly to interpose his smaller DD between the attacking Japanese fleet and the already besieged *Vincennes*. Walker quickly ordered up General Quarters, rang up 20 knots, and swung the bold fighting ship *Patterson* hard over left rudder to close quickly with the American cruisers in her immediate charge. Closest to her in the coming moments was the large CA *Vincennes*, and the dauntless *Patterson* moved to her side as quickly as she could.

Chicago herself would be far less fortunate, and *Canberra* would fare worst of all in the fleeting moments yet to come. In the rocky, bare-knuckled brawl that followed, at least four of Mikawa's seven cruisers opened up with all guns almost as one, ruthlessly targeting both Getting's *Canberra* and Bode's own *Chicago*. Aided entirely by the overhead starshell flares and the cascading orbs that quickly turned night sharply into most brilliant day, the Japanese *Kako*, *Tenryū*, *Aoba*, and even Mikawa's own flagship *Chōkai* opened with full salvos, and with deadly precision, as they bombarded the Allied ships' positions without pause or thought of clemency. With initial hits either falling short or only "bracketing" the two American "heavies," the Japanese cruisers quickly found their range out to them and adjusted fire, each warship fine-tuning its target azimuth for a most concentrated fire. Soon the incoming large-caliber shells were all raining in and dead-on accurate, with damaging, impactful hits that took a heavy toll on each of the Allied cruisers of that Southern force.[166]

Canberra was savaged and soon overwhelmed by Mikawa's attack force, having been spotted by the Japanese lookouts as early as 0134, and even at a distance of some 12,500 meters (7.7 miles). Some minutes later, by 0143, the ship was again fired on by the combined batteries of at least four of the IJN cruiser division ships—and perhaps even five with the great guns of *Kinugasa* itself—and would suffer massive combined hits from the many salvos visited on her by each of the enemy's 8-inch batteries. In mere seconds, then, *Canberra* had been hit unrelentingly some twenty-four times and pounded with as many as nineteen *Type 93* Long-Lance torpedoes that had been fired from Mikawa's prowling, night-shielded fleet.

In the careless blink of an eye, even the combined salvos from all of the IJN ships' batteries would have already claimed the lives of *Canberra*'s gunnery officer and mortally wounded her brave commander, CAPT Frank Getting himself. The pride-of-fleet Australian cruiser, *Canberra*, might now only be seen with a 5–10° list to starboard and grinding to a halt, her powerplants and electrical systems no longer operational. Indeed, many of the enemy's hits had been at (or below) the ship's waterline, leaving *Canberra* with little or no navigability and exposed to even greater attack. In the end, casualty estimates for the ill-fated *Canberra* would be tallied at 84 dead, and some 109 wounded. It might be noted here, however, that those casualty citations (with controversy) do seem to alternate from an initial 74–84 dead to as many as 193, as indeed noted by other sources that may presumably have been closer to the action of that time (and such that seem to have persisted even to the present day).[167]

Bode's own *Chicago* could only be next as second in line, and by 0145 hours his ship was also being fired on by that same IJN attack force that was still finishing off Getting's *Canberra*. By 0147, the first fast-moving spread of Long-Lance torpedoes reportedly fired from the third-in-line *Kako*, sharply impacted on *Chicago*'s bow, sending a thunderous shockwave throughout the ship and causing major damage while also decimating the ship's main battery director. As a result, *Chicago* would now have that many less guns with which to fight back, but her luck still held—this even as a second torpedo impacted close abaft of the first hit—but seemingly malfunctioned on the spot and failed to explode.

Shortly afterward, however, several large high-explosive 8-inch rounds began to rain in on her as well—with a clear and telling accuracy—all being fired almost in tandem by the multiple enemy cruisers now encircling her that then took out *Chicago*'s top mainmast, killing two crewmen outright. Then, almost as abruptly as the attack had begun, it was over—and the brave *Chicago* would see no further action in the battle. Event duration for the entire horrific attack (and resulting battle) would be measured, in the end, in mere minutes, yet within the gape and maw of that brief span the Allied Southern fleet had already lost one heavy cruiser and had seen another savaged in the bow—and such that even left the scrappy *Patterson* herself battered but unbowed.

VADM Mikawa's brilliant orchestration of his battle force, and the deployment and use of all his ship assets during the course of the battle, would become the main set piece for the rousing defeat of Crutchley's Southern force, such that it would so leave those warships smoldering like so much burning flotsam and jetsam on a roiled sea. Therefore, in cause and effect, this would indeed be the *Iron Hammer* to the head of the Allied force. Then Mikawa's fast-moving attack force swung slowly away, soon forming up into a tandem twin-axle assault column that now set its sights on its next target of opportunity—Riefkohl's unsuspecting screening force far to the north. This secondary attack would now be Mikawa's own "killing blow," as it were—the *Spiked Mace* that would now be positioned to break that enemy's back.

The fate of Bode and *Chicago* would be far, far worse, however, as soon the captain would embark on a mysterious and unexplained voyage of his own undertaking: one that would seemingly seal the man's fate forever and enroll his name on a wall of infamy and sad suspicion. Bode's greatest misstep would now begin with his own "40-minute trek" into the unknown, which would begin at almost the very instant the battle itself had been joined.

CAPT Bode: A Lapse in Judgment: Departure of the USS *Chicago*— The "Lost 40 Minutes"

Fortuna secundat audaces, it has been said—*Fortune favors the brave.* But if indeed true, what might be said of the good CAPT Howard Douglas Bode and his "post-action" activity on the night of 9 August 1942? Can the captain's seemingly calculated movements during and after the initial battle in fact be interpreted as either fight or flight? And, by extension, was he pursuing his Japanese attackers—or in fact being pursued by that same force? Much indeed would be noted of this curious topical discussion point, and of Bode as the commanding officer of both *Chicago*, and of the de facto Southern screening force itself at the time of that action. The man's perplexing and wholly secretive trek aboard the stricken *Chicago*, on a curious heading of 263° (T) and well to the northwest—and his own accounting for the "lost 40 minutes"—has inextricably remained the subject of much sharp commentary, and the near-"villainy" of it survives even to the present day and continues to deepen the mystery of what actually might have occurred.

What *is* known of Bode and his trek, and the events that took place on that night, might at least include the following:

- Alerted by the sharp and unscheduled turn to port of CAPT Getting's *Canberra* in line before him—and by the action of the nearby destroyer *Patterson*—Bode orders

Chicago to General Quarters and prepares to engage at best speed any targets of opportunity found. *Patterson* reports spotting a "*Mogami*-class heavy cruiser, and a single *Jintsu*-class light cruiser,"[168] both of which were actually Mikawa's own CLs, the *Tenryū* and the *Yubari*.

- Shortly after *Canberra*'s violent demise, as seen by *Chicago* herself, Bode orders two four-gun starshells "to port" to be fired, and two four-gun starshells "to starboard," to illuminate the area, and "to determine enemy disposition." In point of fact, Bode might only have succeeded in illuminating himself instead and could have been either causal or, at the very least, contributive to the position-compromise situation itself.

- Moments later, a starboard bridge lookout on *Chicago* warns Bode of a torpedo wake detected on the starboard side that was even then quickly tracking its way toward his ship. Bode only rings up an increase in speed and responds with an order of "right rudder full."

- A report of a second torpedo wake, now detected on *Chicago*'s port quarter, results in yet another sharp and evasive maneuver, this time a quick reversal of course and a full over to port rudder change.

- *Chicago* is hit in the port bow by a single *Type 93* Long-Lance torpedo presumably fired from the IJN heavy cruiser *Kako*, which impact staggers Bode's ship, but he is still able to maintain control and stay his course, now in pursuit of a "phantom" IJN contact at the lag-end of Mikawa's exiting column.

- *Patterson* and *Chicago* both shadow and engage a "contact bearing WNW," gauging that ship to be on an approximated heading of 263°. Reportedly, both American warships briefly engage one or more IJN warships within that enemy's departing column as it left the battle zone—this again being either the *Tenryū* or the *Yubari* (or indeed *both*). The errant captain would later report "scoring some hits" on at least one ship, which of course could not be borne out in full by the skipper of the *Patterson* or any other ship in the immediate vicinity. Oddly enough, much, much later, when questioned about the events of this same engagement, however, the old crew of the Japanese light cruiser *Yubari* would themselves recall the incident almost in full but shirked off the claim and could only recall "receiving some scratches" from an unknown American warship in the melee.

    For Bode on *Chicago*, it would sadly already be too late. Now locked on a false pursuit track and fully committed to his attack enterprise far to the north and west for some untold (and otherwise unaccounted-for) forty minutes, Bode had by now fully detached his ship from the main task group element—and his own screening ships—leaving far behind the troop transport and landing vessels he was tasked with protecting imprimis. And Bode had done so without due notice to the others of his move away from the battle arena, now on a dubious chase-down of a "ghost ship" that may or may not have even been there at all. Was that ship in fact either the *Yubari* or the *Tenryū*, or was it nothing more than an over-the-horizon glimmer of light dancing on the fired waters on that one particular night?

In fact, could it have been as Bode himself was "fictionally" portrayed at his mock Board of Inquiry hearing, as he now stood before an enraged ADM Arthur Japy Hepburn and his equally ravenous pit-bull interrogator LCDR Ramsey, as seen in author Sandy Shanks's excellent book *The Bode Testament*, at which point Bode is heard to say:

> Moments after the ship was struck by shell [*sic*], I observed the *Patterson* being illuminated by two enemy destroyers. I engaged these targets, with *Patterson*'s aid, and obtained hits on one of them, or at least I think so. Life was rather confusing at the time. Five minutes after being struck by the torpedo, it was determined that maximum safe speed was 25 knots.[169]

The single bow-shot to his *Chicago* from the torpedo fired from the IJN *Kako*, under the capable command of one CAPT Chihaya Takahashi, would cause Bode's cruiser to shudder underfoot from the single-detonation impact of that enemy "torp." Maneuvering to avoid what he was certain to be any number of follow-on secondary, and even tertiary, hits to his ship from the attacking enemy column, Bode held steady on *Chicago* and steered away from the Southern screening force, continuing to track on until about 0236 hours—an action that is itself borne out and carefully plotted in the Mackenzie J. Gregory map of "The Battle of Savo Island."[170] This is an integral part of the earlier discussion in this book that also touched on the movements of the USS *Jarvis* on 9 August, and as seen in the earlier Table 8.

Whether intentional or inadvertent—premeditated or wholly unplanned—Bode would nonetheless leave behind the stricken *Canberra*, the wounded *Patterson*, and a circling defense-posturing *Bagley* at the scene of the battle's last contact. *Chicago* would later briefly catch sight of the tail-end of Mikawa's now-departing surface fleet as those ships began exiting the area and decided to give chase. In a later response, as the captain appeared before an informal hearing convened to examine his actions on that fateful night, Bode's explanation would continue precisely where it left off:

> After obtaining this assessment, I again observed gun action between two unknown ships lying to the west of Savo. This being the only fight I thought I could join in, I ordered what was now a max speed of 25 knots, continued on to the northwest, reloaded the 5" turrets, and attempted to close with the enemy. Unfortunately, the enemy was not to be found.[171]

And that was it. So indeed, whether pursuing a phantom contact or simply locked on the hot trail of the *Tenryū* or the *Yubari* themselves, Bode's departure from the Southern force might later seen as nothing less than a damaging and near-unforgiveable act of abandonment of both post and station . . . and perhaps most so to the men of the *Canberra* and the *Patterson*. That he would do so without informing any of the other ships of his decision to leave would later resonate loudly and add only more fuel to the fire to which the man's feet would later be held. Decidedly, Fate Itself would soon again step in and ordain that Bode indeed have his full day of reckoning . . . and even that far sooner than he might ever have imagined.

Indeed, whether a fiery engagement or simply an ill-advised "fool's errand" on an unsanctioned flight of fancy in pursuit of what could only have been a faint image of a trailing ship in the Japanese column, the *Chicago*'s skipper had nonetheless continued firing all secondary batteries at that target, purporting to have "scored at least one or more hits" on that departing IJN cruiser. Then only, to his further detriment, had Bode, at any time prior to his departure or since, sought to assert any level of command and control over any of the other Allied ships in that Southern screening force—a force of which he was still technically in command, since Admiral Crutchley had earlier placed him at the helm of that same Task Group 62.2 *pro tempore* in his (the senior admiral's) absence to attend the Turner Conference aboard *McCawley*.

Therefore, compounding an already bad decision to depart the area in the first place, Bode would make no significant attempt to warn the other warships or transports—which were then offloading at both Guadalcanal and Tulagi—of the initial attack itself, even as *Chicago* continued to make steam and move at best speed away from the battle area. So what indeed might the good CAPT Bode's own "take" have been on what actually occurred during the battle? What might the very man in command have to say? Could it in fact have been as simple as that portrayed in Shanks's dialogue in his book *The Bode Testament*? Here, in a quite classic style of wit and dry terseness that was not too uncharacteristic of Bode's signature style, he would have only this to add to his closing statement:

> Unfortunately, for all intents and purposes this was the end of the involvement of the *Chicago* in this engagement. For the *Chicago*, it was all over in five minutes. It is to my everlasting regret that we could not have done more. I am sorry.[172]

While of course the Shanks account is—by the author's own advisory disclaimer—only "an historical novel" in part, it is nonetheless "historical" in its perspective and a highly accurate accounting of the events as they clearly must have unfolded for the much-maligned Howard Douglas Bode. The remarkable Shanks account has found a lost key that can actually open a small and hitherto unseen portal—for however short a period of time remarkably and through which readers may peek in to get a glimpse of Bode and his subsequent "trial," had there indeed ever been one. Still, many questions would remain—which very questions seem to beget an only greater interlocking puzzle that might itself never be solved—in a seemingly never-ending cascade of events and actions on the part of Bode on the night of 9 August 1942.

So indeed, whether friend or fiend, hero or villain, defiant attacker or simply a besieged and crippled target now bolting for the safety of open seas in an imperiled and desperate attempt to flee Mikawa's fierce attacks—not one of us can ever know for certain. And yet the tale doth linger, with questions still awaiting answers—decidedly now with much of a bad taste and a certain disreputable staining of the captain's otherwise good name.

Later, on the afternoon of 19 April 1943, in the face of almost-certain "formal" charges being lodged against him in ADM Arthur Hepburn's Board of Inquiry—which had been formed to investigate the debacle at Savo Island and Bode's role in it—a troubled and now-dejected captain of *Chicago* would return to his BOQ, enter his bathroom, raise a .45 pistol, and simply shoot himself in the head. To the world at large, this would effectively close out the final chapter on the ever-curious story of "Ping" Bode. To the saddened few who might indeed have been interested in hearing more of the man and his proposed defenses, it would be a harsh blow to we few, and in that same instant, a door closed with a great finality on that last chapter of Bode's life.

CAPT Bode: The Dark Legacy—Forever More Questions

In the end, therefore, what would it be? What might indeed be said of the dark CAPT Howard Douglas Bode . . . and how would the entire affair later be viewed? Would a chagrined and clearly incensed Navy in fact call it a "dangerous shirk of duty . . . a refusal to stand and fight . . . desertion in the face of the enemy? Or would they go as far as allowed and simply see it as a kind of "bald cowardice" . . . a crude act of cut-and-run? And what were this man's innermost secrets, and what could he have been thinking about—or, worse, even then hiding? Was the ill-fortuned, ill-favored commander of the *Chicago* simply not suited for the command of that ship—or any ship—let alone a full task group operation like that seen on the night of 9 August? And what (if anything) would then be Bode's dark legacy, if not a darkening bequest that would linger long after he was gone?

Decidedly, little good at all would come of it, and Bode would be called to task from virtually every quarter, clicking his heels and standing snappily on many a shagged carpet, and before so many inquisitive admirals, such as to rival a marching band stepping off in cadence. And would not RADM Crutchley himself—the captain's first-line commander—have fairly demanded an explanation within days of the event? And would he not have also insisted on a fully detailed after-action report being penned and set before him—and even that with undue haste? Decidedly, it may not have happened like that at all and could well have gone in a completely different direction.

On the very next day, 10 August 1942, at 0600 hours, little time would go by before Crutchley summoned the good CAPT Bode to his flagship *Australia* for a "breakfast chat" to discuss the events of the previous night. To at least Bode, this request was in direct opposition to the firm "ass-chewing" he must clearly have been expecting at the hands of his otherwise irate superior officer, but such was apparently not the case. Once aboard *Australia*, the admiral's "chat" would entirely be couched in the nicety of "tea and crumpets," as was indeed the senior British admiral's wont. Author Sandy Shanks's curious, almost amusing portrayal of Crutchley and Bode calmly discussing the extraordinary turn of events centered on the debacle at Savo over "scrambled eggs, sausage, bacon, toast, juice . . . and an inexhaustible supply of coffee,"[173] all of it setting the stage for Bode's first explanation of the events of just the night before—and of his errant track to the north for a hefty forty minutes. Certainly, it would not be his last.

Bode feared no reprisal at this time—or at least during the days immediately following Savo—and believed indeed that both he and the men of *Chicago* had performed commendably in the face of the previous night's action. Now only a self-assured Howard Bode might be heard to opine that *Chicago* was probably (and right-fully) more victim than culprit in the whole affair, having been so brutally attacked herself! What need he fear more than a lack of his own conviction that he had done his utmost to save both ship and men? Bode's suave, but decidedly gruff, attempt at being straightforward with the senior admiral seemed to be working, now with only minor embellishment, causing Bode to almost relax his guard and lunge into a series of curt, off-putting descriptive phrases such as "We got creamed"[174] and "We got caught with our pants down."[175] Not too surprisingly, none of this would sit very well with the already incensed admiral, who, now perturbed and not as well taken by the man's smarmy, almost arrogant presentation and explanation—and by his apparent lack of concern for being found culpable in any way—would soon see the niceties of their "breakfast chat" fast wearing thin, with Bode continuing to rankle and tear at the senior flag officer's last nerve.

By "breakfast's" end, the hapless Bode was summarily dismissed by a miffed and quietly ignited Crutchley and ordered to sail the damaged *Chicago* to a repair facility at distant Noumea in New Caledonia, and later to Sydney Harbor itself for further emer-gency repair of that cruiser. Beyond that, it was not at all clear where Bode might be ordered to next. What is clear, if not yet entirely to Bode himself, is that these "investi-gations," as it were, were far from over, and soon enough the second shoe would hit the floor with a sickening thud. That "sickening thud" would be none other than the navy's newly appointed chairman of the General Board, one RADM Arthur Japy Hepburn—and his equally contentious pit-bull interrogator, LCDR Donald J. Ramsey—in their hastily convened Naval Board of Inquiry set to review, in full, the actions and events of the 1BOSI, with a specific eye toward Bode's complicit role in its deadly outcome. Neither of the two men were in much of a good mood, nor would Bode's encounter with them in the near future in any way involve breakfast, tea, or crumpets.

Clearly, someone's head must roll off the block, so indeed why not his? It was now becoming clearer and clearer. Hepburn and the "pit-bull" inquisitor would soon convene their fact-finding (and perhaps only *fault-finding*) inquiry with the swiftness of a peregrine diving on its unsuspecting target, and Bode was nothing if not their solitary prey.

CAPT Bode: *Mea Maxima Culpa*—The Hepburn Board of Inquiry

The year is still 1942, and Bode and the crew of *Chicago* have indeed already been to both Noumea and Sydney for ship's repairs and are now slowly coursing back across the southwest Pacific to safe portage in the United States. Reportedly, Bode's *Chicago* finally does arrive on 13 October 1942 at a naval repair facility in San Francisco. But months would slip by without further note or notice, and no official discussion of the entire Savo affair, save that of the news of the fiasco itself—centered on the great naval night battle and its heavy losses—that had already begun to filter back to the home-front American news media. Would Bode in fact be touted as a hero, or as a villain, by that same *vox populi*? Would he get a fair shake or simply be vilified by the news and media outlets, as being in fact causal to the entire action itself? And what would the American people themselves—a hungry mass yearning for any string of victories in either the European or the Pacific theater—have to say about the feckless and ever-blameful Howard Douglas Bode? In how high a regard would they have held him?

Soon enough, however, as Bode himself must have already suspected, many of the highly read media outlets back home—such as the *New York Times*, *Time* magazine, and *Life*—were already quickly beginning to piece together the story of what really had occurred. And it was a story that was being told in the clear voice of the many first-person accounts of the harried crewmen who survived the battle and from any number of "leaked" sources came the scattered after-action reports from the few ships that were either directly or indirectly involved in the battle—or those that may only have been in close proximity to the action itself. But the reports coming in were already indeed not too favorable.

Time continued to pass since the fearsome rout of the U.S. Navy at Savo, and the scorching losses suffered by the Allied fleet itself, when Bode was shortly (and duly) notified that he was being summarily relieved of his command of *Chicago* and instead being ordered back to the Balboa Naval Base, in the far-away Panama Canal Zone in Central America. While it was not immediately clear why, the hapless Bode could only surmise that his head was on the chopping block . . . if not right at that moment, then soon enough somewhere down the road. In fact, he did not need to wait too long at all to confirm his worst fears and suspicions, as soon he received his summons to appear before a formal Naval Board of Inquiry to explain, "in far greater detail," his role (or even non-role) in the First Battle of Savo Island. He now had to stand before the "Admiral's Table" and have his day of judgment.

Bode was an intelligent and intuitive man. He had risen carefully—and calculatedly—through the ranks of the navy's prestigious intelligence community, and the ONI itself, and indeed was no one's fool. Stunned by the relief of his command of *Chicago* and astounded by the summons to appear before Hepburn and Ramsey, he was left to ponder only the stark imponderables themselves: a formal charge recommendation being brought against him by Hepburn's Board of Inquiry. Shanks probably best captures the essence of the captain's sad, sad fall from grace, and perhaps his most soulful lament in *The Bode Testament*, where a man standing all alone is almost naively heard to say unto himself, "And now the sonsabitches are going to blame me for the whole thing."[176]

And whereas the good Admiral Crutchley's "kinder and gentler" recommendation might indeed have been stated as "It is my preliminary finding that you and your ship, its officers and crew, acted bravely and intelligently. At this time, I do not see any reason to pursue this (matter) any further. However, it is assumed that there will be many more questions asked before this is over. Be prepared to answer questions from your naval intelligence service. It has been my pleasure, CAPT Bode. You are dismissed,"[177] the grave and scorching comments he would later receive from a fully enraged Ramsey, and his equally ruffled boss Hepburn, would do anything but soothe and console—and clearly none of it would have anything at all to do with breakfast, tea, or crumpets. Just Bode's ass on the line, as he stood with heels locked once again on the good admiral's carpet.

Certainly, after much hot and probing dialogue and several unkind "near"-interrogation moments of the former captain of *Chicago*—and of his actions on the night of 9 August—a beleaguered Howard Bode must have come away from the entire session feeling friendless, utterly persecuted, and entirely dejected. *Gone in an instant* was his command of the *Chicago* and shuttled quickly in within the next moments was his rapid reassignment to Balboa in remote Panama.

And worse—oh, far, far worse than all else that might have gone before—Bode would now never realize his life's ambition and greatest dream to one day achieve his flag rank and wear the shoulder-boards of a rear admiral. Instead, the ill-starred captain would be just lucky enough to get out alive, and only by the skin of his teeth—and even less so with his pride intact.

Fairly spuming with contempt and coupled with an almost palpable and immediate dislike of CAPT Howard Bode (the man and the career naval officer), Hepburn's assistant, the ever-efficient and by-the-book LCDR Ramsey, may have been unrelenting in his dogged push to unmask Bode's real truths. One might almost see the furrowed brow thus knit in anger, the grit of teeth and flash of eye, as the pit-bull interrogator continued to hammer away at Bode, targeting his often less-than-credible recitation of events that had occurred on the night in question. And what indeed may have started off poorly now only devolved rapidly to a near-nightmarish proportion, or at least so for the hapless Bode. Speaking in shortened clips that were quickly honed to either a barbed question or an acid retort, the taut Ramsey and the laconic Bode might at all times have observed military protocol, and only the greatest of decorum, while otherwise thoroughly hating each other's guts. It was an ugly fight, about an ugly turn of events that had claimed the lives of far too many, and a kind of ugly ordeal that sought only an open backyard and ample room to move about and slug it out to settle all.

In fact, it simply would not end for the star-crossed Bode, and much like a jagged fang that at once rankles even as it bites, the conclusion of Hepburn's investigation, and of his heated Board of Inquiry, must have been of no great comfort to him at all. All he might recall of the entire affair was the lingering bitter taste of the fired exchanges between him and the board reviewers, their crafty turn of a phrase used again and again to try to trick an admission out of him about something he had said, or something he had done—or perhaps only something he had "reportedly" said or done. The often-vituperative attacks on his very character, and the none-too-subtle chin-wagging defiance shown by each man to the other, as each struggled to stand his ground. Admiral Hepburn's terse findings and final recommendations, however, would be nothing if not short and to the point and would be summed up in four terse findings emanating from that formal inquiry (see Table 35).

Table 35. CAPT Bode: A Dark Legacy—Hepburn's Initial Findings

The Admiral Hepburn Investigation Findings		Finding Valid? (Y/N)
Finding	**The Hepburn Observations**	
❶	**Finding:** The primary cause of defeat during the First Battle of Savo Island would be the element of complete surprise achieved by the attacking Mikawa surface fleet.	Y
❷	**Finding:** An inadequate state of readiness on all ships to meet and counter the night attack.	Y
❸	**Finding:** A failure to recognize the implication of enemy planes in the vicinity prior to the attack.	Y
❹	**Finding:** A fatal and misplaced confidence in the functional capabilities of the radar screening units used on the "radar pickets" DDs USS *Blue* and *Ralph Talbot*.	Y

Table 36. CAPT Bode: A Dark Legacy—Supplemental Causal Findings

The Admiral Hepburn Investigation Findings		Finding Valid? (Y/N)
Finding	**The Hepburn Observations**	
❺	**Finding:** A failure in communications, on many levels, which resulted in the lack of a *timely* protocol for the send-and-receive of crucial enemy contact data.	Y
❻	**Finding:** A failure in communications to provide timely information regarding any reconnaissance of the enemy's approach prior to 9 August 1942 (i.e., on the evening of 8 August 1942).	Y
❼	**Finding:** The abrupt and ill-advised withdrawal of Fletcher's carrier task force on the evening before the battle, effectively removing all of those capital ship assets from the battle area and leaving only a small light and heavy cruiser force to guard the entire expanse of the Sound.	Y
❽	**Finding:** The *McCawley* Conference itself, hastily convened by ADM Turner, which heedlessly summoned both MG Vandegrift and RADM Crutchley away from their duties. This absence, compounded by his very withdrawal of the CA *Australia* itself (Crutchley's own flagship), would also contribute to the resulting disaster that would later take place at Savo Island.	Y

At Whom the Finger Points. Admiral Hepburn's findings at this interval had not yet "named names," but surely full culpability could not be too far behind, and by late August of the same year the second shoe dropped with a crashing blow. In the report's findings, some measure of accountability would soon find its way and land squarely at the feet of several of the senior admiralty, those with specific leadership responsibilities and deep culpability for their "shirked" command and control tasks for all operations in and around Guadalcanal and the Solomons. Clearly, then, such a scathing rebuke might need to include Admirals Fletcher, McCain, Turner, and even the ever-retiring Victor Alexander Crutchley himself. None of these senior officers, however, would ever be "officially" censured or severely rebuked—and other than Bode and Riefkohl themselves, none would immediately be reassigned. Truth told, virtually all would be dropped just at the doorstep of Howard Bode, and the man's life would never again be quite the same.

CAPT Bode: When, Where, and Why—A Confluence of Heady Questions

And with its final curtain, much like the Japanese imponderable, the great *Kōan*—or great "unanswerable riddle" itself —so, too, a myriad of questions would be indelibly etched in stone surrounding the good CAPT Bode *and* his actions on the night of 9 August 1942. Many questions would remain unanswered for many years to come, and many would never be answered at all, it might seem. Of the many questions asked, few would ever yield any viable answers, per se, but would beget only more questions. In truth, then, had the ill-fortuned captain in fact survived, one can only speculate as to how he might have responded to any of the questions that might be posed to him were he even available to answer them. So yes, the riddles do persist and the questions still abound, and decidedly after some better reflection, these few questions could still be tabled before the man.

The Bode Questions

- What was your pre-battle disposition on *Chicago* on the night of 9 August 1942?
- What happened on the night of 9 August 1942 beginning at a time from 0138 to 0150 hours?
- Where were you at the time of the initial attack at Savo?
- When were you first aware of an attack in progress?
- How long did it take you to get to the bridge from your quarters?
- What happened when you arrived on the bridge? Did you have an altercation with your watch officer?
- Why did you not assume a lead position "in the vaward" of Getting's *Canberra* immediately after the departure of RADM Crutchley to attend the *McCawley* Conference on his own flagship *Australia*?
- When the attack commenced, why did you not specifically warn RADM Riefkohl's Northern screening force of that attack—or of the proximity of those Japanese ships?
- During the time of the attack, did you at any time speak with CAPT Getting on *Canberra*?
- During the time of the attack, did you at any time speak with CAPT Greenman on *Astoria*?

- During the time of the attack, did you at any time speak with RADM Riefkohl on *Vincennes*?
- During the time of the attack, did you at any time speak with RADM Scott of the Eastern screening force patrolling near cross-channel Tulagi?
- During the time of the attack, did you at any time notify or communicate with either of your own escort units, the DDs *Patterson* or *Bagley* just off your starboard and port beam positions?
- Why would you so errantly take such a westerly course—*away* from the Southern screening force—and away from the very troop transport and supply ships you had specifically been tasked with protecting?
- Why did you find yourself distracted by what may have been only a minor skirmish to the northwest of Savo Island, instead of proceeding directly east, where the action was already under way?
- Were you in fact aware of a predetermined "secondary destroyer rendezvous point" some five miles to the northwest of Savo Island, and why would you not have at least proceeded to that point?
- Might there have been more you could have done in the face of the Savo attacks of 9 August 1942?
- Do you have any regrets, personal or otherwise, about your actions on the night in question?

And finally . . .

- What did you know, and *when* did you know it?

To the bitter end, the now-shamed CAPT Bode would maintain his long-suffering innocence for all the world to know and hear. Barring, however, an expansive clearing of his name, or a full "exculpation" of charges coming down from the senior admiralty itself, the man's choices appeared to be whittled down to little else than a rock and a hard place at this time. Might it get worse? Might it indeed have been as Shanks speculates in his *Bode Testament*, in which an incensed and highly volatile Fleet Admiral Ernest J. King—then serving in his capacity as both the CINCUSFLT and CNO—is alleged to have contemptuously contacted Bode by telephone, only to spew out his one final and most vituperative message yet:

> Bode, I have completed a review of the reports submitted to me regarding your inexcusable performance at Savo and am issuing you a fair warning that I'm going to court-martial your ass at the earliest opportunity I have. Is that clear to you, Bode? You got any questions? Good—now, get the hell out of my Navy!![178]

So far a fall, and so far a fall from grace. Now facing full dishonor, a possible reduction in grade, becoming the scourge of an already irate American public, and even dismissal from his beloved naval service with a dishonorable discharge—Bode would inevitably take the path of least resistance. And thus it was, on the afternoon of 19 April 1943, that that path of "least resistance" would be nothing less than a cold and hefty .45 clutched in his hand and held to his head, which would soon end his own life. Oddly, he would survive the single gunshot wound to the head but would expire the very next afternoon at the Balboa Naval Hospital, marking the end of the sad and contentious life of CAPT Howard Douglas Bode. To the world at large he would be dead, and only the ingenious Sandy Shanks, with his creative largess, might ever be able to revive the man again—if only for a brief period of time—in a masterstroke historical novel that would shed some unseen light on the man and allow us to more cautiously hear at least *his* side of the story.

CAPT Bode: The Sad Conclusions

And so indeed we have come full circle with the ill-fated CAPT Howard Douglas "Ping" Bode. We began with the early underclassman years at Annapolis; marked his advancement and ventured with him through his ONI team leadership years. We saw bold conspiracies unfold even as we sat privy to the coded, cryptic messages and raw intercepts that foretold of an attack on Pearl Harbor—even if none would listen to his warnings. Indeed did we swagger along with his youthful pomp and circumstance, as we, too, watched the dashing Naval Intelligence officer making his cordial rounds throughout many of the great European capitals—and even envied him his seemingly never-ending list of high-brow tête-à-têtes and grand appointments. Together, we have uncovered audacious bomb plots, explored dangerous liaisons, and even praised his first command of the *Oklahoma*. When tragedy struck on a date etched in infamy as 7 December 1941, we, too, stood in awe with Bode at short distance and watched him watch his own ship go down at anchorage. And, finally, we have embarked with him on his long journey off to the South Pacific, traveling with him on brave *Chicago* through his several ports of call and great naval exploits at Sydney Harbor, and even his later push far north to Savo Island and the Solomons.

We have seen Bode as the unseasoned and somewhat timid cruiser commander go on to make any number of foolish missteps, and we witnessed the rank and blundering miscalculations that may (or may not) have led to the demise of both *Canberra* and his own *Chicago* and that then led to the loss of several capital ships and lives of men themselves. We stood in awe of his actions on the night of 9 August 1942 and struggled to ourselves understand the man's unplanned and ill-advised trek on 263° and well to the northwest for 40 minutes, well away from the battle main in Iron Bottom Sound. And finally, we have also stood by and watched a now wholly dejected Howard Bode at his time of reckoning during the Hepburn–Ramsey Board of Inquiry, as we, too, sought a full accounting of those same actions on that one occasion. Bode would remain defiant to the bitter end, and, barring moments of dulling weakness and doubt when most locked in his own solitude, he would remain convinced that he had done all that he could have done and that the attacks on the *Canberra* and his ship, and the even later attack on Riefkohl's Northern screen itself, were not of his doing . . . and not at all of his own causation.

In the years leading up to the present day, few kindnesses would be afforded Bode, and history would still not forgive him the grave indiscretions of that one dark night at Savo—not at that cost. In his time, Bode had been (to at least his superiors) a bright, intelligent, and promising young naval officer, a well-credentialed overachiever with (at all times) seemingly good intentions and only the highest of aspirations. He would have been both meticulous and well manicured, tyrannical and tailored to a tee, every button buttoned and every brass insignia buffed to its highest sheen, as he would always demand of his men (who, it is also known, would later poignantly remember him only as a gruff, inflexibly strict, and seldom-liked despot). Seen as best being a stern disciplinarian, and a stickler for good order and sharp detail, the dark legacy left behind by the good CAPT Bode would sadly shed no further light on either the man himself or his actions on the night of the battle itself on that one hot night in August 1942.

When first this author launched this very discussion of Bode, there was admittedly a minor and nagging natural predilection to judge the man at face value only, an ugly predisposition to perhaps assume guilt. As such, and clearly factored into the whole equation, was a pestering undercurrent of doubt that indeed might give one pause and compel one to arrive at an almost-expected verdict both about the man and his actions. And there are still those who say yes, he may have been guilty of any number of grave and capital offenses, such that might not entirely exclude a "gross negligence of duty," "desertion in the face of the enemy," or even its older and far uglier triplet, "cowardice" under fire.

To this, the author might indeed take *bold* exception, as I have since come to wholly revise my humbled opinion of the good CAPT Bode, and now offer this instead: Bode may truly have been many things, at many times, on many ships—and indeed in many places—but I am far more inclined to now stand firm on the point that Bode was never any man's "coward"—and this by no means. He was but a victim of circumstance and timing, an inexperienced captain of a fighting ship caught in a horrid battle in dead of night. He was a man in too far over his head.

So once again we are left to only ask ourselves more and more questions about the curious CAPT Bode: Was he in fact *hero* or *villain* . . . brave voyager, or simply a hapless victim tossed about in a sea of fire? Was he a mere pawn shuffled about on a slick slab of sea as part of a greater gambit in the opening battles for Guadalcanal itself . . . or simply a man misguided and lost in the heat of battle when perhaps most needed? And would he be severely upbraided for his actions, or in fact praised for his tenacity in pursuing the lagging enemy ships even as they sped off after the killing battle itself? Was the man in fact *any* of these things, or simply *all* of them . . . or was it something else indeed? It is not entirely clear to many, but what is clear is the fact that Bode was perhaps one of the most haunting and enigmatic of personas in all of World War II, and certainly during the Guadalcanal naval campaign, and it has indeed been well worth the effort and academic pursuit the author has undertaken to learn more and more of the man. Truly, one might not soon forget the sad and lingering tale of the woeful CAPT Howard Douglas Bode.

CAPT Bode: Additional Reading

Regrettably, there is very little information available on the ill-fated CAPT Howard Douglas Bode, and very little may be gleaned from general online research either. The dogged researcher may be tasked with instead pursuing the subject the "old-fashioned way": by following the winding paper trails that will inevitably lead them through the many government archives and scanning the arcane (and often still-sealed) naval records that may not yet even be in public domain, and by visiting the stacks and carrels of the best possible libraries and records centers that can be found, based on the area of topical pursuit. For the edification of my readers here, however, I can offer some measure of assistance in this area, having found at least these key research sites where one can obtain further background information on this most curious and misunderstood of career naval officers throughout all of World War II.

General Information Websites

Axis History forum: http://forum.axishistory.com/viewtopic.php?t=125903
Review: Sandy Shanks, *The Bode Testament* (with link to interview): http://www.microworks.net/PACIFIC/library/review_bodetestament.htm
Ahoy—Mac's Web Log: http://ahoy.tk-jk.net/Savo/Savo11HepburnsConclusions.html
Human Performance Engineering: "Heroes" (Wesley W. Stillwagon): http://www.hallowquest.com/heros.htm
UBoat.net (Allied Warship Commanders): http://uboat.net/allies/commanders/4343.html
The Free Republic Foxhole Remembers the Battle of Savo Island: http://www.freerepublic.com/focus/f-vetscor/1042631/posts
Pacific War of WW2: The Battle of Savo Island—9 August 1942: The Hudson Pilot Report: http://www.ww2pacific.com/hudsonrep.html
AcePilots.com—World War II and Aviation History (IJN *Yūbari* Report): http://www.acepilots.com/ships/Yūbari.html
About.com—Military History: http://militaryhistory.about.com/od/worldwari1/p/battle-of-savo-island.htm
Impasse webpage: http://www.pearlharboronline.com/mpasse.htm#Captain_Howard_D._Bode

Wikipedia Information Websites

Attack on Sydney Harbor: http://en.wikipedia.org/wiki/Attack_on_Sydney_Harbour
HMAS *Canberra*: http://en.wikipedia.org/wiki/HMAS_Canberra_(D33)
USS *Oklahoma* (BB-37): List of Commanding Officers: http://en.wikipedia.org/wiki/List_of_commanding_officers_of_USS_Oklahoma_(BB_37)
USS *Chicago* (CA-29): http://en.wikipedia.org/wiki/USS_Chicago_(CA-29)
The Battle of Savo Island: http://en.wikipedia.org/wiki/Battle_of_Savo_Island

CAPT FRANK EDMOND GETTING, RAN

CAPT Getting: Submariner Deep

CAPT Frank Edmond Getting[179] would enjoy a distinguished but somewhat abbreviated naval career, entirely owing to his own untimely demise during the outset of the First Battle of Savo Island on 9 August 1942. At that time, he was killed almost instantaneously during the opening salvos of the attack while standing on the bridge of his heavy cruiser HMAS *Canberra* (D33). It would be a matter of some great irony, then, that as a young officer, Getting would have initially set himself on a distinguished course as an avowed submariner, much preferring the depths of the ocean to service with any surface fleet above.

Historically, of course, Getting had been born in Sydney, Australia, before the turn of the century in 1899, and had indeed been one of the first enrollees (or "intakes," as they were called at that time) in the newly founded Royal Australian Naval College (RANC) at Osborne House in Geelong, Victoria (Australia). In due course, he would graduate from that sage institution in 1917, at the very close of World War I. This meant that the young officer had just missed the war probably by mere months, yet he and many of the other midshipmen would still go on to distinguish themselves in other battles yet to come—in yet another war.

By 1939, a twofold event did seemingly solidify his interest in submarine warfare: his promotion to the rank of full commander and an appointment as the operations officer to the RAN Fleet Commander himself. As such, he was now of a grade that made him eligible to opt for an "open-sea" command, and at the outbreak of World War II he would indeed do so, as he was soon given full command of the HMAS *Kanimbla* (F95), an aging and converted passenger ship that had been designated as a Landing-Ship, Infantry (LSI), and even later as an armed merchant cruiser. And on that same *Kanimbla*, Getting would sail Australian waters throughout all of 1939, pacing about on turbulent seas, seemingly ever on the threshold of a full outbreak of hostilities, with war on the near horizon.

By 1940, Getting and his ship could already be found in waters off the coast of Saigon in French Indochina seas, cautiously bearding the Vichy French to boost their own naval presence in the region: the better to extirp the rude interlopers now, the young naval officer must clearly have thought, than to later have to deal with them in full. It would also be on this mission that he would meet and serve in the company of Admiral Sir Percy Lockhart Noble, the erstwhile commander-in-chief of the Royal Navy's famed "China Station," which at the time was based in multiple locations in Singapore, Hong Kong, and mainland Weihai.

Recalled from sea duty in 1940, CAPT Getting would be placed (if but for a short time only) in the prestigious office of the deputy chief of naval staff (or the DCNS) for the RAN. However, soon pressed on by the urgent call of war that was even then looming over Australia itself, Getting would shortly be rotated back to sea and given command of the prized Australian heavy cruiser, HMAS *Canberra* (D33/I33).

In fact, this would be his very last ship and his last command, as soon he and his ill-starred warship sailed from New Zealand waters to rendezvous with ADM Fletcher's Operation Watchtower fleet that was even then assembling at Fiji for their first all-out offensive on a little-known piece of real estate called Guadalcanal. With a sense of great pride and dutifulness, *Canberra* too would join that same Task Force 62—a collective fleet of some seventy-five ships and combined assets from both the American and Australian/New Zealand navies. His time with TF62, however—and with his proud *Canberra*—would only too soon be cut short by the very fatal events of 9 August 1942.

CAPT Getting: Savo Island and the Attack on the HMAS Canberra

On the eve of the attack near volcanic Savo, the Allied Southern screening force would be part of a larger element of ships under the aegis (and command) of RN RADM Sir Victor Alexander Crutchley and designated as Task Force 62.2. His force of warships would this night only consist of three Australian heavy cruisers and five American equivalents. And, with this scant force, he would indeed be tasked with the near-impossible job of screening all of the approaches to and from Iron Bottom Sound, while also guarding the unloading troop transport and supply ships that were even then anchored at Tulagi and Honiara, and with securing the shipping lanes between the loosely grouped islands. Therefore, much to his merit, Crutchley would do the only thing he could do at the time: divide his meager fleet elements to guard only *four* "marginally defensible" screening areas that would now be set as: ❶ a Southern screening force; ❷ a Northern screening force; ❸ an Eastern screening force; and finally ❹ the two radar pickets themselves, the destroyers USS *Blue* and *Ralph Talbot*, both set on elliptically shaped patrol patterns far to the north of Savo.

The admiral's Southern screening force, within which he would also carry his flag, would itself be only a subgroup of the larger Task Force composite, consisting of only his HMAS *Australia*; the more seasoned RAN heavy cruiser HMAS *Canberra*; and an American CA equivalent, the USS *Chicago*. This primary screening force would then further be supported by the two flanking escort destroyers *Bagley* and *Patterson*.

On the night of 9 August, however, Mikawa's interloping cruiser divisions would in fact slip around a darkened Savo and fully elude the American pickets *Blue* and *Ralph Talbot* with seeming ease. Only moments later, however, CAPT Getting and his crew would be rudely awakened and alerted by the now-aggressive posturing of the *Patterson* itself at about 0143 hours. The smaller destroyer escort had just spotted enemy ships at a range estimated to have been no more than 5,000 yards out, and it soon became clear to Getting on *Canberra* that something was amiss. His crew now at full action stations, Getting ordered an immediate increase in ship's speed and reversed his initial turn to port to engage Mikawa's attacking forces.

In this instance, the scrappy *Patterson* was still able to send out her own terse advisory, "Warning! Warning! Strange ships entering the harbor!" to all ships operating within that screening force area, but it might truly have been the harsh illuminants fired by the attacking Japanese ships themselves that would have been a dead giveaway to a commencement of battle. Clearly, to both Getting and the men on *Canberra*, the battle was now afoot. Soon hemmed in by a four-fold assault group led by Mikawa's own flagship *Chōkai*, the *Tenryū*, the *Aoba*, and the *Kako* as well, Getting in mere moments would find himself embroiled in the battle of his life and struggling desperately to initiate a viable strike response, while frantically attempting to fend off the killing attack itself. That killing attack would commence at about 0145, and with *Canberra* set as the lead ship in column, would have been wholly focused on her first by Mikawa's practiced gunners and torpedomen.

The attack would be swift, complete, and wholly devastating for Getting on *Canberra*, and before her crews could even plot their own firing solutions out to the first two of the four attacking ships—namely, *Chōkai* and *Tenryū*—those same IJN cruisers had already found their own range out to her. In the next critical three minutes, the doomed Australian cruiser would suffer a staggering twenty-four combined hits from all four Japanese ships firing on her close-in position. Of nineteen torpedoes allegedly fired at her that night, only two would be recorded as having hit their target, and yet those two hits would be more than enough to cripple the now-stricken *Canberra*.

On the occasion of the battle at Savo, in the opening attacks alone, Getting's flagship *Canberra* would endure sustained enemy fire from numerous incoming 8-inch high-caliber shells, all of which quickly razed the cruiser's boiler rooms, virtually knocking out power to the rest of the ship. Hit by a combined flurry of salvos from all of the main guns on the four Imperial Japanese Navy warships that were even then consuming her with full broadsides, the crew of *Canberra* would soon witness the death of their own gunnery officer, as well as the loss of the ship's captain, who—now injured by shrapnel from the near-in explosions all about him on the bridge—would soon himself be stricken.

Later, to all attempts to evacuate the officer to an American hospital ship operating in near waters just off Lunga Point, CAPT Getting continued to wave off assistance, insisting instead that others be seen to first. All too soon, however, the defiant commander of *Canberra* would indeed succumb to his own wounds and, with due ceremony for both himself and his fallen comrades, would later be buried at sea. Many years later, on a date of 11 November 2011, the Honorable Jason Clare, MP, the Minister for Defence Materiel (Australia), in a commemorative speech given to honor all the brave souls who had fought and died in defense of their Australian homeland, would have the following to say of the good CAPT Getting:

> One of the men who died that [night] was the Captain of the *Canberra*, Frank Getting. As he lay dying on the bridge of his burning ship, he told the ship's surgeon who was trying to save him to look after the other wounded men. His last order to his second-in-command was only "Carry on; carry on."[180]

Figure 40.   HMAS *Canberra* (D33/133): Before and After the Savo Island Action of 9 August 1942

And so Getting himself said only "Carry on . . ."—and perhaps therein lies the greater measure of the man.

The damaging loss of the *Canberra* would be second only to the loss of the entire Northern fleet later that same night, and in the ensuing surprise attacks that would claim the lives of the three American heavy cruisers *Vincennes*, *Quincy*, and *Astoria*. In her prime, however, *Canberra* had truly sported a far different look—an "air of majesty," as it were—than the later images seen of the smoky, flame-engulfed ship in her final, post-battle death throes. Seen clearly in the dual images here is all that would be left of the embattled *Canberra*, now hobbling along with a severe list to port and nearly all main guns out of action. Later, in spite of untold offers of assistance from the arriving American DDs *Patterson* and *Bagley*, the *Canberra* would soon be determined to be wholly "unsalvageable," and with engines that could not be repaired, her sealed fate would now be that of being scuttled in full.

CAPT Getting: Farewell to an Old Friend—The Sinking of the *Canberra*

It is a known fact that many of the ships in close proximity to the now-crippled *Canberra* had indeed rushed to her aid as quickly as they could and moved at best speed to render some measure of assistance. In fact, in quick succession, both the *Patterson* and the *Bagley* were known to have remained on station with her, extracting the wounded and lending a hand with fighting the several unchecked fires that still raged onboard. Later, even the former radar picket *Blue* would return and also join in the search for men in the water, and to help with general ship evacuations. Dutifully, then, almost as if paying a last respect or mourning a fallen comrade of the highest order, did each ship circle and circle again the gravely wounded heavy cruiser, but all to no avail.

CAPT Getting's time on the *Canberra* had been cut short, and now she, too, was compelled to retire. At a slight tick past 0800 on her final morning of 9 August 1942—deemed wholly unseaworthy and unrecoverable—the U.S. Navy dispatched its own attack destroyer USS *Selfridge* (DD-357) to sink the dying *Canberra*. Yet it would not be; even after an initial spread of four torpedoes and some 263 shells fired from her mid-range 5-inch guns, the scrappy, almost-defiant Australian ship *still* would not go down. The final deathblow would soon be delivered by a second destroyer dispatched to the area, the USS *Ellet* (DD-398), with a final single torpedo run that would send the Australian cruiser down to her final resting place.

Of note, the stricken but still noble *Canberra* remains to this day almost exactly where she sank—in a dark and silent place that thereafter could only be called Iron Bottom Sound—at an estimated coordinate fix of 9°12'29" S–159°54'46" E. Her brave captain, Frank Edmund Getting, had perhaps perished much as he would have wished: in command of his great ship and leading his men into battle while fighting for his country. It would be a wholly enigmatic view of the loss of a man and his ship, both brought about in a single, horrific event on one embattled night in 1942.

VADM GUNICHI MIKAWA, IJN

VADM Mikawa: A Bright Star on the Horizon

In his brilliant capacity as COMCRUDIVEIGHTEEN and COMCRUDIVSIX—or Commander, Cruiser Divisions 18 and 6—VADM Gunichi Mikawa was himself the gallant luminary and IJN naval strategist who orchestrated the well-prosecuted twin attacks on both the Allied Southern and Northern screening forces, then under the command of RADM Victor Alexander Crutchley on the night of 9 August 1942. The IJN admiral's masterstroke, *coup de grâce* victory over both the American and the Allied forces that one befogged night near volcanic Savo Island, would result in the critical loss of four Allied heavy cruisers of the line and the damaging of a fifth—the fallout effect of which would leave a string of tumbledown ships smoldering in the scorching dead of night, all seeking shelter from the storm.

And while much (if not all) of the historical information, biographical data, and collected writings about this bold strategist, naval planner, and vice admiral of the Imperial Japanese Navy—along with many of the ships' own after-action reports—would be penned in his native Japanese language, much information would still survive in English to recount at least some of the IJN naval officer's life and times. And truly much from that background seems to unerringly indicate that here was a man predestined for some measure of greatness, and a man preordained to command great ships: the cunning Gunichi Mikawa.

Indeed, historically might we find, on the one hand, a brilliant career naval officer known both for his cunning shrewdness and his driven command of his renowned IJN Eighth Fleet and, on the other, a flawed commander known to also be overly cautious and retiring—as noted in his ubiquitous (and perhaps well-reasoned) fear of the American aircraft carriers. In his time, he had been the commander of fleet destroyers and of large battleships and heavy cruisers, a man who had proven himself time and again to be a superior tactician, a keen-eyed planner, a crafty strategist, and a master of the full-on naval night attack. But all of this would come much, much later in his career, as the very here and now of his time could only begin well before the turn of the last century.

Born on 29 August 1888 in his beloved Hiroshima prefecture, cozily nestled on the coastline of the Japanese home islands fronting its vast Inland Sea, Mikawa would eventually go on to be a vice admiral of the highest old-school order. Certainly by as early as 1910, at the age of twenty-two—with still some four years to go before the start of World War I—it would have been a young and exuberant Gunichi Mikawa who would have already completed his enrollment and graduated in the 38th class at the prestigious Eta Jima Imperial Japanese Naval Academy (IJNA). Mikawa would do so with the greatest honors and graduate with a ranking of third in a class of 149 cadets—*third*—a feat that must not have been too easy a task to undertake or even see through to completion.

Immediately after his stint at the IJNA, then, between the years 1910 and 1912, Mikawa would enjoy his first midshipman posting to service aboard the aging twin-masted protected cruiser (CP) *Asama*, and on the even more curious *Soya*—which was effectively a "spoils-of-war" confiscate vessel left over from the one-sided Russo-Japanese War of 1904–1905, and which in Tsarist Russia would have been known as the former protected-cruiser *Varyag*. On a step-stone path to prominence, and now finding his place within the Imperial Japanese Navy hierarchy itself, Mikawa's next two assignments seemed to move him directly into the "big leagues" of the battleship heavies themselves and propel him directly into service aboard the dreadnought *Satsuma* and the battlecruiser *Kongō*.

Mikawa would further excel, both in his work and in his studies of naval strategy and planning, and it would not be long before he would catch the eye and scrutiny of the IJN "nobility" of the time—which clearly included not only the leadership at the Academy itself but also the many commanders under whom he had served up to that point in time in his early career. Later, again opting for a return to formal schooling for yet a second time, Mikawa would enter the still-nascent IJN Naval Torpedo and Gunnery School (NTGS) between the years 1913–1914, and it would be here that he would later return for even a third time during the late 1920s, only this time as a "preferred" and fully certified instructor, by such time being an already seasoned naval combat operations officer with considerable experience under his belt.

The interim years, of course, would see the start of the brutal Sino-Japanese War, and Mikawa—now with a newfound wisdom and scholarship gleaned from his training at the NTGS and elsewhere well in hand—would make sail again, and by late 1914 was assigned to the armored cruiser *Aso*, itself another "holdover" captured ship from Japan's turn-of-the-century war with Russia. He would sail this ship for the next year before returning once again for additional training at the prestigious Naval War College, or *Kaigūn Daigakkū*. Here, one might take critical note that unlike in our own counterpart U.S. Naval War College (USNWC), an officer of the IJN could not even apply to that higher institution of learning until first having completed a full ten years of active-duty service. Part and parcel of that ten-year requisite would also have been the numerous specialized training classes and technical schools that such an officer would be expected to complete, each of which might last some six months in full. The final IJN NWC class—with its accelerated and highly focused areas of specialized study—would last no less than a full year, and Mikawa would excel yet again in virtually all areas of study, and soon (as with his beloved IJNA) an invitation would graciously be extended him to return once again as one of the college's instructional cadre in later years.

Soon enough, however, it was now a well-respected *Lieutenant* Mikawa who would once again return to open-sea duty to do what he knew best to do—command ships—and he would soon indeed serve in various capacities that included chief navigator aboard the *Kongō*-class battleship *Haruna*, and service on the unprotected cruiser

Tatsuta and *Tsukuba*-class *Ikoma*, as well as a return to the *Aso* of previous assignment in 1914. But first he had more important tasks at hand, as within the span of a single year, from 1919 to 1920, a wholly astounded Gunichi Mikawa found himself embarking on perhaps the first of many such momentous overseas assignments, as he happily accepted his appointment to the representative delegation that would attend the famed Treaty of Versailles in June 1919. In and of itself, this would be the very treaty that would end World War I.

VADM Mikawa: A Rumor of War: *Kido Butai*—Japan's Striking Force

On the morning of 26 November 1941, therefore, Admiral Yamamoto did indeed order his fleet to a full sortie, boldly setting sail from Tankan Bay in the southern Kuriles with a high expectation of victory—and only the slightest fear of early detection before he could get his full attack force into place. Due to the location's very remoteness, its total removal from the prying eye of "foreign watchfulness," and its known natural cloaking of "pea-soup fog" throughout its close expanse—it offered at best only a localized view and poor visibility to an enemy—and the good admiral knew he had chosen wisely and well. This very spot would now be the prime staging point for virtually his entire Imperial Japanese Navy force—totaling some fifty-six surface and sub-surface warships, all told. Tankan would now indeed be the jump-off point for perhaps one of the most ambitious of military undertakings—and one of the most momentous of all world-altering events—the surprise attack on Pearl Harbor.

On 1 December 1941—after due consideration of all intelligence, facts, and innuendo of the American Secretary of State Cordell Hull's demand that certain concessions be made "in good faith" by Imperial Japan—a greatly incensed Emperor Hirohito was finally persuaded by the command staff of his Imperial Conference to indeed go to war, lest the rabid Western powers literally have them "destroy the fruits of the China incident, endanger Manchukuo and undermine Japanese control of Korea." The great Japanese Empire was not at all in the mood to relinquish any (and certainly not all) of their recent ill-gotten gains and land cessions in China and Manchuria—and certainly not without a fight. And now that fight would include the joint forces of Admiral Yamamoto's massive Combined Navy, and Admiral Nagumo's 1st Air Fleet. That overall attack force—known to the Japanese simply as the "Striking Force," or *Kido Butai*—would itself consist of all of the major fleet elements discussed in the Table 37 matrix.

Table 37. *Kido Butai*: ADM Yamamoto's Pearl Harbor Striking Force (General Ship Deployments)

ADM YAMAMOTO PEARL HARBOR TASK FORCE: MAJOR FLEET ELEMENTS	TASK GROUP COMPOSITIONS AND SHIPS' NAMES
FIRST-WAVE COMPOSITION	
(6) × CV (Aircraft Carriers)	*Akagi, Kaga, Sōryū, Hiryū, Shōkaku,* and *Zuikaku*
(2) × BB (Battleships)	*Hiei* and *Kirishima* and initially four BBs; however, the battleships *Kongō* and *Haruna*, under the aegis and able command of ADM Nobutake Kondō, are redeployed at the last minute and dispatched to the South China Sea to support troop landings during the invasion of Malaya
(2) × CA (Heavy Cruisers)	*Tone; Chikuma*
(1) × CL (Light Cruiser)	*Abukuma* (Flag for DDs below)
(9) × DD (Destroyers)	*Tanikaze, Hamakaze, Urakaze, Kasumi, Arare, Kagero, Shiranuhi, Akigumo, Isokaze* (or *Asakaze*)
(8) × AT (Tankers)	*Kyokuto* (Flag): *Kenyo Kokuyo, Shinkoku, Toho, Toei, Nippon, Kyokuyo* (or *Akebono*)
FIRST-WAVE COMPOSITION	
(23) × SS (Submarines)	(a) (3) × Units for fleet reconnaissance: *I-19, I-21, I-23* (b) (20) × Units to be positioned in Hawaiian waters, as noted below: Squadron 1: *I-9, I-15, I-17, I-25* Squadron 2: *I-1, I-2, I-3, I-4, I-5, I-6, I-7* Squadron 3: *I-8, I-68, I-69, I-70, I-71, I-72, I-73, I-74, I-75*
(5) × SSM ("Midget" Submarines)	Five attack submarines with "Midget" subs attached, as noted below: *I-16, I-18, I-20, I-22, I-24*
(189) × Combined Aircraft Elements	**FIRST-WAVE COMPOSITION** *(1st Group)* (50) *Nakajima* B5N *Kate* bombers (w/AP bombs) (40) *Nakajima* B5N *Kate* bombers (type 91 torpedoes) **FIRST-WAVE COMPOSITION** *(2nd Group)* (54) *Aichi* D3A *Val* dive bombers (w/GP bombs) **FIRST-WAVE COMPOSITION** *(3rd Group)* (45) *Mitsubishi* A6M *Zeke* (or *Zero*) fighters (Defense and strafe format)

(continued)

Table 37. *Continued*

ADM YAMAMOTO PEARL HARBOR TASK FORCE: MAJOR FLEET ELEMENTS	TASK GROUP COMPOSITIONS AND SHIPS' NAMES
SECOND-WAVE COMPOSITION	
(171) × Combined Aircraft Elements	**SECOND-WAVE COMPOSITION** *(1st Group)* (27) *Nakajima* B5N *Kate* bombers (Ford Island, Kaneohe, Barber's Point) (27) *Nakajima* B5N *Kate* bombers (Hickam Field) **SECOND-WAVE COMPOSITION** *(2nd Group)* (81) *Aichi* D3A *Val* dive bombers (in four groups) **Second-Wave COMPOSITION** *(3rd Group)* (36) *Mitsubishi* A6M *Zeke* (or *Zero*) fighters (defense and strafing formats)
THIRD-WAVE COMPOSITION	
Third-Wave Composition (Optioned Out)	Attack option is declined by VADM Nagumo, and later ADM Yamamoto himself, as being "tactically infeasible" due to the task force's depleted fuel situation and an overall fear of being too close to any of the American land-based bombers and/or carrier-based attack aircraft

With the attack on Oahu's Ford Island unfolding at about 0748 hours on the morning of 7 December 1941, all speculation was suspended, all rhetorical dialogue halted on the spot, and every debated question answered in total . . . the "rumor" of war had in fact become rumor no more. Oddly enough, the opening salvos of that war would in fact not even come from any of the ships' large guns, but rather from the great carrier's planes. And, as was his wont, Admiral Mikawa was already set to lead "from the front."

Mikawa's Battleship Division 3, or BATDIV3, would this day be composed of only two battleships, the *Hiei* and the *Kirishima*—along with a flotilla of support ships—since indeed the admiral had previously detached two other BBs, the *Kongō* and *Haruna*, to proceed south into the South China Sea in support of Japan's other invasion force landings, focused on their assault on Malaya. Therefore, to fully enlarge his still-considerable large-gun battleship force—and to offset the loss of the other two departing BBs—Mikawa would unquestionably need to ensure that his covering screen was in fact more than adequate to face the coming enemy. To such an end, therefore, Mikawa would not only command his own BATDIV3 but also have direct oversight over RADM Hiroaki Abe's own CRUDIV8. This action would now guardedly place both the heavy cruisers *Tone* and *Chikuma* at his immediate disposal as well, along with the CL *Abukuma*, which also fortuitously brought with her a fast, lethal, and already intact nine-ship destroyer force.

Mikawa would now task those escort ships, and all his submarine assets, to run patterned patrols across all shipping lanes well ahead and around the main body of his fleet to provide a solid protective screen for Yamamoto's vast, primary *Kido Butai* strike force. Proudly riding his command flag on the great battlecruiser *Hiei*, Mikawa's prime directive at all times would have been that of orchestrating a cast-iron wall of defense around not only his own BATDIV3 and CRUDIV8 elements but ultimately the entire six-carrier task force as well. As such, it was clear that the good admiral's work might indeed be cut out for him. Would the good Admiral Mikawa in fact be equal to the task?

Long a student of Sun Tzu and his insightful and widely read writings in *The Art of War*,[181] Admiral Mikawa could never quite forget the words that had been so clearly spoken so many years before: "If you know the enemy and know yourself, you need not fear the result of a hundred battles. If you know yourself but not the enemy, for every victory gained you will also suffer a defeat. If you know neither the enemy nor yourself, you will succumb in every encounter." Embracing the bold dogma of the ancient military strategist, therefore, Mikawa knew very well that it would never be his intent to ever succumb to any such deficit or shortfall . . . and so pushed on cautiously with only the greatest resolve.

The battle main would commence from two of Nagumo's carrier groups, the *Akagi* Striking Force 1 (SF1) and the *Kaga* Striking Force 2 (SF2), with SF1 initiating its first launch just north of the American-run Opana Radar Station on the northern edge of Oahu. Of needs, the SF1 attack squadrons would be compelled to launch in only unsettled seas, even as the great carriers themselves were rocked by a rude and choppy upsurge in mid-Pacific waters—now pitching and rolling as wave on wave swelled almost to the very flight decks themselves. Onboard, harried crewmen worked feverishly to chock down and secure the many flight-ready planes already on deck just to keep them from crashing over the side.

For now, Mikawa dutifully stood by on his hulking flagship *Hiei* and must too have watched the orchestrated launching of aircraft with the greatest interest, even as the great IJN carriers turned one by one into the wind as their planes shuttled down their flight decks and leapt into the sky. Far and away, however, the man's true focus could only have been elsewhere. Air operations, he might quietly have mused to himself, was one thing; screening the great carriers themselves was another thing entirely. And indeed the latter would most have constituted the admiral's greater responsibility, and truly one he would not have taken lightly.

Therefore, once the strike force aircraft were fully aloft, the fullness of the attack on Pearl Harbor would essentially be carried out by Fuchida's VTB, VT, VB, and VF air attack squadrons, and the good Admiral Mikawa would not otherwise figure in the attack itself at all. Yet, ever loyal to his great admiral, Isoroku Yamamoto, the IJN battleship commander would nonetheless remain on station beside the large carrier groups to continually guard their flanks, and to watchfully peruse the skies above for any retaliating American planes.

The attacks, once fully prosecuted against key areas on the island of Oahu, to include Ford Island, Battleship Row, and the airfields at Hickam, Bellows, and Wheeler—as well as multiple American Naval Air Stations (NAS)—were essentially over in a span of little more than two hours. And, by 1000 hours, Fuchida's fighters, bombers, and torpedo aircraft had all formed up at a predetermined rendezvous sector just north of Opana Point, and simply headed back to each of their respective carriers. Still perched high atop the *Pagoda* mast of his great BB *Hiei*, Mikawa must also have watched those same planes so triumphantly return. Out of an initial 414 sortied planes from the combined Japanese carriers, only 29 of them would not come back. The kicker would itself be the overwhelming disparity between the combatant losses—on at least the American side—that would be staggering and entirely disproportionate, as we can clearly see in Figure 41.

Nagumo's decision to foolishly decline a "third-wave" attack against several additional American hard targets on Oahu—such as the naval dockyard facilities, the oil depots, and maintenance bays that clearly dotted much of Ford Island—would in the

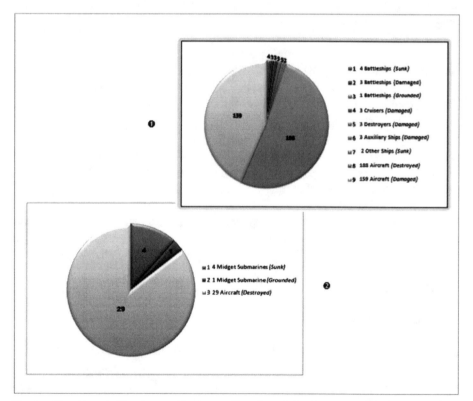

Figure 41. Excel Charts on Comparative Pearl Harbor Losses (❶ American/ ❷ Japanese)

end not at all be unlike Mikawa's own later decision not to prosecute his own follow-on attacks on any of the American troop transport and supply ships off Lunga Point on the night of 9 August 1942 during the First Battle of Savo Island itself. To this extent, the uncanny parallel here is not lost on us and would be eerily precognitive in its very occurrence.

Yamamoto's Japanese fleet then quickly disengaged and moved from Hawaiian waters and well to sea for a time, then looped sharply back to the northwest. By 11 December,[182] with the attack on Pearl Harbor already behind them, yet another target still loomed starkly over the near horizon: Wake Island. Now the full might of the Imperial Japanese Navy would stage its largely "punitive raid" on this island as well, this to simply oust the entrenched U.S. Marine forces already in place, severely punishing those forces for their interloping transgression. Therefore, in a fevered, five-day sprint between the dates of 11 and 16 December 1941 (❶ and ❷ as seen in Figure 42), Yamamoto and Nagumo's forces would make a virtual straight-line run to the southwest, driven by a dogged revenge and poised for yet more victories in the great Pacific. And so it was indeed that early on the morning of 11 December, VADM Mikawa would authorize the "detachment" of a small surface ship task force that would then be known as the IJN "South Seas Force," which detached force then immediately set sail at best speed away from the main body of the carriers, making fast headway toward the tiny coral atoll of Wake Island.

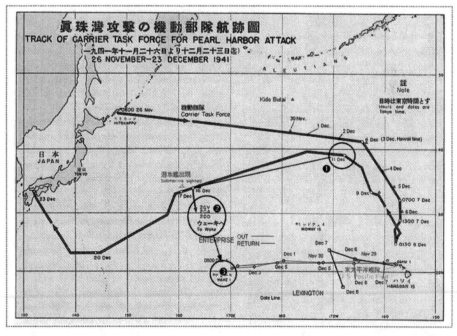

Figure 42.   IJN CTF Track during Attack on Pearl Harbor (Assault and Retirement)

The good Admiral Mikawa, meanwhile, on the successful conclusion of the IJN's previous attack on Pearl Harbor, felt far more confident and assured, and thus prompted, soon authorized the release of the three light cruisers *Yubari*, *Tenryū*, and *Tatsuta*, as well as six destroyers (*Oite*, *Kisaragi*, *Hayate*, *Mutsuki*, *Asanagi*, and *Yayoi*) to the overall command of RADM Sadamichi Kajioka. It was wholly believed the planned assault on Wake (seen as ❸ above) would itself be swift and fierce, but much to the force commander's surprise, it would instead meet with an even more fierce resistance from the dug-in Marines and shore batteries placed about on that island. In fact, Kajioka's first-wave assault would fail miserably, and his forces were compelled to retire from the attack with significant first-action battle losses. Of those at sea, already both the *Kisaragi* and *Hayate* had been sunk almost in situ, and Mikawa's own flagship peppered with shrapnel and numerous bullet holes from those opening actions.

Later, with the carriers *Hiryū* and *Sōryū*, the heavy cruisers *Tone* and *Chikuma*, and two fast destroyers sent to reinforce his fleet, Kajioka's "second-wave" attack on the entrenched U.S. Marines on Wake would be far more calculating and deadly, and it would soon in fact result in the vanquishing of those American forces and all the men who had fought so bravely to hold that ground. The struggle for such a jagged shard of real estate would last a daunting fifteen days—indeed, fifteen arduous days—but the resulting "possession" of that island by the dominant Japan's forces would thereafter last for the rest of the war until, in fact, 4 September 1945.

The battle for Wake Island would also go on to be the subject of an even greater infamy, and indeed become the very stuff of later war crime tribunals, when it was found that some ninety-eight captured American "civilians" were summarily executed in situ by the imprisoning Japanese captors on that same island—executions that would be ordered by an irate (but still fearsome) Japanese Admiral Shigematsu Sakai-bara, who is thought to have "panicked" in the face of what he thought might be a retaliatory strike by the soon-alerted American forces.

Mikawa, however, did not take this circuitous route, and did not participate in the warships' southern turn to storm the Wake Island fortress, instead continuing with the greater carrier force, escort cruisers, and fast destroyers, accompanying each back to the home waters of Japan-proper. And by 23 December—only sixteen days after the initial attack on Pearl Harbor itself—Yamamoto's fleet would indeed arrive back in Japan almost wholly intact and was met by cheering crowds, well wishers, and clearly exuberant onlookers. Elsewhere, throughout the whole of the Western world itself, it would now in fact be Christmas in slightly less than two days.[183]

VADM Mikawa: Heavy Ships, Heavy Guns: The Great Eighth Fleet

Having distinguished himself in numerous naval campaigns subsequent to the successful attacks on Pearl Harbor and Wake Island, RADM Mikawa would next be ordered to support the invasion-force landings during Japan's infamous Operation C (or the

"Indian Ocean Raid" of March–April 1942) and even be present during the three-day debacle at the Battle of Midway. There, the sharp ignominy that the Imperial Japanese Navy must have faced after Midway, due to the total destruction of their four major carriers *Akagi*, *Kaga*, *Hiryū*, and *Sōryū*—and the heavy cruiser *Mikuma*—must have been deep and unfathomable. That the feared and mighty Imperial Japanese Navy would come away from Midway with far more than just a bloody nose, Mikawa (as overall commander of the Second Fleet's Midway Invasion Force) must, to some extent, have been relieved that his own force elements (namely, his own BATDIV3, Kondo's CRUDIV4, and Takagi's CRUDIV5) had all returned virtually unscathed from the action. The single heavy cruiser loss suffered by the IJN (the *Mikuma*) had in fact been a Midway Support Force screening ship from CRUDIV7, under the command of VADM Takeo Kurita, not Mikawa. Therefore, the loss of the single heavy cruiser, however unfortunate, had thankfully not been directly his.

Rewarded for his actions and dogged gallantry throughout all of the major naval campaigns up to that point, Gunichi Mikawa would now be in line for even further advancement. And with quiet ceremony on 14 June 1942—at IJN headquarters at Rabaul, in the east New Britain province of Papua, New Guinea—he would finally be given a full command of the newly formed Eighth Fleet,[184] soon to be known as the "Outer South Seas Force." The new vice admiral almost at once designated his flagship to be his old favorite, the *Takao*-class heavy cruiser *Chōkai*, which floating fortress incorporated a 10-battery, 8-inch naval gun platform that would then go on to serve both as his command ship and as the very nerve center for orchestrating his many naval engagements yet to come. For the time being, however, Mikawa would form up his new fleet and, when ready, mercilessly go about the business of taking the fight to the enemy. And, as seen here in Table 38, Mikawa's firm intent was to sail his deadly warships into battle and to pack one hell of a punch wherever he had occasion to encounter his foe. It was also his avowed intent to place all of those ships well in harm's way.

VADM Mikawa would scarcely have been in place in his new post as Commander, Eighth Fleet (COMEIGHTHFLT), when on 20 July 1942, CAPT Toshikazu Ohmae—the admiral's own newly appointed chief of staff—would announce the tenor of his own less than reassuring report following a quick layover at Simpson Harbor in distant Rabaul. Commissioned by Mikawa to cautiously "go out to the forward areas for a first-hand look at the war situation, and [to] survey local conditions at our bases,"[185] Ohmae spoke at length of his time spent with VADM Shigeyoshi Inoue's Fourth Fleet in the Japanese-held Truk Islands and dryly reported his findings as follows:

❶ Elements of the IJN's famed 3rd Special Naval Landing Force, supported by a small naval screening force, had landed in the Solomons and met only negligible resistance, and now fully occupied the islands of both Tulagi and Gavutu, both of which were cross-channel from the even larger Guadalcanal.

Table 38. Compositional Makeup of VADM Mikawa's Eighth Fleet (Pre-Savo Island Attack)

Ship	Size/ Tonnage	Armament	Command
Flagship — VADM Gunichi Mikawa (Eighth Fleet from Rabaul, New Britain)			
Chōkai (CA) **(Flag)**	661 feet 15,781 tons	10 × 20 cm/50 *3rd Year* type naval guns 4 × 4.7-inch (120 mm) guns 66(±) × 25 mm AA guns 8 × 24-inch tubes for the Type 93 torpedoes	CAPT Hayakawa Mikio
Tenryū (CL)	468 feet 4,350 tons	4 × 14 cm/50 *3rd Year* type naval guns 1 × 8 cm/40 *3rd* year type naval guns 2 × Type 93 13 *Mm* AA machine guns 6 × 533 mm (21.0 in) torpedo tubes	CAPT Mitsutaru Gotō (No relation to RADM Aritomo Gotō)
Yūbari (CL)	455.7 feet 4,075 tons	6 × 140 mm (5.5 in) guns (2x2, 2x1) 1 × 76.2 mm (3 in) AA gun 2 × machine guns 4 × 610 mm (24 in) torpedo tubes (2x2) 34 × mines	CAPT Masami Ban
Yūnagi (DD)	320 feet 1,720 tons	3 × Type 3 120 mm 45 cal naval gun 10 × Type 96 25 mm AT/AA Guns 4 × 21-inch torpedo tubes 16 × naval mines	LT Okada Seiichi
Flagship — RADM Aritomo Gotō (CRUDIV8 from Kavieng, New Ireland)			
Aoba (CA) **(Flag)**	607.5 feet 8,300 tons	6 × 8-inch (203mm) 50-cal guns (3x2) 4 × 4.7-inch (120mm) 45-cal (4x1) 8 × 24-inch (610mm) torpedo tubes (2x4) 50 × 25 mm AA guns	CAPT Narita Moichi

Ship	Size/ Tonnage	Armament	Command
Furutaka (CA)	580 feet 9,150 tons	6 × 8-inch (203mm) 50-cal guns (3x2) 4 × 4.7-inch (120mm) 45-cal (4x1) 8 × 24-inch (610mm) torpedo tubes (2x4)	CAPT Araki Tsutau
Kako (CA)	580 feet 7,950 tons	6 × 8-inch (203mm) 50-cal guns (3x2) 4 × 4.7-inch (120mm) 45-cal (4x1) 8 × 24-inch (610mm) torpedo tubes (2x4)	CAPT Chihaya Takahashi
Kinugasa (CA)	607.5 feet 8,300 tons	6 × 8-inch (203mm) 50-cal guns (3x2), 4 × 4.7-inch (120mm) 45-cal (4x1), 8 × 24-inch (610mm) torpedo tubes (2x4) 50 × 25 mm AA guns	CAPT Masao Sawa

❷ A further element of that Tulagi Landing Force, also supported by a small naval screening element, had been able to land on the main island of Guadalcanal, and now fully occupied Lunga Point. Some eleven days later, an "airfield survey team" had already been dispatched by both the 11th Air Fleet and Inoue's Fourth Fleet to begin work on a brand-new landing strip at that same site.

❸ A garrison-sized unit (84th Garrison Unit) had then been left in place on Guadalcanal to guard that airfield, just then under construction, and that significant progress was being made even at that moment.

❹ That the "general situation in the Solomons was quiet."[186]

On 7 August 1942, however, all of this would change, and what would indeed begin with a smash-and-grab series of initial victories for the great Mikawa would later end in crushing defeat as the battle for the Solomons itself began to heat up. Mikawa's time was finally at hand, and his most immediate place of business would be nowhere else if not Guadalcanal.

Hotly incensed by the very audacity of the bold and foolish American attempt to wrest control of Guadalcanal from his defending garrison forces on the morning of

7 August 1942, Mikawa would receive only more bad news of simultaneous attacks being carried out in the Solomons, even as the two naval officers spoke. It would therefore regrettably fall on Chief of Staff Ohmae to be the one to brief the admiral. The man's best and only hope, however, was that the "messenger" would himself not be shot simply for the tenor of his message. At that time, Ohmae would only inform him that the calm of the following morning had been shattered with the arrival of an urgent dispatch at headquarters—one that read, in part:[187]

> 0430. Tulagi being heavily bombarded from air and sea. Enemy carrier task force sighted.[188]

This statement would almost immediately be amplified to further read:

> One battleship . . . two carriers . . . three cruisers . . . fifteen destroyers . . . and thirty to forty transports.[189]

What followed was the even more dire report from his own IJN naval infantry forces in the field, still attempting to hold the small, tropical island of Guadalcanal against a much stronger secondary Allied force. That "force," of course, would have been the American 1st Marine Division itself, and their brave onslaught had already been swift, decisive, and wholly unforgiving:

> [We have] . . . encountered American landing forces and are retreating into the jungle hills.[190]

Then, almost as abruptly, that same message would end with the even more ominously defiant codicil:

> The enemy force is overwhelming. We will defend our positions to the death.[191]

Mikawa vowed a silent revenge and hastily set about the task of working out a viable plan of counterattack. That plan of action would be deceptively simple, and nothing less than a full-on "punitive raid" that would probe deeply down into the waters fronting Tulagi and Guadalcanal, this to slake his now growing anger. His plan would also be fast-paced and devoid of great complexity: find the enemy, engage them, and blow them the hell out of the water . . . then boldly sail through the blazing wreckage on our way to the next objective in full. And two days later, without fanfare or embellishment from this initial idea, Mikawa would do precisely that.

VADM Mikawa: A Long Day's Journey into Night—Sailing the Slot

On 7 August 1942, therefore, the great flagship *Chōkai* would depart from Moewe Passage, near Papua/New Guinea, and make way for Rabaul, where VADM Mikawa would board his command ship and set sail with three cruisers and a single destroyer

(*Yunagi*), which unit would now be designated as his own CRUDIV18, under the captaincy of RADM Mitsuhara Matsuyama. En route, he would rendezvous near Cape St. George with RADM Aritomo Gotō's own CRUDIV6 task group and would soon add four more heavy cruisers to his surface force. Mikawa's Eighth Fleet was now fully intact and on the move, and its next stop would be Iron Bottom Sound—and directly into a battle main. On the way, however, he and his ships would still face innumerable obstacles.

Ever fearful of detection by either the Allied air or naval forces known to be prowling the areas throughout the hotly contested channel called the Slot (waypoint marker ❹ in Figure 43), Mikawa would cautiously approach under the fading light of day, his forces anxious to avoid engagement with the enemy until they were fully prepared and so disposed. By sunset on 7 August, carefully navigating his fleet through the narrowed straits pinched on both sides by the islands of New Britain and that of New Ireland, the bold admiral forged ahead riding a swift current through the St. George's Channel. It would be here that his force would encounter its first real threat of discovery, this time in the guise of the American *S*-class submarine, the USS *S-38* (*SS-143*) ❶.

Mikawa wisely declined any engagement with the American sub and instead opted to simply continue in his hastened foray to the south. The admiral's objective this night was not a single submarine but the *bulk* of the Allied surface fleet itself. To fire on the intruding submarine at this time would only serve to alert the Americans of his approach, in a scenario where stealth and a still-intact element of surprise would become the staple of his perilous drive down the Slot. Sailing north of Buka Island ❷, Mikawa was compelled to halt his column during the remaining six hours of daylight, then—off the eastern coast of Kieta—the wily admiral split his forces and dispersed them widely, again deciding to mask his full force composition from prying enemy eyes above. Better, he might have reasoned, that his full number not be known, than to be spotted and remove all doubt of his ships' organization, position, and ultimate point of traverse.

Therefore, to continue to further deceive the enemy at large, Mikawa would now only feint a passage on the western edge of Choiseul ❸, when in fact he quickly re-corrected that heading and made instead for the eastern side of that same island. Later, once the flotilla had again entered the security of open waters, and as night began to fall, Mikawa was compelled to order his surface fleet into its standard "night-battle formation," which formation would indeed have been its classic "line-ahead" single-column format, with 1,200-meter (4,000-foot) intervals between each ship. And now, for only the second time that day, he would again order a launch of several *Mitsubishi* F1M2 "Pete" floatplanes to scan the gray horizon ❺, and to reconnoiter the areas south and east of Savo Island.

By 2130 hours, therefore, having sufficiently rested his ships and waited out the fade of daylight, the admiral now increased his speed to a new 26 knots—up from its previous 22; the earlier-catapulted reconnaissance planes began piping back their nervous reports that now told of two formations of large American warships dead ahead and set in patrol patterns off both Tulagi and Guadalcanal. Clearly, then, Mikawa

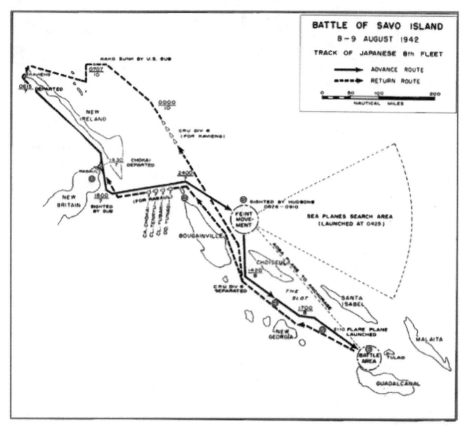

Figure 43.   The First Battle of Savo Island: Track of Mikawa's CRUDIV6/18 Task Force *(USNI Proceedings, 1957)*

might correctly have reasoned to himself, not only were the Americans here, but they had indeed landed in force and appeared to be hunkering down for an extended stay. The acid news rankled the man, adding fuel to Mikawa's already blistering fire and further compelling him to steam ahead at best speed, with stealth, and in relative silence—but always with the deadliest intent. By 2200 hours, therefore, Mikawa ordered "all hands to battle stations,"[192] as each ship in turn prepared for the battle that would soon be on them. By 0054 hours, with Savo now some 20 degrees on her port bow, Mikawa's *Chōkai* was first to spot the distant American radar picket, the destroyer USS *Blue* ❻. His force had now arrived at a point just north of Savo.

VADM Mikawa: Approach to Savo Island

The call quickly went out to Mikawa's two cruiser divisions almost at the moment of detection of the silhouette identified only as "a destroyer at 10,000 meters," which seemed "about to cross our bow from right to left."[193] Now approaching the

American radar picket ship *Blue*, Mikawa ordered left full rudder and slowed to 22 knots. Shrewdly, he declined to engage the passing ship, noting that its sudden and unexpected turnabout no longer posed an immediate threat to his contingency of warships. Then, some three minutes later, a second, even more harried call would go out: "Ship sighted, ship's hull down to port—20 degrees!"[194] This would have been the other radar picket ship, the *Bagley*-class DD USS *Ralph Talbot*. Neither screening ship would spot Mikawa's cruisers that night, even as the IJN commander's naval force simply slipped the noose and silently passed through the eye of the needle past both pickets.

Years later, it would be recounted by Ohmae and others that in spotting those same American warships, virtually every gun on every cruiser had already been trained out and locked on in the ready at all times, even as the ships of CRUDIV6 and 18 sluiced by. Had either ship twitched or swung about a single turret in his direction, Mikawa was prepared to simply obliterate them and would not for a moment have hesitated to do so. But, as with the *Blue*, the *Talbot* had apparently reached the end of its patrol perigee and so also swung about and moved off into the night again—*away* from Mikawa's great ships—and would pose no further threat to his group.

The men on flagship *Chōkai* breathed a collective sigh of relief for not having to engage either ship and so sped off with an even greater momentum and a cloak of darkness into the dead of night. Relieved, but still steeled in his resolve, Mikawa ordered, "Right rudder. Steer to course 150!"[195] as his bold ships now lined up for the kill on their first run in on the Allied fleet just to the south of Savo. From high atop his grand *Pagoda*-mast perch on the great *Chōkai*, Mikawa was now prepared to lead from the front—as always—and his approach to Savo had so far been marked with covertness, plain old good luck, and an element of nondetection by the Allied surface fleet itself. Shortly thereafter, with a near full-throttle push back up to a full cruiser-attack speed of 30 knots, Mikawa's rough-and-tumble charge into Iron Bottom Sound was finally at hand.

VADM Mikawa: The First Battle of Savo Island: "Iron Hammer"— Attack on the Southern Fleet

Admiral Mikawa's battle fleet approached in a single-column, "line-ahead" format that stretched a full two miles. Led by the mighty CRUDIV flagship *Chōkai* came Gotō's own *Aoba*, followed in loose proximity by the *Kako*, *Kinugasa*, *Tenryū*, *Furu-taka*, and *Yubari*. *Yunagi*, the lone destroyer accompanying the cruiser convoy that night, had already been detached from the main body by Mikawa, with specific orders to circle back to guard the "gateway" at Savo . . . and to dutifully "watch the back door" while the primary force moved in to prosecute their several attacks. *Yunagi* would also be expected to serve as Mikawa's own countermeasure against either the *Blue* or the *Ralph Talbot* (or both), should either American DD indeed later "wake up" in the face of the action. Thus, only seven IJN "heavies" would now make up that CRUDIV6 and 18 force, but each sped on nonetheless, soon flicking on their large searchlights and firing starshell flares into the blackness of night at near-distance. The waters fairly glimmered with a shadowed brilliance as the darkened skies were soon themselves lit up in full.

The attack on the Allied Southern screening force would be nothing if not quick and coordinated, well orchestrated, and almost flawlessly executed. Shortly past 0130 hours, on the night of 9 August, the IJN battle fleet would no sooner have sailed past Savo itself when the ships' lookouts found what they had been looking for . . . and once again Mikawa's own chief of staff and right-hand man, Ohmae, would have been right there at the precise moment of that sighting:

> I stood beside Admiral Mikawa. Before me was a chart on which were plotted the locations of [the] enemy ships. We peered into the darkness. The voice of a lookout shattered the tense silence: Cruiser, 7 degrees to port! The shape which appeared in that direction seemed small, and could only be a destroyer. It was still a long way off. Then came the further aviso: Three cruisers, 9 degrees to starboard, moving to the right![196]

Unquestionably, Ohmae could only be alluding to the *Canberra*—misidentified as a "*Kent*-class cruiser"—sailing in consort with *Chicago* and the escort destroyers *Bagley* and *Patterson*. In fact, it would be this latter ship, the *Patterson*, that would be the first to spy the intruding ships and to engage them almost on sight. On *Chōkai*, the order from its skipper, CAPT Mikio Hayakawa, quickly went out to all on the ship: "Torpedoes fire to starboard! FIRE!!"[197]

> Almost immediately, the deadly weapons were heard to smack the water one by one. While we waited for them to hit, the radio announced that our following cruisers had already opened fire with [their own] guns and torpedoes as well.

Within minutes, *Chōkai* and *Tenryū* opened fire with all main guns and had launched several Long-Lance torpedoes in the direction of the "American cruiser," which was in fact Australian. As Mikawa's lead ships passed by, the other heavy cruisers behind them now also swung about in tandem and unleashed their own furies on the enemy warships as well. Then *Aoba* and *Kako* both joined the fray with their own coordinated attacks on Crutchley's unsuspecting Southern fleet, almost in tandem. The gunners and torpedomen on Mikawa's ships could probably not have known that the target ship was in fact the *Canberra*, nor might they have made any real distinction between her and the *Chicago*, the *Quincy*, or the *Astoria*. She was instead simply a target, an enemy ship . . . and this night an object of war utterly to be destroyed.

Mikawa's cruisers now in turn swung their attention toward the second loitering Allied target—also thought to be a cruiser-class ship (and indeed the *Chicago*)—even while still engaging both *Canberra* and the scrappy escort DD *Patterson*, the latter of which was indeed continuing to put up quite a fight—much to the awe and bewilderment of the attacking Japanese sailors.

Caught up in the orchestrated mayhem of the moment, *Canberra* might have been mistakenly hit by either the *Bagley* or the *Chicago* (or both) in the heat of battle, the subject of which would later become an item of some outrage and discussion, centered on the several misguided "friendly-fire" incidents that appeared to have occurred on the occasion of that one night. For further information on other such known incidents involving friendly cross-fire during the battle, see the earlier discussion on *Close Encounters and the Cost of Friendly Fire*.

In the near view, *Canberra* was wholly stunned by the surprise attack, and even CAPT Getting struggled to maintain control of his ship, which was initially still able to respond to the attacking IJN force. Getting ordered a sharp increase in speed and a rapid reversal in course from the ship's initial shunt to port to fully unmask his own guns and train out all batteries. Desperately, he sought out any targets of opportunity but was already too late, as four of Mikawa's seven heavy cruisers had already found *him*—and found their range *out* to him. The next three minutes would witness a total of some twenty-four consecutive hits fired "with good prospect and high confidence" on this one single ship. In the end, the beleaguered *Canberra* could do little else than stagger about the Sound on an apparent evasive zigzag course, her gunnery officer killed outright and CAPT Getting himself now mortally wounded. The cruiser would soon slowly and mechanically grind to a halt and was engulfed in flames with a 5°–10° starboard list. Her time left in battle could now be measured only in minutes and not in hours.

Similarly, Bode's *Chicago*, some 600 yards astern of *Canberra*, would be next in column—and next in the Japanese gunners' crosshairs as well. With no mercy, Mikawa unleashed all guns on his ships, as soon the *Kako* and *Tenryū* themselves moved in to take aim at the lone American cruiser. A single torpedo, thought to have been fired from the *Kako* at a range of about 2½ miles (3,600 meters) at what she had identified only as a "battleship," would now impact *Chicago*'s bow and send shockwaves throughout the entire ship from the resulting blow. A second torpedo would then almost immediately hit the ship in approximately the same location, but simply penetrated the hull of the cruiser but did not detonate. *Chicago* was now locked in a head-to-head matchup with Mikawa's crack cruiser divisions—practiced night fighters all—and soon found itself outgunned, outmatched, and outmaneuvered. By the time Bode realized what had happened, or that his ship was even under attack, Mikawa's forces had already scored their hits and were preparing to disengage from the fray, as soon they began to slowly move off to the northeast. For Bode and *Chicago* it would all be over in minutes, with the hapless captain's ship riddled with shrapnel and sporting a dark, gaping hole that rudely adorned its mangled bow.

This "bloody nose" was all *Chicago* would suffer in the battle, and she would in fact see no further action that night. By 0150 on the morning of 9 August, she would last be seen moving away on a course heading of 263° and crippling off at a cautious 12 knots as she unwittingly continued on well to the northwest. Inexplicably, she would do so for the next *forty* minutes, allegedly pursuing only a "phantom contact" that itself always seemed to be just over the next horizon and quite out of reach—one that Bode thought might be a Japanese destroyer that he later swore he had hit. Indeed, it could have been either the destroyer *Yunagi* or the light cruiser *Yubari*, since, when later questioned back at their home port in Japan, the crew of *Yubari* would recall both the pursuit and the fire-on incident but otherwise appeared to shrug off the claim in principle, noting only few hits and the fact that they had "received some scratches" and nothing more.

Back on *Canberra*, at the moment of the initial attack, the Australian cruiser had sharply turned to starboard to parallel the track of one of the incoming torpedoes she had seen, and to unmask her own guns. In so doing, she would almost run afoul of Mikawa's ships—which action would then inadvertently cause the "splitting" of Mikawa's column at precisely that moment. As a result, the *Furutaka*, *Yubari*, and *Tenryū* would all sharply swerve to avoid an imminent collision, and now found themselves fully detached from the main column and veering slowly forward on a more westerly course, this to form a "second," even deadlier attack column. Mikawa now quietly swung his ships about and sailed north in pursuit of more prey. Well to the north and east, the second American surface fleet—RADM Riefkohl's own Northern screen—sat undisturbed at Readiness Condition Two, its crew seemingly at rest and only mildly oblivious to the attacks going on to the south. As a result, Round One had unquestionably gone to the Imperial Japanese Navy, and Mikawa's own concocted Round Two might itself not be too far behind.

VADM Mikawa: The First Battle of Savo Island: "Spiked Mace"— Attack on the Northern Fleet

Mikawa's abrupt turnabout after the successful attack on Crutchley's Southern fleet would now fortuitously result in the "splitting" of his column into a two-pronged assault force. Within RADM Riefkohl's Northern group, however, the ships were only marginally aware of any action at all taking place to the south of their position. All three captains—Riefkohl on the *Vincennes*, Moore on the *Quincy*, and Greenman on the *Astoria*, along with most of their crews—had already bedded down for the night and were asleep at the time of the attack on *Canberra* and *Chicago*. After multiple days of standing alert watches at a heightened Condition One, the welcomed relaxing of each ship's status to Condition Two must have been itself a breath of fresh air and perhaps their best opportunity to catch up on some much-needed rest. None of the ships' commanders, therefore, would have had much of an inkling of what had already occurred, or even what was just about to befall them. The screening force inched along at a measured 10 knots on the northern leg of its box-like patrol pattern, steadying along on a course heading of 3-1-5° (T). Now, the hour rolled past a dark and dampened midnight and sauntered lightly into a date of 9 August.

Fresh from the deadly victory that had just been centered on the destruction of Crutchley's Southern fleet, Mikawa now arrived in waters fronting Admiral Riefkohl's Northern group at a time as early as 0144 hours. Due east of Savo Island, the crafty

IJN commander now launched his cruiser-based floatplanes to reconnoiter the seas before him and set them to drop illumination orbs from their airborne seat. This illumination was immediately augmented by the ships' own searchlights and starshell flares fired from the cruisers' smaller, 5-inch guns. What had formerly been a securing curtain of darkness enshrouding the Northern screen cruisers was now rudely stripped away, fully exposing those ships to almost certain detection. That detection was of course quickly followed by Mikawa's full-on attacks—which attacks would decidedly not at all wait—and by 0150 he had already ordered all ships to attack. And, as always, Ohmae would himself stand close at the side of Mikawa on the bridge of *Chōkai*. Their element of surprise had indeed been complete, even to the stunned amazement of the Japanese attackers themselves, who could only look on in dismay:

> For incredible minutes, the turrets of the enemy ships remained in their trained-in secure positions, and we stood amazed yet thankful that they did not bear [in] on us.
>
> Strings of machine-gun traces wafted back and forth between the enemy and ourselves, but such minor counter efforts merely made for a colorful spectacle, but gave us no real concern. Second by second, however, the range decreased and now we could actually distinguish the shapes of individuals running along the decks of the enemy ships. The fight was now quickly moving on to close quarters.[198]

Spotting the American cruiser force some 30° to port, *Chōkai's* initially established firing range of 7,000 meters now closed with amazing swiftness, as soon Mikawa's twin-axial attack bracketed the American ships in tandem. All three American cruisers were only then coming alert on the moment and switching on their own searchlights, when the full attack commenced. For the Americans, it would already be too little too late—as truly Riefkohl's Northern ships stood not a chance, and none would be able to escape their fate. Second by second, the range between Mikawa's two columns of warships and the American screening force dissolved quickly, as noted in Ohmae's own words when he said, "we could actually distinguish the shapes of individuals running along the decks of the [burning] enemy ships." Far quicker than thought itself, the battle would be joined at close quarters and was already exacting casualties on both sides, though clearly more so for the Americans than the ships of the IJN.

Proceeding in good formation, with an interspersion of some 2,000 yards between ships, the American *Vincennes* would have been first in line and was immediately followed in column by the *Quincy*—with *Astoria* coming up in her third position—while flanking them would have been the two escort destroyers *Helm* and *Wilson*. As such, each of the three "heavies" would be hit in virtually this same order as they came into view of the Japanese gunners and torpedomen. By 0155, therefore, the *Vincennes* would be the first to succumb to Mikawa's sharp attack, suffering some eighty-five combined hits from the attacking IJN CRUDIV warships. An hour later, almost to the very minute, she would be lost, taking with her some 332 men, and the bold *Quincy* would herself be next in line.

Now CAPT Samuel Nobre Moore, the skipper of the *Quincy*, faced with his own conundrum as to whether he should engage any of the attacking ships, fearing yet another possible "friendly-fire" incident—not at all unlike Bode had on *Chicago* in the earlier attack—may also have been a dime short and a moment too late in his own response. Indeed, by the time his crew had been roused from sleep, fully alerted, and ordered to stations, the battle main was now under way and his ship was already coming under heavy fire. Caught in a deadly crossfire between Gotō's *Aoba*, the *Tenryū*, and CL *Furutaka*, the second American cruiser would be hit with numerous HE shells fired from both the IJN's 5-inch and 8-inch guns and hit with no less than three Long-Lance torpedoes.

The shells alone would almost immediately impact *Quincy*'s pilot house and bridge area, killing outright or wounding virtually all of the officers and crew manning those stations. Sadly, even CAPT Moore himself would be counted among those casualties, and yet the *Quincy* would continue to fight to her dying breath. With virtually all main batteries out of commission, she did the only other thing she could do—she prepared to "ram" the attacking Japanese ships full on. Observing this action, CAPT Ohmae on *Chōkai* would himself note the following:

> From a group of three enemy ships, the center one bore out and down on us, as if intending to ram. Though her entire hull, from midships to aft, was enveloped in flames, her forward guns [were] still firing with great spirit. She was a brave ship, manned by brave men. But the ship immediately took a heavy list as our full firepower came to bear and struck her.
>
> It appears now, from post-war accounts, that this was (in fact) the U.S. heavy cruiser *Quincy*, and she certainly made an impression on the men of our force. At short range, she fired an 8-inch shell which hit and exploded in the operations room on *Chōkai*, just abaft of the bridge, and knocked out our No. 1 turret. We were all shocked and disconcerted momentarily but returned at once to the heat of battle as *Chōkai* continued firing, and directing fire, at the many targets [found].[199]

By 0238 the intrepid *Quincy*—now itself mortally wounded—would sink, taking with her some 370–389 souls, including her captain, Samuel N. Moore. Now next in the almost predictable column-like screening formation being led by Riefkohl, the great *Astoria* might not fare much better.

On *Astoria*, CAPT Greenman seems to have reacted fairly immediately, perhaps far sooner than the others, and quickly ordered General Quarters by at least 0149, almost as soon as the ship spotted the cascading flares in the near distance. The throaty rumblings heard from the decks of the brave *Nasty Asty* were in fact the sounds of the large guns on the Japanese ships themselves, as at once they all barked to life, each seeking their own deadly range out to the stricken American cruiser. It would not take long at all to walk their way out to Greenman's ship, as soon she too was being hit by a heated barrage of high-caliber rounds from the combined batteries of at least four of Mikawa's ships, thought to have been the *Chōkai, Kako, Aoba,* and *Kinugasa.*

Astoria would quickly begin to succumb to those attacks as well, and rapidly began losing speed and steerage. Pounded unmercifully by all four of Mikawa's "heavies," the proud American cruiser would be hit a staggering sixty-five to seventy times and suffer a loss of life that would thereafter number between 216 and 268 men, with some discrepancy. She would be left fighting for her very life, but would somehow survive the battle and the night, only to be later lost at sea in waters just south-southeast of Savo Island. By 1216 hours early on the afternoon of 9 August 1942, *Astoria* would increase her list from 10° to 15° in only minutes, turn slowly on her port beam, and then roll slowly and settle by the stern, disappearing completely into the darkened waters of the Sound, where she remains to this day at a position that is approximated to be at 9°12'-33' S–159°52'-3' E.

Mikawa's twin victories would now be wholly complete, and the sly IJN admiral might now indeed be allowed a brief moment of congratulatory emotion. Having successfully prosecuted not one, but *two* full-scale attacks on two of three Allied screening groups patrolling Guadalcanal that night—and ever fearful of retaliatory airstrikes that might be launched at any time from any of Fletcher's carriers, thought to still be in the area—Mikawa simply reassembled his forces and prepared to depart the area. By 0220, Mikawa therefore issued one final order for all ships to retire, urging them to proceed at best speed back to the north from whence they had come. History would indeed record the events of this day, as soon the men on the American ships might now only see to their dead and tend to their wounded. But now it was an enraged U.S. Navy that would never forget the harsh lessons learned. Full payback and a sharp backlash would come soon enough in the several months to come.

VADM Mikawa: Response to Ohmae—Admiral Mikawa's Statement

Shortly after the release of the interview account of CAPT Toshikazu Ohmae (see also endnote 7), Gunichi Mikawa's chief of staff on the force's flagship *Chōkai* on the night of the Savo attacks, the now-retired VADM Mikawa was asked to review that account and to apply whatever fitting addendum comments he might wish to add to validate, amend, or refute that account. The following is a presentation of the verbatim text of that Mikawa response to Ohmae's statement, as published in the same USNI *Proceedings* journal in that same December 1957 article. The response would be presented in full, complete with an opening observation by editor Roger Pineau: "Since Admiral Mikawa had been in command of the Japanese forces engaged in the First Battle of Savo Island, he was requested to read CAPT Ohmae's article to ensure its very accuracy. His comments follow in the narrative below."[200]

I have read Toshikazu Ohmae's article, "The Battle of Savo Island",* and find it well-written and complete. It covers all the important facts of the battle as I remember them. There are a few points, however, which I wish to emphasize.

Upon my arrival at Rabaul in late July 1942, as C-in-C Eighth Fleet, there was no indication that the quiet Solomons was soon to be the scene of fierce battle. Nevertheless, I recognized the mobile capability of the U.S. carrier task forces, and accordingly ordered my heavy cruisers to the safer rear base area at Kavieng, rather than Rabaul.

It was a serious inconvenience and a shortcoming that my command extended only to sea and land operations in the area. Air operations were entirely outside my responsibility and control. I found, for example, that there was no program or plan for providing planes to the new base at Guadalcanal, and there was nothing that I could do about it.

As soon as the U.S. landings at Guadalcanal were reported [early] on 7 August, and the invasion strength was apparent, I determined to employ all of the forces at my command to destroy the enemy ships. My choice of a night action to accomplish this purpose was made because I had no air support on which to rely—and reliable air support was vital to anything but a night action. On the other hand, I had complete confidence in my ships, and knew that the Japanese Navy's emphasis on night battle training and practice would insure [sic] our chances of success in such an action, even without air support.

My two major concerns for this operation were that the enemy carriers might repeat against my ships their successes at the Battle of Midway before we reached the battle area, and our approach to Guadalcanal might be hindered by the poorly-charted waters of the Solomons. But both of these worries were dispelled once we had passed the scouting lines of enemy destroyers to the west of Savo Island [clearly the American radar pickets *Blue* and the *Ralph Talbot*], and I was then assured of success in the night battle.

The element of surprise worked to our advantage and enabled us to destroy every target taken under fire. I was greatly impressed, however, by the courageous action of the northern group of U.S. cruisers. They fought back heroically despite heavy damage sustained before they were ready for battle. Had they even a few minutes' warning of our approach, the results of that action might indeed have been quite different.

Prior to the action, I had ordered the jettisoning of all shipboard flammables, such as aviation fuel and depth charges, to reduce the chance of fire from any anticipated shell hits. While my ship sustained no fires, we did observe that the U.S. ships, immediately as they were hit, burst into flames which were soon uncontrollable.

The reasons given by Mr. Ohmae for *not* attacking the transports are indeed the reasons which influenced my decision at the time. Knowing now that the transports were vital to the coming American foothold on Guadalcanal; knowing now that our army would be unable to drive American forces out of the Solomons; and knowing now that the (American) carrier task force was not in fact in position to attack my ships, it is easy to say that some other decision would have been wiser. But I believe today, as then, that my decision—based on the information known to me (at the time)—was not a wrong one.

/s/ **G. Mikawa**

---

*The Ohmae interview was rendered in translation by article editor Roger Pineau in that same USNI *Proceedings* article titled "The Battle of Savo Island"—as initially penned by Ohmae in December 1957—and as seen in Vol. 83, no. 12.

VADM Mikawa: Requiem for a Fallen Admiral

In the wake of the stunning successes of VADM Gunichi Mikawa and his naval forces at Savo Island—just north and west of Guadalcanal in the Solomons—even more fierce battles would be yet to come. The admiral's "failure," and perhaps most glaring error, would clearly point to his refusal to further prosecute his attacks during the early morning hours of 9 August on any of the other Allied warships within that zone of attack. Since the IJN commander had been tasked imprimis with the destruction of the American screening forces and the transport and cargo ships themselves, which were even then unloading at both Tulagi and Honiara, it would come as no great surprise that the Japanese high command would later find grave fault with the commander's decision not to do so. The bold strategist's attempts to later offer his reasons for not pursuing those follow-on attacks seemed to fall on deaf ears, and indeed few would listen. If not wholly a full dereliction of duty, as seen from the perspective of his superiors, it nonetheless had the appearance of such and did not at all sit well with the Japanese admiralty of that time.

Thus it was to great extent that the good IJN admiral would later be looked on as the sole source of responsibility for not just the later battle losses and full expulsion of Japan's forces from the Solomons but also the loss of so many critically needed ship assets that would soon be forfeit in the several naval battles to come later between the years of 1942 and 1943—and even for the lack of success (and ultimate killing) of the great "Tokyo Express" itself. By February 1943, Japan's forces, both on land and at sea, would have been all but fully routed from the island groups, and their death-grip hold on the area all but relinquished. Indeed, it was already known that Yamamoto himself was greatly displeased with Mikawa's "no-attack" decision on the occasion of the battle at Savo, and it might therefore have come as no surprise that Mikawa would later be reassigned to duties in "rear-echelon" areas and thanklessly relegated to minor "ship escort duties" in the Philippines.

Sadly, that escort duty would not be with his famed Eighth Fleet constituents, or even with any of his former cruiser division heavies from Savo, but would instead find the admiral commanding a much smaller unit identified only as the "Second Southern Expeditionary Fleet." He would go on to spend the years 1943 to 1944 in this post, perhaps pining deeply for his former open-sea command, which was now almost assuredly beyond his reach. Savo had perhaps indeed been more shortfall than victory—and in at least the eyes of the Japanese Navy's high command, it was forever thereafter seen as only a job half done.

In October 1944, Mikawa would return to his homeland proper, immediately on the heels of the crushing defeat of Japan's Central, Southern, and Northern forces during the volatile encounters that would make up the Battle of Leyte Gulf. Now quite apparent—not just to himself and a distressed Japanese high command but also to the nation at large—all could almost sense that an end might soon be at hand. It would therefore be in the year 1945, at an age of fifty-seven, that a now-fatigued VADM Gunichi Mikawa would formally retire from active duty from the Imperial Japanese Navy and sadly return to his beloved Hiroshima, seemingly with only more regret for that not done than any gratifying feeling of contentment for having accomplished all that he had during his naval career.

In the dark years after the war, now in a post-Restoration Japan—and with the dawning of a new era for that emerging country—Mikawa would in fact go on to live a long and retiring life in Japan, passing at the somewhat incredible age of ninety-two on 25 February 1981. Truly, therefore, the crafty, ever-inspired Mikawa would go on to outlive virtually all of his contemporary Allied and American commanders from World War II and Savo Island. That list would read much like a startling introduction to a military *Who's Who* that would go on to include not only ADM Chester W. Nimitz himself but also Ernest J. King, William F. "Bull" Halsey Jr., and Raymond A. Spruance, as well as Generals Douglas MacArthur, Dwight D. Eisenhower, Henry "Hap" Arnold, George C. Marshall, and even George S. "Blood and Guts" Patton.

The only other senior flag officer from that Solomons campaign—and from that grand era of massive battleships, fast cruisers, and deadly destroyers from those many great blue-water battles of its time—that he might not outlive would be ADM Victor Alexander Crutchley himself, who would also live on to the age of ninety-two. Admiral Crutchley, however, would still be Mikawa's senior and outlive the good IJN admiral by some five years, expiring in 1986. With the passing of both men, therefore, a quiet and dusty curtain would finally (and quite heavily) be drawn on all the former ships, the men, and the bloody battles of Savo Island.

VADM Mikawa: Combat Appraisal of the Naval War College

The following observational statement was provided by historian Richard W. Bates as an addendum to his exhaustive 400+-page analysis of the 1BOSI in his Naval War College report dated 1950 (AD/A-003 037) and titled *The Battle of Savo Island, August 9, 1942. Strategical and Tactical Analysis. Part I*, as coauthored with Walter D. Innis, for the NWC's own Department of Analysis. The statement was set as the book's chapter XXIV.

Combat Appraisal of the Japanese Commander, Cruiser Force

VICE ADMIRAL GUNICHI MIKAWA[201]

Vice Admiral Mikawa was an active, quick thinking, competent commander of naval forces so long as his functions were essentially administrative and where the possibility of losing his naval forces by air attack was more or less remote. He thought clearly and had considerable initiative. His decision to repel the Allied attacking forces immediately, by the employment of both air and naval power, was correct. His decision to attack the Allied amphibious forces at Tulagi-Guadalcanal at night, employing his available cruisers and destroyers, was also correct. His concept embraced boldness tempered with considered discretion.

(continued)

His tactical handling of his cruiser force up to the time of his entrance into Iron Bottom Sound was excellent. He had successfully formed up his cruisers and his lone destroyer into a fast, powerful striking force. He had succeeded in moving this command to Savo Island without damage and in so doing, he had so deceived the Allies as to his probable operations as to completely surprise them. He thoroughly understood the value of correct intelligence and made every effort by the employment of land-based search planes as well as through reports from his land-based attack planes to ascertain the true composition and location of the Allied forces at Tulagi-Guadalcanal. He correctly employed his cruiser-based planes in the early evening of August 8th to give him the latest information concerning those Allied forces, and, based on the information given by these planes, he decided to carry out his attack. He also correctly employed his cruiser-based planes at the moment of attack to provide flares for illuminating and silhouetting enemy forces and to contact scout Allied screening forces.

However, once he had succeeded in reaching Savo Island, he no longer acted with that intelligence, understanding and courage which his previous operations had forecast. For he completely ignored the objective which he had assigned his command. Instead of heading toward either Tulagi or Guadalcanal (or both) to destroy the Allied shipping there, he engaged the Allied screening forces in battle. Although he succeeded in so seriously damaging the principal units of those screening forces as to cause them to sink or be sunk later, he did not assure himself that they had been annihilated. Finally he retired, while his ships were in an excellent combat condition, having suffered little damage, without having made any effort to disrupt the Allied operations at either Tulagi or Guadalcanal. Content with a tactical success he failed to exploit the strategical situation by destroying the transports and cargo ships.

He had such apprehension of carrier-based air power as to allow it to seriously affect his judgment. This apprehension was principally responsible for his decision to retire and it may have been responsible for his decision to attack the screening forces in lieu of the transports and cargo ships. He did not seem able to evaluate properly the possible loss of his ships in accomplishing his objective against the adverse effect which the failure to disrupt Allied operations might have on the Japanese [long-range] strategical plans. He was more of a tactician tha[n] a strategist, and, in his mind, the possible loss of his warships seemed too high a price to pay to accomplish the destruction of mere merchant shipping. When this conception is compared with that of the Commander in Chief, Combined Fleet, the reduced caliber of Commander Cruiser Force becomes marked indeed.

From the above, it is apparent that there were serious frailties in Vice Admiral Mikawa's military character. Whereas he was probably successful as a surface ship commander, he was lacking in that resolute spirit ever found in commanders of the first rank. In addition, he does not appear to have been a deep military thinker, nor does he appear to have had a proper appreciation of the relationship between strategy and tactics and of the necessity for insuring [sic] that his tactical successes contributed fully to the aims of the strategy. Had he had this appreciation, is there any doubt that he would have attacked the transports and cargo ships as his [primary] physical objective?

As with Vice Admiral Takagi at the Coral Sea, and Vice Admiral Nagumo at Midway, this failure in command of Vice Admiral Mikawa augured well for future Allied successes.

VADM Mikawa: Further Reading

Reference Recommendations: Bibliographic

The author found only a paucity of books and materials written about VADM Gunichi Mikawa in English, and indeed my expectation is that the vast majority of information available on this key figure of the 1BOSI might rightly only be found in his native Japanese language. As such, without the use (or availability) of viable translation services for all such materials, much of this information might remain somewhat inaccessible to the average researcher in the Western world.

Regardless, I was able to identify (and focus in on) at least these few excellent reference books and articles that have been penned in English. Those items below were found to offer particularly insightful views into the life and times of one of the most enigmatic of central characters of all of World War II.

Dull, Paul S. (1978). *A Battle History of the Imperial Japanese Navy, 1941–1945*. Naval Institute Press.

Frank, Richard B. (1990). *Guadalcanal: The Definitive Account of the Landmark Battle*. New York: Penguin Group.

Lacroix, Eric, and Linton Wells. (1997). *Japanese Cruisers of the Pacific War*. Naval Institute Press.

Loxton, Bruce, and Chris Coulthard-Clark. (1997). *The Shame of Savo: Anatomy of a Naval Disaster*. Australia: Allen & Unwin Pty Ltd.

Ohmae, Toshikazu (Captain, IJN, Ret.). (1957). "The Battle of Savo Island." *Proceedings* 83, no. 12 (December 1957). United States Naval Institute.

Tameichi, Hara. (Captain, IJN, Ret.). (1957). Edited by Fred Saito and Roger Pineau. *Japanese Destroyer Captain*. Naval Institute Press.

Reference Recommendations: Electronic

In sharp contrast, a virtual plethora of information (and personal biographical data) could almost immediately be found "online" for VADM Mikawa, much to the author's surprise and satisfaction. That almost all such accounts would be wholly "repetitive" of the preeminent Wikipedia springboard account, however, was at once both surpring and disappointing, and the word *rehash* might have come to mind on more than one occasion. The almost innumerable online references and citations found on the good Admiral Gunichi Mikawa seemed to generate a search argument results list that simply ran on and on and on. The key sites presented below, however, should at least provide a spectrum of starting-point material available on this most inscrutable of IJN commanders during the battle for the Solomon Islands and the greater South Pacific area.

World War 2 Plus 55 website at http://worldwar2plus55.com/?c8b51080

Wikipedia biographical account of Admiral Gunichi Mikawa at http://en.wikipedia.org/wiki/Gunichi_Mikawa

Wikipedia account of Admiral Gunichi Mikawa and the IJN Eighth Fleet at http://en.wikipedia.org/wiki/IJN_8th_Fleet

Wikipedia account of Admiral Gunichi Mikawa and the Guadalcanal Campaign at http://en.wikipedia.org/wiki/Japanese_cruiser_Ch%C5%8Dkai#The_Guadalcanal_campaign

World War II Database website at http://ww2db.com/person_bio.php?person_id=15

Discussion of Mikawa and flagship *Chōkai* at http://www.combinedfleet.com/chokai_t.htm

Mikawa on 8–9 August at http://worldwar2plus55.com/

Admiral Mikawa general info at http://english.turkcebilgi.com/Gunichi+Mikawa

Japanese Cruisers Operational Histories at http://www.combinedfleet.com/Junyokan.htm

Chōkai Flag command at http://www.combinedfleet.com/chokai_t.htm

http://www.combinedfleet.com/battles/Guadalcanal_Campaign#Savo_Island

Information on Admiral Gunichi Mikawa's birthday may be found at http://www.trueknowledge
.com/q/when_was_gunichi_mikawa%27s_birthday

Naval History and Heritage Command website at http://www.history.navy.mil/photos/prs-for/japan
/japrs-m/g-mikawa.htm

Imperial Japanese Navy website at http://homepage2.nifty.com/nishidah/e/px38.htm#v025

The Battles for Guadalcanal website at http://battlesforguadalcanal.com/Leaders/Japanese/Mikawa
/mikawa.html

RADM ARITOMO GOTŌ, IJN

RADM Gotō: A Man for All Cruisers

Not unlike many of the commanders on the opposing side—and on his own—
RADM Aritomo Gotō's naval career would also tragically be cut short as a result of
the many fiery naval battles for control of Guadalcanal and, by extension, the greater
Solomons. Born in 1888 in coastal Ibaraki in the prefecture of Honshu, Gotō would
curiously attend the same Imperial Japanese Naval Academy (IJNA) as the later
VADM Gunichi Mikawa (of acclaim in the later First Battle of Savo Island)—and
even within the same time frame. Indeed, might the two underclassmen have been
classmates within the same years, and would they not have fraternized—or at the least
have met and "compared notes" on various theses? Though unclear, it is certain that
they might indeed have known of each other within the environs of the close-knit
body of students at the Academy. Graduating in 1910 in the thirty-eighth class of
cadet nominees, Gotō—unlike his compatriot and naval strategist Mikawa—would
do so with a ranking of "30th" in a class of 149 (this in sharp contrast to Mikawa's
rather outstanding ranking of *third* in a class of that same number). Would this then
in fact speak more to the men—or more to the soon-to-be young naval officers themselves—or indeed to both at once?

Now an enthusiastic midshipman graduate, eager to please his superiors even as he
"learned his way and earned his stay," Gotō would luck out almost immediately with
duty on the "heavy boys," serving both on the protected cruiser *Kasagi*, and later on
the dreadnought-class battleship *Satsuma*. For Gotō, this could only have been one of
his highest honors and greatest of opportunities to serve within the ranks of the aging
but still powerful Asiatic fleet.

In short order, and based on the man's meritorious performance, the young IJN
officer would soon enough be promoted to a rank of Ensign in 1911, after which he
would continue on with the battleship fleet aboard the fast *Iwami*, a ship that had
itself been reborn from the ashes of its origins as a *Borodino*-class battleship of the
Imperial Russian Navy. And, like so many of the other ships that almost wholly made

up the Imperial Japanese Navy of its time, the reconstructed ship had in fact been a "spoils-of-war" holdover from the previous Russo-Japanese War of 1904–1905, and which (before her capture) had begun its life as the Russian *Oryol*. This same *Oryol* would itself have been badly mauled during the course of the blockade action at Port Arthur (Manchuria) during the Battle of Tsushima Strait in early 1905. *Oryol* would be compelled to suffer the indignity of "surrender" during the latter half of the stormy war with Czarist Russia at the hands of the Imperial Japanese Navy, now only too glad to take the battleship in hand and to rebuild her as the new *Iwami*. Gotō's involvement with her would now stretch on for almost a full year of service.

Later, during the interspatial years between wars, Gotō would be dispatched on other, shorter assignments aboard the torpedo-boat destroyer *Murakumo*, and the first-in-class heavy cruiser *Makumo*. This would be the taste that, in the not-so-distant future, Gotō could neither shake nor avoid, and indeed the cruiser heavies would become the very signature and mainstay of his greatest commands. Now a full lieutenant by the year 1917—on the cusp of World War I—Gotō would be assigned active sea duty on several IJN warships in seeming rapid succession, each serving as a stepping-stone for the soon-to-be flag officer, who would rightly enough command his own fleet of cruisers one day. With honor he would therefore sail on the great battle-ship *Kongō*, and later the fast destroyer *Tanikaze*, before returning to his true love, the "cruisers" themselves—which in this last instance would be the aged three-stack armored cruiser *Yakumo*.

Soon enough—with the due adding of "weight" to the still-young naval officer's shoulder-boards—now with a promotion to Lieutenant Commander in 1923 well in hand, Gotō would assume his first full captaincy and in short order commanded the IJN destroyers *Tsuta*, *Urakaze*, *Numakaze*, *Nokaze*, *Uzuki*, and even the fleet *Nada-kaze*. And in the short span of only three years, he would receive yet another bump in grade, up to the rank of full commander but nonetheless still keep a cautious eye on that even higher aspiration: advancement to a full flag rank, that of rear admiral.

His love of the faster, far more maneuverable cruiser and destroyer-force ships of the IJN would overtly drive Gotō forward, keeping him well focused on his studies of the activities, provisional roles, and responsibilities of exactly those types of support ships in any number of deployment settings. Clearly, this would ultimately lead to an even greater understanding of the ships' individual and collective offensive capabilities in battle as well. If any one naval officer of his time could be said to have had a clearer and more distinct view of the several battle tactics, strategies, and deployments centered on the use of both light and heavy cruisers—and the fast-attack destroyers that screened them—it might indeed have been both Gotō and Mikawa themselves.

It would therefore not come as any great surprise when later, on 19 November 1939, Gotō would finally achieve his coveted ranking of rear admiral, or *Kaigūn Shosho*, of the Imperial Japanese Navy. And, for his unflagging dedication and superb leadership skills in service to that same IJN, the naval high command gave him Cruiser Division 2, and less than two years later, in September 1941—only months before their attack on Pearl Harbor—they gave him all of Cruiser Division 6.

It would therefore be this same CRUDIV6 force (then and seemingly forever made up of Gotō's own flagship *Aoba*, the *Kako*, the *Kinugasa*, and the *Tenryū*) that would then bring these four ships together as an almost inseparable entity, even throughout some of the deadliest and most heated actions that each would face just over the near horizon in the distant South Pacific.

For even then, shortly after the American ships at Pearl Harbor had been attacked by Yamamoto's main body of attack planes, which left those ships fully in ruins or heavily damaged—most engulfed in flames and capsizing with men still trapped belowdecks—Gotō's own CRUDIV6 would have an entirely different task at hand, that of providing close-in support for a second-wave assault on Wake Island. And it would in fact be this second wave that would be the most successful attempt by the Japanese to fully overrun and capture the island, later resulting in the discreditable surrender of that garrison by Navy Commander Winfield Cunningham some fifteen days after the start of the enemy's raid on that island.

Departing from Wake Island, and now emboldened, and fresh from their rabid kills and still flush with the successes at now both Pearl Harbor and Wake Island, Gotō's cruiser division made for yet another region of the Pacific—far, far to the south—at a place called *Gadarukanaru*, or Guadalcanal. It was a wedge of dense jungle growth nestled in a loose and scattered archipelago of some 890-plus islands that Gotō and his capable crew would soon come to know as the Solomons.

RADM Gotō: Charging the "Slot"—Kavieng and Rabaul

The Imperial Japanese Navy, understanding fully the importance of a firm global presence in the southern and western waters of the Pacific, now moved to gain a solid toehold in all of the areas they might later need for the resources that would keep their gears of war grinding ever forward, and to keep the impetus of their military drive moving ahead. Therefore, as early as 21 January 1942, it might indeed have come as no surprise that a massive, two-carrier strike force would hit the Papua/New Guinea coastline and attack both New Ireland and New Britain almost simultaneously.[202] In fact, it would take an already over-strength Japanese landing force little or no time to overpower (and displace) the nearly 1,400 poorly armed Australian defenders at that location, and to land their own assault forces on the northernmost island of New Ireland on 22 January. By the following day, they would assault and only too quickly take the adjacent New Britain as well.

The little-expected twin-pronged assault on both islands now effectively sealed their fates, and the captured ports of Kavieng and Rabaul would almost immediately be cast as both primary and secondary home-port facilities for the already thinly stretched Imperial Japanese Navy. Unquestionably, the well-planned and coordinated attacks on both strategic locations enabled the IJN surface fleet to cover virtually all the approaches to and from the islands . . . from both the north and the south. That both the coastal port cities of Kavieng and Rabaul would soon become the very head and spring of virtually all future IJN naval operations in the region was almost certain, if not already apparent to most. Included in that dreadful Japanese push, and their near-in plans to build both airstrips and staging areas throughout many of the islands north of their intended goal, it would not take the leery Allied observers long at all to realize that this might indeed be only a build-up for an even greater planned attack on the Australia mainland itself. And to further invest their chances to do so, Japan would obviously need supply centers, airstrips, and ample-sized deep-water naval ports at which to berth their largest of warships. To Gotō and the Imperial Japanese Navy's high command at both Kavieng and Rabaul, clearly Guadalcanal seemed to offer all three.

Therefore, by 14 July of that same year, VADM Gunichi Mikawa, friend and classmate of RADM Aritomo Gotō from their days back at the IJNA—and now his very commander—boldly set sail from Kavieng (Figure 44 ❶) with an avowed aim to rendezvous with Gotō's CRUDIV6, assume flag command, then charge full on into Iron Bottom Sound to attack both Tulagi and Honiara. At a point near Cape St. George, therefore—fronting the narrowed St. George's Channel that was itself geographically pinched on both sides by the two large islands—the two armadas finally met up and joined forces ❷. With the bold Eighth Fleet "Japanese Striking Force" now intact, Mikawa rode his great flagship *Chōkai* in the company of two light cruisers and a single fast-attack destroyer—as seen in the Table 39 matrix.

In short order, with Gotō's forces now arriving, three more heavy cruisers and the rear admiral's own flagship *Aoba* would be added to the battle main. Arriving with them would also be some 519 naval infantry forces from the rugged "battle-tested"

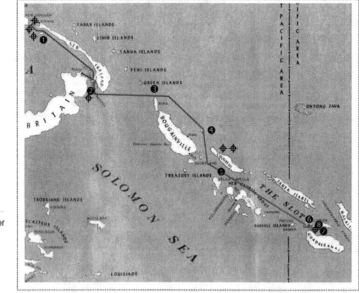

LEGEND

❶ = Waypoint Marker

⊕ = Allied Sightings

Figure 44. Advance of the Mikawa-Gotō CRUDIV6/18 Elements on 8-9 August 1942 (Morison Map)

Table 39.   Composite Makeup CRUDIV6/CRUDIV18 (Under Admirals Mikawa, Gotō, and Matsuyama)

Ship	Complement	Position	Command
Flagship — VADM Gunichi Mikawa (Eighth Fleet) from Rabaul, New Britain			
Flagship — RADM Aritomo Gotō (CRUDIV6) from Rabaul, New Britain			
Chōkai (CA) (Flag)	773	Line-ahead column format: 1st position	*VADM Gunichi Mikawa* CAPT Hayakawa Mikio
Flagship — RADM Mitsuhara Matsuyama Gotō (CRUDIV18) from Kavieng, New Ireland			
Aoba (CA) (Flag)	657	Line-ahead column format: 2nd position	*RADM Aritomo Gotō* CAPT Narita Moichi
Kako (CA)	616	3rd position	CAPT Chihaya Takahashi
Kinugasa (CA)	657	4th position	CAPT Masao Sawa
Furutaka (CA)	616	5th position	CAPT Araki Tsutau
Tenryū (CL)	327	6th position	CAPT Mitsutaru Gotō
Yūbari (CL)	328	7th position	CAPT Masami Ban
Yūnagi (DD)	168	8th position (Rear Guard at Savo)	LT Okada Seiichi

Japanese 38th Infantry Division, and the entire newly formed surface fleet would merge all of their forces into both CRUDIV6 and CRUDIV18, and now began its long stalk into night, its most singular objective being that of vanquishing any opposition and occupying the Solomons. And with this singular purpose in mind, Admirals Gotō and Mikawa ventured slowly down and into the northern sluice points of an area simply known as the Slot.

Ever hopeful of keeping their ships' furtive actions close to the vest without themselves being spotted, Gotō and Mikawa both knew their worst enemy at any time during the push south might be "detection" itself. If seen at any time by either the Americans or their Allies—or by any of their planes, subs, or surface ships—it might be expected that the enemy response would be nothing if not swift and certain: a fast attack and a full neutralization of their fleet.

Therefore, Gotō would have continually advised Mikawa—flag officer to flag officer—to (as often as possible) take a more circuitous and less-traveled venue to the south. That route would now lead both senior admirals' cruiser divisions first to the north and east of jutting Buka Island ❸, then over to the eastern side of Bougainville[203] to a point off Kieta ❹, as plotted on the previous Morison map. Here, Gotō and Mikawa would pause in their savage thrust south and—ever fearful of enemy air attack from any of the American carrier-based forces thought to still be in the area—would halt their fleets to wait out the remaining fading hours of daylight.

Better it would be, the two must clearly have reasoned, to engage the enemy on our own terms in a classic surprise night engagement, than to meet his force full on and do battle with him ship to ship. Their journey would resemble that shown in that same Figure 44 map, on which the author has also superimposed a number of key waypoint markers (❶ to ❺) and known points of "observed movement" by both American and Australian forces (⊕).

On their approach from Kavieng and Rabaul, there would indeed be multiple sightings of the Gotō–Mikawa CRUDIV surface fleet (though not always known to either admiral at the time)—most notably that of the American submarine USS *S-38*, three separate RAAF Hudson reconnaissance overflights, and even a long-range patrol of two Taffy 61 B-17s passing over the northern half of Choiseul (pronounced *Shwä-zool*). All of this notwithstanding, having indeed occurred, few (if any) of the messages and alerts allegedly sent forward by each of those mobile observation units operating that day would even arrive in time back to the Naval Intelligence command centers that might most be in need of that intel.

Through rampant SNAFUs and "procedural derailments" that included everything from poor communication venues to bad weather, and from poor timing to equipment that simply did not work, little in the way of an advisory warning from the crews of the RAAF Hudsons, the B-17 bombers, or even LCDR Munson's USS *S-38* sub itself would ever cross the desks of the command and control hubs in time, or be received by the Allied naval screening ships, each now couched like "sitting ducks" in Iron Bottom Sound.

By nightfall on 8 August, however, Mikawa's cruiser divisions were clearly back on the move and heading south while riding the corridor passage between the Shortland Islands and the large land mass of Choiseul itself. By Vella Lavella ❺, the force was already fast approaching the very top of an area that most mariners simply called the Slot. Having dodged the bullet of detection by the slow-moving B-17s at Choiseul, Admirals Gotō and Mikawa would perhaps breathe a small sigh of relief and now go full throttle with all ships in order to quickly transit the exposed and dangerous waters of the Slot leading down to Guadalcanal itself.

Soon approaching the "gatekeeper" island of Savo—itself a small volcanic land mass squatting on dark haunches at the bottom of New Georgia Sound—CRUDIV6 and 18 would have already spotted the first of two radar picket ships, the American destroyer USS *Blue* ❻, within a ten-minute window between 0044 and 0054 hours on 9 August. Mikawa's ships sailed cautiously on at measured pace and at preset 1,300-yard intervals, moving at a reduced 22 knots. The die had now been cast, and Mikawa's element of surprise was still intact, well guarded, and almost virtually assured.

In Table 40, we see the 0150 hours ship positions of VADM Gunichi Mikawa's attacking force on the night of 8–9 August, in relation to dead center of Savo Island. This reflects the IJN task group's secondary position as they began to approach and prepare to attack RADM Lois Riefkohl's Northern screen that same night.

Table 40.   Position of CRUDIV6 and CRUDIV18 at 0150 Hours, 8–9 August 1942 (by Attack Group)

CRUDIV Asset (Ship)	Designation	Bearing/Distance from Savo Island
Position Relative to Dead Center of Savo Island		
Eastern Group (4)		
IJN Chōkai (Flag-VADM Mikawa)	**CA**	**Bearing 130° (T); distance 13,500 yards**
IJN Aoba (Flag-RADM Gotō)	**CA**	**Bearing 135° (T); distance 13,000 yards**
IJN Kako	CA	Bearing 140° (T); distance 13,000 yards
IJN Kinugasa	CA	Bearing 147° (T); distance 13,250 yards
Western Group (3)		
IJN Furutaka	CA	Bearing 153° (T); distance 12,150 yards
IJN Tenryū	CL	Bearing 151° (T); distance 10,900 yards
IJN Yūbari	CL	Bearing 156° (T); distance 10,100 yards
Destroyer Screen (1)		
IJN Yūnagi	DD	Bearing 205° (T); distance 8,150 yards

In waters just north of quiet Savo, the IJN cruisers would soon spy the American destroyers *Blue* and her sister ship *Ralph Talbot*, and quickly positioned themselves to engage either (or both) of them had it not been apparent that both ships were in fact moving away from their task force position at measured speed on their own predetermined patrol vectors. That Mikawa's force would be able to penetrate the picket screening line at precisely the location that marked the perigee—or nearest point of their patrol corridors—was a matter of history and plain dumb luck, but still a hearty measure of luck for the admiral nonetheless. Therefore, sluicing silently through the gap left open by the two oblivious American picket ships, Mikawa and Gotō navigated their ships to best advantage and steeled themselves for the fast run-in.

RADM Gotō: Springing the Trap—A Deadly Surprise at Savo

Attack on the Southern Fleet (IJN Perspective)

Skirting the volcanic island of Savo, neither Mikawa nor Gotō could have known what lay in wait for them and their CRUDIV fleet just over the next horizon. In fact, it might all have mattered not, for truly the two men were now in their element and milieu, doing best what each had trained to do. After all, what need they fear from the bungling and always unprepared Americans? And, already "owning the night," what need they fear from a poorly practiced American navy or even a retaliatory strike from any of the carrier-based aircraft that only operated during daylight hours? If indeed it was Japan's design to possess the island group at Guadalcanal, it now became Mikawa's mandate as well, and each of his ships would simply become the instruments to achieve that very objective. At 0131 hours on the night of 9 August, therefore, Mikawa increased his column speed back up to a quickened 26 knots and gave his now-famous order: "Every ship attack!"[204]

RADM Gotō's flagship *Aoba*, trailing defensively in its secondary position behind the *Chōkai*, would also receive the order to engage, and quickly moved to "Condition Red–Weapons Hot," with all guns trained out and torpedo tubes swung away to make ready for deployment. By 0134, lookouts on *Chōkai* would spot the Allied Southern screening force at a remote distance of some 14,000 yards ❼, and an order to deploy illuminants quickly went out to all ships. By 0138, under a shimmering cascade of light from the flare orbs and starshells fired from the decks of his cruisers, the first of a spread of torpedoes shuddered the ships and lurched out of the launch tubes on *Chōkai* and *Aoba* and then splashed with lethal precision into the waters to port of each ship ❽. The near-in tracks of the outbound torpedoes ran true and knifed through the water for as far as could be seen by the lookouts perched high aloft the *Pagoda* masts of Mikawa's heavy cruisers, but they were soon lost to the graying mantle of night as they moved off in the distance—right up to the time of impact and first explosion.

Now a combined orchestration of murderous crossfire, dead-on accuracy, and high-explosive shells rained down on the first of the hapless American ships, in a convoy of what appeared to host three such warships. Unbeknownst to Gotō and Mikawa at the time, of course, this was none other than the Australian *Canberra* herself—this indeed as *Chōkai* and *Tenryū* opened up on her almost on the instant. Soon, they would also be joined by the large guns of the *Aoba* and *Kako*, but it is also known that a still-anxious RADM Gotō had to actually sit and wait for several interminable moments for *Chōkai* to clear a firing lane within which the *Aoba* could then unmask her own guns (which soon enough she would indeed be able to do).

Pummeled by the combined attacks of Mikawa's heavy cruisers now all firing in tandem, *Canberra* would be left a smoldering wreck and settling to starboard at what clearly was a 5°–10° list. The Australian ship was now all but lost, in effect simply left as she was by the marauding IJN cruiser force as they now moved on. Almost dismissively did Gotō slide past the scorched hull of the Allied cruiser while also allowing the other ships in column to plot their own firing solutions out to the stricken warship. *Canberra* would be fully decimated in the resulting barrages and torpedo strikes launched by Mikawa's attacking cruiser divisions. Then, Gotō would quickly shift his gaze and his weapons onto the second ship in column—CAPT Bode's own *Chicago*—mistakenly identified by the IJN as a "battleship-class" warship. CAPT Ohmae, aboard flagship *Chōkai* with Mikawa himself, would only have had this to say:

> Our course was now northeasterly. *Chōkai* launched a second set of torpedoes, and
> following the first great explosion, there seemed to be a chain reaction. Within ten

minutes after the first explosion, there were explosions everywhere. Every torpedo and every round of gunfire seemed to be hitting its mark. Enemy ships seemed to be sinking on every hand![205]

Now the secondary attack on the elusive *Chicago* would also begin and was nothing if not explosive and highly concentrated, and cut short only by the movements of the American ship itself, which now mysteriously veered to the north and west and actually moved away from the battle area. This must indeed have been a matter of great puzzlement for both Gotō and Mikawa on their respective flagships, but it was in fact only Bode on *Chicago*, with his famed trek off on a curious heading of 263, that would quite illogically go on for the next forty minutes in pursuit of a "possible phantom contact," reportedly at the lag-end of that exiting Japanese column.

The only remaining American warship still in the fray during the attack on the Allied Southern screening force, and indeed still holding her own while continuing to engage the CRUDIV attack force, was the *Patterson* itself—the scrappy, indefatigable escort destroyer that had ridden the flanks of the *Canberra* and *Chicago* and had been first to sight and do battle with that same approaching force even at the moment they approached.

Fighting to the bitter end to shield her two great wards, the Allied heavy cruisers from that same Southern force, *Patterson* must have been much like a rabid, frenzied dog nipping at the heels of the great bear, but the American destroyer nonetheless fought on until the very last moments, when Mikawa in fact disengaged and swerved back to the north and east, away from the current zone of attack. *Patterson* would never leave the side of the stricken *Canberra*, and for the latter ship's remaining hours she would quickly set about the grueling tasks of search and rescue, plucking survivors and wounded sailors from the deep. Of the *Canberra*'s initial 819-strong complement of men aboard her on that fateful night, 84 would be killed outright—with a stunning 74 lost during the battle main, and 10 later succumbing to their mortal wounds . . . that number, however, would still not include the 109 men who had also been wounded in that same scuffle.

Attack on the Northern Fleet (IJN Perspective)

To avoid an almost-certain collision with the now heavily damaged *Canberra* as she staggered from the attack on the Southern force, both the *Tenryū* and the *Yubari* veered sharply around the stricken ship, which then suddenly placed them on a more westerly heading away from Mikawa's primary strike force column. Following in close proximity behind the two errant IJN cruisers that had split away came the *Furutaka* as well—perhaps believing she, too, should follow suit—and so set out on the same course as the *Tenryū* and *Yubari* without second thought. These three cruisers would now inadvertently form a second column that would sweep far up to the north and effectively "bracket" the ships of the Northern screen. Soon, all of RADM Riefkohl's ships would find themselves almost fully enveloped by Gotō and Mikawa's pincer movement.

The twin-axial assault on the American Northern force would commence at 0144, or indeed as rapidly as plotting solutions could be laid out to the enemy ships. The *Type 93* Long-Lance torpedoes would first be launched and quickly tracked their way out to their intended targets. Those targets would inevitably be the *Vincennes*, the *Quincy*, and the bold *Astoria*. Each ship, in its turn, was already doomed right where they sailed.

The ships that composed the IJN cruiser task force this night were seemingly at peak performance and executing all of their attacks with practiced precision. The three American screening ships (*Vincennes*, *Quincy*, and *Astoria*) would all be repeatedly hit by both the *Type 93*s and by the large 8-inch guns of the heavy cruisers that now so mercilessly pounded them. The four cruisers *Chōkai*, *Aoba*, *Tenryū*, and *Kako* took their hot turns in firing on the Allied ships in an almost ordered sequence,[206] with each ship passing quickly by and then moving free to allow the ship behind to unmask its own guns to rain down still more lethal volleys. The attack would last no more than ten minutes for that *Vincennes* group, and less than thirty-one minutes overall for the attack on both Allied screening forces, from 0144 to 0216, the point at which Mikawa finally withdrew his forces.

The smoking, embering wreckage of all three American warships must surely have lit up the night sky and fired the waters below. *Quincy* alone would be hit a staggering thirty-six times by Mikawa's massive guns and struck by no less than three Long-Lance torpedoes. The *Astoria* would be hit some sixty-five to seventy times, and the *Vincennes*—perhaps savaged worst of all—would be hit by as many as eighty-five rounds fired from at least four of the IJN CRUDIV ships at once. The loss of life between these three ships alone would be an astonishing 918(±) men who would perish during the course of the Northern group assault. The words of Mikawa had now come full circle and resonated in the ears of his entire crew: "Our plan will be simple and devoid of complexity: first we will steal upon their ships, locate our targets, then blow them out of the water . . . then our gallant task force will boldly sail on through the wreckage." And they had done precisely that . . . on at least this one darkened night in early August 1942.

The attack was now at the downside of its height, and Mikawa continually conferred with Gotō and his other staff officers to explore the viability of a "continued attack" on other shippage in the area. In fact, the troop transport and landing ships were still discharging both men and supplies throughout the course of the raging sea battles themselves, and Admiral Mikawa understood the importance of halting—or at the very least impeding—the progress of those American landings, and the delivery of supplies and munitions that could then be used against his forces. Attacking the transports had imprimis been one of his key directives, as set forth by ADM Yamamoto himself. Still, he must have thought long and hard as he anxiously paced the pilot house and bridge, perhaps seeking his answers somewhere in the dark of night: *Should I attack again now and risk the loss of even one ship in an extended battle—or do I simply disengage my forces while all are still intact?*

Clearly, history would show that he would opt for the latter, and by 0216, did indeed give the order to cease fire on the remnant Allied force—this only with a final surge of hot lead and volley. Then, almost as abruptly as he had come in to prosecute his attacks in full, the admiral would just as quietly slink back out under the hooding veil of night. Now on great *Chōkai*, her signalmen worked feverishly as they clackered out Mikawa's final command to all ships in column: "All forces withdraw . . . force in line ahead, course 320 degrees; speed 30 knots."[207]

Minutes later, the seven warships from both CRUDIV6 and 18—with scorched guns still smoking, and the acrid, lingering smell of gunpowder in the air—gradually reformed their ranks in its standard line-ahead column format and increased speed to quickly exit the area. The dark land mass each ship now saw to port on their way out might have seemed faint and indistinguishable, but it was in fact the northern edge of Savo Island. Their mission complete and the twin attacks on the American fleet now so stunningly successful, Gotō and Mikawa knew they had struck a deep blow for the Imperial Japanese Navy, and had gotten clean away with it, as indeed all its ships would live to see yet another day of action.

RADM Gotō: Defeat at Guadalcanal—The Battle of Cape Esperance

The naval butchery at Savo was now far behind both combatant forces, but not so soon forgotten by the Americans or their Allies, and the very next battle sequence in the Solomons—after the Battle of the Eastern Solomons itself in late August 1942— would find the occupying Allied forces once again pitted against a fierce thirteen-ship naval power under the able command of RADM Aritomo Gotō, just south and east of dark Savo. The battle would simply be named after a promontory landmark cape that adorned Guadalcanal's northeastern coast, off which the sea battle would take place. And, on 11 October, that encounter would come to be known to all as simply the Battle of Cape Esperance (BOCE).

Still smarting from the punishing defeats suffered at the hands of Mikawa and Gotō's first assault during their previous battles at Savo, the Allies could now only lick their wounds and bide their time, while also planning their next move. That the Japanese would once again return to lay bold claim to the islands, deep-water ports, and anchorage areas—and especially to the strategically placed (and still only partially completed) airstrip on Guadalcanal itself—was certain . . . when that bold force would do so was, as always, not so clear. In the days and weeks immediately following the triumph over the Allies during their first encounter with the IJN's fierce cruiser divisions, the great Admirals Mikawa and Gotō—soon joined by a third force commander, RADM Takatsugu Jojima—boldly cruised the Slot with swagger and seeming bombast, the action itself made all the more irksome to the Allies by its very audacity.

Now almost fearless of interdiction, Mikawa's great battle force cruised with impunity, fairly inviting the Americans out to fight, but always preferring their hallmark night engagement to any full-on attack during actual daylight hours. Fresh from their "twin kills" at Savo, the two senior Japanese admirals were simply spoiling for another fight, but so, too, were the Americans, who had far more at stake. It was therefore inevitable that the two powers might again meet on a field of battle . . . that field of battle, of course—at least in and around Guadalcanal—would be nowhere else if not the watery passages just off the southern edge of windward Savo, on a date that would thereafter be recalled to history as 11 October 1942.

Pained and grief-stricken—and still reeling from the staggering loss of so many men and ships at Savo, in that single thirty-one-minute night battle—the Americans were still smarting from the last scuffle but by now had indeed learned some valuable lessons as well, and they had done so the hardest way possible, by a school of hard knocks. Now those lessons would be all-enduring, perhaps even lifted directly from Lao Tzu's own *Art of War*, even as a now-beleaguered Allied admiralty sought to embrace an entirely new attack strategy. And much like those teachings of Lao Tzu, those new strategies would need to include the ability to learn to engage the enemy at night—and when he least expects it; to know best when to engage, and when not to engage—and when to retire; to know how to survive against overwhelming odds if at an ill-favored disadvantage; to understand the inestimable value of intelligence and communications flow to ensure that they could get that same intel back to those very field commanders who might most be in need of it; and, finally, to know when to spring a big trap to catch a large prey. Soon all of these sly precepts would be put to good use and later executed to near perfection by the Americans—this time in the dashing persona of the American RADM Norman N. Scott. And it would be Scott's bold actions on *San Francisco* that would this night be the hard pivot and sweet turning point in the battle for Guadalcanal itself—and for the greater Solomons. It would also result in the utter undoing and untimely demise of Admiral Gotō, as the senior IJN flag officer soon lay dying on the mangled bridge of his own besieged and beloved heavy cruiser *Aoba*.

The decisive BOCE might indeed have been one of the greater set piece battles that would now begin to break the very back of the rabid Japanese push to occupy the Solomons, and its even greater plans for a later invasion of Australia. It would effectively mark the death of the great "Tokyo Express" supply line as well. For the Americans, much lay in the balance, and breaking the Japanese stranglehold on both the outlying waterways and shipping lanes up and down the Slot would have been foremost in the minds of all of the Allied commanders almost to a man. Deciding therefore not to wait for the enemy's next incursion event, RADM Scott quickly set about the task of fashioning his own trap, and now lay in wait for his own "big prey" to approach. True to form and expectation, the good admiral need not wait too long at all.

VADM Mikawa's naval powers would this night be twofold and set in a two-pronged assault format—a single force of two light-carrier seaplane tenders that would be escorted in the company of a flotilla of six destroyers, and a secondary force—operating fully independently of the first group—that would consist of an assault column of three heavy cruisers and two destroyers. Each would have separate missions in separate locales, and each would have radically differing outcomes and losses, but neither group would emerge totally unscathed, and sharp losses would be experienced on both sides.

On the night of 11 October 1942, therefore, Mikawa's first naval power would be split between his old friend and seasoned cruiser combatant, RADM Aritomo Gotō, and a compatriot flag officer, the newly joined RADM Takatsugu Jojima—a fellow IJNA alumnus from a class of Academy cadets who had graduated some two years after Mikawa himself. At Mikawa's command, then, Jojima would have full charge of a light carrier task group that would be called the "Reinforcement Force" and would consist of the CVLs *Nisshin* and *Chitose*, which would themselves be escorted by no less than six fast-attack DDs, in the ships *Akizuki*, *Asagumo*, *Shirayuki*, *Murakumo*, *Natsugumo*, and *Yamagumo*.

To reference a full data matrix on the above information, see the composite Table 41 matrix for a detailed view of those IJN ships involved in the BOCE, and their ultimate end-state statuses.

Mikawa's strike force, involving Gotō's own *Aoba* and the CAs *Kinugasa* and *Tenryū*—which still made up that same deadly CRUDIV6 that had so savagely triumphed earlier at Savo—would this night also be tasked with the naval bombardment of Henderson Field on the large main island of Guadalcanal. The field had formerly been held in Japanese hands just prior to 7 August but had been captured and held by Vandegrift's 1st Marine Division, whose arrival on 7 August quickly wrested control of that real estate from a loosely entrenched Japanese defending force. They would then drive that infantry force into the jungle and up into the mountain areas, then rapidly went about the business of setting up camp and resuming construction of the very airfield the Japanese had themselves so feverishly been working on. Much of the equipment that had so hastily been left behind by those former occupiers was now only too gladly put back to good use by the new American owners to precisely complete this one, all-consuming task: finishing the Henderson airstrip—then holding it by any means necessary.

Reportedly enraged by the "displacement" and rude ousting of his own forces from land already held, Mikawa and the Japanese high command now simply wanted their airstrip back, and this as quickly as possible, and at all costs. RADM Gotō's job this night, therefore, was to see that action brought to fruition. And the 8-inch guns he brought with him on the heavy cruisers in his charge were a clear indication that the hot-collared admiral might truly mean business. Those same big guns, now preloaded with a newer and far deadlier kind of high-explosive (HE) charge, were now in fact his own navy's best "persuaders," and it was clear to Mikawa that the shaken and still hotly routed Americans would in the end be compelled to simply leave or die. And, in

Table 41. IJN Force Composite Matrix: The Battle of Cape Esperance (11–12 October 1942)

	FORCE COMPOSITE FOR THE BATTLE OF CAPE ESPERANCE (11–12 OCTOBER 1942)		
SHIP/NAMESAKE	SPECS DATA	MISSION/ASSIGNMENT	OUTCOME (FATE)
	OVERALL TASK GROUP 1 AND 2 COMMANDER (COMEIGHTHFLT AND COMCRUDIV6): VADM GUNICHI MIKAWA		
Task Group 1 (Reinforcement Group): RADM Takatsugu Jōjima			
Nisshin City: Nisshin Aichi	Light carrier/seaplane tender 11,320 tons (w/20 seaplanes)	Deliver first increment of a full complement of 728 soldiers from the 2nd and 38th Infantry Divisions (and related light and heavy artillery/equipment) to Guadalcanal	Sunk 22 July 1943 *Bougainville Strait*
Chitose City: Chitose	Light carrier/seaplane tender 15,300 tons (w/24 floatplanes)	Deliver a secondary group of a complement of 728 soldiers from the 2nd and 38th Infantry Divisions to Guadalcanal	Sunk 25 October 1944 *Battle of Leyte Gulf*
Asagumo "Morning Cloud"	Asashio-class DD 2,370 tons	Provide near-in and outbound screening for Jōjima's light carrier task group	Sunk 24–25 October 1944 *Battle of Surigao Strait*
Natsugumo "Summer Cloud"	Asashio-class DD 2,370 tons	Same operational orders as stated	Sunk 11 October 1942 *Battle of Cape Esperance*
Yamagumo "Mountain Cloud"	Asashio-class DD 2,370 tons	Same operational orders as stated	Sunk 24–25 October 1944 *Battle of Surigao Strait*
Shirayuki "White Snow"	Fubuki-class DD 2,050 tons	Same operational orders as stated	Sunk 3 March 1942 *Battle of the Bismarck Sea*
Murakumo "Massed Clouds"	Fubuki-class DD 2,050 tons	Same operational orders as stated	Sunk 11 October 1942 *Battle of Cape Esperance*
Akizuki "Autumn Moon"	Akizuki-class DD 3,700 tons	Same operational orders as stated	Sunk 25 October 1944 *Battle of Cape Engaño*

Task Group 2 (CRUDIV6): *RADM Aritomo Gotō*

IJN *Aoba* Mount Aoba	*Aoba*-class CA Heavy cruiser (8,300 tons)	Conduct punitive raids and area bombardment of the "pirated" American Henderson Field, then still under construction. Gotō's massive 8-inch guns were all preloaded with deadly HE rounds for just such a task	Sunk 28 July 1945 in Kure Harbor during homeland aerial bombardment
Kinugasa Mount Kinugasa	*Aoba*-class CA Heavy cruiser (8,300 tons)	Provide near-in and outbound screening for Gotō's CRUDIV6 armored cruiser task group	Sunk 14 November 1942 *Naval Battle of Guadalcanal*
Furutaka Mount Furutaka	*Furutaka* -class CA Heavy cruiser (7,950 tons)	Same operational orders as stated	Sunk 12 October 1942 *Battle of Cape Esperance*
Fubuki "Blizzard"	*Fubuki*-class DD (2,050 tons)	Same operational orders as stated	Sunk 11 October 1942 *Battle of Cape Esperance*
Hatsuyuki "First Snow"	*Fubuki*-class DD (2,050 tons)	Same operational orders as stated	Sunk 17 July 1943 *Shortland Islands*

anticipation of the great sea battle soon to come, the following compelling words of verse by the author might fully describe the coming action:

> So at Iron Bottom Sound we wait, few ships at anchor found;
> Our great destroyers well at sea and screening through the Sound.
> By 10 PM on ticking clock, no moment left to gain,
> Gotō's ships approach the Cape at 30 knots in rain.
>
> And thus to Savo Isle we go, to east of Russells fall;
> Gotō's ships disperse themselves—all quiet, couched in squall.
> Southeast due they move their column, driving down the Slot;
> While up from South sails "64", the Task Force of brave Scott.[208]

With great cunning and an iron will—and with an excellent stealth of his own—the bold Scott also had his own ideas about strategy, preemption, and ultimate victory, and he would not sit idly by awaiting the next attack by Mikawa and his ever-persistent heavy cruiser divisions but would instead lay a trap of his own. Hoisting his own battle flag high above the mast of his heavy cruiser *San Francisco*, therefore, Scott would successfully lead his fellow CAs *Salt Lake City*, *Helena*, and *Boise* into a pitched battle late on the squally, misted night of 11 October 1942. Riding flank and steady "shotgun" for the fleet of cruisers would be a bevy of American fast-attack destroyers, none the least of which would be the proud *Laffey*, *Buchanan*, *Duncan*, *McCalla*, and *Farenholt*, and each ship would this night taste the glory of victory in battle.

Approaching dark Savo on that night, visibility had at best been poor due to an early moonset, leaving little ambient light and no real visible sea horizon. Gotō's aggressive CRUDIV6 could have had no idea just what lay in wait for them on the southern end of the island. Admiral Scott—alerted to the presence of "two cruisers and six destroyers"[209] that had been spotted some 210 miles north of Guadalcanal—now made his own preparations for a full interception of that very force. Picked up by far-ranging American reconnaissance planes as they sailed through the open passage of Choiseul and Kolombangara, this would undoubtedly have been Jojima's force of transport ships and the destroyer escorts, and not those of Gotō's actual CRUDIV6. In fact, for all intents and purposes, Gotō's CRUDIV6 had once again slipped the guarded noose of detection and was even then rapidly approaching the "western" edge of Savo Island, its avowed and final destination being nothing other than Henderson Field itself.

Only minutes before midnight on that same night, therefore, several American ships under the command of Admiral Scott began to pick up faint contact signatures on their prototype radar systems at about 2344, those signatures coming from a point still some 27,000 yards north of their current position. Waiting patiently and biding his time, Scott cautiously selected a battle he knew he could win and then set his brave flagship *San Francisco* on a direct heading of 310° to interdict the Japanese force, but he continued to check his ship's fire all the while, unwilling to tip his hand or reveal his ships' position.

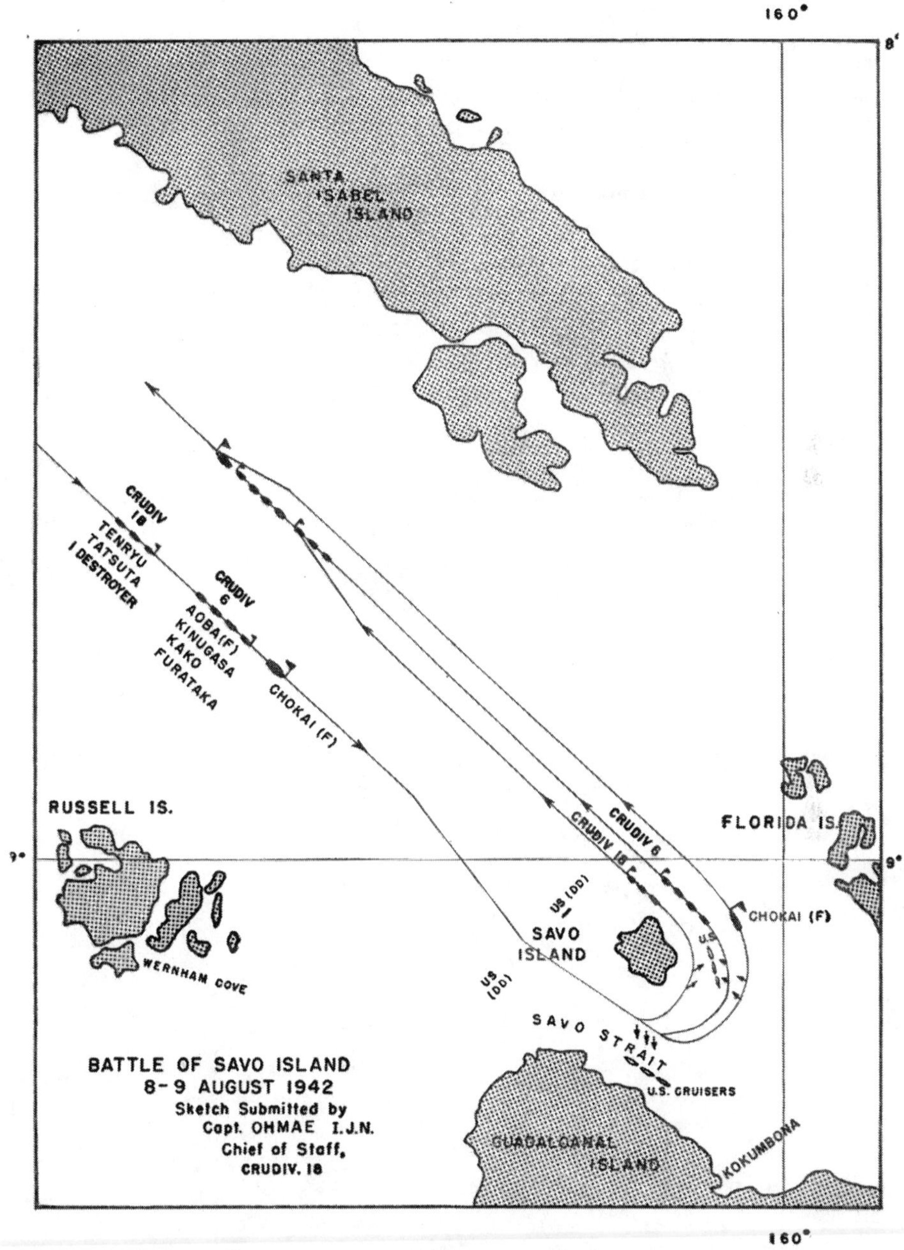
160°
8°
SANTA
ISABEL
ISLAND
CRUDIV
18
TENRYU
TATSUTA
I DESTROYER
CRUDIV
6
AOBA(F)
KINUGASA
KAKO
FURATAKA
CHOKAI (F)
RUSSELL IS.
FLORIDA IS.
CRUDIV 6
CRUDIV 18
9°
9°
US (DD)
CHOKAI (F)
SAVO
ISLAND
U.S.
WERNHAM COVE
US (DD)
SAVO STRAIT
BATTLE OF SAVO ISLAND
8-9 AUGUST 1942
Sketch Submitted by
Capt. OHMAE I.J.N.
Chief of Staff,
CRUDIV. 18
U.S. CRUISERS
GUADALCANAL
ISLAND
KOKUMBONA
160°

Figure 45. BOCE: Japanese Approach and American Response (11-12 October 1942)

What followed was a SNAFU of double magnitude: one on the part of Gotō and his fleet, and one on the part of the American heavy cruiser *Helena* itself . . . and both would happen at about the same time. Gaffe number ❶ would indeed lie with the Americans and might once again be faulted by inadequate communications between ships—and a failure to heed a specific order—in this case as issued by RADM Scott at about 2346. At that time *Helena*, a sister ship of that same *San Francisco*, had requested permission to open fire on a detected column of Japanese warships that was then seen to be approaching. The request was specifically for an "Interrogatory Roger," which in the Navy jargon of its time had queried, "Are we clear to engage?" RADM Scott keyed his radio with the response "Roger," indicating an acknowledgment of only the receipt of the message itself—but not a consent to fire. The light cruiser *Helena* in fact understood the response to be instead an order to engage, and did so on the instant, as shortly did the *Salt Lake City*, the *Boise*, and—much to the American admiral's astonishment—even his own gun crews on the *San Francisco*. With all guns now firing independently and thinking they were correct in doing so, Scott's cagey element of surprise might otherwise have been fully blown, yet the fortuitous Americans were still able to execute their famed "crossing the T" maneuver (Figure 46) and emerge victorious, while also exacting heavy casualties on that enemy's surface fleet. The maneuver itself would be a "textbook" combat positioning action that would have almost no other parallel, in fact occurring only very infrequently in naval history.

Gaffe number ❷ could only be Admiral Gotō's own apprehension in preemptively engaging the Americans in the first place. Having had ample alert from *Aoba's* lookouts as early as 2343, Gotō incautiously opted to disregard the men's advisory and assumed

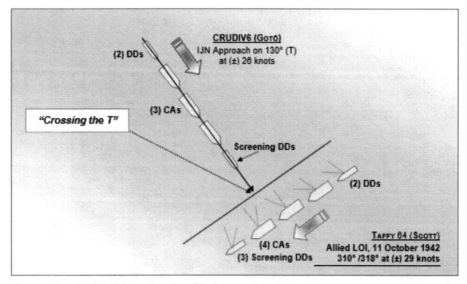

Figure 46.   BOCE: "Crossing the T": Encounter at the Cape
Visio diagram developed by Lawrence A. De Graw.
(**LOI**= **L**ine **o**f **I**nterdiction)

that the fleet spotted was only Jojima's other transport force, known to also be operating in the area. The lookouts on *Aoba* irrefutably confirmed for a second time that the ships were indeed thought to have been American, but a still-obstinate Gotō continued to hold fire and ordered his ships to instead only "flash ident," which perilously gambled away much of the admiral's remaining time before his own planned opening gambit. Therefore, before his "flash ident" order could even be carried out by the harried crews of *Aoba* and the other CRUDIV ships in column, the Americans had already opened up in full on his force in a perfectly aligned "cap-the-T" formation, as soon each of Scott's ships found their own range out to those in Gotō's unsuspecting column.

The very first of the American salvos would hit with deadly impact and decimate *Aoba*'s superstructure—her formerly regal *Pagoda* mast soon a tangled mesh of steel beams and coiled cables. Seemingly in the blink of an eye she was hit in rapid succession by no less than forty incoming rounds fired from the heavy guns of the *San Francisco*, the *Helena*, the *Salt Lake City*, and the DDs *Laffey* and *Farenholt*. Reportedly seven rounds passed directly through Gotō's bridge on his *Aoba* flagship that night, all indeed in a trigger-hot span of minutes.

While it might be reported that many of the rounds fired would not even explode, the impact and concussion of those that had passed through the bridge would leave several killed outright, and Admiral Gotō himself now gravely wounded, even as the man slumped to the deck and bravely accepted his grim circumstance with quiet resignation and a certain dead resolve. The good Japanese admiral must indeed have been a true *Bushi* samurai to the very end, and so might he die much as a hero, standing his ground and station and perishing at his post.

The Japanese would lose *Tenryū* that night, and the great destroyer *Fubuki* as well, each ruthlessly peppered by the combined naval forces under RADM Norman Scott during the course of his own "crossed-T" attack strategy. Both IJN warships would be sunk almost in situ—virtually right where they were struck—and would never sail again. Having had enough indeed, the forces of Cruiser Division 6 simply broke off the engagement, aborted their own incursion plans, and veered sharply back to the north from a point just east of the Russell Islands; the admiral's ships would never even reach Savo Island. Defiant but still badly mauled, the *Aoba* could now only limp away in the vaward position, leading its remnant tattered forces back to the north. Even as they retreated into the night, it was clear to all that they had just been handed their first and most routing defeat, but few could have thought it might be only the first of many yet to come.

Of the good Admiral Gotō's demise, perhaps much can be gleaned from CAPT Tameichi Hara's account from his book, *Japanese Destroyer Captain*.[210] In it, Hara mournfully recalls the inconsolable and deep depression of his own commander, VADM Hiroaki Abe, on hearing of the news of the death of his close friend and naval comrade in arms, RADM Aritomo Gotō:

> Abe's mood was bad—particularly after learning of the October 11 Battle of Cape Esperance, in which his lifelong friend, Rear Admiral Aritomo Gotō, was killed. Sur-

vivors told Abe that they had been caught off guard by the enemy's radar-equipped ships led by Rear Admiral Norman Scott. Abe also knew that Gotō had died believing he [his ship] was the victim of friendly gunfire. On the smashed bridge . . . he breathed his last murmuring "*Bakayaro! Bakayaro!*" ("Stupid bastard!").[211]

Convinced that it had indeed been the *Tenryū* that sunk his ship—and not at all the Americans—the dying IJN admiral spat out the uncharacteristic profanity at those he believed to be most responsible for his ship's death. In contrast, one can only speculate as to whether he was also deriding himself for blundering his ships into the ambush in the first place. To the latter assertion, however, it may be assumed that history might lend no further insight.

RADM Gotō: Somewhere *Aoba* the Rainbow—Fate of a Great Warship

Gotō's bold *Aoba*, even after the demise of her captain during the untimely and deadly Battle of Cape Esperance in late 1942, would go on to play a steadied role of offensive support for multiple Japanese landings throughout the South Pacific and would be tasked with defensive escort duties during many of the battles yet to come in the Philippines and off Okinawa. In fact, it would only be in 1945, in a final defense of her homeland islands at the Kure Naval Facility in Japan, that she would again be harshly attacked, and—almost in view of the fair majesty of Mount Tobisakoyama itself, looming in the far distance like a shadowed backdrop—she would finally succumb to her mortal hits. Pounded repeatedly by a combined assault by elements of the American Task Force 38 and its carrier-based bombers, and the even deadlier low-flying B-24 *Liberators*, with their 500-pound bombs, the fearsome *Aoba* would be feared no more. On 28 July 1945, therefore, after initial (and sustained) attacks by all of those Allied planes, the IJN heavy cruiser—perhaps one of the last of her class still operational at that time—would shallow in some 25 feet of water east-southeast of the port of Kure, and sink heavily at an approximated positional fix of 34°14' N, 132°30' E, where she would indeed remain for some many years to come.

Years later, extremely rare color footage would be found in archive that purportedly depicted the IJN CA in a "refloated" position; however, that same video would soon fall into sharp dispute and may in fact have been only an image of the converted/reclassified *Ise*-class battleship *Hyūga* instead. The short, two-minute clip of footage is captured in very weak color or is perhaps entirely colorized. The moving-image video appears to have been shot from the vantage point of an unidentified motor pan circling the mangled wreckage itself, yet there still seems to be a general consensus that the footage might erroneously be titled "The Wreck of the *Aoba*, April 1946." As such, however, that footage may nonetheless be seen at the following website: http://www.youtube.com/watch?v=KkxNUOV91sk.

Combatants and Damage Assessments

ALLIED SURFACE FLEET: DAMAGE ASSESSMENTS

Table 42. The First Battle of Savo Island: Combatants and Damage Assessments (Allied Naval Forces)

	THE BATTLE OF SAVO ISLAND: COMBATANTS AND DAMAGE ASSESSMENTS (ALLIED NAVAL FORCES)		
HULL #	**SHIP NAME**	**LOSS SUMMARY**	**FINAL DISPOSITION DATA**
AMERICAN NAVAL SURFACE FLEET			
1,077 to 1,083 Men Lost; Four Heavy Cruisers Sunk; One Heavy Cruiser Damaged; Two Destroyers Damaged			
DD-387	**USS Blue**	No sustained damage in this engagement; later torpedoed and scuttled in late August 1942 **9°7'11"S** by **159°56'44"E**	**DD picket radar patrol ship positioned north of Savo:** *Did not detect approach of the Mikawa CRUDIV surface fleet.* The USS *Blue*, having helped to recover survivors from the stricken *Canberra*, saw no real action in the 1BOSI but would be pounced on some thirteen days later, on 22 August, by a single *Kawakaze* torpedo plane. The resulting impactful blows would cripple all main engines, damage *Blue*'s shafts and steering gear, and claim the lives of nine of her crew while wounding twenty-one. After repeated attempts to tow the ship to Tulagi for emergency repair, the *Blue* would later be scuttled at 2221 hours on 23 August 1942 after all attempts to save her had failed. She would sink in waters due east of Savo Island, where she remains to this day.
DD-390	**USS Ralph Talbot**	No sustained damage in this battle, but later sunk in waters off Kwajalein in March 1948	**DD picket radar patrol ship positioned north of Savo:** *Did not detect approach of the Mikawa CRUDIV surface fleet.* The USS *Ralph Talbot* would see only limited action in the 1BOSI herself but would later be fired on by the Mikawa task group as they exited Iron Bottom Sound after the twin attacks on both Crutchley's Southern and Northern screens.

(continued)

Table 42. *Continued*

		The Battle of Savo Island: Combatants and Damage Assessments (Allied Naval Forces)	
Hull #	**Ship Name**	**Loss Summary**	**Final Disposition Data**
American Naval Surface Fleet			
			This famous "parting-shot" encounter with the tail elements of the IJN cruiser force just north of Savo Island would become well known over time. Critically illuminated by searchlights from the passing enemy warships, *Talbot* would be fired on and take near-immediate hits to her chart house, destroying radar equipment and fire control circuits, resulting in major fires that threatened to quickly get out of control. More concussive shells come in at extremely close range and hit in rapid succession, slamming into the starboard quarter, wardroom, and virtually all of gun turret number 4. The *Talbot*, however, would go on in fact to survive *both* the 1BOSI and all of World War II, only to later serve as a "proximity target" during atomic bomb tests off the Bikini Atolls, and was soon found to be non-operational due to a condition of extreme radioactivity. Of needs, she would later be decommissioned in August 1946 and sunk in waters off Kwajalein on 8 March 1948.
CA-29	**USS Chicago**	Moderately damaged during the 1BOSI; then sunk in a later action on 30 Jan 1943 **11°25'S** by **160°56'E** **11°417'S** by **160°933'E**	*Chicago* is torpedoed in the bow while escorting the *Canberra* and withdraws from the area for emergency repair. This "bow shot" event would later itself become an item of some mild controversy as to the source of the initial torpedo launch itself. Partially restored to service at Nouméa, *Chicago* would return to battle in January 1943, only to be attacked that same month and torpedoed by Japanese aircraft, then later sunk in a secondary action during the later *Battle of Rennell Island*. Of curious note, Bode was no longer that CA's captain on that later occasion, as he had already been relieved of command after his questioned actions aboard her during the battle at Savo.

| CA-44 | USS *Vincennes* | Lost in battle east of Savo; 0250 hours, 9 August 1942 **9°7'17"S** by **159°52'48"E** | *Vincennes* is sunk by a deadly workable combination of superior gunfire and Long-Lance torpedoes launched from the cruisers *Chōkai, Kako, Aoba, Kinugasa,* and the CL *Yūbari* itself. Still showing much fight, however, *Vincennes* continued firing volley after volley from her remaining batteries, hitting and destroying the *Kinugasa's* steering gear, and causing that IJN cruiser to critically lag behind her other sister ships.

A shower of deadly accurate salvos had ranged in on the hapless *Vincennes*, hitting the bridge, hangar areas and engine spaces, starting fires virtually on contact. As the fire from the Japanese ships stepped up, *Vincennes* soon ruptured her fire mains and then would take two more torpedoes to her port side. By the time the IJN had disengaged from the battle and switched off their searchlights, *Vincennes* was already fully ablaze and listing heavily to port.

The ship would suffer an astounding eighty-five impact hits—truly the worst of all the cruisers—and would sail off in roughly a westerly direction. *Vincennes* would shortly thereafter roll and sink at about 0250 hours on the morning of 9 August 1942, some two and a half miles due east of Savo in an estimated 3,000 feet of water.

Not unlike the *Quincy* itself, the *Vincennes* would remain wholly unrecoverable, even to the present day, and the wreckage of all three ships are truly only accessible for wreck-diving purposes by either DSRV or other deep-sea submersible craft.

(continued) |

Table 42. *Continued*

	THE BATTLE OF SAVO ISLAND: COMBATANTS AND DAMAGE ASSESSMENTS (ALLIED NAVAL FORCES)		
HULL #	SHIP NAME	LOSS SUMMARY	FINAL DISPOSITION DATA
AMERICAN NAVAL SURFACE FLEET			
CA-39	USS *Quincy*	Sunk ENE of Savo at either: ❶ **09°04'32"S 159°58'30"E** ❷ **09°07'5x"S 159°48'3x"E** ❸ **Directly south of Savo Island—very close ashore**	*Quincy* is sunk by gunfire directed from the IJN CAs *Aoba*, *Kako*, *Furutaka*, and the CL *Tenyū*, then further hit by a single follow-on torpedo fired from the group's only other CL, *Yūbari*. Fully illuminated and taking heavy fire from all quarters, *Quincy* quick-turned sharply to train out her guns, bringing her stern directly through the enemy's line of fire. Two IJN Long-Lance torpedoes were then fired at the ship at near point-blank range and hit her port side, smashing the bridge, number 1 and number 2 gun turrets, and much of the ship's own aircraft hangar. In fact, by 0215 hours, the *Mighty Q* is all but doomed. With all guns out of action and fires engulfing areas of the ship itself, and with water cascading over upper deck areas, and casualties mounting rapidly, the ship would soon cripple off to the north and east, attempting to pursue a standard evasive zigzag course, trailing oil and smoke as she retired heavily from the battle zone in full. Now inclined to a near-45-degree list, the *Mighty Q*—the great *Quincy* herself—would settle at the bow and nose over, sinking in less than ten minutes at about 0238 hours on the morning of 9 August. The ship would suffer a total of some 36 deadly hits all told and would go down with a complement of crewmen that numbered (controversially) from 370 to 389 souls lost.

CA-34	USS *Astoria*	Lost in battle SW of Savo; 1216 hours, 9 August 1942 **9°12'33"S** by **159°52'3"E**	*Astoria* is sunk by a deadly crossfire of gunfire and torpedoes launched from the IJN heavies *Chōkai, Aoba, Kinugasa,* and the *Kako.* Shells fired from the heavy 8-inch guns of the attacking enemy cruisers began to exact a measured toll, igniting fires on the boat deck, aircraft hangar, and paint lockers, in addition to setting off much of the ship's service-ready ammunition stores in the vicinity of gun turret 8. Under a withering and deadly accurate fire, the gallant *Astoria* would completely lose all fire main controls by 0206 and was able to continue only under limited power to a position southeast of Savo Island.
			In fact, the great *Nasty Asty* would continue on well into the next day but began to settle by the stern at about 1216 hours, listing some 10°–15° before slowly sinking, having suffered some 65–70 hits and a loss of some 216 men during the brief course of that one battle.
DD-388	USS *Helm*	Sold for scrap, 1947	*Helm* would sit on the port beam of the heavy cruiser *Vincennes* and was reported to have turned back immediately after the initial attack to help at least one or more of the stricken cruisers. The curious movements of the *Helm* would now also become an item of some mild interest and discussion among analysts thereafter. She is alleged to have stood by *Astoria* and carried many of the survivors to transports off the coast of Guadalcanal and then was said to have withdrawn with the remainder of the force to Nouméa on 13 August.[212] Yet other reports seem to more clearly indicate that this rescue ship might more likely have been either the *Wilson* or the *Bagley.*
			Helm would go on to survive both the 1BOSI and World War II but would later be rendered dangerously radioactive and non-operational after also serving as a "proximity target ship" during the *Operation Crossroads* atomic bomb tests in the South Pacific. *Helm* would later be decommissioned in June of 1946 and sold for scrap to the Moore Dry Dock Company at Oakland, California, in 1947.

(continued)

Table 42. *Continued*

	THE BATTLE OF SAVO ISLAND: COMBATANTS AND DAMAGE ASSESSMENTS (ALLIED NAVAL FORCES)		
HULL #	SHIP NAME	LOSS SUMMARY	FINAL DISPOSITION DATA
AMERICAN NAVAL SURFACE FLEET			
DD-408	USS *Wilson*	*Sunk off Kwajalein Atoll, 1948*	The *Wilson* would see only *limited* action during the course of the 1BOSI but would best be remembered as one of several SAR vessels that were stationed on hand to at least assist survivors of the stricken CAs *Vincennes, Quincy,* and the *Astoria.* *Wilson* would also go on to survive both the 1BOSI AND World War II but would later be tagged as yet another "proximity target" ship that would soon be made radioactive and rendered non-operational by one (or a series of) atomic bomb tests at Bikini Atoll. She too would sadly later also be decommissioned in August 1946 and sunk in waters off Kwajalein on 8 March 1948.
DD-393	USS *Jarvis*	Sunk, East Solomon Sea, 1942 **09°42'S** by **158°59'E**	*Jarvis* is historically said to have bravely interposed herself and maneuvered between *Vincennes* and several attacking planes during the initial 7 August battle. In so doing, a single torpedo hit the ship's starboard side near the forward fire room, effectively stopping her dead in the water and killing some fourteen men in that action. An alert crew was on hand to jettison the ship's port torpedoes before they could detonate and to quickly gain control of the fires caused by the impact explosion. Later, the USS *Dewey* (DD-349) was finally able to tow the *Jarvis* to shallow anchorage near Lunga Point. Still on the fringes of any of the actual battles raging in Iron Bottom Sound, *Jarvis* would begin to retire westward to Sydney, Australia, for further repair, however, en route to that location the ship would again come under heavy attack by some thirty-one Japanese attack planes based out of Rabaul, who, mistaking her for a retreating heavy cruiser of the line, then attacked her *en masse.*

			Last seen moving to the west some 40 miles off the northern coast of Guadalcanal, *Jarvis* was said to be "trailing fuel oil, and cruising low by the bow"; then she reportedly "split and sank" at about 1300 hours on 9 August in the East Solomon Sea. Of the 233 crewmen remaining onboard who had survived the FIRST *Jarvis* attack, *none* would survive the second.
DD-392	**USS Patterson**	*Sold for scrap, 1947*	The *Patterson* would go on to survive both the 1BOSI and World War II, and in 1945 would arrive at the New York Naval Shipyard on 11 October of that year, where she would be decommissioned on a later date of 8 November. With *thirteen* Battle Stars to her good name and ship's credit, *Patterson* would nonetheless be stricken officially from the Naval Registry in 1947 and later sold for scrap to the Northern Metals Company of Philadelphia on the 18 August 1947.
DD-386	**USS Bagley**	*Sold for scrap, 1947*	The *Bagley* would also go on to survive both the 1BOSI and World War II, and in 1945 she would leave Sasebo, Japan, for Pearl Harbor en route to the U.S. Although initially slated to also serve as a "proximity target" for the Bikini Atoll atomic bomb tests, she would escape this ignoble fate only to be deactivated/decommissioned back at Pearl, and summarily struck from the Naval Registry on 25 February 1947. She would later be sold for scrap to the Moore Dry Dock Company of Oakland, California, in September of that same year.

(continued)

Table 42. *Continued*

HULL #	SHIP NAME	LOSS SUMMARY	FINAL DISPOSITION DATA
AMERICAN NAVAL SURFACE FLEET			
I-33/D-33	**HMAS *Canberra***	Lost in action south of Savo, RADM Turner then ordered the scuttling of the ship if it could not keep up with the column. At 0800, the *Canberra* was torpedoed by the DDs *Ellet* and *Selfridge* after an extended barrage of some 260 5-inch shells fired from the two DDs failed to sink the ship. **9°18 5x S by 159°37 2x E**	At 0143 on the night of 9 August, *Chōkai*'s 8-inch guns would indeed open up in full on the Australian cruiser. Curiously recounted, in fact, is the first-person account of seaman Henry Hall that portrays the man as talking on the phone when the first shells began to hit home. "Stupid bloody Yanks," the man muttered. "What the hell are they up to? Why are they dropping flares?" Then, in seconds, his telephone headset disintegrated and the man next to him was killed outright. A second shell then hit the ship's boiler room, fully knocking out ship's power. The great *Canberra* simply glided to a halt, her guns still trained out and essentially useless, where she now lay dead in the water. CAPT Getting's *Canberra* had in fact been mauled and severely damaged by superior gunfire from the IJN surface fleet and several possible hits from her own escort ship *Bagley*, and the larger *Chicago*, itself piloted by the somewhat questionable CAPT Howard Bode. Unable to remain seaworthy, the ill-fated *Canberra* would later be sunk by tandem shellfire and a single torpedo from the DDs *Ellet* and *Selfridge*, at about 0800 hours on the morning of 9 August 1942. The rediscovery of the *Canberra* wreckage would later stun a curious and disbelieving world in July–August 1992 by Dr. Robert Ballard, when she would be closely examined for perhaps the first time since her very sinking, then some fifty years after her scuttling. To this day, the great cruiser still lies upright on the ocean floor nestled some 2,500 feet below mean sea level. The great Australian heavy cruiser still bears the same scars of that same Savo battle, with visible signs of shell hits and heavy fire damage well amidships. And, just as they were during her brief and fatal engagement with Mikawa's own task force more than eight decades ago, virtually all of her main guns still hauntingly remain trained out to port.

| D-84 | HMAS *Australia* | Sold for scrap, 1956 | The *Australia* would serve as both Admiral Crutchley's flagship, and as the lead ship of the *Southern* screening force set by his own order. The Australian CA would survive the 1BOSI and go on to distinguish herself well in the *Battle of Lingayen Gulf* in the Philippines in January of 1945. On station in that battle arena, the ship would be hit one last time by at least "5" kamikaze aircraft and subsequently forced to withdraw to home waters in Australia for repair. This action would therefore effectively have been her last, as she would still be undergoing ships' repairs when World War II itself would officially end and a celebration of V-J day would soon thereafter begin.

In the years following the war, *Australia* would go on to serve as a training ship, but was soon thereafter sadly sold for scrap and dismantled by the end of 1956. |
| D-63 | HMAS *Hobart* | Sold for scrap, 1962 | The RAN *Perth*-class destroyer *Hobart* would go on to receive a distinguished "eight battle honours" (equaling our own "battle stars") for service in the Mediterranean and Indian Oceans, the Coral Sea, the Battle of Savo Island, the Naval Battle of Guadalcanal, and general Pacific theater operations between the years of 1942 on through to 1945, and in the area of the East Indies and even Borneo.

Found unsuitable for further upgrade to any of the newer cruiser formats of the time, the *Hobart* was slated for conversion to an interim "aircraft carrier" until funding (and apparent interest) simply fizzled out. Sadly, she too would later be sold for scrap in February 1962 to the Japanese firm Mitsui & Company and would arrive in Osaka, Japan, on 2 April of that year for full dismantling. |

IJN NAVAL SURFACE FLEET: DAMAGE ASSESSMENTS

Table 43.   The First Battle of Savo Island: Combatants and Damage Assessments (IJN Naval Forces)

		The Battle of Savo Island: Combatants and Damage Assessments (IJN Naval Forces)	
Number	Ship Name	Loss Summary	Final Disposition Data
		Imperial Japanese Navy (IJN) Naval Surface Fleet	
Fifty-eight Men Lost; Two Cruisers Moderately Damaged Only			
CA	IJN *Chōkai*	Sunk in actions during the Battle off Samar on 25 October 1944 **11°22'N 126°22'E**	**Sunk on 25 October 1944, in the Battle of Samar** After months of terrorizing the Allied warships in both the Indian Ocean and South Pacific waters—from the Andamans to Guadalcanal and on to the Philippines—the mighty *Chōkai* would finally be attacked and crippled by torpedoes and small-caliber shells fired from the 5-inch guns of the famed DE, USS *Samuel B. Roberts*[213] during the greatly one-sided *Battle off Samar* in 1944. On scene at that time were also several American light bombers, one of which would drop a 500-pound bomb directly onto the ship's forward machinery room. The resulting fires would rage unchecked throughout what had formerly been Mikawa's flagship, and she would eventually go dead in the water. Unable to move under her own power, and by now more liability than asset, the *Chōkai* would finally be scuttled by one of her own, the DD *Fujinami*, in deep waters several miles east of the *Batang* Peninsula in the Philippines. It might even be assumed that the ship remains at that location to this day.
CA	IJN *Aoba*	Sunk by combined Taffy 38 air attack on 28 July 1945 **34°14'N 132°30'E**	**Sunk on 28 July 1945, after a sustained air attack from *Taffy-38* (TF-38) short-range bombers, and a force of B-24 Liberators, off the coast of Kure, Japan** Battered by multiple direct hits from Task Force bombers and several 500-pound bombs dropped from the Allied B-24s, *Aoba* would end its high reign of terror on the high seas—and its long combative career—at 2200 hours, 28 July 1945, when her stern snapped off and the ship reportedly settled "with great noise" to the bottom of the Inland Sea, sinking in what was then estimated to have been a mere (25) feet of water.

| CA | IJN *Furutaka* | Sunk in actions with American CAs near Savo Island on 12 October 1942 **09°02'S 159°33'E** | **Sunk on 12 October 1942, in the Battle of Cape Esperance, near Iron Bottom Sound** |

When the IJN heavy cruiser *Aoba* force was being engaged by RADM Scott's TF 64, the *Furutaka* was momentarily turning from the line of battle to counter the American CA *Salt Lake City* during the later Battle of Cape Esperance in October of 1942. Insodoing, she reportedly moved into the path of the American DD USS *Duncan*, who had already quick-fired a spread of two torpedoes, but apparently missed with both. With a cumulative bombardment, however, of some (90) shells fired from the *Duncan's* batteries, the *Furutaka* would shortly meet its watery end in waters northwest of Savo and sink at about 0228 hours on the date of 12 August 1942.

| CA | IJN *Kako* | Sunk by U.S. submarine USS *S-44* on 9 August 1942 **02°28'S 152°11'E** | **Sunk on 10 August 1942, after the Battle of Savo Island** |

A final successful attack on the *Kako* would occur as Mikawa was withdrawing his surface fleet from Iron Bottom Sound after his highly successful twin attacks on the occasion of the 1BOSI. The American attack submarine USS *S-44* would probably be the last vessel to spot the now-retreating cruiser force, and so responding quickly fired a calculated spread of four torps—three of which would score direct hits on the *Kako* in rapid succession.

By 0810 of the same day, therefore, the IJN heavy cruiser—a combat veteran of multiple actions throughout the southwest Pacific—would keel to starboard and explode at sea as waters soon began to breach her boilers. The ship would perish with a loss of some seventy-one men, and some fifteen wounded, in 130 feet of water near Simbari Island in the Tabar group just north of Papua/New Guinea. this on the day *after* its own attacks on the Allied ships at Savo on 9 August. It might therefore perhaps be said that payback itself had very much been a bitch indeed.

(continued)

Table 42. *Continued*

	THE BATTLE OF SAVO ISLAND: COMBATANTS AND DAMAGE ASSESSMENTS (IJN NAVAL FORCES)		
NUMBER	SHIP NAME	LOSS SUMMARY	FINAL DISPOSITION DATA
		IMPERIAL JAPANESE NAVY (IJN) NAVAL SURFACE FLEET	
Fifty-eight Men Lost: Two Cruisers Moderately Damaged Only			
CA	IJN *Kinugasa*	Sunk by critical air attack near Rendova Island, 14 November 1942 **08°45'S 157°00'E**	**Sunk on 14 November 1942, in the Solomon Sea, during the Naval Battle of Guadalcanal** Relentlessly attacked by a deadly combination of Dauntless and Avenger dive-bombers from the Marine air groups, and those from the carrier *Enterprise*, the *Kinugasa* would suffer a staggering number of hits, killing the ship's commander and executive officer outright in a single fatal instant. Listing slowly to port, *Kinugasa* would soon roll at 1122, capsize and sink just WSW of Rendova Island in the New Georgia group. She would reportedly take with her an almost full complement of 511 crewmen who would sadly go down with their ship.
CL	IJN *Yūbari* **(CL-14)**	Sunk in actions by the American CAs with American sub USS *Bluegill* (SS-242) on 27 April 1944 **05°38'N 131°47'E**	**Sunk on 27 April 1944, near the *Sonsoral* Islands, Palau, by the American submarine USS *Bluegill* (SS-242)** For the duration of the attack, and after significant damage had been inflicted upon her, the IJN CL *Yūbari* could no longer move under her own power. The captain ordered the ship's battle colors stricken from the mast and she was allowed to scuttle—her crew standing solemnly by and looking on from the decks of the two nearby IJN rescue ships, the DDs *Samidare* and *Yuzuki*. Reportedly grief-stricken to no end and with tears held in check, survivors of the *Yūbari* now watched in horror as their ship sank with great finality bow-first into the deep of the southern Philippine Sea on 27 April 1944.

CL	**IJN *Tenryū***	**Sunk on 19 December 1942, off Papua/New Guinea in the Bismarck Sea, by the U.S. submarine USS *Albacore* (SS-218)**
	Sunk in action by the American sub USS *Albacore* (SS-218) on 19 December 1942 **05°12'N 145°56'E**	*Tenryū* would in fact go on to survive the attacks at Savo and continue to be based out of Rabaul. Later, by the end of August 1942, she would already be far away, in fact covering the landing of troops at Milne Bay, New Guinea.
		On 19 December, *Tenryū* would reportedly be spotted by the attack sub USS *Albacore* (SS-218) and would receive a single impact hit from a threefold spread of torpedoes fired from that sub. *Tenryū* would thereafter go down in the Bismarck Sea.
DD	**IJN *Yūnagi***	**Sunk on 25 August 1944, after the Battle of the Philippine Sea**
	Sunk in action with American sub USS *Picuda* off Luzon, Philippines, on 25 August 1944 **18°46'N 120°46'E**	On a return trip to Manila from Taiwan, *Yūnagi* would be abruptly attacked by the American *Balao*-class attack submarine USS *Picuda* (SS-382) in the South China Sea and sunk some twenty miles off the northeasternmost tip of Luzon in the Philippines.
		On her third war patrol, and under a new command, the *Picuda* had been tasked to form up with a wolf-pack made up of two other subs, which had spotted some ten unidentified ships suspiciously perusing the coastline some 4,000 yards off the Luzon peninsula.
		Having already slipped past five escort ships and a number of enemy attack aircraft—the *Picuda* was still able to loose a spread of six torpedoes to sink the merchant vessel *Kotoku Maru*. Then, as if to further capitalize on her very non-detection and shot-positive positioning, *Picuda* skillfully maneuvered herself into a secondary kill zone for a single "down-the-throat" shot that would soon spell a certain end for the then hotly pursuing IJN destroyer.
		The *Yūnagi* would later sink in waters north of Cape Bojeador, Luzon, in the Philippines, with a loss of some thirty-two souls still remaining onboard.

Sunken ships

Allied

- *Aaron Ward* (US *Gleaves*-class destroyer)
- *Astoria* (US *New Orleans*-class cruiser)
- *Atlanta* (US *Atlanta*-class anti-aircraft cruiser)
- *Barton* (US *Benson*-class destroyer)
- *Blue* (US *Bagley*-class destroyer)
- *Canberra* (Australian *Kent*-class cruiser)
- *Colhoun* (US *Wickes*-class destroyer)
- *Cushing* (US *Mahan*-class destroyer)
- *De Haven* (US *Fletcher*-class destroyer)
- *Duncan* (US *Gleaves*-class destroyer)
- *George F. Elliot* (US *Heywood* class transport)
- *Gregory* (US *Wickes*-class destroyer)
- *Jarvis* (US *Gridley*-class destroyer)
- *John Penn* (US miscellaneous class Attack Transport)
- *Kanawha* (US *Kanawha/Cuyama* class fleet oiler)
- *Laffey* (US *Benson*-class destroyer)
- *Little* (US *Wickes*-class destroyer)
- *Moa* (New Zealand *Bird* class corvette)
- *Monssen* (US *Gleaves*-class destroyer)
- *Northampton* (US *Northampton*-class heavy cruiser)
- *Preston* (US *Mahan*-class destroyer)
- *PT-37* (US PT boat)
- *PT-44* (US PT boat)
- *PT-111* (US PT boat)
- *PT-112* (US PT boat)
- *PT-123* (US PT boat)
- *Quincy* (US *New Orleans*-class cruiser)
- *Seminole* (US *Navajo*-class oceangoing tug)
- *Serpens* (United States Coast Guard-manned Liberty ship)
- *Vincennes* (US *New Orleans*-class cruiser)
- *Walke* (US *Sims*-class destroyer)
- *YP-284* (US Yard Patrol craft)

Japanese

- *Akatsuki* (Japanese *Akatsuki*-class destroyer)
- *Ayanami* (Japanese *Fubuki*-class destroyer)
- *Fubuki* (Japanese *Fubuki*-class destroyer)
- *Furutaka* (Japanese *Furutaka*-class cruiser)
- *Hiei* (Japanese *Kongō*-class battleship)
- *Hirokawa Maru* (Japanese military transport)
- *Kasi Maru* (Japanese freighter)
- *Kinugawa Maru* (Japanese military transport)
- *Kirishima* (Japanese *Kongō*-class battleship)
- *Makigumo* (Japanese *Yugumo*-class destroyer)
- *Takanami* (Japanese *Yugumo*-class destroyer)
- *Teruzuki* (Japanese *Akizuki*-class destroyer)
- *Toa Maru* (Japanese military transport)
- *Yudachi* (Japanese *Shiratsuyu*-class destroyer)

Figure 47.   List of Ships Lost during Combined Operations at Guadalcanal/Iron Bottom Sound (Unofficial)

The Battle of Savo Island: Lessons Learned

So what did we not know then—before, during, and after the First Battle of Savo Island—and what were the failings and inadequacies pointed up and brought to light as a result of the cascade of sharp analyses and after-action reports that would inevitably soon follow? And what new information might be presented and gleaned from the otherwise stop-gap explanations and ad hoc findings offered by an already tarnished Navy Department? And finally, what indeed were the general conclusions offered by the several boards of inquiry and government-appointed investigative subcommittees that would only too soon be convened with but one, single purpose in mind: to investigate and find fault in the tragedy and critical losses suffered by the Allies during the battle at Savo? Would there be fault—or no fault? Would there be "collective culpability" or only individual blame? And were these all simply random acts of fate, bad luck, and poor timing . . . or was it something else? Perhaps in retrospect, it would decidedly be all of the above—and far, far more.

The battle for control of the Solomons would be one of the key turning points of World War II, and for at least the soon-retreating Imperial Japanese Navy, the fall of Guadalcanal (and surrounding environs) would effectively turn the tide of the war in the South Pacific and almost certainly begin to place victory in the hands of the tenacious Allied coalition navies that would so doggedly pursue that enemy force in full. It would truly be these very naval battles then that, between the years of 1942 and 1943, would soon break the stranglehold of Japan's dominance and supremacy on the high seas, even as the American battle fleet began its long and arduous "island-hopping" push to north. The dauntless American and Allied naval forces would soon begin their own gritty and steadfast thrust up and into the heartland of the *Land of the Rising Sun*, up toward the home islands of Japan itself.

WHAT WE DIDN'T KNOW THEN—WHAT WE KNOW NOW

Truly there might be much that we can only see *now* that we did not see *then*—at the time of the savage attacks at Savo—and that we may only now, at leisure, view with the unstained eye and impeccable clarity of 20/20 hindsight. A myriad of hot discussions would later ensue that would directly center on the shortcomings of the American fleet and their level of ill-preparedness, the apparent lack of any viable command structure, and even the absence of a workable battle plan. And almost all of these bald observations would begin and end with the massacre at Savo. If viewed rightly, it was only then that an aggrieved and now-crestfallen U.S. Navy Department would begin to hotly scramble for answers to quell the outpour of inquiries, those demands being made first by their own (the Navy Department's) command and control hierarchy and those by the Washington-based Pentagon officials controlling those forces, ultimately answering to those within an already harried and incensed Roosevelt administration. After all, just what the hell could have gone so wrong for the Allies that could bring about such a deadly and unforeseen outcome for its combined naval forces—and in such an untimely manner? And oh, the damnable ignominy of it all, a chagrined presidential administration must clearly have thought in summation of the whole affair. Clearly, there'd be hell to pay for some—and for some others, nothing less than their lobbed heads rolling off the executioner's stump would suffice.

So what, precisely, might we assume the Allied naval forces knew of their foe—or of that enemy's wily tactics—or even of the very battle arena itself in which they found themselves fighting? Looking ahead, the discourse narratives that follow can only "ambitiously" attempt to define only some of the key points of the *what* and the *why* of the battle, and just how much we knew—or simply *assumed* that we knew—of our enemy at the time. And although the discussion itinerary may not itself be the most definitive analysis of all such factors and considerations, the author is confident that it will at least address most (if not all) of the more widely accepted findings and key lessons learned from the deadly encounter at Savo.

NO EFFECTIVE BATTLE PLAN

Background/Premise

In the wake of the brief but savaging battles at Savo, it might have been widely upheld that the risks endured—and the losses suffered—may have been appropriate to the overlying Allied action of fully denying Japan (and her Imperial Navy) even toehold access to Guadalcanal, or any of its surrounding islands. Given a clear chance to do so, Japan would inevitably have used those islands as both staging points and resupply areas to further back her own stepped-up moves to fully occupy the main island as well as several of its outlying islands, such as Tulagi and Tanambogo—both for purely tactical reasons.

If the clear and unimpeachable aim of Japan, and its fearsome IJN Combined Fleet, had been that of using the Solomons as a "stepping-stone" launch-point for a further planned move against the Australian mainland itself, then it was just as clear that it would now fall to the United States and its Allies to negate any such strong-arm takeover attempt within precisely that same arena by any such IJN invasion force—and that by any means necessary.

The United States would move on to do precisely this—and with its tripartite Allied force of British, Australian, and even New Zealand naval ships, sought to sustain and solidify their long-range *strategic* goals by paying an inordinately high *tactical* price at Savo on the night of 9 August. Clearly, the Allied battle plan might be flawed, and VADM Gunichi Mikawa and his two cruiser divisions knew best how to exploit those weaknesses. The Imperial Japanese Navy's own vice admiral was arguably the best man for the job and Japan's greatest cruiser commander bar none. A brilliant tactical strategist who rode the crests of his own waves in his own time, he would soon realize his twin victories at Savo not just by skill but admittedly much by chance as well . . . and even that with a wink of good fortune and the simple luck of the draw. And, on the night of 9 August 1942, Mikawa would hold the winning upper hand and truly realize both.

Lesson(s) Learned

❶ History seems to support the thought that many of the "tactical" decisions made by the Washington-based Joint Chiefs of Staff (JCS) who, at least in 1942, were gravely concerned about the seemingly uncheckable encroachment and rapid hostile advance of Japan's land and naval forces into the Solomons, with their sharpest focus being the island jewel of Guadalcanal. Such a concern would clearly have filtered down to the COMSOPAC and COMSOWESPAC theater commanders (Ghormley and Fletcher, respectively) as well, and each seemed to uphold the greater strategic goal of getting in first, seizing Guadalcanal and its surrounding islands outright, and holding them at all costs for themselves. The Allied force commanders may have been convinced that it was simply the duty of the *tactical* to directly support (and perhaps even be appropriate to) the *strategical*: that of ensuring a positive and desired outcome for the Americans and their Allies. That desired outcome was nothing less than full control of the Solomons as quickly and as quietly as could be accomplished—if not by "precedence," then by all means by "force." Sadly, for the U.S. naval planners of the time, this was only a "best-case" scenario and an unspoken wish—with all things being quite favorable—and would not at all be reflective of what would actually occur at the later massacre at Savo.

❷ In fact, the attacks at Savo would be characteristic of anything *but* favorable conditions—occurring both at night and at a time of sopping inclement weather and a heavy presence of fog. The Washington high command knew that such an Allied invasion of Guadalcanal, and a later defense of same, would in and of itself be a costly undertaking, and could be expected to come only at high price—in both casualties and capital ship losses. Yet the risk itself might actually have been acceptable to the JCS, who were then overseeing the deployment of all area forces and, charged with the orchestration of its navy's movements, clearly must have had a greater purview and perspective of the combat arena. Perhaps to them the considered "tactical" losses that might be suffered up front might indeed be appropriate to the greater "strategical" advances that might later be realized by that same Allied force. "Area domination," after all, was the key call of the day, and the Americans and their Allies intended to get in first, dig in deep, and then *hold* that real estate with a bulldog tenacity that would make that effort famous for all time. The battle plan would now become far more complex and far more fluid for the Allies and would more carefully weigh the enemy's intent with his capability—and never again mistake the two a second time.

COMMAND STRUCTURE: A FAILED LEADERSHIP

Background/Premise

Bad decisions, poor timing, absent leadership, and the removal of Fletcher's carrier assets—even RADM McCain's own failure to provide adequate air cover requested by RADM Turner when specifically asked to do so—might all be key examples of the failed leadership factors that seemed to nip and rankle at the heels of the Allied command during at least the opening salvos of the battle for control of the Solomons. The almost compartmentalized command structures that were already in place (or simply assumed to be in place) were rigid and fixed, and oft set along lines of cultural and national origin (i.e., for the Americans, for the British, for the Australians, etc.); truly a full command orchestration of such a size, and of such a multi-national force, might indeed have been difficult, even under the very best of circumstances.

The removal and final sequestration of some of the Allied forces' own leaders would also be pivotal to the later losses at Savo, since several of the key task group leaders would not even be available for consultation when the battle began, and would in fact be found elsewhere, locked in conference with Turner to discuss Fletcher's withdrawal of the Allied carrier force. This action alone would seriously impinge on any viable first-line understanding by those key commanders of just what was going on, even precisely at the very moment it was. It further disallowed any degree of flexibility in the rapid deployment of the meager fleet assets at their disposal—or time to perhaps reposition those ships to enlarge the screening force they had already hastily set in place in and around Guadalcanal. Some key considerations of the effects of such a failed leadership ability, therefore, might be widely assumed to include all of the following:

- The removal of Admiral Fletcher's Carrier Task Force late on the afternoon of 8 August. The admiral's CTF 61 would comprise some eighty-two ships at full strength, and yet none of those ships would ever be any closer than eighty miles from the scene of battle—far too far away for intercession—and far too removed to lend any real level of direct, or even logistical support.
- RADM McCain's poorly reasoned decision *not* to fly the additional reconnaissance overflights as previously ordered on 8 August by Admiral Turner in his capacity as COMPHIBFORSOPACFLT.
- Poorly established communication links between Turner and many of his key force commanders.
- Poorly established communication links between each of the group commanders within the Southern, Northern, Eastern, and "radar picket" screening groups, the latter of which was made up solely of the DDs USS *Blue* and *Ralph Talbot* just north of Savo.

- The departure of RADM Crutchley and the Marine Corps' own commanding general, MG Vandegrift, to attend the "Turner Conference" aboard Turner's interim flagship USS *McCawley* on the night of 8–9 August. Clearly, the untimely departure of both commanders would come at a time when both might most be needed, just when the battle itself would commence.
- A lack of a full command and control structure—or even competent oversight—of the full multi-national naval task force in play that night, as seen at Savo during at the opening gambits of the battle main.

Lesson(s) Learned

The Americans and their allies would learn hard and pressing lessons in the wake of Savo, and would learn those lessons through a school of hard knocks that would be served up in a manner so unsettling and unforgiving as to not soon be forgotten. Indeed, those same high-priced lessons would also involve the critical loss of some 1,100 men and at least four heavy cruisers sunk, and one additional CA, the *Chicago*, left ablaze and sailing erratically off from the battle area for at least the next forty minutes.

ADM Fletcher's tenuous position of having withdrawn his CTF 61 carrier assets on the day just before the Savo attack would be among the first of many protocols and command responsibilities to be shored up in the aftermath of the dreaded night battle that had cost too many lives, on both the American and the Australian sides. Almost immediately, it had become abundantly clear to the naval high command that the COMSOPAC, even in his most generic command role, should no longer be based on a carrier asset only (due entirely to its somewhat limited range of operation) and that such a commander's flag should be transferred instead to a smaller (albeit faster) warship, such as a fast BB or CA. This change would quickly allow for added mobility for that force commander and a far greater degree of flexibility with which to respond to any call—in any area—as needed and to immediately be on scene in the event of an unexpected encounter with any such large enemy force. In form and effect, then, America was simply but quite clearly saying, "Nothing like this horrid Savo must ever be allowed to occur again."

In addition, individual task group commanders, such as the captains and rear admirals who drove the very CAs, CLs, and DDs that were themselves often directed into the thick of battle, soon carried new mandates designed to improve on current communication protocols for notification of an enemy's presence, or sudden action within any quadrant of their assigned areas of operation.

Crutchley's circumstance as the involuntary "absentee warrior" on the night of 8–9 August, due to Turner's call to his late-night powwow aboard *McCawley*, would not be allowed to occur again, and the grip of command exercised by those same key force leaders would only tighten further over the course of the coming weeks and months after Savo.

DEPLOYMENT OF FORCES: CRUTCHLEY'S SCREENING ASSETS

Background/Premise

In the absence of a firm directive, or even a further promise to later augment his subordinate British admiral's already scant naval force, Admiral Turner set Crutchley's screening forces to a task so strict that it might itself be nearly impossible: patrol and guard "hundreds of miles" of open blue-water ocean fronting Guadalcanal—in and around Iron Bottom Sound—and screen the even smaller inland seas around Tulagi and Florida Island, all of it with only a handful of heavy and light cruisers, a small flotilla of DDs, and a motley assortment of support and coastal patrol craft. And with this meager screening force, Crutchley was expected to guard all of the sea lanes and approaches into and out of the Guadalcanal area. A near-monumental task by any standard for any commander, Crutchley nonetheless set himself about the business of placing his screening forces just so, stationed in and around the two major troop embarkation points at both the Lunga Point X-Ray landing zones and cross-channel port of Tulagi.

Crutchley therefore split his meager screening elements into five effective battle groups, as best he could, as noted: ❶ a positioning of two "radar picket" DDs *Blue* and *Ralph Talbot* far to the north of Savo, as a first line of defense; ❷ a Southern screening force, under the command of Crutchley himself, just off the Lunga Point landing area; ❸ a Northern battle group under the aegis of the somewhat inexperienced RADM Riefkohl just north and west of Nggella Sule (Florida Island); ❹ an Eastern screening element, led by RADM Scott, that would itself be stationed nearer into the Tulagi-side staging area; and finally, ❺ a small and little-known screening element of DDs and localized patrol craft set to guard the inlets and watery approaches fronting the smaller southern port areas of Tulagi and Tanambogo.

Lesson(s) Learned

❶ As a result, a poor (or less than optimum) deployment of Allied naval assets under Crutchley's command on the night of 8–9 August 1942 would play right into the hands of Mikawa's own cruisers during their sly push into the area that night; almost as quickly, the Allied naval strategy for the entire region would need to change virtually overnight. Therefore, in later battles and defensive strategies centered on Guadalcanal, it was no longer unusual to see many of the Allied screening forces set at points even farther north—well above Savo—to intercept the encroaching enemy fleet well before they could even sail through the upper reaches of the Sound. Better to head them off at the pass—the American admirals must clearly have reasoned—well above the Allies' current zone of operation, than to later have to tangle with those same deadly ships in one's own home port area right there in the Sound.

❷ The Allied naval screening forces defending Guadalcanal and the cross-channel Tulagi and Tanambogo staging areas would not make this mistake again, and they immediately set about the business of augmenting their own force-presence in the region. Replacement BBs, CAs/CLs, DDs, and many other support ships were quickly redeployed from other theater venues—some even pulled from ETO operations areas a full ocean away—and sent immediately to the Guadalcanal arena to boost the overall number of post-invasion warships available to guard the still-offloading troop transport and supply ships at each of those coastal ports.

❸ Allied commanders might have also unavoidably been distracted by their insistence in following the initiative of the enemy's "intentions," rather than the reality of the enemy's actual "capabilities." A clear understanding of just what the IJN might intend to do, juxtaposed to what they might in fact be *capable* of doing, could unquestionably be two different considerations and could allow one to arrive at two separate conclusions. Crutchley and his limited screening resources—at least on the night of 9 August—must clearly have misread both the intent and the capability of their Japanese counterparts, and were therefore entirely surprised by the devastating attacks that would commence at Savo only two hours after midnight. Those attacks would themselves be sharp, brief, violent, and near-flawlessly executed—and all occurring in a curt span of thirty-one minutes or less.

PROVISIONING OF AIR COVER

Background/Premise

❶ No unsustainable naval task force (of any significant size) should feasibly undertake any major at-sea offensives with only *limited* (or, even worse, *no*) air cover provisioned for that attack effort. Nearly an unthinkable deficit for any mission undertaking, this was precisely what Crutchley had been ordered to do by Turner on the night of 8–9 August. In fact, the subordinate British officer attempted to sortie his meager ships out with only a scant screening force of eight cruisers and five DDs—all with no air cover—then set them up into logical defense perimeters in and around the Guadalcanal–Tulagi defense line.

❷ With the removal of the one cohesive mainstay element in the area that had been Fletcher's Carrier Task Force 61 on the day just before the Savo attack, the provisioning of viable air cover would over time become only more problematic. Concerned over the loss of twenty-one of his own carrier aircraft in multiple actions over Guadalcanal between 7–8 August, and cautious lest his exposed Watchtower task force be attacked by enemy torpedo bombers or by prowling IJN subs with their deadly Long-Lance torpedoes, Fletcher abruptly made his decision to simply weigh anchor and depart the area on the evening of the second day. Perhaps considering his area screening duties essentially fulfilled (at least to his own satisfaction), the admiral simply left Iron Bottom Sound and moved to reposition his ships to a more secured reassembly point well to the north and away from the hotly disputed area of Guadalcanal.

In so doing, Fletcher not only left the troops being landed from those same transport ships at Lunga entirely exposed and unprotected but also left the still-unloading cargo ships with insufficient air cover. Later, an exasperated RADM Crutchley, the commander in charge of that same transport task group, would himself be compelled to discontinue his own unloading operations as well, and, with no appreciable CAS (Combat Air Support) brought to bear by Fletcher's now-absent CTF, Crutchley would also pull up stakes and move away from the Lunga staging area to make for the more secure open waters of the Sound. As a direct result, all unloading activities—both cargo and transport—would be suspended in full.

❸ In arguably one of the most curious shows of widening acceptance, history would later seem to more favorably view Fletcher's grave decision to remove his carrier assets from the area as being more faux pas than grave error. Fletcher's concern over the vulnerability of his fleet and its weakened state of fueling and general combat readiness, as well as its need to at least partially repair its damaged ships after two days of significant air and sea attacks stemming from the invasion landings of 7–8 August, all ultimately won out in the commander's mind, who thought it far better to err on the side of caution than to remain in the Sound as essentially little other than a raft of sitting ducks. It might not be surprising, then, that the later battle at Savo would go on to assume the rather ignoble colloquialization of "The Battle of Five Sitting Ducks" that—in at least the minds of the aggrieved sailors who had survived its stark terrors—would sadly bespeak the loss of four heavy cruisers from the Allied fleet, and yet a fifth—the *Chicago* herself—left smoldering and staggering blindly off to the northwest in that same action.

❹ RADM John S. McCain Sr., the extant commander of all naval air forces within the South Pacific Fleet—alternately known as the COMNAVAIR at the time of the attacks at Savo—would be only mildly rebuked in the wake of the naval debacle at Savo. In fact, the admiral would be found negligent only to the extent that he did not immediately obey the "extra reconnaissance overflights" order issued by Turner earlier on the afternoon of 8 August—missions that should have been conducted in and around the Sound and points north of Savo (and perhaps even up and down the Slot itself).

In fact, had such a reconnaissance effort been launched by McCain as instructed, his planes might clearly have noted the approach of Mikawa's cruiser force long before it skirted around the northern edge of Savo and entered the Sound—wholly unchallenged and virtually undetected. All of this notwithstanding, the good Admiral McCain would nonetheless remain in place as the COM-NAVAIRFORSOPACFLT for at least the foreseeable future and would go on to further solidify his position. The good admiral would almost fully redeem himself by providing optimum air support for virtually all the remaining Allied offensives that were now centered on first subduing, then holding the Solomons at all costs.

But on far too many occasions the admiral's planes, like so many of the other grounded aircraft at the time, were essentially "blind" at night and would subsequently seldom engage in any significant air actions during either the hours of darkness or inclement weather.

Lesson(s) Learned

The U.S.-led coalition of forces that included the United Kingdom, Australia, and an oft-forgotten New Zealand would go on to beef up its "air presence" in the region, and the COMNAVAIR would see to it that adequate land and carrier-based air assets could always be brought to bear at any time, sortied out to any location, and flown in support of any mission . . . and would do so thereafter on an ongoing and as-needed basis.

Clearly a daunting task even for RADM McCain, resupply aircraft were quickly reassigned from virtually every location in close proximity to the area of most critical operation in the southwest Pacific, diverted to both Guadalcanal and Tulagi, corralled onto secured areas in and around Henderson airfield, and ordered to fly any number of combat and reconnaissance missions over Iron Bottom Sound in support of the continued landing of the Allied occupational forces. This action alone would lift the overwhelming onus of responsibility from the backs of the fleet's own light and heavy cruisers (and their screening DDs) as the sole measure of screening protection being offered the transport and cargo ships that were continuing to operate in and around Lunga and Tulagi. In the wake of Savo, even greater air assets would arrive at the scene of battle—many planes with faster engines, more powerful weapons systems, and even extended operational ranges—and each in turn was quickly assigned to various CAP (Combat Air Patrol) duties over Guadalcanal and its watered environs. Response times would markedly change for the better, and the number of "committable" combat aircraft that could quickly be made available and mustered out on short notice in defense of a specific battle area, or established defensive position, would measurably increase nearly twofold.

BATTLE PREPAREDNESS: RESPONDING TO THE ELEMENT OF SURPRISE

Background/Premise

Clearly the odds-on favorite for being able to develop and (entirely exploit) a full element of surprise in attacking an enemy force time and again in seemingly every open-sea naval engagement initiated against an already beleaguered U.S. naval fleet that had been all but decimated at both Pearl Harbor and Ford Island—and later Coral Sea encounters—the Imperial Japanese Navy, under Marshal Admiral Isoroku Yamamoto, had indeed become the definitive masters (and true practitioners) of precisely such a tactic. And while Pearl Harbor had itself been a rude wake-up call for the Americans, it is still possible that the U.S. Navy had not yet learned its lessons in full at that time and so fell prey to such tactics again and again in other battles, at other times—and all within the same theater of operation.

This same strategy would unceasingly be put to quite effective use by an emboldened Japanese navy in battle arenas everywhere, ranging from Midway to Attu, and from Wake to Tassafaronga. But Savo itself would soon become the true cut-off point for the Allies, as truly now they had had enough, and by the later battles at Santa Cruz and Cape Esperance, RADM Norman Scott would do everything in his power to turn that tide in a tidy and timely fashion.

And so it was, late on the night of 11 October 1942, that the sly American admiral found himself sitting patiently on the southwestern edge of volcanic Savo waiting for the IJN fleet to once again sortie down the Slot on another of their nightly forays, prepared to spring a trap of his own making. The USN had finally caught on and was now poised to lower the boom and counterstrike an unsuspecting IJN, only this time the gloves would completely come off. In the interim, however, leading up to these later battles in and around Guadalcanal, the incontrovertible effect of each of those IJN surprise attacks on Allied shippage was almost always the same, as seen here in the brief (but tragic) cause-and-effect synopses noted below:

★ Each surprise attack seemed to leave Allied commanders utterly flustered and bewildered, causing them to confuse many of the developing situations even as they were unfolding and further lure them into making incorrect assumptions, bad situational assessments, and even worse decisions.

★ Commanders would continue to be plagued by the always deadly IFF issues of confusing friend with foe and adversary with ally, either withholding fire when they should have engaged—thereby opening themselves up to only greater attack by an interloping enemy force—or, worse, firing on a "friendly" assuming that they were in fact the enemy. For greater insight into this topical discussion point, see the earlier module titled "Close Encounters and the Cost of Friendly Fire."

★ Commanders would continue to make effectively bad decisions that would too often result in further tragic circumstances that might cause an even greater loss of lives and critical ship assets.

★ The actions at Savo would occur as a result of a serious lack of communication among the Allied fleet's forces in the heat of battle, and time and again had they failed miserably in even alerting the other screening ships in the Sound of that enemy presence even as it was occurring. And finally:

★ Events unfolding even at the moment of battle seemed to cause some of the Allied commanders to completely ignore the task group's "prime directive"—that of safeguarding the unloading troop transport and cargo ships that they had been tasked with safeguarding imprimis.

The IJN element of surprise was at least for them certainly a "win-win"; for the Americans, perhaps not so much at all. It was a sly and stealthy tactic that apparently worked only too well to the enemy's favor time and time again, and the Allies soon realized that they must urgently find a way to turn the tables to thwart the killing effect of that enemy's recurring element of surprise.

Lesson(s) Learned

Author/historian Richard Bates quite aptly stated, "Surprise is the injection of the unexpected for the purpose of creating an unfavorable military situation for the enemy."[214] Unfortunately, the Americans had already learned this lesson the hard way at Pearl Harbor, then thwarted its success at both Midway and Wake, only to once again fall victim to its harsh pronouncements during the opening gambits in the battle for control of the Solomons. Well after the attacks at Pearl Harbor and Ford Island, Savo would become that secondary wake-up call for all of the Allied naval commanders, who then began to more clearly anticipate (and counter) that very IJN tactic of surprise and entrapment.

It would be precisely this countertactic that would serve the Allied naval forces only too well in later battles at Cape Esperance and Tassafaronga, when the American navy would begin to stage its own series of surprise attacks on the ever-encroaching forces of the IJN with a greater and more measurable success. Clearly anticipating the Japanese ships' movements—coupled with a fair guess of just *where* they might be coming from and *when* they might arrive—much would now play directly into the hands of the Americans and their coalition navies. It might even be fairly stated that Guadalcanal, and the nightly surprise attacks orchestrated by the wily IJN in and around Savo, would be the last time the Americans would fall prey to such a tactic, and it would become increasingly difficult for the Japanese to fully exploit such to any real advantage in the coming months of war.

In fact, those same Americans would quickly become so practiced and so accomplished at exploiting such a deceptive ploy, that by June 1944 the tactic would even be used at the start of the Normandy invasion landings in the ETO (European Theater of Operations). In that latter scenario, the Allies would carry out perhaps one of the greatest deceptions of all time, feigning a move toward France's northern *Pas de Calais*, when in fact the actual targeted landing area had all along been the southernmost beaches of Normandy. This sly element of surprise, and the greater gambit of feinting to the north while attacking to the south, would now work only too well against the German defensive forces then guarding coastal France. In fact, it would be precisely this—the enemy's preoccupation with the Allies' anticipated move on Calais and not Normandy—that would soon shift Operation Bodyguard into a much higher gear and make Operation Neptune possible. On this point, consider Bates's own thoughts as presented here:

> Surprise must not be counted on too strongly in planning, although it should be considered as the soul of nearly every operation. There must be sufficient means available to insure [sic] success even though surprise may not be obtained. In considering surprise the enemy's intelligence potentialities [sic] should not be overlooked.

There are, of course, occasions when surprise may not (at all) be desired, as exampled in an intended deception operation where it is hoped to entice enemy forces into a definite area and away from another area.[215]

Such would indeed be the case on the beaches of Normandy later in the war, but for now—in at least a 1942 time frame in the Solomons—the Allies could only counter the effects of the IJN's oft-used element of surprise by fully anticipating those actions themselves, and by lying in wait for them in areas where they (the Americans) might least be expected to be. This must clearly have been the reasoning behind RADM Norman Scott's series of successful attacks on Gotō's fleet at the time of the Battle of Cape Esperance—and the even later naval encounter just off coastal Tassafaronga. The die had been cast anew for the American forces both through hardship and attrition, and the pendulum of war was now beginning to sway in favor of the Allied navies. The color of war had somehow changed, but perhaps even the Americans themselves did not know this for sure.

EARLY RADAR: A SHORT HORIZONAL VIEW

Background/Premise

For the early part of World War II, from 1941 and well into 1942—precisely up to the time of the First Battle of Savo Island—American radar technology would still have been both elemental and functionally primitive. In fact, the two specific types of radar that may have been in use by both of the Savo radar pickets *Blue* and the *Ralph Talbot*, at the time of their first major naval campaign in the Solomons, might indeed have been the SC and its close derivative SC-1 radar systems, both of which were long-range air radar detection platforms. From the outset, however, both would be met at best with mixed emotions, and among the men on the ships there was only a basic understanding of the systems' somewhat arcane workings, followed closely by a general reluctance to ever rely on their quirky functionality. Units broke down often, parts were scarce, arrays were sometimes unworkably "frozen" (or indeed not moving at all), and the radar's seek capability was itself often compromised because of the systems' inability to distinguish between actual targets and general landscape (ground and sea) clutter.

SC and SC-1 radar systems used an almost identical set of electronics, both fitted with a smaller antenna array that featured only a minor 6×2 spread of dipoles that might have only been some 15 feet tall and 5 feet wide, allowing the unit to provide a scan that could be focused out on a narrow horizontal beam only. This same SC-series array boasted only a 60 Hz range and was found to essentially be of better use on the smaller DD ships. SC-1, a variant of the earlier radar prototype, would marginally improve on the unit's overall reach factor but still left far too many gaps and blind spots in the unit's horizontal sweep.

Figure 48. Early U.S. Navy Radar Detection Systems: SC, SG, and CXAM (Circa 1942-1943)

Subsequently, the new "SG" surface search radar would soon become its own quantum leap forward from those earlier systems, and could easily work in a higher 775, 800, and even 825 Hz range, as needed. The system was also found to be more desirable to the men who had to use it—and by the commanders on whose ships they would later be deployed—but were still somewhat limited and could only see out to the near horizon. In a scenario where an advance warning of an enemy's approach was most critical—certainly during at least some of the earlier Solomon campaigns—the American navy knew it needed something that could see over that horizon and provide ample warning of that enemy's encroachment before they even got close. Regrettably, that new SG system would not be rolled out until October 1942, already some months after the battle at Savo, so clearly it might be expected that neither the *Blue* nor the *Ralph Talbot* would have carried this later-versioned screening radar. Indeed at Savo, later after-action reports filed by both American destroyers would seem to indicate that neither ship's radar appeared to work optimally, which might account for why all of Mikawa's CRUDIV forces were able to simply "sluice through the gap" created by the two American screening ships without the slightest detection by the SC radar units on either picket radar.

Lesson(s) Learned

Later CXAM radars would in fact be considered a vast improvement over its SC and SG predecessors, and it was soon found that it could also function quite effectively in a mid- to high range, with a VHF frequency band that could reach up to 200 MHz. CXAM was designed to replace the earlier Naval Research Laboratory's NRL (1937) and XAF (1938) systems, and even RCA's later CXZ system developed in 1939, and would now become a fusion melding both those XAF and CXZ technologies. It was therefore understandably a quite eager and enthusiastic U.S. Navy that would then order thirty such units be made and delivered in 1942. It would be the first production radar system deployed on multiple USN ships of the time, to include many of the "heavies" themselves, such as the CAs USS *Pensacola*, *Northampton*, and later even Bode's former command ship *Chicago*.

At Savo, however, before any such radar systems had even been installed, most skippers still far and away preferred to rely on their own tried-and-true fire control systems—systems they felt still capably (and routinely) provided them with not only accurate target azimuth data but elevation, range, and velocity as well—and that then fed the data directly into the ship's fire-control systems to quickly plot a dead-on firing solution out to that (or any) target.

Therefore, only by the later Battle of Cape Esperance—and the several other battles that would follow that conflict—far more destroyers, light and heavy cruisers, battleships, and carriers of the line would now be smartly arrayed with just such radar technology, a technology that would time and again detect, effectively neutralize, and confound IJN ship movements in and around Iron Bottom Sound. Now finally, the Allies would be more and more empowered to catch the sly and stealthy Japanese at bay, often before they even came into view over the short horizon. Now payback would indeed be a bitch, and it would soon be Japan's own time to squirm.

Technology had already begun to play its first and greatest role in the battle to reclaim (and hold) the Solomons, and would aid both the Americans and their Allies to forge ahead in their push north, as they feverishly sought to drive the Imperial Japanese Navy all the way back to their homeland ports. It was also the clear and certain intent of that Allied fleet to attack those forces there, in fact allowing them no safe haven from the growing storm of the dogged Americans' advance.

TRAINING AND EFFECTIVENESS OF LOOKOUTS

Background/Premise

Standing watch and wide awake, the masterful IJN ships' lookouts—on not just Mikawa's own flagship *Chōkai* but also Gotō's cruiser *Aoba* and their sister-ship *Kinugasa*—were all hand-picked men who were very well trained, its chosen cadre of petty officers made up of a group of shipboard sailors who would themselves be called simply the "Masters of the Lookout." These lookouts were probably the earliest of the "early-warning systems" of that time, at least for the IJN, and each would soon make good use of the new stanchion-based 20 cm binoculars—the deck-mounted version of which had far better optics than its American counterpart. And the new "Big Eyes" binocs would be used far more effectively by the seasoned IJN lookouts, each designed to provide both the gunnery and torp crews with even greater advantage to the deadly accurate ships of Mikawa's cruiser force.

The enhanced binoculars could see over far greater distances, and identify the potential threat of a horizonal ship within a far shorter period of time. The Japanese Masters of the Lookout were rotated in set, rested intervals and working in settled shifts, each man bearing no additional (major) shipboard duties other than that of their one task: Watch and keep a wary eye. See the enemy before he sees us. And so indeed they would do precisely that, in battle after battle, as the Japanese naval commanders sought to further exploit a deadly combination of not just stealth, speed, reconnaissance, and practiced night-fighting skills alone but, in great measure, also the alertness of the ships' own lookouts on which they each so critically depended.

Reportedly at a point in time occurring just before 0000 hours—itself but a changing-point witching hour that embraced neither dawn nor dusk—Mikawa's forces had already spotted the two American radar pickets *Blue* and *Ralph Talbot*, both nestled in their northernmost patrol quadrants well above Savo, and this without being detected themselves. On the *Blue*, now patrolling in calm seas on an otherwise moonless night, the commander of that ship, a lieutenant commander named Harold N. Williams, would later report that visibility out from his ship's vantage point was only about 8,000 yards; however, as later borne out by reports from others on the *Chōkai*—and second-in-column *Aoba*—visibility for the IJN ships was estimated to have been far greater and more in a range out to 11,000 yards. With near-certainty, it might be argued, then, that this 3,000-yard differential was due almost entirely to not just the "trained alertness" of the Japanese lookouts themselves but also the superior optics they used, with a proven ability to detect and identify enemy ships at far greater distances, and even at night. Thus, even with all manner of luck factors set aside, the advantage almost always seemed to ride with the Imperial Japanese Navy when it came to "seeing first without being seen."

This is but one example of the effectiveness and inherent advantage of being able to first spot the enemy before he sees you, and until the Americans and their Allied co-alition forces could learn the true value of this premise, they would remain susceptible to virtually all (and any) such surprise attacks in and around the Guadalcanal area by day, and simply everywhere else by night.

Lesson(s) Learned

The U.S. Navy's lack of due diligence and disciplined training vis-à-vis its own ship-based lookouts—like those that had been set to screen the far northern horizon for enemy ships—would now improve markedly both by day and by night. America's unwarranted reliance on technology must end, or at least cease to be the only means by which to detect an approach of (or intrusion by) any IJN warships into the Sound, as it had earlier proven to be both foolish and ill advised and would serve as only another contributing factor that would decidedly not work at all to the favor of the Allies.

Such a reliance on the technology of the day, such as the prototypical radar-equipped ships screening the waters north of Savo Island—in lieu of actual human assets that had in the past proven themselves invaluable through several naval operations in the Pacific, was probably just another key factor that would facilitate the attacks at

Savo, and probably one of the gravest errors the American and Allied fleets could have made. In fact, the point is sharply driven home in Bates's own reporting of the events of that time when he noted:

> Complete reliance should not be placed on technological devices. This is especially important when such devices have not been fully proven. And while such devices, when operating correctly, can give an unusual—and in some instances an almost insurmountable advantage to those who have them—they can also, when operated incorrectly, be seriously disadvantageous as they may entirely present a false impression as to the accuracy of their performance. It is of great importance, therefore, that commanders understand the full utility of both the capabilities and limitations of those technological devices, and that they make a provision, when practicable, for paralleling the more vital technological devices by other means.[216]

The Americans would soon take quick measures to rectify both problem areas with priority, as they now sought a twofold solution to the ever-present attack strategies used by the deceptive IJN forces. That twofold strategy was generally quite simple: ❶ work quickly to shore up the training and essential capabilities of its nightly lookout crews, and ❷ continue to fine-tune the technology of the radar systems themselves, on which they seemed to so heavily rely. Still in its prototypical infancy, however, the American radar systems were still "glitchy" and often unworkable in the hands of sailors who simply did not entirely understand their full workings and capabilities.

The Americans would simply need to go back to the basics of trained seamanship for the men who would be tasked with serving as those ships' lookouts. Radar technology would come apace in its own time, indeed just not quite yet, and until such time as it had been fully perfected, it simply swung the pendulum back to that of continuing to scan the far reaches of sky and sea from the bridge, the deck lookouts, and the trained human eye.

TRAINING AND EFFECTIVENESS OF NAVAL NIGHT FIGHTING

Background/Premise

For their highly effective, almost impeccable skills in the operational deployment of their seemingly unlimited fleet assets, the exacting battle tactics they used, and the scalable naval night attacks that the IJN had by now perfected (and that almost always resulted in quite excellent successes), the Imperial Japanese Navy must truly have stood alone during this period of time in 1942. Their proven ability to engage an enemy fleet in open-sea battle, preferably in a "post-midnight" time frame in dead of night, was both *notable* and well *noted* by the commanders of the Allied surface groups. Small wonder, then, that following immediately on the heels of the surprise attacks at Savo, the U.S. naval fleet would now become ever more vigilant and would retool itself, quickly adapting to—and even further exploiting—the very tactics that had been so effectively used against them by their wily adversary, the bold IJN.

Lesson(s) Learned

Set to good use almost immediately after the debacle at Savo, the Allied surface fleet would learn their hard lessons through a school of hard knocks and now began reversing the tide and springing their own traps on an unsuspecting IJN naval force in the many deep-water encounters that would follow, specifically that of the Battle of Cape Esperance and an even later encounter at Tassafaronga. And each minor victory, and each stepping-stone win, would soon become a measured success that sought to further fine-tune itself over time. The Americans would become quick learners and shortly turn the tables to their own advantage in many of the later battles that would unfold in and around Guadalcanal. Naval night fighting—rightly extended to further include both naval night gunnery and torpedo crew training cycles—would now take on a whole new dimension for the U.S. Navy and its Allies and finally be taken far more seriously than it had been at any other time in the past.

The Allied naval brass—from ADM Ghormley on down to the more localized theater commanders themselves, as seen in the personas of Admirals Fletcher, Turner, and Crutchley—would now more seriously embrace the concept of naval night training and see to it that each of the individual ships' commanders in their charge observed an even higher degree of alertness, especially during the daunting, trickster hours between twilight and dawn. Stepped-up training in night naval warfare would, at least for the Allies, come apace and enjoy a far greater priority. Training scenarios would be one thing, real-world actions quite another, and the U.S. Navy had by now had quite enough of being bested by a naval force they inherently considered to be far less superior to their own. It was simply time to buckle down and perfect new methodologies and new technologies if they were to survive the coming storm at Guadalcanal and beyond. In brief, the American navy simply needed a new plan, and a new prime directive, and thankfully in short order they would soon have both.

TRAINING AND EFFECTIVENESS OF NIGHT GUNNERY CREWS

Background/Premise

In Bates's exhaustive report of 1950 on the First Battle of Savo Island—as commissioned by the Naval War College[217]—the celebrated naval historian correctly summed up the essential differences between ADM Yamamoto's Imperial Japanese Navy and the U.S./Allied Navy's battle posturing at the time. And at its core, those key differences would almost always begin and end with the practiced and effective training of those Japanese ships and crewmen in naval night-fighting tactics. It would be precisely this training that would also allow that same IJN naval force to so successfully prosecute attack after attack, night after night, during the opening salvos in the battle for control of the Solomons—and this with an almost flawless, practiced execution throughout the latter half of 1942. To this end, Bates offers us at least this much:

> The difference in night gunnery performance between the Japanese cruisers and the Allied cruisers was SO marked as to show plainly what success can be achieved by correct training in night firing, and what disaster can result from a lack of such training, particularly when complicated by the effect of surprise.[218]

In his summation, Bates further calls to mind the sheer numbers and statistics that only too clearly seemed to point up the key differences (and core competencies) of both navies in being fully empowered to carry out just such a night naval engagement—on at least the occasion of the 1BOSI. And if indeed the estimates bear out even a *small* measure of truth, those numbers plainly would not lie. That the IJN gunnery crews packed a hell of a wallop and could provide a far more effective level of firepower—with much greater accuracy and far more time-on-target hits—was itself almost irrefutable, and soon enough might simply be a foregone conclusion, at least if the estimates borne out in the Table 44 calculations are even close to being true.

Of note, we also see other variant totals and breakdowns of those same IJN shell consumption figures, these based on the CAPT Toshikazu Ohmae accounting of all such shell expenditures[219] on the same night in question, as noted in Table 45.

Table 44.   1BOSI Night Gunnery Performances: IJN Shell Consumption (Bates Perspective)

Ship's Battery / Armament	IJN Ship(s)	Rounds Expenditure	Rounds Totals
8-inch	*Chōkai*	302	**1,014**
	Aoba	183	
	Kako	192	
	Kinugasa	85	
	Furutaka	152	
5.5-inch	*Tenryū*	80	**176**
	Yūbari	96	
5.0-inch	*Chōkai*	120	**120**
4.7-inch	*Aoba*	85	**534**
	Kako	130	
	Kinugasa	224	
	Furutaka	94	
3.0-inch	*Tenryū*	23	**23**
Total (in Rounds Expenditures):			**1,867**
Total (in Hits):			**159**

Table 45. 1BOSI Night Gunnery Performances: IJN Shell Consumption (Ohmae Perspective)

IJN Ship and Type	20cm Gun	14cm Gun	12cm Gun	8cm Gun	8cm AA Gun	25cm Gun	Torpedoes	Depth Charges	Casualties
Chōkai (CA)	308		120			500	8		34 killed 48 wounded
Aoba (CA)	182		86			150	13	6	
Kako (CA)	192		130			149	8		
Kinugasa (CA)	185		224				8	6	1 killed 1 wounded
Furutaka (CA)	153				94	147	8	6	
Tenryū (CL)		80		23			6	20	2 wounded
Yūbari (CL)		98					4		
Yūnagi (DD)			32				6	1	
Totals:	**1,020**	**176**	**592**	**23**	**94**	**946**	**61**	**39**	**35 killed 51 wounded**
				Aggregate Total of IJN Shells Expended:					**± 1,844**

Clearly, the numbers simply do not add up, or coincide in any way with the Bates estimate, which in and of itself, might be wholly attributed to both "perspective" and the often-exaggerated computations of the IJN to the aggrandizement of their own postured gains. Therefore, whether Bates has *under*estimated his calculated figures, or Ohmae has *over*estimated his own, we cannot be 100 percent certain, but one can easily note a major discrepancy between the 1,867 rounds expenditure figure in the Bates account and Ohmae's total of 2,951. Clearly, there might be no accounting for some 1,084 shells fired during the battle that were not reflected in the first Bates tally, and indeed one is left to wonder why.

In sharp contrast, note the correlated shell expenditure numbers for the American and Allied ships during this same time frame, as seen in this Table 46 recap, with an estimate of far fewer impactful hits (shown as an interrogatory "?" in the table) than its opposing IJN force. Could such a high degree of accuracy on the part of the IJN crews be directly attributed to the practiced night gunnery training exercises that the Japanese naval forces were known to have carried out with near regularity? Or were those numbers simply "juggled" and inflated by an often-self-promoting Imperial Japanese Navy to only feign superiority? In all probability, we may never know for certain.

To be sure, it must also be noted that only a few of the primary Allied warships that would later be involved in the skirmish at Savo would have been adequately trained in naval night-fighting tactics at all. Historically, both the heavy cruiser *Quincy* and her sister ship *Vincennes* had only recently been redeployed from the European Theater of Operations (ETO) and had just arrived in Pacific waters near Guadalcanal.

Table 46. 1BOSI Night Gunnery Performances: Allied Shell Consumption (Bates Perspective)

Ships' Battery/ Armament	IJN Ship(s)	Rounds Expenditure	Rounds Totals
8-Inch Main Batteries	Canberra	0	107
	Chicago	0	
	Vincennes	33	
	Quincy	21	
	Astoria	53	
5.0-Inch Secondary Batteries	Chicago	25	361
	Vincennes	20	
	Quincy	0	
	Astoria	59	
	Patterson	33	
	Ralph Talbot	12	
	Wilson	212	
4.0-Inch Secondary Batteries	Canberra	3	3
Totals (In Rounds Expenditures):			471
Totals (In Hits):			10 (?)

Therefore, neither of the two ships would have taken part (as yet) in any real joint Pacific maneuvers preceding their arrival.

Further, even during the time both cruisers had spent with that Atlantic fleet, neither ship had conducted any level of naval night-fighting training for at least the past eighteen months. Only *Astoria* had done so recently (if only marginally) in Pacific waters but may still not have been prepared for the skilled effectiveness of Mikawa's crack gunnery teams and torpedo crews of the IJN, and it was clearly no match for Japanese cruiser divisions at Savo. Similarly, within the Allied naval coalition itself, only the HMAS *Australia* had really carried out night training exercises as recently as May of that same 1942. Of course, all of this would soon change as time and opportunity would allow, but clearly the first responsibility for those Allied navies would have been that of ❶ protecting the troop transport and cargo ships that were then still offloading at Lunga and Tulagi, ❷ deterring the ever-present threat of nightly incursions by an ever more determined Japanese surface fleet, and ❸ nullifying the full element of surprise in which that enemy seemed to so much delight. With much on their collective plates, however, stepped-up training in naval night fighting might not have been the Allies' first (or even highest) priority, even if much still needed to be done in the coming months of war.

Lesson(s) Learned

The admiralty and high command in charge of naval operations in and around Guadalcanal could now more clearly see the urgent need for additional training in naval night fighting, both for themselves and for their Allies, that—though warranted—might not be so easily accommodated due to the immediacy of the tasks already at hand. Overwatching the deployment of troops at both Guadalcanal and Tulagi (as well as other locales), and the offloading of critically needed troops, munitions, and supplies for Vandegrift's 1st Marine Division, must certainly have been the prime focus for all of the navy ships that had been tasked with specifically guarding those very activities. Had the Allied naval elements in play at the time been afforded any leisure to carry out any such "on-the-fly" training they would have done so, but in the face of the daytime attacks, and the nightly harassment raids that came in the form of Mikawa's stealthy cruisers, the combined navies truly had all they could do to simply carry out that specific task.

This would nonetheless continue to be a matter of some grave concern not just for the COMSOPAC himself (Ghormley) but also for Fletcher as COMSOWESPAC, and Turner as COMPHIBFORSOWESPAC, as certainly some measures must be taken to quickly ensure a heightened awareness—and a greater degree of combat flexibility—that would then allow those forces to do battle both during daylight hours and at night. To precisely this end, historian Richard Bates would later observe the following on the "practiced efficiency" of the IJN's night gunnery crews:

> Gunnery effectiveness in war stems not only from frequent battle experience, with its resulting improved fire disciplines, but also from intensive training in day and night

gunnery exercises in the combat areas as well as in [otherwise] rear areas. It is only by such continuous training that units can be kept ready for battle. Type commanders, task force and group commanders, and commanding officers [themselves] are responsible for insuring that their commands are trained as necessary to maintain this specific combat efficiency.[220]

Such an observation was already assumed to have been made even at the time of the battle at Savo—or certainly at least in the wake of that battle—but must have been little more than a foregone conclusion, as any such night-fighting training would probably have been undertaken only if and when it was expedient to do so. Savo was that rude wake-up call, that harsh slap in the face and brutal kick in the pants that would only too clearly drive its point home—to wake up and get in the game. The Americans and Australians would soon be on a slow road to recovery, however, and both would only intensify their night-fighting training exercises to sharpen their skills, such that in actual battle they might more capably defend themselves and make every shot count in their many later encounters with the cunning IJN.

FLEET COMMUNICATIONS

Background/Premise

Fleet communications between the American and Allied fleets, at least at the time of the first attack at Savo, might arguably have been only middling to poor at best. From the opening run of Mikawa's cruiser fleet from points north in Kavieng and Rabaul to the distant detection of that force by the American attack submarine USS *S-38* in the St. George's Channel (who did in fact spot the IJN cruiser division but was slow in reporting the finding), to the three RAAFR Hudson reconnaissance planes that likewise would note the IJN fleet's presence but would also be slow to report that discovery, to an overflight of B-17s from Espiritu Santo that would again spot that same surface fleet near the large island of Choiseul, it was already quite apparent that there might still be some troubling issues found with the existing communication protocols in place between the Allied surface ships and between the very air and naval assets that they were to put in play in and around Guadalcanal.

Seemingly countless were the number of SNAFUs and "problem-injected moments" that seemed to find the Americans and their Australian counterparts only too often bungling simple communiqués from air to ground or ground to air—or even simply ship to ship. Worse yet were the critical "omissions" and outright failures to even attempt to report a sighting imprimis, the failure of which would almost always be catastrophic. It would in fact be precisely this one quintessential failure—that of effectively communicating (in a timely manner) the intel reports that each of these reconnaissance units knew they should send forward to the high command at Guadalcanal—at precisely the moment they had it in hand. This situation would later cause immeasurable harm and grave damage to those same Allied ships of the Southern and Northern screens that would themselves become the targets of that enemy's attack.

In fact, perhaps both attacks might have been wholly prevented. Yet, oddly, this same scenario would occur but a month later during both the hot Battle of the Eastern Solomons (in late August of 1942) and the even later Battle of the Santa Cruz Islands in October of the same year, when the issue of communications on the part of the Americans (or lack thereof) would again play a critical role in the outcome of both battles, as observed by author Jack Coombe when even he flatly observed that "once again, poor communications would hamper U.S. Air operations,"[221] and which again would entirely affect the outcome of both later naval encounters.

The information matrix shown in Table 47 depicts only a few of the known instances of miscommunication and/or *no* communication at all, and it clearly continued to dog the heels of the surface fleets of both the Americans and their Allies then operating in the region.

Lesson(s) Learned

The American and Allied naval powers in the region now sought only to strengthen and more carefully unify the diffuse (and often speckled) bands of communication protocols already in place within the operational areas in and around Guadalcanal, but swallowing the bitter pill that might offer the cure did not seem to be working to any advantage of the Allies. Of two CAs and two DDs that had, on the night of the Savo attack itself, made up the *Chicago* group—and the three CAs and two DDs of Riefkohl's own *Vincennes* battle group far to the north—only one ship, the *Bagley*-class *Patterson*, even attempted to sound the alarm, as the small destroyer immediately set about the business of reporting her contact with Mikawa's ships both by TBS and by open-network radio.

In addition, *Patterson* augmented its broadcasts by using an alternate "visual" means of reporting the sighting, such as the ship's blinkers, to report on both the initial attacks and the ensuing battle developments unfolding immediately after. *Patterson* would have had just enough time to get off her first series of messages to her charge ships before she herself would be hit by several 5- and 8-inch shells fired from Mikawa's now-withdrawing cruisers and was immediately compelled to evade the even deadlier long-range Long-Lance torpedoes being fired at her by those same IJN warships. Indeed, it would only be *Patterson*'s gritty and well-disciplined gunners that would hold her out to a deadly defense of the larger CAs that would save her, as she zigzagged a jagged course to throw the attacking enemy ships off her trail.

The dastardly truth and hard lessons learned by the Allies as a result of the battle at Savo would now hinge on a key understanding of the importance of clear and effective communications between *all* of the participants in that multi-national naval coalition—that same coalition that had by now already grown to include the United States, the United Kingdom, Australia, and now even New Zealand. It was no longer

Table 47. Communications Issues: Actions, Decisions, and Impacts

COMMUNICATION OPPORTUNITY: ACTIVITY	STATUS OF COMMUNICATION (OR LACK OF): RESULT
	LEGEND: C = Communication / LOC = Lack Of Communication
Fletcher Withdraws CTF 61 from *Iron Bottom Sound*	Fletcher's sudden and unexpected decision to remove his CTF-61 air and naval assets from the Guadalcanal area would later have a major impact on operations in the vicinity. The carrier force withdrawal—due in great measure to the admiral's concern over IJN long-range bombers and torpedo attack planes, fuel shortages for his task force, and a need to effect at least minor ship repairs from damages sustained in the previous day's battles—all caused him to make the fatal decision to reposition his fleet.
	C OR LOC Result: Little or no air cover is provided to ❶ effectively screen Turner's amphibious landings at both Lunga and Tulagi; ❷ support the entrenched assault forces of Vandegrift's own First Marine Division, just then landing on Guadalcanal, Tulagi, and far Kolombangara; or even ❸ assist Crutchley's own scant number of screening ships set to patrol the *Sound* that night.
	Fletcher's decision to remove that CTF force was not made clear to many of the key area commanders until only well after the fact. It would later also become the most pivotal reason that would compel ADM Turner to convene his late-night conference aboard the USS *McCawley*. Fletcher's action would soon then also go on to engender the all-too-familiar (and not-soon-forgotten) sentiment that would soon be recorded to history as the "Great Navy Bugout"—the result of which would bring about a deep and unrelenting enmity and feeling of mistrust between the two armed services (the Navy and the Marines) for some many years yet to come.
American Attack Submarine USS *S-38*	The American attack submarine USS *S-38* also spots the southbound cruiser divisions led by Mikawa as far up-channel as the convergence of the St. George's Channel into the passageway known as the *Slot*. The boat's commander, one CAPT Munson, does in fact dutifully report the sighting but has difficulty routing the message through his own "regional" COMSUBDIV5 command echelon, to have that intel relayed to the admiralty awaiting its arrival in Guadalcanal. In due course, the information would in fact stagger in from COMSUBDIV5 but would arrive only much later, effectively rendering those data as utterly useless, as only "stale" intel.
	C OR LOC Result: Communication was thwarted, delayed, and received far too late for area commanders at Guadalcanal to find it at all useful or even "actionable."

Espiritu Santo B-17 Overflight	A CTF-assigned squadron of B-17s out of Espiritu Santo spot the approaching Mikawa fleet near the island port city of Kieta and advise their base of a sighting of "four cruisers and a destroyer headed westward at 1231."

C or LOC Result: The B-17s communications are delayed and not received until much later, and once again the failure to quickly forward that sighting intel in a timely manner to the high command south of Savo would be yet another causal factor and keen example of the appalling lack of (any viable) communication link between ADMs Fletcher, Turner, Crutchley, and McCain—and the other individual force commanders operating in and around Guadalcanal at that time. |
| **McCain's Failure to Conduct Air Searches** | Turner requests that RADM McCain—in his role as COMNAVAIRSOPACFLT—conduct extended (and far more reaching) air searches of the Guadalcanal operational area and even north to points beyond Savo Island itself. McCain in fact does *not* carry out the order and instead further compounds his contumacy with a non-communication of that fact to his superior, by failing to inform that commander that the order had not been carried out and that the extra reconnaissance flights had not been accommodated as ordered by Turner.

C or LOC Result: Communication was not readily forthcoming from McCain to Turner, causing the superior officer to falsely operate under the unsound assumption that the task had in fact been carried out, and that all air and shipping lanes leading into the transport areas at Guadalcanal had indeed been screened and cleared. Believing the task done in fact, Crutchley and Turner would continue with their amphibious landing duties, only to later be made extremely vulnerable to attack by Mikawa's now quickly advancing attack column that was even then just coming out of the Slot. |

(continued)

Table 47. *Continued*

COMMUNICATION OPPORTUNITY: Activity	STATUS OF COMMUNICATION (OR LACK OF): Result
	LEGEND: *C = Communication / LOC = Lack Of Communication*
Crutchley Leaves Southern Screening Force (SSF) for Turner's Conference Aboard the USS McCawley	RADM Crutchley departs the Southern screening area late on the evening of 8 August and leaves CAPT Bode in command pro tempore, in what was thought to be but a brief absence to attend the "Turner Conference" aboard the APA *McCawley*. In so doing, Crutchley would foolishly take his entire ship, the heavy cruiser *Australia*, with him, in lieu of the ship's simple launch or admiral's barge.
	C OR LOC Result: Crutchley would do so effectively without informing the task group commanders of the Northern, Southern, or Eastern screens of that intended action, and in fact left Bode in command with no clear operational mandate in hand. When the action began shortly after 0138 hours, a bewildered Bode did not know how to assume command of that task group, and in truth, left his own screening force mid-battle and moved off on a forty-minute trek to the northwest in pursuit of an alleged "phantom" contact. He would further do so without informing any of his own peer commanders of that departure, thereby leaving the already stricken *Canberra, Bagley,* and *Patterson* open to attack by Mikawa's now-encroaching ships. This level of negligence and lack of communication would become one of the cornerstone accusations that would later be hurled at Bode and the even later basis of an in-depth investigation into the captain of *Chicago's* own actions on the occasion of that one battle. Bode would later only escape indictment and imminent prosecution by ADM Arthur Japy Hepburn, and his intended special courts-martial, by the sudden taking of his own life in Panama in April 1943.
Crutchley Remains at X-Ray Staging Area Overnight	Crutchley, not wishing to navigate dangerous and unfamiliar waters during the night hours of 8 August, opts to *remain* at anchorage in the vicinity of the *X-Ray* transport area near Turner's flagship *McCawley*, the site of the previous late-evening conference. He again decides to do so without appropriately informing his subordinate Bode—or any of his other force commanders—of his decision to do so. Crutchley would also later be heavily questioned on this matter in the aftermath of Savo but would suffer no significant rebuke for his actions.

	C or LOC Result: A full lack of communication surrounding Crutchley's intent to remain at the *X-Ray* transport area effectively left Bode with the idea that the commander might in fact still be returning shortly; however, Bode had no way of knowing if he had already done so, or if he had in fact even moved his flagship back to station to rejoin that Southern screening group. Again, the sad result of this lack of communication was that Crutchley's removal of his own CA *Australia* essentially left that Southern screening force "one ship down," leaving that group with that much less punch and firepower with which to then oppose the interloping IJN surface fleet. Doing away with the *Canberra*, and badly damaging Bode's own *Chicago*, was perhaps made only that much easier by the non-presence of Crutchley's one additional ship, the heavy cruiser *Australia*.
The Mystery of the *Helm*	The *Bagley*-class destroyer USS *Helm* (DD-388) was one of two DDs escorting the small American cruiser force on routine box-like patrol pattern within the northern area of the Solomons at the time of the 1BOSI (First Battle of Savo Island). VADM Mikawa had just fully prosecuted his carefully orchestrated attack on Crutchley's Southern fleet, then swung about to turn his full attention to the north to Riefkohl's own *Vincennes* group.

By 0152, just at the time of the attack on his Northern screening force after some delay, operational orders were finally issued by Riefkohl to the two flanking DDs that then ordered them to immediately engage the attacking IJN force with torpedo spreads that would then be laid out from the port side of the column and out to those enemy ships, but did not provide any bearing data on those ships. Even without such data, both *Helm* and *Wilson* still dutifully moved off in an attempt to engage those enemy ships, and to plot effective firing solutions for each of their torpedo runs, but in fact both ships were for the most part only firing in the blind with only negligible impact on that enemy fleet.

Without communicating her next move to the *Vincennes* or any of the other ships in the area at the time, *Helm* would continue on an erratic bearing of 102° (T) at a distance of some 10,500 yards from dead center of Savo Island. The DD then proceeded north for the next two minutes before turning back toward Savo at about 0154. Meanwhile, Mikawa's cruiser divisions were now moving at a clipped speed of 15 knots (up from 10 knots), to a point SE of *Helm*'s position, even as the American DD continued moving at best speed back toward Savo. That "point" was in fact a predetermined reassembly area that had earlier been set by Crutchley as a "destroyer rendezvous point" that would be used in the event any of the escorting DDs became separated from their flotilla groups. That rendezvous point was just to the north and west of volcanic Savo, at an approximated 159°42' E–9°08' S; as a result, *Helm* would only sit at that location and see no further action in the battle. |

(continued)

Table 47. *Continued*

COMMUNICATION OPPORTUNITY: ACTIVITY	STATUS OF COMMUNICATION (OR LACK OF): RESULT
	LEGEND: *C = Communication / LOC = Lack Of Communication*
The "Coastwatchers"	"Coastwatchers" themselves were the daring operatives, the clandestine outpost watchers, and the ever-vigilant lookouts who, on many occasions, were the very "eyes and ears" of the Allied forces—and were often employed by local Australians who used their keen first-line spotting skills to best advantage. Perched high on hilltops on remote island locations throughout the Channel— each with a commanding view of most of the shipping lanes past Choiseul and on down the *Slot*— these Coastwatchers regularly reported on any large (or otherwise suspicious) Japanese shipping activity (and/or air incursions) passing through the Channel en route to points south. On at least two occasions, however, Coastwatchers Jack Read and Paul Mason were known to provide widely discrepant accounts of the *same* sighting event, even as each presented their own version of the same sighting, engendering a level of confusion for the Allies far below who were planning a defense of that same Guadalcanal area.

C OR LOC RESULT: Reliance on (or unvetted use of) inherently unverifiable data from an unknown third or fourth-party source later proved impactful to the screening forces operating in Iron Bottom Sound and in and around Guadalcanal, leading up to the night battle at Savo. Differing *strength* and *type* sighting reports such as these would only too often crop up—more as an unwanted confusion than actual assistance—especially in a scenario where the number and types of such ships would so critically vary between multiple Coastwatcher reports.

This aside, the orchestrated activities of those very Coastwatchers were more often quite helpful to the Allied commanders and would seldom have been turned away as not being reliable. They were, in fact, our very "eyes in the hills." |

TBS Overload: "Jamming the Waves"	In its final analysis, perhaps the degree to which all (or any) of the above communication and IFF issues might have played any kind of significant role in the unfortunate events leading up to Savo itself, might have been negligible and worth only small view when compared to the sideband jamming activity that was going on from ship to ship on the American side—this just at the height of the attack. *Patterson* had been struggling desperately to both engage the enemy and simultaneously get her message out to the fleet elements around her current position, but could not initially do so due to the overwhelming amount of general "chatter" across the TBS ("Talk Between Ships") comm system.
	With virtually every deck and every room, of every ship, constantly reporting and updating statuses while also receiving orders; and every commander on every ship now also hearing the dire *sitreps* for each of their own ships—some indeed still under attack at that very moment—to their own next-level commands as well, comm lines were only too quickly bogged down to almost zero capacity. And all of it had literally flooded the airwaves in seconds, seemingly all at once; each call seeking orders and instruction, or perhaps just assistance—from the many trapped and perishing souls now looking for any quick-fix answer to their most immediate of needs—*survival* in the face of the blistering IJN attack even then under way.
	C or LOC Result: In all events, so significant were the TBS overuse problems, during at least the early-on attacks at Savo, and so significant had it later been to the *Patterson* to even get her warnings out, that new recommendations were soon forthcoming that would now restrict ships' use of that TBS comm system to report on the "day-to-day" minutiae and routine "chatter" that might otherwise be inappropriate (and even unnecessary) in the actual heat of battle. Fletcher and Turner's new mandates would now clearly sweep the decks clean and bar the unsanctioned use of the TBS for "petty or only minor communications," which might then preempt its greater use when most needed for emergencies purposes.

sufficient to simply have an equal or superior naval force in a state of readiness, if that command was widely diffused and further compromised in its ability to communicate with those forces for control, area security, and deployment of the group's joint assets—and this at precisely a time when perhaps most needed during that (or any) naval night engagement.

Quickly now would newer and heftier measures be taken and bold new initiatives laid out that would be crafted for consideration by all—and all springing up from the drawing boards of a distraught USN department now doggedly shadowed by a mantle of mild disfavor as it struggled to understand just what had happened—and what precisely had gone wrong at Savo. It would take that naval high command weeks, perhaps even months, to even begin to unravel the very puzzling questions that centered heavily on the deadly events at Savo. In addition, stricter and far more carefully disciplined radio and TBS communication protocols would now be set in place between ships, as noted in this commentary extracted from Franks's Battle Experience Information Bulletin of 1942:[222]

> Regarding the failure of the TBS report [of *Patterson*'s contact with the enemy] getting through, comments indicate that there was a tendency to use such a convenient and rapid means of communication for "purely" "routine" matters instead of reserving it for strict emergencies. Therefore, while it is being used for such routine matters, it cannot be used for emergencies; and apparently the loudspeaker on the bridge served only to distract people's attention from other more weighty matters on that occasion. It might therefore have been more of a hindrance than a help.[223]

Perhaps adding only more fuel to the fire, the Bulletin continued to even more carefully fine-tune its point, observing that the excessive (and often unauthorized) use of that Talk Between Ships (TBS) broadcast system might have further engendered any (or all) of the following problem scenarios:

❶ Facilitate an overall poor degree of discipline due to an overall lack of communicative clarity.

❷ Cause possible undue circuit overload situations that might then render entire networks inoperable, or otherwise inaccessible, due to the unsanctioned use of same for simple ship-to-ship "chatter."

❸ Exacerbate an already heightened level of confusion both for the commanders, and for the combatants involved, precisely at a time when clarity is most needed.

❹ Cause any number of serious disjoins and disruption of the otherwise precisely timed tactical operations already in play in and around Guadalcanal.

❺ Create an inadvertent opportunity within which the enemy might more fully exploit a misstep, a known or simply found weakness within the system, that might then allow them to glean critical operational intel otherwise broadcast "in the open."

❻ Create an even secondary opportunity for that same enemy—now in possession of that intel—to plan a counteracting or deceptive ploy of their own.

❼ Actions, such as those involving the misuse of localized comm systems, might also be expected to clearly reflect unfavorably on the individual ships' commanders themselves, the very seat of naval power that should otherwise be empowered to curb precisely that kind of activity.

SHIPS IN THE NIGHT: IDENTIFICATION FRIEND OR FOE

Background/Premise

During the course of the battle at Savo, there had indeed been multiple reported instances of near (and, unfortunately, some very *real*) encounters between ships of the Allied force, as they sought to maneuver about to best advantage during the opening salvos of that encounter. In a post-0130 time frame, in dead of night and the sparking heat of battle, the *Astoria* and the *Quincy*, the *Bagley* and the Australian *Canberra*, Bode's own *Chicago*, and again that same *Canberra*—and even the escort DD *Patterson* itself—would each endure near-fatal encounters with one another at various intervals during the heated exchange. But were these actual Identification Friend or Foe (IFF) issues or simply random isolated acts of ships caught up in battle under the very worst of fighting conditions: under severe and concentrated fire, at night . . . at sea . . . and in the rain?

Several known encounters involving just such IFF issues seemed to rear their ugly heads again and again to further plague the Allied navies at Guadalcanal and to wreak a certain havoc that would itself end up as one of the very worst of incidents— this time between the enemy-pursuing American DD *Bagley* and the ill-fated Australian *Canberra*, the latter under the able command of CAPT Frank Edmond Getting. At some point after 0143 hours on the morning of 9 August, *Canberra*—already hit by numerous 8-inch shells fired from both the IJN *Chōkai* and the *Kinugasa*, and again during the joined attacks of both the *Aoba* and the *Kako*—would shudder and stagger to a slowed halt with a 5°–10° starboard list and was no longer able to move under her own power. In the span of three minutes, the proud Australian cruiser had already suffered some twenty-four hits, including a single torpedo strike to her starboard side.

Here the greatest point of contention surrounding this single event was the fact that since all of the attacking Japanese cruisers were situated to her port side, the single bow shot to *Canberra*'s starboard forequarter might actually have come from the *Bagley* itself—that same *Bagley* who—in her own haste to respond to the attack and to protect the cruisers in her charge—had just loosed a spread of torpedoes that were aimed at those same enemy ships. In the hot frenzy of battle, on the very shank of night in early August, was this in fact an instance of "failed" IFF, or simply a poorly aimed and poorly timed shot fired from ship to ship, and sadly even from friendly to friendly?

Lesson(s) Learned

An always problematic sticking-point during the First Battle of Savo Island, and the "newer" strategy sessions that would later be taken up in the wake of Savo, commanders were now understandably hard-pressed to make rapid life-and-death decisions "on the fly" and especially while engaged in any such deadly, transient open-sea battles.

It might therefore be these same commanders who would in fact be damned if they *did* check fire—in a scenario where the other ship is the enemy—and damned if they *didn't* and the other ship was in fact a "friendly." As a result, such a thought might place a tremendous (and undue) burden on the ships' commanders while also continuing to place them in a serious situational quandary—to either hold or open fire—this even as precious seconds ticked by in a deadly pitched battle at night. A poor showing of a ship commander's action/reaction response time to any such scenario could easily mean the difference between vanquishment and survival, victory and defeat—or perhaps even between life and death itself. The Allied naval high command badly needed a bold assurance that such a battlefield tragedy would not happen again, and to a man each concluded that there must simply never be another Savo.

After the terrible losses suffered during the thirty-one-minute melee on the night of 9 August, both Admirals Fletcher and Turner knew that something must be done to offset the number of near-misses (and several resulting in dead-on hits on their own ships) that had in fact occurred with at least two of the Allied coalition naval ships operating in and around the Sound that night. The post-Savo warships that now filled the ranks of the Allied surface fleet set to replace those just lost in battle became the aggregate stand-ins in a revitalized and newly refitted U.S. Navy, as soon word came down to individual ship captains instructing them to more carefully clear and verify all targets about to be engaged before doing so in earnest. Watch your target, and be damned sure of what you hit. The battle at Savo had been costly, in both lives and in capital ships, and had witnessed as many deadly incidents of friendly fire and IFF misidentification as any blue-water naval contingent might ever wish to see or experience. It was now quite evident that a clearer and more optimal solution must be found . . . and that much sooner than later.

FIRE DAMAGE

Storage of Deckside Flammables

Background/Premise

From the fiery impact of the first Long-Lance torpedoes jettisoned off the decks of Mikawa's flagship *Chōkai* and Gotō's own second-in-column *Aoba*, the Allied surface fleet truly had not a chance, either in advancing their own offensives against the attacking IJN force or in defending the very positions they so tenuously held, with even that being but for the moment. It is already generally agreed that the American DD *Patterson* might indeed have been the first ship of that Southern screening force to be spotted and engaged by Mikawa's advancing column during the early morning hours of 9 August, and on which several of their ships quickly opened fire in hot sequence. Almost as quickly, however, that same IJN cruiser force broke off its attack on the *Patterson* and instead swung its full-force attention (and follow-on salvos) onto the larger, heavy cruisers that were then maneuvering nearby. Those ships were, of course, the Australian CA *Canberra* and the American *Chicago*—both from Admiral Crutchley's own Southern screening element—with the Japanese only much later revealing that they had actually mistaken both American warships for "small battleships" and had thus coordinated their harsh attack strategies based on that false assumption.

That aside, the two Allied ships would soon be rocked unmercifully by the tandem, twin-axial attacks from at least four of Mikawa's heavily gunned cruisers, all now firing independently at them—and almost at once—raining down blow on blow of high-caliber shells on the fully illuminated targets that unavoidably gave them away with the blazing backdrop of their own burning hulks in situ. In dead of night, the ships' fires soon cast deep and ghastly silhouettes on each of the Allied heavy cruisers and seemingly set a curious dancing interplay of shadow and light on each. It was also a light that now made it that much easier for the enemy's gun batteries to fix a sighting on, seek a range out to, and soon visit a deadly rate of fire on those same "sitting-duck" cruisers—now almost at a measured leisure—so in control of the attack seemed the Japanese that night.

Then, only minutes later, at a tick of the clock past 0144, the unsuspecting ships of Riefkohl's own Northern screen would also fall prey to a heavy and sustained fire from Mikawa's ships, in a secondary surprise attack by that same force. In short order, the American "heavies" *Vincennes*, *Quincy*, and *Astoria* were savagely set on by a two- (or even three-) pronged assault column that was spearheaded by Mikawa's northward-moving fleet. The hot and determined charge of the two columns of Japanese cruisers would be led, on the one hand, by Mikawa's own *Chōkai* and, on the other, by Gotō's secondary flagship *Aoba*, while yet another assault column had inadvertently formed up behind a "course-straying" *Tenryū* and *Yubari*. Soon, all three of the targeted American Northern force ships had been effectively bracketed and torpedoed and then pummeled unmercifully with a killing barrage of some 175 shells.[224]

Caught completely off-guard, the American warships immediately burst into flames, against which lighted backdrop those same ships became mere free-for-all targets in a shooting match in which they simply had no place to hide. Within a span of mere minutes, two of the three American screening ships had already been routed, left entirely ablaze and already sinking. But within both screening groups, what did they all have in common that had so drastically ensured their mutual undoing? Why did so many of the ships (in both groups) simply go up like a tinderbox of combustibles held near open flame—which indeed they were—and that then led to the oil-fed fires that consumed those ships once struck by any of the incoming IJN torpedoes and high-explosive rounds?

In almost all events, it was probably indeed due to the deadly admixture of chemicals, aviation fuel, and deckside flammables; the ordered stacks of high-caliber live rounds (for both the 5-inch and the 8-inch guns); and the concentrations of other service-ready ammunition being stored on deck that would most account for the conflagration mishaps. Much of this ammo had been ill-advisedly stored right at (or nearby) the very batteries and gun turrets they would be called on to service once in battle. As a result, countless were the number of secondary, tertiary, and even later explosions that would themselves bring about perhaps the worst damage of all to the Allied screening ships—which by now had already been hammered heavily topside and torpedoed belowdecks—with many of those hits breaching just below some of the ships' waterlines.

Clearly, the most telling effects of the uncontrolled fires that would only too quickly besiege the Allied ships, however, would only later be analyzed in greater detail, as noted in this extract from the U.S. Navy's Chief of the Bureau of Ships Assessment Report (CBSAR), dated 2 September 1943, that would come more than a year after the attacks at Savo:

> Smoke and glare rendered directors, range finders and [other] spotting instruments useless even when personnel were physically capable of remaining at their stations. On all three ships, these fires were fed by topside paint, life jackets, signal flags, airplanes, airplane spare [parts], wings, parachutes, ships' boats, lubricating oil and kerosene; [all of] which made the area between the bridge and the after hangar an inferno beyond human endurance.[225]

And what of the taut findings of that same report that would not stop there, and that would in fact be found elsewhere in other assessments of the dire conditions aboard the similarly stricken *Astoria*?

> Fires, particularly the one in the wardroom area, were the direct cause of the loss of *ASTORIA*. Excess equipment, paint on bulkheads, records and so forth in officers' spaces—and in ship's offices—provided fuel for a fire which gradually worked downward exploding ammunition in the 5" hoists. From there the heat of the fire eventually reached and exploded the unflooded 5" magazines. This [action alone] blew a hole in the ship's side below the waterline and she began to rapidly take on water.[226]

Or again, as a sad continuum of that same report's observation of *Quincy*'s own comparable damage assessment:

> Numerous hits on the [*Quincy*'s] main and second deck amidships started fires which soon resulted in the ship becoming a blazing inferno from turret II to the aft bulk-

head of the hangar. Nearly all of the fire main risers were cut by either direct hits or fragments. This rendered the ship incapable of fighting the fires except by a few CO_2 extinguishers which were all too soon exhausted.[227]

These same reports would not exclude any mention of the damage suffered by Riefkohl's own *Vincennes* during that same battle, as noted here as well:

> Besides the damage suffered by gunfire, it appears as though one [or possibly *two*] torpedoes struck the port side of *VINCENNES*. One torpedo probably struck under the sick bay in way of the lower handling room near the number II turret, around frame 38. The deck in sick bay was reported ruptured and blown upward. This torpedo hit probably resulted in the flooding of all magazines on the second platform deck, between frames 30 and 45, and the crew's space . . . resulting in a series of horrendous fires.[228]

So, what indeed might be said of these deckside flammables that were stored so indiscriminately aboard each of these American heavy cruisers?

Damage Control Responsiveness and Training

Background/Premise

In almost every event, fires—and the techniques used to combat those fires—would later define just who might survive and who might not, which ships might indeed remain salvageable and which might later need to be scuttled as a result of the harsh night attacks of 9 August. Emergency response team training aboard all of the affected ships of the time had been intensive and was crucial to each ship, the drills for which were almost always sternly mandated. The response teams still able to mobilize their recovery units would have set virtually every able-bodied seaman available to combat the resulting ships' fires, and it should indeed be these men who should, in the end, be commended for their actions, as team after team aboard the Australian *Canberra* and the American *Chicago, Astoria, Quincy, Vincennes, Patterson*, and even the slowly exiting *Jarvis* herself, would all have valiantly battled the raging fires that threatened to get out of control on each of their respective ships. At all times, the teams would have had their hands full, working feverishly into the night to save their ships, as indeed it is already known that the men on at least the *Canberra, Astoria*, and *Jarvis* were the only reason why those ships were not immediately lost to the ravages of the battle that night.

Of Crutchley's original *Australia* screening group, *Canberra* would continue with her own shipboard battles as well, her crew desperately seeking to fight the damaging fires for some time after the initial attacks, thought to have occurred at about 0145 hours. She would later be aided by a quick-responding *Patterson*, who would pull alongside her to assist in any offloads. *Canberra*'s death knell would later be rung at about 0630 hours on the following morning by Admiral Turner himself, who—concerned that the stricken heavy cruiser would not be able to keep up with the other withdrawing ships at the time—would order her scuttled and sunk by the combined fire of the DDs *Ellet* and *Selfridge*.

Likewise, CAPT Greenman's own *Astoria* would survive the night's action, again due in great measure to the uncompromising efforts of her firefighting crews, who defiantly fought a pitched battle around the clock to stem the dangerous spread of fires aboard that ship, this even as "bucket brigades" of men reportedly battled blazes on the gun deck and starboard passages[229] of that cruiser, but sadly to no avail. Overwhelmed by the extent of damage and the still-raging infernos aboard the ship from the number of flammables stowed above and below decks, and within their holds, each was essentially a powder keg just waiting to blow. From the excessive layers of lead-based paint on the ships' bulkheads to the amount of upholstery, linoleum, and wood trimmings fashioned on many of those same ships, each was a ticking time bomb just waiting to go off. Therefore, in spite of the combined efforts of the assisting DDs *Bagley*, *Hopkins*, and *Wilson*—each in short order arriving on scene to assist the sinking CA—the *Astoria* itself could not be saved, and by 1216 on the morning of the same day, she too would be ordered sunk by Turner, who soon dispatched the *Buchanan* to see that grim and final task carried out.

The scrappy *Jarvis*, however—the bold escort destroyer that had been badly damaged as she interposed herself during the earlier attacks of 7 August between several IJN torpedo-bombers and their intended target, the much larger CA *Vincennes*, and would herself suffer a massive hit from a single Long-Lance torpedo that would impact near her forward fireroom—would not fare much better than the other ships that had also been attacked.

Now with a gaping 50-foot hole in the *Jarvis's* side, the crew stood fast and valiantly fought the raging fires that were even then scorching her decks, successfully quelling those fires, to the extent that the DD might actually remain seaworthy enough to undertake her fateful southwest journey to Sydney for repairs. It would only be much later, during her trek on the afternoon of 9 August, that she would be attacked a second time by a sortie of some thirty-one IJN attack planes that had been dispatched from the Japanese airbase at Rabaul. She would in fact be sunk on that occasion and lost in the vast deep of the East Solomon Sea. She would go down at about 1300 hours that same day, yet her fire teams had performed their duties brilliantly as they sought to battle the ship's fires, even gaining somewhat of an upper hand, if only for a while—only to lose all in the wake of that unchecked secondary attack.

Lesson(s) Learned

The finding of the Bates report prepared for the NWC in 1950 states clearly that "damage control is the responsibility of all hands,"[230] which would indeed have held true, at least for the men on the ships of Crutchley's screening forces who were even then patrolling the Sound on the night of 9 August. Speaking precisely to the matter, Bates goes on to tell us:

> War experience has shown that inexperienced, untrained, personnel are prone to attach exaggerated importance to flooding following an explosion and to become unduly alarmed; to give undue weight to fires which can often be quickly brought under control; to be unduly concerned by a heavy list and to thereby become fearful of the danger of capsizing, which danger often does not, at the moment, exist; and to abandon ship before it is necessary to do so. War experience has also shown that in many cases ships which appeared to have been damaged beyond saving were often saved because the personnel had been well trained and put forth the same determined efforts towards saving the damaged ship that they exerted in fighting her.[231]

In even greater support of this theory, a later in-depth examination of the events at Savo by a number of oversight agencies, and boards of inquiry of the time, seemed to uphold at least the following findings as also being "wholly causal" to the ultimate demise of the Allied navies, and the loss of the four Allied ships on the occasion of that battle.

Table 48. Lessons Learned: Damage Control Deficiencies and Remediation

DAMAGE CONTROL ASSESSMENTS AND RESPONSIVENESS	
DEFICIENCY FINDING/ISSUE	**REMEDIATION**
Storage of Paints and Flammables	Deckside combustibles must *not* be stowed in concentrations in or around otherwise highly flammable areas (or materials) on the ship. Combustibles should instead be stored in secured and well-sequestered locations throughout the ship, and in the event a sea action is in fact joined, all such unneeded combustibles should either be further secured *or* jettisoned over the side in full anticipation of that battle—this to minimize the possibility of secondary or follow-on explosions from a hit to any of those prime turret or munitions storage areas.
Non-readiness of Mechanical Aids	Critically needed damage control apparati, accessories, and vital mechanical tools that might be needed to quell ships' fires in battle (i.e., fog nozzles, fire mains, risers, and fire-fighting hoses) must be maintained in fully accessible areas and in a complete state of readiness at all times while on patrol in potentially hostile zones. Such must be the responsibility of each ship's commander (or designated senior subordinate) and might easily mean the difference between survival and recoverability and the full loss of that ship, if indeed hit by enemy fire during the course of that (or any) battle.

(continued)

Table 48. *Continued*

DAMAGE CONTROL ASSESSMENTS AND RESPONSIVENESS	
DEFICIENCY FINDING/ISSUE	**REMEDIATION**
Destruction of Facilities	If engaged in pitched battle, or other open-sea engagement, it might be expected that any ship may encounter some degree of damage during the course of that battle from incoming rounds, AP shells, torpedoes, or aerial bombardment.
	Commanders must have in place certain countermeasures and unimpeachable contingency plans to offset the effects of the destruction of critical ship resources, again such as fire mains and risers, and to avoid a compromise of that ship's very integrity—this as best as possible in the time allotted. The anticipation of just such a loss in heated battle might better prepare that ship to more capably respond to any such situations with a higher level of competence and a greater assurance of recoverability/survivability.
Inoperability Factors Due to a Loss of Power	During the steeped battle at Savo, with the extremely high level of hits received by each of the affected Allied ships on the night of 9 August, the unexpected loss of power to key areas of those ships would greatly hamper their ability to fight the resulting fires—or to even effect a recovery of that ship. Functional equipment, such as risers, fire mains, and bilge pumps, were reportedly found to be inoperable on many of the ships, further exacerbating an already bad situation—a situation that itself could only threaten to further spiral out of control and make matters even worse.
	Commanders would thereafter be urged to ensure that there were effective backup and "triply redundant" recovery plans in place to handle many of these critical functions, in the event any of that ship's primary systems or apparati were rendered inoperable by any such naval attack.

DAMAGE CONTROL ASSESSMENTS AND RESPONSIVENESS	
DEFICIENCY FINDING/ISSUE	REMEDIATION
Untimely Abandonment of Station	The keen human factors of fear and apprehension, especially in the face of any such series of harsh and sustained night attacks, would of course seize hold of some of the men on the stricken ships, causing them to abandon their stations far too soon, even before being sanctioned to do so. This might especially have been true within many of the ships' confined spaces, such as engine rooms, bilge areas, and other belowdecks levels on each of the affected ships.
	Commanders were therefore now urged to re-instruct subordinate officers and senior enlisted personnel to ensure that all duty stations remain manned in full and to ensure that all of the men did so until a valid order to abandon ship had been issued by the ship's captain. A failure to do so might place both the ship and the men in a greater state of peril and advance the untimely loss of the entire ship due to the lack of personnel standing by station to carry out specific recovery tasks when perhaps most needed.
Inaccurate or Incomplete DCA* Reporting	Both the present and the future actions of any well-functioning commander will always only be as good as the information they receive, both from his subordinate officers and from the senior enlisted men tasked with ensuring that those orders are in fact carried out in a timely and actionable manner. Late situational estimates, "stale" intel, misrouted reports, inaccurate damage assessments, fact omissions, and many other types of misleading tactical and damage control data presented to the commander before, during, and even after a battle, might cause that commander to make any number of false asssmptions, and to take any number of flawed (or even ill-advised) actions based on those initial inaccurate assessments given him.
	Commanders would therefore be urged to ensure that each of those subordinates did in fact provide both preliminary and follow-on reports on damage assessments, progress of recovery efforts, and any other "state-of-the-ship" matters that might critically impact the optimum performance of that ship during the course of any joined battle. Updates must also be timely and made at periodic intervals as time and actions allow, and reporting channels left open and available for the critical dissemination of orders and operational data that must be allowed to get through to the commanders and senior chiefs of those warships.

(continued)

Table 48. *Continued*

DAMAGE CONTROL ASSESSMENTS AND RESPONSIVENESS	
DEFICIENCY FINDING/ISSUE	REMEDIATION
Combat Inexperience of DCUs** and Crews	Ships' commanders must be tasked with fully ensuring that all crews—especially those that make up the ship's damage control response teams—have been fully trained in all aspects of those same DCA* procedures, fire control, and expected response scenarios under pressure, which rigid training might indeed make all the difference in that ship's recovery when later operating in battle. Such action would ensure a proper and well-actioned response to any unfolding crisis should that ship come under attack at any time in the rage of battle.
	In and of itself, experience would be the *best* teacher in all events—this during the course of the conflict unfolding even then in the southwest Pacific at that time—and which would come soon enough to Guadalcanal. Ships' firefighting crews and DCUs** would only improve over time, reaction times become more dutifully optimized, and a full understanding of just *what* must be done *when*, and by *which* team, would now become more and more a pre-battle priority in subsequent confrontations with the IJN in the wake of that same battle at Savo Island.

*DCA = **D**amage **C**ontrol **A**ssessment(s)
DCU = **Damage **C**ontrol **U**nit(s)

MINDSET AND ATTITUDE: AN ASSUMED SUPERIORITY

Background/Premise

Tempering the Edge: An Assumed Superiority in Battle

In the aftermath of the atrocities at both Pearl Harbor and Ford Island on 7 December 1941, the American attitude toward the Empire of Japan would quite understandably morph into a more deeply seated antipathy and a bitter rage that was directed mainly toward that country's military. Gone was the avowed and certain "hands-off" neutrality that our country had once enjoyed during the opening gambit of the war in Europe. Gone was the isolationist indifference we had so carefully cultivated, now transformed *on the spot* to a rabid hatred and a deadly intent to strike back at the island nation of the Land of the Rising Sun—and at the very heart of Japan. America's navy now pulled itself up off the charred decks of its own sunken ships at Pearl Harbor, and soon knit the brow and set the teeth, as it rolled up its sleeves and prepared to do battle with greater resolve. The end of Americans' neutral stance in the Pacific (as in Europe) was now finally at hand, and the all-too-famous war cries of decades past of *Remember the Alamo!* and *Remember the Maine!* were almost overnight changed to *Remember the Arizona!* and *Remember Pearl Harbor!*

Now with the scant remaining naval forces that the United States did have, or at least those remaining *intact*, America's military set sail for southern Pacific waters with but one aim in mind: full payback in kind. The Americans would enter the war against an emboldened Japan and what was thought to be its "Paper Navy"—and would do so with a hot swagger and a certain avowed belief that they simply could not lose. But before Savo, there would first have to be a Midway, a Wake Island, and yet another crippling tragedy at Coral Sea. And, almost as expected, America's naval forces would have different results in different battles.

Midway, of course, would be a most decisive victory for the Americans; Wake, a thwarted surprise attack that would in short order be turned back against the very Japanese attempting to execute that initial failed strike; and Coral Sea would nearly witness a complete and unparalleled decimation of our carrier strike force in but a single afternoon's battle. But America's fighting men would simply never rid themselves fully of the unshakable belief that they were still far superior to the Japanese fighting machine they now faced, at least in any one-on-one encounter with them, and the men seemingly never gave up on that single, unreasoning belief.

On this, noted author and naval historian Jack D. Coombe, who had himself served on the scrappy DD *Patterson* on the night of the attack, made his own bold observation when he noted the following:

> Though it was known that Japan had a sizable fleet, the prevailing impression among us Navy men at the time was that the Imperial Navy was inferior to ours. The feeling was only strengthened by purposeful visits to Western ports by Japan's decrepit training ships, which gave the impression of a third-rate fleet that was no match for the modern navies of the United States and Britain.[232]

In fact, Coombe saunters on even further in his narrative, recalling an even more curious conversation he had with a buddy while they both stood leaning over the stern rail of the American destroyer *Patterson* in the year 1941, well before the fated DD even sailed into the hotly contested waters just off Guadalcanal:

Coombe: "Do you think we'll go to war with Japan?"

Shipmate: "*Mebbe.* But I hear if we do, we'll sink their Navy in six months."[233]

Clearly, the men of the *Patterson*—in consort with the many sailors on each of the other American warships—may have been well off the mark, but the sentiment was still clear. We were supposed to be the guys on top . . . if not *always*, certainly most of the time. And so America's overconfident navy now set hard the jaw and sailed off to war but would only too soon find out just how horrid that war might actually be. And Savo would be nothing itself if not a full end-state affirmation of just how horrid war could be, especially when it also meant a major win for the bold IJN.

So, just what did happen at Savo that would so radically check the resolve and standing of that same American navy after the sudden loss of three of its best heavy cruisers in a single night's battle? Perhaps it was the very torpor of the assumption itself, an inherently "faulted" assumption brought on by an idea of always feeling superior to one's enemy: in effect, then, a poor underestimation of the enemy and a dread overconfidence of one's own standing and capabilities. Even as the extant COMPHIBFORSOPAC (Turner)—the admiral in control of all screening forces at Guadalcanal—did himself observe, one of the key reasons why his ships may have been so roundly defeated at Savo was exactly this same feeling of false bravado, this same overweening presumption of an assured victory, and an unwarranted "they-wouldn't-dare" American attitude toward a Japanese counterpart that was not at all interested in standing on ceremony, or even playing by the rules, were there indeed any to begin with. Thus Turner's message on precisely this sentiment was nothing if not short, clear, and to the point when he said:

> The Navy was still obsessed with a strong feeling of technical and mental superiority over the enemy. In spite of ample evidence as to the enemy's capabilities, most of our officers and men despised the enemy, and felt themselves sure victors in all encounters under any circumstances. The net result of all this was a fatal "lethargy of mind" which induced a confidence without readiness and a routine acceptance of outworn peacetime standards of conduct. I believe that THIS psychological factor, as a cause of our defeat, was even more important than [Mikawa's own] element of surprise.[234]

In later years, a like sentiment would echo further in the findings of the noted author and naval historian Richard B. Frank, in his epic book *Guadalcanal: The Definitive Account of the Landmark Battle*, where he, too, would clearly note:

> This lethargy of mind would not be completely shaken off without some more hard blows to [the U.S.] Navy pride around Guadalcanal, but after Savo the United States picked itself up off the deck and prepared for the most savage combat in its history.[235]

Lesson(s) Learned

America's navy would now be compelled to perhaps "bring it down a notch" in their perceived view of their enemy—and of themselves—as they soon began to realize just how critically they may have underestimated the tactical capabilities of that adversary. America's predominant "Iron Will" would be tempered with a greater caution, its jaunty swagger more moderated by the kick in the teeth suffered at both Pearl Harbor and Ford Island, and again at Savo. But America still kept coming on, soon with a greater dragged-through-the-mud determination—now with clenched teeth and a steely resolve that kept our ships (and the brave men who sailed them) ever hot on the trail of the IJN fleet, only more cautiously so and without counterfeit presumption.

Now was the time for a clearer understanding of just how cunning, how elusive, and how deadly that enemy surface fleet could be, and to recognize that it might in fact not be just a "Paper Navy" as purported after all, and America's struggling Pacific fleet would simply need to reload, readjust its sights, and cock back the trigger one more time, as it primed itself to join that enemy in a battle that would turn into an all-out, island-by-island hop across the vast Pacific Ocean.

Clearly factored into this heavy equation may also have been America's ill-advised reliance on its prototypical radar systems, like those seen on both of the American radar pickets USS *Blue* and the *Ralph Talbot*, this on at least the occasion of the night battle at Savo. Now that very "reliance on technology" would enjoy a decidedly far more diminished favor, and commanders on many of the ships of the line would still much prefer the sharper and more keen-eyed "human assets" who stood their watchful lookouts from station to station on those vessels.

The sheer gallantry of America's navy, and the bold bravado that seemed to drive that force, would become the very embodiment of a mental state that would effectively carry it through conflict after conflict in the continuing war across the Pacific. The clear lesson learned during the opening gambits of the war would now more rationally settle down to a quieted self-assuredness and a certain dead intent; gone were the boastful strut and taut presumption of assured victory in each and every battle encounter. In fact, all such victories would now be hard fought and hard won, and only achieved through the sweat and blood of the American sailors, and the ships on which they fought, and would never again be taken lightly as a foregone conclusion of a supposed (or even *assumed*) superiority.

For additional information on this topical discussion point, see the earlier section titled "Finding 15: A Confidence Untested: An Unfounded Certainty."

SUPPLY AND REPLENISHMENT

Background/Premise

From the very outset of hostilities in the Solomons, the critical issue of supply and replenishment for that effort would almost immediately be a problem for the Allied forces attempting to boldly gain (and hold) a foothold in the region. Alerted to the idea that there might be an intent by the Japanese to invade the area, and to annex it in full to exploit the region's vast natural resources—and to perhaps even prepare for an ultimate invasion of the Australian mainland itself—the American response was both swift and decisive . . . seize that "real estate" first and in full, then hold it at all costs. And, on the morning of 7 August 1942, the combined Allied forces would do precisely that.

That Allied task force, now dubbed Operation Watchtower, would consist of some seventy five multi-national Allied ships and a landing force of some sixteen thousand troops—most of which were preeminently cut from the cloth of the rugged MG

Alexander A. Vandegrift's own 1st Marine Division. There was also the U.S. Army's contingency troops, the crack XIV Corps units, which would land on the islands of Guadalcanal and at cross-channel Tulagi and far Tanambogo, nestled at the very southern tip of Florida Island.

Almost immediately, then, the logistics of supply and replenishment for all of these forces would become an organizational nightmare, a quite daunting task that seemed to continue to escalate and plague every inch of the multi-national undertaking—and one that would seemingly begin and end with Rear Admirals Fletcher and Turner just before the events at Savo itself. Now, on the day before Savo took place—with Crutchley's screening ships not yet fully deployed in the Sound, and most of Vandegrift's men still hunkering down in and around Henderson Field—it would be VADM Fletcher's own ill-advised move to withdraw his carrier task force from Iron Bottom Sound that would most clearly ring a death knell for "supply and replenishment," and that almost all at once.

With Fletcher now pulling the plug on his carrier-based strike force prematurely and taking away the concomitant air cover that would have come with it, Turner—as the second in command in the area as the extant COMPHIBSOPACFOR, or commander of all amphibious operations then in play at Guadalcanal—was compelled to do likewise with his own troop transport and supply ships as well. And so stranded were the ships that were still busily unloading their precious cargoes of ground troops, materiel, and munitions at each of three key disembarkation points.

Fearful of no longer having adequate screening (air) cover that would normally have been provisioned by Fletcher and McCain's air assets from both the carriers and nearby islands, it was now a far more edgy and tentative Admiral Turner who soon did the only thing that made sense at the time: cease all unloading operations himself and pull out all of his transport and supply ships as well. But even pulling the plug, Turner was not at all happy, and he earnestly hoped to return as soon as he could safely afford to do so.

Both of these withdrawal actions would clearly leave the land-based infantry forces in dire straits, since only about half of the desperately needed supplies and munitions slated to provision them had been unloaded from the ships, and half still remained carefully stowed away in cargo holds deep within each vessel. And all of it was now forfeit to Admiral Fletcher's miscalculated uncertainty, and his reserved caution over possible air attacks by an IJN force that was suspected of already being in the area. Gone now was the very supply line that the men on Guadalcanal might most need—precisely at the moment they might most have needed it—as they now sat at the crossroads of having essentially one foot in and one foot out of their precarious entrenched positions in and around Guadalcanal and a still-smoking Henderson Field.

Many of the troops from both the 1st Marine Division and the Army XIV Corps were themselves fresh out of training and had only recently been scurried off to fight on some hell-hole piece of island real estate called Guadalcanal, with only an older model M1903 .30-06 Springfield rifle in hand and a meager ten-day supply of ammunition on which to rely.

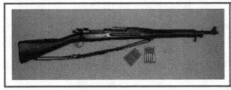

Figure 49.   M1903 Springfield .30-06, Model 1903 (r.) and M1 Garand .30 Caliber Semi-Automatic Rifles (l.)

That meant few (if any) Garand-generation rifles,[236] only slight ammo, and even less food with which to feed the troops already in place. Perhaps lacking foresight into the matter, the operational planners behind the invasion effort had effectively reduced the soldiers' munitions from an original ninety-day supply to a sixty-day supply of those same munitions. Now a bitter sarcasm began to simmer and emerge among the dog-faces and dug-in Marines that soon rankled the resolve and attitude of the men of the rank and file. On the ground, many of the disenchanted soldiers referred tongue-in-cheek to the poorly executed plan as Operation Shoestring, and even fewer gave any credence to its success.

Fletcher's unheralded and unwise actions with the carrier withdrawals, and his untimely removal of the critical air assets that all of the ships so badly needed, would be further exacerbated by Turner's later decision to withdraw the supply ships in response to those actions, and the entire fiasco (at least to the men who had to live through it) would very quickly come to be known as the "Great Navy Bugout." Indeed, it was a "bugout" that would be neither forgotten nor forgiven by those men who had been left stranded on the beachheads dotting the island footholds in and around Guadalcanal, Tulagi, and Tanambogo. If the tide were in fact to turn for these men, Turner needed to get those supply ships back to shore and offloaded—and *that* as quickly as possible.

Lesson(s) Learned

Almost immediately, over a period of the next four days of only mildly contested occupation of key island areas on Guadalcanal, Turner would indeed return with his supply ships, finally redocking and resuming the offloading tasks he had so recently abandoned with undue haste. The crucially needed supplies were now swiftly being unloaded from the cargo ships and hustled inland to predetermined staging points for use by both the Marine and the army infantry units already in place and anxiously awaiting their arrival. In the interim, however, many of the landed troops, on at least Guadalcanal, had been astounded to discover just how intact and fully operational much of the equipment had been when left behind by the enemy.

Soon indeed, Vandegrift's men were able to salvage and commandeer many of the supplies that had been abandoned in place by the fast-retreating soldiers of GEN Harukichi Hyakutake's 17th Army, a unit that had only too rapidly taken to heel and fled in the face of the American invasion and beach assaults of 7 August. And now they were on the move yet again, scurrying inland and up into the mountains just beyond the American lines at Henderson. Much of that captured equipment was in truth found to be a virtual "gold mine," ranging from bulldozers to leveling planers, and from tankers to large road-toughened trucks and other heavy equipment pieces that had been used to construct the very airstrip that the Americans had just commandeered and which they now so tenaciously held.

Found almost immediately were communications equipment and parts, building tools, and heavy construction machinery—and better still, wine, rice, and basic foodstuffs that had all been left behind during the Japanese push to abandon their positions at Lunga in an all-out effort to flee the American storm cloud invasion. The discovery of these patchwork caches of supplies and "found" goods was nothing less than fortuitous and a thing of wonder to behold (if even for the moment). As such, the unexpected provisions would now work to at least hold the American fighting men together until Turner could complete his final unloading tasks at Lunga Roads, and the long-awaited supplies that the men so desperately needed could finally be outsourced and sent ashore.

Supply and replenishment would continue to be a problem, both for the men and the ships at Guadalcanal, but in the wake of the travesty at Savo, both Admirals Fletcher and Turner would now more seriously go about the business of beefing up the reduced force-presence in the area—especially from the Allied naval perspective—which had just faced the loss of *four* heavy cruisers in a single chance encounter with Mikawa's two cruiser divisions. In short order, additional light and heavy cruisers of the line, along with their attending DDs—and even several BB-class warships—would all soon be reallocated by Halsey (or others acting on his behalf) to the Guadalcanal operational area.

Soon, ships such as the massive BB USS *Washington*, the CAs *Salt Lake City*, *Minneapolis*, *New Orleans*, and *San Francisco*—and even the CLs *Boise*, *Helena*, and *Honolulu*—would all be dispatched to the area to replace those ships lost at Savo—and to further augment the Allied naval presence in Iron Bottom Sound and points north up through the Slot. Foremost of these would be RADM Willis Augustus "Ching" Lee's own *Washington*—which ship would shortly go on to "even up the score" for Savo by sinking one of Japan's greatest battleships, the *Kirishima* itself, in a later deadly one-on-one skirmish off the southern edge of Savo during the Naval Battle of Guadalcanal in November of that same year. On at least that one occasion, the great *Washington* would bravely stand her ground and fire all guns at full broadsides as she engaged the Japanese battleship . . . a heroic and terrifying moment that would not soon be forgotten by the men who served on her.

Regardless, the clear and irrevocable truth was that the hotly contested battle for the Solomons was still far from over. A measured standoff in the region would now exist between both combatant navies—navies that were each struggling to extend their operations in the area—and by September 1942 Yamamoto's Imperial Japanese Navy, the great *Kaigun* itself, would further step up its almost-predictable nightly supply-side runs and troop reinforcement forays into key areas just north of Guadalcanal. In a desperate run to obtain a more solid foothold in the region, and to regain control of the large (Henderson) airfield at Lunga—from which they had only recently been so rudely ousted, precisely at a time when they were almost done with its construction—the Japanese fleet would simply keep coming on and coming back, much to the dismay of the Americans and their Allies. Area dominance, however, had already begun to swing in favor of the dauntless Americans and their combined Allied navies, and the beleaguered Imperial Japanese Navy—now beaten back time after time—would never again regain the strategic advantage it might once have enjoyed had they been able to fully occupy and control all of the Solomons.

SOURCES

❶ Cited from the Naval War College report, dated 1950 and titled *The Battle of Savo Island, August 9, 1942: Strategical and Tactical Analysis.· (Part I)*. Authored by Richard W. Bates and Walter D. Innis for the Naval War College (Department of Analysis) and distributed by the National Technical Information Services (NTIS) organization; Chapter XXIII: Battle Lessons, pp. 343–65.

❷ Cited from the Navy Department Bureau of Ships Assessment Report (C-FS/L11-1(374)-C-EN28/A2-11); Subject: USS *Quincy*, USS *Astoria* and USS *Vincennes*: Report of Loss in Action; dated 2 Sep 1943; cf. Conclusions (94 and 95): 21–22.

❸ From the detailed Office of Naval Intelligence discussion titled *The Battle of Savo Island: 9 August 1942: Combat Narrative*, found as an appendix entry under a topical heading of "Observations," 44. From the *HyperWar* website at http://www.ibiblio.org/hyperwar/USN/USN-CN-Savo/USN-CN-Savo-11.html.

The Battle of Savo Island: Slipping the Hounds

A PUSH TOO FAR—THE DEATH OF THE "TOKYO EXPRESS"

The Battle of Savo Island: Slipping the Frightful Hounds of Hell

Savo would be that one critical turning point in the battle for the Solomons that—although a series of savaging battles that from time to time appeared to be a tactical victory for the Japanese—would in the long run often be a clear strategic win for the United States and its Allied coalition forces. The clear "denial of access" to both the region—and to the vast resources contained within that region—that Japan had so desperately sought to possess to further its own expansionist endgame, would now serve as but one more nail in the coffin of the Imperial Japanese Navy's avowed attempt to push into the southwest Pacific, in their ultimate drive to get to the true gem and capstone of the area—the vast continent of *Australia*!

Later battles between the two powerful navies would soon be ushered into the region as well, to be sure, and the not yet fully tested Americans would clash again and again with Yamamoto's own battle-hardened navy over the coming months, on the later occasions of the Battle of the Eastern Solomons, Battle of Cape Esperance, Battle of Santa Cruz, Naval Battle of Guadalcanal, and even the distant endgame confrontations at both Tassafaronga and the Rennell Islands, the last battle occurring as late as January 1943. But the scorching result would almost always be the same: either "stalemate" or outright victory for the American naval forces and their toughened Allied coalition. After a series of great *tactical* losses during the opening gambit of hostilities at Guadalcanal, the Americans would ultimately win the grand *strategical* battle of disputed access to the area against the Japanese and its great Imperial Navy. It would also finally witness the death of the notorious "Tokyo Express," stopping *cold* the persistent supply-side runs and thwarting Japan's every effort to provision and bolster its forces in the region once and for all. The end of Japan's aggressive, ever-engorging bid for occupation and control of the islands of the Southwest Pacific might finally be coming to a close.

America had summarily picked itself up off the blackened decks of the sunken ships at Pearl Harbor and Ford Island and had feverishly thrown itself back into the game—and into the war—soon gaining an even greater momentum that would make its push deeper into the northern regions of the Pacific, and into other areas held by Japan, all but unstoppable. Now securing one of the true gemstones of the southwest Pacific with the acquisition of the new Guadalcanal "real estate," the Allied ground and naval forces were soon able to both seize and *hold* the area, while at the same time preempting an IJN move toward ascendancy in that same region. This would then allow the U.S. Corps of Engineers an even greater window of time within which to fully concentrate their efforts on repairing the heavily peppered Henderson Field, which would itself further the Allies' own battle posturing in the region and bring the fight right to the enemy's doorstep that much sooner. And it would be Halsey, Fletcher, and Turner's ships that would lead that vanguard charge, with its own measured push to north as it tenaciously battled its way from island to island in its ultimate drive toward Okinawa and the Japanese homeland itself.

Savo would be that one harsh slap in the face, that one swift kick in the pants, and that sharp rap on the knuckles that would quickly mobilize America's navy. It would unquestionably also instill that navy with an even greater resolve to avenge the fearsome actions at Pearl Harbor, at Coral Sea, and now again at Savo—this to finally put an end to Japan's expansionist activities in the region, and to fully ravage and destroy any Japanese shippage found. The war would rage on for some three more years, but the Imperial Japanese Navy's dominance on the high seas, in at least this southwest Pacific theater of operations, would have become far more stunted than it had ever been in the past, and an end to the ever-tormenting "Tokyo Express" would be at hand that much sooner.

There would indeed be other "dog days of August" as well, as soon the world would sit up and take note, as witnessed only some three years down the road, well after the 9 August attacks at Savo in 1942. For indeed at its later time, with only a three-day calendar differential, the poignant fallout of the American attack on Hiroshima would come first on 6 August 1945 and would be desperately sequenced some three days beyond that by the second "Fat Man" fusion bomb that would be dropped on an unwary Nagasaki. That following date would be 9 August, some three years "to the day" after Savo, and both nuclear events would then bring a horrific and final end to the second-theater Pacific War with Japan for all time. Therefore, it might be said that from "August to August" within those incredibly diverse years spanning 1942 through 1945, neither military power would ever again be quite the same.

For additional reading on the subject of the "killing of the Tokyo Express," and the certain end to the nightly supply-side runs that Japan had sought with such seeming desperation to carry out time and again in Guadalcanal, the author might recommend the insightful book by historian Jack D. Coombe, *Derailing the Tokyo Express: The Naval Battles for the Solomon Islands That Sealed Japan's Fate.*[237] A precarious and fascinating view of all of the battles for the Solomons, Coombe's book might be expected to serve as both a personal recounting of that author's own time spent on one of the participants of that battle—the American destroyer USS *Patterson* itself—and of the events occurring precisely during the time of the deadly night encounter at Savo.[238]

BATTLE STATIONS: A POET'S COMMEMORATIVE— AND PROUDLY WE SERVED

In all events have I continued to pursue a solid and historical purview of the many naval battles that would occur during the arduous years of 1942 and 1943 during World War II in the Pacific, but I did so with a particular emphasis on the heated battles for the Solomons. A devoted naval historian with a specific interest in each of the series of naval encounters that took place in and around the waters surrounding Guadalcanal (and Florida Island), the author has penned several such historical poem pieces on just such naval battles—each a set piece commemorative with a different topical theme—but all indeed military in tenor and tone. And in every instance have I only humbly attempted to recapture the pith and essence of what must actually have occurred within each of the battle scenarios described, as much as one can, since indeed no one—save those who lived, fought, and survived the deadly close-in encounters themselves—might ever know or understand in full.

As such, all of the following first-person, period-piece narratives have tried to become the very voices of war—the voices within and without, as it were—all set to embrace the full grit and action of those many battles. As such, the compilation currently includes all of the following titles:

NAVAL ENCOUNTERS: The First Battle of Savo Island (1942)
NAVAL ENCOUNTERS: The Hunt for the *Quincy* (1942)
NAVAL ENCOUNTERS: Tale of the USS *Quincy* (1942)
NAVAL ENCOUNTERS: The Battle of Cape Esperance (1942)
NAVAL ENCOUNTERS: The Battle of Tassafaronga (1942)
NAVAL ENCOUNTERS: The Naval Battle of Guadalcanal (1942)
NAVAL ENCOUNTERS: The Battle of the Coral Sea (1942)

NAVAL ENCOUNTERS:	The Battle of the Jutland Sea (Dogger Bank, 1916)
NAVAL ENCOUNTERS:	USS *Nebraska* (SSBN-739) (2009)
NAVAL ENCOUNTERS:	Tale of the USS *LST-342* (2012)
NAVAL ENCOUNTERS:	Tale of the USS *Pueblo* (AGER-2) (1968)
NAVAL ENCOUNTERS:	The Sand Pebbles (USS *San Pablo*) (1926)
THE AIR WAR:	Call to Quarters: No Deed Unheralded (2005)

Far and away, however, my most intriguing and most consuming passion has been that of researching, interpreting, and fully understanding the very nature and fullness of the First Battle of Savo Island itself. Taken even further, it would be the specific movements of the American heavy cruisers in RADM Crutchley's own screening groups—namely, the USS *Vincennes*, the *Quincy*, and the *Astoria*, as well as the *Helm*, the *Chicago*, and the *Patterson*—and truly all of the many other brave ships that were so hotly embattled (and many lost, during the scattered, random actions on that one tepid night in August 1942).

It is therefore the author's best hope that at least the first such commemorative piece, presented here on the 1BOSI, might at least lend some insight into why I found *these* times, and *these* battles, to be of such great import. For me, it became important enough that I would never thereafter forget the crewmen—or the great steel ships that carried them into battle—and through the very jaws of death. To perhaps ensure that we never forget those that did so sadly perish on high seas that one night under a dark and moonless sky at a shadowy place called Savo Island.

Naval Encounters: The Battle of Savo Island, 1942—Iron Bottom Sound

Early morning, sleeve of night, sleek and wary mile by mile,
Down the "Slot" they push their warships, never doubting all the while,
The smack of success, the timing of surprise;
Battlecruisers close at "ten," now horizoned to our eyes.

Aboard the *Quincy* first we go—a Cruiser less than none—
Fearless tasks she'd undergone, but nothing like this one
Harsh naval night, with velvet shroud around;
A blackened sea, with blackened sight, at Iron Bottom Sound.

Off Guadalcanal this place we'd find, of battles long ago;
With names like Florida and Lunga Point, Tulagi and Savo . . .
Itself a slice of isle in channel center—a cork in ocean blue;
But on this night, and on these seas . . . 'tis August '42.

For on this slab of southern sea, the best of fleets collide,
And gun-to-gun and ship-to-ship, barrage and full broadside
Of full thirty ships of war, converging for the clash;
Now down the Slot the great foe steams, forged by storm and lash.

But *Quincy* waits, its orders fast: "To set the Northern screen."
So, off deep Savo shoals we sit, our enemy unseen.
"Patrol, patrol . . . and keep your lookouts sharp!", we hear;
So, scan we well the reach of sky and all our waters near.

To be alert—to keep our ken—to set a klaxon knell;
And to a man we'd stand our ground, and hold our station well.
We'd sound the alarm and salvo back, and bear the bites of war,
Engaged in forward battle like no pitchèd fight before.

So, sweep away, sweep away, sweep away far . . .
Main guns training in tandem and aiming "on-bar."
With "8-inchers" hot loaded and guns swiveling free,
We wait for great fleet of Japan, both by air and by sea.

With calculation then they come; with cunning and iron will,
Great Mikawa stealthy sweeps his course from Bougainville.
In Solomons—a world apart—they push the mighty fleet,
Quick and quiet now they speed, their movements all discreet.

Now battlecruisers, warships—dread escorts all—in shipping lanes of two,
Head undetected south by east—hot course "140-true."
Seeking . . . searching . . . looking for a kill, they slice the waters blue;
Mikawa's ships so soon arrive, and number ten less two.

Thus, north and west of Savo Isle the mighty ships do perch,
Each locked in dead of night, while each with each do search
The brackish waters dead ahead, and screening all about—
Engines scream in muted pitch, destroyers placed well out

In van of main Battle Force as they carve their way southeast;
Like ravaged mongrels and rankling curs, gluttoned by the feast
Of former routs and shallow wins—defeat upon high seas;
But even the loss of Guadalcanal would not bring us to our knees.

Now, *six* thousand Marines hold on *seven* thousand as told;
Securing the airstrip, watching sea battles unfold.
Some standing on shore as skirmish rages through night;
The burning silhouettes of ships they see, engagèd in this fight

Of fights—like never fought before; they push the dauntless run
And down the Slot advance the ships in a battle lane of one.
Mikawa on his Flagship slows and orders, "Hit them with the light!"
Now, searchlights scan horizon, trapping *Quincy* in their sight.

So, *outgunned now* we stand in way, proud *Quincy* soon is sought,
Vincennes and fleet *Astoria* now veering hard to port;
To guard our flank and "check our six," they push themselves to stern;
Quincy now quick-turning well to starboard, while all our engines burn.

Now, heavy Cruiser cannonades are shot, that tear into our hull;
We sound "GQ" and move to guns, and brave our fate in full.
Deadly caught in fire crossed from three Mikawa ships,
"*Full ahead!!*", our Captain roars, but to heel she slowly tips.

We turn and charge the very fleet—with intention now to ram;
We answer back with volley full, from men who gave no damn.
Now, gun directors come alive, men scrambling all in tandem;
"Ack-Ack" guns and fifty cals, with shells jacked back at random.

But even as we veer to angle, nosing out to come up true,
Lookouts clapped to masts on high yell, "Watch! Torpedoes two!!"
Their tracks well seen in flare of fight, we watch their silent running,
While still on deck our men stand fast with guts and deadly gunning.

In seconds then, this bout was through—a date for hardship known,
Vincennes was gone, the *Quincy* too; and proud *Astoria* blown.
In minutes thirty—maybe more—this deadly fight did claim,
Three heavy cruisers from our fleet, and destroyers well in name.

The day would go to Mikawa; the action hot and fast;
The night would swallow up its ships, the men at peace at last.
And some would live a shallowed life, whilst some would fight anew;
To set the teeth and flash the eye, and prep for Battle Two . . .

APPENDIX A

The Map Series

FORCE DEPLOYMENTS, TIMELINES, TABULAR RECORDS OF MOVEMENT

In the wake of the vicious attacks at Savo, all of the topographical representations—to include the drawn-to-scale maps and plotting charts depicting the events, chronology, and ships' positions before, during, and after the First Battle of Savo Island—would be numerous and compelling. From the archives of the Naval War Center, and even from the sober overseeing ONI agency itself, would come the highly sophisticated and tightly scaled mappings that would fully incorporate not just the orders of battle but also illuminating date and time stamping, progressive chronologies, and TROM (Tabular Records of Movement) positioning data for all ships, as well as key areas of conflict. Some of the maps would be meticulously crafted—the drawn and detailed representations set down by the several admirals and commanders who might later recall their roles in the battle; other maps would only surface as a result of the untiring work of the many investigators and researchers, emerging decades later, that would be far more roughly cast and hand-drawn, "approximating" actual events and ships' movements. For more on this subject of TROMs, reference the later section titled "A Word about TROMs," to be found at the end of this module.

All such presentation issues set aside, the author has been both fascinated and overwhelmed by the seeming abundance of cartographic images available on the 1BOSI. Indeed, each of the images in the map series that follow seem to present their own interpretations, as it were—their own depictions and extrapolations—and only the informed viewer might be able to make a final determination as to which map, or map type, can best serve their analytical needs. In fact, the map images shown here and on the following pages represent only a handful of those available on the 1BOSI, beginning with the otherwise unattributed chart shown in Figure 50 (from the *Hyper-War* Combat Narrative series).[239]

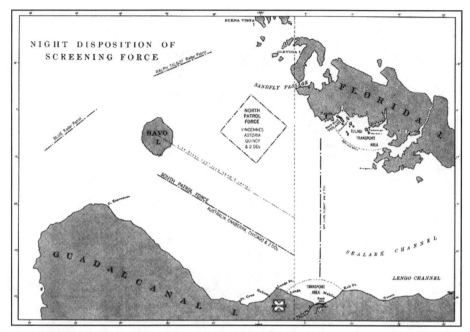

Figure 50.   Map ➊: Prelude to Battle: Dispositioning of American Surface Forces, 9 August 1942

In the mapped image seen here, we can clearly see all of the key deployment areas of the Allied warships on the night of 8–9 August, with the notable exception of RADM Norman Scott's Eastern screening force itself, just southeast of Tulagi. From this, it might be reasoned that since that same Eastern group was the only Allied naval force not involved in the night action that took place only shortly after midnight on 9 August, such an omission may indeed have been wholly intentional.

Clearly noted on that same map, however, are the two radar picket patrol ships USS *Blue* and USS *Ralph Talbot* (DDs both) well north of Savo, with RADM Riefkohl's Northern screening force made up of the USS *Vincennes, Quincy,* and *Astoria* (and accompanying DDs *Helm* and *Wilson*)—and RADM Crutchley's own Southern screening element—patrolling just off the coast of Guadalcanal in a line that ran almost parallel to that island's northern coastline, and leading all the way up to Cape Esperance. It might therefore be the author's opinion that the map rendering may be marginally accurate at best, with a primary intent to depict only "general" deployment areas for the defending Allied naval assets at Guadalcanal at the time, but not necessarily relying on any precision plotting of the ships' actual movements.[240]

The map in Figure 51 is but the *first* of two of the most well-known and most well-referenced maps published by the Office of Naval Intelligence (ONI) and was itself extracted from an even larger work titled "The Battle of Savo Island: 9 August 1942: Attack on Our South Cruiser Force," as released by that Department of the

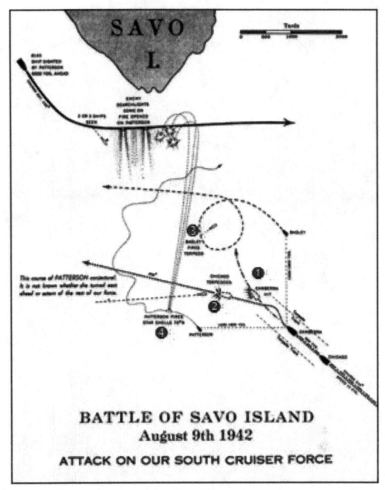

Figure 51. Map ❷: Battle Phase: Attack on the Southern Screen, 9 August 1942

Navy office. Further information on this map, and others in a series of such representations, may be seen on the *HyperWar* website, information for which may be found in better detail in the book's endnotes section.[241]

In it, we can clearly see the full attack by VADM Mikawa's CRUDIV6 and CRUDIV18 battle elements during the early morning hours of 9 August 1942. Shown also are each of the engagements of not just the HMAS *Canberra* ❶, which later had to be scuttled and sunk, but also the *Chicago* ❷, the *Bagley* ❸, and the *Patterson* ❹. Of the four ships cited here, one would in fact be critically damaged (the American cruiser *Chicago*) and one lost (the Australian *Canberra*), with the former *Chicago* itself under the questionable command of CAPT Howard Douglas "Ping" Bode.

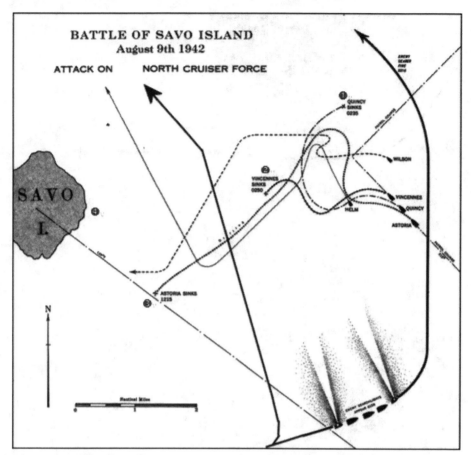

Figure 52.   Map ❸: Battle Phase: Attack on the Northern Screen, 9 August 1942

In Figure 52,[242] note the "tentative" positioning (and reported "last-knowns") for each of the capital ships of the Allied Northern screen on the night of 9 August 1942. Shown here are a series of approximated positions of the American heavy cruisers USS *Quincy* ❶, USS *Vincennes* ❷, and USS *Astoria* ❸, before, during, and even after the attack by Mikawa's cruiser division task force. If drawn with an intent to show a reasonably accurate scale of the events that took place, the map seems only to call into more serious question each of the actual (and later confirmed) locations of the *Vincennes* and *Astoria* themselves. Simply put, the two "heavies" should simply not be found anywhere near any of the locations actually shown here. In sharp contrast, the *Quincy* herself might actually be closest to its correct last-known plotting location, shown here as being in waters roughly east-northeast of Savo Island ❶, as plotted against the eastern edge of Savo ❹, where in fact the American heavy cruiser would later be found—and indeed remains to this day.

Perhaps the most prominent of all maps depicting the 1BOSI, however, is the concise rendering of the map seen in Figure 53 that connotes both the movement and

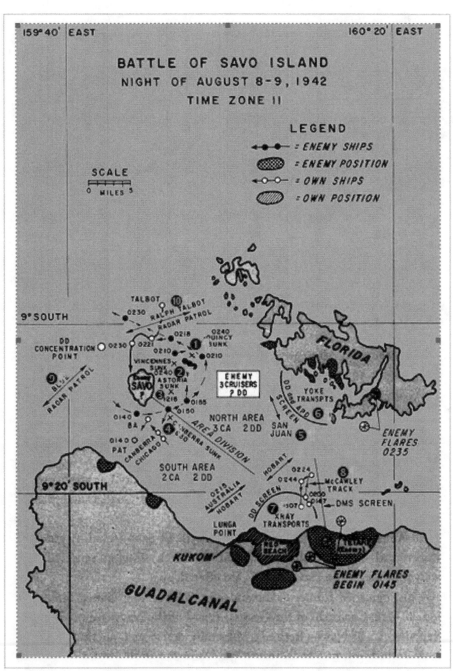

Figure 53. Map ❹: Battle Phase: Attack Scenarios and Transitions, 9 August 1942

the attack posturing of the IJN surface fleet in actions sustained during the surprise attacks launched both to the south and east of Savo Island. As a result of the well-timed, well-executed twin attacks that occurred within a time frame not exceeding some thirty to thirty-one minutes in duration, Crutchley's Southern and Northern screens were dealt several critical deathblows when attacked by both Long-Lance torpedoes and concentrated shellfire from the massive 8-inch main guns of Mikawa's cruiser division forces. Lost outright in the skirmish would be the Australian *Canberra* and the American heavies, *Vincennes* and *Quincy*, with a third cruiser (*Astoria*) being lost the following day shortly after noon.

Included in Figure 54 is the ever-ambitious and somewhat loosely interpreted Wolfgang Wolny map of June 2005: one of the most intriguing maps that I have to date been able to uncover—and indeed the first such map ever seen by this author, one that would indeed go on to become the impetus and inspirational springboard that would set me on a path to undertake a full investigation of the 1BOSI imprimis. Curiously, this Wolny map interpretation seems to again indicate only "approximate" plotting points for many (but not all) known shipwrecks dotting the area around Iron Bottom Sound. As a result, the chart seems to essentially present only a "cumulative" mapping of all ships lost—not just during the First Battle of Savo Island itself but fully incorporating all other capital ship losses as well—occurring during the later battles of Cape Esperance and Tassafaronga. Decidedly, then, the plotting cycle here must presumably also be set in a time frame ranging from late 1942 to early 1943.

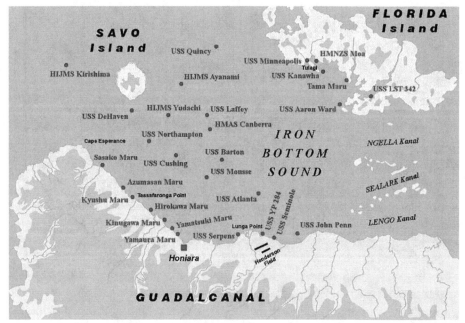

Figure 54.   Map ❾: The Wolny Map (2005)—Allied and IJN Naval Losses at Iron Bottom Sound

Missing from the image, however (almost conspicuously so)—in addition to its scant attention paid to any level of geographic detail—are both the USS *Vincennes* and its sister ship, the American heavy cruiser USS *Astoria*, with several of the other warships simply being plotted in areas where they actually should not be. Key among these "lost" ships might clearly be the USS *Aaron Ward*, the *Minneapolis*, the *Atlanta*, and even the scrappy fighting-ship USS *DeHaven* itself. Note also that the ship name USS *Monssen* (DD-436)—a *Gleaves*-class destroyer seen in the lower-center area of the map—has somehow been truncated to that of simply *Monsse*, which in and of itself might simply be a typographical error and a minor oversight by the chart developer but is nonetheless indicative of the work noted herein. The overall "impact" of the map rendering might nonetheless still serve as a dark reminder of precisely how many Allied (American, Australian, and New Zealand) ships, along with their IJN counterparts, were in fact lost in just this one primary battle zone . . . that of Guadalcanal, in the Solomon Islands of 1942 and 1943.

The map representation seen here in the sparse depiction of this chart seems to be directly attributable to CAPT Toshikazu Ohmae himself, as the extant chief of staff to VADM Gunichi Mikawa, then commander of the IJN's formidable Eighth Fleet, made up of his Cruiser Divisions 18 and 6 (as CRUDIV6 and CRUDIV18) at the time of the actual attack. Perhaps little more than a tool-aided, hand-drawn sketch wholly crafted from memory, the chart nonetheless effectively depicts the First Battle of Savo Island from the Japanese perspective before, during, and after the post-midnight attack of 9 August 1942. Unique in its purview of both the IJN ships' deployment and battle formations at the time, we also see the chart's depiction of Mikawa's task force splitting into three battle elements (at position ❶) before slowly reforming into additional battle group columns at ❷, ❸, and ❹. This, then, sharply contrasts the more conventionally proposed "two-column" attack format, especially as seen here as being just southeast of Savo Island, and just prior to the attack on Riefkohl's Northern screening force. Also noted in this chart markup is RADM Gotō's own CRUDIV18 battle group, noted at ❺, which included both the CLs *Tenryū* and *Yubari* but only generically refers to a "DD" as the third member of that group. That DD was in fact the lone straggler, *Yunagi* herself, a lowly destroyer that had been left behind by Mikawa to "guard the back door" at Savo.

The large-scale, high-angle overview map in Figure 56 can be attributed to the celebrated researcher and naval historian Samuel Eliot Morison,[243] and it depicts the movement and approach of VADM Gunichi Mikawa's CRUDIV6 and 18 attack fleet from Rabaul, Kavieng, and other points north. Set in a time frame ranging from 7 August (**A**), to 8 August (**B**), to 9 August (**C**) of 1942, the map shows the clear transit points of the IJN battle element as it sailed south past both New Britain and New Ireland, around the large island of Bougainville, then returned south and into the Slot as it then cruised past Choiseul and Vella Lavella. The force's next waypoint would now push it past Savo Island and into Iron Bottom Sound, where the small surface fleet would quickly carry out its twin attacks on both Crutchley's Southern and Northern fleets.

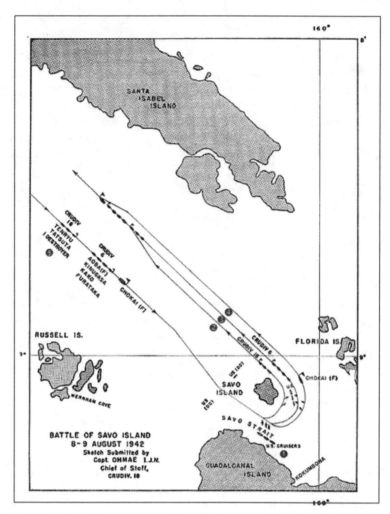

Figure 55.   Map ❻: Battle Overview: IJN Surface Fleet Deployment and Battle (Japanese Perspective)

The author can only speculate that the intent here was not to show the detailed particulars of the attacks, but rather simply the sortie itinerary and "course of best approach" for that IJN force as it approached its final zone of attack on the morning of 9 August.

Quite conversely, we see here in sharp contrast this sparse rendering that seems to have been but a smaller part of a larger official ONI report on the 1BOSI,[244] and may have been drawn only to show scale, movement, and patrol patterns of Crutchley's screening forces on the night of 8–9 August 1942, just prior to the surprise attack at Savo. Prepared and submitted as part of their massive post-action analysis of the events of the battle, the map (and the findings report that accompanied it) seems to entirely

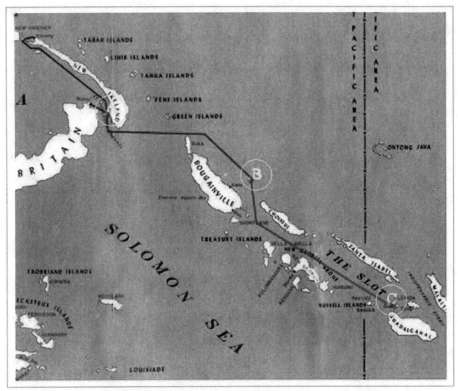

Figure 56.   Map ❼: The Morison Map—Transiting Itinerary of the IJN

omit any of the transit points or areas of approach for any of the Imperial Japanese Navy ships on the date in question.

To its credit, clearly visible here are not just the two patrol corridors of the DD radar pickets *Blue* and *Ralph Talbot* but also the screening activities of Crutchley's own Southern force, Riefkohl's Northern element, and even Scott's own Eastern screen. This unfortunately seems to be, however, the full extent of the map, since it appears not to depict any of the actual blue-water naval encounters that later took place on 9 August.

Curious and highly inventive, Figure 58 is essentially only a screen-captured "still" of an otherwise highly animated and interactive website that meticulously presents a full-spectrum view of the order of battle for the 1BOSI, from beginning to end. The carefully crafted animations shown on the site appear to have been developed by webmaster J. Cagney as recently as 2012, and present multiple cause-and-effect sequences that portray the strength, dispositioning, and transitional movements of all surface ships involved, both Allied and IJN forces, during the course of the short but violent attack on the Allied fleet at Savo on 9 August. Shown here, therefore, is essentially but a "freeze-frame" image of one of the final animated sequences that show the deployment, posturing, and interaction of the combatant forces as they faced off during that battle main.

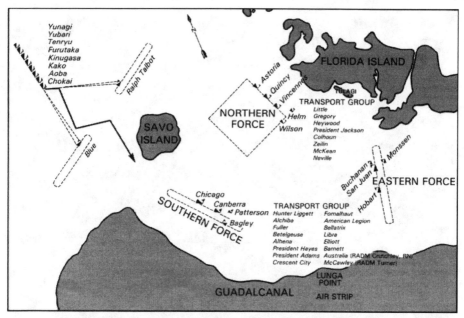

Figure 57.   Map ❸: The ONI Map—Night Disposition of the Allied Screening Force

Here, we can easily see not only the troop and transport ships busily unloading at Lunga and Tulagi under the watchful and protective eye of Vandegrift's 1st Marine Division but also at least two of the three Allied screening elements that we know to have been both the Southern and Northern forces (❶ and ❷). Conspicuously absent, however, is any plotting of RADM Norman Scott's own Eastern battle group that (in the author's opinion) seems to be depicted here as simply "Ships guarding transports" ❸. Note also the discrepant placement of the two radar picket ships *Blue* and *Ralph Talbot* (❹ and ❺), and the erroneous positioning of Riefkohl's own Northern fleet. Clearly, no account, past or present, of the patrol sector of the *Vincennes*, the *Quincy*, and the *Astoria*—and their escort DDs *Helm* and *Wilson*—can support a patrol corridor this far north of Savo Island. To exacerbate the problem further, the developer of the map seems to depict them as not being on their correct initial northbound heading of 315°, instead showing them as being positioned elsewhere at a point well north of Nggella Sule (Florida Island), which we know is not entirely correct.

Viewers of the site, and its animated maps, might also take note of the inset photographs of the two opposing combatant commanders, as shown in the upper right-hand corner, depicting both Admirals Mikawa and Turner. Therefore, a presentation of both the opposing ships, and the opposing naval commanders leading those ships, make this animated "historical walkthrough" of the battle that much more interesting for both the astute researcher and the casual viewer.

For further viewing, the reader is urged to access the *History Animated* website noted below and then click on *The Battle of Savo Island* link under its greater *The*

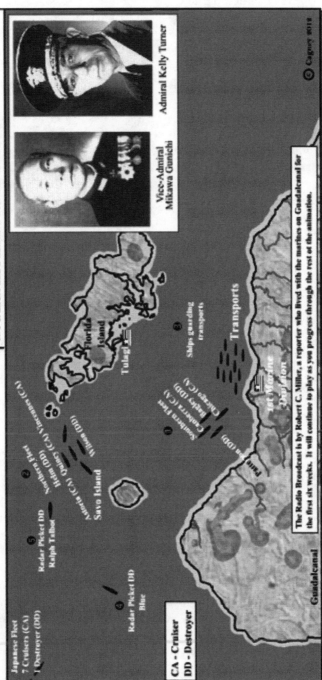

Figure 58.   Map ⑨: The HistoryAnimated.com Map—Opposing Naval Forces

Battle for Guadalcanal heading to enjoy the full presentational display: http://www .pacificwaranimated.com/Guadalcanal_Savo_Island.html

The scale-drawing map in Figure 59 is yet another from the *HyperWar* website (http://www.ibiblio.org/hyperwar/USN/USN-CN-Savo/index.html) and is accurate and detailed enough to pique the researcher's interest and to provide viable answers to many long-standing questions. Clearly shown here are the placements of all four of the targeted (and later ill-fated) heavy cruisers of the Allied surface fleet, to include "last-knowns" for the *Quincy* ❶, *Vincennes* ❷, and *Astoria* ❸, as well as the Australian heavy cruiser *Canberra* ❹. It is widely accepted that the *Quincy* did in fact go down just east-northeast of Savo Island almost precisely as she is shown here, and that the *Canberra* was sunk in a position almost due south of the island. Both assumptions appear to be well supported in this map depiction, and the chart image also appears to include solid referential time stamps to walk the researcher through each of the battle scenarios as they occurred.

Of note, and seen also in this plotting map, are the movements of not only RADM Scott on his *San Juan*, as part of the Eastern screen ❺, but also the DDs guarding the Yoke transports at Tulagi ❻; the DD screens protecting the X-Ray landing areas near Red Beach at ❼; the unexplained movements and track of Admiral Turner's own flagship *McCawley* (APA-4) on the occasion of the night battle itself ❽; and even the concurrent patrol patterns of Crutchley's two radar pickets, the *Blue* and the *Ralph Talbot*, at both ❾ and ❿.

This most excellent and incredibly detailed battle map can be attributed to the eminent naval historian Bruce Loxton in his notable work, *The Shame of Savo: Anatomy of a Naval Disaster*,[245] and is probably the most exceptional plotting chart of all found by this researcher. The concise rendering and "minute-by-minute" recap quite capably show the full end-phase (secondary) attack on RADM Riefkohl's own Northern fleet, presenting ❶ transitional track movements; ❷ positional ship placements and course change headings; ❸ impeccable date and time stamping; and even ❹ "last-knowns" for virtually all of the ships involved in the lag-end attacks of the 1BOSI. Found to be a truly inspirational study piece and an excellent accounting of the attack on the American Northern screen in full, researchers will easily find this chronological depiction to be most valuable, with a scale of "one-to-ten" rating almost peaking out at twelve.

Note also the curious presence of the blurred, cloud-like image that is shown just south of Savo Island, tagged simply as "Heavy Cloudbank." This one, single depiction of inclement weather, known to have been in situ just prior to (and even during) the battle itself, is not often shown on other maps of the time depicting this same naval scenario, and is therefore somewhat unique in its presentation. Only the much later Ohmae map seems to depict this "fogbank" as being a somewhat contributing factor, at least in this place and at that time, and was in fact the very means by which a harried *Ralph Talbot*, then under extremely harsh attack, was able to escape the battery of shells fired on her by Mikawa's own cruisers (the *Furutaka*, *Tenryū*, and *Yubari*) even as they disengaged their attacks and began to clear Savo Island at an approximated 0216 hours.

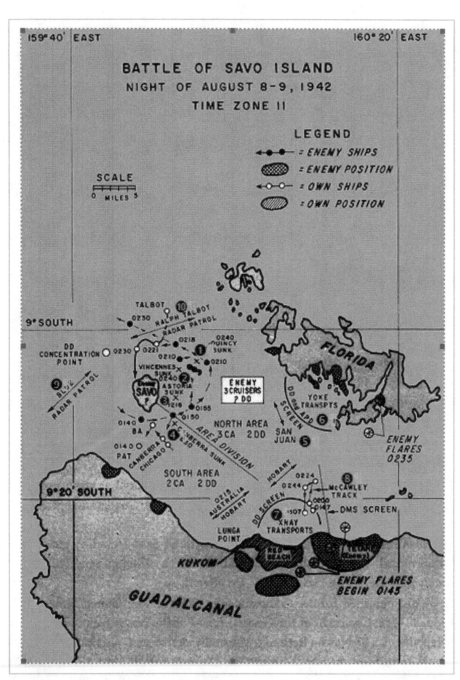

Figure 59.   Map ⑩: The _HyperWar_ Map

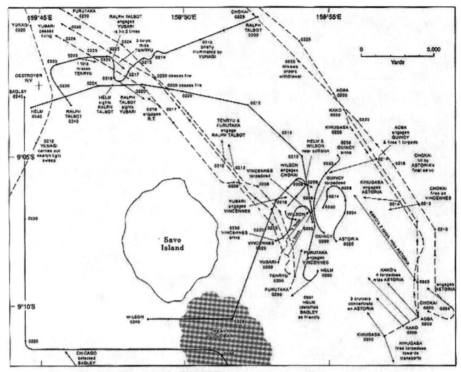

The final phase—Battle of Savo Island: 0200–0240

Figure 60.   Map ⓫: The Loxton Map (1994)

Seen in Figure 61 is yet another exacting diagram of the 1BOSI in full—here a cartographic depiction that again shows the attack on both Crutchley's Southern and Northern fleet, transitional track movements, time stamping, and positional ship coordinates as the two combatant navies moved from battle to battle. The scale drawing is from the Mackenzie J. Gregory website[246] and titled "The Battle of Savo Island: 8 August 1942"; however, the only other attribution that can be found on the image is that of an otherwise obscured tagging of "N. W. Grosen," in the lower right-hand corner, identifying the individual who may (or may not) have crafted the original map outlay.

Of note are the curious tracks of both the DD *Jarvis* ❶ and Bode's own CA *Chicago* ❷, as the two ships proceeded far to the north and west—seemingly away from the battle itself. And, while it was clearly understood at the time that the *Jarvis* was in fact en route to Sydney, Australia, for badly needed repairs after its scathing attack on 7 August, there would be hell to pay for the far less fortunate CAPT Howard Douglas Bode for his actions on the night in question, and his unexplained move to the north and west for some *forty* unaccounted-for minutes.

Also quite visible are the actual (and correct) "box-like" patrol pattern of RADM Riefkohl's Northern screening force ❸; the activities of Crutchley's own Southern force that was made up of the *Canberra* and *Chicago*, as well as the DDs *Patterson* and

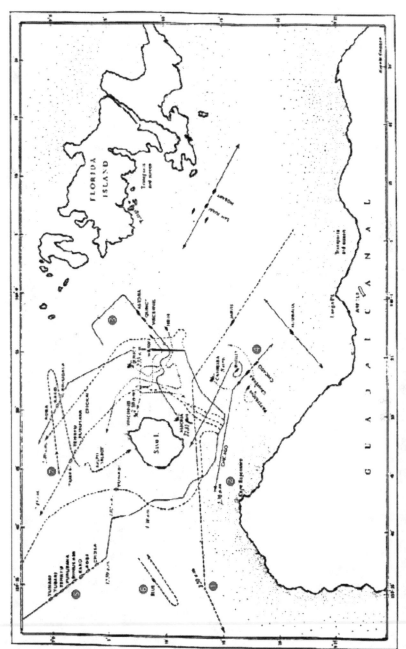

Figure 61. Map 12: The N. W. Grosen Map (Undated)

Bagley ❹; and the incursive movements of Mikawa's IJN battle group ❺ as it in fact approached the battle arena and as carried throughout the course of both skirmishes. Note also the elliptical patrol patterns of both of the American radar pickets *Blue* and *Ralph Talbot* at ❻ and ❼.

The last map image (Figure 62) is again one of the finest and most meticulously developed maps of the 1BOSI, as presented here by the Naval War College (NWC) in (then) LTC David E. Quantock's in-depth analysis of the battle.[247] Here, the inset citation shown at left seems to suggest that the chart may have been entirely based on a previous rendering that had itself been prepared by a CDR W. D. Innis, who had apparently worked within the Analysis Section of that same NWC. Clearly, the "Innis/Quantock" interpretation is easily seen to be not only smartly rendered in its representation but also complete in its detailed depiction of the orders of battle, attack scenarios, and transitional movements of those surface fleets, as well as their post-action dispositioning. Also seen clearly in this map, the researcher might once again note the bizarre navigational activities of both the *Jarvis* and the *Chicago*, as each ship appears to have exited the area almost at the very height of the battle; indeed, while the overall movement of the *Jarvis* may in and of itself have been well known, the activities of Bode's own *Chicago* would very soon come under sharp scrutiny by the RADM Hepburn and the naval high command of that time.

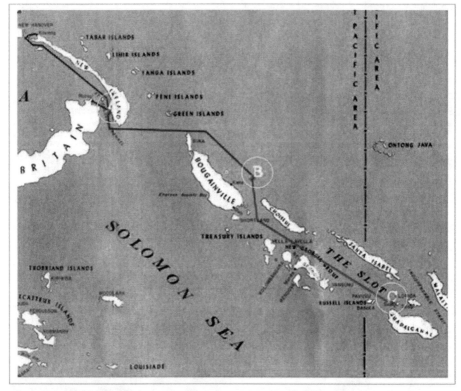

Figure 62.   Map ⑬: The Innis/Naval War College (NWC) Map

A Word about TROMs:
A Special Acknowledgment

In form and effect to the researcher of naval history, a "TROM" profile is simply an arcane and somewhat unique "Mil-speak" term for a ship's "Tabular Record of Movement." It is a term that is essentially applied to the movements and activities of a specific (or an entire class or formation) of naval warships, as it might relate to Imperial Japanese Navy vessels—especially before and during World War II. Seemingly unsubstantiated by any "official" U.S. Navy records, the term itself seems to be wholly unique to the *Nihon Kaigūn*—an English language venue for the study of the Imperial Japanese Navy Combined Fleet webpage (found at http://www.combinedfleet.com/kaigun.htm), and the site's two major contributors, Bob Hackett and Sander Kingsepp, both from that same online source.

Of inestimable value to researchers, naval historians, and chroniclers of ships' service histories, TROMs are—in at least this one author's opinion—almost as important as the ships' action reports themselves and are entirely gleaned from extant American and Japanese source materials, then compiled into chronological accounts of a ship's movements and activities, to include the before and after of many of those ships' major naval engagements.

Of interest, one can indeed find TROMs for virtually all of the American CVs, BBs, CAs, CLs, and DDs, and for many of the more major and minor IJN warships of the time as well. In fact, entries were found for all of the ships of the 1BOSI encounter, to include chronological timelines that had been captured for not only Mikawa's own *Chōkai* but also the *Aoba, Furutaka, Kinugasa, Tenryū,* and *Yubari.* The information for each seems to be impeccable, all-conclusive, and all-encompassing for virtually all of the "original" participant ships from the battle at Savo. To illustrate exactly this point, note the TROM extracts shown here, for the IJN heavy cruisers *Aoba* and *Tenryū,* representing but a brief span of time from July 1942 and leading up to the First Battle of Savo Island.

> 5 July 1942:
>> *Aoba* arrives at Kieta, Bougainville.
>> 7 August 1942: American Operation Watchtower—The Invasion of Guadalcanal, Solomons:
>> RADM (later ADM) Richmond K. Turner's (former CO of *Astoria,* CA-34) Amphibious Task Force 62; covered by VADM (MOH, later ADM) Frank J. Fletcher's (former CO of *Vermont,* BB-20) Task Force 61, and RADM (later ADM) John S. McCain's (former CO of *Ranger,* CV-4) Task Force 63's land-based aircraft; and MAJ Gen (later GEN/MOH/Commandant) Alexander A. Vandegrift's 1st Marine Division on Florida, Tulagi, Gavutu, Tanambogo and Guadalcanal during the opening campaigns to take the island.
>> That same day, CRUDIV6 and *Chōkai* depart the Moewe Passage through the Slot toward Guadalcanal with light cruisers *Tenryū* and *Yubari* and destroyer *Yunagi.* At Rabaul, *Chōkai* embarks the Commander of the Eighth Fleet, VADM Mikawa Gunichi (former CO of *Kirishima*) and his staff.

8 August 1942:

> At 0625, each of Mikawa's six cruisers catapult a sortie of floatplanes. Three fly to search waters N of the Solomons. *Aoba*'s floatplane—probably an E13A1 *Jake*—flies S to the landing area and reconnoiters Tulagi. Avoiding fighters and flak, the crew returns at noon and reports "one battleship, one auxiliary carrier, four cruisers, seven destroyers and 15 transports" off Lunga Point. Mikawa now knows that the Allied force is divided and that he can deal with them separately.
>
> 9 August 1942: The Battle of Savo Island.[248]

14 July 1942:

> The IJN undergoes a major reorganization. The Eighth Fleet is created under VADM Mikawa Gunichi (former CO of *Kirishima*) and based at Rabaul.
>
> 14–26 July 1942:
>
> IJN CA *Tenryū* and *Kinugasa* pay call at various IJN bases in the Solomons, New Britain and New Ireland arriving at the Moewe Passage, near Kavieng.
>
> 27 July 1942:
>
> CRUDIV6 is reassigned to the Eighth Fleet.

7 August 1942:

> CRUDIV6 and *Chōkai* depart the Moewe Passage toward Guadalcanal with the light cruisers *Tenryū* and *Yubari* and destroyer *Yunagi*. At Rabaul, *Chōkai* embarks the Commander of the Eighth Fleet, VADM Mikawa and his staff.

9 August 1942:

> Both naval elements clash on the occasion of the First Battle of Savo Island.[249]

A very special note of thanks and acknowledgment must be extended to Bob Hackett and Sander Kingsepp of the *Nihon Kaigun* (Imperial Japanese Navy Combined Fleet) site (http://www.combinedfleet.com/kaigun.htm), for both their superb compilation efforts and a most excellent presentation of that empirical data, as seen in their *Junkoyan* TROM database for each of the classes of IJN light and heavy cruisers that were in service during World War II in the great Pacific.

The author cannot offer high enough praise to the developers of the database venue itself, both for the ease of access and the wealth of information they have made available to all serious naval history researchers. It is highly recommended that any serious analyst of the time, the events, and the ships—both on the American side and on that of the Imperial Japanese Navy—make good use of that resource. A special thanks, therefore, is extended to the illuminating and important work being done on that site.

APPENDIX B

Table of Terms, Definitions, Acronyms, and Abbreviations

The following list is provided for ease of reader cross-referencing and to promote a clearer understanding of much of the topical discussion points presented within the full treatise. Therefore, shown below (and on the following pages throughout the extended table matrix) is a concise listing of all terms, definitions, acronyms, and abbreviations used in the context of this book.

Acronym	Definition
AAR	**A**fter-**A**ction **R**eport
ABC	**A**ustralian **B**roadcasting **C**orporation
ABCD	**A**merican, **B**ritish, **C**hinese, and **D**utch (forces); defined as the *primary* major military powers that would oppose the formidable Empire of Japan and its IJN, and that was agreed on in principle before the extended war in the Pacific in World War II. (See also **(N)WPL** and **Rainbow 5**).
ADM	**Adm**iral
"Angel's Mile"	The author's own honored appellation for the area of Sealark Channel (or Sealark Lane or even Canal) that would later come to be known only as Iron Bottom Sound. See the author's commemorative poem, "The Battle of Savo Island."
AO	Fleet Oiler (U.S. Navy ship classification naming convention)
AP(A)	**A**mphibious **T**ransport (**A**rmed)
ANZUS	**A**ustralian–**N**ew **Z**ealand–**U**nited **S**tates (Treaty Organization)

Acronym	Definition
AT	**A**mphibious **T**ransport (Variation)
ATF	**A**mphibious **T**ask **F**orce
BATDIV or **BatDiv**	**Bat**tleship **Div**ision Admiral Gunichi Mikawa's 3rd Battleship Division at the time of the attacks on Pearl Harbor and Ford Island on 7 December 1941. This small but powerful group consisted of the BBs *Hiei* and *Kirishima*.
BB	**B**attleship Official naval designation for a Battleship-class vessel, built in a format to contain a series of multi-turreted main gun armaments, usually in a 16- to 18-inch range. Here, for the sake of phonetic consistency, the first **B** is indeed meant to mean "Battleship," while the second **B** is simply added to effect a degree of "alliterative repetition" (as seen also in **DD**).
Betty	To the American (and Allied) forces, this was a medium-range, land-based bomber that was officially the *Mitsubishi* G4M (and later G4M1), widely used by the Japanese Naval Air services to conduct forays and attacks on Guadalcanal and other locations throughout the Solomon Islands. The twin-engine light bomber was maneuverable and highly nimble, boasting two *Mitsubishi* MK-4A-11 powerplants and twin 14-cylinder radial engines.
BOCE	**B**attle **o**f **C**ape **E**sperance A famed night naval battle in the Solomons that would take place just off the northern coast of Guadalcanal near a landmark promontory called Cape Esperance, the night naval action would involve the forces of ADMs Mikawa, Gotō, and Jōjima, as counterpoised against those of RADM Norman Scott. The BOCE would later be seen as a considerable (and key) defeat for the Japanese Navy's surface fleet. See ***Cape Esperance*** below.
BOSAMAR	**B**attle **off** **Samar**
1BOSI	**1**st (First) **B**attle **o**f **S**avo **I**sland
"The Great Navy Bugout"	This "dripping-with-sarcasm" phrase was probably first coined by U.S. Marines entrenched on the main island of Guadalcanal, and it dryly

Acronym	Definition
	refers to ADM Fletcher's ordered pull-out of his CTF naval screening forces from Iron Bottom Sound on the afternoon of 8 August 1942. This decision then caused Crutchley to withdraw his own cargo and support ships from the area, leaving the men already dug in ashore with scant munitions and supplies, effectively stranding them for a period of time until they felt it safe to return. Furious with the Navy's decision to pull virtually all of its forces from the area, almost in tandem, the U.S. Marines used the rather tongue-in-cheek catchphrase "The Great Navy Bugout" to thereafter to refer to the incident in full.
CA	**C**ruiser, **A**rmored
CAP	**C**ombat **A**ir **P**atrol
CAPT	**Capt**ain
Cape Esperance	The northernmost coastal point on the main island of Guadalcanal in the Solomon Islands. Well north of the capitol city of Honiara—and the always hotly contested Henderson Field—this area would host one of the most vicious sea battles to be unleashed in all of the World War II Pacific area, the Battle of Cape Esperance. For more detailed information, refer to the Wikipedia website (http://en.wikipedia .org/wiki/Cape_Esperance). See **BOCE** above.
CAS	**C**ombat **A**ir **S**upport
CBSAR	**C**hief of the **B**ureau of **S**hips **A**ssessment **R**eport
CDC	**C**ruiser **D**ivision **C**ommander
CDR	**C**omman**der**
CDRE, COMO or **Cdre**	**C**ommo**dore**
Choiseul	Pronounced (*Schwä-zool*), this is a large island mass that was one of the northernmost islands in the nearly 900-island archipelago of the Solomon chain. Bounded on its north by the Pacific Ocean, and on its southern coast by the New Georgia Sound, Choiseul was highly desirable as a strategic base of operations for both the Allies and the Japanese, the channel of which sluiced past its location and would later be called the Slot. That channel would serve as a key avenue of approach for VADM Mikawa's surface fleets on many of their forays to the south.

ACRONYM	DEFINITION
CINC	Commander-in-Chief
CINCAF	Commander-in-Chief, Asiatic Fleet
CINCPAC	Commander-in-Chief, Pacific (perhaps interchangeable with CINCPACFLT)
CINCPACFLT	Commander-in-Chief, Pacific Fleet (perhaps interchangeable with CINCPAC)
CINCUSFLT	Commander-in-Chief, United States Fleet
CINCPOA	Commander-in-Chief, Pacific Ocean Area
CL	Cruiser Light
CNO	Chief of Naval Operations
CO	Commanding Officer
Coastwatcher	"Coastwatchers" were the daring operatives, the clandestine outpost watchers, and the vigilant lookouts employed by local Australians who used their keen first-line observational skills to best advantage. Perched high atop remote island locations throughout the Channel—each with a commanding mountain view of most of the shipping lanes past Choiseul and the Slot itself—the Coastwatchers regularly reported on any large (or otherwise suspicious) Japanese shipping activity (and air incursions) passing through on their way south to Guadalcanal.
COM13NAVDIST	Commander, 13th Naval District
COMAIRSOSPAC	Commander, Air Forces South Pacific
COMCRUDIVSIX or COMCRUDIV6	Commander, Cruiser Division 6 Under the command of RADM Aritomo Gotō
COMCRUDIVEIGHTEEN or COMCRUDIV18	Commander, Cruiser Division 18 Under the command of RADM Mitsuhara Matsuyama, but one that ultimately fell under the umbrella of VADM Mikawa's greater charge
COMEIGHTHFLT or COM8THFLT	Commander, Eighth (8th) Fleet
COMFIFTHFLT or COM5THFLT	Commander, Fifth (5th) Fleet
COMNAVAIR	Commander, Naval Air Truncated abbreviation for below
COMNAVAIRFORSOPAC	Commander, Naval Air Forces South Pacific

Acronym	Definition
COMNAVAIRFORSOPACFLT	**Com**mander, **Nav**al **Air For**ces **So**uth **Pac**ific **Fl**eet
COMPACFLT	**Com**mander, **Pac**ific **Fl**eet
COMPHIBFORSOPAC	**Com**mander, Am**phib**ious **For**ces **So**uth **Pac**ific
	This command (and its somewhat lengthy designation) was held, at the time of the 1BOSI, by RADM Richmond Kelly Turner, Crutchley's superior, a position he would hold until well after the invasion of Guadalcanal and the twin attacks at Savo.
COMPHIBFORSOPACFLT	**Com**mander, Am**phib**ious **For**ces **So**uth **Pac**ific **Fl**eet
	The command (and its somewhat lengthy designation) was held, at the time of the 1BOSI, by RADM Victor A. Crutchley (RN).
COMSOPAC	**Com**mander, **So**uth **Pac**ific (often with word "Area" appended to its functional title)
COMSOWESPAC	**Com**mander, **So**uth**wes**t **Pac**ific
	Revised command structure for the American and Australian military command during the early part of World War II, which on 18 April 1942 appointed GEN Douglas MacArthur as the Supreme Commander of Allied Forces in the Southwest Pacific (SOWESPAC) area.
COMSOWESPACFOR	**Com**mander, **So**uth**wes**t **Pac**ific **For**ce(s)
COMSUBDIV5	**Com**mander, **Sub**marine **Div**ision 5
	The command reporting structure, set for the S-class USS *S-38* and *S-44* diesel subs during the 1942 campaigns in and around Guadalcanal area and the St. George's Channel. The misinterpretation and *sluggish* reporting of the *S-38* sighting of Mikawa's fleet by this same COMSUBDIV5 would later go on to quite negatively affect the outcome of the 1BOSI.
CRUDIV or **CruDiv**	**Cru**iser **Div**ision
	One of Admiral Gunichi Mikawa's Eighth Fleet force elements. At Guadalcanal, two such units would be combined and would bring together the famed CRUDIV6 (RADM Gotō) and CRUDIV18 under the aegis and operational command of Mikawa for both forces.

Acronym	Definition
CBSAR	**C**hief of the **B**ureau of **S**hips **A**ssessment **R**eport
	U.S. Navy organizational report
CTF	**C**arrier **T**ask **F**orce
CV	**C**arrier **V**essel, General Purpose
	U.S. Navy ship designation
CVL	**C**arrier **V**essel, **L**ight
CXAM	The RCA Corporation's first-production radar system deployed on some U.S. Navy ships, such as the USS *Pensacola* (CA-24), the USS *Northampton* (CA-26), and even the later USS *Chicago* (CA-29) itself, which operated in a mid- to high VHF frequency band of 200 MHz range.
DANFS	**D**ictionary of **A**merican **N**aval **F**ighting **S**hips
DCNS	**D**eputy **C**hief of **N**aval **S**taff
DD	**D**estroyer
	Official naval designation for a Destroyer-class vessel, built to be extremely swift and low in the water, again with a series of multi-turreted main gun armaments, usually in a 5-inch range. Here, for the sake of consistency, the first **D** is meant to mean "Destroyer," while the second **D** is added for the sake of alliterative uniformity. Compare also **BB**.
DE	**D**estroyer **E**scort
DESRON	**Des**troyer Squad**ron**
Doma or **Doma Reef**	An area of heavy reef formation off the coast of Tassafaronga and Guadalcanal and just north of Honiara. This was the location at which the Japanese quite unsuccessfully "dumped" their cargo and munitions crates (often in 55-gallon drums) under due scrutiny and the heavy fire of American and Allied naval forces during the fierce Battle of Tassafaronga on 30 November 1942. For further information, see http://en.wikipedia.org/wiki/Battle_of_Tassafaronga.
DNC	**D**o **N**ot **C**oncur
	A converse, optional response by the author to that of *Concur* as regards the findings of Admiral Hepburn's investigative report of 1943. Of the several separate and distinct charges (and allegations) read before Captain Howard Bode of the USS *Chicago*—as a result of the

Acronym	Definition
	1BOSI—the author notes that not all findings may have been included, or even brought to bear initially, during that formal Hepburn inquiry. The **C** or **DNC** tagging, therefore, has simply been used here to connote either a *new* finding or a variance of agreement with a specific finding relating to Bode's conduct on the night in question.
DSC	**D**istinguished **S**ervice **C**ross
FADM	**F**leet **Adm**iral As noted in FADM Chester William Nimitz and FADM Ernest J. King
FCS	**F**ire **C**ontrol **S**ystem(s)
F/L	**F**light **L**ieutenant (RAAF/RAAFR ranking of some Hudson pilots)
F/O	**F**light **O**fficer (RAAF/RAAFR ranking of some Hudson pilots)
Fortuna secundat audaces	Latin: *Fortune favors the brave.*
Gadarukanaru	The quaint Japanese-enunciated name set to approximate "Guadalcanal."
Gotō	Rear Admiral Aritomo **Gotō** Gotō's Cruiser Division 6 (CRUDIV6) directly supported Japanese naval operations during the first several months of the Guadalcanal campaign, especially during the 1BOSI on the night of 9 August 1942. A second sortie of even deadlier heavy cruisers known as Cruiser Division 18 (or CRUDIV18) would soon enter the fray and go on to play an integral role in that 1BOSI outcome in particular. On that occasion, VADM Mikawa would have assumed effective command of *both* cruiser divisions.
GQ	**G**eneral **Q**uarters
Henderson Field	Initially, a minor Japanese-constructed airstrip near Honiara on the main island of Guadalcanal, the "real estate" was almost easily wrested from the clutches of Japan's ground forces on 7 August 1942—the area seized in a series of bold and almost uncontested assaults on the island itself. For further information, see http://en.wikipedia.org/wiki/Honiara_International_Airport.
HMAS	**H**er/**H**is **M**ajesty's **A**ustralian **S**hip

Acronym	Definition
HMNZS	Her/His Majesty's New Zealand Ship
Honiara	A major city on the main island of Guadalcanal in the Solomon Islands, its location was always hotly contested during at least the initial phases of the Allied invasion of 7 August 1942. USMC assault forces would continue to fight a series of battles against a ragged and disorganized Japanese infantry force that was quite fluid and less dug in hard. For further information, see the detailed account at http://en.wikipedia.org/wiki/Honiara.
HR	Hepburn Report Findings gathered and presented by Admiral Arthur Japy Hepburn and his second in command, LCDR Donald J. Ramsey—then chairman of the General Board of the Navy—regarding Captain Howard Douglas Bode and his actions on the USS *Chicago* (CA-29) on the occasion of the 1BOSI during the early morning hours of 9 August 1942. The Hepburn Report would go on to scathingly investigate Bode's actions and conclude much to his disfavor.
IBS	Iron Bottom Sound
IFF	Identification Friend or Foe (Naval/Air Force identification confirmation query protocol)
IJN	Imperial Japanese Navy
in actum	Latin: *in actuality* (i.e., served in place)
Iron Bottom Sound	Geographically mapped as Sealark Lane (or Sealark Channel or even Canal), this large sound was the principal arena for multiple sea battles and ship-to-ship engagements, such that when all was said and done the sunken hulls of some 50+ warships would dot that ocean floor. Virtually all naval battles of any significance would take place in and around this watery arena, most often ending in disaster for either the Americans or the Japanese (and most often *both*). (See also **IBS**.) For further information, see the account at http://en.wikipedia.org/wiki/Ironbottom_Sound.
Itto-Junkoyan	A literal translation for the IJN heavy cruiser class warships of World War II.

Acronym	Definition
JMSDF	**J**apan(ese) **M**aritime **S**elf-**D**efense **F**orce
Jōjima	Rear Admiral Takatsugu **Jōjima** A key naval force commander during the Battle of Cape Esperance, a battle that would later come to be known to the Japanese as the Second Battle of Savo Island.
JN	**J**apanese **N**avy See also the **IJN** abbreviation as the more appropriate use for the Imperial Japanese Navy.
JN-19	**J**apanese **N**avy Code #**19** A precursor of the later equally secret **JN-25** code, the **JN-19** was all too often intercepted and decoded by American cryptanalysts, thereby rendering that code—and all of the data that flowed thereafter between commands—fully compromised. (Compare **JN-25** below.)
JN-25	**J**apanese **N**avy Code #**25** The name given by American cryptanalysts and codebreakers to the secretive (and thought to be secure) command and control communications coding scheme used by the IJN during (and even before) World War II, tagged as such because it was the twenty-fifth Japanese Navy system identified. First introduced in 1939 to replace its even older code *Blue* and JN-19, JN-25 was itself an enciphered code with (5) separate and distinct numeric groupings presented in its *send* traffic. The code would be changed from time to time without announcement, and it had again been modified as early as 1 December 1940 and again, three days before the attack on Pearl Harbor, on 4 December 1941. Curiously, it would be this very coding sequence that would be cracked by American eavesdroppers just before the Battle of Midway. The possession of such key intelligence and vital information would later work out much to the advantage of the Americans and would virtually ensure victory for its naval forces during the short but decisive battles on that one occasion. (Compare **JN-19** above.)

ACRONYM	DEFINITION
Junkoyan	A literal translation for the IJN cruiser-force warships of World War II. See also http://www.combinedfleet.com/junyokan.htm.
Kei-Junkoyan	IJN Light Cruiser class warships of World War II (literal translation).
"King Kong"	Refers to the IJN Vice Admiral Chūichi "King Kong" Hara, the podgy but highly aggressive nemesis of Vice Admiral Frank "Jack" Fletcher himself, this during the hotly contested Battle of the Eastern Solomons and later Battle of the Santa Cruz Islands, both occurring in mid-1942. He would best be remembered for the surrender of the controversial *Takahashi* sword, an historic and exquisitely crafted samurai blade that was surrendered in 1945, at the close of the war, aboard the USS *Portland* (CA-33). At Hara's specific request, the highly sought-after fifteenth-century sword would later be set on display at the USNA Museum in Annapolis, Maryland.
Kido Butai	The Japanese name of the 1st Air Fleet of the IJN. At the time of the naval campaigns at both Guadalcanal and the Eastern Solomons, this force would have been under the aegis of two commanding admirals, VADMs Chuichi Nagumo and Gunichi Mikawa himself.
Kōan	Seen as a story, dialogue, or statement—indeed, generally a question—that is used in Zen practices, often to test a student's astuteness and keenness of insight. One of the most famous of these "unanswerable" Japanese *Kōans* (or "riddles," as it were) has come to be typified by the classic *What is the sound of one hand clapping?* question, to which there is seldom a ready answer.
Kondō	Vice Admiral Nobutake **Kondō** Led the battleship *Kirishima*, four cruisers, and nine destroyers into the disastrous Battle of the Santa Cruz Islands in October 1942, against the American ADMs Halsey and Kincaid and their own force of twenty-three warships. The battle would later be seen as a tactical victory for the Japanese but a clear strategic win for the Americans.

Acronym	Definition
Lat	**Lat**itude Defined as the arc (or segment) of the Earth's equator that intersects between the meridian of a given place and the prime meridian (one that is also expressed in a measurement of both degrees and time).
LCDR	Lieutenant **C**omman**de**r
Lex	Shortened name of the USS **Lex**ington (CV-2)
LOC	❶ **L**etter **o**f **C**ommendation ❷ **L**ack **o**f **C**ommunications
Long	**Long**itude Defined as the angular distance from a specified circle, or plane of reference, as in an angular distance north or south from the Earth's equator measured through 90 degrees.
LOI	**L**ine **o**f **I**nterdiction Seen as the line drawn by an opposing force and the time at which they will interdict (and attack) an enemy fleet. This would most notably be used during the rare "crossing of the T" naval maneuvers seen during both the Battle of Cape Esperance and the later Battle Off Samar.
LST	**L**anding **S**hip, **T**ank
LT	**L**ieutenant
LTC	**L**ieutenant **C**olonel
Lunga or **Lunga Point**	A large promontory point jutting out from the main island of Guadalcanal just northwest of Honiara and Henderson Field. Many American transport and service ships would be ruthlessly attacked by the constantly encroaching Japanese ships and planes dispatched from Rabaul and Kavieng, to the north. For further information, see http://en.wikipedia.org/wiki/Lunga_Point.
MG	**M**ajor **G**eneral (Marine Corps and U.S. Army rank)

Acronym	Definition
Mikawa	Vice Admiral Gunichi **Mikawa** Commander of the IJN Eighth Fleet, based in Rabaul, the admiral would brilliantly lead the surprise attack on the Allied surface fleet (specifically, Crutchley's ill-fated Southern and Northern screening ships) in Iron Bottom Sound off Savo Island on the night of 9 August 1942.
MOBAIRFORPACOA	**Mob**ile **Air For**ce, **Pac**ific **O**cean **A**rea
Mothball Fleet	An area of storage for multiple retired, but not yet fully decommissioned, older USN ships. While many such vessels are saved by *vox populi* petition to perhaps serve as training vessels and/or museum ships, most such mothball fleet ships sit in close mooring in secured inlets to await a further fate of final scrapping.
NAS	❶ **N**avy **A**ir **S**ervice ❷ **N**avy **A**ir **S**tation ❸ **N**aval **A**ir **S**tation
New Britain	Seen as the largest of the island groups making up the Bismarck Archipelago near Papua/ New Guinea. During the Guadalcanal naval campaigns, this locale would be a major base and a key launch site for the Japanese throughout much of the war. Control of these islands was, in the end, wrested from Japanese control by force and would change hands in late 1945.
New Ireland	Another adjacent island group in the widely dispersed Bismarck Archipelago near Papua/New Guinea. The Japanese would exert considerable control over this entire geographical region and would hold on to both this island group and New Britain until 1945—the very last year of the war.
Nihon Kaigun	Imperial Japanese Navy's Combined Fleet. For more information, see http://www.combinedfleet.com/kaigun.htm.
NSF	**N**orthern **S**creening **F**orce (i.e., *Vincennes*, *Quincy*, and *Astoria*)
NWC	**N**aval **W**ar **C**ollege
ONI	**O**ffice of **N**aval **I**ntelligence

Acronym	Definition
Operation Watchtower	The officially sanctioned name for all operations surrounding the invasion and capture of Guadalcanal and the greater Solomon Islands region. The heated individual battles that would later make up this greater campaign would rage on from August 1942 to February 1943 and would go on to claim some 7,100 casualties in full on the Allied side.
Pagoda Mast	The mast superstructure atop many of the massive IJN heavy cruisers, as seen in ships like the *Chōkai*, *Tenryū*, *Kinugasa*, and *Kako* in 1942. It was the "stacked" effect of the level-on-level structures that extended upward from the bridge to smaller and smaller-scaled platforms that was most intriguing, such that it seemingly presented a "pagoda"-like effect.
PBY	An official U.S. Navy initialism, as set forth in accordance with the Aircraft Designation System of 1922. Here, the **PB** stood for "**P**atrol, **B**omber," while the **Y** was simply set as a coded entry to connote the aircraft's general manufacturer—in this instance, the Consolidated Aircraft Company.
Picket	A familiarized name assigned to any of a series of ships tasked with guarding the outer perimeter of a shipping lane, or a set defensive position. Usually assigned to ships of a DD (destroyer) class, these "pickets"— much like the USS *Blue* and USS *Ralph Talbot* themselves on the night of 9 August 1942— often carried "new" radar units with the best leading-edge technology available at the time built in to optimize those screening duties. The term itself is oddly reminiscent of the evenly spaced white picket fences of old, each stave and board serving to guard its separate but equally important quadrant (or, in this instance, patrol sector).
PO1	**P**etty **O**fficer **1**st Class
RAAF	**R**oyal **A**ustralian **A**ir **F**orce
RAAFR	**R**oyal **A**ustralian **A**ir **F**orce **R**eserve
RADAR	**R**adio **A**ssisted **D**etection **a**nd **R**anging
RADM	**R**ear **Adm**iral

Acronym	Definition
Rainbow 5	This idea formed the core of American (and later Allied) strategies during World War II and maintained a then-unchallenged assumption that the United States would always be allied with Britain (and France), to ensure (and enhance) offensive operations led by those forces on the European and African continents—or, as it turned out, *both*. It might clearly have been understood, however, that the United States would assume a leadership role in any such undertaking, as indeed it later would. (See also **ABCD**.)
RAN	**R**oyal **A**ustralian **N**avy
RANC	**R**oyal **A**ustralian **N**avy **C**ollege
Recomm	**Recomm**issioned (brought back into naval service, as with a temporarily retired ship)
Rengō Kantai	A native appellation for the Imperial Japanese Navy's *Combined Fleet*
RN	**R**oyal **N**avy (United Kingdom)
RNZAF	**R**oyal **N**ew **Z**ealand **A**ir **F**orce
S	**S**ubmarine Early *S*-class submarines, affectionately called Pigboats, Sugar Boats, or simply S-Boats. There were at least fifty-one of this early class of diesel-electric submarines built from 1920 to 1925, many of which would go on to serve quite distinguished campaigns and careers well into World War II.
S2C	**S**eaman **2**nd **C**lass
Samar	Geographically the easternmost island of the Philippines, Samar was the focal point and centerpiece of the Battle of Leyte Gulf in October of 1944. Here, naval elements led by VADM Takeo Kurita would roundly defeat VADM Clifton A. "Ziggy" Sprague's own *Taffy 3* (*TU 77.4.3*) in a wholly mismatched, one-sided battle that would find the Americans somewhat unprepared for the encounter. For specific details and further information, see http://en.wikipedia.org/wiki/Battle_off_Samar.
SAR	**S**earch **a**nd **R**escue

Acronym	Definition
Savo or **Savo Island**	The name (or abbreviated name) of the location of the night naval action during the First Battle of Savo Island on 9 August 1942, during which four heavy cruisers of the Allied fleet were decimated and sunk by an encroaching Japanese surface fleet led by ADMs Mikawa and Gotō. For further information on the 1BOSI, view the full and detailed account at http://en.wikipedia.org/wiki/Savo_Island.
SC and **SC-1**	Long-range air search radar and detection systems (U.S. Navy)
Sealark Lane or **Sealark Channel**	The actual (original) name of the expanse of water fronting Guadalcanal on one side and cross-channel Tulagi on the other. The area, alternately called Sealark Channel (and even Canal), would later be renamed as the far more ominous Iron Bottom Sound, soon becoming a hotbed of action and a focal point for virtually all of the great naval campaigns that would follow throughout the Guadalcanal area.
SECNAV	**Sec**retary of the **Nav**y
SF1	**S**triking **F**orce **1**
	One of the main strike-force elements of the Imperial Japanese Navy task group that was under ADMs Yamamoto and Nagumo, during the morning attacks on Pearl Harbor and Ford Island on 7 December 1941.
SF2	**S**triking **F**orce **2**
	The second main strike force element of that same IJN task group that was under the joint commands of ADMs Yamamoto and Nagumo, on the occasion of the dawn raids on Pearl Harbor and Ford Island on 7 December 1941.
SG	Surface Search Radar (U.S. Navy)
SGT	**S**er**ge**an**t**
Shackle-Unshackle	Embedded data code format used by Americans over extant TBS networks from ship to ship.

Acronym	Definition
"The Slot"	The somewhat-colloquialized name given to the channel area of New Georgia Sound in the Solomon Islands by American and Allied forces in 1942. This curious appellation referred to the narrowed channel area that ran geographically from Bougainville (to the north) to Makira (to the south). An area always contested by the American and IJN surface fleets throughout the years of 1942 and 1943, the channel separated the main islands of Guadalcanal from Florida Island (Nggela Sule), with a southern terminus ending in Sealark Channel itself. For further information, see http://en.wikipedia.org/wiki/The_Slot.
SNAFU	**S**ituation **N**ormal **A**ll **F**ouled **U**p (Polite Utterance) Considered a somewhat comical military vernacular term that is used to connote any situation that is seemingly out of hand or irresolvable. The phrase, of course, also came with its far more vulgar and unseemly alternate for that famed letter "F," which of course shall bear no mention here. Seen also as a distant cousin of FUBAR.
SNLF	**S**pecial **N**aval **L**anding **F**orce An IJN naval infantry unit deployed from Sasebo, Japan.
SOPAC	**So**uth **Pac**ific
SSF	**S**outhern **S**creening **F**orce (i.e., the HMAS *Australia*, HMAS *Canberra*, and USS *Chicago*)
(T)	**T**rue (for a true heading at sea) Seen as a course heading for a ship on an absolute and fixed directional compass point, as shown in the earlier **NW**, **NNW**, **SE**, and **SSE**.
Taffy	Task Force (familiar Navy term) A task force may be subdivided into several integral subgroup hierarchies. Therefore, below a *task **force*** might be a *task **group***—identified (and separated by) decimal points, as in TG **3.2**. Thereafter, even smaller units would then be called *task **units*** (TU **3.2.1**), and individual ships could be designated as *task **elements***, as seen in TE **3.2.1.4**, which would itself connote that this was the fourth ship within Task Element TU 3.2.1.

Acronym	Definition
Tassafaronga	An area of coastal expanse to the north and west of Honiara, Guadalcanal, Tassafaronga Point would be the scene of perhaps one of the greatest naval battles of the entire campaign for the Solomons. After a series of actions spanning from 1942 to 1943, no less than seven large IJN transport and supply ships would be sunk (and beached), virtually *in situ*, and would thereafter "dot" the coastline around that point area. In fact, known to have been lost in the area were the *Sasako Maru*, *Azumasa Maru*, *Kyushu Maru*, *Hirokawa Maru*, *Kinugawa Maru*, *Yamatsuki Maru*, and *Yamaura Maru*. For more information on Tassafaronga Point, and the key naval battle just off its coast, see: ❶ http://en.wikipedia.org/wiki/Tassafaronga_Point ❷ https://en.wikipedia.org/wiki/Battle_of_Tassafaronga
TBS	**T**alk **B**etween **S**hips
Ten Ichi Go	Seen as perhaps the last major naval operation by the IJN in the Pacific arena during World War II. A nearly preposterous operational plan concocted by a now-desperate Japanese military elite, *Ten Ichi Go* had at its core a doctrine of full attack on any advancing American battle force, even as those same elements quickly approached Okinawa, with the ultimate aim of crossing the very doorstep of the Japanese homeland. The bizarre plan, with its even more grotesque outcome, called for a naval battle group of ten ships—centered around the massive IJN battleship *Yamato*—to approach as closely as they could to the island of Okinawa, already under heavy siege by the Americans, and engage the enemy on all fronts. Thereafter, odd but seemingly strict contingency orders were set in place to beach the BB and use its large 18.1" guns as a makeshift "land battery" until either the ship itself was destroyed or the ammunition fully expended. Should the former scenario indeed occur, the remaining sailors still aboard *Yamato* had been ordered to disembark

Acronym	Definition
	the ship and join the ranks of the common infantry foot-soldiers onshore. Tragically, *Ten Ichi Go* would fail miserably, resulting in the loss of not only the *Yamato* but also at least one light cruiser and as many as four destroyers.
	It is only now, with the clarity of hindsight, that we may look back on the flawed reasoning behind the doctrine's theorization and even consider the imponderables, yet only continue to ask ourselves *why*. Ultimately, it would be an ignoble end for an otherwise noble ship—perhaps the finest ever of her class—and by 1420 hours on 7 April 1945, the bold *Yamato* would be struck, capsized, and sunk 120 miles WSW of Kagoshima, Japan, at an approximate coordinate fix of 30°22'N 128°04'E.
	For further information, see http://en.wikipedia.org/wiki/Operation_Ten-Go.
TE	**T**ask **E**lement (See *Taffy* explanatory note above)
TF	**T**ask **F**orce (See *Taffy* explanatory note above)
TG	**T**ask **G**roup (See *Taffy* explanatory note above)
"Tin Can"	The highly stylized name given to a specific class of naval ship, generally proudly reserved for "destroyer" force vessels. So named for its lower-grade armoring (or perhaps lack thereof) applied to the skeletal framework of the ship itself, these destroyers willingly sacrificed armor for speed, enabling them to serve in the crucial roles they would go on to play in World War II as both battle group and convoy escorts. In time, the men who served on these fast-attack escort ships would themselves be tagged as *Tin Can Sailors*, who, to a man, were proud to be called such.
"Tokyo Express"	The fanciful name given by the American and Allied forces to the IJN use of stealthy submarines, transport and cargo ships, and fast destroyers to deliver personnel, fresh supplies, and badly needed equipment, usually under the cover of night, to the entrenched IJA infantry forces then operating on Guadalcanal during the hotly contested years of 1942–1943.

Acronym	Definition
	With good fortune and a trick of luck, good timing, and effective deployment of ships, the U.S. Navy would rout the Japanese from these islands and stop the "Tokyo Express" virtually dead in its tracks. By late 1942, Japan would have already been handed a series of crippling defeats in the several open-sea battles that would later take place in the area and had begun to lose its expansionist taste for running that same supply line.
	By 1943, the "Tokyo Express" was all but shut down and forgotten, almost as soon as all Japanese forces had been expelled from the region, their terrifying stranglehold and expansionist design on the region foiled yet again by the tireless Allied surface fleets. It was to be a time of great indignity and loss for both the Imperial Japanese Navy and its disaffected admiralty. For further information, see http://en.wikipedia.org/wiki/Tokyo_Express.
TROM	**T**abular **R**ecord **o**f **M**ovement A "mil-speak" term for "**T**abular **R**ecord **o**f **M**ovement," this term was most applied to the movements and activities of a specfic (or an entire class) of naval warships, as it might relate to both American and Imperial Japanese Navy vessels—especially during the operational periods of World War II.
TU	**T**ask **U**nit (See **Taffy** above)
Tulagi or **Tulaghi**	Tulagi (less commonly referred to as Tulaghi) is a small island in the Solomon Islands group, just off the south coast of Florida Island (Nggella Sule). This location figured significantly in many of the sea and land battles centered just opposite of Guadalcanal in the Solomon Islands. For additional information on Tulagi, view the link at http://en.wikipedia.org/wiki/Tulagi.
USN	**U**nited **S**tates **N**avy
USNA	**U**nited **S**tates **N**aval **A**cademy
USMCNCTA	**U**.S. **M**arine **C**orps–World War II **N**avajo **C**ode-**T**alkers **A**ssociation
USNWC	**U**nited **S**tates **N**aval **W**ar **C**ollege

Acronym	Definition
USS	**U**nited **S**tates **S**hip (formerly **U**nited **S**tates **S**teamship)
VADM	**V**ice **Adm**iral
Val	*Aichi* D3A dive-bomber aircraft belonging to the Imperial Japanese Navy, which also came in two subversions: the D3A1 and the D3A2.
Vought 03U-3	A type of floatplane carried by many older American heavy cruisers, especially CA warships of a *New Orleans* class. These 03U-3 planes would have been fully mounted on short-skid catapults and fired—at astonishing speeds—off the decks of the cruisers and literally hurled directly into flight from the ship's decks. The 03U-3-class planes were used for reconnaissance and screening, deploying illuminants, and limited aerial combat and bombardment missions.
WWI	Common abbreviation for World War I
WWII	Common abbreviation for World War II
ww2db or **WW2DB**	**W**orld **W**ar II (**2**) **D**ata**b**ase Prolific data mining website that offers extensive information on World War II—the people, battles, events, date and time chronologies, participant (opponent) countries and forces, reference books, period photographs, useful weblinks, and *more*—provided for both the mildly curious researcher and the serious naval historian.
WYZYWYG or **WYSIWYG**	**W**hat **Y**ou **S**ee **I**s **W**hat **Y**ou **G**et
XO	**E**xecutive **O**fficer
YP	**Y**ard **P**atrol Smaller civilian commercial craft that were quickly pressed into service by a harried USN at the outset of World War II. Many of these small "littoral" ships were clippers, trawlers, and even "tuna boats," all of which were placed into service to patrol inlets and ships' berthing areas that were close in to shore, and all were painted with a standard gull-gray Navy color and given a USN designation of "YP." Indeed, many such vessels are still in service to this day and are used as at-sea training vessels in today's modern Navy.

Acronym	Definition
Zeke	Term used to describe Japan's long-range fighter aircraft, the *Mitsubishi* A6M *Zero*, which was wholly in use by the Imperial Japanese Navy Air Service (IJNAS) from 1940 to 1945. Again, with its stylized name that was seemingly interchangeable with that of the *Zero*, these planes were the terrors of the skies between the years of 1942 and 1943, as wave after wave of these attack aircraft continually strafed and attacked both shippage and entrenched land forces throughout all of the campaigns of the Solomon Islands.
Zero	The official (yet colloquialized) Allied name for the above type of aircraft, which was itself virtually interchangeable with the earlier-mentioned *Zeke* name.

Endnotes

1. Extracted from an early United States Naval Institute's *Proceedings* article titled "The Battle of Savo Island," by CAPT Toshikazu Ohmae, extant chief of staff to VADM Gunichi Mikawa from June 1942 to December 1943; edited by Roger Pineau; December 1957 (Volume No. 83, No. 12), 1272.

2. Dull, Paul S. (1978). *A Battle History of the Imperial Japanese Navy, 1941–1945*. Naval Institute Press.

3. Op. cit., Ohmae account, 1273.

4. Coombe, Jack D. *Derailing the Tokyo Express*. (1991). Stackpole Books, 24.

5. Morison, Samuel Eliot. (1958). *The Struggle for Guadalcanal, August 1942-February 1943. Volume 5 of History of United States Naval Operations in World War II*. Boston: Little, Brown and Company.

6. From Toland, John (1970). *The Rising Sun: The Decline and Fall of the Japanese Empire 1936–1945*. Random House; as cited in the article at http://en.wikipedia.org/wiki/Battle_of_Savo _Island#cite_note-Toland-13.

7. Op. cit., Ohmae account, 1270.

8. Extracted from the official Naval War College report, dated 1950 (AD/A-003 037) and titled *The Battle of Savo Island, August 9, 1942. Strategical and Tactical Analysis. Part I*, authored by Richard W. Bates and Walter D. Innis for the Naval War College (Department of Analysis), and distributed by the National Technical Information Services (NTIS) organization (U.S. Department of Commerce), 98.

9. Cited from *The Amphibians Came to Conquer: The Story of Admiral Richmond Kelly Turner*, by VADM George C. Dyer (Ret.), Chapter 10: "Savo: The Galling Defeat," 362.

10. Op. cit., Dyer, 365.

11. Op. cit., Ohmae account, 1272.

12. Ibid., 1271.

13. Ibid.

14. Ibid.

15. Ibid., 1272.

16. Op. cit., Dyer, 364, footnote 21, citing a specific memorandum from the Communications Officer of the Australia-based COMSOWESPACFOR, dated 19 February 1943. For additional information, view the excellent website at http://www.ibiblio.org/hyperwar/USN/ACTC/actc-10 .html#fn21.

17. Op. cit., Dyer, 365, footnote 22.

18. Op. cit., Bates/Innis, 101.

19. Ibid., 102.

20. Op. cit., Bonnot.

21. To view the Naval Warfare Simulations forum, and historian Richard Morgan's 2008 notes on the Hudson overflights, see the *Savo Island Project* link at http://forums.navalwarfare.net/archive/index.php/t-449.html.

22. Note that while some source documents (i.e., Dyer) refer to these B-17 patrol zones as "Sectors," yet other reports seem to refer to them as "Reconnaissance patrols" for Areas A, B, C, D, and E. The patrol sector most in question regarding the sighting of the Mikawa surface fleet that day was that of Area C patrol.

23. From VADM George Carroll Dyer's embedded report, as noted in his writings in *The Amphibians Came to Conquer: The Story of Admiral Richmond Kelly Turner* (Vol. 1), U.S. Department of the Navy (FMFRP 12-109-1).

24. Op. cit., Dyer, Chapter 10: "Savo: The Galling Defeat," 363.

25. Op. cit., Bates/Innis, 99.

26. Ibid., 100.

27. Ibid., 99.

28. Ibid., 98.

29. Ibid., 103.

30. View the full David H. Lippman account on the *World War II Plus 55* website at www.WorldWarIIPlus55.com.

31. Cited from CDR James C. Shaw, "Jarvis: Destroyer That Vanished," *Proceedings* 76, no. 2 (February 1950): 122. USNI.

32. Ibid., 123.

33. Op. cit., Bates, 114.

34. Ibid.

35. Loxton, Bruce, and Chris Coulthard-Clark (1997). *The Shame of Savo: Anatomy of a Naval Disaster*. Allen & Unwin Pty, Ltd.

36. Op. cit., Ohmae account, 1273.

37. It is curious that the USNI *Proceedings* article by Shaw should note the time of the *Blue–Jarvis* encounter west of Savo as being precisely 0308, while the NWC Bates/Innis account clearly cites 0325 as the more correct time. Further, in commenting on the encounter even within the Wikipedia account, it seems to indicate a time closer to 0132, immediately after the IJN destroyer *Yunagi* had been detached by Mikawa to serve as a rear guard.

38. Op. cit., Bates, 298.

39. Op. cit., Loxton, *The Shame of Savo*.

40. Cited from the Wikipedia article "The Battle of Savo Island," subsectioned as "Action North of Savo," at http://en.wikipedia.org/wiki/Battle_of_Savo_Island#Action_north_of_Savo, and based in full on the Loxton account itself. Retrieved 8 February 2013.

41. Op. cit., Coombe, *Derailing the Tokyo Express*, 140–41.

42. Ibid.

43. Ibid.

44. Op. cit., Loxton, *The Shame of Savo*.

45. Op. cit., Ohmae, 6.

46. Map courtesy of Mackenzie J. Gregory (*Map of the Battle of Savo Island—9 August 1942*) and can be viewed at http://ahoy.tk-jk.net/Savo/SavoMap.html.

47. Map courtesy of Shaw, "Jarvis: Destroyer That Vanished," 125.

48. Ibid.

49. Ibid., 126.

50. Ibid.

51. Ibid., 8.

52. The *Chicago* had previously operated with both the *Australia* and the *Canberra* in early 1942, when all three ships had been the victims of yet another close-in attack by Japanese warships. The action at that time would have been in Sydney Harbor, Australia, yet no appreciable damage and few injuries would result from the encroaching IJN midget submarine attack that day.

53. For additional insight into CAPT Howard Bode's involvement with the ONI, and his plea with CAPT Alan Kirk to have ADM Husband Edward Kimmel investigate the infamous "Bomb Plot Message," see authors Shanks and Lanzendoerfer's interview in their book *The Bode Testament* at http://www.microworks.net/pacific/library/shank_interview.htm.

54. For additional information on the USS *Chicago*—and the IJN submarine attack on that American CA—and other ships at portage in Sydney Harbor, see the website at http://en.wikipedia.org/wiki/Attack_on_Sydney_Harbour.

55. Note here the curious tale of the American diesel submarine USS *Bowfin* (SS-287) firing at a suspected convoy of four Japanese ships near the small island of *Minamidaitō* (now a prefecture of Okinawa) on a date of 9 August 1944. On that occasion, the *Bowfin* either sunk *outright* or damaged three of the four enemy vessels but missed with her fourth shot. In fact, that fourth torpedo is actually alleged to have errantly run its course, careened itself ashore and climbed the beach to hit a dock facility instead, taking out both a *crane* and a *bus* parked on that pier. This by now almost *comical* image would later indeed be memorialized and fully incorporated into the sub's own battle flag, which, in addition to the many kills and tonnage of convoy ships sunk, would now proudly emblazon an image of both in the lower right-hand corner of that flag. No other submarine (or other capital ship of the line) would ever boast of any such acquired "kills" throughout the course of the war in the Pacific.

56. Source is cited as the Mackenzie J. Gregory *Naval, Maritime and Australian History* website, as seen at http://ahoy.tk-jk.net/Savo/Savo11HepburnsConclusions.html.

57. It should be clear that the title "A Report of Suicide" is not added with any intent to either confound or confute; instead, it is more to serve as an elective portal to an even higher historical plane—that of *The Bode Testament* itself—as written years later by Sandy Shanks and Tim Lanzendoerfer in 2001. The book would meet with a tidal wave of acclaim for its foresight and clever invention, and it would go on to present a detailed historical account of the "trial and prosecution" of CAPT Howard Douglas Bode, had the man indeed survived and stood before a formal Naval Board of Inquiry.

58. For additional information on "The Bode Testament Interview," by Shanks and Lanzendoerfer, see the excellent website at http://microworks.net/pacific/library/shank_interview.htm.

59. Quantock, David E. (LTC, USA, Ret.). (2002). *Disaster at Savo Island, 1942.* U.S. Army War College, PA. Retrieved 29 January 2013 from http://www.ibiblio.org/hyperwar/USN/rep/Savo/Quantock/index.html#illus. Cited from a report under the section titled "Tactical Disposition," 24.

60. Cited from the Wikipedia article "Victor Crutchley," subsectioned as "Battle of Savo Island," at http://en.wikipedia.org/wiki/Victor_Crutchley#The_Battle_of_Savo_Island. Retrieved 29 January 2013.

61. Op. cit., Bates, 6.

62. Ibid., 347–48.

63. Op. cit., Ohmae, 1273.

64. The destroyers referred to here were the *Porter*-class USS *Selfridge* (DD-357), and the *Bagley*-class DDs USS *Henley* (DD-391) and USS *Mugford* (DD-389). Any one (or *both*) of these DDs could easily have been reassigned and used by Crutchley to supplement his understrength radar picket screening force that had been positioned just north of Savo.

65. Op. cit., Loxton, 214–15.

66. Ibid., 234–35.

67. Ibid., 56.

68. The number cited here as "three" might more accurately be represented as "four," which must include the individual (and combined) navies of not just the United States but also Great Britain and her two commonwealth states of Australia and New Zealand. It was therefore not at all unusual to find ships operating together that were tagged as being of a mixed USS, HMS, HMAS (and even HMNZS) designation origin.

69. The men of the 1st Marine Division, fighting in jungle-rotted locales like those around the Tenaru River, Matanikau, and Edson's Ridge, would all soon become aware of the major naval battles happening just off the coast of Guadalcanal at places like Lunga Point and Tassafaronga, and would later learn of the crushing defeat at Savo, the loss of the four heavy cruisers, and the damaging of a fifth (the *Chicago*). It would therefore not be long before those same Marines, with a typically gruff turn of phrase, would come up with the more colloquialized term "The Battle of Five Sitting Ducks" to describe what had indeed occurred that night.

70. Op. cit., Bates, 56–57.

71. Ibid.

72. Frank, Richard B. (1990). *Guadalcanal: The Definitive Account of the Landmark Battle*. Penguin Group.

73. Cited from *The Amphibians Came to Conquer: The Story of Admiral Richmond Kelly Turner*, by VADM George C. Dyer (Ret.), Chapter 10: "Savo: The Galling Defeat."

74. Op. cit., Dyer, Chapter 10: "Savo: The Galling Defeat."

75. Op. cit., Coombe, *Derailing the Tokyo Express*, 22.

76. Op. cit., Dyer, Chapter 10: "Savo: The Galling Defeat."

77. Worth noting is the fact that at least one of VADM Mikawa's ships would indeed be attacked later that same (9 August) date, and in fact sunk by the American attack sub USS *S-44*, piloted by LCDR Munson. The incident would occur during the victorious return trip of Mikawa's force when, at a point just seventy miles from their home port of Kavieng, the American *S*-class diesel sub was indeed able to spot, track, and plot a solution out to that IJN CA. Successfully firing a spread of four *Mark 10* torpedoes at that ship—then still some 700 yards away—three of the four torpedoes would run true and find their mark, exploding into the rear hull of the Japanese cruiser, sinking her virtually in situ, and claiming the lives of some seventy-one crewmen during that brief action.

78. Map courtesy of OnWar.com website and titled *Map of the 1st Battle of Savo Island, 09 August 1942*. From the website at http://www.onwar.com/maps/wwii/pacific2/savo42.htm. Retrieved 31 January 2013.

79. Map courtesy of Wikipedia from its article titled "Battle of Savo Island," and subsectioned under "Action South of Savo," at http://en.wikipedia.org/wiki/Battle_of_Savo_Island#Action _south_of_Savo. Retrieved 31 January 2013.

80. Cited from the Wikipedia account of the *Type 93* Long-Lance Torpedo, under a subsectioned heading of "History and Development," at http://en.wikipedia.org/wiki/Long_Lance#History_and_ development. Retrieved 16 January 2013.

81. Extracted from an early USNI *Proceedings* article titled "The Battle of Savo Island," by CAPT Toshikazu Ohmae, VADM Gunichi Mikawa's chief of staff from June 1942 to December 1943. Edited by Roger Pineau, December 1957 (Volume No. 83, No. 12), 1269.

82. Cited from the *Clash of Arms* website at http://www.clashofarms.com/ATReadinglists.html, and extracted from the Admiralty Trilogy Reading List; subsectioned as "IJN Cruiser and Battleship Doctrine"; document titled "Battleship and Cruiser Doctrine, Imperial Japanese Navy," by W. D. Dickson. Retrieved 23 January 2013; article undated.

83. Several such IJN cruiser surface actions were found to be remarkably detailed and set apart into even smaller subcategories such as day actions, dusk actions, night actions, and dawn actions— each time-of-day element mandating markedly different tactical approaches for those IJN light and heavy cruisers to locate, identify, and engage an enemy force, this almost always with target acquired and a virtually assured victory over that enemy fleet.

84. Here, of course, *Visio* refers to the Microsoft *Visio* program, a development platform used for extensive and detailed process flow mapping, hierarchical diagramming, organization charts, topologies, scale drawings, and, in this instance, the mapping of critical naval deployments and night actions in and around Savo Island and the Sound.

85. Cited from Wikipedia at http://en.wikipedia.org/wiki/Battle_of_Savo_Island.

86. Cited from Wikipedia at http://en.wikipedia.org/wiki/Second_Battle_of_Savo_Island.

87. Cited from Wikipedia at http://en.wikipedia.org/wiki/Naval_Battle_of_Guadalcanal#First _Naval_Battle_of_Guadalcanal.2C_November_13.

88. Cited from Wikipedia at http://en.wikipedia.org/wiki/Naval_Battle_of_Guadalcanal#Second _Naval_Battle_of_Guadalcanal.2C_November_14.E2.80.9315.

89. Cited from Wikipedia at http://en.wikipedia.org/wiki/Naval_Battle_of_Guadalcanal.

90. Cited from Wikipedia at http://en.wikipedia.org/wiki/Battle_of_Tassafaronga.

91. Frank, Richard B. (1990). *Guadalcanal: The Definitive Account of the Landmark Battle.* Penguin Group, 437–38. Cited from the Wikipedia article titled "The First Naval Battle of Guadalcanal" and subsectioned under "Action."

92. Cited from the PBS.org presentation, *The War,* subtitled *Guadalcanal (August 1942–February 1943),* further subsectioned under "Guadalcanal Naval Campaign." The comment, and additional reference information, may be viewed in full at the website: http://www.pbs.org/thewar/detail_5210 .htm. Retrieved 27 January 2013.

93. Op. cit., Ohmae account, 1270.

94. Ibid., 1269.

95. Ibid., Ohmae account, subtitled *Admiral Mikawa's Statement,* 1278.

96. Cited from Frank, Richard B. (1990). *Guadalcanal: The Definitive Account of the Landmark Battle.* Penguin Group; as noted on the website: http://en.wikipedia.org/wiki/Battle_of_Savo _Island#Aftermath.

97. Ibid.

98. Op. cit., Office of Naval Intelligence account, *The Battle of Savo Island.*

99. Ibid.

100. Ibid.

101. Cited from the USS *Ralph Talbot* (DD-390). After-Action Report, dated 1 September 1942.

102. Ibid.

103. Diagram created by the author using the Microsoft *Visio* development platform, which serves to illustrate the deployment and positioning of all five ships that composed the Northern screening force on the night of 8–9 August 1942.

104. Cited from Bates, Richard W., and Innis, Walter D. (1950). *The Battle of Savo Island, August 9, 1942. Strategical and Tactical Analysis. Part I.* Naval War College (Department of Analysis). U.S. Department of Commerce.

105. Ibid., 200.

106. Ibid.

107. Ibid.

108. For a somewhat clipped account of the history, timeline chronology, involvement, and movement of the USS *Helm* itself, view the web-based article at Wikipedia: http://en.wikipedia.org /wiki/USS_Helm_(DD-388).

109. Op. cit., Coombe, *Derailing the Tokyo Express*, 26.

110. For additional information on the *Opentopia* historical account of the USS *Helm* (DD-388), view the website at http://encycl.opentopia.com/term/USS_Helm_(DD-388).

111. For additional information on the *Dictionary of American Naval Fighting Ships* (DANFS), and its historical account of the USS *Helm* (DD-388), view the website at http://en.wikipedia.org/wiki/Dictionary_of_American_Naval_Fighting_Ships, and the Haze Gray website at http://www.hazegray.org/danfs/.

112. Cited from the "NAVY DEPARTMENT BUREAU OF SHIPS Assessment Report (C-FS/L11-1(374)-C-EN28/A2-11). Subject: USS *QUINCY*, USS *ASTORIA* and USS *VINCENNES*: Report of Loss in Action, dated 2 September 1943, 4.

113. For additional information on the Wikipedia historical account of the USS *Helm* (DD-388), view the website at http://en.wikipedia.org/wiki/Battle_of_Savo_Island#Action_north_of_Savo.

114. Ibid., Wikipedia, USS *Helm* (DD-388): http://en.wikipedia.org/wiki/USS_Helm_(DD-388).

115. Ibid., Wikipedia.

116. Quantock, David E. (LTC, USA, Ret.). (2002); *Disaster at Savo Island*, 1942. U.S. Army War College, PA. Retrieved 7 December 2012 from http://www.ibiblio.org/hyperwar/USN/rep/Savo/Quantock/index.html#illus.

117. The sources mentioned here are preeminently cited as Wikipedia, with other supporting narratives citing the Richard B. Frank book, *Guadalcanal: The Definitive Account of the Landmark Battle* (1990): New York: Penguin Group.

118. Op. cit., Bates/Innis, *The Battle of Savo Island*.

119. See the Wikipedia account of the USS *Helm* at http://en.wikipedia.org/wiki/USS_Helm_(DD-388).

120. Map rendering extracted from the Bruce Loxton book titled *The Shame of Savo: Anatomy of a Naval Disaster* (Allen and Unwin, St. Leonard's, NSW, 1994). Retrieved 11 December 2012, as extracted from the Elmer Smith letter at http://ahoy.tk-jk.net/Letters/ElmerSmithwasalsolostatth.html.

121. As noted from the website, *Ahoy! I Saw It: Naval Reminiscences* (http://tenika.tripod.com/). The specific Grosen map charting the full naval night encounter at Savo Island is more readily depicted at http://tenika.tripod.com/savo1023.jpg. As approximated on this map, the end-point position for the *Helm*—now finally at the DD rendezvous point—is estimated as having been more at a position of (±)159°30' E–9°02' S. Retrieved 16 December 2012 from: http://tenika.tripod.com/savo1023.jpg.

122. Op. cit., Bates/Innis NWC report, *The Battle of Savo Island*, 34.

123. Ibid., 35.

124. Ibid.

125. Ibid., 158.

126. Op. cit., Frank, *Guadalcanal: The Definitive Account of the Landmark Battle*.

127. Op cit., Loxton, 234.

128. The four ships under the command of RADM Norman Scott on the night of 9 August 1942, and that wholly made up Crutchley's hastily contrived Eastern screening force, would have been that of Scott's own flagship, the USS *San Juan* (CL-54), the Australian CL HMAS *Hobart* (D-63), and the two escort destroyers USS *Buchanan* (DD-484) and USS *Monssen* (DD-436). All of these ships would play no role in the events of the 1BOSI, and all would remain essentially unscathed throughout the course of that single night battle.

129. Photo courtesy of Robert Hurst and DANFS, at http://www.navsource.org/archives/05/388.htm, and Warship Boneyards, by Kit and Carolyn Bonner.

130. Op. cit., Bates, 362.

131. Cited from the World War 2: Pacific website from an article subtitled as "A Slur Upon Australian Air Force" by Morison, based on the Morison account titled *The Struggle for Guadalcanal: History of United States Naval Operations in World War II* (Vol. 5 of 15), 25–26. Retrieved 19 March 2013.

132. Op. cit., Bates, 363.

133. Cited from the BOSAMAR (Battle Off Samar) website at http://www.bosamar.com/pages/bosTBS, as noted in the table and Figure 33, as well as the full topical discussion of Talk Between Ships (TBS). Retrieved 26 March 2013.

134. For additional information, view the excellent and highly informative website presented by the U.S. Marine Corps (World War II) Navajo Code-Talkers Association (USMCNCTA) at http://navajocodetalkers.org/the_code/. Retrieved 26 March 2013.

135. Quantock, David E. (LTC, USA, Ret.). (2002). *Disaster at Savo Island, 1942*. U.S. Army War College, PA, at the website http://www.ibiblio.org/hyperwar/USN/rep/Savo/Quantock/index.html#illus.

136. Ibid., 26.

137. Cited from the Navy Department Bureau of Ships Assessment Report. (1943). (C-FS/L11-1(374)-C-EN28/A2-11). Subject: *USS Quincy, USS Astoria, and USS Vincennes: Report of Loss in Action*; dated 2 September 1943, 8.

138. Cited in official Action Reports from the USS *Sargo* (SS-188) in 1941, the *Seadragon* (SS-194) in 1942, and the *Tunny* (SS-282) and the *Tinosa* (SS-283), both in 1943, with each sub citing one or more such known problematic malfunctions as discussed.

139. Cited from Loxton's *The Shame of Savo: Anatomy of a Naval Disaster*, 43.

140. Here, the "Mahanian Naval Philosophy" represents those theories and naval strategies advanced by RADM Alfred Thayer Mahan (1840–1914), the brilliant naval strategist and authority on sea power and general naval tactics spanning many centuries. A devout student of doctrine, strategy, and historical naval encounters, his views and advanced theorems would propel him to the forefront of naval tacticians and planners, and he would often later be called "the most important American naval strategist of the 19th century."

141. Extracted from an early USNI *Proceedings* article titled "The Battle of Savo Island," by CAPT Toshikazu Ohmae, VADM Gunichi Mikawa's chief of staff from June 1942 to December 1943; edited by Roger Pineau, December 1957 (Volume No. 83, No. 12), 1272.

142. Op. cit., Ohmae account, 1272.

143. Cited from the account offered at the World War 2 in the Pacific website and titled "The Pacific War, 1942: The Battle of Savo Island—August 9, 1942, Off Guadalcanal, Solomon Islands." Retrieved 28 December 2012 from http://www.ww2pacific.com/savo.html.

144. Cited from Bates, Richard W., and Innis, Walter D. (1950). *The Battle of Savo Island, August 9, 1942. Strategical and Tactical Analysis. Part I*. Naval War College (Department of Analysis). Distributed by National Technical Information Service (NTIS). U.S. Department of Commerce, 139.

145. Op. cit., Bates/Innis NWC report, 140–41.

146. Ibid.

147. Mikawa's probative contingency of ships this night would be assigned as CRUDIV18, consisting of the *Chōkai* (the Mikawa flagship), the light cruisers *Furutaka* and *Yubari*, and the destroyer *Yunagi*—out of Rabaul. Augmenting this already formidable force would also be Admiral Gotō's *Aoba, Tenryū, Kako*, and *Kinugasa* from that admiral's CRUDIV6, arriving from the only other major IJN port of embarkation at Kavieng, also in Papua/New Guinea.

148. For additional source material, see http://en.wikipedia.org/wiki/Battle_of_the_Bismarck_Sea.

149. Op. cit., Ohmae account, 1276.

150. Map courtesy of About.com and may be viewed at http://militaryhistory.about.com /gi/o.htm?zi=1/XJ&zTi=1&sdn=militaryhistory&cdn=education&tm=20&gps=208_124_822_443 &f=00&tt=11&bt=1&bts=1&zu=http%3A//www.battlesforguadalcanal.com/Story/Battles/savo /savo.html.

151. For a clearer understanding of the hierarchical organization of ADM Crutchley's multiple screening force elements on the night of 9 August 1942, see the full *Visio*-based organization chart shown in Figure 3, beginning on page 8.

152. Cited from the USS *Vincennes* (CA-44) in an undated after-action report, as attributed to the Wikipedia account of the *Vincennes* at http://en.wikipedia.org/wiki/USS_Vincennes_(CA -44)#Loss_at_the_Battle_of_Savo_Island.

153. Op. cit., reference Wikipedia account of the *Vincennes* at http://en.wikipedia.org/wiki /USS_Vincennes_(CA-44)#Loss_at_the_Battle_of_Savo_Island.

154. On the night of 9 August 1942, CAPT William Garrett Greenman would be the command-ing officer of the USS *Astoria* (CA-34), while CAPT Samuel Nobre Moore was the corresponding CO of the American cruiser USS *Quincy* (CA-39). Both officers would perish with their stricken vessels once sunk. Only Riefkohl on the *Vincennes* would survive the brutal tragedy of that night.

155. Cited from the Morison account titled *The Struggle for Guadalcanal: History of United States Naval Operations in World War II*. Retrieved 17 July 2015.

156. Op. cit., Morison.

157. Op. cit., reference, http://en.wikipedia.org/wiki/Battle_of_Savo_Island#Action_north_of _Savo.

158. For additional reading on the USS *Samuel N. Moore* (DD-747)—the commemorative DD named in honor of the good captain of the lost USS *Quincy*—see the following excellent online resources:

❶ http://en.wikipedia.org/wiki/USS_Samuel_N._Moore_(DD-747)

❷ http://www.hullnumber.com/DD-747

❸ http://www.destroyersonline.com/usndd/dd747/

159. These passages have been collected from the David H. Lippman account of the *1st Battle of Savo Island* on his *World War II Plus 55* website at http://usswashington.com/worldwar2plus55 /dl09au42.htm.

160. For additional insight into CAPT Howard Bode's involvement in the First Battle of Savo Island, see the Shanks and Lanzendoerfer interview and presentational follow-up in their acclaimed historical novel, *The Bode Testament*. A more in-depth discussion of that interview may be seen at http://www.microworks.net/pacific/library/shank_interview.htm.

161. Dull, Paul S. (1978). *A Battle History of the Imperial Japanese Navy, 1941–1945*. Naval Institute Press.

162. Extracted from the official Naval War College report, dated 1950 (AD/A-003 037), and titled *The Battle of Savo Island, August 9, 1942. Strategical and Tactical Analysis. Part I*, authored by Richard W. Bates and Walter D. Innis for the Department of Analysis, Naval War College, and distributed by the National Technical Information Services (NTIS) organization (Department of Commerce), 116.

163. Extracted from an early United States Naval Institute's *Proceedings* article, dated December 1957 (Volume No. 83, No. 12), titled "The Battle of Savo Island." This well-received piece might easily be found to provide a wealth of information to the dedicated researcher, to include that of a detailed critique of the battle itself, preparations leading up to that battle, and truly walks in the shoes of the author by providing a good first-person narrative and account. That man was CAPT Toshikazu Ohmae, the naval officer who distinguished himself as VADM Mikawa's chief of staff during a period ranging from June 1942 to December of that same year.

Clearly, Ohmae might indisputably have had his finger well on the pulse of the events as they unfolded on the occasion of the 1BOSI and would surely have both issued and carried out many of those same attack orders given him by Mikawa on the night of 9 August 1942.

164. Op. cit., Coombe, *Derailing the Tokyo Express*, 24.

165. Op. cit., Loxton; *The Shame of Savo*.

166. Graphic image, "Ships." *CanStock*.

167. For additional information on the discrepant casualty figures noted for the armored cruiser HMAS *Canberra*, view the report at this Navy.gov website at http://www.navy.gov.au/w/index.php /HMAS_Canberra_%28I%29.

168. After-Action Report, USS *Patterson, Engagement with Enemy Surface Ships, Night of August 8–9, 1942; Guadalcanal-Tulagi Area*; Serial 001, dated 13 August 1942.

169. Op. cit., Shanks, 94.

170. For additional information on this account of action and this specific map, view the excellent MacKenzie J. Gregory website, *Ahoy-Mac's Web Log*, at both http://www.ahoy.tk-jk.net/Solo mons/BattleofSavoIsland.html and http://ahoy.tk-jk.net/.

171. Op. cit., Shanks, 94.

172. Ibid.

173. Ibid., 57.

174. Ibid., 54.

175. Ibid., 57.

176. Ibid., 129.

177. Ibid., 62.

178. Ibid., 132.

179. For additional information on CAPT Getting, and his time on the HMAS *Canberra*, review the information available at the following websites:

❶ http://www.hmascanberra.com/crews/Getting.html

❷ http://en.wikipedia.org/wiki/HMAS_Canberra_(D33)#Loss

❸ http://en.wikipedia.org/wiki/Royal_Australian_Navy

180. For further information on the verbatim text of the speech titled "Minister for Defence Materiel—Remembrance Day Commemoration, Honiara, Solomon Islands," presented by the (Right) Honorable Jason Clare, MP, Minister for Defence Materiel, on 11 November 2011, see the Australian Government Department of Defence website at http://www.minister.defence.gov .au/2011/11/11/minister-for-defence-materiel-remembrance-day-commemoration-honiara-solo mon-islands/.

181. Refers to the epic thirteen-volume tome, *The Art of War*, by Lao Tzu. Chapter 3: *Attack by Stratagem (Stratagem 6)*; Spring/Autumn Period; Period of Warring States (515 BC–512 BC). English translation by Lionel Giles.

182. Public Domain chart is available from Wikipedia and Wikimaps, and extracted from the "Reports of General MacArthur, Prepared by his General Staff," printed by the GPO, 18 October 2005. View the full detailed image at http://en.wikipedia.org/wiki/File:PearlHarborCarrierChart .jpg#filehistory.

183. For more complete information on the attack on Pearl Harbor and Ford Island, initial orders of battle for each combatant force, fleet dispositions, attack itineraries, and post-action damage assessments, refer to all of the excellent web resources at

❶ http://www.teacheroz.com/PearlHarbor.htm

❷ http://www.ww2pacific.com/pearljp.html

184. For additional information on Gunichi Mikawa and his command of the newly formed Eighth Fleet on 14 June 1942, review the information available at

❶ http://en.wikipedia.org/wiki/IJN_8th_Fleet

❷ http://en.wikipedia.org/wiki/Gunichi_Mikawa#World_War_II

❸ http://www.combinedfleet.com/chokai_t.htm

185. Op. cit., USNI *Proceedings* article by CAPT Toshikazu Ohmae, 1264.

186. Op. cit., Bates/Innis NWC report, 1275.

187. Ibid., 1268.

188. Ibid.

189. Ibid.

190. Ibid.

191. Ibid.

192. Ibid., 1273.

193. Ibid.

194. Ibid.

195. Ibid.

196. Ibid., 1275.

197. Op. cit., Bates/Innis NWC report, 1275. The command issued at that time is actually attributed to CAPT Mikio Hayakawa, the captain of the IJN heavy cruiser *Chōkai*. Though the CA was Mikawa's flagship on at least the occasion of this one night attack, overall command of the ship remained with CAPT Hayakawa.

198 . Op. cit., Bates/Innis NWC report, 1265.

199. Ibid., 1275.

200. Ibid., 1278.

201. Extracted from Bates, Richard W., and Innis, Walter D. (1950). *The Battle of Savo Island, August 9, 1942. Strategical and Tactical Analysis. Part One.* Naval War College (Department of Analysis). Distributed by National Technical Information Service (NTIS), U.S. Department of Commerce, 367–69.

202. For additional information on the assault on both Kavieng and Rabaul—and the reported atrocities known to have occurred in both areas—see the detailed information presented at the following informative websites:

❶ http://en.wikipedia.org/wiki/Battle_of_Rabaul_(1942)

❷ http://en.wikipedia.org/wiki/Japanese_war_crimes

203. Off the northernmost coast of Bougainville, just before arriving at Kieta, it is known that VADM Mikawa did shrewdly attempt to mask his contingency's composition by dispersing his ships widely in a broadened patrol pattern, thereby ensuring a lesser degree of visibility as a group to any enemy search planes or patrolling Allied ships.

204. The order, issued by VADM Mikawa by 0131 hours on the morning of 9 August, would have followed closely on the heels of his previous instruction to "Release all ships" to operate independently of his own flagship *Chōkai*. In this instance, the comment is attributed to Dull, Paul S. (1978). *A Battle History of the Imperial Japanese Navy, 1941–1945.* Naval Institute Press. The comment may also be seen at http://en.wikipedia.org/wiki/Battle_of_Savo_Island#Action_south_of_Savo.

205. Op. cit., Bates/Innis NWC report, 1275.

206. Ibid., 1277.

207. Ibid., 1276.

208. Poem extracted from the author's longer collection titled *Naval Encounters: The Battle for Guadalcanal.* To read the full saga of the clashes between Admirals Mikawa, Gotō, Fletcher, and Crutchley as a quatrain narrative, see the commemorative literary poem on the First Battle of Savo Island, beginning on page 442.

209. Cook, *Cape Esperance*, 19 and 31; Frank, *Guadalcanal*, 296; Morison, *Struggle for Guadalcanal*, 150; Dull, *Imperial Japanese Navy*, 226; and Hackett, *IJN Seaplane Tender Chitose*.

210. Hara, Tameichi (Captain, IJN Ret.). (1961). *Japanese Destroyer Captain*. Edited by Fred Saito and Roger Pineau. Naval Institute Press.

211. Op. cit., Hara, 127.

212. For additional information on the curious movements of the USS *Helm*, see Finding 17 on "The Mystery of the Helm," beginning on page 188.

213. The DE USS *Samuel B. Roberts*, the "destroyer that fought like a battleship," bravely engaged a far superior IJN surface fleet and fought through a one-hour slugfest with the IJN *Chōkai* and the *Chikuma*, causing serious damage to both CAs. Raked by continual fire from the heavy 8-inch guns from both ships, the American DE would dauntlessly fight on until hit by the combined 14-inch guns of the great battleship *Kongō*. Now with a gaping 40-foot hole in her port bow, the *Sammy B.* would finally sink at about 1000 hours on the morning of 25 October 1944. Survivors from the wreckage of the *Roberts* would be forced to remain in the water some fifty hours before rescue.

For additional information on the USS *Samuel B. Roberts*—and the ship's most valiant exploits during the Battle off Samar—see the Wikipedia account at http://en.wikipedia.org/wiki/USS_Samuel_B._Roberts_(DE-413)#The_Battle_off_Samar.

214. Op. cit., Bates/Innis account, 444.

215. Ibid., 344.

216. Ibid., 350.

217. Ibid., 408.

218. Ibid., 356.

219. Op. cit., Ohmae account, 1277.

220. Op. cit., Bates/Innis account, 358.

221. Op. cit., Coombe, *Derailing the Tokyo Express*, 102.

222. Cited in the narratives of the *Battle Experience Information Bulletin #2* titled *Solomon Islands Actions; August 1942*. HQs CINC, U.S. Fleet, 11–20.

223. Ibid.

224. The USS *Vincennes* was cited as having been hit an overwhelming seventy-four times, the *Quincy* some thirty-six times, and the great *Astoria* a staggering sixty-five times from the large-bore 8-inch projectiles fired at them by the IJN cruiser fleet on that occasion. Source is from the official U.S. Navy Department Bureau of Ships Assessment Report (C-FS/L11-1(374)-C-EN28/A2-11). Subject: USS *Quincy*, USS *Astoria* and USS *Vincennes: Report of Loss in Action; dated 2 September 1943*; from Summary, page 1.

225. Op. cit., Frank, official U.S. Navy Department, Bureau of Ships Assessment Report, B. Fires, 81(b), 18.

226. Ibid.

227. Ibid., 11.

228. Ibid., 15.

229. For additional information on the sinking of the USS *Astoria* (CA-34), see the Wikipedia account at http://en.wikipedia.org/wiki/USS_Astoria_(CA-34)#The_Solomons_.28Battle_of_Savo_Island.29.

230. Op. cit., Bates/Innis account, 361.

231. Ibid., 362.

232. Op. cit., Coombe, *Derailing the Tokyo Express*, 2.

233. Ibid.

234. Op. cit., Frank, *Guadalcanal*, 123.

235. Ibid.

236. Both images made available courtesy of the www.becuo.com website.

237. Coombe, *Derailing the Tokyo Express.*

238. Ibid.

239. Op. cit., Office of Naval Intelligence, *The Battle of Savo Island: 9 August 1942: Combat Narrative* from the *HyperWar* website at http://www.ibiblio.org/hyperwar/USN/USN-CN-Savo/maps /USN-CN-Savo-1.jpg.

240. Op. cit., ONI narrative.

241. Op. cit., Office of Naval Intelligence, The Battle of Savo Island: 9 August 1942: Combat Narrative from the website series as noted:

❶ http://www.ibiblio.org/hyperwar/USN/USN-CN-Savo/USN-CN-Savo-5.html, page 16

❷ http://en.wikipedia.org/wiki/File:SavoIslandMap2A.jpg

242. Op. cit., Office of Naval Intelligence, *The Battle of Savo Island: 9 August 1942: Combat Narrative* from the website at http://www.ibiblio.org/hyperwar/USN/USN-CN-Savo/USN-CN-Savo-5. html, 16.

243. Morison, Samuel Eliot (1958). *The Struggle for Guadalcanal, August 1942–February 1943, Vol. 5 of History of United States Naval Operations in World War II.* Little, Brown and Company, 21. See also http://en.wikipedia.org/wiki/File:SavoMikawaApproach.jpg.

244. Op. cit., *HyperWar* website at http://www.ibiblio.org/hyperwar/USN/USN-CN-Savo /index.html, under a topical discussion heading of *Disposition of Screening Force, Battle of Savo Island [Chart]*, page x of Appendix. See also http://en.wikipedia.org/wiki/File:SavoIslandMap.jpg.

245. Op. cit., Loxton, *The Shame of Savo: Anatomy of a Naval Disaster.*

246. For additional information on this account of the action, and this specific mapping chart, view the excellent MacKenzie J. Gregory website, *Ahoy-Mac's Web Log,* at http://www.ahoy.tk-jk.net /Solomons/BattleofSavoIsland.html and http://ahoy.tk-jk.net/

247. Op. cit., Quantock, *Disaster at Savo Island,* 1942; from *List of Illustrations,* Figure 4, *The Battle Savo Island.*

248. Extract from Tabular Record of Movement (TROM)–IJN *Aoba.* From the Imperial Japanese Navy Combined Fleet website, which can be viewed in full in the *Junkoyan* heavy cruiser listings at http://www.combinedfleet.com/aoba_t.htm.

249. Extract from Tabular Record of Movement (TROM)–IJN *Tenryū:* From the *Imperial Japanese Navy Combined Fleet* website, which can be viewed in full in the *Junkoyan* heavy cruiser listings at http://www.combinedfleet.com/furuta_t.htm.

Bibliography, Reference Links, and Further Reading

The following information resources and research websites have, over time, proven to be quite insightful to the author, and might be expected to provide both a level of thoroughness and accuracy for all applied researchers. These resources are provided primarily to assist the reader in research efforts in the event that further information is desired for any topical discussion point presented in the book. I have found these resources to be extremely helpful, presenting both an unbiased and objective summarization of events as they must have occurred before, during, and after the battle. In the case of multiple historical presentations, with each account describing essentially the same event from different vantage points, the author is pleased to present each interpretation to allow you, the reader, the option to develop and arrive at your own conclusions.

Also, for the sake of convenience and practicality—and to perhaps point out resource similarity—the listings have been compiled and grouped into two logical media formats, those of both print and electronic. As such, the reader is invited to review each of the book and electronic media resource listings below.

PRINT MEDIA: BOOKS

The following resources are all text-based and might truly be considered "required reading" for both the serious naval historian and the evolving researcher of this time period of World War II—and of the Battle of Savo Island specifically. Each book uniquely presents its own authentic account of events as they must have taken place at the time of the battle, and each might indeed be considered an excellent and informative read.

Bix, Herbert P. (2000). *Hirohito and the Making of Modern Japan*. Diane Publishing Company.
Calhoun, C. Raymond. (2000). *Tin Can Sailor: Life Aboard the* USS *Sterett, 1939–1945*. U.S. Naval Institute Press.
Coggins, Russell S. (1972). *The Campaign for Guadalcanal*. Doubleday Books.
Coombe, Jack D. (1991). *Derailing the Tokyo Express*. Stackpole Books.
Crenshaw, Jack D. (2009). *South Pacific Destroyer: The Battle for the Solomons from Savo Island to Vella Gulf*. Naval Institute Press.
Custer, Joseph J. (1944). *Through the Perilous Night: The* Astoria's *Last Battle*. The Macmillan Company.

Domagalski, John J. (2010). *Lost at Guadalcanal: The Final Battles of the* Astoria *and* Chicago *as Described by Survivors and in Official Reports.* McFarland.

Domagalski, John J. (2012). "Abrupt End and Then Aftermath; United States Naval Institute (USNI)." In *Composure Amid a Naval Disaster* (chapter); *Naval History* 26, no. 4 (August 2012).

Frank, Richard B. (1990*). Guadalcanal: The Definitive Account of the Landmark Battle.* Penguin Group.

Hara, Tameichi (Captain, IJN Ret.). (1961). *Japanese Destroyer Captain.* Edited by Fred Saito and Roger Pineau. Naval Institute Press.

Hornfischer, James D. (2012). *Neptune's Inferno.* Bantam Books.

Kilpatrick, C. W. (1987). *Naval Night Battles of the Solomons.* Exposition Press.

Loxton, Bruce, and Chris Coulthard-Clark. (1997). *The Shame of Savo: Anatomy of a Naval Disaster.* Allen & Unwin Pty Ltd.

Morison, Samuel Eliot. (1958). *The Struggle for Guadalcanal, August 1942–February 1943.* Vol. 5 of *History of United States Naval Operations in World War II.* Boston: Little, Brown and Company.

Newcomb, Richard F. (2002). *The Battle of Savo Island: The Harrowing Account of the Disastrous Night Battle off Guadalcanal That Nearly Destroyed the Pacific Fleet in August 1942.* Holt Paperbacks.

Ohmae, Toshikazu, and David C. Evans (Eds.). (1986). *The Battle of Savo Island. The Japanese Navy in World War II: In the Words of Former Japanese Naval Officers.* Naval Institute Press.

Shanks, Sandy, and Lanzendoerfer, Tim. (2001). *Bode Testament.* Writers Club Press.

Stile, Mark. (2011). *USN Cruiser vs. IJN Cruiser: Guadalcanal 1942.* Osprey Publishing Books.

Toland, John. (1970). *The Rising Sun: The Decline and Fall of the Japanese Empire 1936–1945.* Random House.

Tregaskis, Richard. (1970). *Guadalcanal Diary.* Modern Library Publishing.

Tzu, Lao. (1994). *The Art of War.* Basic Books.

PRINT MEDIA: ARTICLES

Bates, Richard W. (1950). The Battle of Savo Island, August 9, 1942. Strategical and Tactical Analysis. Part I. Naval War College (Bureau of Naval Personnel—AD/A-003 037). (Distributed by National Technical Information Service (NTIS), U.S. Department of Commerce.

Bonnot, Emile I. (Captain, USNR, Ret.). Historian General Emeritus—Naval Order of the United States). (1988). Were the Hudsons to Be Blamed for the Naval Disaster at Guadalcanal? *Independent* (February 23, 1988).

Lanzendoerfer, Tim. (2006). *Opening Salvos: The Battle of Savo Island, August 9, 1942. The Pacific War: The U.S. Navy.*

Office of Naval Intelligence. (1943). *The Battle of Savo Island, August 9, 1942.* Combat Narrative. Publications Branch, Office of Naval Intelligence, United States Navy.

Ohmae, Toshikazu (1957). *The Battle of Savo Island.* United States Naval Institute (USNI). *Proceedings* 83, no. 12 (December 1957).

Shaw, James C. (CDR, USN, Ret.). (1950). *Jarvis: Destroyer That Vanished.* United States Naval Institute (USNI). *Proceedings* 76, no. 2 (February 1950).

U.S. Navy Department Bureau of Ships Assessment Report (C-FS/L11-1(374)-C-EN28/A2-11). *Subject: USS Quincy, USS Astoria and USS Vincennes: Report of Loss in Action*; dated 2 September 1943.

ELECTRONIC MEDIA: BATTLE OF SAVO ISLAND–SPECIFIC

Bing search facility, *Battle of Savo Island* (Images). Retrieved 19 November 2012 from http://www.bing.com/images/search?q=Battle+of+Savo+Island&id=A5C16D79DB344CF873F833AAF392 71F943D19F80&FORM=IGRE1#x0y0.

Bauer, James. *How the End of World War I Led to World War II: World War II Pacific*, subtitled "The Pacific War, 1942: The Battle of Savo Island-Aug 9, 1942: Off Guadalcanal, Solomon Islands." Retrieved 19 November 2012 from http://www.ww2pacific.com/savo.html.

Cagney, James. (2012). Interactive Animation of the Battle of Savo Island, August 9, 1942. Retrieved 19 November 2012, from JavaScript at HistoryAnimated.com, at http://www.pacificwaranimated.com/index.php/savo-island.

Friedman, Kenneth I. (2007–2012). *The Battles for Guadalcanal*, subtitled "The Battle of Savo Island." Retrieved 19 November 2012 from http://battlesforguadalcanal.com/Story/Battles/savo/savo.html.

Lanzendoerfer, Tim. (2012). *The Pacific War: The U.S. Navy*. Retrieved 19 November 2012 from http://microworks.net/PACIFIC/battles/savo_island.htm.

Office of Naval Intelligence, Department of the Navy. *Combat Narrative: The Battle of Savo Island: 9 August 1942*; subtitled, *The Battles of Savo Island: 9 August 1942 and the Eastern Solomons: 23–25 August 1942*. Retrieved 19 November 2012 from http://www.ibiblio.org/hyperwar/USN/USN-CN-Savo/index.html.

Quantock, David E. (LTC, USA, Ret.). (2002). *Disaster at Savo Island, 1942*. U.S. Army War College, PA. Retrieved 19 November 2012 from http://www.ibiblio.org/hyperwar/USN/rep/Savo/Quantock/index.html#illus.

Wikipedia, "The Battle of Savo Island." Retrieved 19 November 2012 from http://en.wikipedia.org/wiki/Battle_of_Savo_Island.

ELECTRONIC MEDIA: COMBATANT SHIPS: ALLIED FLEET

The author is pleased to share the following insightful website resources for several of the participant ships, many of which were found during the course of the research undertaken for this very book. The development journey itself had been both arduous and rewarding, challenging and uplifting, and often fraught with impediments and roadblocks. Whether an unconfirmable source, a seemingly untagged citation, or simply a series of conflicting map images, there were always far more red lights than green. And whether a striking iconic graphic of the great IJN battleship *Kirishima* that cannot fully be ascribed to a specific artist, the haunting image of the USS *Laffey* battling the much larger BB *Hiei*, or a single viable photograph of CAPT Howard Douglas Bode as the skipper of the USS *Chicago*, it was almost always an uphill battle that was made that much easier by the repositories of information made available on these key websites.

It is therefore my great hope that these sites can be of some use to other researchers—for those who may follow in these footsteps—to perhaps ultimately arrive at their own conclusions.

Wikimedia Foundation, Wikipedia online encyclopedia: List of U.S. Navy losses in World War II at http://en.wikipedia.org/wiki/List_of_U.S._Navy_losses_in_World_War_II

Wikimedia Foundation, Wikipedia online encyclopedia: USS *Vincennes* (CA-44) (and others) at http://en.wikipedia.org/wiki/USS_Vincennes_(CA-44); http://www.ussvincennes.org/vincennes/ca-44/index.htm; http://www.history.navy.mil/photos/sh usn/usnsh v/ca44.htm

Wikimedia Foundation, Wikipedia online encyclopedia: USS *Quincy* (CA-39) (and others) at http://en.wikipedia.org/wiki/USS_Quincy_(CA-39); http://www.ussquincy.com/; http://www.history.navy.mil/photos/sh-usn/usnsh-q/ca39.htm

Wikimedia Foundation, Wikipedia online encyclopedia: USS *Astoria* (CA-34) (and others) at http://en.wikipedia.org/wiki/USS_Astoria_(CA-34); http://ussastoria.org/; http://www.navsource.org/archives/04/034/04034.htm

Wikimedia Foundation, Wikipedia online encyclopedia: USS *Helm* (DD-388) (and others) at http://en.wikipedia.org/wiki/USS_Helm_(DD-388); http://www.destroyersonline.com/usndd/dd388/; http://www.navsource.org/archives/05/388.htm

Wikimedia Foundation, Wikipedia online encyclopedia: USS *Wilson* (DD-408) (and others) at http://en.wikipedia.org/wiki/USS_Wilson_(DD-408); http://www.navsource.org/archives/05/408.htm; http://www.hullnumber.com/DD-408

Wikimedia Foundation, Wikipedia online encyclopedia: USS *Blue* (DD-387) (and others) at http://en.wikipedia.org/wiki/USS_Blue_(DD-387); http://www.navsource.org/archives/05/387.htm; http://www.destroyersonline.com/usndd/dd387/

Wikimedia Foundation, Wikipedia encyclopedia: USS *Ralph Talbot* (DD-390) (and others) at http://en.wikipedia.org/wiki/USS_Ralph_Talbot_(DD-390); http://www.hullnumber.com/DD-390; http://www.navsource.org/archives/05/390.htm

Wikimedia Foundation, Wikipedia online encyclopedia: USS *Chicago* (CA-29) (and others) at http://en.wikipedia.org/wiki/USS_Chicago_(CA-29); http://www.history.navy.mil/photos/sh-usn/usnsh-c/ca29.htm; http://www.navsource.org/archives/04/029/04029.htm; http://www.pacificwrecks.com/ships/usn/CA-29.html

Wikimedia Foundation, Wikipedia online encyclopedia: USS *Patterson* (DD-392) (and others) at http://en.wikipedia.org/wiki/USS_Patterson_(DD-392); http://www.destroyerhistory.org/goldplater/usspatterson.html; http://www.navsource.org/archives/05/392.htm

Wikimedia Foundation, Wikipedia online encyclopedia: USS *Bagley* (DD-386) (and others) at http://en.wikipedia.org/wiki/USS_Bagley_(DD-386); http://www.navsource.org/archives/05/386.htm; http://www.destroyerhistory.org/goldplater/ussbagley.html

Wikimedia Foundation, Wikipedia online encyclopedia: HMAS *Australia* (D84) (and others) at http://en.wikipedia.org/wiki/HMAS_Australia_(1927); http://www.navy.gov.au/HMAS_Australia_%28II%29; http://www.history.navy.mil/photos/sh-fornv/austral/aussh-ag/austr2.htm

Wikimedia Foundation, Wikipedia online encyclopedia: HMAS *Canberra* (D33) (and others) at http://en.wikipedia.org/wiki/HMAS_Canberra_(D33); http://hmascanberra.com/; http://www.navy.gov.au/HMAS_Canberra_(I)

ELECTRONIC MEDIA: COMBATANT SHIPS: IMPERIAL JAPANESE NAVY

Gone are the years of 1942 and beyond, to war's end in 1945, when a researcher's best friends were still an old manual typewriter, a pile of dusty old books, and a sheaf of sea-worn maps and charts from any of several military archives. The naval historian then in search of a viable truth would have to wade through stacks of chronicled information such as ships' logs, TROMs, mounds of first-person accounts, uncounted after-action reports, and even proceedings and findings from extant courts of inquiry that may have been convened at the time.

In and of itself, the research process will almost always be long and grueling, demanding a certain dogged will on the part of the examiner, added to which must be a sound determination to ferret out the facts (with some degree of certainty) surrounding the specific events that occurred during a sketchy South Pacific campaign near a small island in the Solomons called Guadalcanal, during a now almost-forgotten World War II battle.

So thus have we ardently tried to keep the memories alive and pass on the lore and heroic tales from generation to generation, much as my own urgent need to seek out each of the truths about Savo, probing me almost to the soul and urging me to pursue all as far as I could. Only now may we leap light years ahead from that battle, arriving at a point in time when there is a veritable *wealth* of information right at our very fingertips. With the introduction of the World Wide Web and the far-reaching resources it makes available to historians and researchers alike, we can seriously seek out at least some of these vanishing truths—these arcane and little-known truths that are understood by only a few who may actually have been there at Savo on the night of that one scorching battle in August 1942.

The following research and reference sites have, on many occasions, served to provide impeccable and easily understood information about the operational posture of the Imperial Japanese Navy of 1942. Indeed, throughout the course of my own research, I was able to find site after site that freely offered keen elements of data, first-person accounts, event timelines, area maps, and even hierarchical organizational charts that addressed the First Battle of Savo Island. The puzzle pieces quickly came together, and a greater picture emerged surrounding the events of that battle.

Presented as high-level categories only, therefore, the following reference sites are offered to aid the serious historian and researcher alike in their own course of study of both the battle itself and its resulting great losses.

The Imperial Japanese Navy: General Information Sites

Kaigūn: The Imperial Japanese Navy Webpage: http://www.combinedfleet.com/kaigun.htm
"The Imperial Japanese Navy" (Wikipedia): http://en.wikipedia.org/wiki/Imperial_Japanese_Navy, http://www.ww2pacific.com/japbb.html
Japanese Battle Fleet of World War II: http://www.ww2pacific.com/japbb.html
The World War II Multimedia Database: http://www.worldwar2database.com/html/kaigun.htm
Imperial Japanese Navy (IJN—*Nihon Kaigūn*) (Global Security.org): http://www.globalsecurity.org/military/world/japan/ijn.htm
List of Ships of the Imperial Japanese Navy (IJN): http://en.wikipedia.org/wiki/List_of_ships_of_the_Japanese_Navy

The Imperial Japanese Navy: The IJN Carrier Force

http://en.wikipedia.org/wiki/Imperial_Japanese_Navy#Aircraft_carriers
Japanese Carriers of World War II: http://www.ww2pacific.com/japcv.html
World Aircraft Carriers List: Japanese Aircraft Carriers (Haze Gray): http://www.ww2pacific.com/japcv.html

The Imperial Japanese Navy: The IJN Cruiser Force

Aoba-class heavy cruisers: http://en.wikipedia.org/wiki/*Aoba_class*_cruiser
Mogami-class heavy cruisers: http://en.wikipedia.org/wiki/Mogami_class_cruiser
Tone-class heavy cruisers: http://en.wikipedia.org/wiki/Tone_class_cruiser
Takao-class heavy cruisers: http://en.wikipedia.org/wiki/Takao_class_cruiser
Myoko-class heavy cruisers: http://en.wikipedia.org/wiki/Myoko_class_cruiser
Heavy Cruisers of World War II: http://www.chuckhawks.com/heavy_cruisers_part3.htm

The Imperial Japanese Navy: DESRON, the IJN Destroyers

Akizuki-class destroyer: http://en.wikipedia.org/wiki/Akizuki_class_destroyer_(1942)

Super *Akizuki*-class destroyer: http://en.Wikipedia.org/wiki/Super_Akizuki_class_destroyer

Asashio-class destroyer: http://en.wikipedia.org/wiki/Asashio_class_destroyer

Fuyuzuki-class destroyer: http://en.wikipedia.org/wiki/Akizuki_class_destroyer_(1942)#Fuyuzuki_class

Kamikaze-class destroyer: http://en.wikipedia.org/wiki/Kamikaze_class_destroyer_(1922)

Kagerō-class destroyer: http://en.wikipedia.org/wiki/Kager%C5%8D_class_destroyer

Matsu-class destroyer: http://en.wikipedia.org/wiki/Matsu_class_destroyer

Michizuki-class destroyer: http://en.wikipedia.org/wiki/Akizuki_class_destroyer_(1942)#Michizuki
_class

Minekaze-class destroyer: http://en.wikipedia.org/wiki/Minekaze_class_destroyer

Moni-class destroyer: http://en.wikipedia.org/wiki/Momi_class_destroyer

Shiratsuyu-class destroyer: http://en.wikipedia.org/wiki/Shiratsuyu_class_destroyer

Wakatake-class destroyer: http://en.wikipedia.org/wiki/Wakatake_class_destroyer

The Imperial Japanese Navy: IJN Command Structure

Commanders of the IJN Combined Fleet: http://en.wikipedia.org/wiki/Combined_Fleet#Com
manders_of_the_IJN_Combined_Fleet

Naval Ranks of the Japanese Empire during World War II ❶: http://en.wikipedia.org/wiki/Na
val_ranks_of_the_Japanese_Empire_during_World_War_II

Naval Ranks of the Japanese Empire during World War II ❷: http://www.enotes.com/topic/Na
val_ranks_of_the_Japanese_Empire_during_World_War_II

Ranks, Appointments and Units in the Japanese Navy (Naval Air Force): http://orbat.com/site/ww2
/drleo/014_japan/_ijn_ranks.html

ELECTRONIC MEDIA: MISCELLANEOUS RESEARCH WEBLINKS

Throughout the course and venue of the research conducted for this book, the author has truly enjoyed the "journey" far more than the actual "destination." Embracing the full empowerment of being able to access a robust assortment of technical reference materials online—in an incredible age of technology—has made that journey that much shorter in tenure, but not at all in content. During the course of the development of the narratives for this book, the author has made use of (and gratefully acknowledges) all of the above-listed web-based resources for the valuable data they have provided the researcher. To this end, all of these excellent and highly pertinent sites have been compiled and are provided for general researcher use as needed.

WEBSITE RESOURCE	RESOURCE WEBSITE ADDRESS	BRIEF RESOURCE DESCRIPTION
Wikipedia	http://en.wikipedia.org /wiki/Battle_of_Savo_Island	Wikipedia is uniquely a multilingual, web-based, and free-content encyclopedia resource that can provide the serious (or even *casual*) researcher with a uniquely focused view of virtually every major battle scenario, beginning with the 1BOSI and moving on to the battles off Cape Esperance, Tassafaronga, and the naval encounters, including even the final Battle of Rennell Island. Expect to find a series of excellent maps, charts, illustrations, and B&W period photographs that are available for all to access and use.
Wikimapia	http://wikimapia.org /country/Solomon_Islands/	Wikimapia is another powerful and invaluable tool, one that can provide both online mapping and satellite imaging resources that utilize Google Maps. One highly desirable feature is that of allowing users to add (and even manipulate) information about a specific global location, a shipwreck site, or even a specific battle arena itself. Seen as an excellent tool for all users and researchers.
DANFS	https://www.history.navy .mil/research/histories/ship -histories/danfs.html	*Dictionary of American Naval Fighting Ships*: This superlative repository contains a summary of (and TROM historical activity for) many USN ships, conveniently presented in an A–Z listing. Individual ship listings are concise and informative.

WEBSITE RESOURCE	RESOURCE WEBSITE ADDRESS	BRIEF RESOURCE DESCRIPTION
Haze Gray & Underway	http://www.hazegray.org/danfs/destroy/dd408txt.htm	Excellent naval history website, with ship types and name listings, date and timeline chronologies, and TROM service records, as well as source photographs of the period itself. It also contains a handy link directly to the DANFS database.
World War 2— Plus 55	http://usswashington.com/worldwar2plus55/dl09au42.htm	Account of the Naval Battle of Guadalcanal and other battles as experienced from the deck of the American BB USS *Washington* (BB-56), at the time under the command of RADM Willis Augustus "Ching" Lee.
World War 2— Pacific	http://www.ww2pacific.com/savo.html	Citing the Hudson pilots' sightings report of the IJN fleet on 8 August 1942, this web page avowedly proclaims the "non-culpability" of the two Australian reconnaissance plane pilots who allegedly did *not* report having spotted Mikawa's task force until it was too late for any preemptive action by the Allied navies then operating at Guadalcanal. For more information, see the full topical discussion on the "Teacup Controversy."
History Animated	http://www.historyanimated.com/newhistoryanimated/index.php	To see a multi-phase animation of the 1BOSI, click on the screen's "Pacific War Animated" link, then the secondary "The Battle for Guadalcanal Island link," followed by the site's "View Battle Animation" link to see the full battle main.

Website Resource	Resource Website Address	Brief Resource Description
W R E C K Site	http://www.wrecksite.eu/wreck-search.aspx?alpha	Search the full website database of shipwrecks and sites of "last knowns" in an alphabetical ordering—or by a more specific search argument.
NavWeaps	http://www.navweaps.com/index_oob/OOB_WWII_Pacific/OOB_WWII_First-Savo.htm	The *Naval Weapons* website offers the Richard Worth repository of highly relevant information on the order of battle for the 1BOSI. Seen as a valuable tool.
Brad Sheard Deep Sea Photography	http://bradsheard.com/GCanalwrecks.html	This well-acclaimed Brad Sheard website chronicles many of the current-day dive activities for various 1BOSI (and later) shipwrecks that can be found in and around the Guadalcanal area, with a keen focus on Iron Bottom Sound itself.
The Battle of Guadalcanal Foundation	http://www.guadalcanal.com.sb/	This site may be used for tourism groups (or individual) charter information, touring itineraries, and commemorative anniversary observances that may be taking place in and around the Guadalcanal area.
Solomon Islands Board of Tourism	http://www.visitsolomons.com.sb/wwii-stories/savo-fight	Official Solomon Islands website, offering a wealth of information on dive sites, military tours, viewable wreck sites, amenities, and accommodations, as well as all pertinent travel information for anyone who may wish to visit the area.

Website Resource	Resource Website Address	Brief Resource Description
Tulagi Dive	http://www.tulagidive.com .sb/Index1.htm	This website is dedicated to more experienced divers, specifically those interested in wreck-diving the *Aaron Ward* and many of the several sunken Japanese *Maru*-class transport ships that were lost during and after the 1BOSI.
Greg Goebel: **In The Public Domain**	http://www.vectorsite.net /tw2guad_1.html#m3	The Greg Geobel "Vector" website provides a unique and informed perspective of the Mikawa attack itself in a seven-volume online repository of documents titled "August–September 1942: Are You Going to Stay Here?"
Publication Semaphore	http://www.navy.gov.au /Publication:Semaphore _-_Issue_12,_2007#The _Battle_of_Savo_Island	The official Royal Australian Navy website, with a link to "Australians at Guadalcanal, August 1942," the invasion landings of 7 August, and the 1BOSI itself.
Together We Served	http://navy.together weserved.com/usn /voices/2010/4/Galvin _voices.html	View an up-close and verbatim interview with Petty Officer Daniel Galvin, one of the few remaining survivors of the USS *Quincy* (CA-39) crew after the ship's sinking on the night of 8–9 August 1942.
USS Quincy Website	http://www.ussquincy .com/quincyws121200 /index.html http://www.ussquincy .com/quincyws121200 /CA39.html	Excellent roster and reunion page for those who served on either the initial (CA-39) *Quincy* or the later "vengeance ship" incarnation of that same *Quincy* as CA-71.

WEBSITE RESOURCE	RESOURCE WEBSITE ADDRESS	BRIEF RESOURCE DESCRIPTION
USS Astoria Website	http://ussastoria.org/USS_ASTORIA_CA-34.html	A home for all "Nasty Asty" veterans, with key information about the ship and its crew, along with excellent period photographs of the CA-34 in action.
USS Vincennes Website	http://www.ussvincennes.org/vincennes/ca-44/index.htm	Contains a substantial presentation of the ship's TROM data and history, as well crew rosters, reunions, updates, and general research resources.
USS Chicago Website	http://www.usschicago.org/ http://en.wikipedia.org/wiki/USS_Chicago_(CA-29) http://ww2db.com/ship_spec.php?ship_id=335	Official USS *Chicago* (CA-29) web page is preeminently dedicated to the later CA-136 *Chicago*, which was itself later converted to its even newer incarnation as CG-11 Guided Missile Cruiser status in 1958. The best source of information on the CA-34 would generally be either Wikipedia or the Naval Historical Center (NHC) website. Some excellent technical data on this specific CA is also available on the World War II Database site at www.ww2db.com.
USS Wilson Website	http://www.hazegray.org/danfs/destroy/dd408txt.htm	General website references for the USS *Wilson* (DD-408) only.
USS Helm Website	http://www.hazegray.org/danfs/destroy/dd388txt.htm	General website references for the USS *Helm* (DD-388) only.

WEBSITE RESOURCE	RESOURCE WEBSITE ADDRESS	BRIEF RESOURCE DESCRIPTION
USS Blue Website	http://wikimapia.org /11129545/Wreck-of -USS-Blue-DD-387 http://en.wikipedia.org /wiki/USS_Blue_(DD-387) I http://www.destroyer history.org/goldplater /ussblue.html	General website references for the USS *Blue* (DD-387) only.
USS Ralph Talbot Website	http://en.wikipedia.org /wiki/USS_Ralph_Talbot _(DD-390) http://www.navsource.org /archives/05/390.htm http://www.destroyer history.org/goldplater /ussralphtalbot.html	General website references for the USS *Ralph Talbot* (DD-390) only.
USS Patterson Website	http://www.navsource.org /archives/05/392.htm http://www.hazegray.org /danfs/destroy/dd392txt .htm http://www.destroyer history.org/goldplater /usspatterson.html	General website references for the USS *Patterson* (DD-392) only.
USS Bagley Website	http://en.wikipedia.org /wiki/USS_Bagley_(DD-386) http://www.navsource.org /archives/05/386.htm http://www.history.navy .mil/photos/sh-usn /usnsh-b/dd386.htm	General website references for the USS *Bagley* (DD-386) only.
USS De Haven Website	http://www.ussdehaven .org/first.htm http://en.wikipedia.org /wiki/USS_De_Haven _(DD-469)	Official website for the first (earlier) USS *De Haven* (DD-469), complete with maps, photos, links, and even a suggested bibliography for all. This site also contains a secondary link to a full Wikipedia data mine, and pertinent info can be found on the later DD-727 incarnation as well.

WEBSITE RESOURCE	RESOURCE WEBSITE ADDRESS	BRIEF RESOURCE DESCRIPTION
HMAS Canberra Website	❶ http://www.hmas canberra.com.au/ ❷ http://en.wikipedia.org /wiki/HMAS_Canberra _(D33) ❸ http://www.pacific wrecks.com/ships /hmas/canberra.html ❹ http://ahoy.tk-jk.net/ macslog/H.M.A.S .Canberraand theBat.html	❶ Info on diving the *Canberra* wreckage site, with FAQs and tour bookings. ❷ Full Wikipedia coverage of the *Canberra* and its sinking in 1942. ❸ Info on MIAs and an excellent forum for survivor families. ❹ *Ahoy!* naval (and general maritime) site offers good historical background on the D33.
World War II Database	http://ww2db.com/ship .php	This World War II data mining website offers users great info on ships of all types and classes. Seen as a prolific data mining resource, this site can provide extensive information on World War II, the combatants, battles, events, chronologies, books, photos and more—this for both the serious period researcher and the casual reader as well.
Old Blue Jacket Website	http://oldbluejacket.com/	Site provides a wealth of information and links in an icon image format, with connections to information on World War II, Korea, Vietnam, and even present-day Middle East conflict areas. Pages viewed come complete with accompanying martial music.
Hull Number Website	http://www.hullnumber .com/	This concise website provides a series of ship-silhouetted links that can easily navigate the user out to any number of ships and ship types.

WEBSITE RESOURCE	RESOURCE WEBSITE ADDRESS	BRIEF RESOURCE DESCRIPTION
Destroyer History Website	http://www.destroyer history.org/	Contains some great technical data on all DD-class ships that are sorted by ship name and hull number. Provides a curious "Find a Ship" link for these same DD vessels in a later 348–420 hull number classification range, which include many of the earlier World War II-era DDs.
Destroyers Online	http://www.destroyers online.com/usndd/	Seen as an above-average compilation (and presentation) of *all* information relating to DDs by "class," presented with a glossarial database and an extensive bibliographical listing.
Ahoy—Mac's Web Log	http://www.ahoy .tk-jk.net/Solomons /BattleofSavoIsland.html	Provides a full and in-depth review of the several naval battles of Guadalcanal from August to November 1942. Preeminent focus seems to be that of the involvement of the HMAS *Canberra* during the IJN attack on Crutchley's Southern screening force during the 1BOSI on the night of 8–9 August. Researchers can also find several excellent "first-person" accounts and narratives from surviving crewmen who were aboard the Australian CA during the night battle at Savo.